PUBLIC
PHILOSOPHER

Also by John Morton Blum

Joe Tumulty and the Wilson Era

The Republican Roosevelt

Woodrow Wilson and the Politics of Morality

Yesterday's Children (Editor)

The National Experience (Editor)

The Promise of America

From the Morgenthau Diaries

    I. Years of Crisis, 1928–1938

    II. Years of Urgency, 1938–1941

    III. Years of War, 1941–1945

Roosevelt and Morgenthau

The Price of Vision (Editor)

V Was for Victory

The Progressive Presidents

PUBLIC PHILOSOPHER

Selected Letters
of Walter Lippmann

JOHN MORTON BLUM
EDITOR

TICKNOR & FIELDS   NEW YORK   1985

For Yale University

Library of Congress Cataloging in Publication Data
Lippmann, Walter, 1889–1974.
  Public philosopher.

  1. Political scientists—Correspondence.
I. Blum, John Morton, 1921–   II. Title.
JC251.L468   1985   320.5'092'2   85-9830
ISBN 0-89919-260-2

Printed in the United States of America

P 10 9 8 7 6 5 4 3 2 1

Contents

Preface

THIS VOLUME includes a comprehensive representation of the historically significant comments and thoughts of Walter Lippmann as he expressed them in
his letters. Like other busy public figures, Lippmann received more correspondence than he sent. Nevertheless, between 1906 and 1974 he wrote an estimated twenty thousand letters. Those published here constitute a selection of
several kinds: letters about public affairs, domestic and international; letters
about politics and political ideas; letters about other ideas that engaged
Lippmann; letters, particularly those from his youth, that revealed his thinking while he was maturing. The letters gathered here express the mind of the
committed journalist, the political and social critic, the confidant of statesmen,
the influential commentator — the "public philosopher" of his generation of
Americans. Like his published writings, the letters of Walter Lippmann constantly addressed the history of his times. That quality and their inherent
interest make the letters worthy of publication.

No routine or intimate letters appear in this volume: Lippmann's letters
about the purchase or sale of real estate or automobiles; letters to publishers
about contracts and royalties; letters about lectures he agreed or declined to
give; letters confirming professional or social engagements; love letters to his
second wife. Because Lippmann was not given to self-searching in his letters,
there are no letters of that kind in his correspondence; nor are there letters
designed for posterity, for Lippmann wrote none of those either. Rather, the
public letters chosen for this volume, like his public letters in general, have
about them much of the casual quality of good conversations. Indeed, transcribed tapes of Lippmann's luncheon conversations, were they available, would
probably read much the same way, for in talking to men of affairs at luncheon,
as one listener observed, Lippmann spoke about nations the way less Jovian
men discussed mutual friends.

*

Lippmann gave his correspondence to the Yale University Library, where it constitutes two of the ten series that make up the Walter Lippmann Collection. Series I (1428 folders) includes his correspondence from 1906 through 1930; Series III (2760 folders), correspondence from 1931 through 1974. Both series are arranged alphabetically by correspondent, except for sixteen "general" folders of little historical significance. The arrangement of both the correspondence and the rest of the Lippmann Collection fell primarily to Robert O. Anthony, who also made significant additions to the library's Lippmann holdings from his own extensive collection of works by and about Walter Lippmann. Anthony prepared the indexes to the Lippmann Collection and to his own, and he produced the Lippmann chronology that I have adapted, with his permission, for the appendix to this volume. Both Anthony and Ronald Steel, Lippmann's capable biographer, discovered letters not in the original Lippmann gift which they persuaded the owners to add in typed or photoduplicated copies. The Lippmann correspondence, now in that enhanced form, provided the source for the letters published here. This volume also contains occasional references to Lippmann's diaries. He never kept a consecutive diary for any significant length of time, but the Lippmann Collection contains fragments of an intermittent diary from his youth, daybooks of later years that record an occasional comment, and rather extensive day-by-day accounts of conversations he held while traveling abroad for part of most years in the quarter century after 1945. Those conversations served primarily as sources for his syndicated columns, not as expressions of his own views about world affairs.

I have altered the letters I have selected from Lippmann's correspondence in several cosmetic ways. I reorganized them in chronological order — the order in which Lippmann filed them and the only order that places the letters in their historical context. I also divided the letters for convenience into four chronological periods, each roughly representative of biographical and historical phases in Lippmann's life. I have excised the letters to eliminate redundancies and irrelevancies. Where excisions occur, they are marked by an ellipsis, three dots (. . .) in a line. Most often excisions fall at the end of letters that Lippmann concluded with an expression of good wishes or a remark about some private matter. But I have also, without the use of ellipses, eliminated Lippmann's sign-offs, such as "Sincerely yours," except where a usage of that kind constituted an integral part of the last paragraph of the letter, as in some telegrams. Other excisions cut out personal material irrelevant to the basic content of the letter, or repetitive comments about events that Lippmann addressed more directly and extensively in other correspondence included in this volume.

Since Lippmann dictated most of his letters, I have corrected and standardized the spelling in the typed originals. The errors in spelling in those letters were made by his secretaries, whom he never bothered to correct. The punctuation and capitalization, also the work of his secretaries, departed so consistently from any discernible criteria that I have let them remain as they were, for they defy standardization according to current practice, which varies so often from the practices of earlier times. Lippmann was himself erratic about both spelling and punctuation, as his handwritten letters reveal. I have indicated which of the letters in this volume were written by hand and have left Lippmann's orthographic errors intact in these.

The headings that I have added designate the recipient of each letter. My notes to the letters identify the recipients as well as the men and women mentioned in the letters and describe, as economically as feasible, the issues and events to which the letters refer. Some of the notes suggest judgments of my own that I considered pertinent to the issues Lippmann raised. Other notes cite historical or biographical studies that I found particularly salient for the subjects under discussion. Still others refer to books, articles, and columns that Lippmann wrote. The notes and the citations within them are intended to help readers who do not recall the history of the years in which Lippmann lived; they are not intended as critiques of his letters.

I have seen no need to provide a list of all the books and other sources I consulted. Such a list would resemble a working bibliography of sixty years of American history, a bibliography outside the purpose or the scope of this volume. In preparing the notes, I often consulted standard reference works that I have not cited — indispensable compilations such as *Who's Who in America* and *The Readers' Guide to Periodical Literature*, as well as that extraordinary compendium of historical information by William L. Langer et al., *The Encyclopedia of World History* (4th ed., Boston, 1968). More than any other title, I have cited the essential biography of Walter Lippmann by Ronald Steel, *Walter Lippmann and the American Century* (Boston, 1980), which I could have cited twice as often.

This volume begins with an introductory essay that provides my own interpretation of the sources and nature of Lippmann's thought. It offers one way — by no means the only or necessarily the best — to find a developing and coherent pattern in the content of Lippmann's letters, both in themselves and as they relate to his voluminous published writings. The many critics who have analyzed Lippmann's works disagree at least in part with one another, and in some respects I disagree with each of them. With Lippmann, as with other men and women who wrote much of significance, no interpretation can be final or definitive. The interpretation provided here may nevertheless help readers unfamiliar with books by and about Lippmann better to understand and evaluate his letters. My own understanding has profited especially from several studies, no two of them alike. Apart from the Steel biography, they are: the essays, particularly that of Arthur M. Schlesinger, Jr., in Marquis Childs and James Reston, eds., *Walter Lippmann and His Times* (New York,

1959); Charles Forcey, *Crossroads of Liberalism: Croly, Weyl, Lippmann and the Progressive Era, 1900–1925* (New York, 1961); and D. Steven Blum (who is not a relative of mine), *Walter Lippmann: Cosmopolitanism in the Century of Total War* (Ithaca, 1984).

Though none of them bears any responsibility for any of my errors of commission or omission, a number of friends have given me significant help in the preparation of this book. Chester Kerr encouraged me to undertake the editing of Lippmann's letters, as did Arthur Schlesinger, Jr., who confirmed my belief that those letters had a historical importance, and Theodore H. White, who reassured me that the letters of so eminent a journalist deserved the kind of attention ordinarily reserved for statesmen and literary figures. Ronald Steel gave me unrestricted access to the rich and valuable notes and transcripts he used in his biography of Lippmann. The late Frances Davis permitted me to read and to publish letters in her possession from Lippmann to Hazel Albertson, letters Davis herself quoted in *A Fearful Innocence* (Kent, Ohio, 1981). Robert O. Anthony, to whom all scholars interested in Lippmann owe a special debt, gave me his duplicate copies of several of Lippmann's books no longer in print and the benefit of his informed advice. Frank M. Turner made several useful suggestions about the introductory essay. Janet Barnes Lawrence transcribed much of Lippmann's difficult handwriting. The staff of the Division of Manuscripts at the Yale University Library, particularly Lawrence Dowler and Judith Schiff, responded with unfailing patience and generosity to my continued requests. The A. Whitney Griswold Fund of Yale University provided the funds for photoduplication of the letters I selected for study, some twice the number published here, and the Sterling Fund of the same university defrayed the cost of typing the manuscript of this book. The letters in it are published with the permission of the Yale University Library. The Rockefeller Foundation granted me the privilege of a month at its conference center in Bellagio, Italy, where I began the editing of the letters under conditions of memorable comfort and beauty. Most important, Anne S. Bittker, in effect the assistant editor of this volume, not only typed the manuscript but also helped with the editorial procedures I have described and, during several months while I was incapacitated, kept up the necessary research for the notes for the letters. Without her solicitous collaboration, I could not have completed the task.

John Morton Blum

New Haven, 1985

Introduction

WALTER LIPPMANN AND THE
PROBLEM OF ORDER

EVEN IN HIS CHILDHOOD, at the turn of the century, Walter Lippmann led an ordered life. A grade school classmate recalled that "what made Walter special was his extraordinary intellectual capacity and discipline."[1] Six decades later, Lippmann's "reflective and disciplined life" impressed a fellow journalist: "His life is not commanded by events. . . . If you ask him on New Year's Eve what he is going to do the coming year, the chances are that he has a fully detailed plan worked out."[2] By the 1950s Lippmann's days in Washington had come to follow a strict routine: before nine o'clock, breakfast and the morning papers; then two or more hours of concentration in the uninterrupted silence of his soundproof study, where he drafted his columns before dictating them for transcription; then the mail, luncheon with a friend or notable, and an early afternoon of recreation; thereafter a rest, reflection about future columns or books, and dinner, often in the company of men and women of station and influence. Appointments with the same kind of people punctuated the days he spent traveling in Europe, days planned in deliberate detail long before his journey. So firm were those plans that Lippmann in 1961 declined a request to change the date of his appointment with Soviet Premier Nikita Khrushchev, who then bent to Lippmann's convenience.

The order that Lippmann imposed on himself and his circle had long seemed to those who knew him to reflect his inner being. Mabel Dodge, the keeper of New York's most celebrated salon, one Lippmann often frequented, found him "in possession of himself. There was no incontinence there, no flowing sensuality."[3] And John Reed, his radical and romantic Harvard classmate, had characterized the young Lippmann's manner in lines of bemused verse, appropriate both when they were written and indefinitely thereafter: "But were there one / Who builds a world, and leaves out all the fun — / Who dreams a fragrant gorgeous infinite, / And then leaves all the color out of it — / Who wants to make the human race, and me, / March to a geometric Q.E.D. — / Who but must laugh, if such a man there be? / Who would not weep, if Walter L. were he?"[4]

Yet the young Lippmann, as Mabel Dodge discerned, had a capacity for deep and spontaneous sympathy for the impoverished and the oppressed. To his intimates, he also revealed a guarded romanticism redolent in expression of the Germanic cultural set of his childhood home. He felt that sentimentality himself in his response to music. "I am," Lippmann wrote, "the perfect example for Santayana's remark about musical appreciation being for most persons 'a drowsy revery interrupted by nervous thrills.' "[5] He romanticized his first courtship. "You're the only girl I ever knew," he wrote Lucile Elsas when he was eighteen, "who loved beauty, not for the sake of languorous dreaminess, but because beauty was a part of existence, — tell me if this attitude towards nature is not the last word in idealism."[6] Lippmann's own dreamy idealizations outran their relationship, for though he apparently never kissed her, much less proposed to her, he resented her decision to marry another man.

He had a second crush on a somewhat older woman, Hazel Albertson, the young wife of his friend Ralph Albertson, who was the father of Lippmann's future bride. Hazel, "a superior flirt," charmed the Harvard undergraduates who lounged about the Albertson farm near Boston during their long discussions about politics and life. She liked Lippmann, so articulate, so carefully distanced from the others, so formally attired even at leisure in the country. On account of his rather chubby appearance and his shy detachment, she called him "Buddha." She also warned him against self-satisfaction while she allowed him to address her by pet names and in his letters to trade affectionate "pinches" with her. For his part, Lippmann overlooked Hazel's endemic disorganization in his gratitude for her fond understanding. He also outgrew her. Her romantic attachment to good causes conflicted with his sense of reality, particularly with his decision, after a brief experience with socialism in practice, to organize his life for other purposes.[7]

The young Lippmann — the Buddha, on the surface serene, already wise — became the older Lippmann, renowned, organized, prophetic. But neither young nor old did Lippmann lack normal human qualities: ambition, sentiment, passion. The last of these he controlled so tightly that it did not much mark his life until his love affair, in his middle years, with Helen Armstrong, who became his second wife. Lippmann always knew that passion was there, and almost always he succeeded in disciplining it. His control satisfied his sense of the fitness of things, not for himself only but for mankind, for he was like other social critics in seeing human nature largely through the lenses of his own experience. From that sense of self, perhaps as much as from the study of politics and philosophy, Lippmann fashioned his public discourses and devised his own humanistic ethic. In the process, he had to come to grips with himself, his past, and his preferred social role.

*

In the formulation of his beliefs and the development of his style, Judaism, the religion of Lippmann's youth, had little influence. By the time he was an undergraduate at Harvard, he had turned away from his parents' synagogue, Temple Emanu-El in New York City. There, in his view, the tenets of Reform Judaism wrapped a conventional moral code in an antiseptic creed. That creed he considered to be divorced from the zealous faith of traditional Jewry and adapted to the outlook of a socially mobile middle class acculturated in American secularism. Lippmann, as he wrote Lucile Elsas, would have none of it: "Can we tell them that the Temple Emanu-el exhibition is a piece of blatant hypocrisy? that its mechanical service, its bromidic interpretation, its drawing room atmosphere of gentility, its underlying snobbishness, which makes it an exclusive organization for the wealthy, strangle all the religion that is in us? Can we tell our friends — pillars of the Church, all of them — that . . . a visitor in New York on Yom Kippur, fled from the temple to St. Patrick's Cathedral to find there a religious atmosphere?"[8] Religion, Lippmann continued, had to "make life richer, fuller, more splendid . . . touch life at every point, thus creating a harmony between the soul of man and the stars. . . . The scheduled prayer . . . is no prayer at all. . . . The truly religious man needs only the bright sun . . . and the blue beyond blue of the clear night to make him happy and worshipful." The beauty of friends and art increased devotion, as did "a passion for deed," for progress.[9]

Lippmann felt uncomfortable alike with "the dead hand of the past," which he found in Judaism, and with "that rather Jewish feeling of not belonging." As he wrote Helen Armstrong years later, "I have never been oppressed by it. . . . I have never in my life been able to discover in myself any feeling of being disqualified for anything I cared about, and . . . I can find nothing in myself which responds to the specific Jewish ethos in religion or culture as it appears in the Old Testament. . . . I have understood the classical and Christian heritage and feel it to be mine, and always have."[10]

That was a perceptive statement. As a schoolboy, Lippmann had excelled at Latin and Greek. The heritage he described infused Harvard — especially in the courses Lippmann took, in his informal friendship with William James, who had taught at the university, and in his association with James's celebrated colleague George Santayana, the skeptical philosopher whose acid analyses of conventional religion floated on his own humane convictions. Discontented with Judaism, involved in the larger world of American culture, Lippmann for most of his life was an assimilationist, a Jew who renounced both the sustaining certitudes and the constraining proscriptions of Judaism. He could validly claim a classical Christian heritage, for he absorbed one. Not surprisingly, the wives he chose were one a Protestant, the other a Catholic.

Assimilation did not necessarily imply anti-Semitism, though the two sometimes resembled each other. In Lippmann's case, positions that on occasion appeared anti-Semitic may have had different origins, usually political. For example, he was never a Zionist, because he believed that the presence of an independent Jewish state in the Middle East was bound to create a disequilibrium potentially threatening to American interests. Some of his critics considered his columns culpably silent about the Holocaust, for he chose to write about other matters — those that he believed American policy could affect. The United States could not, in his view, prevent Hitler's "final solution" except by winning the war. Lippmann's indifference, during World War II, to the civil rights and human rights of Jews and Japanese-Americans stemmed not from calculated anti-Semitism or racism but from his preoccupation — like Franklin Roosevelt's and Winston Churchill's — with the strategy of victory and of peace making. As Lippmann saw it, he was a realist; some other men discerned a different reality.

Lippmann's posture suggested at least a callousness, which had earlier assumed an anti-Semitic form in his remarks about Harvard's quota on the admission of Jews.[11] Though he said that he disapproved of quotas, he supported restricting the number of Jews admitted in order to facilitate mutual accommodation among various student groups, a process he considered necessary in undergraduate life. To that end, he proposed an admissions test that would have militated against the admission of Jews. The idea was at best disingenuous.

Lippmann's rejection of Judaism left him, as he had suggested it should, with no faith in any church, or indeed in any supernatural authority, though he remained persuaded of the religious experience available in nature. He consciously substituted secular beliefs for conventional faith. As he had put it to Lucile Elsas, religion for him was "expressed in Socialism, Pragmatism, and poetry," a trinity a bright undergraduate might well have admired; disdainful of "the tinsel of the uppercrust of society with its enormous wealth," Lippmann had "come around to Socialism as a creed."[12] He had rejected not just Judaism but the haute bourgeoisie and, as it worked out, his family as well as their conventions. Privileged though he had been as an only child, Lippmann as an adult revealed little affection for either his mother, "a little too ambitious and worthy," or his father, a successful businessman "without much color or force."[13] Neither provided an attractive model. Lippmann selected instead, though always only briefly, models of his own from among the progressive reformers, the intellectuals, and the avant-garde of his young manhood. Then to them, to their goals — which also became his, temporarily to socialism as well as to pragmatism and poetry — he attributed at times a mystical aura. It was as close as he came to having a religion.

Though Lippmann was loath to talk about his inner self, his understanding of that self and of society rested on a foundation of modern psychology, including Freudian psychology. He could become tiresome about that subject. "I wish Walter Lippmann would forget Freud for a little," Harold Laski, the British political scientist, wrote in 1916, "— just a little."[14] But Lippmann considered Freud a successor in insight and influence to Sir Isaac Newton, whose theories about physics had shaped so much of eighteenth-century political thought, and to Charles Darwin, whose ideas about evolution had similarly affected the nineteenth century. In the twentieth century, an understanding of politics depended on "an objective understanding of what we really are."[15] On that account, Lippmann wrote *A Preface to Morals* (1929), his effort to establish a basis for morality in the absence of traditional faith.

"We can begin to see," Lippmann wrote near the end of *A Preface to Morals*, ". . . that what the sages have prophesied as high religion, what psychologists delineate as matured personality, and the disinterestedness which the Great Society requires for its practical fulfillment, are all of a piece, and are the basic elements of a modern morality."[16] "The Great Society," a phrase Lippmann had borrowed from Graham Wallas, would objectify the social ideas he valued. "A matured personality," in a Freudian sense, would discipline its impulses to social use. Both polity and individual would substitute a humanism rooted in science and reason for now implausible religious belief.

"An understanding of what we really are" occupied Lippmann in *A Preface to Morals*, of which the first quarter continually struck apparently autobiographical notes that disclosed much about the author, perhaps inadvertently on his part. Critics at the time remarked that the book spoke the mind of an unbelieving Jew making a nonreligious case for the Judeo-Christian ethic. The text seemed to start that way: "Among those who no longer believe in the religion of their fathers, some are proudly defiant, and many are indifferent. But there are also a few, perhaps an increasing number, who feel that there is a vacancy in their lives. This inquiry . . . is concerned with those who are perplexed by the consequences of their own irreligion."[17]

Those who were no longer bound by orthodoxy, Lippmann observed, confronted "the greatest difficulties." They missed "the gifts of a vital religion," the conviction that there was "an order in the universe which justified their lives because they were part of it." As he put it, "the acids of modernity have dissolved that order for many of us," but without dissolving the needs religion had satisfied. He sought, therefore, a substitute for religion.[18]

In the past, "the search for moral guidance" independent of "external authority" had invariably ended in the acknowledgment of some new authority. Now modern science made it impossible to "reconstruct an enduring orthodoxy, a God of the ancient faith . . . God the Father, the Lawgiver, the Judge." Modern churchmen no longer believed literally in the God of Genesis, and modern biblical criticism had eroded belief in "an historic drama . . . enacted in Palestine nineteen hundred years ago." Quoting Santayana, Lippmann repeated his point: " 'The idea that religion contains a literal, not a symbolic representation of truth and life is simply an impossible idea.' "[19]

Modern men, nevertheless, did not lack a "sense of mystery, of majesty, of terror, and of wonder." What was missing was "the testimony of faith." As Lippmann characteristically understood it, faith had always related to men's experience with government. Since an Asiatic people naturally imagined a divine government as despotic, Yahweh in the Old Testament was "very evi-

dently an oriental monarch inclined to be somewhat moody and vain." Lippmann
had long since disavowed that God. He had never put credence in the feudal
lord whom God resembled, as he saw it, in medieval Christianity, or in the
God of the Enlightenment, who reigned without ruling. He was equally dissatisfied with that modern God who was deemed to be "the élan vital within
the extraordinary person." "With the best will in the world," Lippmann held,
modern man (of whom he was one) found himself "not quite believing."[20]

To that point, *A Preface to Morals* had dwelt upon Lippmann's personal
predicament, which was by no means his alone. From that point, Lippmann
suggested for modern man his own solution, one that postulated an intellectual basis for morals and an intellectual order, a "disinterestedness," essential
for moral behavior. Traditional moral commandments, he argued, had worked
in "some rough way" as long as people had lived close to the soil. But ways
of life had changed; morality could no longer be imposed by faith or by habit.
Instead the "difference between good and evil" had to become a difference
"which men themselves recognize and understand." Happiness had to be an
"intelligible consequence"; virtue, to be "willed out of conviction and desire."
That was a Jamesian assertion demanding not belief but testing. "Such a morality," Lippmann wrote, "may properly be called humanism, for it is centered
not in superhuman but in human nature." In that formulation, man faced the
difficult but unavoidable obligation of making the will conform to "the surest
knowledge of the conditions of human happiness." The orderliness, the control so important to Lippmann, imbued the last sentence of his analysis. When
men, he wrote, "find that they no longer believe seriously and deeply that
they are governed from heaven, there is an anarchy in their souls until by
conscious effort they find ways of governing themselves."[21]

Modern man, Lippmann continued in the second half of his study, freed as
he was from superstition, had no further cause to be afraid of evil. Evil continued to exist "only because we feel it to be painful," a condition, once understood, that allowed man to dissociate that feeling from evil. That was "a momentous achievement in the inner life of man. To be able to observe our own
feelings as if they were objective facts, to detach ourselves from our fears,
hates, and lusts, to examine them, identify them, understand their origins,
and finally, to judge them, is somehow to rob them of their imperiousness.
. . . They no longer dominate the whole field of consciousness . . . no longer
. . . command the whole energy of our being."[22]

The psychological mechanism he was describing, Lippmann wrote, had been
commended by the philosophers of antiquity and elaborated by the discoveries
of Freud. "To become detached from one's passions," he went on, "and to
understand them consciously is to render them disinterested. A disinterested
mind is harmonious with itself and with reality." The principle of humanism,
he concluded, was "detachment, understanding, and disinterestedness in the
presence of reality itself."[23]

In the last chapter of *A Preface to Morals,* Lippmann examined the idea of disinterestedness as "implicit and necessary" in "the great phases of human interest, in business, in government, and in sexual relations." On the subject of love, he concluded that "by the happy ordering of their personal affections" (his stress on order again), men and women could "establish the type and the quality and the direction of their desires for all things." In a parallel passage, he had written that "the prime business of government" was not to divert the affairs of the community, but "to harmonize the direction which the community gives to its affairs." To that purpose, the great statesman was "bound to act boldly in advance of his constituents. When he does this, he stakes his judgment as to what the people will in the end find good against what the people happen ardently to desire. This capacity to act upon the hidden realities of a situation . . . is the essence of statesmanship." It was also, for Lippmann, the essence of an individual life.[24]

As a political theorist, as a journalist and columnist, Lippmann strove to realize his ideal of disinterestedness. He recognized a moral responsibility to base his commentaries upon reality divested of the distortions of emotions. Of course he did not always succeed, but his continuing effort made his failures at the worst those of a temporarily lapsed humanist, a secular sinner. Lippmann would never have denied his fallibility or his susceptibility to emotions common to all men. At the simplest level, he found pleasure in graceful entertainments — in the heaven that was "Green Pastures," in the bear who was Winnie-the-Pooh. On a grander scale, the "happy ordering" of his inner self took expression, both before and after he wrote *A Preface to Morals*, in his continual assay in political theory.

Even as a young man, only several years out of college, Lippmann revealed the exceptional intelligence and broad learning that marked him always. Those traits, along with his concern for the nonrational, the instinctive, marked *A Preface to Politics* (1913), his first book, published when he was twenty-four. A youthful work, it catalogued, sometimes indiscriminately, the ideas of authors who had aroused his interest, among them William James, George Santayana, the French philosopher Henri Bergson, Sigmund Freud, and especially Graham Wallas, the most influential of Lippmann's teachers. Following Wallas, Lippmann took human nature as the basis for politics and read human nature as illogical. On that premise, he departed, of course, from eighteenth- and much nineteenth-century political theory, with its assumption of rationality in politics and other forms of human behavior. James, Santayana, Bergson, and others familiar to Lippmann had questioned that assumption, while Freud, whose early work much impressed Lippmann, demolished it.

Writing, as Lippmann was, in "an attempt to sketch an attitude toward statecraft,"[25] not to define a constitution or a program, he tested his approach not only in theory but in the context of concrete political experience — his own especially. He had served briefly as an assistant to the newly elected

Socialist mayor of Schenectady. His quick disenchantment with the banal practicalities of local politics provided the foundation for his criticism of socialism. His view of the nature of man ("all the passions of men are the motive powers of a fine life")[26] underlay his dismissal not just of a socialism he found dull but, more important, of Marxist doctrine altogether — though he praised Marx's own prophetic genius.

Most often Lippmann cited examples of his contention that "human nature seems to have wants that must be filled. If nobody else supplies them, the devil will."[27] Consequently, he reasoned, taboos were ineffectual. Building on James's concept of a "moral equivalent of war," Lippmann called for a moral equivalent of evil, a device to redirect human impulses that could not be contained. The mayor of Milwaukee, he wrote, had to that end provided public dance halls to compete with the sleazy private dance halls of that city. The Chicago report on vice, to which Lippmann devoted two chapters, showed "that lust has a thousand avenues."[28] The report proposed the suppression of prostitution. That would do no good, Lippmann argued, unless new routes were opened for the release of lust. The report, in his opinion, "studied a human problem but left humanity out." Sex, Lippmann explained, here following Freud, was an instinct "which can be transmuted and turned into one of the values of life."[29] Jane Addams at Hull House had abetted that transformation by providing access to the arts and crafts, "other methods of expression that lust can seek."[30]

That, for Lippmann, was the essence of statecraft. Practical moralist that he then was, he turned Freud's theory of sublimation, as he would later turn it again and again, into a lesson in politics. He recommended to his readers his own self-conscious purpose: to "ventilate society with frankness, and fill life with play and art . . . with passions which hold and suffuse the imagination"[31] — a revolutionary task.

For Lippmann, those who merely followed precedent, "the routineers," the keepers of conventions, could not adapt government to modern conditions. For that task he looked to the "inventors," of whom he saw himself as one. Those inventors, in the manner of William James, regarded "all social organizations as an instrument."[32] They provided the natural leadership society needed, as Theodore Roosevelt had during his presidency. Under the control of inventors, Lippmann wrote, modern corporations, modern labor unions, indeed even the federal government would serve as instruments for social, economic, and political reforms. The inventors — Lippmann himself not the least — were, like Roosevelt, committed opponents of the status quo.

A Preface to Politics commended at once a politics of sublimation and a politics of energy, of dedication. Metaphorically, in his own striving, Lippmann practiced both. "If we have the vigor," he had written while he was at work on the book, "we find joy in effort itself. . . . An odyssey that never ends — it's not an unmixed joy. . . . In a personal way I am very happy — now especially. There is so much to love and do in the world — so much that after all does answer to our needs."[33] A man of emotions was the young Lippmann, but a man of intellect and morality, too, a man of emotions under control.

The condition of control seemed to Lippmann, as his next book indicated, no less desirable in politics. "Scientific invention and blind social currents," he wrote in his introduction to *Drift and Mastery* (1914), "have made the old authority impossible. . . . The dominant forces in our world are not the sacredness of property, nor the intellectual leadership of the priest; they are not . . . Victorian sentiment, New England respectability, the Republican Party." On the contrary, he asserted, enlisting with youth in its political discontents, *"the rebel program is stated. . . .* Our time . . . believes in change." But even youth was "somewhat stunned by the rarified atmosphere" of the day. Consequently the "battle for us . . . lies against the chaos of a new freedom."[34]

That disorder arose because "human beings . . . cling passionately to the emotion of certainty" in their social and political as well as their personal behavior. Bothered by the resulting "unrest," or "drift," Lippmann searched "for the conditions of mastery" that would "contribute to a conscious revolution."[35]

In large measure, *Drift and Mastery* spoke directly to the political issues of the day. It attacked President Woodrow Wilson's program, the New Freedom, which Lippmann considered anachronistic. Conversely he commended Theodore Roosevelt's program, the New Nationalism, the progressive charter to which he, like the other founders of *The New Republic*, subscribed. As he did as an editor of that journal, so in his new book Lippmann criticized private commercialism. Based on the profit motive, it had inaugurated modern industry but become "antiquated" and "feeble" as a method of realizing the promise of industry. Labor unions and consumer cooperatives expressed the social dissatisfaction with commercialism, as also did the changing structure of industry itself.

"The huge corporation, the integrated industry, production for a world market," Lippmann contended, echoing Graham Wallas, were part of "a general change of social scale." That new scale had produced "a new kind of businessman," for the giant corporation had to have managers of broad interests and abilities — managers able "to preserve intimate contact with physicists and chemists . . . to deal with huge masses of workingmen . . . to think about the kind of training our public schools give . . . to consider . . . the psychology of races . . . the structure of credit."

Managers had also to educate and pacify "thousands of ignorant stockholders," the owners of corporations. Consequently administration was "becoming an applied science, capable of devising executive methods for dealing with tremendous units." Since shareholders lacked the competence to exercise that function, the great corporations had separated ownership from management and concentrated control under the managers. In that sense, "most of the rights of property had already disappeared."[36]

With that conclusion, Lippmann defined a satisfying substitute for the un-dergraduate socialism he had abandoned. As he often remarked, he had never been a Marxist. His youthful socialism had derived from the beliefs of the English Fabians, Wallas particularly. It envisaged a humane society with pub-lic programs to combat poverty, with institutional restraints (such as labor unions) on predatory capitalism, with ample public support and social space for the arts — all under the direction of men and women of exceptional intel-ligence and generous sympathy. Lippmann both sought and expected a place within that elite. His experience with urban socialism in Schenectady had been disillusioning because he had found himself a petty bureaucrat, not a philos-opher prince. In *Drift and Mastery,* he joined the new royalty of industry, the managers who gave direction to the vital institutions of modernity. They had altered the nature of property ownership more to his satisfaction than could conventional socialism.

That alteration took many shapes. "The right to fix rates," Lippmann wrote, "has been absorbed by the state; the right to fix wages is conditioned by very powerful unions." Those changes so threatened traditional prospects for profit that stockholders in railroads might soon be eager "to give up the few vestiges of private property which are left to them, if they can secure instead govern-ment bonds." Government ownership in that case would provide a haven for rentiers. What had happened to the railroads, Lippmann predicted, "is merely a demonstration of what is likely to happen to the other great industries. . . . Private property will melt away; its functions will be taken over by . . . salar-ied men . . . government commissions . . . labor unions."[37]

Obviously then, the "collectivism" of the modern corporation was due, not to the institution of private property but "to the fact that management is autocratic, that administrators are . . . given power adequate to their respon-sibility. When governments are willing to pursue that course, they can be just as efficient."[38]

But Lippmann recognized a major problem for government. Because of the diffusion of stock ownership, corporate management had escaped a challenge from "decadent stockholders." Governments would be less free of their con-stituencies. "The real problem of collectivism," Lippmann wrote, "is the dif-ficulty of combining popular control with administrative power."[39] Lippmann had no confidence in the populace. "The existence of great masses of unorga-nized, perhaps unorganizable workers" imperiled the nation, he believed, for they would foment "street fights . . . beatings . . . sabotage . . . threats to order." Consequently he was convinced of the indispensability of leadership by an administrative elite who would introduce "order and purpose" in busi-ness and government alike.[40]

A modern nation, Lippmann continued, could not be built "out of Georgia crackers, poverty-stricken negroes, the homeless and helpless of great cities. They make a governing class essential." That class alone could provide the essential guidance for society: "This is what mastery means: the substitution of conscious intent for unconscious striving." Only those who could govern themselves qualified as members of the governing class: "What civilized men aim at is . . . a frank recognition of desire, disciplined by a knowledge of what is possible, and ordered by the conscious purpose of their lives."[41]

The mastery that Lippmann sought was obviously incompatible with popular democracy, just as the self-discipline he practiced was beyond the reach of most men and women. As one of Lippmann's shrewdest critics put it: "Never was he able to think of himself as a man no more important than other men."[42] And never was he at ease with the emotions of the mass of men.

The depth of those emotions, and the federal government's facility in arousing and exploiting them, characterized American experience both as a neutral and later as a belligerent in World War I. Lippmann was involved in those years both in generating official propaganda and in devising terms for an enduring peace, terms that were lost in the heat of clashing chauvinisms. The experience provided both desolate confirmation of his earlier doubts about the populace and a disturbing contradiction to his earlier confidence in the organized intelligence of a governing class. The problem of order became more exigent in the glare of the furnace of war.

Like almost all Americans and many Europeans, Lippmann was not prepared intellectually or emotionally for the outbreak of war in Europe in August 1914. "It all came so incredibly fast," he wrote from England in September.[43] He had been "overcome with a general feeling of futility," he confided to his diary, where he went on to define his own self-constituted role: "My own part in this is to understand world-politics, to be interested in National and Military affairs, and to get away from the old liberalism which concentrates entirely on liberal problems. We cannot lose all that but see now that our really civilized effort is set in a structure of raw necessity."[44]

A year of study led Lippmann to conclude that the great issues of world order resembled those of domestic order. "I've learned a lot," he wrote Graham Wallas on August 5, 1915. "I feel now as if I had never before risen above the problems of a district nurse, a middle western political reformer, and an amiable civic enthusiast. . . . I've come to see that international politics is not essentially different from 'domestic' politics. . . . They are phases and aspects of one another."[45]

As Lippmann also said, he distrusted simplistic analogies. It did not necessarily follow, as so many British and American statesmen seemed to think, that world federation would develop as federalism had among the thirteen original American states. Those states, for one example, had governed property common to them all during the period of the Articles of Confederation. Since the Western nations had no such property, it would be necessary in the postwar settlement to establish a number of "internationalizations." Further, "the dangers of perverted nationalism" would threaten the making of peace and the establishment of order.[46] The breakup of Austria, Lippmann believed, was "a real world tragedy. Perhaps one should say, the conquest of Austria by Hungary."[47] The ethnic aspirations to nationhood of the several peoples of the Hungarian kingdom constituted exactly the kind of nationalism Lippmann feared. Ethnic particularism, he wrote, resembled the traditional profit motive among firms in American industry. That particularism impeded the kind of collectivism subject to intelligent management that he had so praised in *Drift and Mastery*.

Most of all, Lippmann in 1915 began to stress sea power. The use of sea power by the belligerents had come to command diplomacy by provoking American efforts to limit Great Britain's blockade of Germany and to control German submarine warfare. The German definition of freedom of the seas, Lippmann wrote Wallas, meant "freedom in time of war" — by implication freedom to use submarines without restriction. That was a freedom of chaos, Lippmann continued, because Great Britain would struggle to prevent it. "The whole discussion," he added, "is vitiated . . . by the old notion that freedom can be had by competition rather than cooperation." British sea power, he concluded, "is the decisive factor in the future arrangement of the globe but I personally prefer its semi-benevolent autocracy to the anarchy of 'equal.' And I am prepared to have the U.S. join with Britain in the control of the seas, rather than see a race of 'sovereign states' oscillating in insecure 'balance.' "[48] He had come to support an Anglo-American alliance, a position from which he never departed.

Lippmann's reflections about the war during its first year formed the basis of his book *The Stakes of Diplomacy* (1915). The substance of that work followed the contours of his letters, especially about sea power and his concept of internationalizations. The latter prospect seemed to him the best basis for postwar world order. "The crux of our problem," he wrote, "is whether the flag is to follow trade . . . the essence, the power, the prestige of imperialism depend upon the theory that the flag covers its citizens in backward territory."[49] The task of internationalism was to destroy that excuse. Further, any postwar organization could "command a world patriotism," an essential sentiment, only by "proving its usefulness."[50] To attain the objectives he had described, Lippmann proposed the establishment of a number of continuing conferences to solve regional problems — as the Algeciras Conference temporarily had in its decisions about Morocco in 1906.[51]

He also suggested establishing protectorates like that of the United States in Haiti. "The chief task of diplomacy," Lippmann maintained in a characteristic assertion, was the organization of disorderly areas. Protectorates would create "efficient authority in weak states." Concurrently, the development of international political agencies, his continuing commissions, would control "imperialistic competition" and "reorganize the country under joint supervision." In that role, the commissions would proceed by "employing experts from the developed nations" who would be responsible to the "Diplomatic Body" of the supervised nation. From that experience "would arise the beginnings of a world state."[52]

As Lippmann saw it, that world state would not soon resemble a "Federation of Mankind." Rather, at the outset, it would consist of a federation of Western powers. It was "likely to be unequal, coercive, manipulative, and unsatisfactory." Only after demonstrated usefulness could it become more inclusive and benign. Yet peace was "to be had as a result of wise organization" and of a beginning that would lead, as in the United States under the Constitution, to the peaceful resolution of differences between nations by means of elections. "We do by elections," Lippmann said of the forty-eight states, "what sovereign states do by war." Consequently "the supreme task of world politics" was "a satisfactory organization of mankind." Peace would then prevail not because of "the abolition of force" but because of "its sublimation."[53]

With that conclusion, Lippmann, at least by implication, drew concentric Freudian rings.[54] Sublimation would create order for the individual, the state, and the world of nations alike. For all of them, sublimation, as he conceived of it, was a necessary means to protect the civility and rationality essential to their well-being.

As the war drew toward its close, Lippmann's formulations for an enduring peace clashed in several respects with those of Woodrow Wilson, particularly with Wilson's notions about absolute freedom of the seas, with his support for ethnic self-determination, and with his advocacy of a world confederation — his League of Nations. Lippmann had served on Colonel Edward M. House's Inquiry, the semi-official group preparing analyses of international problems for Wilson's use in making peace, but the president did not much consult the resulting studies during his tribulations at the Paris Conference. The treaty negotiated there and signed at Versailles fell short of Lippmann's expectations. In an article in *The New Republic*, later reprinted as *The Political Scene*, Lippmann mounted an attack that was part of a larger charge against the treaty.

The Treaty of Versailles, Lippmann held, would not prevent disorder in Europe. *The Political Scene* exhorted the Western democracies to "devote themselves unreservedly" to making a cooperative peace in the face of "international revolution." With bolshevism gaining in Russia and spreading westward, Wilson's proposals lacked "the precision and downrightness" of both the revolution and the strenuous resistance to it among European powers. In destroying the German Empire, Lippmann argued, the Allies had torn down "the authority which rules in central and eastern Europe. . . . It was a vile authority, but it was the existing authority in law and fact." Its demise left "chaos . . . wild and dangerous, perhaps infectious." Because the military campaigns of 1918 had become revolutionary in their effect, Wilson's proposals provided an insufficient basis for a stable peace. Both in international and domestic affairs, Wilson's ideas rested on "the Old Manchester" — the mechanistic conceptions that Lippmann had long considered anachronistic.[55]

Like Jan Smuts, the South African statesman, Lippmann viewed Wilson's League as both essential and inadequate. On the broadest scale, the League, Lippmann wrote, would assume the functions he had assigned to his continuing commissions. But along with many, perhaps most, other Americans, Lippmann disliked many of the terms of the Treaty of Versailles, particularly the ethnic particularism it endorsed (though much of that particularism could not have been prevented). He also criticized the Covenant of the League, especially Article X. That article guaranteed the political independence and territorial integrity of members of the League. Wilson believed that guarantee would make the League an instrument for the effective mobilization of the opinion of the world against any aggressive nation. In contrast Lippmann feared the guarantee would make the League an instrument for preserving an unsatisfactory status quo (and by and large, he proved correct). Lippmann also argued that if the United States approved the treaty and the League, Congress would be forced to "abandon power over foreign affairs." He therefore urged the Senate to "insist upon representation of the legislature in the structure of the League"[56] — a demand Wilson would not contemplate.

As he had in 1915, so again in 1919 Lippmann contended that Anglo-American sea power would best provide a foundation for a lasting peace. He did not mean to restore the nineteenth-century balance of power. Rather, as he saw it, the victory of 1918 had left Great Britain and the United States as "the two great states with the resources and the wealth for really modern munitions manufacture." If the two nations worked out "their common purposes, then such a preponderance of power is created as to make all notion of a balance impossible. An Anglo-American entente means the substitution of a pool for a balance, and in that pool will be found the ultimate force upon which rests the League of Nations. The reason for this is that they exercise a form of force — sea power — which is irresistible in conflict." Sea power, Lippmann went on, "can be all-powerful without destroying the liberties of the nation which exercises it, and only free peoples can be trusted with sea power."[57]

The Covenant of the League provided the procedure "to insure delay accompanied by publicity" in the event of a dispute between nations. During that delay, a democratic power uninvolved in the dispute, probably the United States, could generate the publicity that would convince the members of the League to use the "pooling of force" — Anglo-American sea power — to end the emergency. Here Lippmann was linking Wilson's League with an Anglo-American alliance, a combination designed to establish and maintain world order — to serve, as it were, as a substitute for the sublimation that the rival powers of Europe and Asia were still too hostile to experience.

In his letters, Lippmann had referred to the decisions at Paris as "an impossible settlement"[58] that would "provoke a class war."[59] That conviction and a growing bitterness about Wilson, as well as his own ideas, prompted him to cooperate with Senator Hiram Johnson and others in their fierce opposition to the treaty and the League. But Lippmann was never an isolationist. No one concerned about world order could be. Possibly his political behavior detracted from his trenchant analyses, but he was not alone. The passions generated by the war and by the fight over the treaty temporarily cost many men, Lippmann not the least, their normal civility.

During the war, Lippmann had been prepared to forgo absolute freedom of speech for the sake of suppressing disloyalty or imposing a tolerant censorship, but he had also warned against official repression of criticism and poisonous official propaganda. "Freedom of thought and speech," he wrote in 1919, "present themselves in a new light and raise new problems because of the discovery that opinion can be manufactured."[60] That discovery, a part of his own experience with the dissemination of propaganda, led him to explore the interaction of public opinion and government in *Liberty and the News* (1920). Because government could control opinion and thereby avoid its negative impact, Lippmann concluded that freedom of expression was no longer enough. It was necessary also for the public to have access to accurate information. His investigations had disclosed that newspapers, even the *New York Times*, had supplied biased accounts of bolshevism in Russia. He made a plea, therefore, for "unaltered data . . . disinterested fact." Apparently satisfied that men would respond rationally to accurate facts, Lippmann, in a typical recommendation, proposed the creation of an independent research organization to build a system for supplying neutral information.[61]

An interpreter rather than a reporter of news, Lippmann in 1922 became the chief of the editorial page of the *New York World*, a Democratic newspaper notable for its sprightly style and social consciousness. His new role reflected his new focus. The bias of the reader, he now observed, would filter even trustworthy news. That insight informed *Public Opinion* (1922), probably his most enduring and most completely original book. There he began by contrasting reality and illusion. Freud's study of dreams, he wrote, had illuminated the process by which a pseudo-environment was put together. "Whatever we believe to be a true picture," Lippmann observed, "we treat as if it were the environment itself." So it had been in recent years: "We can best understand the furies of war and politics by remembering that almost the whole of each party believes absolutely in its picture of the opposition, that it takes as fact, not what is, but what it supposes to be fact."[62]

Symbols, particularly stereotypes, which Lippmann addressed at length, were the carriers of those pictures. The symbols were subject "to check and comparison and argument" in ordinary times, but not in times of stress, especially when the government used the symbols to promote its own objectives. During the war and the postwar period of hysteria, individuals had succumbed to a distorted pattern of behavior: "the casual fact, the creative imagination, the will to believe, and out of these three elements a counterfeit of reality to which there was a violent instinctive response."[63] An analysis of public opinion had to take into account "the triangular relationship between the scene of action, the human picture of that scene, and the human response to that picture."

The fictions men substituted for reality, moreover, "determined a very great deal of men's political behavior."[64]

Even after wartime propaganda and censorship had ended, Lippmann continued, an artificial censorship persisted because of "the limitations of social contact, the comparatively meager time available each day for paying attention to public affairs." Distortions resulted "because events have to be compressed into very short messages," because of "the difficulty of making a small vocabulary express a complicated world," because of "the fear of facing those facts which seem to threaten the established routine of men's lives. Consequently representative government could not work successfully "unless there is an independent, expert organization for making unseen facts intelligible to those who have to make the decisions."[65] Lippmann had altered the diagnosis since his *Liberty and the News* but prescribed the same remedy, one in which he could assume a major role.

He also returned to a theme that he had used before. Popular democracy, he maintained, could not provide the check necessary to separate illusion from reality, a check necessary also for making decisions about important matters of state. "The mass of absolutely illiterate, of feeble-minded, grossly neurotic, undernourished and frustrated individuals," he wrote, "is very considerable, much more considerable . . . than we generally suppose." Since that had been the case even in Thomas Jefferson's time, Jefferson had been deluded in putting his faith in the people. Now it was "no longer possible . . . to believe in the original dogma of democracy: that the knowledge needed for the management of human affairs comes up spontaneously from the human heart."[66]

"The specialized class" to which Lippmann looked instead to "report the realities of public life" would replace the "augurs, priests, elders" of earlier eras (the very group he condemned in *A Preface to Morals*). The new specialized class consisted of "statisticians, accountants, auditors . . . engineers . . . scientific managers . . . research men." They and their equivalents in other callings constituted the only group trained to make the "Great Society intelligible to those who manage it." They served to "prepare the facts for the men of action."[67]

In *The Phantom Public* (1925), an important sequel to *Public Opinion*, Lippmann rephrased the argument of the earlier book and again denied any "ethical superiority" in majority rule. Repeating a Freudian metaphor he had used earlier, he wrote that an election "based on the principle of majority rule is historically and practically a sublimated and denatured civil war, a paper mobilization without physical violence." Though elections were only a social tranquilizer, public opinion in a time of stress served as a "resolve of force. . . . Public opinion in its highest ideal will defend those who are prepared to act on their reason against the interrupting force of those who merely assert their role." But that kind of result would be neither spontaneous nor continuous: "When power, however absolute and unaccountable, reigns without provoking a crisis, public opinion does not challenge it. Somebody must challenge arbitrary power first. The public can only come to his assistance."[68]

Only with help, then, would public opinion recognize a crisis. It would have reached the "limits of its normal power if it judges . . . rule to be defective, and turns then to identify the agency most likely to remedy it." Ordinarily the public should remain neutral: where events were confused or hard to understand, the probabilities were "very great that the public can produce only muddle if it meddles."[69]

Though the body of experts he had recommended in *Public Opinion* was not revived as a solution in *The Phantom Public*, Lippmann remained skeptical about majoritarian rule. He provided no clear role for representative government as a constraint on the authority of those holding high office. There was no way, he wrote, to educate public opinion for self-government: "This democratic conception is false because it fails to note the radical difference between the experience of the insider and the outsider . . . it asks the outsider to deal as successfully with the substance of a question as the insider. He cannot do it. No scheme of education can equip him." It was a liberal fallacy to believe otherwise. "In the struggle against evil," philosophers had avoided that fallacy — Plato wrote his *Republic* "on the proper education of a ruling class"; and Dante, "seeking order and stability," had "addressed himself not to the conscience of Christendom but to the Imperial Party."[70]

Lippmann, the exemplification of the insider, placed his trust, as he always had and as he wrote in his conclusion to *The Phantom Public*, chiefly in the individuals who initiated, administered, and settled affairs.[71] But he continued to trust only those who held to the kinds of standards he had set in his earliest books. He loathed Mussolini. Though he supported the candidacy of Alfred E. Smith for the presidency, he had grave doubts about Smith's understanding of several major issues. With the coming of the Great Depression and the international crises that accompanied it, Lippmann, now a syndicated columnist for the Republican *New York Herald Tribune*, deplored Herbert Hoover's management of affairs. Dubious as he was about the public and its educability, by 1932–33 Lippmann was equally dubious about the visible ruling class — the lawyers, financiers, and politicians who were failing to make their Republican party a useful instrument of positive government; their counterparts who had done no better as Democrats. He was as eager as other responsible observers for new, informed, energetic leadership. He did not expect that kind of leadership from Franklin D. Roosevelt, but he welcomed it when it came; and he began immediately to weave Roosevelt and the New Deal into the tapestry of his political thought.

Looking at the world in the summer of 1933, Lippmann could not avoid feeling that "the regime of liberty is almost everywhere on the defensive."[72] The Japanese had wrested Manchuria from China. Mussolini retained his authoritarian rule in Italy, as did Stalin in the Soviet Union. Both were potentially dangerous states. Hitler and his Nazis, even more threatening, had come into power in Germany. The industrialized nations remained in the depths of the worst depression they had ever experienced. That depression had left some 25 to 30 percent of Americans unemployed, millions of families in or close to poverty, thousands of banks threatened, many of them bankrupt. Franklin Roosevelt's exhilarating first months as president had won Lippmann's applause and lifted the spirits of a frightened people, but that brave and productive beginning had left international problems unaffected. Indeed, the Anglo-American entente that Lippmann believed essential to international order had suffered severe strains at the London Naval Conference of 1930, where the two nations could not reach a peaceful agreement. Agreement again eluded them at the London Economic Conference of 1933, when they failed to work out an acceptable formula for international monetary exchange.

After that failure, Lippmann began to assemble his thoughts about both the international and the domestic developments of the previous several years. He prepared a preliminary statement for the Godkin Lectures at Harvard which he delivered in 1934. Published later that year as *The Method of Freedom*, those lectures linked the renascent militarism of the Fascist and Communist states to the domestic absolutism they had embraced. In the face of that threat, and as in other periods of great disorder, Lippmann wrote, men needed positive convictions to defend freedom, indeed to defend civilization itself. He set out, therefore, to provide "a statement of principles by means of which . . . a nation possessing a highly developed economy and habituated to freedom can make freedom secure amidst the disorders of the modern world."

Lippmann built *The Method of Freedom* on the social psychology of *Public Opinion* and *The Phantom Public*, as well as on the inspiration of celebrated defenders of an orderly and principled freedom — particularly Edmund Burke and Edward Coke. As before, he had no confidence in the mass of the electorate or in "legislative supremacy," though he considered legislative consent to executive initiatives essential to political liberty. More than ever, Lippmann rejected what he again defined as the anachronistic ideas of nineteenth-century laissez-faire economics.[73] He was most concerned with the question of the proper role of the state in the crisis of the time.

With the end of the war in 1918, Lippmann argued, "the mass of people . . . wished to recover the peace, the plenty, and the liberties" the war had denied them. But with the depression, the failure to achieve "a restoration of the pre-war economy" brought about a generally revolutionary condition. The disruption of previous customs left men in such confusion that they listened to "unfamiliar ideas." After the financial panic of 1931 and its related developments, the international economy collapsed as "each state seized the control of that part of the cosmopolitan economy which lay within its frontiers or the reach of its army and navy." Managed economies replaced what remained of the "regulating mechanism of the market" and destroyed "the separation of political and economic power" so vital to the old order of "free capitalism and political democracy."[74]

That order, only marginally affected by public supervision before the war, was now gone forever: "Capitalism has become so complicated that private initiative is insufficient to regulate it; the democratization of political power had made collective initiative imperative. . . . The state is now compelled to look upon the economy as a national establishment for which it is responsible." Consequently "the assumptions of laissez-faire have given way to the assumptions of collectivism."[75]

"Collectivism" for Lippmann implied collective responsibility and collective action, not authoritarianism. He cited in that connection the ambiguous case of Herbert Hoover, who while celebrating laissez faire had nevertheless regarded it as the government's duty to spend public funds to protect banks, to try to maintain the price of wheat and cotton, and in other ways also to influence the economy in the first years of the depression. Hoover had acted on a doctrine, collectivism, which he professed to reject. In so doing, he had anticipated many of the major policies that Franklin Roosevelt adopted.

Much of what the New Deal had undertaken was essential, both in the United States and in other democratic countries. In the absence of remedy, debtors facing foreclosure on their homes, workers thrown out of their jobs, depositors threatened by loss of their savings, would "fight back," if necessary "overturn the government and the social order when their own security is destroyed." The state had, therefore, to intervene to prevent unemployment and to protect the standard of living: "Only by making its people economically secure can a modern government have independence, wield influence in the world, preserve law, order, and liberty."[76]

Yet government had also threatened liberty. During the war, in most belligerent countries, national plans were imposed on production and enforced by military law. After the war, "military collectivism" perpetuated itself as communism and fascism. The military pattern abolished freedom. It allowed no room for "argument, persuasion, bargaining and compromise." In an economy "which is directed according to a plan and for definite national objectives," Lippmann warned, "the official must be superior to the citizen. . . . The citizen is conscript." A state of that type had to control public opinion and therefore also education and the press, for it could not permit disloyalty or dissent. That was "the logic of absolute collectivism," which turned naturally to violence "to suppress the contrariness of free men."[77]

Fortunately it was not necessary to choose between laissez faire and military collectivism. There was a third, "a radically different method" to insure both freedom and security. The English-speaking people, the people most experienced in self-government and economic enterprise, had developed that method, "the method of free collectivism." It acknowledged the responsibility of the state for the standard of living and the operation of the economy as a whole, and it also preserved "within very wide limits the liberty of private transaction." Its object was not to direct individual behavior but to "redress the balance of private actions by compensating public actions."[78]

In the compensated economy of free collectivism, the state prevented fraud between buyer and seller, enforced "equitable contracts," equalized "the bargaining power of the consumer and of the employee," regulated public utilities as well as conditions of work in factories, and set minimum wages. The state also broke up monopolies, restricted speculation, and prevented "a too rampant individualism in the use of property." Since the crash of 1929 and the ensuing depression had revealed that "individual decisions were not sufficient to create a lasting prosperity," the state had to provide a "compensating mechanism" to offset and correct private economic judgments. That mechanism would require public management of money and credit, the planning and timing of public works, and the utilization of taxation to encourage or curtail consumption in order to smooth the business cycle by preserving a sufficient "equilibrium between saving and investment."[79]

Lippmann had drawn together the agenda of American progressivism and the developing policies of the New Deal. He had also placed that agglomeration within the broad context of the emerging economics of his friend John Maynard Keynes, who was at work on his momentous *General Theory of Employment, Interest and Money* (1936). Though Lippmann had reservations about some New Deal programs, he believed — as did Roosevelt and Keynes — that financial panic and economic instability created the mood on which fascism fed, that "the existence of plenty is a condition of liberty."

The "special concern" of free collectivism, Lippmann wrote near the end of *The Method of Freedom*, was "to bring as many as possible" to the "middle condition" — a phrase from Aristotle that translated in 1934 as "the middle class." "Free men," Lippmann continued, "with vested rights in their own living: men like these alone, and not employees of the state or the disinherited who today walk the streets . . . can constitute a free society. . . . With them peace and order are most likely to prevail against the violence of faction and the stratagems of adventurers." To be sure, the bourgeois were often dull, but they had hold "of the substance of liberty and they cling to it"; they were stubborn and careful and "of their fate, though it be a small one and private . . . the masters."[80] In the modern world, the authority of the state had to be enlarged. About that enlargement, free men were cautious, "in the knowledge that it is expedient but not glorious, that it is necessary but dangerous, that it is useful but costly." About free collectivism and about the New Deal, Lippmann was cautious himself. Within two years, the dangers that he perceived had come to command his continuing inquiry into the process of governing men.

By the spring of 1937, when Lippmann completed *The Good Society*, Hitler had reoccupied the Rhineland; Japan had invaded China; in Germany, Italy, and the Soviet Union, totalitarian regimes had turned to systematic brutality in order to hold and enlarge their authority. "The dominant fact in the contemporary world," Lippmann wrote, was "the return of the European and Asiatic great powers to the conception of total war."[81]

The Good Society, a treatise on political economy, was intended to set forth,

Lippmann later recalled, the enduring principles on which a postwar reconstruction should be based. In his discussion of those principles, Lippmann criticized some programs of the New Deal, particularly those of the National
Recovery Administration and the Agricultural Adjustment Administration,
agencies created during the emergency of 1933 and since abandoned or modified. He had come to believe that the president was excessively fond of authority, and he had opposed his re-election in 1936. But *The Good Society* was
only incidentally a criticism of the New Deal. It was primarily a condemnation
of "the increasing ascendancy of the state" — of fascism, whatever its guise —
and a plea for personal freedom under the law. In writing it, Lippmann drew
upon the idea he had developed in *Public Opinion* and *A Preface to Morals*,
expanded and refined his argument in *The Method of Freedom*, and dispelled
the potential confusion of that book's distinction between two kinds of collectivism. Indeed, *The Good Society* departed only toward its end from the main
contention of its immediate predecessors.

In *The Good Society*, Lippmann gave up the phrase "free collectivism." He
now reserved "collectivism," unmodified, for Fascist and Communist states.
He also wrote less about the international than the domestic market, but he
wrote with his characteristic criticism of laissez-faire doctrines. As he so often
had, he expressed his reservations about majoritarian democracy, though now
he was at least equally dubious about governments not subjected to constitutional limitations. Where earlier he had hoped for the sublimation of the passions of the governors, he now looked instead to the rule of law, to a controlling superego, as it were.

The Good Society affirmed the first "and most fundamental" of the principles on which Lippmann was building his case: "that the politics, law and
morality of the Western world are an evolution from the religious conviction
that all men are persons and that the human person is inviolable." The second
principle held that the continuing industrial revolution "posed all the great
issues of the epoch" and arose "primarily from the increasing division of labor
in ever-widening markets." He intended to reconcile those principles.[82]

Lippmann immediately rejected "the gigantic heresy of an apostate generation," the mistaken belief in the authoritarian principle and the collectivist
state as somehow indispensable for controlling modern technology. That apos-
tasy grew out of a confusion about the development of "concentrated corporate capitalism," which Lippmann considered (in a reversal of *Drift and Mastery*) a transitory and correctable distortion of the free market. The functioning
of that market, he maintained, had released the energy of men and permitted
their inventiveness to lift the bondage of "authority, monopoly, and special
privilege." Regrettably, since the war the leaders of the world had lost their
way and "abandoned the method of freedom" for intensified national rivalries. They had been able to do so because "the acids of modernity" (a phrase
from *A Preface to Morals*) had unsettled prewar routines: "In the disorder,
men became . . . bewildered . . . credulous . . . more anxiously compulsive,"

ready to turn to a government of technicians to restore the order they missed. "To magnify the purposes of the state," they had to "forget the limitations of men." They were deceived because no device of social control could approximate "the mastery" once attributed to "God as the creator and ruler of the universe" (though Lippmann had himself once attributed mastery to talented men, technicians included). Men were incapable, he now argued, to construct a planned society consciously directed.[83]

The movement toward collectivism, Lippmann continued in a familiar vein, had fed on the invocations by "great corporate capitalists" of "the shibboleths of liberalism." Those shibboleths erroneously equated the free market — essential for the release of human energy — with laissez-faire government, a transient and expendable theory. Laissez faire, in that self-serving view, had come to connote freedom for monopolies, which in fact were corrupting the free market. Reformers and labor leaders, for their part, while talking about liberty, had actually tried to obtain control over the monopolies for themselves. "In their belief that popular majorities must be unrestrained," Lippmann went on, "in their persistent demands for the magnification of government, in their fundamental aim to dominate . . . the private collectivism of the corporate system, rather than to break up monopoly and disestablish privilege, they became the adversaries of freedom and the founders of the new authoritarian society."[84]

In support of his case, Lippmann cited the Soviet Union, Germany, and Italy. The absolutism of those countries, he argued, was the outgrowth of "the essential principle of a full-blown collectivist society." Its "ultimate ideal" had been defined by Mussolini; it was the state, "nothing outside the State, nothing against the State." Lippmann then returned to a theme of *The Method of Freedom*. "All collectivism," he wrote, "whether . . . communist or fascist, is military in method, in purpose, in spirit, and can be nothing else." Therein lay "the tragic irony" of the time: "The search for security . . . if it seeks salvation through political authority, ends in the most irrational form of government . . . in the dictatorship of casual oligarchs."[85]

Collectivism, Lippmann argued, had perverted nationalism. In the early nineteenth century, nationalism had originated in "a passion to overcome the particularism of petty states." Later it became a reaction against the free market, an effort, as in high tariffs, to provide exclusive privilege for a particular state and the economic interests within it. Almost simultaneously the perpetuation of special interests had spawned collectivism, which sought further to insulate the state from its neighbors. "Collectivism," Lippmann wrote, "moves toward autarchy, the totalitarian state toward isolation."[86]

In the collectivist state, rulers used instruments of terror to indoctrinate the masses "with the view that their real enemies were not the privileged classes at home but the privileged nations abroad." The proletarian became imperialist. Thus arose the dreadful prospect of "total war . . . fought not for specific objects but for supremacy."[87] In that observation, Lippmann had succeeded, so he wrote a friend, in "relating domestic and foreign policy organically one to the other."[88]

Lippmann went on to warn against the dangers of gradual collectivisms and the related assumption, so often his target, that majorities expressed the will of society. He differentiated gradual collectivism, which inhered in intrusive microeconomic programs such as that of the New Deal's National Recovery Administration, from what he now called "liberalism," which many New Deal policies advanced. The liberalism he promoted was not the liberalism of laissez faire but the program of the compensatory state. "The first principle of liberalism," he held, ". . . is that the market must be preserved and protected."[89] To that end, he again advocated the very policies he had praised in *The Method of Freedom*, including the outlawing of monopoly; the provision of equal bargaining power to farmers, workers, and consumers; and the redistribution of income toward "a middle-class standard of life."

The liberal state recognized that the "populace had the power to rule" and "the right to rule." It was necessary also to structure the government so as to enable the populace to rule. That was the purpose of the Founding Fathers, who "conceived of the people as subjecting themselves to a legal system in which their power to rule was carefully organized." The Constitution protected both the masses and American society "from the hypnosis of the moment." The Constitution refined the will of the people.[90]

It did so partly through the role assigned to the judiciary, though the courts were not devised to obstruct the popular will. Rather, the courts were a part of "the oldest, the best established, the most successful" method of social control necessary for a civilized order, the Anglo-American common law. The common law, Lippmann wrote, which the framers of the Constitution had taken for granted, defined "the reciprocal rights and duties of persons" and invited them to enforce the law by proving their case in a court. In contrast to collectivism, liberalism under the law sought to govern "primarily by applying and perfecting reciprocal obligations." Liberalism operated "chiefly through the judicial hearing of individual complaints and the provision of individual remedies." The agencies of the liberal state, unlike the agencies of collectivism, while hospitable to "all manner of concerted action," would function only "as creatures of the law invested with special rights and duties which . . . may be repealed or amended."[91]

Lippmann's emphasis on the rule of law carried him beyond the argument of *The Method of Freedom* and the books that preceded it. The rule of law, as he described it, solved many of the problems that he had contemplated so long. It checked the will of the majority. It guarded against the tyranny of the governor. It permitted established, informed, and accountable public agencies to shape the economy of the state. The liberalism Lippmann advocated continued "the persistent search by the noblest men of our civilization for a higher law which would bind and overcome the arbitrariness of their lords and masters, of mobs at home and barbarians abroad, and the vagrant willfulness of their own spirits." The denial "that men may be arbitrary," Lippmann held, "*is* the higher law," a higher law particularly important in the period in which he wrote, one of the "great periods of disorder."[92]

With that conclusion, Lippmann, involved as ever with the problem of order, reached toward a conception of a secular natural law that emerged fully only after almost two more decades of reflection. In the intervening years, the coming of World War II and the issues arising out of the tenuous settlement of that war — issues of American foreign and military policy — commanded Lippmann's attention and analysis. Those issues took him back to his work during the Wilson years and forward to the exigent questions of national power and national survival.

The European war that began in 1939, in contrast to the war of 1914, came to Americans as no surprise. At the outset, most of them hoped and expected to avoid involvement in the war. Lippmann, distressed by the concessions that Britain and France had been making to Hitler and saddened by the foreseeable horror of war, nevertheless believed that the time had come to stand up to Germany and its allies, and that the United States could not avoid the predictable challenge to its own interests. American anxieties soared in the spring of 1940 when German divisions overran most of Western Europe. That conquest left Britain alone between the victorious Nazis on the western coast of France and the inadequate and ill-equipped American forces on the eastern coast of the United States. War overspread the Atlantic in 1940–41 as the United States attempted to supply Great Britain in the face of the growing German submarine fleet. In that time, the long coast from Argentina to Labrador remained substantially undefended.

The surprise Japanese attack on Pearl Harbor in December 1941 demonstrated a parallel vulnerability across the Pacific, while it also precipitated the declarations of war that made the United States a belligerent in the global struggle against Germany, Italy, and Japan. For almost another year, however, the United States and its major allies — Great Britain, the Soviet Union, and China — continued to suffer shattering defeats from advancing German and Japanese forces. In that grim time, with the civilization he cherished everywhere in danger of extinction, Lippmann wrote *U.S. Foreign Policy: Shield of the Republic* (1943).

"This is the time of reckoning," he warned. "We are liquidating . . . at our mortal peril, the fact that we made commitments, asserted rights, and proclaimed ideals while we left our frontiers unguarded, our armaments unprepared, and our alliances unformed and unsustained."[93] Consequently, as he wrote the French philosopher Jacques Maritain, Lippmann devoted his book, his "speech of a public man at a critical juncture in public affairs," to the specific purpose of "showing how the people of the United States could unite quickly on a decision which, if it is not taken within the next twelve months, would leave us paralyzed and would render impossible an orderly solution of the war."[94]

Rejecting the views of American isolationists, as he always had, Lippmann located the proper foundations of American foreign policy in the insights of the first national statesmen, Washington and his early successors in the presidency. They had recognized the American stake in a European balance of power that would prevent a potentially hostile nation from controlling the eastern Atlantic. That stake required alliances of convenience to sustain the balance of power and with it the security of the Atlantic Ocean. The Monroe Doctrine, Lippmann wrote, drawing upon the best historical account of its origin, appeared to extend the beneficent protection of the United States over the whole of the Americas. The preservation of the American continents from European encroachments remained an essential purpose of foreign policy. But the Monroe Doctrine during the nineteenth century depended upon the unacknowledged domination of the Atlantic by the British navy.

The failure of Americans to acknowledge and formalize that dependency contributed to the national illusion of superiority. That failure, as Lippmann saw it, was immoral as well as deluding. "Unearned security," he wrote, ". . . had the effect upon our national . . . mind which the lazy employment of unearned income so often has on the descendants of a hard-working grandfather. It caused us to forget that man has to earn his security and his liberty. . . . We came to think that our privileged position was a natural right . . . the reward of our moral superiority."[95]

Misled by that belief, convinced of their exceptional virtue, most Americans had "come to argue . . . that a concern with the foundations of national security, with arms, with strategy, and with diplomacy, was beneath our dignity as idealists." That fallacy resembled the "vice of the pacifist ideal": that peace was the "supreme end of foreign policy." A surrender to Germany or Japan, as Lippmann argued, would bring no real peace. Rather, the "true end" of foreign policy was "to provide for the security of the nation in peace *and* in war."[96]

A nation that had security did not have to sacrifice its legitimate interests to avoid war and was able to maintain those interests during war. But during the interbella years, the United States, Great Britain, and France had neglected the essential elements of national security, "armaments, suitable frontiers, and appropriate alliances." In those democratic countries, the pacifist ideal had led to military weakness and the appeasement of aggressor nations, who were thereby encouraged to turn to war. The Wilsonian ideal, for Lippmann a variant of the pacifist ideal, had falsely identified collective security with an antipathy to alliances. In reality the League of Nations could have enforced peace only if it had been led by "a strong combination of powers"[97] (a contention similar to Lippmann's conclusion in *The Political Scene*).

"Americans in particular had ignored the basic principle of foreign relations" — that a foreign policy consists in bringing into balance, "with a comfortable surplus of power in reserve, the nation's commitments and the nation's power."[98] That postulate guided Lippmann's approach to foreign policy through the rest of his life. In 1943 he defined it in terms from which he

afterward never deviated. A foreign commitment, he wrote, was "an obligation, outside of the continental limits of the United States, which may in the
last analysis have to be met by waging war." Power was "the force . . . necessary to prevent such a war or to win it." "Necessary power" included both
American military force and reinforcements from "dependable allies."[99]

A solvent American foreign policy, one that balanced power and commitments, had to be formulated by "responsible statesmen" whose decisions would
unite "the common sense of the nation."[100] As he expected them to, so did
he identify the vital interests of the United States. The first of those interests,
the defense of "the continental homeland . . . against foreign powers," had
been extended by the Monroe Doctrine to "the whole of the Western Hemisphere." That region had "to be defended against the invasion, intrusion, and
absorption by conspiracy within; and if lost, would have to be liberated." The
Americas could not be defended "by waiting to repel an attack . . . by a formidable enemy." Rather, strategic defense reached "across both oceans and to
all trans-oceanic lands from which an attack by sea or by air can be launched."
North America had become most accessible from "the British Isles, Western
Europe, Russia, and Japan." Consequently relations among Great Britain, Russia,
and Japan "as foes, as allies, or as neutrals" regulated "the issues of peace and
war for the United States."[101]

As Lippmann saw it, Germany affected the Americas as the enemy or ally
of those three powers. In 1917, he wrote, the United States went to war when
Germany threatened to conquer Great Britain and "to become our nearest
neighbor." In 1940 neutrality had become impossible for the same reason. In
those as in all cases, the paramount concern of American foreign policy related
to the alignment of the great powers. Foreign policy was solvent only when
the combination of powers allied with the United States was stronger than the
combination allied against it. In the latter event, American commitments would
exceed American means. Consequently the makers of foreign policy had to
"organize and regulate the politics of power."[102]

National interest, the Monroe Doctrine, and, so Lippmann argued, the Open
Door policy, which guaranteed China's political and territorial integrity, taken
together committed the United States to defend half the globe. Standing alone,
the nation could not do so. It had, therefore, to turn to dependable friends in
the Old World, as Woodrow Wilson and Franklin Roosevelt had by joining
alliances already in the field. In the future, in "the postwar order of the great
powers," it would be the business of diplomacy to form similar dependable
alliances. Victory in the war would destroy the effective power of Japan and
Germany. China had little available strength. The postwar order would, therefore, rest in three "great military states," Britain, the Soviet Union, and the
United States. Unless their alliance persisted after victory, one of them would
seek realignment with Germany or Japan and then rearm that new ally and
disrupt the order of power necessary for peace.[103]

Lippmann went on to focus, as he had in *The Political Scene*, on the importance of the alliance between the United States and Great Britain with its dominions. American commitments in Europe and Asia "dictated the need" for that alliance, which was "natural" because the "overthrow of the American position in the world would mean the break-up of the British community of nations," just as the overthrow of the British position would revolutionize the system of American defense. As Lippmann saw it, the Anglo-American connection was the product of "the facts of geography and . . . historic expedience" of a community of interest. Other European nations bordering the Atlantic belonged to the same community, whose security turned upon the Anglo-American alliance. It provided "the nucleus of force . . . of the whole region."[104]

Lippmann also perceived a complementarity of interests between the United States and the Soviet Union. In spite of American dislike of czarist autocracy and Soviet dictatorship, the two nations had, "each in its own interest, supported one another in the crucial moments of their history." Now both nations retained an interest in the European settlement. It would require the willingness of both the Soviet Union and the Atlantic community to neutralize the border region — Poland, Czechoslovakia, and other "remains" of ancient empires. Neutralization would protect the interests of the partners to it, the most powerful states, and provide the basis for general peace.[105]

In 1943 the outcome of the war remained too uncertain for Lippmann to proceed beyond his "guessing and hoping" about the future. But by 1944, great decisions had been made, and he was ready to add to his analysis another chapter, which built on the major points of *U.S. Foreign Policy* and considered their application in the foreseeable postwar world. That sequel, a brief hortatory book, Lippmann entitled *U.S. War Aims* (1944).[106]

The four-power alliance that was winning the war — the alliance of the United States, Britain, the Soviet Union, and China — was "not an international order" but the "nucleus around which order can be organized." First it would be necessary to define and stabilize "the strategic defenses and the foreign relations of all states within the same strategical system." The Atlantic community constituted one such system. The Soviet Union provided the nucleus for a second that was already grouping; China, for an incipient but still inchoate third.[107]

The Atlantic community, Lippmann held, was the "historic center of the international exchange economy." From that condition there followed "the essential political character which fits our way of life . . . that the state exists for man, and not man for the state; that the state is under the law, not above it." No social program that violated that heritage, Lippmann wrote, citing *The Good Society*, would "long be endured." Among the Atlantic nations, war had to be outlawed, and "any idea of preparation for such a war . . . excluded from all plans." The security of the weaker members of the community would be assured by their participation in a common defensive system and its combined force and combined command.[108] The nations of the community would also, he wrote — with more logic than European nationalisms permitted — have to agree to pursue a "common foreign policy in their relations with the non-Atlantic world." That policy would require " 'organic consultation' . . . something more elastic than a formal treaty of alliance, and . . . much less than political federation."[109]

The alliance faced the immediate task of working out with the Soviet orbit a settlement with Germany — as Lippmann saw it, a neutralization of Germany so that it would not become an object of a dangerous rivalry.[110] As he observed, the Russians, after German invasions in two wars, were bound to consider the region east of Germany as part of their own strategic system. The eastern frontier of the Atlantic community would, therefore, follow a fluctuating line through central Europe. There, as in Asia (where the future remained opaque), the relationship between the Atlantic and the Soviet orbit would "decide the outcome of the war."[111]

The European settlement Lippmann envisaged depended on Soviet as well as American self-restraint, for which in 1944 he had considerable hope — as did many Americans, the president among them. But Lippmann also understood the possibilities of international disorder. "It will disrupt the peace of the world," he wrote, "if the Soviet Union and the Atlantic nations become rivals and potential enemies in respect to China, India, and the Middle East." The Atlantic region, therefore, could permit no nation to act on its own in those areas. "Colonial policy," he warned, "can no longer be the sole prerogative of the imperial state, and will have to be set by consultation and agreement."[112] That was a wise admonition that few nations were then ready to accept.

"Under the regional principle," Lippmann also wrote, " . . . it would be . . . an overt act of aggression for any state to reach beyond its own strategical orbit for an alliance with a state in another orbit." If the Soviet Union, for one example, made an alliance with a Latin American country, the peace would be "troubled," as it would also be if the United States made an alliance with Iran or Romania. Further, ideology could create disorder. Unless "the ideological conflict over the elemental civil rights of man" were resolved, Lippmann predicted, secrecy and repression would prevail in the Soviet Union and breed reciprocal redbaiting within democratic societies afraid of subversion. There would then follow not peace but "only a *modus vivendi*, only compromises, bargains, specific agreements, only a diplomacy of checks and counter-checks."[113]

U.S. War Aims in general prescribed self-contained regionalism as the basis for postwar order. It also related that order to the prevalence of the liberal rule of law Lippmann had earlier advocated. But even before the victories over Germany and Japan, the rivalry between the Atlantic and the Soviet communities made possible only the modus vivendi Lippmann had hoped the settlement would transcend. Once the Cold War began, *U.S. War Aims* perforce became in large part a catalogue of his prescient fears.

*

The exhaustion of British strength during World War II left the United States and the Soviet Union as the only great military powers in the world. That condition alone might have produced the antagonistic bipolarity of the early Cold War. As it happened, both great powers acted in a manner that bred distrust. In the perceived interest of national security, the United States acquired a ring of air bases from which a new generation of conventional bombers could reach Soviet territory and, theoretically at least, deliver an atom bomb — a weapon then still an American monopoly. For its part, the Soviet Union, while encouraging the Communist revolution in China, also closed its grip on the countries of Eastern Europe, including the Soviet eastern zone in Germany, which was also to become a satellite nation. That European development reflected the traditional Russian concern about the security of the western border, so often crossed by invading armies. Now a resurgence of activity by Communist parties in both Eastern and Western Europe seemed to reach beyond the Soviet needs for security toward subversive threats to established governments in Western nations already disturbed by the immediate postwar economic distress.

In the resulting climate of anxiety and suspicion, of accusation and counter-accusation, President Harry S Truman devised the policies through which the United States pursued its ends in the Cold War. In 1947, with England no longer able to sustain an amicable order in the eastern Mediterranean, Truman pledged the United States to provide immediate assistance in Greece and Turkey, countries with obviously shaky economies and allegedly threatened, non-Communist governments. The Truman Doctrine also promised everywhere "to support free peoples who are resisting attempted subjugation of armed minorities or by outside pressures." That commitment, which far exceeded American means, drew Lippmann's predictable attack; just as the announcement of the Marshall Plan, designed to provide American assistance for the rebuilding by Europeans of their economies, predictably drew Lippmann's praise. The former violated, while the latter advanced, the principles of his wartime reflections about foreign policy.

Characteristically, Lippmann directed his critical analysis of American policy against the theory that provided its rationale. That theory had received its most influential expression in an article published in July 1947 in *Foreign Affairs:* "The Sources of Soviet Conduct," written by one "X." In reality, as most informed readers knew, "X" was George F. Kennan, the director of the policy planning staff of the Department of State. Earlier Kennan, while stationed in Moscow, had put forth similar ideas in a secret "long telegram" that both affirmed and provoked the anti-Soviet feelings of most of Truman's advisers. Addressed to a wider audience, the X article ascribed to Marxism, as Lenin and Stalin had reinterpreted it, an intense, inherent antagonism to the capitalist world that was accentuated by the internal insecurities of the Stalinist regime and armed with religious fervor. Yet Soviet doctrine, Kennan wrote, in its certainty that Marxism would prevail in the end, encouraged accommodation to transient barriers to that ultimate triumph. Consequently Kennan argued that the American policy toward the Soviet Union should be "long-term, patient but firm and vigilant containment of Russian expansive tendencies." By containment he meant "the adroit . . . application of counter-force at a series of constantly shifting geographical and political points, corresponding to the shifts and maneuvers of Soviet policy." Properly applied, that policy would promote "either the break-up or the gradual mellowing of Soviet power."[114]

Though Kennan later asserted that in the X article he had not meant to recommend military counterforce, Truman did give containment a distinctly military cast across a global reach. Both the military and the global aspects of the Truman Doctrine and its implications dismayed Lippmann. He was not deluded about the nature of the Soviet state. As he wrote in *The Cold War* (1947), his criticism of Truman's policy did "not arise from any belief or hope that our conflict with the Soviet government is imaginary or that it can be avoided, or ignored, or easily disposed of. . . . I agree entirely that Soviet power will expand unless it is prevented from expanding because it is confronted with power, primarily American power." But the concept of containment that he ascribed to Kennan struck Lippmann as "unsound," bound to "cause us to squander our substance and our prestige."[115]

After criticizing Kennan's reasoning, Lippmann proceeded with his own case, little modified since 1944. The continual application of a counterforce at shifting points all over the world, he contended, would require unlimited money and military power. Congress, however, could not provide a blank check on the Treasury or a blanket authorization for the use of the armed forces without violating the Constitution. Further, if the United States awaited Soviet initiatives before responding, American forces would always enter the field too late and with too little. "A policy of shifts and maneuvers," he believed, though perhaps suited to the Soviet system, was "not suited to the American system of government. . . . It is even more unsuited," he continued in the spirit of *The Good Society*, "to the American economy which is unregimented and uncontrolled, and therefore cannot be administered according to a plan."

Unsound in its domestic ramifications, containment was also a "strategic monstrosity," for there was "no rational ground for confidence that the United States could muster 'unalterable counterforce' at all . . . sectors." American military power, great though it was, could not cover all of Europe. American reserves of infantry, difficult to transport across the ocean, did not match Soviet reserves. Indeed American power was "peculiarly unsuited" to the policy of containment. It was, instead, "distinguished by its mobility, its speed, its ranges and its offensive striking force," characteristics inappropriate for a strategy "of waiting, countering, blocking, with no more specific objective than the eventual frustration of the opponent. As Lippmann foresaw, Americans "would themselves . . . be frustrated by Mr. X's policy long before the Russians were."[116]

Lippmann also predicted (wisely, as it developed) that, because of the limits of American power, a policy of containment could "be implemented only by recruiting, subsidizing and supporting a heterogeneous array of satellites, clients, dependents and puppets." The resulting coalition would be disorganized, a loose combination of "feeble and disorderly nations, tribes and factions around the perimeter of the Soviet Union." That disorder would require "continual . . . intervention by the United States in the affairs of all the members of the coalition," an impossible task in the face of Soviet resistance. The Russians, Lippmann realized, "can defeat us by disorganizing states that are already disorganized . . . and by inciting discontent which is already very great." The United States would then have to disown its puppets or "support them at incalculable cost." [117]

In 1947, as Lippmann observed, the United States had not yet consolidated "the old and familiar coalition of the Atlantic Community." That task deserved immediate priority. Fortunately the nations of the Atlantic community were not yet occupied by the Soviet army and could not be unless the Kremlin was "prepared to face a full scale world war, atomic bombs and the rest." Though "impoverished and weakened," those Western European countries were "incomparably stronger, richer . . . more democratic and mature than any of the nations of the Russian perimeter." The United States should therefore concentrate, as George Marshall had proposed, on reconstructing the "economic life" of the members of the Atlantic community. It was necessary also for the United States to promote a German settlement on which the Western Europeans could agree — an objective spelled out in *U.S. War Aims*. But now Lippmann gave Western Europe a new role. Reconstructed along the lines he recommended, Western Europe would "hold the balance of power between Russia and America," would become the mediator of their conflict. [118]

Reconstruction, however, was not yet possible. The threat of the Red army, "not the ideology of Karl Marx," gave "the Kremlin and the native communist parties of western Europe an abnormal and intolerable influence in the affairs of the European continent." Consequently the "immediate and decisive problem" of American relations with the Soviet Union was "whether, when, on what conditions the Red Army can be prevailed upon to evacuate Europe." [119] That evacuation would require, too, the removal from Europe of British and American forces. Lippmann recognized the difficulties of accepting a settlement in which the nations of Eastern Europe "lost all independence," but he deplored the entanglement of American and British diplomacy "in all manner of secondary issues . . . in the Russian borderlands." In that preoccupation, Britain and the United States "failed to see . . . that until the Red Army evacuated eastern Europe and withdrew to the frontiers of the Soviet Union, none of these objectives could be achieved." [120]

In 1944, in *U.S. War Aims*, Lippmann had feared that a conflict in ideologies between the Atlantic community and the Soviet orbit would prevent a world settlement. Partly because his fears had materialized, in 1947 in *The*

Cold War he was proposing a settlement based upon two worlds, each separate and secure, each willing to allow the developing nations ultimately to form an orbit of their own. At both times, with consistent emphasis, he looked to negotiations, rather than to confrontations, to establish international order; and he stressed the importance of solvency in national foreign policy. Americans, he wrote in *The Cold War*, had "to reduce, not to extend, our commitments in Asia, to give up the attempt to control events which we do not have the power, the influence, the means, and the knowledge to control." If the Soviet Union refused to evacuate Europe, the Atlantic community would be no worse off than it already was, "but our energies will be concentrated, not dispersed all over the globe, and the real issues will be much clearer." The policy of containment, he concluded, had to give way to a policy of settlement.[121]

In those views Lippmann persisted. They accounted for his criticisms of the adventurism of Dean Acheson, for his attacks on John Foster Dulles with his alarming threats and multiple regional pacts, for Lippmann's later dismay about American involvement in Vietnam, for his continual advocacy of a neutralized settlement in Germany. The makers of American foreign policy and their supporters during the two decades and more that followed the end of World War II frequently shared a trinity of illusory beliefs. They believed too often in the exceptional virtue of the American people and, therefore, of American policy. They believed too often in the necessity for opposing communism everywhere, in a universal American commitment. They believed too often in the omnipotence of American power. Lippmann had no such illusions. Predictably, in one administration after another, those who held power in the United States became restless with his continual demands for negotiation. Had they tried more often to negotiate, even if they had failed, the United States, as Lippmann had suggested, would have been no worse off for the effort. In the absence of continual and successful negotiations, the tension between the United States and the Soviet Union persisted, and with it the disorder that Lippmann deplored.

U.S. Foreign Policy, U.S. War Aims, and *The Cold War* — all tracts for their times — advocated a consistent conception of international order that did not materialize during Lippmann's life. Though his ideas were no less cogent on that account, he had to explore an issue other than foreign policy with its somber expedients if he was to complete the task he had long since undertaken — the definition, at once theoretical and practicable, of the foundations of a beneficent political order.

Almost immediately after publishing *The Good Society*, Lippmann embarked in 1938 on a study that took various shapes during the next decade and a half. At times he worked on a new manuscript designed to carry his analysis of the state beyond anything he had yet done. At other times, he contemplated revising *The Good Society* or commissioning some younger but sympathetic friend to do so for him. Even while addressing foreign policy, he never abandoned his project. In the end, he finished a new book, his last major work, *Essays in the Public Philosophy* (1955). Deeply rooted in his earlier work, it also ventured onto ground he had not previously staked.[122]

"During the fateful summer of 1938," Lippmann undertook his "effort to come to terms . . . with the mounting disorder in our Western society." "I was filled with foreboding," he recalled, "that the nations of the Atlantic Community would not prove equal to the challenge, and that . . . we should lose our great tradition of civility, the liberties Western man had won for himself after centuries of struggle . . . now threatened by the rising tide of barbarity." The war did not cure the continuing "sickness of the Western liberal democracies." During the postwar years, Lippmann still discerned "a deep disorder in our society which comes not from the machinations of our enemies and from the adversities of the human condition but from within ourselves." As he saw it, "we were . . . not wounded but sick . . . we were failing to bring order and peace to the world, and we were beset by those who believed they have been chosen to succeed us."[123]

In that dour humor, Lippmann turned to eminent philosophical conservatives who had in their own way admonished their contemporaries, to political theorists such as Aristotle, Edmund Burke, and Alexander Hamilton. Consulting also celebrated diagnosticians of the modern condition, he borrowed again from Freud's interpretations of dreams; from Vilfredo Parato's theory of social equilibrium; and from Emile Durkheim's concept of anomie, particularly as the concept informed Erich Fromm's discourses about modern man's proclivity to "escape from freedom." In one way or another, all of those theorists shared Lippmann's distrust of popular majorities and his related belief in rule by an elite responsible to society but uninfluenced by transient opinion.[124]

So armed, Lippmann began *The Public Philosophy* by examining the "decline of the West" as revealed in the incapacity of the democracies to "cope with reality, to govern their affairs, to defend their vital interests." As he had before, he dated that decline from 1917, the devastating year of the First World War in which "there had occurred . . . an unrecognized revolution within the democratic states." After their cumulative losses, their "institutional order . . . gave way under the strain." In the defeated countries — the Hohenzollern, Hapsburg, Ottoman, and Romanoff empires — revolution toppled established order. Within the victorious nations — France, Italy, Great Britain, and the United States — "the constitutional order was altered subtly and yet radically."[125]

That order had arisen during the antecedent century while democratic governments were "spared the necessity of dealing with the hard issues of war and peace, of security and solvency, of constitutional order and revolution." In that time, liberals had become "habituated to the notion that in a free and progressive society it is a good thing that the government should be weak."

But in the crisis of 1917, "the old structure of executive government with the consent of a representative assembly" could no longer function. The existing governments had "exhausted their imperium"; they could not carry on the war except by "democratizing" its conduct and "by pursuing total victory and . . . promising total peace." Then occurred the subtle revolution as a "cession of power to representative assemblies," which further ceded powers to "the masses of voters," who in their turn passed them on to "the party bosses, the agents of pressure groups, the managers of the new media of mass communication" — all in all the development Lippmann had long deprecated.[126]

Earlier he had ordinarily attributed the collapse of constitutional order primarily to economic changes, to the persistence of nineteenth-century laissez-faire doctrines into the oligopolistic and protected markets of the twentieth century. *The Public Philosophy* emphasized a different but not unfamiliar theme, the "hyperbolic" war as it had emerged in 1917. That condition had caused "the paralysis of government" and the resulting "functional derangement of the relationship between the mass of the people and the government." The "malady of the democratic states" arose when "the executive and judicial departments, with their civil servants and technicians" lost "their power to decide."[127]

For Lippmann the solution to the problem he had again identified lay, as it had before, partly in restoring the executive as "the active power in the state" and using the "representative assembly" only as the consenting power. The health of the constitutional system depended upon that relationship, for "the government must be able to govern and the citizens must be represented in order that they shall not be oppressed." Indeed for Lippmann that relationship was "rooted in the nature of things."[128] That conclusion inhered in his historical argument; but not for the first time, he had used history perhaps better than he had understood it — used it, in spite of the astonishing variety of the past and of its unpredictability, as if history were metaphysics. On that account, his case for a strong executive was less than wholly persuasive, even in the context of representative government.

Yet his conviction carried him on. Citing Edmund Burke, he also warned against the ephemeral demands of the masses, demands threatening to "the connected generation" — the links Burke was "talking about when he invoked the partnership 'not only between those who are living' but also with 'those who are dead, and those who are to be born.' " That community gave "rational meaning to the necessary objectives of government," Lippmann continued. He also bemoaned the lost capacity of democratic peoples to believe in the intangible realities that had once sustained royalty — the "imponderable authority . . . derived from tradition . . . consecration, veneration . . . prestige . . . hierarchy."[129] Here by projection he seemed to cloak his strong executive in trappings that could become ludicrous in American practice, trappings that served as an odd substitute for the obligations, now omitted, that he had once attached to that strong executive and his technicians in the compensatory state.

Still, Burke's community of generations and its traditional venerations had, as Lippmann contended, checked those impulses for chaos which the Jacobin revolution had unleashed. The Jacobins were his targets, and the Founding Fathers still his models, for unlike the revolutionary French in the eighteenth century, "Jefferson and his colleagues . . . were interested in government" — thus the American Constitution. In contrast Jacobin doctrine was nihilistic: "The peculiar essence of the dogma is that the revolution itself is a creative act." So, too, with Karl Marx, who also preached a fallacious doctrine of redemption. The Marxist heresy held that, with revolution, "men who were evil were to be made good" — a delusion of demagogues who thought they were gods. That delusion, an expression of our "uncivilized selves," called for a revolution against "freedom . . . justice . . . the laws . . . the order of the good society . . . as they are contained in the traditions of civility, as they are articulated in the public philosophy."[130]

By extension, then, in the good society the strong executive would venerate the values of the historical community that was the polity. A legislature, involved not with initiatives but with consent, would also protect those values, among them the freedom of the people. For those values, for the preservation of civility — of civilized order — Lippmann used a name, "the public philosophy," which expounded tradition and undergirded the good society. "The public philosophy," he wrote, "is known as *natural law*. . . . This philosophy is the premise of the institutions of the Western society, and . . . unworkable in communities that do not adhere to it."[131] Here were his two worlds. But here again, his use of history had become overtly metaphysical; here his logic, so convincing to him, was uncharacteristically reductionist, its conclusions inherent in its premises.[132]

Lippmann's natural law was secular, not supernatural. As such it violated none of his personal canons, while it also satisfied his concern for rational order. His conception of natural law closely resembled the constitutional principles he had earlier derived from a similar logic. Rational man, he believed, could "produce a common conception of law and order which possesses a universal validity." Alexander the Great had done so, as had the Stoics and Cicero, and as had Anglo-American constitutional theorists who understood "that a large plural society cannot be governed without recognizing that, transcending its plural interests, there is a rational order with a superior common law."[133]

Modern man, Lippmann wrote, had forgotten the natural law of civility. Indeed nineteenth-century populist democracy had been hostile to that law and its rhetoric. Nevertheless, until the devastation of 1917, "the loneliness and anxiety of modern man had been private, without public and overt political effect." It remained private so long as "public order provided external security." But the breakdown of public order intensified private anxieties. "The inner disorder provoked the impulse to escape" from freedom to authoritarianism.[134] Patently the metaphor of sublimation could no longer serve for Lippmann in the condition he described, a condition of "anomic man," lawless states, and by extension a lawless world. The solution to those related disasters could not spring up from within but had to be summoned from without, from a revivified past.

It followed, as he went on, that only a renewal of the public philosophy, of secular natural law, would restore public security. That renewal could not be accomplished by force. It was necessary, rather, to "demonstrate the practical relevance . . . of the public philosophy."[135] Its practicality, Lippmann argued, not some supernatural faith, would establish its validity. Here he seemed to be applying a Jamesian test for a singularly un-Jamesian ideal. He had always felt that Santayana had saved him from a total conversion to James, but now he appeared implicitly to have tried to merge them. He took one test, as he often had, in the case of property. Since the rights of property, he wrote, were "a creation of the laws of the state," no man had "an absolute title." Rather, owners of property, beholden to the state, were obligated to promote, in Blackstone's phrase, "the grand ends of a civil society." "Private property," Lippmann continued, "is . . . a system of legal rights and duties. Under changing conditions the system must be kept in accord with the grand ends of civil society." That conclusion, he wrote, would be self-evident to a lucid and rational man. In that sense, it was a natural law, a "principle of right behavior in the good society, governed by the Western tradition of civility."[136] In his test, Lippmann had come full circle.

He moved on to familiar territory. He did not expect, he wrote, that many individuals would master the public philosophy: "Most people . . . may have heard almost nothing about it." No matter, for "if among the people of light and leading the public philosophy has, as the Chinese say, the Mandate of Heaven, the beliefs and habits which cause men to collaborate will remain whole."[137] As ever, Lippmann put his faith in an elite of intelligence and character; as ever, he wrote for them and counted himself among them.

As ever, too, Lippmann anchored his argument in his view of human nature. A good citizen in a good society, a man fit to rule, was himself ruled by "his second and civilized nature," not by his instincts. He was "the noble master of his own weaker and meaner passions," as he always had been in Lippmann's chain of being. That mastery was "the aristocratic code," which was not inherent in prerogative and birth "but functional to the capacity to rule."[138]

But Lippmann did not expect a new Jerusalem. "The ideals of the good life and of the good society," he warned, would fall short of perfection. They were "worldly ideas concerned with the best that is possible among mortal . . . men." Words such as "liberty, equality, fraternity, justice" had various meanings "which reflect the variability of the flux of things." That was a phrase from William James, whom Lippmann continued to quote: " 'The essence of life is its continually changing character . . . our concepts are all discontinuous and fixed.' "[139] That was the human condition, in its nature imprecise and inconclusive. That admission of fluidity made *The Public Philosophy* not Lippmann's final statement of a universal truth but his latest statement in a long series of intellectual ventures. As his letters and his newspaper columns continued to reveal, he had not lost in a monistic natural law his lifelong hopes for a liberal state.

He had not lost his old preoccupation: "The principles of the good society call for a concern with an order of being," an order, like the order he had continually sought, where "the human being is inviolable . . . reason shall regulate the will . . . truth shall prevail." That order, which had to rest upon a constitutional system, also had to be earned: "The public philosophy is addressed to the government of our appetites. . . . The regime it imposes is hard."[140]

As some of his friends had warned him before the publication of *The Public Philosophy*, the book was vulnerable in several respects. Even his admirers found it so — Arthur Schlesinger, Jr., for its monism and its too simplistic confidence in a strong executive; Reinhold Niebuhr on those grounds as well as because of the book's presupposition of "a classical ontology, which equates history with nature and does not allow for the endless contingencies of history."[141] Lippmann felt that they and other critics had "not wholly understood or sympathized with" *The Public Philosophy*; but he agreed with Schlesinger's description of his quest, of "a long search and much turmoil," that had begun even before the publication of *A Preface to Politics*.[142]

Though Lippmann published no major book after *The Public Philosophy*, his search, his Jamesian testing, had brought him to conclusions inherent in his earliest formulations about individual and social morality, about civility, order and their relationship — conclusions now more prudent and less unconventional than had been his youthful views. Essentially he had always been a conservative, for he had never trusted the mass of people or had much confidence in their elected representatives. He had always had a shaping faith in the basic values of Western civilization, though not always in their contemporary focus or expression. Never a Jeffersonian, he had believed consistently in a strong federal government, particularly a strong executive, in an active but not intrusive government directed by alert and intelligent managers resolved to promote efficient and equitable social and economic policies. To be sure, he had described the compensatory functions of government as characteristics of a liberal state, but he was a liberal only in that special meaning of the word, and only if government operated within the constitutional restraints that he commended. Those related principles drew strength from his interpretations of the continual crises in American foreign policy. In every context, his observations about the fallability of governors (as well as the fallability of those they governed) moved him increasingly to stress the necessity of protecting human freedom by constitutional means, and consequently of holding government to that higher law. As he wrote, Lippmann had embraced the conservatism of Edmund Burke, and like Burke, he cherished the continuity between generations. "The question you are asking yourselves," he wrote to a group of student rebels of the 1960s, "is whether 'revolution' is not the only way of achieving the good life. I had asked myself that question when I . . . was a student in college. . . . In the advanced nations of the modern age, the old conception of revolution — the overthrow and the replacement of an established governing class — is . . . antiquated. . . . I believe that society can be improved and reformed but not transformed by disruption."[143] So he had long believed. And he had long since concluded, though his argument changed with his times, that reform and improvement were essential for preserving order, without which man could not lead a good life.

Notes

1. Carl Binger in Marquis Childs and James Reston, eds., *Walter Lippmann and His Times* (New York, 1959), pp. 23, 28.
2. James Reston in Childs and Reston, pp. 230–33.
3. Mabel Dodge as quoted in Ronald Steel, *Walter Lippmann and the American Century* (Boston, 1980), p. 51.
4. John Reed as quoted in Steel, p. 55.
5. Lippmann to Helen Armstrong, February 12, 1938, Lippmann Collection, Yale University Library. Except for the letters to Helen Armstrong, all letters quoted in this introduction are published in the text of this book.
6. Lippmann to Lucile Elsas, undated, 1907.
7. Frances Davis, *A Fearful Innocence* (Kent, Ohio, 1981), pp. 70–74.
8. Lippmann to Lucile Elsas, undated, 1908.
9. Ibid.
10. Lippmann to Helen Armstrong, February 12, 1938, Lippmann Collection.
11. Lippmann to Lawrence J. Henderson, October 27, 1922. See also Steel, ch. 15.
12. Lippmann to Lucile Elsas, undated, 1908; and May 10, 1908.
13. Binger in Childs and Reston, pp. 23, 28.
14. Harold Laski in Mark D. Howe, ed., *Holmes-Laski Letters*, v. 1 (Atheneum Edition, New York, 1913), p. 28.
15. Lippmann to Newton D. Baker, May 15, 1929.
16. Walter Lippmann, *A Preface to Morals* (New York, 1929), p. 323.
17. Ibid., p. 3.
18. Ibid., pp. 3–10.
19. Ibid., pp. 20–35.
20. Ibid., pp. 53–55.
21. Ibid., pp. 135–37.
22. Ibid., p. 219.
23. Ibid., p. 220.
24. Ibid., pp. 231, 283, 313.
25. Walter Lippmann, *A Preface to Politics* (New York, 1913), introduction, n.p.
26. Ibid., p. 52.
27. Ibid., p. 42.
28. Ibid., p. 127.
29. Ibid., p. 138.
30. Ibid., pp. 150–51.
31. Ibid., p. 152.

32. Ibid., p. 8.
33. Lippmann to Hazel Albertson, September 18, 1912.
34. Walter Lippmann's *Drift and Mastery* was first published by Mitchell Kennerly in 1914 and republished in 1961 by Prentice-Hall, Englewood Cliffs, New Jersey, with an introduction by William E. Leuchtenburg. Notes refer to the latter edition, here pp. 16–17.
35. Ibid., pp. 19, 114.
36. Ibid., pp. 38–44.
37. Ibid., p. 49.
38. Ibid., p. 50.
39. Ibid., pp. 50–51.
40. Ibid., pp. 64, 85.
41. Ibid., pp. 148–49.
42. Leuchtenburg in introduction to *Drift and Mastery*, p. 14.
43. Lippmann to Hazel Albertson, September 25, 1914.
44. Diary entry for August 2, 1914. Lippmann kept a diary only intermittently. Usually it was merely a record of appointments. Various parts of it are in the Lippmann Collection, Yale University Library.
45. Lippmann to Graham Wallas, August 5, 1915.
46. Lippmann to Alfred E. Zimmern, June 7, 1915.
47. Lippmann to Alfred E. Zimmern, June 23, 1915.
48. Lippmann to Graham Wallas, December 8, 1915.
49. Walter Lippmann, *The Stakes of Diplomacy* (New York, 1915), p. 159.

50. Ibid., p. 179.
51. Ibid., p. 181.
52. Ibid., pp. 168–69.
53. Ibid., pp. 211, 224.
54. Though he had yet to write *A Preface to Morals*.
55. Walter Lippmann, *The Political Scene: An Essay on the Victory of 1918* (New York, 1919), pp. x, xii, 8.
56. Ibid., p. 61.
57. Ibid., pp. 41–42.
58. Lippmann to Norman Hapgood, July 28, 1919.
59. Lippmann to Ralph Pulitzer, July 30, 1919.
60. Lippmann to Ellery Sedgwick, April 7, 1919.
61. Walter Lippmann, *Liberty and the News* (New York, 1920), here briefly summarized.
62. Walter Lippmann's *Public Opinion* was first published in New York in 1922 and was reprinted by the Free Press, a division of Macmillan, in 1965. Notes refer to the latter edition, here pp. 4–5, 17.
63. Ibid., pp. 8–10.
64. Ibid., pp. 11–13.
65. Ibid., pp. 18–19.
66. Ibid., p. 158.
67. Ibid., pp. 196, 236–37.
68. Walter Lippmann, *The Phantom Public* (New York, 1925), p. 58.
69. Ibid., pp. 124, 141.
70. Ibid., p. 146.
71. Ibid., p. 198.
72. Walter Lippmann, *The Method of Freedom* (New York, 1934), p. viii. Lippmann began the book a year before it was published.
73. Ibid., pp. ix, 78, 85.
74. Ibid., pp. 8, 10, 16.

75. Ibid., p. 28.
76. Ibid., pp. 35–37.
77. Ibid., p. 44.
78. Ibid., p. 46.
79. Ibid., pp. 46–53.
80. Ibid., pp. 112–14.
81. Walter Lippmann's *The Good Society* was first published in Boston in 1937 and was re-printed in 1943 by Grosset and Dunlap, New York. Notes refer to the latter edition, here p. ix.
82. Ibid., pp. x–xi.
83. Ibid., pp. 6, 17, 23, 26, 33.
84. Ibid., pp. 46–47.
85. Ibid., pp. 51, 67, 105.
86. Ibid., pp. 133, 138, 140.
87. Ibid., p. 148.
88. Lippmann to Hamilton Fish Armstrong, November 9, 1935.
89. *The Good Society*, p. 174.
90. Ibid., p. 256.
91. Ibid., pp. 266, 268, 307.
92. Ibid., pp. 338, 346, 369 (emphasis Lippmann's).
93. Walter Lippmann, *U.S. Foreign Policy: Shield of the Republic* (Boston, 1943), p. 8.
94. Lippmann to Jacques Maritain, July 1, 1943.
95. *U.S. Foreign Policy*, p. 49.
96. Ibid., pp. 49–51 (emphasis Lippmann's).
97. Ibid., p. 74.
98. Ibid., p. 9 and ch. VI.
99. Ibid., pp. 9–10.
100. Ibid., p. 85.
101. Ibid., pp. 88, 89, 95.
102. Ibid., pp. 95, 100, 101.
103. Ibid., p. 114.
104. Ibid., pp. 129, 136.
105. Ibid., p. 147.
106. Walter Lippmann, *U.S. War Aims* (Boston, 1944), p. vii.
107. Ibid., p. 65.
108. Ibid., p. 69. This was a foreshadowing of NATO, of course.
109. Ibid., pp. 69, 76, 87.
110. Ibid., p. 65.
111. Ibid., p. 89.
112. Ibid., p. 95.
113. Ibid., pp. 136, 141.
114. Ronald Steel wrote the introduction to a short, paperbound booklet published by Harper and Row in New York, and elsewhere, in 1972. That booklet reprinted the columns by Walter Lippmann that, taken together, constitute *The Cold War* (New York, 1947). The booklet also reprinted the article "The Sources of Soviet Conduct," described in the text. Quotations here are from the 1972 booklet.
115. *The Cold War*, p. 4.
116. Ibid., p. 13.
117. Ibid., pp. 14–16.
118. Ibid., pp. 17–21.
119. Ibid., p. 26.
120. Ibid., pp. 28–30.

121. Ibid., pp. 36, 42–47, 50–52.
122. Walter Lippmann's *Essays in the Public Philosophy* was first published in Boston in 1955 and was reprinted in 1956 by Mentor Books, New York. The following notes refer to the latter edition.
123. Ibid., pp. 12–13.
124. Ibid., p. 13.
125. Ibid., p. 14.
126. Ibid., pp. 17–18.
127. Ibid., p. 19.
128. Ibid., p. 31.
129. Ibid., pp. 35, 47, 49.
130. Ibid., pp. 49, 60.
131. Ibid., p. 79 (emphasis Lippmann's).
132. Though much less significantly, reductionism marked parts of both *A Preface to Morals* and *The Good Society*.
133. *The Public Philosophy*, pp. 81, 83.
134. Ibid., pp. 85, 86.
135. Ibid., p. 89.
136. Ibid., p. 94.
137. Ibid., p. 114.
138. Ibid., p. 107.
139. Ibid., pp. 110, 113.
140. Ibid., pp. 113, 127, 128.
141. Childs and Reston, eds., chs. X, XI, and p. 170.
142. Lippmann to Edward Engberg, November 7, 1961.
143. Lippmann to Donna M. Reichel, December 15, 1969. (Reichel had written Lippmann on behalf of the group of students.)

I

Preface to Mastery

1907–1920

To Lucile Elsas[1]

HANDWRITTEN

[c. 1907]

My dear Lucile,

. . . Tell me, for you're the only girl I ever knew who loved beauty, not for the sake of languorous dreaminess, but because beauty was a part of existence, — tell me if this attitude towards nature is not the last word in idealism. . . .

You have asked for my confession of faith — Here it is:

The people are too busy and too much blinded to care about the beauty of nature or the works of the masterbuilders; our critics with singular depths of visions have shown us the hollowness of our social fabric, the farce and absurdity of its ceremonials. Ibsen and Shaw have shown us with perfect truth that morality is not respectability, that the Life force is above marriage laws, that society is against the individual. We have seen that the curse of great fortunes is the degradation of the poor, that social position is built upon the slum.

And our duty? Surely it is not in business, not in an effort to multiply the family fortune. The path has been cleared. We must build upon it. In the work of uplifting we cannot do too much. No glory for us, perhaps not even the glory of accomplishment. But this is our ideal of happiness everlasting: To build a citadel of human joy upon the slum of misery — to raise the heads bowed in degradation to the blue and gold of God's sunshine — to give to human hearts their heritage of happiness — to raise upon the ruins of infamy the purity of the hearth — to give to the world not a doctrine but a fact — to give to the words "the brotherhood of man" a meaning. Contemplation has been done; realization is our work.

There you have me, Lucile: there is the first time in my life that I have dared to put into words what I have been dreaming. It's been hard work: the

Lady Godiva act is distressing to me. You see I have some modesty, for I, unlike my poetic friends, would have preferred to express my dreams not in words but in the enmity everlasting of a slum landlord. I have written this to you because your friendship is blood red. . . .

I have obeyed your orders: eight pages, closely written, about myself !

1. Lucile Elsas, a young woman whose social background resembled Lippmann's, commanded his sentimental attachment during his years at Harvard. In 1910 she married Horace Liveright, who was to become a successful publisher.

To Lucile Elsas   HANDWRITTEN

May 10, 1908

Dear Lucile,

. . . I believe in the old, old saying "That he who would save his soul — must love it." The cultivation of one's own garden usually produces mushrooms; but he who cultivates the whole world necessarily has a beautiful garden. The irony of conscious and deliberate individualism is that it is never individualistic; the paradox of socialism is that it is highly individualistic. . . .

A very inspired man said at Harvard the other day: "Do everything well — do your work supremely well." He was right: we must make our choice of the largest life and then live it supremely well. No act is insignificant in this world: a clean collar is a religious duty under certain conditions, and the tragedy of a whole life may lie in an unfulfilled dance card. The sum of it all lies just here: In the richest fullest expression of the highest instincts of our nature, interpreted through action or beauty, which are in essence the same, we are cultivating our garden, not our backyard. . . .

I have come around to Socialism as a creed. It is not the half-baked, naive faith of the man who sees in it the universal panacea. I have come to it rather through hard work and painful thinking. I began from two ends: The tinsel of the uppercrust of society with its enormous wealth which ought to mean life gone nowhere; the hopelessness of the bourgeoisie with their pitiable Eighteenth Century ideals; the degradation of the wage slave to such depths that today 1,700,000 children work at least twelve hours a day — these evident and obvious vices of our civilization produced the usual reaction in me. Had I stopped there I should be simply a muck-raker. Now muck raking is a form of intellectual search light which any one can turn on. The revelations are amazing — conditions are disgusting. (May I go on to a less satisfactory sheet of paper). . . .[1]

1. That sheet of paper, the rest of this letter, has been lost.

To Lucile Elsas

[c. 1908]

Dear Lucile —

. . . We come to New York and we find ourselves in a strange position. We have to choose between insincerity and rudeness. Politics are discussed by the gentlemen of the houses: can we tell them that their political ideas are of the Eighteenth century, and that their business methods of competition are worthy of a savage in the jungle? that modern business life with its theory of the devil take the hindmost, its abnormal concentration of wealth, which is Life, and its million unemployed leaves nothing to turn to but Socialism?

Religion comes up: can we tell them that the Temple Emanu-el exhibition is a piece of blatant hypocrisy? that its mechanical service, its bromidic interpretation, its drawing room atmosphere of gentility, its underlying snobbishness, which makes it an exclusive organization for the wealthy, strangle all the religion that is in us? Can we tell our friends — pillars of the Church, all of them — that Carb,[1] when a visitor in New York on Yom Kippur, fled from the temple to St. Patrick's Cathedral to find there a religious atmosphere? Can we tell them that a religion, which doesn't make life richer, fuller, more splendid than it now is, which doesn't touch life at every point, thus creating a harmony between the soul of man and the stars in heaven, is no religion at all. The only religion is one of joy — we worship when we are happy and when we are beautiful. Joy and Beauty are God's inner consciousness — we live in God when we realize His nature. The scheduled prayer which comes rain or shine on Saturday at 10:10 A.M. is no prayer at all. God isn't so vain that we have to tell Him he is great. There is something naive and childish about the adoration of God. It's like the child who asks whether God wears Alexander shoes, and who cuts God's hair?

The devoutest people are not church-going. The truly religious man needs only the bright sun, the gossamer tints of the twilight and the blue beyond blue of the clear night to make him happy and worshipful. The beauty of our friends, in the full meaning of the word beauty, works of art, and music those are the things that make life still more devout. Add to this religion a passion for deed, a Faust-like "Streben," even a dissatisfaction, which leads to progress, expressed in Socialism, Pragmatism and poetry, and you have a "Theory of Life," which the young never outgrow. Such an expression of youth is inspiring and gives the lie to pessimism. . . .

---

1. David Carb, a Harvard friend of Lippmann's.

To Lincoln Steffens[1]

May 18, 1910

Dear Mr. Steffens,

Do you remember our correspondence some time ago in regard to my accepting a position with the *Boston Common*? You said that while there were no journalists connected with it, the opportunity to see various departments of a paper at once might compensate. I decided to accept the offer as I was exceedingly enthusiastic about the ideal, anxious to help, and able to do so without leaving college.

I have been with the paper since the beginning and I see clearly that it would be a waste of time on my part to stay with it after the summer. Philip Fiske, under whom I am working, is to put it flatly a man from whom I don't want to learn journalism. His notion of fairness is that it is identical with the baldest statement of facts. . . . Any attempt to find the meaning, or the tragedy, or the humor of the story is rigorously edited out as an expression of opinion which belongs only in the editorial columns. . . .

My complaint is, in short, that the work is so mechanical that I am learning nothing. I might as well be attached to a clipping bureau. . . .

What I have dreamed of doing is to work under you. Can you use me in your work? There is no position I should go at with more eagerness, because there is no kind of work that appeals to me as much as yours does. Money does not happen to be an important consideration for me at the present time. Opportunity to work and to learn is the thing I am looking for. . . .

1. Lincoln Steffens, the celebrated muckraker, had advised Lippmann to enter a career of writing. For his part, Lippmann seized the chance to begin as a reporter for the *Boston Common*, a weekly paper of which his old friend Ralph Albertson, a former clergyman and sentimental Socialist, was publisher. Neither Albertson nor his associates were the "good journalists" Steffens had urged Lippmann to seek out for an apprenticeship.

To Lincoln Steffens

April 17, 1911

Dear Mr. Steffens,

Before I left,[1] I wanted badly to tell you a little of what this year with you has meant to me. But of course, I flunked; it's so devilish easy to say what you think, and so devilish hard to say what you feel. No matter how much I meant to say, I'd probably have talked about the Insurgent prospects in 1920 while I meant to be telling you how deeply, deeply grateful I am to you.

Writing it down while you aren't looking on makes it a little easier. You often asked me whether the year had been worthwhile. Lord, if I could tell you and make you believe it. You'd know then why "Everybody who knows you loves you." You gave me yourself, — and then you ask me whether it has been worthwhile. For that I can't write down my thanks. I shall have to live them.

But whenever I understand a man and like him, instead of hating him or ignoring him, it'll be your work. You've got into my blood, I think, and there'll be a little less bile in the world as a result. It was like letting loose a hungry man in Park & Tilfords. You gave me a chance to start — you know what that means to a fellow who has an indifferent world staring him in the face.

There are only two things more I want from you. One is to see you very, very often, and the other is the chance to do you a service. I almost wish you'd take it into your head that you needed some thing that was only to be had in Peru. I'd like to make the trip there just to show you how ready I am at any moment to work my head off for you. . . .

1. Lippmann was leaving his post as Steffens's assistant. They had worked together primarily on a study of the structure of American banking and business.

To Graham Wallas[1]   HANDWRITTEN

November 9, 1911

Dear Mr. Wallas,

I met Zimmern[2] last night for the first time — I had been away from the city. Of course, I liked him immensely. I know that the five hours we spent together were incredibly short. I wanted to embrace him for he was the first human being I've met for ever so long who wanted to see in America the things I've been trying to see for the last year and a half. And of course, we talked at length about you and the very deep things to be got out of you.

Our policies here are largely concerned with the new alignment which is bound to come between 1912 and 1916. La Follette in the Republican party and Woodrow Wilson among the Democrats are moving closer together — they already have some kind of understanding. Bryan, who is still important, broke all precedent by speaking for La Follette the other day. The support for La Follette is made up of all kinds of liberals and radicals. In the East, only social workers and various propagandists — single taxers, collectivists, etc. — are supporting him. Wilson is strong everywhere — even in the East. His academic prestige is helping him a good deal.

Syndicalism is becoming something of an issue here among the brave unionists. The McNamara case at Los Angeles[3] is really the first example where all kinds of labor interests are united. They expect to carry the city for socialism. . . .

1. Graham Wallas — eminent British social critic, earlier a Fabian Socialist, author of *Human Nature in Politics* (London, 1908) — much influenced Lippmann, who with several of his friends attended the courses Wallas gave while visiting Harvard. As his first two books revealed, Lippmann

had large intellectual debts to Wallas, who for his part became intrigued with his young friend's quiet intelligence. Theirs was to be a long and close relationship.   **2.** Alfred E. (later Sir Alfred) Zimmern, British political analyst and outstanding lecturer, was author of *The Greek Commonwealth: Politics and Economics in Fifth-Century Athens* (Oxford, 1911). A classic of its kind, the book embraced various reform causes, including the dismantling of the British Empire and, in time, the creation of a league of nations.   **3.** The brothers John J. and James B. McNamara had confessed to bombing the *Los Angeles Times* building in October 1910, an incident that caused twenty-one deaths. Their lawyer, Clarence Darrow, had made a secret arrangement, never wholly divulged, which guaranteed a life sentence instead of a death sentence for John, and a shorter sentence for James. In Los Angeles, a strong antiunion city, the Socialist candidate for mayor lost.

To Hazel Albertson[1]   HANDWRITTEN

January 8, 1912

Dear Hazel,

. . . Being in Schenectady isn't as inspiring as it sounds.[2] I don't mean for a minute that I'm bothered at all by being away out here in a city which is a mere adjunct to two factories. What appalls me is the smallness of our power and our knowledge and our ability in the face of the problems we are supposed to solve. It's really pathetic to see as I do every day twenty-five to fifty men out of work, hungry, cold, come here with shining eyes to participate in this new heaven on earth which socialism promised them. Many of them lost their jobs because they worked for the victory. And we can't do anything essential for them. Inspect them a little closer for disease — give them a municipal skating rink and a concert! Tabulate a few more statistics of unemployment! Install what goes by the name of efficiency, talk in whispers about possible municipal ownership if the state legislature allows us, and hide our impotence in as sympathetic a face as we can put on.

We are, dear Hazel, a ridiculous spectacle. Between keeping the half hearted in line, and proving to the country that we're safe and sane, between the ignorance of real conditions which we share with everybody else, and the old blunderbusses which go by the name of political machinery, I have all the sensations of a man trying to tie a string around a sunbeam. I'm becoming more and more sure that political victories are comparatively insignificant; that we must know more before we can do more; that the obstacles are not the greed or bad will of capitalists one half so much as the unimaginative, dry, timid, mechanical boxes of wood which go by the name of brains. . . .

1. Hazel Albertson, Ralph Albertson's second wife, presided over the informal fellowship at their farm in West Newbury, Massachusetts — something of a haven for Lippmann and a small company of his Harvard friends, among many others. She was little older than they, a wise and a warm woman who played for them the role of confidante and charmer. About Hazel, her husband, and the farm, the most incisive account is in Frances Davis, *A Fearful Innocence* (Kent, Ohio, 1981).   **2.** Lippmann had become assistant to the Reverend George R. Lunn, the Socialist candidate elected in 1911 as mayor of Schenectady, New York.

To Hazel Albertson

HANDWRITTEN

March 4, 1912

Dear Hazel,

I wish I could watch your face when you read this letter: I'm going to resign my position here in a few weeks.

The reason is complicated because it lies in circumstances outside of myself and in certain determinations within myself. From what I've written already you must have seen that the socialism in Schenectady was more of a name than a reality. A mushroom victory to begin with, based on a whirlwind campaign of personalities, the socialists are in power over a city almost entirely unconverted. They have won votes but they have not taken the trouble to make socialists. The result is what might have been expected: the development of ring rule and machine politics with the frank objects of staying in power. In six weeks we had the stand-put psychology in full bloom. You know I am no impossibilist, but I know machine politics and political disloyalty when I see them.

The situation in Schenectady is a very dangerous one for the socialist movement: having got the name without the substance, it has created hopes which it must dash to pieces. If Schenectady is to stand for Socialism, there is nothing left for the workers but direct action. If that is what ballots achieve, they will have to turn to bullets.

It seems to me that if political action is to be saved, we must turn our faces away from the socialism which works for immediate success. And political action must be saved: it is the only way that creative statesmanship can find expression. The general strike, sabotage and propaganda of the deed are dramatic and compelling, but they are dust and ashes in the long run.

Yet nothing is so clear than that the sham politics of Schenectady mean despair with political action. We must not take political power till the people understand what we are up to, that is the rock of truth on which democracy is built.

Education, talk, persuasion aiming to make socialists — that is worth doing. But sitting tight on political jobs — that is not worth doing, it seems to me. I know it isn't worthwhile for me at any rate. And so I'm resigning. Lord knows I shall be roasted for it.

I'm not going to make any public attack just now at any rate. If I published anything it would make trouble, and that wouldn't be quite fair at this time.

But as to my own position I'm quite sure. My work isn't arranging compromises, covering up mistakes, putting on a front of steel to cover a heart of butter, and living in an atmosphere of grand phrases and petty intrigue.

I've about made up my mind to get away from everything until the fall. The last two years have been so tremendously crowded that I positively long for fresh air. That book of which I read you the beginning[1] in your den interests me more than anything else just now, and so I'm going to cut away from all committees, conferences and muckraking to do that.

When the break comes in Schenectady I'm going to come up to the farm for a week. How good that will be. In the meantime I'm keeping this a dead secret from everyone but a few very dear friends. . . .

1. That book became *A Preface to Politics* (New York, 1913), on which Lippmann worked while in Maine during the summer of 1912.

To Hazel Albertson   HANDWRITTEN

March 11, 1912

Dear Hazel,

You do not know how much I appreciate your letter or how deeply glad I am that you were so honest with me. But there is no use denying that it left me feeling considerably bruised. It was all so true — yet so untrue for me.

These things — lunches, streets, playgrounds — are worth doing, possibly more worth doing than anything I shall ever do. But they are not the things for me to do. We cannot sit down and think out rationally what is worthwhile — then turn and do just that. We have a bent — all wisdom consists in knowing it and all service in developing it. It often seems to me that the biggest tragedy in life is that so many people are determined by necessities instead of being guided by their own aptitudes, that is the real curse of our civilization — misery, hunger and pain become bearable when we follow our own bent — that's been shown again and again — they are unbearable when we are simply borne down by the weight of them and tortured for a reason we cannot understand. There is no use trying to make rooks white, says Galsworthy in "the Pigeon."

"It's too much like giving up," you say, dear Hazel. I have had that out with myself and the thing is clear to me. It will seem that way to everybody, and in a worldly way it will hurt me. It will destroy what confidence people have had in me — But it's not true anyway, and that's all that can be allowed to count. I know that staying on would be the easy thing to do — the lazy, acquiescent thing — the tempting, the softest thing to do.

When you tell me I have skipped such a lot of life for my age, I cannot answer. I know it and that's why I shall always fight an easy rut. Schenectady is becoming something of a rut, and I know at least what I do not know.

There is not much for me to do in Schenectady for a year to come. The program is made, the budget finished — only the execution remains. That is for the experts to do — we know what we are going to build — the rest is technical work until next January. Oh to be sure, there's politics to play, and public opinion to swing — but in the matter of the concrete things you mention my part is done — and all I can do is watch.

I shall probably stay until the first of May. By that time I am satisfied the lesson will be learnt. And I am going to take advantage of your splendid faith to ask you to believe I am doing what I must. . . .

To Hazel Albertson

July 19, 1912

Hazel dear,

Those pinches arrived and I'm almost well. Today I played a little tennis and read Henry James — both slightly convalescent amusements I admit — but still convalescent.

I know I'm not sixty-five, and I haven't one white hair, and of course I'm not wise — but must one wait that long for understanding? Le coeur aussi plut comprendre un peu.

Just now I am pretty far behind on the book — the first chapter and the second are done in rough drafts — It's a big job of organization — a book is — and I'm an awful amateur at it — the thing constantly overflows its banks — thinking in chapters is really a very curious experience — I'm going to do the whole thing in the rough so that I can find out what it's all about, and then perhaps I'll grow one gray hair like yours, and be wise enough to — not sleep — but live on the book for a year or so. But until it's all written out I shall have the fidgets. . . .

To Graham Wallas

HANDWRITTEN

July 31, 1912

Dear Mr. Wallas,

John Graham Brooks[1] was kind enough to lend me the outline of your lecture on Syndicalism. I have wanted often in the last few months to write to you in order to draw a letter out of you.

I have had some interesting political experience in the last half year. The Socialists carried their first eastern city last November — the City of Schenectady in upper New York State. Victory came as a revulsion against two corrupt machines after an eloquent campaign by a young minister who had recently turned to socialism. He came down to New York last December and picked me up to act as his Secretary. On January first we went into office. It wasn't long before I discovered that the desire to raid saloons and brothels, to keep taxes below the usual rate, and to ignore the educational problem were the guiding principles of this "socialist" administration whose real ambition was to be re-elected. I cannot go into details. It would take too long. But the point is that the victory was a purely negative accident — they are occurring constantly in America Mr. Brooks tells me. On every vital question, the socialists ignored their own point of view and fell in with what we have come to know as "good government" or "goo-goo" politics.

I fought as hard as I could within the "organization" without any result. When I saw that the policy and program were settled, as under our charters they naturally are in the first few months, I resigned and attacked the administration in a socialist paper.[2] This brought down upon me the wrath of the leaders — my analysis was ignored, but I was the subject of the most careful and bitter attention for several weeks.

The whole affair is very objective to me. I have a splendid little collection of letters informing me that I have "botched" my political career. But as the only interest a "career" would have is the chance to understand politics a little more directly, I really feel elated that mine was so compressed that I can already look back upon it.

Seriously, though, I have been writing what may be a little book — at least a series of essays, and no small part of it is aimed at popularizing your "Human Nature in Politics".[3] You do not know how eagerly I am looking forward to the sequel. For the rest I have been reading a good deal in the Freudian psychology and puzzling about socialism, syndicalism and the complexities of our political situation.

We are all elated that Wilson got so far.[4] He is lucid and imaginative, and above all intellectually honest. You know how rare that is in national politics. But his perceptions are not very wide. The labor situation which is becoming very urgent is not very vivid, I fear, in Wilson's mind. But he grows as no other politician we have. If elected we all expect him to outgrow his party in short order. For once he begins to handle the situation he must face, his conglomerate supporters will drop off. . . .

1. John Graham Brooks, American Socialist and reformer of a progressive temper, advocate of trade unions and social security legislation.   2. The *New York Call*, June 9, 1912.   3. In *Human Nature in Politics,* Wallas had stressed the irrationality of politics and the significance of prejudice and habit in political behavior.   4. Woodrow Wilson had won the Democratic nomination for president.

To Hazel Albertson   HANDWRITTEN

September 18, 1912

Hazel dear,

. . . Some day I must tell you all about myself. I know more than I used to about that person. But one thing you say — and this isn't the first time — puzzles me a good deal — my 'protected existence.' Surely you cannot mean that I have had comfort and no worry about necessaries. That protection doesn't go very far. Protected against what? How can a person be protected against the banes of life if he sees them. Only an elephant's hide will do that, and I'm only a partial elephant, you know.

I have never cared for an upholstered life, and, please God, I never shall. The protected existence, as I see it, is to refuse the risks, to be prudent and acquiescent, to sit tight, perhaps to climb cautiously, but never to plunge. I have had perhaps ten chances for a career that would have been useful and honorable and certain. Just that I couldn't endure. I'd rather be squashed at the bottom of the heap than planted at the top. The thing that is easy to do isn't worth doing when you've done it.

How flat it seems to write out these things. And how can I answer your question? There is a deep sadness in things, a persistent vein that sounds to me like mockery. "Even not quite" — yes, one can rejoice in that, but not altogether. Perfection is a want that stays with us, philosophize about it as we will. Some beautiful things give it, children promise it, there are moments in love and friendship. For the most part we have to lay aside this dream; if we have the vigor, we find joy in effort itself, and cease to think about its results. In laying that hope aside, in a willingness to love life as a finite gift, skepticism enters into your soul. The great faiths are built on absolutism, and when they have gone men have merely their own courage to beat off loneliness. An odyssey that never ends — it's not an unmixed joy.

These things lie in the back of my head. Sometimes they come forward and ask disturbing questions. I can't answer them, though I can shut them up. In a personal way I am very happy — now especially. There is so much to love and do in the world — so much that after all does answer to our needs. The futilities — well, we are what we are. . . .

To Graham Wallas   HANDWRITTEN

October 30, 1912

Dear Mr. Wallas,

Your letter gave me great pleasure. After such a lapse of time — yours is dated Sept. 17 — a direct answer becomes awkward. Your "preaching" about the "element of uncertainty in looking forward" and the danger of fixed formulae is in line with what I have been writing all summer. That surely is the great difficulty in all complicated thinking — to understand that the concept is a rough instrument that stands in place of adequate perception — to see that abstract thinking is a short cut, a continuance, and of no value in itself. The more I see of "machine politics" the more certain I become that metaphysics is a very real and important pursuit. The epistemological problem, especially, is one that has tremendous consequences. James[1] always felt that, and I'm just beginning to see concretely what he meant. . . .

Are you in your new book making much use of the Freudian psychology? I have been studying it with a great deal of enthusiasm for several months now, and I feel about it as men might have felt about "The Origin of Species." The Freudian psychology is truly "Ailfenpsychologie" — a dynamic conception of the mind. I went back and read some of James with a curious sense that the world must have been very young in the '80's! The dream interpretations, the book on wit, the esthetics, the child psychology do for the first time in any psychology I know furnish a picture of human nature in the act, so to speak, of venting and expressing its character. Moreover there is the immense recommendation that this psychology is receiving a constant clinical test, and in finding so much justification in its results. Its political applications have hardly begun, though there are a few stray articles here and there. . . .

1. William James, the great American philosopher, whom Lippmann had come to know at Harvard.

To Max F. Eastman [1]   HANDWRITTEN

April 24, 1913

Dear Max,

I have just finished reading your book. I love you for it. I love it because it is so much more than a book about something else; it's the revelation of a very vivid and loving human being. I can testify to a complete achievement. You do increase enjoyment. I have been extraordinarily happy with your book.

Over the philosophy which saturates it, I gurgled with delight. It is so clear a proof that the new temper of mind enriches whatever it approaches. The best of modern feeling is in this book: it's fertile and human, and large with what James called 'aerial perspective.'

Thank you heartily. I'd like without cant to sign myself,

Fraternally yours,

1. Max F. Eastman, then editor of the *Masses*, Lippmann's contemporary and fellow participant in New York salons of "the lyrical left," had just published his *Enjoyment of Poetry* (New York, 1913).

To Theodore Roosevelt

May 30, 1913

Dear Colonel Roosevelt,

Thank you very much for your kind letter in regard to my book, "A Preface to Politics."[1] You can readily see from it that it owes a great deal to you, and for that reason I was very eager to have your opinion of it. I hope, when I return from abroad in the Fall, to have the opportunity of talking over some things with you. . . .

1. "I have only had a chance to glance at it," Roosevelt wrote on May 22, "but what I have seen I greatly liked." That response was predictable. Lippmann had written, for one example, "The Roosevelt regime gave a new prestige to the Presidency by effecting through it the greatest release of political invention in a generation"; *A Preface to Politics* (New York, 1913), p. 24.

To Hazel Albertson   HANDWRITTEN

October 23, 1913

Dear Pat,[1]

I had your letter written on my birthday just a few days before I sailed. Thanks for the wishes given and the pinches — deferred. You know I was very, very glad to hear from you, and that I haven't the slightest excuse for the bad way I've treated you in letters this summer. It wasn't because the soft spot for you is any less soft. I thought of you and the kiddies ever and ever so often. There were times when I'd have given anything to be with you, walking in the mountains or looking at things. But writing was another matter. The things that really counted were too complicated for letters at such a distance, and I really couldn't afflict you with sections of Baedecker — could I, Pat?

It has been a very long time — five months, crowded. First, there's the book I'm working on.[2] It has given me very little peace all summer. The first draft which I did in July and August was a sort of 50,000 word thesis of what I'd been doing last winter. That was no sooner done than the thing began to grow in all sorts of directions — with the standing around and trying to keep up with it. I don't feel for a minute that I've dominated it or that it's really my own. It's as if the idea of the book had a life of its own, making me feel fearfully humble and inadequate. Sometimes I think that I'm just learning what the real tension of thought can be. For six or eight months now I don't believe I've had two hours, lying around or walking, that haven't been stirred or made taut by this book. I may have been in Europe and having a wonderful time, but a vacation (like Center Lovell) I haven't had. When the last proof is corrected, I shall yell. Yell with me, Pat. I positively ache for a fight, for journalism, for literary essays, for anything that doesn't take all of you all of the time.

You ask how I am. That's how I am. You get honest answers, Pat, because you understand them.

I don't know where to begin about what I've seen. It's been the most un-imaginable variety — an airship flying over Venice, a week bathing and baking by the Adriatic, a new play by Wedekind in Berlin with Wedekind in the principal role, a fine talk with H. G. Wells,[3] with Graham Wallas, Alfred Zimmern, John Hobson,[4] the first international syndicalist congress, Shaw's wonderful new play — "Androcles and the Lion", a visit to Sam in Manchester, a feeling that Manchester is the bottom of hell, and a fascinating trip through Ireland. We had the best kind of opportunity there. We were in Ulster and Belfast when the Carson rebellion[5] was on, in Dublin at the time of the Larkin strike,[6] had an evening with George Russell (AE) who is, of course, one of the principal poets of the Gaelic Revival, and at the same time editor of the "Irish Homestead," the organ of the marvellous cooperative movement which is doing revolutionary work. Ireland is a most stimulating country for studying social conditions in their relation to national psychology. I've been doing nothing but read about Ireland for a month. I want to tell you about the cooperative movement there when I see you. . . .

We had a storm at sea about four days ago that would have gladdened your heart. This monster of a ship had to stop, it was so bad. The sea can do things when it tries.

1. One of her several pet names. For her part, she frequently referred to Lippmann, a somewhat plump and precocious young man, as "Buddha." **2.** A draft of *Drift and Mastery*, which Lippmann published the next year. **3.** Frank Wedekind, the notable German playwright, and H. G. Wells, who had just published *The Passionate Friends* (London, 1913). **4.** John A. Hobson had just published *Gold, Prices and Wages, With an Explanation of the Quantity Theory* (London, 1913). **5.** Sir Edward Carson led the opposition in Ulster to Home Rule for Ireland, which the House of Commons had approved but the House of Lords vetoed. By July 1913, he had raised a volunteer force of more than two hundred thousand Ulstermen to resist Home Rule. In 1914 the House of Commons agreed to exempt Ulster. **6.** James Larkin — Irish syndicalist and trade economist, principal organizer of unskilled Irish workers, and the founder of the Irish Transport Workers Union — led his union in a series of strikes that spread through central and southern Ireland during 1912–13. After employers resorted to a lockout that heightened the already considerable level of violence on both sides, the union admitted defeat in January 1914.

To Van Wyck Brooks[1]

HANDWRITTEN

February 5, 1914

Dear Brooks,

It was good to hear from you, especially as my conscience has been bothering . . . me. I read your book as soon as it came, and I started right in to send you word about it. The letter didn't get finished that day, and the next day I had to go out of town. When I came home, the letter was stale, and so between conscience and indolence, I haven't written to you. But I have thought often, and felt glad that we had begun to know each other.

Your book helped that along. It was fine and personal, and rich with intimate experience. It made me feel that the kind of thing I do is rancorous, and noisy, and sweaty. I like a good fight, but it's all so preliminary. It is on the conflicts you've written about that real values and final judgments depend.

I think I have one piece of good news for you. We're starting a weekly here next fall — a weekly of ideas — with a paid up capital — God save us — of $200,000. The age of miracles, sir, has just begun. Our general form will be that of the Saturday Review. The substance will be American, but sophisticated and critical. The editor is to be Herbert Croly, who wrote "The Promise of American Life"; Walter Weyl ("The New Democracy") is to be a regular contributor; Francis Hackett, formerly of the Chicago Post, and a few others are to be regular editors. I'm going to give most of my time to the paper, and while the heaven isn't altogether unclouded, it will pass for excellent weather, I think.

S. K. Ratcliffe, who works for "The New Statesman" and "The Nation" is to be a sort of official English representative; Graham Wallas is very much interested, and we expect to camp steadily on Zimmern's trail. Will you consider yourself elected a contributor? I think you will find the work worth your while. We have every opportunity of focusing the young men in America, and if we succeed we ought to do something that America needs very badly. I wish you'd think of yourself as one of our group, make it a personal interest of yours, and help in the suggestions and ideas, as well as with articles. I should add that we won't publish till next fall, and that our name is to be "The Republic".[2]

We may be able to do what you ask for in your letter — to define the issues on the "robust middle plane", put a critical clinch into discussion, and infuse American emotions with American thought. That is our expressed purpose, at any rate. We have no party axe or propaganda axe to grind. We shall be socialistic in direction, but not in method, or phrase or allegiance. If there is any word to cover our ideal, I suppose it is humanist, somewhat sharply distinguished (but not by Irving Babbitt)[3] from humanitarianism. Humanism, I believe, means this real sense of the relation between the abstract and the concrete, between the noble dream and the actual limitations of life. I hope that every part of the paper will be vivid with the humor and insights and sounds of American life, and yet imaginative enough to point through them to a more finely disciplined and what Wells calls a more spacious order of living.

I wish you would do that article on the windier Americans. They irritate me enormously, so much that I can't treat them with the respect they undoubtedly deserve. They are so damned lazy. Rhetoric is so damned cheap. That man Lee[4] has sold like a novel: he makes every self-righteous business man feel like Julius Caesar and St. George rolled into one. Lee's theory is that businessmen will become that by assuming that they are that. But I think Lee is a toady and a flatterer and a great self-deceiving fraud. I don't know why I should get into a temper about this to you. I guess it's because I've had such a close contact this winter with people like Lee, and I'm raw on the subject. . . .

1. Van Wyck Brooks, whom Lippmann had first met in England, had just published *The Wine of the Puritans* (New York, 1909) and was working on *America's Coming of Age* (New York, 1915). 2. Changed, of course, to *The New Republic*. 3. Irving Babbitt, a conservative humanist and influential literary critic, then also a professor at Harvard. 4. Ivy L. Lee, then near the pinnacle of his career as a public relations counselor to existing monuments of corporate wealth such as John D. Rockefeller and the Bethlehem Steel Company.

To Graham Wallas

May 12, 1914

Dear Mr. Wallas,

I had no idea that you had it in mind to do for me what you have done.[1] Nothing that has ever come to me has meant so much as this chance to be

identified a little with your work. I know what form you want my gratitude
to take — You wrote it on the copy of "Human Nature in Politics" which you
gave me when you were at Harvard — to "be truth's pilgrim at the plough."
I'll keep that faith, and while I know I've done nothing to deserve such a gift,
I can take it as a pupil from his teacher. . . .

I wonder how the Mexican trouble[2] looks to you in England. There is almost no public feeling here: Hearst's most violent efforts have had very little
effect. I've just been out through Western New York and Ohio, and everywhere I found a lack of war spirit. I believe that the real fever is confined to
the Texas and Arizona borders. The rest is rather ineffective newspaper agitation. The refusal of the country to become excited has been a great relief,
and everyone says that the contrast with 1898 is startling.

The most informed interpretation of Wilson's sudden aggression is that
after the fall of Torreón, John Lind returned to Washington and urged the
President that a blockade would enable the Constitutionalists to strangle Huerta,
and that Wilson seized upon the Tampico incident. His greatest ally just now
seems to be time. Incidentally the mediation of the A.B.C. powers,[3] while
meaningless because there is nothing to mediate, has made an immense breach
in the Monroe Doctrine, relieving the United States of a great deal of responsibility in the future.

In the midst of the Mexican trouble we had a civil war in Colorado[4] and it
attracted at least as much enthusiasm as the operations at Veracruz. Nobody
knows the facts here in the East, but it's said that the present strikers who
came from the Balkans, were imported here years ago to break a strike of Irish
and American born miners. . . .

1. Wallas had dedicated his new book, *The Great Society* (London, 1914), to Lippmann in acknowledgment of the younger man's comments about the subject matter, which Wallas had been
addressing while he was teaching at Harvard.   2. Wilson, abandoning his announced policy of
"watchful waiting," had sent American troops into Veracruz in retaliation for a petty insult to an
American naval vessel at Tampico. In part an act of petulance, the seizure and blockade of Veracruz represented also an effort on Wilson's part to prevent the landing of German arms. John
Lind, a friend of Secretary of State William Jennings Bryan and a former governor of Minnesota,
had served as Wilson's confidential agent in Mexico and in that role presented terms to the Huerta
government, which rejected them.   3. Argentina, Brazil, and Chile.   4. The bloody strikes of
coal miners against the Rockefeller interests in Colorado.

To Felix Frankfurter[1]

August 2, 1914

Dear Felix,

—   This isn't a very cheerful day to be writing to you. It's an hour since we
learned that Germany has declared war against Russia. We shall hear of France
later in the day, no doubt. Wallas and Hobson, Gilbert Murray, Hobhouse
and the others are at work trying to stir liberal feeling against immediate

intervention by England.[2] But it's a toss up. We sit and stare at each other and make idiotically cheerful remarks. And in the meantime so far as anyone can see, nothing can stop the awful disintegration now. Nor is there any way of looking beyond it; ideas, books, seem too utterly trivial, and all the public opinion, democratic hope and what not, where is it today? Like a flower in the path of a plough.

Petitions are being signed. We shall march in Trafalgar Square this afternoon, and the madness is seizing us all, so that taking war as we do there is something which makes me feel like getting at the throat of Germany.

I spent this last week in Belgium where the panic was nerve-wracking. Money seemed not to exist. A twenty franc note was practically valueless in Brussels. I had hoped to get on to Switzerland. But that was impossible. So here I am back in England being taken care of by the Wallases and wondering whether to stay in Europe or to come home. There is nothing to 'see' except anxious people buying thoroughly censored news dispatches — you feel this money panic, but all anyone can do is to wait and wait. Jack Reed was bored at the battle of Torreón.[3] I can understand it now. There is the worst event in the world hanging over our heads and all we can do is to read once in twenty-four hours a two-line Reuter telegram entirely surrounded by journalese. . . .

1. Felix Frankfurter and Lippmann, linked by their involvement in *The New Republic*, their interests in social reform, and their enthusiasm for Theodore Roosevelt, were then in the early stage of a long friendship that eventually faltered over differences in their views and essential differences in their temperaments. In 1914 Frankfurter, a contributor and adviser to *The New Republic* and a veteran of public service, became a professor of law at Harvard. **2.** Graham Wallas, John Hobson, Gilbert Murray, and Leonard Hobhouse — "radical liberals" in Lippmann's phrase — were members of the British Neutrality League. As Lippmann noted in his diary for August 2, 1914 — a diary he kept only intermittently — "even today their position seems hopeless." Later that day at Trafalgar Square, he was, he wrote, "overcome with a general feeling of futility, a sense that fighting had to be, and the sooner the better." By the next day, Murray and Hobson, among others, had reluctantly accepted the inevitability of war, which England declared on Germany on August 5, following the German invasion of Belgium. "My own part in this," Lippmann then wrote in his diary, "is to understand world-politics, to be interested in National and Military affairs, and to get away from the old liberalism which concentrates entirely on liberal problems. We cannot lose all that but see now that our really civilized effort is set in a structure of raw necessity." **3.** John Reed, Lippmann's radical and romantic Harvard classmate, had observed as a reporter the capture of Torreón, Mexico, by the Constitutionalists during their campaign against Pancho Villa and his personal following.

To Hazel Albertson

HANDWRITTEN

September 25, 1914

Pat dear,

Here I am back, and it seems as if a good pinch from you would wake me up so as to be able to say: 'That horror in Europe is unreal, but Pat and the kiddies and the Farm and the sanctity of human beings are real.' It all came so incredibly fast. On Thursday in Ostende we were sunning ourselves on the beach; on Friday I was wandering around Fifteenth Century Bruges; on Saturday in Brussels people were weeping in the streets. We crept back to London through hundreds of warcraft — rushing in to the North Sea, and then went through two days of unbelievable suspense while the English Cabinet was deciding for war. The most peaceful people you met were praying for war, praying that England should not stand aside while Belgium was annexed and France crushed.

I lived with Graham Wallas almost the whole time till I sailed last week. We tried to live in the country and read history and think out a settlement. On August 26 we thought the British force had been annihilated, and that the road to Paris was open. I tell you that was the blackest day I ever spent. That week I was having dinner with George Booth when he received word that in his brother's regiment eighteen out of twenty-one officers had been killed at the battle of Mons. The next week the refugees began to pour in — three little French children from Reims came to stay at the Wallas's. They had been running in front of the Germans for two weeks — their father was at the front, their mother a nurse: they had been within two streets of one of the bombs dropped in Paris. The little girl woke up in the night screaming, 'les Taut' — the name of the German armored aeroplane. On the streets of London the kiddies were forever looking up at the sky.

I saw soldiers go: I saw them come back, and as the weeks passed there was noticeable increase of people in mourning. I could go on endlessly with the detailed horrors that began to permeate ordinary life — the line of anxious women waiting at the war office; the terror of German waiters and barbers; the searchlights playing over the sky at night, and this run across the ocean without light through fog and icefields.

We tried to find comfort in what we were pleased to call the "larger historic meaning," but I for one don't find one. If Germany wins the whole world will have to arm against her — the U.S. included, for Germany quite seriously intends to dominate the World: if Germany loses, Russia alone wins, and every country in Europe will arm for a struggle in which Asia is the stake. Two equally uncomfortable horns of the dilemma. Do you see anything hopeful? . . .

To Robert Dell[1]

October 26, 1914

Dear Mr. Dell:

 . . . Our own sympathies here are with the Allies, although we do not accept the British case at its face value, or hold the Allies entirely guiltless. Of course, now that the war is on, we look for a decision that shall not be too crushing for any of the nations. I tell you these more or less obvious matters so as to give you a little better sense, perhaps, of the audience for whom you will be writing. . . .

1. Robert Dell was then *The New Republic*'s Paris correspondent.

To Roy Ogden [1]

December 8, 1914

Dear Mr. Ogden:

. . . What I object to most in Wilson's policy is the fact not that he has kept the peace but that he has intervened. I think that in making the United States responsible for the government of Mexico he took the one most dangerous step toward intervention. He admitted the first item in the doctrine of aggrandizement, which is that you are responsible for the government of your neighbor. It is just what all the people who are talking about the White Man's Burden and the rest of the imperialistic slang always say, and the fact that the President was actuated by pacifist motives does not alter the fact that he played into their hands. . . .

1. Roy Ogden, then a student at Harvard, had written Lippmann to defend Wilson's policies in Mexico, which Ogden interpreted rather curiously as manifestations of the president's opposition to American aggrandizement.

To Marie Hoffendahl Jenney Howe [1]

February 16, 1915

Dear Mrs. Howe:

Even though I may not be able to come,[2] I don't want to be kept out of the discussion, so I shall jot down a few stray thoughts which occur to me on the subject of the evening. Of course, this is like being the first speaker with no chance for plagiarism.

No doubt somebody will define the terms. But definition is not easy. You know the fable of the blind men who tried to define an elephant. One of them took hold of the tusk and said: The elephant is a slender, bony rod. Another took hold of the ear and said: it's a large, shapeless, floppy thing. Another held the tail and said: it's insignificant. That is the human way of making definitions. We all tend to think that the part we know is the whole of the creature.

So with this reservation let me say that I understand by feminism the rebellions, the experiments, and the efforts at readjustment made by modern women in response to the development of capitalism, the application of inventions, the spread of political democracy, and the opening up of education. But in a complicated social movement it is never possible to know how much we are pushed by circumstances and how much we pull because we wish it. So in a rough way one might describe feminism as a virtue made out of a necessity. Women have to readjust their lives. This compulsion has made them dream various ideals. They have pictured themselves as self-governing, self-respecting members of a free community in which they shall have the opportunity not only to live usefully, but to make and to share a more humane culture. In other words, the emancipation of women, which is at bottom the dumb product of social conditions, becomes in a small minority a self-conscious purpose. Women come to desire what they are compelled to be.

But desires, theories, ideals always run ahead of the facts, and a good part of the time they run directly against the grain of the facts. That is why we discuss feminism. It is our attempt to make our theories count in the actual world. It means generally that we modify the world a little, and our theories a great deal.

For what happens, it seems to me, is this: Women have to live differently. Yet society is not decently ordered so they can live differently. They go into industry because they are compelled to, but they find that industry is not conducted so they can live sanely within it. They learn to desire a wiser choice of mates and they are confronted with a class-bound society, in which human selection is subordinated to economic necessities.

These obstacles drive the ablest women to revolt and to reconstruction. But in the very process of revolt and reconstruction they learn to think for themselves, they practice independence, they become sophisticated about the world. In short, the making of a better society is the training ground of feminism.

I call that better society socialism. I don't identify it with the Socialist Party. I don't identify it with government ownership, or the general strike. I think of it as a society in which social opportunity has been equalized, in which property has lost its political power, a society in which everyone has a genuine vote, not only a ballot, but a real share in economic development, and free access to the resources of civilization. Such a society cannot be realized without feminism. It will, I believe, in large measure be made by feminism.

For that reason I am unable to distinguish feminism from socialism, except to say that feminism is the special name we give to the special women's problems in the struggle for socialism. But those problems can never be disentangled from men's problems, or children's problems. They are all parts of one another. It is only for intellectual convenience, for purposes of classification that we make the distinction. For obviously women cannot live well except in a fine society, and a fine society cannot be made without the help of women.

1. Marie Hoffendahl Jenney Howe, feminist founder of "Heterodoxy," Greenwich Village's avant-garde women's club, had married the urban reformer Frederic C. Howe in 1903.   2. To a meeting of the Men's League for Equal Suffrage, of which Lippmann was a member and a luminary on the Publicity Committee.

To Theodore Roosevelt, Jr.[1]

February 18, 1915

Dear Ted:

One of the reasons why I have delayed so long in sending you the suggestions which I promised is that I have not been able to formulate them to myself. Essentially, too, I have not anything much to add to the draft which I prepared for your father last Spring.[2] However, as a matter of approach to an article whose purpose is a confession of faith on labor, it seems to me the most good would be done by beginning right away with a statement of what that faith is.

As I see it, it is a belief that workingmen will learn industrial citizenship from the exercise of industrial power; that the only way the habit and intelligence for industrial democracy can be developed is by the increasing exercise of industrial responsibility. If that faith is pretty strong in us we have got to be prepared to understand failure, disappointment, corruption, and all the other bad qualities which labor shows in such a startling parallel to the political citizen. By "understanding," of course I do not mean indulgence or excuse, or acquiescence. I mean, simply, that we shall look upon labor unions as hard schools of experience in which the lessons gained from experience are of more importance to the community than the immediate comfort of mind of some employer, or the confidence of some factory manager.

Having stated this faith, I should want to go on and discriminate within the labor world. I should want to point out the difference between the old powerful conservative unions based on skill, on long tenure of job, on the exercise of responsibility, on contact with American institutions with the floating here-today-gone-tomorrow type of union made up of men who have no stake in the country, who literally have nothing to lose and who are in an industrial position where the opportunity to develop industrial character and industrial morale is practically denied them.

On the basis of this discrimination I should want to urge that the time is coming when certain industries ought to make an experiment in representative government. Some far-sighted railroad man, for example, ought to try a radical reorganization of the method by which a board of directors is chosen. It seems to me that the proper representation now would be one director from the stockholders, one director from the bankers, one director from the shippers (elected perhaps by the chambers of commerce in the section which the railroad serves), one representative of the working force, and one representative of the executive, who would be the President. Such an experiment if honestly carried out would give us a chance to test our theories and would be a practical demonstration of what we mean by our faith in labor.

There would arise, of course, the question of the financial responsibility of the workers represented. It seems to me that the only fair way to make that responsibility real now is to establish a form of conditional compensation. I use the term "conditional compensation" rather than profit sharing because profit sharing has come to mean giving individual workers individual share in the profits. The only way to share profits, however, and preserve the confidence of the union is to share in a lump sum with the union and let the union make the division of it. The great advantage of this method would be that it would create in the union a collective responsibility for the efficiency of the road. It would become the basis of a public opinion within the union against the individual shirker and it would not have the disadvantage of creating the competition of workmen which tends to disrupt the morale of the union.

This experiment should be adopted slowly and under such conditions that it could be very carefully watched and studied. There should be no attempt to apply it generally at first. However, for the industries where the experiment is not tried, we ought to stand at present simply for collective bargaining. For some unions the bargain might take the form of a legal contract with legal responsibility; for others, where the workers are weak and ill-informed, collective bargaining must simply be an attempt in a friendly way to settle differences with the representatives of the workingmen.

And then, of course, there is a large part for the state to play in the whole question of labor. The first item there, it seems to me, is the organization of the labor market by a system of nationally federated labor exchanges. The second, is the development of sickness, accident, and unemployment insurance. The third, is the development in parasitical industries of minimum wage boards. The fourth, is drastic legislation against child labor, overwork, bad sanitary conditions, and so on.

To support all this the state must create certain positive agencies for improving the efficiency and the character of labor. This means the development of real industrial education along the lines I believe laid down by Professor Dewey[3] and so interestingly developed in Gary, Indiana. Then, too, there must be coordination between the labor exchanges and the schools so that vocational guidance may be based not only on a knowledge of the pupil's capacities but a knowledge of industrial demands.

There remains the question of violence in labor disputes. We ought to stand there, it seems to me, for lawful methods of enforcing the law. That means the elimination of the private detective, the private mine guard, the imported thug, and the provocateur. I don't know whether the necessary police work can best be done by state constabulary or by local police officials, but I want to suggest that if we establish a state constabulary and give the state power to police a strike, that power should always be exercised in conjunction with a scientific inquiry by the state into the causes of the strike. This would mean an industrial commission with power to go in to strike districts, summon witnesses, the books of the company, local citizens and compel a complete ventilation of the issues. However, I believe that no method of policing a strike will really be effective until we deal with the prime cause of violence in a strike, and that cause is the imported strike breaker. He is the real trouble maker and should be clearly distinguished from the nonunionist who refuses to go out on strike. I don't know about the constitutionality of the proposal, but it seems to me that as a matter of social policy it would be wise to forbid the importing of strike breakers until a government commission had sat upon the issues of the strike and attempted mediation. There is a real justice in this proposal for we ought to begin to recognize that the worker has certain property rights in his job. Under this plan that I suggest, he could not be replaced until public opinion in the community had had a fair chance to make up its mind about the causes of the strike. If the strikers are in the wrong but continue to be obstinate, the public will support legal protection to imported strikebreakers. If the strikers are in the right, it should not be in the power of the employer to break the strike through his superior economic position.

I hope this will be of some use to you and any points that you would like to have worked out in greater detail I shall be glad to take up again.

1. Theodore Roosevelt, Jr., Theodore Roosevelt's eldest son. **2.** For the ex-president's use in preparing a campaign against Wilson in 1916. The memo, like this letter, follows the contours of Lippmann's discussion of industrial democracy in his book *Drift and Mastery* (New York, 1914). **3.** John Dewey, the eminent philosopher of pragmatism and champion of social and educational reform.

To Theodore Roosevelt

March 10, 1915

Dear Mr. Roosevelt:

I am writing to you about a case in which the human facts are in conflict with legal right and wrong. A man named F. Sumner Boyd, an Englishman, took a small part in the Paterson Silk strike. He went out there one day to speak to the strikers and thoughtlessly and foolishly, at the request of some of the Italians, he spoke of sabotage. For that he was indicted and sentenced to a term in prison. He will go to prison in a short time now, unless mercy is shown to him.

There are many elements in the case which call for the exercise of charity. For one thing, Boyd has changed his point of view entirely. He knows and admits that he advocated a silly thing. For another, he is a man of frail health, threatened with tuberculosis. So far as I can see no end of justice can be served by making him pay the full penalty of the law. He is now working on the *Metropolitan Magazine,* trying to think straight. It seems like unnecessary cruelty to break up all that, wreck his health, and send him to prison to expiate a folly which had far better be forgotten and buried. Looked at as a matter of public policy, it seems to me pretty clear that class hatred and vindictiveness can only be increased, and that much is to be gained by showing mercy.

The Governor of New Jersey is to hold a hearing on Friday morning in

Jersey City at which a number of people are going to plead Boyd's case. They want a pardon or a commutation of sentence, and they feel that a word from you could do a great deal to avert this unnecessary tragedy. I don't want to be in a position of presuming upon your kindness to ask you to use your influence. I want only to put these facts before you with my own feeling. I feel I should not have done my duty unless I called the matter to your attention.[1]

1. Roosevelt wrote what Lippmann called a "generous letter about Mr. Boyd," but the governor did not commute the sentence.

To John Collier[1]

March 22, 1915

Dear Collier:

I want to write you in regard to the film, "The Birth of a Nation."[2] Would it be possible for you to write for us a statement of the attitude of the Board of Censors in regard to it? We think here that it is the most serious case in regard to the use of the "movies" that has come to public notice and we want to carry on the discussion with every possible fairness to the Board of Censors. I cannot imagine that the people I know on the Board of Censors could possibly have approved of the film, and in my ignorance I am wondering what determined their action.

Quite apart from the Board of Censors I am wondering whether something cannot be done to create public opinion against this film. Don't you think a mass meeting in Cooper Union is needed? I don't see how in self respect we can refrain from taking some action.

1. John Collier, an experienced and muscular social worker, a vocal opponent of racism, at this time with the People's Institute of New York City, later — during the 1930s — the leading champion of federal policies to preserve the cultural and tribal heritage of the American Indian.   2. On March 15, by a vote of fifteen to eight, the board had approved the showing in New York City of *The Birth of a Nation* with only minor changes in the film. In spite of various protests, it was exhibited. Stridently antiblack in content, the film proved also to be a classic in cinematography.

To Alfred E. Zimmern

June 7, 1915

My dear Zimmern:

At last I have had enough time to read "The War and Democracy."[1] And although I still have a chapter or two to read I must write to you and tell you how enthusiastic I am. It is indeed the very best book on the war published so far. A sweet tempered and generous book, such as one almost despairs of securing from a nation in the midst of war. I wish I could believe without any further doubt that your crowd represented enlightened England. It would disperse the last doubt I have about the fairness of the essential issues in this war.

Your opening chapter and your chapter on Germany and Seaton Watson's chapter on Austria-Hungary are I think the best things in the book. They have won me as almost nothing else that has come from England since last August. And with the general philosophy that lies behind them I think I agree too. I have been studying the *Round Table*[2] literature and feel essentially converted.

I would be a little more comfortable if the economic issues were more strongly emphasized and if the relations between commerce and nationalism were stressed. I also feel that the dangers of perverted nationalism are greater than the tenor of your book seems to imply. You do of course make the horror of the German kind of nationalism pretty clear. And I do not accuse you at all of being blind to the equal dangers of Italian or Japanese or even American nationalism. But I do think you slide over the point a little bit as the result of your sympathy for the denationalized groups. You do not quite make strong enough your opposition to the over-nationalized groups. I should have liked for instance to have it made clearer where nationalism ceases to be worth cultivating. Is every little language worth reviving? Ought we to advocate Gaelic revivals in Ireland and dialect revivals all over India, etc.? Ought we to be sympathetic only to the larger and simpler groupings?

We have been going through a bad month here ever since the *Lusitania* went down.[3] Our press has been very misrepresentative. The feeling against war in this country is a great deal deeper than you would imagine by reading the editorials. The feeling is due in part to horror of the war. It is in part due to a fear of what would happen to our own nationalism if we made war on the Fatherland of so large a proportion of our population, and in part I think to general international irresponsibility and shallowness of feeling.

We have all been very much worried about the situation in England. The Cabinet changes shocked us and somehow or other many of us got the sense from the tone of the press that there was something like panic or at least bad morale among the English and I hope there is nothing in that.

Why don't you plan to come over here some time or other? You could do an immense amount of good work for the English cause. . . .

In redrawing the map of Europe have you taken into consideration as much as you should the commercial strategy of frontiers? It does not always coincide with nationalistic frontiers — and ought we not to work for a larger number of internationalizations such as you suggest, quite rightly, for the problem of Trieste?[4]

---

1. Alfred E. Zimmern and Arthur Greenwood, *The War and Democracy* (London, 1914).
2. The *Round Table*, an English periodical, served as the voice of a group of men often referred to by the same name. They believed, in the large, in preserving the British Empire by federalizing

it, in a nationalism that rejected aggression against other nations, and in social reform to remove provocations to disruptive dissent.   **3.** On May 7, 1915, a German submarine sank the *Lusitania*, a British passenger liner carrying both travelers and munitions. One hundred twenty-eight Americans were killed. They had sailed in spite of a published German warning that the voyage would be dangerous. The Wilson administration considered the warning irrelevant to the rights of neutrals, negotiated to hold Germany to accountability for its acts, but assiduously avoided moving toward war. Nevertheless, the *Lusitania* episode provoked a sharp jingoism among Americans such as Theodore Roosevelt and a refreshed pacifism among those already leaning that way. Lippmann, neither jingo nor pacifist, continued to sympathize with the British cause and to oppose proposals for an embargo on all shipments of war materials, which would have hurt both Britain and France.   **4.** The Adriatic city Austria then held and Italy coveted.

To Robert Dell

June 7, 1915

Dear Mr. Dell:

. . . You mention in your letter the current belief in Paris that we propose to declare war on Germany. At this moment the tension is very great. Our press while not advocating war has advocated an attitude towards Germany which makes war very likely. But we here and a great mass of the people besides want to avoid getting into the struggle, if it is at all possible. We have everything to lose and nothing to gain by taking part in it. It would only mean that the last great power was engulfed in the unreasonableness of it all and that American lives far from being safer would be a great deal more in danger. What would happen to the little neutrals if Germany had nothing to fear from us is hard to imagine, and the prospect of deserting Belgium and the noncombatants and leaving them to Germany and Turkey is too terrible. We have got to stay out if there is any way of doing so. . . .

To Alfred E. Zimmern

June 23, 1915

My dear Zimmern:

. . . As for nationalism, I regard the European variety, which sets up the National State as its ideal, as a passing phase, and an anachronism at that. One could not say so at this juncture, because misgovernment and oppression seem to have made it a necessary phase.

But the break-up or rather the failure of Austria is a real world tragedy. Perhaps one should say, the conquest of Austria by Hungary. Anyhow it seems to be irreparable, and that part of the world will have to be built up from its elements. That being so, one must wish them much luck, knowing the pitfalls of independence and narrow nationalism. . . .

To Graham Wallas

HANDWRITTEN

August 5, 1915

Dear Graham Wallas,

A year ago we had just settled down in Surrey. I dread thinking how much pain you have gone through since then. I have just re-read the "Great Society" — I suppose for the tenth time — and nothing impressed me so much as the foreboding of this war which was with you when you wrote it. You were at least intellectually prepared for it. . . .

It seems kind of heartless to say that I've learned a lot. But that's a fact. We are too far away here to dwell long on the human horror of it. We are just near enough to realize that a whole new set of ideas and values has come to dominate our thinking. I feel now as if I had never before risen above the problems of a district nurse, a middle western political reformer, and an amiable civic enthusiast. At first I could make no approach to international affairs. The standard books seem obsessed with unanalyzed concepts like "sovereignty", "national interest", and so on. But in the last few months I've come to see that international politics is not essentially different from "domestic" politics, that there is in fact no division between them. They are phases and aspects of one another. The world problem is an infinitely complicated version of our old states rights controversy, our frontier problem, and negro, tariff, immigration, franchise, federal problems. I've been studying the history of American, German and Italian union, especially the work of men like Bismarck, Cavour, and Hamilton. Within certain territorial limits, and with definite class prepossessions, they grasped the problem of constructive internationalism. They welded, and united, and submerged petty sovereignties. The more I study them, the less faith I have in the kind of thing that the Bryce group is working on.[1] For it seems to me that federalism in order to work must have common things which animate it. Our federalism would never have had much reality if there hadn't been a Northwest Ordinance, an Erie Canal, transcontinental railroads, turnpikes, and so on for a federal government to administer. It was the administration of federal property which gave reality to Congress and the Supreme Court. Had there been nothing but Hague resolutions, and machinery of conciliation, we should never, I think, have been drawn together into federal union.

I've been making notes on all this in order to clarify my notions about it, and in a month or two, I'd like to send it to you for comment. This line of reasoning bears freshly, it seems to me, on the proposals for peace. . . .

1. Lord James Bryce — historian, statesman, unofficial interpreter of the United States to Great Britain — and other British World Federalists.

To Graham Wallas   HANDWRITTEN

December 8, 1915

Dear Graham Wallas,

I can't tell you how relieved I am at your letter. I wrote the book[1] with much misgiving, feeling at every point how much of a novice I was. Had there been any book written in America which was concerned with future organization, I should not have done it.

Now for the points you raise. The "clearing house idea" would clearly be useful, though it would not be possible I think to abandon the exchange of ambassadors. So much of what is "domestic" politics is also "international" politics that nations need to be represented in each other's capitals. Would it be desirable to define the jurisdiction of the clearing house envoys? Definition would be required, because they would have to act much more on their own initiative, owing to the difficulties of communication with sentiment at home. I think this definition would be required.

(a) The terms of representation in any world federation are the crux of the matter, and the biggest opportunity for invention. The problem would also have to be solved in respect to the local world gov'ts which I suggested. Some ratio between volume of trade, population, and geographical position has been suggested, and there are precedents I believe in the Venice Customs service. Much help is to be had by studying how Hamilton and Madison worked for the support of the larger American states.

(b) The question of sea power suffers I think from considerable confusion. When Germans talk of "freedom of the seas," they mean freedom in time of war. The lack of this freedom, they say, gives Britain preponderant diplomatic power in time of peace. They desire — (1) safety of commerce in time of war — (2) "equality (or nearly that) of naval strength." But so far I can see no guarantees in time of peace will hold in time of war if the issue is great enough. If two nations enter some kind of federation, they cannot at the same time make arrangements for breaking it up. And that is what "freedom of the seas" means to the Germans. It is their greater freedom to secure the prizes of the earth's surface. The whole discussion is vitiated, I think, by the old notion that freedom can be had by competition rather than cooperation. Now British seapower is the decisive factor in the future arrangement of the globe, but I personally prefer its semi-benevolent autocracy to the anarchy of "equal." And I am prepared to have the U.S. join with Britain in the control of the seas, rather than see a race of "sovereign states" oscillating in insecure "balance."

The only path that has promise is to go behind the question of what the power is for. If a fairly harmonious arrangement of the globe can be reached, the problem of power will become less important. The size of the states obstructs all our proposals for limiting armaments. . . .

The most interesting thing happening in America is the sudden appearance of Roosevelt as a candidate. The strangest thing of all is that the German-

Americans are swinging to him — their reasons are interesting. "He represents German Kultur" in America, and he is the best man to defeat Wilson. They pretend not to mind what he says about them.[2]

Personally, I have been in bad favor with Roosevelt for a year. We criticized him for his attitude about the Catholic church in Mexico.[3] Last night he sent word that it was time to forget and forgive, that there was great work to do, etc., etc.

It's the most difficult political decision I have ever had to make. Wilson is impossible. He has no sense of organization and no interest in the responsibility of the socialized state.[4] He has no grasp of international affairs, and his pacifism is of precious little help to the peace of the world. The Republican Party, sans Roosevelt, means Penrose and Barnes[5] and Capitalism unashamed. The Progressives are dispersed. The Socialists have become purely negative and orthodox.

Roosevelt alone of men who are possible has any vision of an integrated community. He is always better in action than in his talk. He is the only President in fifty years who gave social invention an impetus. And I am not sure but he is a more realistic pacifist than most.

His talk has often been sickening, but we think we know him well enough to understand that in the opposition he spends his energy in violent utterances, whereas in power that energy goes more largely into constructive effort.

Nevertheless it is the Devil's own choice, but a decision must be reached by the end of February. . . .

1. *The Stakes of Diplomacy* (New York, 1915).   2. Roosevelt was attacking those German-Americans who, in his view, had divided loyalties. He had advocated war against Germany since the sinking of the *Lusitania* the previous May, a position that Lippmann opposed in his new book, as well as in *The New Republic*.   3. Roosevelt had also been advocating armed intervention in Mexico, recently on the ground that the Constitutionalist government there was guilty of violating the property of the Catholic Church and the person of nuns and priests, a development he blamed on Wilson. *The New Republic* had criticized Roosevelt's hyperbole.   4. A theme implicit throughout Lippmann's *Drift and Mastery* (New York, 1914).   5. Boies Penrose and William Barnes, the notorious "bosses" respectively of the Pennsylvania and New York Republican organizations, both political opponents of Roosevelt in 1912 and thereafter.

To Felix Frankfurter   HANDWRITTEN

January 7, 1916

Dear Felix:

. . . I have just got back from Washington and heard lots of interesting things, — too many to write about now. But I will say that compared to the average Congressman and Senator the President is a gallant, dashing cavalier ready to risk his skin in any old cause at any old time.

I had tea with the British Ambassador[1] and a fussier, more hysterical old lady I have not seen for a long time. He thinks maybe he is going to be sent home because of the blockade,[2] and what he does not know about this country is almost all there is to know. I am going to write to Eustace[3] and tell him to discount about ninety percent of what he hears from Washington. He was really beyond belief. . . .

George Rublee's appointment is in a bad way I am afraid.[4] Senatorial courtesy seems to be in command of the situation. . . .

1. Sir Cecil Spring-Rice, an intimate of Theodore Roosevelt's, had perhaps passed the peak of his career, but his qualities of mind and character were considerably more impressive than Lippmann's assessment suggested.   **2.** In March 1915, the British had issued an Order in Council expanding the existing blockade, which already included food, to interdict all neutral commerce to Germany, whether through German or neutral ports. This tightening of the blockade angered the Wilson administration, not the least because the blockade from the first had provided the Germans with an excuse for their submarine warfare in the Atlantic.   **3.** Lord Eustace S. C. Percy, a friend of Lippmann's, was then in the British Foreign Office. He had served in the British embassy in Washington from 1910 to 1914.   **4.** Wilson had appointed George Rublee, a talented progressive lawyer, to the Federal Trade Commission, but the Senate was then on its way to refusing the necessary confirmation. Rublee, who had helped to draft the legislation creating the commission, had a close relationship with *The New Republic* staff.

To Graham Wallas   HANDWRITTEN

January 8, 1916

Dear Mr. Wallas,

I have been in Washington this week, and I feel that I must write you about it. It seems that the Germans have decided to acquiesce in the submarine question in order to give Congress a free hand to develop a munitions and anti-blockade agitation.[1] The situation is extremely serious — very, very serious. I have this on first hand authority.

To handle it you need really adequate representation over here, and you haven't got it. I have talked to Spring-Rice and to officials in our State Department, and the relations are very bad. Your ambassador does not seem to grasp American opinion or to convey it to your Foreign Office. He is an hysterical man, and somewhat bad tempered. In the next months you will need your very best diplomats over here, or trouble may result. I don't want to make suggestions, though of course Bryce's presence would help enormously.

I thought you ought to know this, and perhaps pass it on. . . .

1. Actually the Germans were still embroiled in negotiations with the State Department over the *Lusitania* issue, though that stalemate was soon to be broken. Further, Wilson's confidential adviser and personal emissary, Colonel Edward M. House, was in London, engaged in fruitful conversation with the British government. Those developments were, of course, secret at that time.

To Joseph Lee[1]

January 8, 1916

Dear Mr. Lee:

Personally I have not thought we ought to enter the war on the side of the Allies, and I did not mean to imply that in my article. I do not think the issues of the war are clear enough to justify our participation for we have to remember that this is not alone England's war and France's war, but Russia's, Italy's and Japan's. So I should not criticize the President for having kept us out of war. I should criticize him chiefly on two scores: that he has made neutrality a negative and legalistic thing and that he has not taken to heart the lessons of internal organization which the war in Europe teaches us. Those were his two opportunities for leadership and I fear he has missed them both. I have spent a good deal of time in Washington lately and this impression is very much strengthened by contact with members of the administration. . . .

1. Joseph Lee, a prominent social worker.

To Graham Wallas   HANDWRITTEN

January 12, 1916

Dear G. W.

. . . I enjoy the New Republic though it wouldn't do for a permanent job. Some time when its distractions worry me, I remember your Fabian days and am comforted. The paper is beginning to count here, more than we hoped. It has some influence in Washington and a very good deal among the younger intelligentsia. Our relations with the President are very cordial now. He is really a very considerable man and so is Colonel House. They both have imagination and the courage of it which is a good deal at this time. I suppose Wilson is the most freely speculative mind we've had at Washington, and as disinterested a man as one could wish. If only so many people didn't make it their chief business to distort his phrases. . . .

To Felix Frankfurter

January 17, 1916

Dear Felix:

I have just got back from Chicago, where the most important thing I did was to think over the question of T. R. I had long talks with all sorts of people out there, ranging from Miss Addams[1] to the Roosevelt at any price people, and I am pretty well convinced that T. R. will not do. His latest performance in regard to Mexico has just about cured me of any revival of enthusiasm, and the kind of people who are turning out to support him are a crowd that I do not want to see in power in the United States. After all, you and I have been banking on a theoretical Roosevelt, a potential Roosevelt, but not a Roosevelt who at this moment is actually at work.

It occurred to me after a talk with Walter Fisher[2] in Chicago that he might be the man, and I would like you to think about him. He stands very much closer to us on the preparedness issue than T. R. does, and on the economic questions he seems to be much more sound and better informed. Politically there seems to be a good deal to be said for him. He is a regular Republican but he has good standing with the best Progressives. He comes from the Middle West. He is out for preparedness but he never seems to forget the militarist bogy.

His personal ability is of course very great. I do not know how much of a leader of men he is, but he has a realistic quality and a good deal of iron in his soul. I think we ought to consider him very seriously as an alternative to T. R. and to Hughes.[3]

1. Jane Addams, pre-eminent American social worker, founder of Hull House in Chicago, in 1912 a fervid Roosevelt Progressive.   2. Walter L. Fisher, a Chicago lawyer, municipal reformer, and leading advocate of the conservation of natural resources. He served effectually as secretary of the interior, 1911–13.   3. Associate Justice Charles Evans Hughes, formerly a reform-minded governor of New York, was to be the Republican candidate in 1916.

To Edward B. Burling[1]

January 28, 1916

Dear Burling:

You are probably wondering at my long silence. The fact is I have been in Washington twice since I saw you and have been meaning to write you each day, but the whole Fisher matter has been in such utter confusion that there seemed to be nothing to say that was worthwhile and I have put it off from day to day hoping that at last I would be able to give you a definite answer but I am not able to do so. We have talked over the matter with a dozen people or so who are closest to us, and there is such violent difference of opinion that we have not been able to decide what to do. . . .

This is what the anti-Fisher men say, and they stand about ten to two among the people whose opinions I have asked. They say he cannot work with other men, that he does not know how to delegate power, that he is obstinate about his opinions, that he cannot inspire or lead large masses of ordinary people; that he becomes too absorbed in the details of a job to give it a large setting and to act as a kind of public educator. That his administration of the Interior Department was commonplace; that he has altogether too many personal enemies among the Progressives. People like Stimson and Pinchot[2] will not stand for him I am told. They have been consulted.

I do not myself agree with all these criticisms of course, but I still think there is a good deal in our idea; but of course this is a co-operative paper and any decision would have to be a joint decision. This does not mean, however, that we have given up the idea. Not by a long shot. We spent five hours the other night going over in detail every possible candidate for the Republican nomination. There were Fisher men present and anti-Fisher men and the antis had to confess that apart from T. R. and Hughes, Fisher was still the most available. But several of them said that if they had to vote between Wilson and Fisher they would throw their vote to the Socialists, so you can estimate from that the strength of the opposition.

I would rather you did not show this to Fisher because I want to feel free to write to you with entire frankness. We are meeting twice a week now-a-days at dinner and the main subject is always this one, so we may be able to come to some conclusion within the next few weeks. . . .

1. Edward B. Burling, already an eminent Washington attorney, had earlier practiced in Illinois and knew and admired Fisher. 2. Henry L. Stimson had been secretary of war while Fisher also held Cabinet office. Fisher had defended Gifford Pinchot after Taft dismissed him as chief forester of the United States during Pinchot's celebrated fight with Fisher's predecessor in the Interior Department, Richard A. Ballinger.

To Joseph Lee

February 2, 1916

Dear Mr. Lee:

Thank you for your letter. I must say I do not like the literacy test and I am very much perplexed about the proportional method,[1] but what makes you think that it is so impossible to get it adopted? As a way of dealing with the Japanese difficulty it has considerable political value, at least some of us here think it has, and we have been studying the plan for some time. If you have any light for or against it I wish you would let me know.

1. Advocates of the restriction of immigration had long supported a literacy test, a device that Congress incorporated in legislation passed in 1915 but that Wilson vetoed. (Later a similar bill was passed over his veto.) A literacy test would have discriminated against poorer and less educated immigrants, most of them at this time from southern and eastern Europe. An alternative device for the same purpose, later incorporated in legislation of 1921 and 1924, proposed restricting immigration by imposing quotas for each nation based upon the population from that nation within the United States either in 1890 or 1900. The earlier date usually was more restrictive of the "new" immigrants. Either date would have reduced Japanese immigration to a trickle. The "Gentlemen's Agreement" had already accomplished that purpose, so popular among West Coast groups hostile to Asians. But continuing racial tensions on the West Coast were keeping the issue alive. To the damage of Japanese-American relations, the 1924 act cut off Japanese immigration entirely.

To Mary Ware Dennett[1]

February 4, 1916

Dear Mrs. Dennett:

I do not expect to be in Washington for ten days so I am afraid you had better not count on me.

There is really a much more important reason why I should not wish to undertake the task to get these bills introduced. The reason is that I do not agree with the purpose of the bills. I think your attempt to legalize what amounts to practically any method of conveying this information is simply an invitation to wholesale quackery. We have taken up the matter here in editorial conferences and we are all agreed that if the bill is introduced in the form you propose that we shall have to attack it.

The whole purpose of the birth control agitation can be achieved by permitting physicians and perhaps trained, certified nurses to convey information about contraception. Nothing whatever but evil is accomplished by allowing every patent medicine firm and every quack doctor to write books and pamphlets and mail them broadcast. Not only is your proposal unwise, it is of course utterly impossible to get a hearing for it either in Congress or before intelligent public opinion. As a sheer matter of fighting strategy you are making a mistake. Instead of picking out the easiest place to break the taboo, you choose to make the attack all along the line, and you are bound to fail. Narrow your insistence to the fact that physicians shall be able to instruct their patients and there is some chance, if not for a change in the law, at least for such a change in public sentiment that enforcement of the law would become impossible.

This represents the opinion of all the editors.

1. Mary Ware Dennett, director of the National Birth Control League, previously secretary of the National Suffrage Association. The league, appealing largely to middle-class women, was working for the repeal of state and federal statutes restricting the dissemination of information about birth control, which the league considered a "purely scientific topic" properly to be excluded from obscenity laws.

To Mary Ware Dennett

February 14, 1916

Dear Mrs. Dennett:

Thank you for your frank letter.

I think you underestimate the danger of the quack and have too much faith in the ability of what you call "authoritative information" to drive out the other kind. The idea I had in mind in writing you was that we can hope to attach to ourselves that section of public opinion represented by doctors, nurses, social workers, editors, the moderate conservatives, by saying that we are as aware of the dangers of indiscriminate use of this information and as anxious to control it as they are.

In your last paragraph but one I feel that you are raising a logical dilemma and not a real one. You are right in thinking that the law will become unenforceable through the weight of public opinion, but the way to develop the weight of public opinion is to concentrate on the sanest measure that meets the necessities of the case. For example, I see that Emma Goldman[1] has been arrested for giving some kind of a lecture on the subject. Now, emphatically a lecture of that sort is not the way to give medical information of any kind and if we identify ourselves with that sort of propaganda we shall raise the resistance of people everywhere.

In regard to your question as to whether the cure for the danger of education is more education, all I can say is that I do not believe in running an important public movement on an aphorism. I cannot see why the forces working for this reform should be divided. I cannot see why you do not throw in your lot with the other league[2] which is agitating for a simple change in the law. What they are trying to accomplish is all that the situation requires. It raises the minimum of opposition, whereas your bill supports the forces interested in the control of births and lets us in for that boresome characteristic of radical movements — the tendency to schism.

1. Emma Goldman, American radical champion of many social causes.   **2.** The Birth Control League of America.

To Felix Frankfurter

February 18, 1916

Dear Felix:

I have just got back from Washington with the feeling that *The New Republic* must get into the Brandeis fight[1] with its heaviest guns. I guess there is no doubt that he will be confirmed, but the fight is going to be much bitterer than we anticipated. We had a war council the other day — Norman Hapgood,[2] George Rublee and I, and we decided that *The New Republic* was the paper that ought to do the aggressive fighting for Brandeis. There is no daily paper doing it and *Harper's Weekly* goes to press so late that they are almost out of it. What we have got to do is to take up each one of these charges and assert enough about it to knock it over in the ordinary editor's mind. Of course no one of us knows enough to do that and so we will have to get different people to help. . . .

We need all the telling points in Brandeis's favor as can be used; such for example as the fact that in the United Shoe Case[3] he took no fee. That he is on the visiting committee of the Law School, etc., etc. You know what I mean in this respect. . . .

1. On January 28, 1916, Wilson had nominated Louis D. Brandeis as associate justice of the Supreme Court. That nomination predictably provoked strong protests from business interests, who considered Brandeis an antagonist — as he had been in instances where he had found management corrupt or inefficient. So, too, conservative Republicans resented Brandeis's part in exposing former President Taft's maladroit role in the celebrated Ballinger-Pinchot embroglio. Since Brandeis was a Jew, the nomination also brought to the surface the latent anti-Semitism of the American bar. Lippmann, Frankfurter, Senator Robert La Follette of Wisconsin, and other progressives of both major parties took the contrary view. The debate on Brandeis's confirmation continued in the Judiciary Committee of the Senate until early June, when a favorable report, precipitated by President Wilson's intercession, resulted in a solid majority of approving votes in the Senate.   **2.** Norman Hapgood, editor of *Harper's Weekly*, had known Lippmann for several years and admired his talents, though not without some jealousy. The strategy the two discussed about the role of *The New Republic* in the Brandeis fight cast the journal in a somewhat unfamiliar role. Though a trumpet of progressive causes, *The New Republic* had also opposed Brandeis's beliefs in the efficacy of antitrust policy as a device for controlling business and industry. But Brandeis had begun to modify his previous position, and in any case, for progressives, the man was more important than the issue.   **3.** Brandeis had acted as an adviser to the Justice Department in its antitrust suit against the United Shoe Machinery Company, a corporation for which he had once been counsel.

To Louis D. Brandeis

February 18, 1916

Dear Mr. Brandeis:

I have just received your note after being in Washington two days. Everyone there told me that there was no question but that we were bound to win. I attended part of one session of the committee and . . . was very much impressed with the attitude of Senator Walsh.[1] It seems to me extraordinarily fortunate that he is playing so big a part in this whole matter.

I dined Wednesday night with Justice Holmes[2] and he spoke of you with such affection and admiration that I have come home feeling extremely happy. You know of course that all of us here look upon the fight as the most important one now taking place in this country. The issue opened out seems to me fundamental and it is wonderful to see how many people realize this. You know that if there is anything you think any one of us here can do you must not hesitate for any personal reason. The thing at stake is much greater than our personal affection for you.

1. Senator David I. Walsh, Massachusetts Democrat.   **2.** Associate Justice Oliver Wendell Holmes, Jr., the Olympian of the United States Supreme Court.

To John Reed

February 21, 1916

Dear Jack:

I have read your letter and I am a little sorry that you should have decided to cast me out.[1] I do not suppose that I was entitled to expect any kind of patient fairness from you even though I have tried to be pretty patient and fair with you for a good many years. I continued to believe in you even though many times I have felt that you had acted like a fool or a cad. I would have supposed that the least you would have done after you had come to your weighty conclusion about me was to talk to me about it instead of writing me an hysterical letter. I am not going to try to prove to you that you are totally and ridiculously mistaken about what I believe. But I cannot help saying that you are hardly the person to set yourself up as a judge of other people's radicalism. You may be able to create a reputation for yourself along that line with some people, but I have known you too long and I know too much about you. I watched you at college when a few of us were taking our chances. I saw you trying to climb into clubs and hang on to a social position by your eyelids, and to tell you the truth I have never taken your radicalism the least bit seriously. You are no more dangerous to the capitalist class in this country than a romantic guerrilla fighter. You will prick them at one minute and hurt them at one point perhaps once in a while; but for any persistent attack — for anything which really matters, any changing fundamental conditions — it is not your line. You have developed an attitude which is amusing and dramatic. But do not get the idea that you are one of those great strong men who the vested interests of this country fear.

And I will just make one little prophecy, which may sound to you like a boast. I got into this fight long before you ever knew it existed and you will find that I am in it long after you quit.

1. Reed and Lippmann, never really compatible, had been growing apart. Now Reed, exasperated by Lippmann's views about the war, had accused his classmate and former friend of falling in with Wall Street and the jingoes. Later they had a partial but brief reconciliation.

To Graham Wallas   HANDWRITTEN

February 21, 1916

Dear G. W. —

Your letter of February 2nd has just come. I have not heard from anyone. I agree that Bryce is too old, but if you send anyone it must be a man whose coming would flatter American public opinion — somebody with a big name, a winning manner, and real negotiating power.

I am not surprised that you are bewildered about Washington. There is no doubt that if Germany ever backed down completely on the submarine issue — disavowed the past and started no new entanglements — then the anti-British sentiment in Congress would become formidable. I gather on fairly good evidence that Wilson and Lansing are unalterably opposed to any embargo, so you have nothing to fear except their irritability and tendency to say nasty things. Germany realizes, I believe, that while we shall continue to argue with you, we do not intend to embarrass you. That's why she seems ready to raise a new submarine issue[1] just now a propos of the armed mer-chantmen. If she believed that we seriously intended to break the "blockade", she wouldn't risk another quarrel with us. For, of course, every time Germany makes a threat every bit of anti-British feeling disappears.

Last week in Washington you couldn't have squeezed a drop of embargo talk out of Congress. They were too excited about the new submarine order.

Another great factor is that Roosevelt and Root[2] are forcing Wilson's hand, trying to make him seem afraid of the Germans. This he resents, and you may expect him to act like a good imitation of a bold man as the conventions draw nearer. They are the dominating factor in Washington. Wilson is afraid of Bryan[3] and of a militant Republican — either Roosevelt or Hughes, and his foreign policy reflects both sets of fears. This is not conjecture. I have an intimate friend high up in the State Department who is quite frank about this.

It is extraordinary how the Belgian issue is growing. In October 1914 when Roosevelt first spoke about an American protest, there wasn't anybody who agreed with him. We were practically the only paper that took up the issue, and we were derided more for that than for anything else. To-day there are hundreds of papers talking about what we should have done in August 1914 (when not a soul thought of doing it). For a time this retrospective gallantry seemed to me a bit futile, but of late Croly and I have been thinking that it might be turned to some account in the future.

It is clear that the U.S. had no legal standing in the Belgian matter in 1914. It would have had to cast off all its traditional policy and force its way into a situation which it had no share in creating. But why shouldn't our policy about Belgium, and sense that the period of isolation is over be signalized in the treaty of peace by adding our signature to the new guarantee of Belgian independence? Such an act might have great consequences, for it would draw us closer to you and to France, and would give the Belgian question a more genuinely international character. The British record about Belgium is tainted, it seems to me, by a good deal of purely national expediency. But if we partic-ipated the Germans would not claim that we were using Belgium for American purposes. It would be a risk taken in the interests of the world's security. From our own American point of view it would be a very valuable experience in world responsibility, and an inspiring way of emerging from our isolation. It might also prove the entering wedge to a naval agreement with Great Brit-ain, which from every point of view seems to me the sine qua non of cooper-ation in the future. . . .

1. On February 10, the German government had announced that it would order its submarines to begin on February 29 to attack armed merchant ships without warning. Since those ships were capable of sinking any submarine that surfaced to issue a warning, the threat had a sound basis in naval strategy. Further, the State Department's clumsy antecedent negotiation had more or less encouraged the Germans to turn to the proposed policy. But on February 15, Secretary of State Robert Lansing, while recommending the disarming of merchants, said the United States would continue to insist on conventional maritime rules, which required visit and search by men-of-war before they sank merchant vessels. Lansing also said the United States would not warn its

nationals against sailing on Allied liners, as they had in the case of the *Lusitania,* a still unresolved issue in German-American relations. That response forced the German government again to debate its submarine policy and provoked in Congress a renewed attempt by opponents of American involvement in the war to ban American travel on Allied ships. **2.** Elihu Root, who had been secretary of war and then secretary of state during Roosevelt's administration, had split with the Colonel over the issues of 1912. Now the two old friends were reunited in their opposition to Wilson; see Lippmann to Kenneth Hunter, February 29, 1916, inf. **3.** William Jennings Bryan had resigned as secretary of state in protest against what he considered Wilson's militant posture on the *Lusitania.*

To Graham Wallas

February 21, 1916

Dear Graham Wallas:

 . . . One point of news may interest you. This is of course strictly confidential. I had a very good talk with Lansing the other day and we were discussing the various criticisms made of the American policy in regard to the war. Towards the end I said to him: "There has always been one point in the submarine situation that I find it hardest to excuse. At the time the German Embassy published its advertisement in the American papers concerning American travelers of dangers in the war zone, why did our government take no action? It was published the day before the *Lusitania* sailed and there would have been plenty of time to stop the ship and insist on a clear understanding with Germany." A curious change came over his face and he hesitated a few minutes, and then he said: "We might have saved a great many lives, but to tell the truth, no one of us believed that any government would commit a crime like that. We just did not think of acting at the time." He also told me in strict confidence that he knew it as a fact that the Kaiser was furiously angry at the sinking of the *Lusitania,* and that the Kaiser had always regarded it as one of the great blunders of the war.

To Raymond B. Stevens[1]

February 21, 1916

My dear Stevens:

 . . . I had three hours' talk with Brandeis last night and he treated the whole fight as if it were happening on the planet Mars. I had to rub my eyes every once in a while and remind myself that the whole row was about him. We went over all the cases, especially the Shoe Case in a great deal of detail, and I am convinced that when we talked of it the other day we did not begin to realize how favorable to Brandeis all the facts were. . . .

1. Raymond B. Stevens, New Hampshire Democratic congressman, 1913–15, at this time special counsel to the Federal Trade Commission.

To Kenneth Hunter[1]

February 29, 1916

Dear Kenneth:

. . . A few things have happened that may interest you. After some time in Washington I began to notice that the British Ambassador was making a lot of unnecessary trouble just because he is incompetent and hysterical. I confirmed this when I talked to a lot of people who knew and then wrote the whole situation to Graham Wallas. He got his friends together and they inserted a long editorial in the *Manchester Guardian*, urging that Balfour[2] be sent over to straighten out the blockade. This has made Spring-Rice a little angrier than he was before and he is now convinced that there is a kind of German plot going on to create friendship between the United States and Great Britain.

The other news concerns T. R. When Root wrote his speech for the New York Convention the other day he sent it out to Oyster Bay and got T. R. to revise it. Thus do thieves, scoundrels, poltroons and pacifists come to love each other again when there is a chance to be elected. The Roosevelt clan think it would be fine to have T. R. back in the White House. I suppose that is very disinterested judgment on their part. The only thing they are afraid of is that the country is not good enough for him. Young Ted told me so the other day. There is only one thing to do really and that is to climb up on an oak tree and eat acorns and laugh.

1. Kenneth Hunter, Harvard '11, a close friend whom Lippmann had known during his undergraduate years.   2. Arthur J. Balfour, later Lord Balfour, the head of the British Admiralty.

To Cornelius Vanderbilt[1]

March 13, 1916

Dear Mr. Vanderbilt:

I have just received copy of the resolutions adopted by the conference of Mayors and Mayors' Committees at St. Louis, in which it is stated that: "We believe that the navy should be increased with all speed until we shall have become the first naval power of the world with strength on the Atlantic equal to that of any other power upon that ocean, and with additional strength upon the Pacific to make of us the first naval power upon that ocean."

This seems to imply that you advocate a navy larger than Great Britain's in the Atlantic, and a navy larger than Japan's in the Pacific. It is incredible that any group of thinking men should advocate a program like that — a program which would mean national suicide. I beg therefore, to offer my resignation from the Mayor's Committee.

1. Cornelius Vanderbilt, chairman of the Mayor's Committee on National Defense (New York City), colonel in the New York National Guard, later brigadier general in command of the Twenty-fifth Infantry Brigade in France.

To Felix Frankfurter

March 16, 1916

Dear Felix:

 . . . I had a long talk the other day with His Excellency of Turkey[1] at his invitation. He reminded me of the frog that inflated itself and kept on inflating itself till it splashed all over the place. He doesn't want to go back to Turkey, and the reason he gives is that Wilson must be re-elected, that the Democratic party is shot to pieces, and that he alone of all men is capable of uniting it. He will therefore stay here for a few months and touch it up with his master hand. After that, or during that time, Gerard[2] in Berlin is to be thrown out — his collarbone will not mend or something like that and His Excellency will go to Berlin and touch up that situation with a master hand. His plans include among other things the settlement of the submarine controversy and the bringing of peace in Europe. If he cannot do that he will go into the Cabinet. My, what a peanut politician in the midst of Armageddon. He ended the interview by saying that he was glad he had met me — that he always read *The New Republic* and that some day he would like me to write something for him. He had so many ideas that he did not have time to express and I could be so useful to him! I expect to see him taken off to an asylum soon under the delusion that he is either Napoleon or Buddha.

1. Henry Morgenthau, wealthy New York banker and real estate promoter, and a generous contributor to Wilson's campaign, was then United States ambassador to Turkey.   **2.** James W. Gerard, then United States ambassador to Germany.

To Robert C. Valentine[1]

March 17, 1916

Dear Valentine:

 I am really stumped to give you a definition of industrial democracy. It is so much easier to say what some of the elements of it would be. I should say that industrial democracy exists when every adult has enough education not only to do a job but to know why he is doing the job, and what the circumstances are which make that job necessary; where every adult is sufficiently insured for the primary needs of life so that he is capable of making some kind of free contract with other men. On a basis like this it would not be difficult to erect machinery for the different kinds of control which may be derived. Sufficient education and a sufficient stake in the community are necessary to what in the modern sense we may call a free man. That is all I can think of to add to your very good definition.

1. Robert C. Valentine, Harvard '96, chairman of the first Massachusetts Minimum Wage Board, often an arbiter in major labor disputes.

To Willard Straight[1]

April 6, 1916

Dear Willard:

Your cable about Roosevelt arrived this morning and as Herbert is away this week it is more or less up to me to answer it. Perhaps this is a good opportunity for me to explain to you at least how I feel about Roosevelt and his candidacy.

You know that I started with an immense prejudice in his favor. It goes back a long ways. You know too that in spite of the attitude he has taken towards *The New Republic* no element of spite has entered into our treatment of him. From the very first we have leaned over backwards in his favor, and if my conscience troubled me about our attitude towards him it would be that we have not been as candid about Roosevelt as we have been about Wilson. We not only were the first paper I think anywhere in the country to give full support to Roosevelt on the Belgian question, we have been one of the papers that has persistently pointed out the superiority of his diplomatic method. Except for the one paragraph about Mexico, which I do not need to go into with you now, we have been praising Roosevelt long before the present boom started. At the time of the libel trial in Syracuse[2] we were one of the very few papers in the East here which from the very start played up his side of the case. At other times when he has been grossly unfair, as for example about Mexico last January, at the time when you yourself felt and I believe said that he "will not do," we refrained from criticizing him.

When Root made his speech at the Republican Convention holding up the Belgian issue against Wilson, I began personally to feel that the issue was being used in a cheap partisan way. It seemed to me that since Root was in the Senate at the time Belgium was invaded and since Root said not a word about our duty to protest at that time it was pretty poor performance for him to criticize Wilson on the matter fifteen or sixteen months after the event. Some time after that I first saw the *Outlook* article of September 23rd, which proves beyond the shadow of a doubt that six or seven weeks after the invasion of Belgium Roosevelt was not only not advocating an American protest but was accepting the old policy of isolation. I feel that since *The New Republic* had said so often that Roosevelt would have acted in a different way about Belgium than Wilson did, it was clearly our duty to eat our words and if possible make Roosevelt eat his. This is what we did in the article about which you have evidently heard rumors by cable. The publication of this article was followed by an attempt on the part of Lawrence Abbot[3] to explain the whole matter away, and we got a flood of letters here saying that we had done Roosevelt a great injustice. That made it necessary for us to reply in this week's issue and there our part of the matter rests.

It was not a pleasant thing to have to do. Personally there are few things in Roosevelt's career that have shocked me as much as this revelation of how his mind works, and I feel most strongly that the reputation of *The New Republic* for fair play absolutely required our taking the stand about the matter that we did.

In regard to the future, my feeling is about this: Roosevelt is the best man in sight for the job, but Roosevelt himself is not one man but many men. Now some people and some newspapers think it is their duty to elect Roosevelt and take him any way that he comes. You know that *The New Republic* was not created to play that kind of a game. If Roosevelt is nominated this campaign is going to be the most crucial test of our independence that has ever been presented to us because as I see it we have got to do two things. We have got to lean towards Roosevelt and we have got to keep up a running fire of criticism about him. You realize that a campaign between Wilson and Roosevelt is likely to be one of the most venomous and heated campaigns that we have ever had. The issues at stake are so indefinite that an inordinate amount of bunkum is going to be talked. Now if we refuse to be partisan about him in that situation we are sure to irritate the people closest to Roosevelt — there is simply no way of avoiding that. For example, if he talks foreign policy we are going to have to push him towards the Anglo-American alliance and show that the logic of his position drives us in that direction. Yet in the heat of a campaign there is no issue that he would less like to have pushed upon him. There is no issue so likely to lose him votes. The same is true of his domestic policy. For any kind of real preparedness he has got to be prepared to do things which I believe will outrage the soul of Mr. Root and if not of Mr. Root then surely of the ordinary political leaders in the Republican party. We have to push him to commit just those outrages. In other words, we shall be very inconvenient politically. We are bound to be about the most troublesome friend that he has.

I have written all this because I know we are going to have to talk it over many times in the next month.

---

1. Willard Straight — diplomatist; partner in J. P. Morgan and Company; generous angel, with his wife, Dorothy, of *The New Republic* — had subsidized the magazine since its founding while also promising not to interfere with its editorial policy. He kept his promise, though now and then he complained, as he had about Lippmann's recent criticism of Theodore Roosevelt. **2.** Roosevelt had sued William Barnes for his fatuous but provocative assertion that the Colonel was a heavy drinker. The resulting trial proved an embarrassment to Roosevelt because of the pettiness of the proceedings. **3.** Lawrence Abbot, editor of the *Outlook*, a pro-Roosevelt weekly news magazine.

To Graham Wallas

April 21, 1916

Dear Graham Wallas:

We had a letter here the other day from Willard Straight saying that he had seen you and speaking most affectionately of you but he made one remark that has bothered us a great deal. He said you had been hurt, I think that was his word, by certain parts of our attitude towards the war. He didn't specify and so we are a good deal in doubt as to what he could have meant. My guess is that you have missed in *The New Republic* the emotional warmth toward the cause of the Allies which our real feelings would justify. That would be a true accusation against us, I think, but there are reasons which, in a measure, explain it. In the first place, we have all suffered from an exhaustion of feeling about the war. The thing has left us recently in a kind of lackadaisical condition. There is another reason, however, and that a more rational one. We decided just about a year ago, precisely at the time the *Lusitania* was sunk, to devote the paper to the creation of an Anglo-American understanding. We felt then that the traditional hostility to England in this country could not be overcome by a paper that didn't take what might be called a strongly American view of the situation. The worse enemy of such understanding in this country is the typical Bostonian who is suspected by the rest of the country of being nothing but a colonial and in our anxiety to avoid that charge we have perhaps leaned over backwards. But of our real feeling about the struggle, of the way we've watched the battle at Verdun, our hearts have been with you every minute.

Eustace Percy is here now and we have had some good talks with him.

This is the day on which the President's speech to Congress and the so-called ultimatum to Germany[1] are published in the papers. I was in Washington a good deal lately, in fact, I have been there two or three days ago and saw four members of the Cabinet. There wasn't one of them who had looked beyond the possibility of a rupture with Germany and had tried to think out our policy in case things become still more acute. That's why we are so utterly discouraged about Wilson. Our own emphasis, as you will see from *The New Republic*, is to invent some kind of coercive policy which would have no actual relation to the submarine issue. But from the way things look in Washington and from the talk I had with the President, I haven't very much hope that any discriminating policy will ever be adopted by this administration.

1. The ultimatum threatened a break in diplomatic relations unless Germany gave up submarine warfare against merchant and passenger ships, armed or unarmed. It followed the torpedoing of the French channel steamer *Sussex* on March 24 and precipitated a debate about submarine policy in Berlin that resulted in the Sussex pledge of May 4. Germany then agreed that submarines would follow the rules of visit and search, but warned that it would resume unrestricted use of submarines unless the United States compelled the British to obey international law, by which the Germans essentially meant to lift the blockade. That proved impossible, as many senior German officials had expected, but they had agreed to the pledge in response to the argument of their

colleagues that the effects of submarine warfare on Allied shipping, at least for the near future, would inflict less damage on the Allies than would American entry into the war damage Germany.

To Newton D. Baker[1]

May 5, 1916

My dear Baker:

I have thought a good deal about our talk the other night and the enormity of the job which you have. It seemed to me that the endless amount of administrative work which comes to you must make it very difficult for you to set your mind fully on the kind of subtle, intangible problem which we discussed. If a break comes with Germany or a war, those subtle problems are going to be of very great importance. They are going to be involved not only as matters of policy and police work, but they are involved in the whole conduct of the press bureau and press censorship. I was wondering whether it might not be a good plan to do what I understand the British Treasury Department did at the outbreak of the war. They went to Oxford and Cambridge and got a number of specialists in economics and said to them: "Now you have no administrative work whatsoever — your job is to think out and report on certain large theoretical problems." Mightn't it be a good scheme for you to have a voluntary, inconspicuous number of people whose business it would be to analyze and make suggestions about the kind of thing we talked of and digested — reports about conditions of public opinion in this country and elsewhere? To formulate methods not only of censorship but of positive press agenting and to deal in general with all those matters of morale which army men are not so likely to understand, and for which people like you tied to a devastating task cannot have the time to think about at length. I know that the last year and a half those problems have seemed to be the ones most neglected because they are most difficult to deal with in administrative office. In time of crisis there are endless gestures and subtle influences which can be set at work, which keep people's temper right and help to bolster up those spiritual elements which are at bottom the essence of preparedness.

1. While assisting Lincoln Steffens, Lippmann had first met Newton D. Baker — Cleveland lawyer, successor to Tom Johnson as reform mayor of that city, secretary of war since March 1917, and a moderate on the question of preparedness.

To Felix Frankfurter

May 6, 1916

Dear Felix:

I have just gotten back from Washington and I want to report.

On Wednesday I saw Gregory[1] the Attorney General, at his office. . . .

The theory of Gregory is that if the Committee reports adversely a lot of

Democrats who do not like Brandeis would make it an excuse to vote against him without regarding the charge that they have been irregular. Gregory lays all his faith on the possibility of making the confirmation an administration measure with the test of party loyalty.

In the afternoon I had a long talk with Senator La Follette, who feels about as we do, that the case should have been fought in the open. On the other hand he feels that the time is so late now that the most effective thing that can be done is, first, to apply local pressure in Tennessee and Georgia and New York;[2] and second, to create as much publicity as possible with designs to do two things: first, to reveal the nature of the opposition, and secondly, to convey to the Senate the extent of the pro-Brandeis feeling throughout the country. . . .

With regard to publicity, we are having a luncheon here today . . . and we will get things started along that line. Every single person I talked to is agreed that there is no use whatever in arguing the merits of the charges. The highest estimate anyone made was that thirty Senators had read either the majority or the minority report. The real voting will not be decided by anything that was brought out at the hearings. The chances are that the thing will go into the open Senate. . . . According to present calculations we are pretty certain to have five progressive Republicans. . . . There is also a bare chance that we will get Borah. We shall lose Hardwick of Georgia; that is fixed — and probably Bankhead and Underwood. Also possibly Shields, O'Gorman and Hoke Smith.[3] We still have enough to win. But all this depends on getting an affirmative note into our campaign.

Last night the Attorney General, Lane and Wilson the Secretary of Labor,[4] Norman Hapgood and George[5] and I talked over the thing and we shouted so hard at the Attorney General that this ought to be an administration matter that when he left he said with a confidential voice: "I think something will happen within the next forty-eight hours that will please you boys." Hitz[6] says that in all probability the President is writing a letter to somebody in the Senate. However, the man we are all really counting on is McAdoo.[7] Norman says that they are going to make him take charge of the thing and that he is the only man who knows how to go up to the Senate and shake his fist at them.

In the meantime whatever the people in Washington may say I am convinced that there is no reason why people should not break loose all over the country if they want to. It is perfectly absurd to suppose that the publicity on a matter like this should be controlled from one source by people overimpressed with the traditions and sanctities of this case.

Norman will be in Washington for two weeks at least and he has promised to be the mediating influence, so communicate with him about anything you think of. I am going away on Sunday because I said I would and there is no particular reason why I should stay. I am not going to have any mail forwarded except from a few people, so if you write to me just put your initials in the corner of the letter.

P.S. I had a fine long talk with Baker and a pretty good one with Hughes. We did not discuss anything more recent than New York State politics in 1835, but he did express his horror of the scandal and notoriety of public life. He also inquired most warmly about Brandeis.

1. Thomas W. Gregory.   2. So as to influence Democratic senators from those states, who were wobbling within the Judiciary Committee.   3. William E. Borah, Idaho Republican; Thomas W. Hardwick, Georgia Democrat; John H. Bankhead, Alabama Democrat; Oscar W. Underwood, Alabama Democrat; John K. Shields, Tennessee Democrat; James A. O'Gorman, New York Democrat; Hoke Smith, Georgia Democrat.   4. Franklin K. Lane, secretary of the interior; and William B. Wilson, secretary of labor.   5. Rublee.   6. William Hitz, special attorney in the Justice Department.   7. Secretary of the Treasury William G. McAdoo, Wilson's son-in-law, an effective administrator and, at that time, an articulate progressive.

To Eustace S. C. Percy

May 29, 1916

Dear Eustace:

. . . The main interest here at this moment is in Wilson's speech delivered Saturday evening at the banquet of the League to Enforce Peace.[1] We all think it was a highly significant one in that it is practically the first official statement ever made in America that we were ready to do our part and take our responsibilities in the world at large. And I am looking forward with great interest in seeing how the French papers and yours receive it. Our press is very curious; the violent anti-Wilson people like Frank Simonds,[2] etc. thought it was no good before they had read it. There is considerable outcry about entangling alliances from the provincial newspapers, together with a very powerful body of opinion supporting Wilson. You know that I have not too much faith in the whole of it, but it seems to me that there is an element of real politics in it on which we can base a good deal of hope. Such an arrangement is I suppose the only one in which average American opinion could be induced to break with a tradition of isolation. It is all too evident that our preaching of Anglo-American agreement can reach only a minority. But the people at large I think could be made to accept the plan of a League to Enforce Peace. And after all the core of any such league would be the alliance of French, British and American sea power.

The three great sources of opposition of course are the Germans, the Irish and the Colonial Americans. The hardest of all to reach are undoubtedly the Americans. I really believe it is quite possible that the American Germans would accept some such plan as the League, provided that they could feel that the peace which follows the war is not an unjust peace. In other words, since the League would be a virtual guarantee of the status quo after the war, its stability would depend on creating some sense of contentment in Germany.

So far as the Irish are concerned, the executions have done serious damage to Anglo-American relations.[3] I really believe that the most bitter hatred of the English to be found anywhere in the world is to be found among the leading Irish-Americans. I hope your statesmen realize the international significance of a decent settlement of the Irish question. I hope they realize that the feeling of Irish Americans here with all their political influence is really one of the great factors of that whole problem.

You may be interested to hear that a very good observer whom I happen to know, has just returned from Japan having spent many months there. He has seen all the important Japanese public men. He tells me that the anti-British feeling is a dominant factor there and that the government is extremely active and helpful as regards the Hindu nationalists. He mentioned the case of two men who had taken refuge in Japan and your Ambassador asked to have them deported, and as I understand it the outcry was so great that the government decided to let them stay unofficially.

By this time you have no doubt read Maximilian Harden's article called "If I were Wilson."[4] A translation of it was published in the *New York Times* of Sunday May 28th. It is a most astonishing document. And if it reflects in any measure the state of German opinion in any influential quarter there has been a real conversion. You will remember how violent Harden was at the beginning of the war. He writes now like a pro-Ally pamphleteer. No doubt he is an extremist and rather unsteady, but after all he is a great journalist and his article was passed by the censor.

I am going out to Chicago at the end of the week, with no idea at all as to the outcome of the convention. My preference is for Hughes although I am not at all certain that I shall not line up for Wilson in the end. T. R. gets on my nerve so much these days that I shall become a typical anti-Roosevelt maniac if I do not look out.

1. On May 27, Wilson had addressed the nonpartisan League to Enforce Peace. He then spoke of his, and of the nation's, readiness to abandon the policy of isolation from European affairs. That speech influenced Lippmann's accelerating movement from support for Roosevelt toward support for Wilson.   **2.** Frank H. Simonds, journalist with a specialty in military matters, at this time associate editor of the Republican *New York Tribune* — to which he contributed, as he did to other newspapers, columns on the war. Later he was author of the five-volume *History of the World War* (Garden City, 1917–20).   **3.** The execution for treason of Sir Roger Casement and other leaders of the Easter Rebellion in Ireland, a failed effort for Irish independence that had had German support.   **4.** The article, which the German government had permitted to be published, revealed a deep yearning for peace on the part of the author and other Germans of his mind. Harden also set as one aim of peace the placing of "diplomacy above strategy" and the establishment of "the higher authority of the counsel of statesmen over every . . . interference of those brought up for the work of war." Perhaps a part of the German government's peace offensive, Harden's article also defended Germany's decision to go to war as a "necessary measure of defense."

To S. K. Ratcliffe[1]

June 15, 1916

My dear S. K.:

. . . I returned two or three days ago from Chicago after attending the two conventions. . . .[2]

Although we have not declared ourselves yet, most of us here feel very much inclined to Wilson — a strange business isn't it? But the fact is that the return of the Republican party to power means a return of the most evil-smelling plutocracy that this country has. Hughes is of course an able and respectable and incorruptible man, but he is a pretty conservative man and his party is unspeakable.

There is this to be said for Wilson: that he has learned a lot, has admitted most of his errors and has begun to surround himself with a new and rather more hopeful crowd of men. I came home from Chicago convinced that Wilson had done more for the cause of the Allies than the ordinary American realizes or wished to have done, and the irony of the situation is that the Republican party which has raised the issue of Americanism is going to poll the weight of the German-Hungarian-Irish vote. If Americanism means anything at all Wilson is paying the penalty for it. And at the present moment we have the tragi-comic spectacle of fanatically pro-Ally Boston united with the German-American Alliance to elect Hughes. If ever there was a case in which extremes met, here it is. It is as if the gods had shuffled all the people in the United States in such a way that all those who were fanatical, either pro-German or pro-Ally, were finally collected in one heap. I may add that the heap is glued together by the high-minded and heroic appeal of an increased protective tariff. . . .

1. S. K. Ratcliffe, at this time *The New Republic*'s English correspondent. 2. The Republicans had nominated Hughes. The Progressives, spurned by Roosevelt, had rejected his recommendation of his conservative friend and fellow jingo Senator Henry Cabot Lodge of Massachusetts. The disenchanted delegates went through the motions of nominating Roosevelt anyhow and went home to observe the demise of their party.

To Katherine Philips Edson[1]

June 27, 1916

Dear Mrs. Edson:

I took the liberty of opening your letter and reading it, and I do not a bit feel that you were too angry. I think I share your feeling completely and I am sorry that you should have gotten the impression you did from my article. I am afraid it is a case where my attempt to understate the feeling of the situation in order to give it additional force did not succeed. What I felt was that it was easy to denounce and that was the obvious thing to do, but a more restrained note might be more effective. I have had a good many letters about the article and on the whole most people did not get the same sense of aloofness that you did.

Perhaps there was one thing which did temper my whole feeling, and that was a sense of the folly of the Progressives. Men who were fighting a great battle ought not to be so everlastingly simple and trusting. Nor do I feel that Col. Roosevelt betrayed the Progressives. I have never believed for one moment at any time during the last eight months that he would consent to run on the third ticket. It is beyond me how any one could have supposed that he would lead a lost cause this year. He is not that kind of a man. I blame the Progressives for not realizing this and I blame them still more for pretending to accept his jingo platform and for writing a platform at Chicago which was fundamentally insincere. I can say this with all the more feeling because so many of the Progressives are my personal friends, and also because most of them will admit the truth of all this.

I hope whenever you feel that your soul is full again that you will write.

1. Katherine Philips Edson, a social reformer active in campaigns for women's suffrage and for minimum wage legislation, was serving as a member of California's Industrial Welfare Commission, to which she had been appointed by Governor Hiram Johnson, Roosevelt's running mate in 1912. She was a member of the state central committee of the Progressive party.

To Felix Frankfurter

June 30, 1916

Dear Felix:

. . . But I do not a bit agree with you about T. R. Your attempt to read into his words all the glowing aspirations of your heart simply will not work. He does not understand industrial preparedness; he does not know what he means by social justice. He has no vision of the class struggle and you can not jolly him into an understanding.

As for Hughes, I am ready to be shown, but there is a lot to be shown still. Since his nomination he has not said one word that is interesting; not one word any politician trying to say the conventional thing would not have uttered. He has talked the regular rigmarole about protection, national honor, prestige. There is not an idea in any of his statements which is more recent than Mark Hanna. And I think it is much too early to have faith in him. I think the best that we can say is that we would like to have faith in him. . . .

To Eustace S. C. Percy

July 5, 1916

My dear Eustace:

I just had read your letter of June 16th and I want to write you a few lines about the political situation here.

The actual strategy of the conventions I tried to describe in *The New Republic* of June 17th, and I won't try to go over that part of the ground here. You will be specially interested in the effect of the campaign so far on foreign policy. I think it is possible to make a bold generalization and say right off that European relations play practically no role whatever in the campaign. Hughes has not said, and is not likely to say anything which indicates any constructive foreign policy. He was nominated by the politicians of the Republican party purely on the ground of "availability." That is to say, because he was not in the fight of 1912, because he was semi-progressive by reputation, because there is a great legend about his efficiency, and because he had alienated no body of voters including the German-Americans. His nomination was received with enthusiasm by the German-Americans, and the result of that enthusiasm was to destroy, I think completely, any effort to make the Republican party seem a party which represented a far-seeing European policy. At this moment the Wilson Democrats (I have to distinguish between them and the party Democrats) are prepared to go a good deal further in international arrangements than the Republicans. The prevailing tone of the Hughes supporters is protectionist. Protectionist as regards tariff, as regards large industry, and as regards military affairs. The ideal they preach is that of a self-sufficing, rather aggressive, and somewhat bad-tempered nationalism. Their impulse is to defy everybody, and politically this works out as a defiance of the Allies. You will understand how this comes about. If you preach absolute independence and the destiny of this country hard enough, you are bound sooner or later to align yourself against British sea power and against the internationalizing tendencies of the Entente. I think if the thing had to be phrased you might say the Democrats consist of people who are by tradition isolated, led by a group which in a somewhat naive way hopes to join a European co-operative arrangement; whereas the Republicans consist of people who on the whole believe in aggressive isolation and lean heavily towards imperial expansion in Latin-America and the Pacific. But all these tendencies play a very incidental role in the campaign. I do not think that even Mexico is going to play a very large part in the decision, except that Wilson's policy, such as it is, is on the whole very popular with the people. The mobilization of the National Guard has had a very sobering effect on the belligerent minority in the East.[1] The tremendous cost of the new armament bills, which is to be paid out of taxation on inheritance and incomes, has had a still more dampening effect, and Wilson's tendency to muddle through to peace and some kind of understanding is very deeply approved. The feeling that he has represented the real wish of the people, and the enormous prosperity of the country, are I think decisive factors. We still believe here that Wilson will carry states in the Middle West and North-West which are usually regarded as solidly Republican.

There have been a number of very interesting psychological changes since you were here. Outside of the Wall Street, country house, club element in the larger cities, which is, after all, naturally Republican anyway, no one believes that there is any essential difference between Hughes and Wilson; no one believes that this country is in a crisis, the result of which depends upon the election. No Republican has succeeded in making any kind of an issue which distinguishes him sharply from Wilson, except, perhaps, Roosevelt, and the general feeling is that he has been repudiated by the Republican party. I do not think it is possible to overstate the irrelevance of this election to the issues in Europe. Both parties intend to be neutral. Neither party intends to fight your blockade, and generally there is a sense that the election is not a campaign between two great parties and two great policies, but between politicians who are in and politicians who are out. The country is apathetic in regard to the election, pretty well satisfied with things as they are, and rather cynical about the political noise. My guess is that Wilson will grow steadily stronger as the election approaches; that nothing short of a humiliating disaster in Mexico, or perhaps a resumption of German submarine warfare, can prevent a steady growth in his favor. His political skill is tremendous. Almost every week he remedies some fault and keeps at, what we call here, repairing his political fences.

I spent yesterday out on Long Island with the kind of people who are most violently pro-Ally in this country. I was shocked to find how little the offensive begun in France seems to affect them. Even the interest there seems to have worn down to a kind of apathy.

You speak of some apprehension in regard to the relation between our countries due to the campaign. I think you have nothing really to fear. You can count upon it, I think with absolute certainty, though I realize the danger of making a statement like this, that nothing will be done to impair your military success. There may perhaps be another note or two about the blockade, but no one will take the notes seriously here. If Hughes denounces Wilson for not pressing our claims against England, he will be denounced at once for playing to the German-American vote. If Wilson acts too strenuously, he will be accused of it, and I therefore expect that nothing will be done. Both parties are very much afraid of the open support of the German-Americans.

I have just heard that Gilbert Murray[2] arrives in a day or two and the rumor is that he is to do "propaganda." I think he will do no good by it and a group of us plan to get hold of him in order to tell him so if it is necessary. Anything approaching his pamphlet on Sir Edward Grey's foreign policy[3] would meet with a very cold reception in this country today and before he had been talking ten minutes he would be on the defensive in regard to such matters as Ireland, Greece and the Economic Entente about which our papers have told us something. Anglo-American relations will be improved best by British victories. I think if there has been any diminution of the intensity of feeling it is due to disappointment, but if the present offensive appears effective I expect a revival of the feeling.

---

1. Wilson had mobilized the Guard for duty on the Mexican frontier after Pancho Villa's raids into American territory. The president also sent troops under General John J. Pershing on a futile pursuit of Villa, the unpredictable rascal of Mexican revolutionary politics. **2.** Gilbert Murray, eminent British classicist. **3.** That is, the foreign policy of the British government, of which Grey was foreign minister.

To Maurice S. Amos [1]

July 24, 1916

Dear Professor Amos:

I was very deeply interested in your letter and had I known where to reach you I would have sent you a copy,[2] because I often thought of you while I was writing it and wished I had had a chance to talk to you and get at first hand some of your experience in Egypt.

Let me say first of all that I would not try to maintain that wars are entirely due to the undeveloped countries. There are of course many other factors involved. But I do think that it is possible to maintain that the grand strategy of diplomacy in the world, the diplomacy of the great powers, is determined chiefly by the situation in backward countries. Our own foreign policy for example, depends almost entirely upon the internal condition of the Latin-American states and of China. Given a China which was strong and able to take care of itself and we should have no Japanese problem of any real international significance; because the question of immigration in California could hardly be the subject of an international war. If we choose to exclude the Japanese nothing the Japanese government could do by a victory over us would ever secure a really free admission to the Japanese. What really sets our two countries at loggerheads is the control of commerce and privileges in the undeveloped portions of China. So I think in Europe I cannot imagine any cause for a German attack on France if France had not held a vast Colonial Empire in Africa. Nor the enmity that exists between Britain and Germany if they had not clashed so continuously in the Near East and in the Far East and in northern Africa. It seems to me that the undeveloped country magnetizes all the other causes of friction, and that they would be entirely manageable once these areas of trouble were organized.

My own suggestion for some kind of international control was put forward with very real humility. And I believe I even stated that an international administration would be as you say extremely backward, at least for a long time. I should not urge international administration for countries like India or Egypt, which are admittedly under the control of some other government. The problem is to find some authority for the very highly disputed areas. Wherever a backward country has got an administration which is part of the accepted status quo we do not have to consider it immediately, but within the last ten years there have been certain areas where the Imperial conflict has been so bitter that no other solution presents itself except an international control. The question of the Dardanelles for example, is the one I have most in mind at the present time. I do not see how any Englishman or any liberal person elsewhere can look upon Russia's control of the Dardanelles with any equanimity. It seems to me that with Russia at Constantinople the stage would be set for another war, and I do not see why with all the conflict of interest in the Allied countries some internationalizing of those Straits is not the most hopeful solution.

But as I said before, the particular situation is of no importance — the main point is that we have disputed and unorganized territories without some kind of authority in them which is strong enough to control the rights of traders and financiers and efficient enough to administer and police the territory so that riot and revolution cannot be made the excuse for intervention followed by commercial monopoly.

You mentioned the conflict in England between your liberals and your Prussians. We are watching that rather closely here, because we realize that if America is to participate in the settlement, it will have to be with a Britain governed by liberals and not by your Carsons, et al.

1. Sir Maurice S. Amos, an English judge in Egypt, 1903–12, returned to Great Britain in 1915 as an adviser on foreign contracts to the Ministry of Munitions. He later wrote extensively about the British and American constitutions. 2. Of *The Stakes of Diplomacy* (New York, 1915).

To Newton D. Baker

August 2, 1916

My dear Mr. Baker:

Thank you so much for sending me the material on mobilization.

I attended the Hughes notification meeting on Monday night, and I must say it was a dismal affair. I had never realized before how commonplace his mind is. There is something honest and likable about him, but he is certainly bourgeois, as the Socialists would say.

I wish the President in his acceptance speech might see his way clear to laying considerable emphasis on the very serious problem of the economic war after the war outlined in the Paris conference.[1] It seems to me that this is the biggest item in the statesmanship of the future and Hughes ignored it. Of course it is a very delicate matter for him to touch on, but he is virtually running as a candidate for the Reconstruction Period and he has, it seems to me, a wonderful chance for leadership if he will show that he is vividly aware, first, of the international problem raised by these economic alliances, and secondly, of the fact that tariffs alone, unless coupled with something like the Australian system of wage distribution, will be quite helpless in meeting the situation after the war. . . .

1. At the Paris Economic Conference of June 1916, the Allied governments announced their plans for an exclusive postwar economic union that would have placed imposing barriers against American exports to Europe. The trading bloc the Allied governments contemplated would have led to

common tariff, banking, and shipping policies, common efforts to exploit raw materials throughout the world, and an allocation of shares of the world markets among the signatories. The conference also established a committee to pursue those plans. Secretary of State Lansing considered the agreements "serious, if not critical" for American and other neutral interests. Wilson, rejecting Lansing's suggestion for the creation of an economic bloc of neutrals, called instead for an open world economy, long one of his goals.

To Joseph P. Tumulty [1]

August 8, 1916

Dear Mr. Tumulty:

Thank you for your kind letters, the one promising an appointment with the President when he reaches the Jersey shore, and the other commenting on my letter to Secretary Baker.

I have been wondering whether it would not be a good thing for our government to do what the English government has been doing for some time according to information which I received the other day, viz., to appoint reconstruction committees to study the economic and political problems arising from the settlement of the war and from conditions after the war in order to formulate expert advice for the use of the administration. I understand that in England they have committees not only studying diplomatic problems in order to advise their own Peace Commissioners, but they also have committees of economists representing public, labor, and various interests, studying all the intricate questions of tariff and financial reconstruction. The whole subject is so difficult that no one now is really fitted to formulate any kind of policy, but as a step in the deeper preparedness I should think such a study ought to be made.

1. Joseph P. Tumulty, Wilson's secretary and political adviser, keeper of the president's calendar of appointments, and often unofficial White House press secretary.

To L. Stanwood Menken [1]

August 16, 1916

My dear Mr. Menken:

It seems to me that the National Security League could do its biggest work now if it devoted itself to attacking the theory of diplomatic isolation and making people realize that navy bills and universal service and the rest mean nothing unless we have worked out our relations to the great powers of Europe. I would like to see Congress next winter debate the question of the League to Enforce Peace: What is a virtual offensive and defensive of the western powers; and also the special subjects of our relations to the British Empire and to the weak states of Latin America. On the question of the weak states I would like to see such a gathering honestly face the question of a concessionaire — how far he is to be encouraged and how far he is to be protected, and what his status is to be in the backward countries. That problem and our relations to the British sea power are the two crucial questions of our foreign policy. It seems to me they underlie all the other questions either with Japan or Germany. . . .[2]

1. L. Stanwood Menken, New York lawyer, Democrat, president of the National Security League.   2. As Lippmann had argued at length in *The Stakes of Diplomacy* (New York, 1915).

To Graham Wallas

August 29, 1916

Dear G. W.:

. . . There are ever so many things to write about and I have longed for a real chance to see you. . . . I really think very seriously that there never was a better opportunity, so far as this country is concerned, to get it into some kind of international organization. But a certain amount of wooing from England is required and no one could do it more effectively than you. I have talked to Wilson and to all the people who are closest to him, and there is no doubt that the desire to form a league has grown upon them until it is really their greatest passion. In President Wilson's speech of acceptance, which is to be delivered Saturday, he will make a very effective statement about it, going so far even to accept the doctrine *The New Republic* has been preaching that in the future the United States cannot be neutral in a world war. What this means for an American President you will appreciate and I hope that at least the liberal press in England will give it some kind of cordial reception. As I see it America's participation depends on three things. First, a just and moderate peace. Second, the control of England by liberal minded people. Third, the reelection of President Wilson.

I have come around completely to Wilson. Chiefly because I think he has the imagination and the will to make a radical move in the organization of peace, because the Republican party is disorganized, inarticulate, commercially imperialist and conventional-minded, because the defeat of Wilson in November would mean that for six months following no nation in the world would know what America's policy was, and as I take it those six months are likely to be the most crucial months of our time. Wilson's faults and weaknesses are obvious enough but in the last six or eight months he has developed a power of decision unlike anything he has shown before. You have probably not been able to follow the situation here in regard to the threatened railroad strike,[1] but if you had I think you would agree that Wilson has shown the qualities of a great negotiator. It seems to me that it would be a sheer calamity to throw him out, repudiating and disorganizing the government at this time, and especially since the alternative of Hughes has nothing whatever to recommend it.

Hughes has proved to be a great disappointment. I saw a great deal of him in Washington last winter before he left the Bench to accept the nomination. I dined with him and talked with him and walked with him, and although we never discussed any issue at the time I did get the impression that he was a man of very powerful mind. But when he went on the stump he flattened out, became timid and evasive and dull, and at this moment he is actually engaged in trying to be elected with the help of the tariff vote, the anti-Wilson pro-German vote, and the rather powerful anti-Carranza Catholic vote. Our tories here are supporting him, though they are sick at heart for they are in the discomforting position of voting for a man whose attitude towards the war is far worse than Wilson at his worst. Hughes's trip through the West has been a complete frost. Even the people at the Hughes headquarters admit that he has not gained any votes and that he has lost them steadily.

If the present drift continues it seems very likely that Wilson will be re-elected. Hughes, although he is the opposition candidate, is actually on the defensive and every day brings new evidence of a great popular movement towards Wilson. The prosperity of the country of course helps the administration enormously, but coupled with it there is a great sense that Wilson has kept the peace, that he has avoided a futile war with Mexico, and that while American prestige abroad may not be high enough to suit the temper of people engaged in a great war, it is as high as may be expected under the circumstances. Last winter the current of feeling was one of self depreciation, it was popular to say that this country was cowardly and weak and all the rest. But in the last few months there has been a kind of recession of pride, and you find magazines like the *Atlantic Monthly*, published in the very center of pro-Ally feeling writing caustic sonnets against the Americans who say they are ashamed of America. All this is very interesting and significant because it means a pro-Wilson drift.

Of course the result of the campaign depends above all on what the former progressives do. If Wilson can get 20 percent of their votes he will be re-elected. 30 percent would make it absolutely sure. The Democratic party is unified and powerful and in better condition than it has ever been at any time since the days of Andrew Jackson, and Wilson is by far the best party leader the Democrats have ever produced. The Republicans on the other hand are divided, cantankerous, bulky and without leadership. The only living force they have is Roosevelt and Roosevelt is really sulking in his tent. In private conversation he refers to Hughes as the feather-duster and his private secretary says that privately he hopes Hughes will be beaten. Of course Roosevelt will make a few speeches for Hughes but the main object of those speeches will be to preserve Roosevelt's regularity as a Republican. The theory of the Roosevelt people is that if Hughes is beaten this year Roosevelt will be the unquestioned leader of the Republican party in 1920. . . .

1. Eager to prevent a pending strike by the railroad brotherhoods, which would have disrupted the economy and interrupted the flow of goods to England and France, Wilson had attempted unsuccessfully to mediate between the unions and management. He then, again without success, asked both sides to accept compromise terms he had worked out. On August 28, 1916, he proposed to Congress legislation designed to prevent a strike on equitable terms. The resulting Adamson Act, signed on September 2, imposed an eight-hour day, as the unions had demanded and Wilson had urged, and set up a commission to study the railroad problem. The unions did not get the overtime pay they had wanted, but in return for the extra cost of an eight-hour day, management soon received offsetting increases in rates from the Interstate Commerce Commission.

To Hazel Albertson   HANDWRITTEN

November 10, 1916

Pat dear,

We've lived through a good deal since Tuesday night. It wasn't till yesterday (Thursday) at 11 P.M. that the insiders at the Democratic Headquarters were really sure.[1] At that hour the committeeman from Pennsylvania kissed me in his delirium. We had been waiting all evening for the returns from the Sierra precincts of California. Surely not sure enough.

Vance McCormick[2] was in an heroic frame of mind all evening. One thing he said to me is particularly worth remembering. "We've won without Tammany in New York, without Taggart in Indiana, without Roger Sullivan in Illinois.[3] The Democratic Party is emancipated from its old bogey, that it required corruption to win. . . ."

1. So close was the election that it hinged on returns from Minnesota and California, which were late coming in. Hughes's early lead in the East evaporated west of the Mississippi, and Wilson won re-election by a slim plurality of the popular vote and a majority of the electoral college. **2.** Vance McCormick, chairman of the Democratic National Committee.   **3.** Tom Taggart of Indiana and Roger Sullivan of Illinois, the Democratic "bosses" of their states — whose support had been indispensable to Wilson's nomination in 1912 — represented, as did Tammany, the machine politics so distasteful to the progressives in the party.

To Woodrow Wilson

February 6, 1917

Dear Mr. President:

I was deeply touched to receive a letter from you written last Saturday, and I do not want to take any more of your time than is absolutely necessary. There are two matters, however, that we have talked over here and have very much at heart and that we want to put before you.

The first is that if it becomes necessary to raise a considerable army a recruiting campaign should be avoided. Any army that would be raised would probably be unready to fight before the war was drawing to its close, and the purpose of producing the army could really be for emergencies and to give the country a sense of security. We feel that it would be almost impossible to raise such an army by voluntary enlistment, and there is no prospect of immediate service in view of the present condition of the labor market, except by a newspaper campaign of manufactured hatred that would disturb and distract the morale of the nation. It has always seemed to me that the experience of England in her recruiting campaign acted like poison. We here have never up to this time been believers in compulsory military training, but in view of the immediate facts that seems to be the only orderly and quiet way to accomplish what may be the necessary result. Our idea was to make the training compulsory; call up two or three classes and then make foreign service voluntary.[1]

The other matter is the question of a censorship. We feel very strongly that in this country in view of the temper of the people, the usual military censorship would be of great danger and we were hoping that you could see your way to putting it in civilian control, under men of real insight and democratic sympathy. The danger in America from the press will be far less the danger of the conventionally unpatriotic than it will be the danger of those who persecute and harass and cause division among our people. It will be more important to control untruth than it will be to suppress truth as is done so much in Europe. In case of war the protection of a healthy public opinion in this country will be of the first importance. And after talking over the matter we feel that if he could be spared the ideal man to take charge of a censorship would be Secretary Lane.[2] I hope you will pardon the liberty of my suggesting this to you.

I need hardly tell you I suppose that *The New Republic* and all of us here are entirely at your disposal.

1. Wilson did turn to conscription after the United States declared war on Germany, but service abroad was not voluntary. 2. Franklin K. Lane, then secretary of the interior, a veteran of the Roosevelt administration, did not command Wilson's full confidence. When war came, the president turned to George Creel to head the Office of War Information, which adopted a severe policy of censorship distinctly in contrast to Lippmann's recommendation.

To Felix Frankfurter

February 19, 1917

Dear Felix:

I have just been in Washington and I have not much time to write at length, but I want you to know what I think is the essence of the situation at this moment: When the break[1] came the administration absolutely expected a sensational outrage within a few days and had set its mind in preparation for war on the strength of it. They miscalculated the facts. They did not realize that the present rather unspectacular chain of events would follow. This miscalculation of facts has raised all the old feeling of the country. The pacifist and the isolationist sentiment, and Congress is an enormously difficult problem for the President to handle. He could have carried the country with him had the facts gone as he supposed they would go. The failure of the facts to act up to expectations has put him in a hole; whereas if he acts aggressively and seems to desire war he will lose the very public opinion which he most needs. The reason he broke off so triumphantly was that all the aggressions had come from Germany. If he acts now the aggression will seem to come from Washington. He is really in the position that Sir Edward Grey would have been in had Germany failed to invade Belgium.

1. German resumption of unrestricted submarine warfare had provoked Wilson to break diplomatic relations with the German government. In an address to Congress on February 3, the president nevertheless restated his desire for continuing peace between the two nations. In the ensuing weeks, increasing pacifist agitation against war struck responsive chords among that large body of Americans who hoped their country would remain uninvolved.

To Julius Kuttner[1]

February 19, 1917

Dear Julius:

I think you have got the point just about right. As I see the war in very large outline it is a balance of power war in which England in her traditional role stepped in to redress the balance against the strongest power on the continent. So long as only that was at stake our sympathy and our help and even the bounds of technical neutrality were all that were required, but the moment England is in danger of actual defeat by starvation or the crippling of her sea power, the whole world order in which this nation has grown is imperiled. As I see it a victory by Germany on the high seas would make her not only supreme on the continent but would give her such naval power in the world (negative to be sure) that she would attract to herself Russia and Japan and imperil us as we have never been imperiled before.

1. Julius Kuttner, one of Lippmann's friends at Harvard.

To Oliver Wendell Holmes, Jr.[1]

February 21, 1917

My dear Judge Holmes,

. . . I lunched the other day with Henri Bergson[2] and wondered how even as a college sophomore under the spell of William James I could have thought him a great man. We talked about the war of course and a most discouraging talk it was. The function of philosophy in wartime appears to be confined to making terrible faces at the enemy. Lord knows, I don't feel a bit neutral between the Western Powers and Germany, but I can't believe that Germany is the last and most elaborate effort of Satan to destroy God. I don't understand Bergson nor Brandeis for that matter — they don't seem able to believe in one side without insisting that the cosmos justifies them. Sometimes I wonder whether this elaborate rationalization isn't just squeamishness on the offensive.

1. Associate Justice Oliver Wendell Holmes, Jr., one of Lippmann's heroes, had considerable admiration for Lippmann's energy and intelligence. They were to come to know each other increasingly well during the ensuing years. **2.** Henri Bergson, the French philosopher, had engaged Lippmann's enthusiasm a decade earlier, revealed in *A Preface to Politics* (New York, 1913).

To Norman Angell[1]

March 1, 1917

My dear Angell:

. . . Ever since the Germans proclaimed their new submarine warfare we have had an exceedingly hard time in this country dealing with the pacifists who simply want to avoid trouble, and we feel that an article from you justifying America's entrance into the war on liberal and international grounds would be of immense help to us. You will of course know that with Wilson in office for the next four years there is no danger at all of our taking an Imperialist line in the war. We would use it first of all to resist German maritime aggression. Secondly, to start going America's participation in world affairs, and third, to bring in America to stabilize settlement. To us it looks as if the present opportunity might almost be decisive in the history of the world, because there is a chance by America's entrance into the war to crystallize and make real the whole league of peace propaganda. We all know what we owe to you in convincing us of the justice of this view, and it sometimes makes me boil with anger to think that there are Englishmen who speak bitterly of you when as a matter of fact you have had more influence than any other one Englishman I can think of in preparing the background of ideas which would convince Americans who are now in power of the necessity of their taking an active role in the war. That service though it has been in some measure indirect, has been immense. . . .

1. Norman Angell, whose ideas had attracted Lippmann increasingly, was a frequent contributor to *The New Republic* and had influenced the editors of that journal to adopt their policy of urging economic aid to Britain and France for the purpose of effecting "a just peace without indemnities or territorial aggrandizements."

To Woodrow Wilson

April 3, 1917

Dear Mr. President:

I have tried to say a little of what I feel about your address[1] in the following words, which are to appear in *The New Republic* this week:

"For having seen this (i.e., that this is a war between democracy and autocracy) and said it, for having selected the moment when the issue was so clear, for having done so much through the winter to make the issue clear, our debt and the world's debt to Woodrow Wilson is immeasurable. Any mediocre politician might have gone to war futilely for rights that in themselves cannot be defended by war. Only a statesman who will be called great could have made America's intervention mean so much to the generous forces of the world, could have lifted the inevitable horror of war into a deed so full of meaning."

I would like to take the liberty of saying a few words to you about the military service recommendation: It seems to me absolutely essential to the success of the idea which you have in mind, that this country be spared the worst features of the war psychology, and they are raised more than anything else by a recruiting campaign. I would like therefore to suggest to you the following plan in order to work out the suggestion which you laid down:

A register of all men of military age should be made as soon as possible. That register would of course give information as to their present occupation and alternate abilities. When that is done the government could decide which of the men were already employed in essential industries and which ought to be exempted from military service either because of their physical condition or because of conscientious objections. Then the government might invite the remainder to volunteer, calling them in order by classes. The understanding would be that if by this voluntary method enough troops were not raised compulsion would be resorted to, but it seems altogether probable that a half a million men can be raised in this way. I do not know what practical objections can be raised against the plan, but the arguments in its favor are clearly obvious. It avoids the recruiting campaign; it avoids helter skelter volunteering and misuse of talent; it retains the volunteer principle for the present; and it lays the foundations for compulsion if that should become necessary.

1. Wilson's eloquent address of April 2, 1917, calling for a declaration of war against Germany, which the Senate voted on April 4 and the House on April 6.

To Charles S. Wallace[1]

April 4, 1917

Dear Sir:

I can well understand the difficulties raised in your mind by the contrast between the socialistic German state and the rather individualistic state of England before the war. When we speak of this struggle as a war for democracy we do not mean of course a war for a social democracy. That will be a long time coming. We mean that now after the Russian revolution, the Allies, including ourselves, consist of nations in which the foreign policy is controlled by a public opinion wide enough to make criticism count; but that in Germany as it is organized today a small group consisting of a union between certain of the large capitalists, certain of the large landlords and the upper grades of the military profession, decide absolutely the direction of the German foreign policy. This group is an adventurous and aggressive group and nothing quite like it exists any longer in any of the Allied countries. I think the really reactionary quality of the German ruling class was shown by the inevitable alliance with Russia's autocracy.

1. Charles S. Wallace of Bellingham, Washington, had apparently written criticizing Lippmann's position on the war as expressed in *The New Republic*.

To Edward M. House

April 12, 1917

Dear Colonel House:

I am leaving for Washington tonight and shall see Secretary Lane tomorrow. I want just to take this opportunity to give you an outline of the progress of the work which you asked me to do yesterday:

The chief item of importance is that I have found the nucleus of an organization already in existence which is ready and competent to take up the work of a press bureau. It is an organization built up by Professor Pitkin[1] at the Columbia School of Journalism and is fully trained and ready. Professor Pitkin is going to Washington with me tonight and we shall look over the ground there together. We are also drawing up the budget and the administrative chart, which I shall be ready to give you on Tuesday. The task of the bureau I have tried to phrase for myself somewhat as follows:

"American strategy in this war has raised a peculiar psychological problem. For a year at least the nation's enthusiasm cannot be focused upon great naval and military operations. Bread and boats and training camps, finances and taxes, organization, manufacture, and munitions are all prosaic, but they are the fundamental and decisive things. The enthusiasm which in other wars is reflected from the battlefield will have somehow to be centered on a gigantic industrial operation. Moreover, the objects for which we are at war are delicate and difficult. We are fighting not so much to beat an enemy as to make a world that is safe for democracy. We shall be working this next year for objects which are new to warfare by methods which are new in warfare."

This is the justification and the chief spirit of the bureau I have in mind. As for its more concrete activities, I conceive them as follows:

1. It must be a clearing house of information for the activities of the government.

2. It must invent a form of publicity which will enlist attention in the comparatively prosaic tasks of industrial warfare.

3. It must be able to supply special articles supporting the government policy.

4. It must keep a close watch on the movement of public opinion in this country in order to supply the government with ideas and criticisms and to be able to advise and warn and suggest to editors.

5. It must follow and report upon the allied, neutral and enemy press.

6. It must deal with the moving picture situation.

7. It must be prepared to run down rumors and lies.

The type of organization I have in mind would consist of a very small council, one member of which would be the executive head of the organization. Another member would be the state, military and naval censor; a staff of reporters; a staff of men from the trade journals who can popularize technical news; a group of copy readers and a corps of special writers who would volunteer their services.

All the lower positions in this organization would be easy to fill. The main difficulty will come in selecting the men for the top. My own best judgment is that the ideal man for the chief of this bureau would be Mr. Vance McCormick, and if his services could be secured I feel that the thing would be in the right hands. Mr. Woolley[2] would be just the right man to deal with the distributing end of the organization, and I would like to suggest Mr. Pitkin as the proper man to act as director of the staff. The members of the advisory council would be more difficult to pick. They must be of course men deeply in sympathy with the President's spirit and intention in this whole matter, and I am afraid there are not as many of them as we would like to find.

The main thing I wanted to let you know by this letter was first, that a preliminary plan was in existence and the nucleus of an organization was in existence; that Mr. Pitkin and I were ready to give all our time to the organization of the thing, and that when we can present to you on Tuesday a definite plan the main thing then will be to secure the active approval of the President. Mr. Pitkin and I estimate that we can have the thing started in two weeks if the government will give us the word.

1. Wolcott Pitkin, Jr., a special adviser to the Siamese government, later on the staff Colonel House gathered to develop postwar plans.   2. Robert W. Woolley, in 1916 publicity director of the Democratic National Committee.

To Herbert C. Hoover[1]

May 15, 1917

Dear Mr. Hoover:

I'm going to take the liberty of making a few suggestions in regard to the propaganda bureau in connection with the Food Administration. Your plan, as I understand it, calls for action by great masses of people, humble, out of the currents of public affairs, many of them practically illiterate. The propaganda differs from most in that you must reach deeper than the mere leaders of opinion. It is not enough to convince them, and have the rest inertly acquiesce. The motives that are to be worked are patriotism, social pressure in the local committee, the sense of what is respectable and what isn't, and finally the threat that drastic powers are in reserve.

One might make a list of agencies that are available:

    I. The President —
       Yourself —
       Governors and Mayors and village officials
    II. Commercial organizations — i.e., Chambers of Commerce
                                          Granges
                                          Trade Unions
       Trade Associations — Millers, etc.
       Bankers and Railroads
       Churches
       Women's Clubs — including the Federation, Woman Suffrage,
                      Anti-Suffrage, D.A.R., etc., etc.
       Universities
       National Educational Association
       Social Service Organizations
       Medical Societies
    III. The Press — through the A.P.; U.P., etc.
                 "   the Publishers' Association
                 "   Syndicates-Sunday specials
                 "   woman's pages, boiler plate, cartoons
                 "   direct communication with editors and owners
       The Trade Press
       The Women's Press
       The Foreign Language Press
    IV. Movies
       Advertising

Method of Control

It will be for you to lay out the things you want put over at particular times. I should imagine that you would do this by daily or weekly conference with the head of the whole publicity scheme. He should have under him probably three executives — on organizations, on the press, on movies and advertising. He would give these three executives a written order explaining just what is wanted, which they would transmit down.

Each one of these executives would be in communication with the most powerful person in a particular group. He could then instruct him that beginning on such and such a date the Food Administration desires a certain kind of publicity, either throughout the nation or in a particular district. Sometimes the instructions would be general, sometimes they would dwell on a specific point. The instructions would then go to the publicity head of the Chambers of Commerce, or the American Federation of Labor, or the executive head of agricultural papers, etc., etc. These bodies would work through local publicity, circulars, speeches, etc., and they could be made to give their services free.

In addition there ought to be a central news bureau with a staff of reporters. This would issue reports of progress, news of good work, expose special interests that were obstructing, publish pamphlets of a more scientific character.

At the present time I can suggest no one better for the general executive head than Vance McCormick. For his three immediate subordinates I'd like to make further inquiries, and within a few days I hope to send you a list of men and women who could organize special parts of this work.

I may say also that we have just established a New Republic News Service in Washington which would gladly volunteer.

1. Herbert C. Hoover, organizer of Belgian relief, head of the Food Administration during the war, soon became a frequent visitor at the house in Washington where Lippmann lived later in 1917. Lippmann once said he had "never met a more interesting man, anyone who knew so much of the world and could expound so clearly . . . the . . . mysteries of European politics"; Ronald Steel, *Walter Lippmann and the American Century* (Boston, 1980), p. 123.

To Norman Hapgood

July 20, 1917

Dear Norman:

 . . . You asked how I am enjoying the work here.[1] The answer is, I think, that I am enjoying it more and more as I become busier and busier. I should not want office work for life but at the present time under war conditions I had rather be doing it than attempting to write. I don't believe I shall be interested in doing any journalism now until the end of the war, though I shall have to do some to make up for what the Government doesn't pay me.

The thing that makes the difference between night and day so far as work of this kind is concerned is the association with Newton Baker. I have the deepest personal affection for him mixed with a constantly growing admiration for his real great abilities. I think he is as good a combination of mind and heart as I ever met. . . .

1. Lippmann had left *The New Republic* to serve as an assistant to Secretary of War Baker.

To Newton D. Baker

[c. August 29, 1917]
MEMORANDUM FOR THE SECRETARY OF WAR
-:*Reply to the Pope's proposal:*-[1]

We are conducting the war on the assumption that there is a distinction between the German government and German people. The question is: Why have the German people supported this government in the past and why do they continue to? Among the elements which bound the German people to their government in the past are the following:

    1. The memory of centuries of oppression and poverty which preceded German unity. Germany was the battleground of Europe.

    2. The splendor and prosperity which followed Bismarck's triumph.

    3. The fear of imperial Russia.

    4. The fear that Germany's access to raw materials would be cut by the British fleet.

    1. On the basis of these memories, hopes, and fears a government and educational system has grown up which makes the German people obedient by playing on these motives. The military, financial, aristocratic and large agrarian class maintains its position because it is associated with the fundamental ideas of national security, economic opportunity, human pride.

If the German people are to be weaned from their governing class they must be made to believe that they can be safe, prosperous, and respected without dependence upon their government as it exists. Unless this is done they will continue to regard as their sole means of defense what we regard as an engine of aggression. The mistake of Allied diplomacy has been due to a failure to see that Prussian militarism which looks so dangerous to us looks to the German people like their best defense against a circle of enemies. They hold the handle of the spear which is pointed at us.

In the last year or so another motive has arisen which binds the people to the government — the yearning for peace. The German government has very shrewdly identified itself with that yearning, and the Allies, through the Paris conference and their reply to President Wilson last December, have very unwisely presented themselves to the German people as implacable enemies intent upon imposing a humiliating peace. It is clear by now that the majority of the German people accept the formula of "no annexations and no indemnities," that this formula is in their opinion a disavowal of aggression, and that the Allies disdain of the formula is convincing proof to them that whatever the origins of the war they are now in fact engaged in a war of national defense.

    2. From the American point of view the obstacle to peace is our distrust of the German government. We are not interested in particular territorial settle-

ments; we are interested in the *method of settlement*. "The world made safe for democracy" means concretely not a specific form of government for Germany, not a specific drawing of strategic and nationalist frontiers, but a binding assurance that the future method of settlement between the powers shall be by a civil procedure. We are at war with the German procedure, and we hesitate to negotiate now because we do not see adequate guaranties for the future that the procedure will be different.

3. So long as those guaranties do not exist the nations aligned against Germany are compelled to rely for their safety upon maintaining a balance of power against Germany. The machinery of peace, i.e., a League of Nations accompanied by reduction of armament, cannot be set in motion until Germany becomes, in the President's words, "a fit partner."

4. By a fit partner we understand a Germany in which control of foreign policy and of the military machine has passed to the representatives of the people. We go on the assumption that it is possible to deal in good faith with a democracy.

5. But the progress of democracy in Germany is arrested by the conviction of the German people that a radical change in the midst of war will have results similar to those in Russia, i.e., that it will render them defenseless.

6. *This is the vicious circle which it may be possible to begin breaking by the reply to the Pope.*

Suppose the argument ran as follows:

The American people share his noble desire to see an end of the agony, but they desire even more to end the possibility of its repetition. They believe in the establishment of a League of Peace and reduction of armaments and equal opportunities for all nationalities. They are convinced, however, upon Germany's record in Belgium and in regard to the submarine that it does not respect treaties. The American people, therefore, desire to know what guaranties there are that a negotiation undertaken now would be binding. This is the essential point for which we fight. If those guaranties are forthcoming, the United States will not countenance economic war after the war, will accept Germany as a partner in the League, and as a member of such a league would be prepared to guarantee the German people in the future against aggression.

7. It would be unwise, I think, to specify the terms of territorial settlement for several reasons: Because they are secondary not only from the American point of view but from the world point of view; because it is essential to focus on the method of peace rather than the terms of peace; because such a reply really represents our share in the war. Keeps us clear of entanglements, justifies a continuation of the war if it is rejected, and yet leaves the door sufficiently ajar so that the President cannot be accused either by Germany or by the American people of prolonging the war.

---

1. Pope Benedict XV on August 1, 1917, had issued a call for a peace without spoils. The German government replied cautiously, promising no withdrawal from the areas its armies had taken but seemingly prepared to negotiate. The French and British, encouraged by the American entry into the war, held back. Wilson, too, preferred a peace he could fashion in negotiations, and Lippmann's memo to Baker was designed to assist the president in preparing a reply to the pope.

To Edward M. House

September 10, 1917

My dear Col. House:

I don't need to tell you that I was more than happy at the President's reply to the Pope. It seems to me that events since then have more than justified our best expectations.

I want to write you, however, in regard to a matter which seems to me of a good deal of importance. I have just had a talk with Prof. William E. Rappard,[1] who is an old friend of mine, formerly a professor at Harvard College. He has come to this country as a member of the Swiss mission. His private sympathies are ours. He points out what is clearly an obvious fact, that Switzerland is one of the very best places, perhaps the best place, from which to influence German opinion. The French and Italian parts of Switzerland are, of course, unanimously anti-German in this war. The German part of Switzerland, he tells me, began with the majority sympathetic to Germany. This majority has dwindled but is by no means pro-ally as yet. The German press in Switzerland has a very large circulation in Germany. It is probably the one press of all outside of Germany which actually reaches a large number of Germans and its attitude is of great importance in its influence upon radical elements in Germany. Professor Rappard tells me that this German-Swiss press has been very skeptical about our disinterestedness and our genuine democracy. The fact that this Swiss press is not strongly sympathetic to America has a bad effect in Germany, because it is assumed there that if there is any country in Europe which would have a natural sympathy for our ideas it would be Switzerland.

It follows that it is of the very greatest importance to influence this German-Swiss press by convincing it that we mean what we say. Prof. Rappard has not seen the President, except at the formal reception. I think that it is of genuine importance that he should see you. . . .

1. William E. Rappard — professor of history and public finance at the University of Geneva, formerly an assistant professor at Harvard — in 1917 was attached to the Swiss mission in Washington and had published a long article in the *New York Times*, August 26, 1917, explaining the Swiss position on the war.

To Edward M. House

September 24, 1917

[No salutation]

. . . Nothing has ever pleased me more or come as a greater surprise. The work you outlined is exactly that which I have dreamed of since the very beginning of the war, but dreamed of as something beyond reach. I'd literally rather be connected with you in this work in no matter what capacity than do anything else there is to do in the world.[1]

1. House had invited Lippmann to join the group he was gathering to begin work on plans for a postwar peace conference. Early in October, Lippmann moved to New York to begin that study with the others in what became known as the Inquiry.

To Louis D. Brandeis

October 6, 1917

Dear L.D.B.:

Sidney Hillman[1] was in to see me this morning, fearing that the *Jewish Daily Forward* is about to be denied second class mailing privileges by the post office department. The representatives of the paper have been asked to appear in Washington on Friday of this week.

Hillman insists that the *Vorwaerts* is a moderate socialistic paper and that Cahan[2] would be perfectly ready to moderate his tone if he were advised to, but that the outright suppression of a paper of such influence would have a very bad effect not only on the east side but in Russia as well. The *Vorwaerts* of course is a paper of international reputation and is looked upon by Russian socialists as almost bourgeois in its point of view. Its suppression would give the Russian extremists every excuse for insisting that American reactionaries were completely in the saddle. I imagine I do not need to tell you how great a blunder it would be.

Hillman wants to know whether he should come and see you about it or whether you have any other advice to give. It seems to me a matter that certainly ought to be put before the President and not decided by some petty official or even by Mr. Burleson.[3] It is undoubtedly the most important case of the kind that has arisen since the war began.

I shall speak to Colonel House about it but I know that you can do more than any one else in a matter of this kind if you feel that you can. . . .

1. Sidney Hillman, president of the Amalgamated Clothing Workers, then one of the most radical and vigorous of American unions; the membership was heavily Jewish. 2. Abraham Cahan, editor of the *Jewish Daily Forward* and a leader in the Jewish community of workers in New York. 3. Postmaster General Albert S. Burleson exercised his wartime control over the mail with small regard for the freedom of the press or of expression. A provincial Texas Democrat, he brought to his task a mean oppressiveness.

To Woodrow Wilson

October 8, 1917

My dear Mr. President:

No doubt the seriousness of the political situation in New York City has already been called to your attention, and I feel that I must write to you briefly in regard to it. The certain facts appear to be the indisputable superiority of Mitchel[1] to all the other candidates. There are many things he has done that liberal minded people cannot altogether agree with and there are more things that he has said which are hard to bear, but the tone and quality of his administration has been extraordinarily fine. From the point of view of the city itself his defeat would be something like a political disaster.

In the course of his administration he has of course raised a formidable opposition: much of it is ignorant opposition but a good deal of it consists of petty special interests, and his re-election is at the present time exceedingly doubtful.

As you know, he is making the issue turn on the support of the war, shoving all municipal issues into the background. Now it is true that the disaffected elements in the city are all against Mitchel. There will be a very large vote for Hillquit[2] and of course Hearst's influence in New York is powerful. There can be no doubt that in the opposition to Mitchel will be found all the pro-German, anti-British, anti-war sentiment there is in the city. On the other hand it by no means follows that all the loyal sentiment in the city will be found on Mitchel's side. There will be thousands of men who will follow you on the issue of the war who will vote against Mitchel. In fact Mitchel himself admitted to me on Friday that a word of support from you would be worth seventy-five thousand votes to him. The obvious deduction from that is that Mitchel does not monopolize the support of the patriotic groups of the city. This has put those of us who wish to see him elected but who wish to preserve the national morale, in a very distressing position. Important as it is to reelect Mitchel from the point of view of a New Yorker, it is even more important that the vote in November should not be allowed to appear as a test of the country's support of the war. The *New York World* is the only paper which seems to understand this point.

I should like therefore to put this before you for your consideration. Would it not be possible for you to find some way of saying publicly that the issue in New York was one of good government, putting that issue as strongly as possible and at the same time asserting that the only national issue at stake is the cause of good government. This of course is bound to be a somewhat awkward thing to do, but it does seem important in view of the reaction on the rest of the country and abroad, and that there should be some official record before election making it perfectly clear that the outcome in New York is not to be taken as a test vote. A heavy defeat of Mitchel in the present temper of his campaign would let loose pacifist feeling throughout the country as no other thing would do. I know enough about pacifist feeling to be certain that Mitchel is now identified in their minds with a vigorous military policy. It is therefore highly important that something be done to dissociate the issues.

1. John Purroy Mitchel was running for re-election as mayor of New York City. A fusion candidate, he had won office on a reform platform and brought unusual probity and vigor to his duties. He had also wholly identified himself with the preparedness movement to the dismay of many of the New York German- and Irish-Americans. In 1917 a renascent Tammany Hall, with a characteristic candidate in John F. Hylan, supported also by the Hearst press, both expected and achieved victory.   **2.** Morris Hillquit, New York Socialist intellectual, whom Lippmann some seven years earlier had found too conservative a Socialist for his taste.

To Edward M. House

October 17, 1917

Dear Colonel House,

At your suggestion I am setting down a few impressions of the effect on morale produced by the Post Office campaign against seditious newspapers.

I find on my return to New York that the radical and liberal groups are in a sullen mood over the government's attitude towards the socialist press. Men like Prof. Dewey,[1] who represent the warmest kind of faith in the war and in the President, have told me that they intend to vote for Hillquit if the *Call*[2] and the *Jewish Daily Forward* are excluded from the mails. In the labor movement, apart from those who will support Tammany, the feeling on this issue is at white heat. The position taken by Mr. Burleson is regarded as brutally unreasonable.

So far as I am concerned I have no doctrinaire belief in free speech. In the interest of the war it is necessary to sacrifice some of it. But the point is that the method now being pursued is breaking down the liberal support of the war and is tending to divide the country's articulate opinion into fanatical jingoism and fanatical pacifism.

The thing has worked out about as follows. No one but a man with the President's record of democratic achievement could have united the country as he did last April. It was an utter faith in him, more than anything else which reconciled the humbler people of the country to the war. They accepted conscription because he said it was necessary, and because there were men like Mr. Baker to administer it.

During July and August there was a relaxation, chiefly I think because Washington was too busy to keep the country informed. The President's reply to the Pope completely altered everything however. There has never been a moment since the war began when the country was so thoroughly interested and united. Why even the *Masses* confessed that it could not oppose a war for such purposes! On the basis of that message no pacifist opposition that amounted to anything could survive. Happily this coincided with the brilliantly success-ful mobilization of the draft army.

But two forces are at work to destroy this fine national unity. One is the fierce heresy hunting of a portion of the press and the other is the apparent approval of this bitter intolerance on the part of the Post Office. Liberals can not understand why the government is apparently more apprehensive about what an obscure and discredited little sheet says about Wall Street and muni-tion makers than about Mr. Roosevelt's malicious depreciation of the Ameri-can army. Suppression of course gives these papers an importance that intrin-sically they would never have.

A great government ought to be contemptuously uninterested in such opin-ion and ought to suppress only military secrets and advice to break the law or evade it. In my opinion the overwhelming number of radicals can be won to the support of the war simply by conserving the spirit of the President's own utterances, and by imaginative administration of the censorship and the nec-essary suppression of disloyalty.

Censorship in wartime is one of the most delicate tasks that confronts a government. It should never be entrusted to anyone who is not himself tol-erant, not to anyone who is unacquainted with the long record of folly which is the history of suppression.

1. John Dewey, then a professor at Columbia. **2.** The *Call,* a Socialist newspaper to which Lippmann had earlier frequently contributed.

To Graham Wallas

HANDWRITTEN

October 18, 1917

Dear G. W.

. . . For the first time since the summer of 1915 I am coming to believe that the war will end with a breakdown of the German army and a revolution-ary temper in Central Europe, though I can see no probable end of the war before the last quarter of 1918. Naturally, the Administration is proceeding as if the war would last several campaigns, merely as a matter of pru-dence. . . .

To Felix Frankfurter

October 30, 1917

Dear Felix:

. . . Strictly between ourselves the job goes well but it has not reached a point where you can be drafted into it with any fairness to the work you are now doing. The Colonel has been exceedingly busy on other work and has not been able to give much time to this so we have been going along on our own.[1] "We" consists of Mezes, Shotwell and myself together with a few people like Archie Coolidge and others.[2] We are beginning at the academic level, simply collecting maps, the general statistical material, the obvious historic material and references, etc. etc. of the paper side of the job. That will take eight weeks anyway I imagine and is that part of the work you refer to as the nose of the camel. Of course the job cannot be done on that level but it can be begun that way, and for reasons which I do not need to explain to you, that is the way they wish it begun. I myself am working chiefly on the experience of inter-nationalization. . . . Shotwell is directing the preparation of maps, showing the changes of boundaries, movements of population and so on. Coolidge is trying to chart the Polish problem and the problem of the missing provinces of Russia. I think he will also take up Bulgaria. Pitkin is in general charge of the Far Eastern question. George Louis Beer is going to make a study of Central Africa, trying to get as much wisdom as he can of the general question of the tropical colonies. You know that is his life specialty and it is the best thing he does. We have made only a beginning but it is a beginning I think. The discretion required in carrying on the work is huge, superabundant and over-flowing.

You can see from this that there is nothing on hand at the moment which would induce the chief to pull you out of your present job, much as I should like to see you brought east again. You can be sure of this, however, that the moment I see a break in the line I will telegraph for you.

1. The Colonel did not want Frankfurter on the Inquiry. For his part, Frankfurter was at work on labor problems in the West but eager, as ever, to be at the center of events.   2. Sidney E. Mezes, House's son-in-law, president of the City College of New York, and head of the Inquiry; James T. Shotwell, Columbia historian; Archibald Cary Coolidge, Harvard historian and librarian; George Louis Beer, at this time American correspondent for the *Round Table*, eminent in his generation as a historian of colonialism.

To Maurice S. Amos

November 5, 1917

My dear Amos:

It was mighty good to hear from you just now. Owing to the distance which separates us I cannot expect you to keep track of my kaleidoscopic changes. I was in Washington all summer as assistant to the Secretary of War, but at the present time I am working for Colonel House on the preparation of data to be used at the eventual peace conference, and I should give a great deal to have you in New York in order to talk over all sorts of things. There is no use trying to write about them at this distance.

Our own war preparations have developed on a scale and at a speed that none of us thought possible when you were here. Perhaps the weakest link has been the shipping, and sometimes I fear that the French especially have estimated a little too highly the amount of assistance it is possible to send within the required time. There is no question at all about this country's willingness to send whatever it has, but as one friend of mine expresses it — our situation is a little like that of a great crowd down in the street anxious to take part in a fight on the tenth story of a building to which the only access is a narrow and steep ladder.

The most serious problem at the moment seems to be the lack of diplomatic and administrative unity among the Allies, and of course the events in Italy[1] bring this home most forcibly. It seems to me that the proverbial weakness of coalitions has been unnecessarily increased by our failure in the last year to arrive at a candid examination of war aims. After all, it is not possible to unify administration unless there is complete unity of purpose, and as I think back over the tragedies in Italy and Russia I can't help feeling that the Liberals who asked for specific declarations were the people who really understood the fundamental problem of the Allies. I think we are witnessing the destruction of a great illusion, namely, the illusion that the Jingo is the man who can best conduct a war. Among the men I know who have seen the problems most clearly are those who have bellowed least.

We have reached temporarily a stage in our progress where elderly and impotent people are dethroning the Kaiser by refusing to play German opera. If I had time I would like to write a little book entitled "What Did You Do In The Great War?" It would have chapters on the people who sat in clubs in New York and deplored Kerensky,[2] who spent time writing to the papers insisting that an obviously German musician could be transformed into a patriotic American by hypocritically playing the Star Spangled Banner. But I suppose I won't do it.

You ask in your letter about "priority." There is no doubt that your visit left a deep impression in Washington, and the word was almost as popular as *camouflage*. I sat for a time on the Priority Committee but we proceeded without any success. During August the various committees of the Council of National Defense were reorganized into what was called the War Industries Board, which was the nearest approach to a ministry of munitions which it was possible to make without legislation, and nobody was in a mood last summer to stir up Congress sufficiently to ask for a new department. In the War Industries Board there was a Priority Department . . . but I saw little of its work and I do not know how it succeeded. At present priority questions are being handled, I understand, through a great number of agencies — that is, coal through the fuel administration, tonnage through the Shipping Board, metals through the War Industries Board.

Our labor situation is not satisfactory. Business men on the whole are still worrying about ancient problems such as whether trade unions are seditious or not, and that part of labor which is organized under the American Federation of Labor is almost without leadership. . . .[3]

1. The Italian disaster at Caporetto and the resulting reshuffling of the Italian cabinet deeply worried the British and French, whose decision against reinforcing Italian troops several months earlier seemed to the Italians to have constituted a major factor in the defeat. Inferior Italian military preparation and strategy, and antiwar sentiment among Italian troops, provided a sufficient explanation. The defeat occurred just as the Bolsheviks were seizing power in Russia. 2. Alexander F. Kerensky — a brusque, sometimes arrogant, relatively ineffectual liberal, the chief architect of the Russian Provisional Government that the Bolsheviks were supplanting — had struck conservative Americans as something of a radical, especially after he brought the Mensheviks into his coalition shortly before its collapse.   3. Though Samuel Gompers remained its president, as he had for so long.

To Woodrow Wilson

November 21, 1917

Dear Mr. President:

A fairly large number of utterances published recently indicate that the more far-seeing Germans are assailed by fear which we may perhaps turn to good account. Last June Dr. Dernburg[1] wrote as follows about economic conditions after the war:

> The problem of reintroducing our soldiers into productive activities is vital. It can only be done in proportion as employment, that is to say, raw material and working capital, are available. For even a partial period of unemployment would lead to disastrous manifestations. Demobilization will have to be carefully worked out, and will certainly extend over a long period, however irksome it may be to those with the colors.

The period of demobilization will certainly be critical, for then the exaltation of war will be relaxed and political rebellion cannot so easily be stamped out as treason. For this period Germany must have supplies from beyond Middle Europe. What the Germans are beginning to see is that they are now blockaded in a way that no other nation was ever blockaded. Cessation of hostilities will not mean, as it did in previous wars, the free entry of supplies. In this war the enemies of Germany have done more than intercept overseas trade. They have stopped that trade at its source.

Germany's enemies not only control the sources — they themselves will put forth prior claims on the supplies, and with the utmost goodwill on the part of the anti-German coalition the best Germany can hope for immediately is to be put on strictly limited rations.

Certain inferences suggest themselves: If in addition to a unity of diplomatic and of military strategy, America and the Allies could achieve unity of administrative control over the scarce and essential supplies which German industry needs, a most powerful weapon would be forged. It would make it impossible for Germany to remain outside the society of nations, and it would put the Western Allies and America in a position to state the conditions on which Germany would again be given access to the resources of civilization.

This would be a war measure, not a war after the war. By insisting on a measure of economic unity now, the total strength of the coalition would be increased and the much discussed "new mercantilism" of the European nations made difficult, if not impossible. Unity of purpose and control is not only essential to victory, but to that general purification of aims which must precede a fine peace. Merely selfish purposes cannot survive a movement towards unity, and the spiritual reaction might be very great. It would, I believe, put new heart into the humble if they saw through the war the rise of an international structure. For a unification of diplomatic, military and economic action would give enormous vitality to the idea of a League of Nations.

1. Dr. Bernhard Dernburg — director in chief of German propaganda in the United States from the outbreak of war in Europe until mid-June 1917 — had returned to Germany, where he continued to make speeches and write pamphlets directed in part to American audiences.

To Edward M. House

December 19, 1917

MEMORANDUM ON RECONSTRUCTION [1]

(1) The longer the war lasts and the more deeply the United States becomes involved, the more complex will our internal political, economic, and social problems be at the conclusion of peace.

(2) Here is a partial list of issues that will have to be met:

The return of our army from France.

The demobilization of the expeditionary and home forces.

The reabsorption of these men into industry.

The transformation of many industries from the making of war materials to normal trade uses.

The financing of the war debt.

The revision of tariffs.

The administration of a vast government-owned merchant marine.

The working out of a military and naval policy adapted to the international liberation at the close of the war.

The study of what war-created agencies like the Food Administration, the War Trade Board, etc., should be maintained, or how they should be modified.

The study of methods for meeting and regulating the foreign trade competition which will follow the end of the war.

The planning of a comprehensive immigration policy.

The development of the country's education, especially along the lines of
industrial technique and scientific agriculture.

(3) In France, England, and Germany organs exist for working out after-
the-war problems based on a realization that the return to peace will be accompanied by grave disorder unless it is skillfully and courageously planned. Once
the war-motives are relaxed, governments will not be able to count so heavily
on the patriotism and self-sacrifice of interested groups.

(4) What appears to be needed is a disinterested analysis and forecast of
these issues, together with the preparation of a number of alternative programs which can be put at the disposal of the President.

(5) There are a number of ways in which this might be done. We might
follow the English model and establish a Reconstruction Bureau in Washington. The objections to this are obvious. It would create an immense amount
of gossip and speculation, and would be besieged by dogmatist and special
interests. A better way, it seems to me, would be to do it quietly, along the
lines we are pursuing in collecting reference data for the peace conference.
The method would have this advantage, that it would enable us to consider
international conditions in their relation to internal problems.

(6) In working out the organization of the Inquiry, we are canvassing the
expert resources of the country as they relate to social problems. It would be
entirely feasible, I believe, for the Inquiry to expand into this other field without straining it. The method of assembling data would be much the same, the
machinery for editing and digesting would require no essential change. We
should need a somewhat larger central office force, six or eight more men to
direct the research, and from twenty-five to fifty thousand dollars to cover
payments to specialists, their clerical assistants, and expenses.

(7) If this method were adopted, the procedure would be about as follows:

To plot out the main issues tentatively.

To select scholars of an administrative type and divide the field among them.

To have each of them secure a small staff, say of four or five men, who
would give full time, and associated with them a larger number of collab-
orators working voluntarily or for bare expenses.

To pick out key men in important trade, engineering, scientific, agricultural,
and labor organizations, and stimulate them quietly to form committees
in their organizations which would report needs, problems, and solutions.

To have the reports and researches collated and edited by the directors of
the research.

The results could then be laid before the heads of departments at Washington for criticism and for preparation in the form of legislation.

1. Lippmann sent this memorandum to Colonel House, as he did also the two undated memoranda of December 1917 that follow.

To Edward M. House

[December 1917]

MEMORANDUM

Now that a skeleton organization has been created, it may be well to examine the context of the Inquiry.

In all human probability the war will not at any one moment suddenly terminate in a peace. Demobilization will not precede the peace conference. It is not even likely that hostilities will cease during the early stages of the discussion.

The probable course of events is already indicated. We may expect a peace propaganda from Central Europe of increasing intensity calculated as accurately as possible to allure the groups of the Allied Left at a minimum of concessions. The minimum of actual concession will be covered by formulas which approach more and more the verbal form of the war aims outlined by the Left among the Allies. As the German proposals grow in "moderation" there is a political movement in each of the Allied nations towards its own left. The object of course is the division of the coalition as between the nations and within the nations. Naturally the German peace offensive is aimed at the weak points of the Alliance. Those points are those where the aims of the Allies do not coincide and within the nations the points where the imperialists — nationalist — liberal — pacifist cleavages are least successfully covered.

Thus the Reichstag resolution[1] immensely reduced the war spirit of Russia and opened a schism between Russia and the Western Allies. That same resolution and the propaganda which accompanied it very seriously affected what might be called the reluctant liberal support of the war in the Western Nations. The Stockholm conference[2] plan had a similar effect, and from its failure dates the withdrawal of official labor and socialist support of the French and British governments.

It must be noted that a parallel movement exists in Central Europe. There too the strain within the Allies and between the Allies is serious, and each move to seduce the Left among the Allies involves a heavy pull upon the Right in Germany. How much of the concessive policy of the German government is forced by the German Left and how much is deliberately preventive in order to forestall division at home and how much is carefully calculated to create division abroad it is not possible to estimate exactly. But this we do know.

The German government has succeeded thus far in maintaining a unity in Central Europe which is effective for military purposes and has played with considerable result for the weakening of the coalition.

The counter to this German effort has taken two forms. The first is coercive, and consists in the suppression and ostracism of any opinion which is responsive to the concessive proposals from Central Europe. This policy has had some success in the Western Nations, at least temporarily, and may be even more successful in America as we become heavily engaged in France. But it is a very costly policy in the long run chiefly because it tends to accentuate class division into a militaristic-pacific division as well; because it corrupts the war spirit by inciting mob violence to drive out disinterested idealism; because it establishes a mood which is recklessly hostile to a constructive international policy. The other of the two methods by which the German offensive is countered reached its expression in the President's reply to the Pope. That emphasized those purposes which have the widest possible acceptance; it repudiated those which not only divide the Coalition within itself, but unify Central Europe in a tenacious defense psychology. This method unifies the Allies by attraction, immensely enlarges the constituency of the war, and because it acts to disintegrate Central Europe compels increasing concession by the Right to the Left. These concessions are, of course, minimal and deceptive, but the assumption of power by a Catholic Bavarian,[3] even though an aristocrat, is an important shift in the balance of political power.

In enemy and friendly nations there is at this time a fierce political struggle, not even concealed. The fact that the European Allies did not themselves reply to the Pope is not to be taken as complete acceptance by the governments of the President's reply. It is to be taken as an indication that the domestic political situations are too tense for them to risk a discriminating reply. They were compelled to avoid a debate which would have inevitably revealed grave differences of opinion. The actual governing groups in Britain, France and Italy do not agree with the underlying purpose of the reply to the Pope; they acquiesced because the note was a repetition of peace negotiations. To have said what they believe about it would have involved serious disunity within and without.

These divergences of purposes in the coalition are no doubt the ultimate cause of an uncoordinated strategy. The logic of nationalist absolutism is to stake more and more on victory, and to increase the prize as the effort requires sacrifice. The Western Allies are in the control of absolute nationalists the stability of whose own power depends upon the realization of certain large promises. Therefore in official circles there has been a recession of interest in what may be called the program of enduring peace, the program for which the workers, the farmers, the small capitalists and the liberal intellectuals of Western Europe and America accepted the war. This heavy emphasis on nationalist success in each country has brought its government into conflict with the governments of the Allies. As between Russia and the West it appears to have opened up an era of tragic misunderstanding. For Italy it has meant a curious isolation which appears to have led her to military disaster in a spectacular effort to secure sympathy and assistance. Thus because the allies distrusted Italy's political ambitions, and her uncooperative method of pursuing them, her military zone was in a measure disregarded and the supplies needed for an offensive to complete Italy's purposes were not furnished. To secure those supplies Italy appears to have overextended her front and exposed her flank. A similar political blunder upon the part of Romania appears to have led her to disaster.[4]

Unity of strategy, especially if the war is prolonged, will depend upon a simplification and pooling of purposes in both coalitions, the enemies' and our own. This involves a shifting of political power from those who now control all the nations of Western Europe and Central Europe so that the governments represent both in personnel, in social outlook and in patriotic purpose the middle parties. Unity will involve placating the moderate left even at the cost of opposition from the irreconcilable right. In both coalitions unity will depend increasingly upon this movement towards the left. The movement, of course, need not be parallel or at the same rate. In each country it is relative to the position now occupied by the controlling groups.

But the two movements react upon each other almost like the bidding at an auction. The price of unity is increased in each nation as the liberalism of the enemy increases. But as the governing groups have staked themselves on particular nationalist successes, this competition in liberalism cuts under the whole social regime which they represent. They resist liberalization of purpose and so while they disintegrate their own people they make it easier for the enemy to hold together.

This political situation bears most heavily on our own success in the war. Excluding for the purposes of argument the invention of some brilliant tactical or strategical novelty the military decision must be reached on the Western Front by an attempt to exhaust Germany's reserves. No spectacular success is expected. This involves an unprecedented strain on morale and resources which can be met only by the most successful kind of moral administrative economy in western Europe and the United States. This is to be had only by keeping political power upon the broadest basis of popular consent and by a powerful counter-offensive in diplomacy to reveal deceptive liberalism in Germany.

Without this we may expect Germany's skillful seduction to succeed sufficiently in order to bring about moral disunion followed by administrative waste and military weakness. Larger and larger areas of the front would then grow torpid as the Russian, Romanian, Macedonian, Caucasus, Mesopotamian, and Gaza fronts now are, and as the Italian may very possibly be.

---

1. The Reichstag resolution of July 9, 1917, which the kaiser and the war party disavowed, nevertheless seemed to the war-weary people of the belligerent powers to suggest a German desire for peace. The resolution, emphasizing the defensive character of Germany's war, called for a peace of understanding and reconciliation without forceful acquisitions of territory or economic coercion.   **2.** The International Socialist Conference of June 1917, to which German but neither British nor French delegates received passports, expressed the rising antiwar sentiments of European Socialists generally.   **3.** On October 30, 1917, Count Georg von Hertling had become German chancellor. A septuagenarian, nearly blind, he presided for about a year over a government whose policies the military determined.   **4.** Romania had signed a truce with the Central Powers on December 6, 1917.

To Edward M. House

[December 1917]

PRELIMINARY MEMORANDUM ON GREAT POWERS [1]

The character of the peace conference and the issues it will discuss depend upon the internal situation of the Powers. A question which seems of outstanding importance to a man who has lived all his life among officials is seen in totally different perspective by a workingman, a soldier's wife, or a private soldier. The basic human fact about war is that the governing classes are practically untouched by the burden. Their sacrifices are almost entirely vicarious, and the personal prestige is if anything enhanced. They carry over into war time a set of values collected in time of peace. These values were never seriously questioned while the unofficial masses were absorbed in domestic questions. Masses of people rarely react to distant objects. And the objects of diplomacy in peace time are as remote as possible from the daily life of men.

War is a draft upon the mass to pay for the situation created by diplomacy. In the earlier periods of a war this truth is not disclosed because there is an era of exaltation and party truce. But unless the war is quickly and spectacularly concluded the exaltation and the truce disappear and the antagonism between diplomatic and democratic values grows more bitter. This takes the form of a demand for open statement of war aims. This in itself is a deep challenge to the diplomatic view of the world, and is always resisted for a long time as giving aid to the enemy. It is a convulsive thing because the comparison of diplomatic aims with democratic suffering is disastrous to diplomatic aims. Men will not die and starve and freeze for the things which orthodox diplomacy holds most precious. It follows that a "statement of war aims" is really a "revision of war aims." No government dares to go to its people with an open avowal of its old diplomatic purposes. They are incommensurable with the agony of war.

The public statement of war aims marks the collapse of the historic system of diplomacy. In proof of this it is important to note that the first request for such a statement came from President Wilson, a liberal spokesman of an unentangled nation, that almost the first act of revolutionary Russia was to insist upon it, that in England and France, and even in Germany and Austria, it was the Socialists and radical intellectuals who have been calling for it. And conversely, it is the imperialistic governments which are resisting it now.

As the balance of power in each nation moves towards the left the complexion of international affairs changes. The alignments of the peace conference, the relative order of the questions discussed, will depend upon the degree to which political power has passed to the trade unions and lower middle classes, away from big business and the governing classes. As this cannot be determined now, the only way to anticipate the situation is to start from the diplomatic concepts of the Great Powers and estimate which of them will be mollified and amended by democratic pressure.

What then is the "diplomatic view" of vital interest?

I. Great Britain.

A. Belgium is both a diplomatic and a democratic interest. As a democratic interest it stands as an[2] example of an unoffending nation violated. Int'l pledge. From this point of view the United States has exactly the same interest as the British democracy in the reestablishment of Belgium. Britain also has a diplomatic interest in Belgium, which distinguishes Belgium from any other small nation which might be violated. The possession of the Flanders coast and of access to Belgium is a naval threat. The diplomatic view is that no strong power must ever hold Flanders or the channel ports. This is a diplomatic conception resting on the belief that strong powers contiguous are likely to be enemies. The extreme diplomatic view in England is that some kind of British protectorate of Belgium is essential to prevent renewed German attack. The democratic view is that a democratic England and a democratic Germany need not have a special Belgian policy.

B. France[3]

---

1. The Lippmann papers contain two copies of this memorandum, one typed, the other handwritten, identical in text except that the concluding paragraph printed here (see note 2) appears only in the handwritten copy. Both copies are undated and incomplete. No copy of a completed memorandum exists in either the Lippmann or the House papers. Arthur S. Link, the editor of *The Papers of Woodrow Wilson*, 48 v. (Princeton, 1966–), and the distinguished biographer of Wilson, clarified the dating and importance of this memorandum in a letter of February 18, 1983, to John M. Blum. Link identified the memo as that prepared by Mezes, David Hunter Miller (a senior member of the Inquiry), and Lippmann, entitled "The Present Situation, The War Aims and Peace Terms it Suggests," written about December 22, 1917. "House brought this memorandum," Link wrote, "to the White House on December 23, but . . . Wilson and House did not discuss the memorandum during House's Christmas visit to Washington. Nor is there any evidence that Wilson read the memorandum between December 23 and January 4, 1918.

"House, when he came to Washington on January 4, 1918, brought with him the revised memorandum by Mezes, Miller, and Lippmann [which is not in the Lippmann papers] entitled . . . 'A Suggested Statement of Peace Terms.' This document is in the Wilson papers at the Library of Congress. There is no evidence that Wilson ever read this memorandum. . . . Actually, the document which Wilson and House read first on January 4 was the memorandum of December 22 [printed here]. Wilson wrote the first draft . . . of the Fourteen Points on the margins of the pages of this document."

The December 22 memo, as also the material Lippmann later prepared for Colonel House at the time of the armistice negotiations, suggested that Wilson had been familiar with the series of the secret treaties among the Allies. They obviously indicated that Lippmann and his colleagues were advising Wilson through House to send peace terms wholly different from those the secret treaties contemplated. Lippmann's belief that Wilson had committed himself to do so, and his further belief that the Treaty of Versailles failed in that respect, were later to account for his opposition to that treaty. The failure, if it was that, involved concessions that Wilson deemed necessary; but Lippmann nevertheless felt betrayed. That feeling doubtless owed much to his conviction, expressed to a colleague after Wilson's January 8, 1918, message, that he had "put words into the mouth of the President." An exuberant and self-confident young man, as Lippmann was, came perhaps naturally to that interpretation of a role that others might have found akin to ghostwriting.

Lippmann was partly wrong in his assumptions about Wilson and the secret treaties. As Professor Link's letter observed: "Regarding Wilson and the secret treaties, Wilson and everybody else . . . knew about the Treaty of London. Balfour sent . . . copies of all the secret treaties among Great Britain, France, Greece, and Russia to Wilson in May 1918; however, not the secret treaties relating to the Far East and not the Treaty of Bucharest. Wilson put the copies that Balfour sent him in his private files, and I am convinced that he never read them. For one thing he certainly would have made some marks on the papers, and he did not do this. More important . . . most of the treaties were in French, and I am sure that Wilson would not have trusted his French well enough to read them without having them translated, and this he did not do. . . . Of course, the Bolsheviks . . . published the secret treaties in the possession of the Russian government, and there was much discussion about them at the time." **2.** The balance of this memorandum is from the handwritten draft. **3.** The text in the Lippmann papers ended here.

To Newton D. Baker

January 29, 1918

Dear N.D.B.:

Your statement of yesterday[1] was all that your best friends could have desired. It was convincing and brilliant and rich, and I am deeply proud.

I have thought very earnestly about the situation in the last few weeks, and with a growing sense of the seriousness of the issue involved. No doubt the bulk of what popular support has been given the attack upon the Department was due to what you so generously described as "impatience to do this great thing greatly," and it would not be honest of me not to say that I have often worried in an impatient way at what seemed to me the undue confidence you have placed in some of your subordinates. This somewhat too great faith on your part has given the criticism whatever force it had. Fundamentally I am convinced that it has a different origin.

You have been something more than a Secretary of War. You have incarnated the temper which alone could justify this gigantic enterprise. You have built up a great army, and you are not a militarist; and you have never lost sight of what the President has called the "unprecedented things" which must come out of all this fighting. Your being just where you are has been absolutely fundamental to the democratic character of this war. It has saved us from the situation into which some of our allies have occasionally fallen, it seems to me — of waging a war for liberty through men who are imperialists and militarists at heart. In the minds of such men there are two deadly counts against you: You are unwilling to commit yourself to any particular military policy after the war; and you are known to be the kind of man who would not hesitate to sacrifice many an economic and nationalist superstition in order to insure a good peace.

In each country there has been in addition to the international war a war between imperialism and democracy, and in each country the pendulum has swung as far as possible towards imperialism at some time or other in the course of the war. In France this point has just been reached, I believe. In England the reaction towards democracy is already very strong. To my mind the events of the last few weeks viewed in the long perspective represent at bottom just this same effort to swing the administration of the war out of liberal hands. The way in which permanent universal military service has been tied up with shortages in overcoats and then on to objections to radical taxation is very clear evidence of the real nature of the political movement. When I read that Senator McKellar[2] was deeply concerned about war efficiency, I saw light.

I hope and believe that the attack is scattered, and that nothing will be left but criticism of the kind which will really be helpful. All of our little group here are enthusiastic about the results of yesterday, and many of them were inclined to be very critical before you spoke. If personal affection is of any help to you in these trying times you have it in full measure, from Faye Lippmann as well as myself.

1. Republican congressmen had been attacking what they considered Wilson's mismanagement of the war. There were many problems that seemed to support their case. The shipbuilding program was snarled; the American army in Europe had not received American-made artillery or airplanes; conditions in training camps were sometimes primitive. In January 1918, a crisis in the delivery of fuel to eastern manufacturing areas brought Democrats into the attack. One, Senator George Chamberlain of Oregon, on January 19 introduced a bill that would have moved control of the war effort from the president to a war Cabinet of "three distinguished citizens." Baker testified against the bill before the Senate Military Affairs Committee on January 28. Defending the administration's program, he produced telling data about production and organization for war. His testimony sufficiently stilled criticism to permit Wilson to introduce his own measure, the Overman Act, which enlarged the president's discretion to reorganize executive agencies and made the issue of efficiency Wilson's, rather than his critics.   2. Senator Kenneth McKellar of Tennessee, a Democratic reactionary whose positions on major issues were such, during his long and undistinguished career, that it was generally wise and constructive to oppose him.

To Newton D. Baker

February 26, 1918

My dear N.D.B.:

I have been trying to figure out where we stand as a result of the latest moves in Russia,[1] and it seems to me that pretty nearly everything depends upon the answer to one critical question: Will the control of the eastern area and Russia mean that Germany is to grow relatively stronger in the next twelve months? If not, then the unsuccessful liberal movement in Germany which for a time found expression in the Reichstag majority will revive, and the military party will be forced to seek a decision against the major belligerents in the west before German liberalism and Austrian separation become too powerful. If on the other hand the success in Russia means a growth of German strength as time goes on, then I should expect them to stand on the defensive in the west and try to win victories in minor theaters, that is, in Mesopotamia and Saloniki.

That is, a western offensive by Germany would indicate doubt as to the immediate possibilities in Russia and fear for the solidity at home. It would mean that they had been forced to accept a gamble. Personally there is nothing I should fear so much at the present time as a defensive policy by Germany in the west. It would indicate a most dangerous assurance by the governing classes as to their internal position, and it would mean a determination to consolidate an empire which would carry German influence to Persia and Central Asia that might very conceivably be based on some kind of tacit agreement with Japan. It would also create a profoundly puzzling strategic situation for us. The main theater of war would be in an area in which we are physically ineffective, and without trying to imagine wild things I do not think it at all impossible that such a coherent policy by Germany might include the offer of an imperialistic settlement with the Western Powers.

Taking this dark view, what are our possible lines of action? In addition, of course, to exerting the greatest possible strength on the western front, and in addition to continuing a beckoning policy towards Austria, we must beyond question, I think, maintain as friendly as possible an attitude towards the Russian revolution. We should not scold the Russians, no matter what peace they make. We ought to make it as clear as possible to them that we have not lost faith in the revolution, even though it is costing us so much. We ought to continue to speak to the Russians with charity and understanding, and let them know that we see that they are acting under duress, and that we have no reproaches to offer, no matter what we may feel, that we count the revolution one of the real victories of the war, and that we mean if possible at the settlement to safeguard Russia's interests as much as those of anyone else.

If by any chance some minor offensive action on the part of the Western Allies is contemplated in the near future, it might be a great advantage to couple it with some statement to the Russian revolution which said that we were going on to fight their battles and would count them our friends still. The one note we must avoid in regard to Russia is the insistence that we are interested only in their military aid. . . .

---

1. Though the Bolsheviks had ended the war by proclamation, the Germans at this time were advancing toward Petrograd (Leningrad). On March 3, the Russians signed the Treaty of Brest-Litovsk, by which they gave up to Germany and her allies Poland, the Ukraine, and all of their borderlands occupied by non-Russian peoples.

To Frederick P. Keppel[1]

May 6, 1918

Dear Fred:

I'm going to try to put down a few ideas about universal military training, and see where they lead. As I remember the Secretary's last report, he said that no permanent military policy should be adopted until the international situation at the close of the war could be examined. This seems to me axiomatic — an appreciation of the principle that armaments are an instrument of international politics.

The other side has, I believe, the following things in mind:

1) That this is a propitious moment to enact the legislation, with the added thought that if after the war the world becomes radically pacifist, universal training will be an accomplished fact, something to be conserved rather than achieved.

2) That military training is educational.

3) That it will preserve the country from placing too much faith in the machinery of international organization and a policy of concession and compromise.

The first of these, the argument from opportunity, will not be accepted by a generous leaven of opinion. It is essentially a moral *coup d'état*, founded on distrust — an attempt to bind the future by exploiting the necessities of the moment.

The educational argument stands on a very different level. The physical discipline, the practice of service, the social mixing, are undeniably good. To secure full value in time of peace the prime consideration would be the character of the officers in charge of the training. But the thing is also a matter of quantity — our nineteen-year-old class is, I presume, 1% of the total population. This would produce nearly 1100 thousand. To have a system worthy of the name universal at least 800,000 would have to be trained annually. With due regard to seasonal occupations, and on a basis of six months' training, this would mean 400,000 with the colors at a time. This doesn't seem to be an unmanageable number, though it would be illuminating to know how large a permanent staff would be required to enlist and train and administer.

The question is, how could such a system be integrated with the establishment now conducting the war? The essential thing about the plan, from this point of view, is a transition from selective service among a larger number of age groups to service by classes. There is no prospect, I suppose, of exhausting class 1 now registered, and the new 21-year-old men before June 5, 1919. By that time another class will have become eligible, though possibly an insufficient number to provide for 1919–20 should the war continue. In that case the choice will lie between invading class 2, which covers married and industrially valuable men, raising the draft age, or possibly lowering it to 20 years and six months, with a virtual understanding that these younger men would not see active service till they were twenty-one. This would establish universal *training*[2] automatically, and yet would involve no final commitment as to military policy after the war.

The question then would be, should this training be established "for the emergency" following the Selective Service Act, or should it be made a continuing thing. My own feeling is this: A reduction of armaments after the war is an unavoidable necessity for every great power in Europe except America. We alone can stand the racket. If we are willing to abandon competitive armaments it will be because we genuinely want to, not because we are so bankrupt that we have to. This will give our leadership an indisputable element of sincerity. But these facts would be emphasized enormously to the world if we go to the peace conference with tangible military institutions to reduce, instead of with the prospect of a long, bitter domestic struggle between those who want and those who oppose a compulsory military system. Without wishing to be dogmatic it seems to me now that some such plan I have outlined might fit the facts of the present war and at the same time meet the more thoughtful arguments now being advanced.

I think I'd like to see the Secretary or the President take the lead and embody in the legislation the following points:

That it shall apply to those who have become say 20½ on January 1, 1919, though the call for training shall be within the discretion of the executive departments.[3]

That it shall continue after the war, unless there is an explicit international agreement which conflicts with it.

That a commission of educators, physicians, industrial experts, and military men be created immediately to study means of deriving the maximum educational value out of it after the war, together with plans for improving the national system of education.

1. Frederick P. Keppel, dean of Columbia College, had become Baker's confidential clerk and the third assistant secretary of war in charge of nonmilitary matters concerning the lives of soldiers. After the war, he became head of the Carnegie Corporation. 2. Emphasis Lippmann's. 3. As revised in 1918 according to the administration's preferences, the Selective Service Act increased the pool of men subject to conscription by lowering the minimum age from twenty-one to eighteen and raising the maximum from thirty-one to forty-five. That change provided sufficient manpower for the Army. As the war then came toward its close, sentiment for universal military training, never really strong though often noisy, receded and quieted.

To Edward M. House

May 11, 1918

Dear Colonel House:

In accordance with your suggestion of this morning, I am setting down as briefly as possible a few of the reasons why our government ought now to create a confidential commission for the scientific planning of reconstruction questions.[1]

On the following points it will be essential to act quickly and successfully immediately after the declaration of peace:

1) The return of our army from France. Suppose that we have from one million to two million or even more troops in France. The moment the war is over, the desire of these men to get back home, and the pressure from their families and friends to have them come home, will be enormous. Moreover, it would of course be a great injustice to them to keep them abroad a moment longer than is absolutely necessary. Both the Germans and the English with a far simpler problem have, I am reliably informed, worked out very careful schemes for the return of their armies. As our problem will be complicated by the tonnage question, a great deal of careful planning is needed.

2) Some provision must be made for finding employment for these men as they return. They can't simply be landed in New York and left to shift for themselves. As the Selective Service Act works, it calls into the army chiefly unskilled men, the hardest type of man to find a place for in industry.

3) In order to avoid an unemployment crisis, schemes must be worked out for transforming war industries into peace industries without breaking the continuity of operations.

4) The war has produced a vast number of new government agencies, like the Food Administration and the War Industries Board. Just what their status ought to be after the war ought to be worked out now.

5) Our industrial truce, such as it is, will end when the war ends, and if the demobilization and the transformation of our industries from a war to a peace basis is not skillfully handled, we shall have labor troubles of the first magnitude.

6) Our immigration policy will demand a reconsideration.

7) The foreign trade situation after the war will have to be met.

8) The raw materials problem will be pressing.

9) Something should be done immensely to improve our national system of education, especially along technical and scientific lines.

None of these problems can be dealt with quickly, unless there has been a preliminary period of calm and disinterested study, and above all, study which is carried on without publicity.

I should strongly argue against entrusting the work to what is called a representative committee of prominent people, that is to say, a commission in which the various interests affected are supposed to be represented. No doubt before any action could be taken on anything representatives of different groups should be consulted, but they should not be brought in, in my opinion, until an expert staff with liberal sympathies has had about six months' freedom to explore the different subjects.

I should recommend an organization quite similar to that of the Inquiry, that is, an organization with one man at the head who has the complete confidence of the President; under him two or three assistants guided by the same sympathies who actually administer the detail of the research; and with about fifteen or twenty men of the right kind, clerical assistance, and with proper access to Washington bureaus the trick could, I imagine, be done. The problems are a good deal easier than those which the Inquiry is handling, because there are so many men available who have a good background and there is so much information easily at hand. . . .

1. The federal government undertook no useful planning for the transition to peace, which proved to be chaotic in all the respects to which Lippmann addressed this letter.

To Edward M. House

June 16, 1918

Dear Colonel House:

Yesterday Captain Blankenhorn[1] of the Military Intelligence Branch came up to see me at the Geographical Society. He is to have charge of the "propaganda" over the enemy lines, and he wanted to secure the help of the Inquiry. We showed him some of our material, and he insisted that our organization was the only one in the government which had the kind of information which he needed.

He then asked me whether I would be willing to organize and train the men who are to go abroad with the army in his unit, and work out the lines along which the "propaganda" should be conducted. He wanted me to take a commission in the Intelligence Branch and be detailed to the Inquiry, establishing the new organization in New York, work for both the Inquiry and his unit, keeping them distinct, and yet cooperating. He said, I'm just repeating his argument, that I ought to do it, because I knew the work of the Inquiry and therefore knew where to get accurate information, that I had a journalistic training, and that I would not be likely to misrepresent the President's aims.

The answer I gave him was this: that I was ready to do anything I was told to do; that if the Military Intelligence wished me to do this after thinking it over, I would lay it before you and ask you to decide.

I added that I would want to do this work only in a way which the President and you would approve, that this meant getting away from propaganda in the sinister sense, and substituting for it a frank campaign of education addressed to the German and Austrian troops explaining as simply and persuasively as possible the unselfish character of the war, the generosity of our aims and the great hope for mankind which we are trying to realize. Captain Blankenhorn said that was the spirit in which he wanted it done.

He has returned to Washington to secure the approval of his superior officer to his plan. I told him that I would not move at all in the matter until that came, but on thinking it over last night I felt I must write to you and let you know just what had happened, so that you could tell me whether I had acted correctly, and if you thought it worthwhile that you would perhaps ask the President.

1. Heber Blankenhorn was setting up a propaganda unit for the Army in France, in which Lippmann served as a captain until October. Lippmann was in that time also House's representative to the Allied intelligence offices, in order to coordinate their work and the Inquiry's, and Lansing's envoy to make special economic and political studies.

To Isaiah Bowman[1]

July 24, 1918

My dear Bowman:

I wish I had had a chance to see you before I left, but time was short and it seemed strongly against the national interest to drag you away from your vacation. I hope you are well rested by this time as you have a very heavy responsibility resting on you now. Dr. Mezes will be particularly interested in modes of representation and in the attempt to find solutions for particular problems, it will be for you to see that in the next few months the Inquiry completes in organized form what you and I had come to call the scientific elements of the question. You know, of course, that I always agreed heartily with your theory that we had to have the complete basic data even though their relevancy was not immediately apparent.

The getting up of this material is a very fussy job, and I hope that you will assure yourself of a sufficient number of men . . . to see the stuff through the mill. The last time I saw Col. House I put in another word about the necessity of spending more money. . . .

My thought in general is about this: among the things I can best do over here is to make as detailed as possible a report on the imponderables; *the thing the Inquiry can best do is to lay down a solid basis of underlying fact and get itself so smoothly organized that you and some of the big men in the organization . . . can sit down with my material and integrate it with the American material.*[2]

The layout of my trip is not yet determined, although I shall probably be in London by the time this reaches you. I don't think I shall be there long the first time and in all probability I shan't be able to do more than make a few scratches on Inquiry business. Nevertheless I hope you'll begin sending me memoranda right away of things to do addressed to the American Embassy, London.

You might as well regard this letter as personal. I am writing to Dr. Mezes at the same time covering many of the same points.

1. Isaiah Bowman, political geographer, director of the American Geographical Society, at this time the most powerful member of the Inquiry, had resented Lippmann during their service together on that body. Indeed Bowman was jealous of any rival for authority. **2.** Emphasis Lippmann's.

To Edward M. House

August 9, 1918

Dear Colonel House:

. . . After about two weeks spent in traveling between Paris and Head-quarters and London, attempting to understand the rather complicated and perhaps somewhat confused relations between the Committee on Public Information and the Army, I have got to London and yesterday had my first interview with Sir William Tyrrell.[1] It was not necessary to listen to him very long to realize how wise a man he is. After explaining to him the fact that my immediate task is to report upon the question of propaganda into enemy countries, and that after that to meet the experts in the British Government who are thinking about the settlement, the conversation turned immediately to the question of a League of Nations.

I am to lunch with Sir William again tomorrow and he is to introduce me to the men in the Foreign Office who are working in Political Intelligence. (You know that he is now the head of the recently created Department of Political Intelligence in the Foreign Office.) . . . He was kind enough to say that he would like to have the opportunity of "soaking" me in his ideas and seemed very much pleased with my suggestion that I should finish up the investigation into propaganda as quickly as possible . . . and return here the end of September to spend a month or six weeks with him and the men working in the Foreign Office. I already know a fair number of them personally, and they have all been embarrassing in their generosity and in their willingness to go to any length of trouble in turning over their material. I feel sure that this will be a very useful thing to do, both from the point of view of the Inquiry and propaganda work.

This letter is already very long but I am going to take the liberty of making it a little longer, in order to say a word on the highlights in the propaganda situation. To do the work effectively over here we shall need to create a real center of political information. So far as I can learn no such center of information exists at the present time either in the Army or at the Embassies, or in the offices of the Committee on Public Information.[2] Unless the men who are writing and directing propaganda are in close touch with political developments they cannot of course do anything effective. The second point is that they should be in very close touch with our own foreign policy, as of course the most important propaganda are diplomatic acts themselves. . . .

1. Sir William Tyrrell, director of the nearest British equivalent of the Inquiry.   2. The Committee on Public Information had its own offices in London and in France and took a negative view of the rival unit to which Lippmann belonged.

To Sidney E. Mezes

September 5, 1918

Dear Mezes:

. . . There are just four Americans who exist in the consciousness of people over here. First, of course, the President, a figure of mystical proportions, of really incredible power but altogether out of reach of direct contact. Many of course disagree with him, some like Arthur Henderson[1] and his group are bewildered by him, but it makes no difference who you are or what you want, be it a war of extermination or peace at any price, you always take a kind of immunity bath by prefacing your remarks with a pledge of undying devotion to the principles laid down by President Wilson.

The second figure is Colonel House, and if you and he will forgive me for saying it, his position is that of the Human Intercessor, the Comforter, the Virgin Mary. To him the weak, even in principle, can go and be listened to kindly, and his advice is sought because it is believed to be a little nearer this world than the President's and a good deal nearer heaven than that of Lloyd George or Sonnino.[2]

The third is Hoover, who incarnates all that is at once effective and idealistic in the picture of America. They speak of him everywhere with reverence, and I believe there is no man on our side in the war whose competence is so universally known.

The fourth figure is of course General Pershing[3] about whom there is heartfelt enthusiasm among the troops and a very deep respect everywhere.

The Inquiry seems to be far better known over here than in America because there is the minutest interest in Colonel House's doings. So far as I can make out he is what somebody once called the pantechnicon van of all the tangles and troubles of Europe. . . .[4]

1. Arthur Henderson, British politician, Labourite, formerly an ironworker.   2. Baron Sidney Sonnino, Italian foreign minister and ardent nationalist.   3. General John J. Pershing, the commander in chief of the American Expeditionary Force in Europe.   4. The fragment of this letter here published is in the original in the Edward M. House Collection at the Yale University Library. No full text of the letter appears to be extant.

To Edward M. House

October 26, 1918

MEMORANDUM ON THE INQUIRY

The following recommendations are based on the idea that the time has come to move the Inquiry to Europe.[1] The reasons why this step should be taken now are:

1. It would be a mistake to suppose that the Powers intend to go to the peace table before the main features of the settlement have been worked out.

They all realize that if they leave the big territorial issues entirely open, those issues will be neglected at the conference because of the pressure of time and the necessity of turning as quickly as possible to the problems of reconstruction. They realize too that the peace conference will be an unwieldy body subject to all kinds of unexpected pressure and agitation, once the discipline of war is relaxed.

They are, therefore, each of them now engaged in the making of all kinds of preliminary and provisional arrangements, which may be likened to the pledging of delegations and the holding of caucuses before the opening of a political convention. An example which may be cited is the meeting in London this week of Pasic, Venizelos, Take Ionescu, and Benes[2] for the purpose of trying to arrange a Balkan settlement.

In these preliminary meetings we have presumably had no voice. This may be satisfactory. But what is undesirable is that we should not be thoroughly informed as to the course of negotiations. In order to be thoroughly informed the diplomatic service needs to be supplemented by the men who have specialized upon the detail of the problems for the Inquiry. Another example may be cited in this connection. The Department of State has accredited Mr. Hugh Gibson[3] to the Polish National Committee and the Czecho-Slovak National Council, but before Mr. Gibson can begin to establish the proper relations with these organizations he needs a staff of men who know the problems, or at least have a background of expert knowledge by reason of which they can analyze questions as they arise. We are in a position to exercise a moderating and democratic influence upon Polish aspirations now when we are so essential to them, and it would be a pity to miss the opportunity.

2. The greatest weakness of the Inquiry is its divorce from responsibility and from intimate knowledge of current affairs. That a certain objectivity has been gained from this is undeniable, but the time has come to ask ourselves whether the Inquiry is not now in danger of becoming too academic and out of touch with European ways of thinking. Furthermore, the Inquiry is fast approaching a point where its sources of information are exhausted and need to be strengthened by the great mass of recent information available only in Europe. Finally, the members of the Inquiry staff need to establish personal acquaintances among the men in England, France and elsewhere who will be their opposite members at the peace conference.

3. It would be very desirable from the point of view of Allied unity that so far as possible they should be in agreement upon the main facts in each problem. Thus in the case of Poland we ought now to establish with the Allies a map which represents our common agreement as to the distribution of the Polish population. The same should be done for other problems of a similar character.

The most serious objection to the plan of moving the Inquiry over here now is that its departure would cause a considerable amount of speculation. This might be avoided, in part, by bringing it over in sections, and by instructions to the press that its departure should not be discussed, and by confidential explanation that the move had no significance beyond that of preparation. . . .[4]

1. House had reached Paris on October 25 and transferred Lippmann to his staff. The Germans had appealed to Wilson for an armistice on October 3, and House was negotiating with the British and French about terms.   **2.** Nicholas Pashich, Serbian political leader, and his counterparts, Eleutherios Venizelos of Greece, Take Ionescu of Romania, and Eduard Beneš of Czechoslovakia.   **3.** Hugh Gibson, American foreign service officer who had worked with Hoover in Belgium, had been cooperating with Blankenhorn and Lippmann in France.   **4.** Whatever their merit, the suggestions Lippmann made had little effect, for Wilson had plans of his own for the peace conference.

To Edward M. House

October 28, 1918

MEMORANDUM [1]

I. Open covenants of peace, openly arrived at, after which there shall be no private international understandings of any kind but diplomacy shall proceed always frankly and in the public view.

The purpose is clearly to prohibit treaties, sections of treaties or understandings that are secret, such as the Triple Alliance, etc.

The phrase 'openly arrived at' need not cause difficulty. In fact, the President explained to the Senate last winter that the phrase was not meant to exclude confidential diplomatic negotiations involving delicate matters. The intention is that nothing which occurs in the course of such confidential negotiations shall be binding unless it appears in the final covenant made public to the world.

The matter may perhaps be put this way: It is proposed that in the future every treaty be part of the public law of the world; and that every nation assume a certain obligation in regard to its enforcement. Obviously, nations cannot assume obligations in matters of which they are ignorant; and therefore any secret treaty tends to undermine the solidity of the whole structure of international covenants which it is proposed to erect.

II. Absolute freedom of navigation upon the seas, outside territorial waters, alike in peace and in war, except as the seas may be closed in whole or in part by international action for the enforcement of international covenants.

This proposition must be read in connection with No. XIV, which proposes a League of Nations. It refers to navigation under the three following conditions:

1. General peace;

2. A general war, entered into by the League of Nations for the purpose of enforcing international covenants;

3. Limited war; involving no breach of international covenants.

Under "1" (General peace) no serious dispute exists. There is implied freedom to come and go on the high seas.

No serious dispute exists as to the intention under "2" (a general war entered into by the League of Nations to enforce international covenants). Obviously such a war is conducted against an outlaw nation and complete nonintercourse with that nation is intended.

"3" (A limited war, involving no breach of international covenants) is the crux of the whole difficulty. The question is, what are to be the rights of neutral shipping and private property on the high seas during a war between a limited number of nations when that war involves no issue upon which the League of Nations cares to take sides. In other words, a war in which the League of Nations remains neutral. Clearly, it is the intention of the proposal that in such a war the rights of neutrals shall be maintained against the belligerents, the rights of both to be clearly and precisely defined in the law of nations.

III. The removal, so far as possible, of all economic barriers and the establishment of an equality of trade conditions among all the nations consenting to the peace and associating themselves for its maintenance.

The proposal applies only to those nations which accept the responsibilities of membership in the League of Nations. It means the destruction of all special commercial agreements, each nation putting the trade of every other nation in the League on the same basis, the most favored nation clause applying automatically to all members of the League of Nations.

Thus a nation could legally maintain a tariff or a special railroad rate or a port restriction against the whole world, or against all the signatory powers. It could maintain any kind of restriction which it chose against a nation not in the League. But it could not discriminate as between its partners in the League.

This clause naturally contemplates fair and equitable understanding as to the distribution of raw materials.

IV. Adequate guarantees given and taken that national armaments will be reduced to the lowest point consistent with domestic safety.

"Domestic safety" clearly implies not only internal policing, but the protection of territory against invasion. The accumulation of armaments above this level would be a violation of the intention of the proposal.

What guarantees should be given and taken, or what are to be the standards of judgment have never been determined. It will be necessary to adopt the general principle and then institute some kind of international commission of investigation to prepare detailed projects for its execution.

V. A free, open-minded, and absolutely impartial adjustment of all colonial claims, based upon a strict observance of the principle that in determining all such questions of sovereignty, the interests of the populations concerned must have equal weight with the equitable claims of the government whose title is to be determined.

Some fear is expressed in France and England that this involves the reopening of all colonial questions. Obviously it is not so intended. It applies clearly to those colonial claims which have been created by the war. That means the German colonies and any other colonies which may come under international consideration as a result of the war.

The stipulation is that in the case of the German colonies the title is to be determined after the conclusion of the war by "impartial adjustment" based on certain principles. These are of two kinds: 1. "Equitable" claims: 2. The interests of the populations concerned.

What are the "equitable" claims put forth by Britain and Japan, the two chief heirs of the German colonial empire, that the colonies cannot be returned to Germany? Because she will use them as submarine bases, because she will arm the blacks, because she uses the colonies as bases of intrigue, because she oppresses the natives. What are the "equitable" claims put forth by Germany? That she needs access to tropical raw materials, that she needs a field for the expansion of her population, that under the principles of peace proposed, conquest gives her enemies no title to her colonies.

What are the "interests of the populations"? That they should not be militarized, that exploitation should be conducted on the principle of the open door, and under the strictest regulation as to labor conditions, profits and taxes, that a sanitary regime be maintained, that permanent improvements in the way of roads, etc., be made, that native organization and custom be respected, that the protecting authority be stable and experienced enough to thwart intrigue and corruption, that the protecting power have adequate resources in money and competent administrators to act successfully.

It would seem as if the principle involved in this proposition is that a colonial power acts not as owner of its colonies, but as trustee for the natives and for the interests of the society of nations, that the terms on which the colonial administration is conducted are a matter of international concern and may legitimately be the subject of international inquiry and that the peace conference may, therefore, write a code of colonial conduct binding upon all colonial powers.

VI. The evacuation of all Russian territory and such a settlement of all questions affecting Russia as will secure the best and freest cooperation of the other nations of the world in obtaining for her an unhampered and unembarrassed opportunity for the independent determination of her own political development and national policy and assure her of a sincere welcome into the society of free nations under institutions of her own choosing; and, more than a welcome, assistance also of every kind that she may need and may herself desire. The treatment accorded Russia by her sister nations in the months to

*come will be the acid test of their good will, of their comprehension of her
needs as distinguished from their own interests, and of their intelligent and
unselfish sympathy.*

The first question is whether Russian territory is synonymous with territory belonging to the former Russian Empire. This is clearly not so, because
Proposition XIII stipulates an independent Poland, a proposal which excludes
the territorial reestablishment of the Empire. What is recognized as valid for
the Poles will certainly have to be recognized for the Finns, the Lithuanians,
the Letts, and perhaps also for the Ukrainians. Since the formulation of this
condition, these subject nationalities have emerged, and there can be no doubt
that they will have to be given an opportunity of free development.

The problem of these nationalities is complicated by two facts: 1. That they
have conflicting claims: 2. That the evacuation called for in the proposal may
be followed by Bolshevist revolutions in all of them.

The chief conflicts are (a) Between the Letts and Germans in Courland;
(b) Between the Poles and the Lithuanians on the northeast; (c) Between the
Poles and the White Ruthenians on the east; (d) Between the Poles and the
Ukrainians on the southeast (and in Eastern Galicia). In this whole borderland
the relation of the German Poles to the other nationalities is roughly speaking
that of landlord to peasant. Therefore the evacuation of the territory, if it
resulted in class war, would very probably also take the form of a conflict of
nationalities. It is clearly to the interests of a good settlement that the real
nation in each territory should be consulted rather than the ruling and possessing class.

This can mean nothing less than the recognition by the Peace Conference
of a series of *de facto* Governments representing Finns, Esths, Lithuanians,
Ukrainians. This primary act of recognition should be conditional upon the
calling of National Assemblies for the creation of *de jure* Governments, as
soon as the Peace Conference has drawn frontiers for these new states. The
frontiers should be drawn so far as possible on ethnic lines, but in every case
the right of unhampered economic transit should be reserved. No dynastic ties
with German or Austrian or Romanoff princes should be permitted, and every
inducement should be given to encourage federal relations between these new
states. Under Proposition III the economic sections of the Treaty of Brest-
Litovsk are abolished, but this Proposition should not be construed as forbidding a customs union, a monetary union, a railroad union, etc., of these states.
Provision should also be made by which Great Russia can federate with these
states on the same terms.

As for Great Russia and Siberia, the Peace Conference might well send a
message asking for the creation of a government sufficiently representative to
speak for these territories. It should be understood that economic rehabilitation is offered, provided a government carrying sufficient credentials can appear at the Peace Conference.

The Allies should offer this provisional government any form of assistance it may need. The possibility of extending this will exist when the Dardanelles are opened.

The essence of the Russian problem then in the immediate future would seem to be:

1. The recognition of Provisional Governments.
2. Assistance extended to and through these Governments.

The Caucasus should probably be treated as part of the problem of the Turkish Empire. No information exists justifying an opinion on the proper policy in regard to Mohammedan Russia — that is, briefly, Central Asia. It may well be that some power will have to be given a limited mandate to act as protector.

In any case the treaties of Brest-Litovsk and Bucharest must be canceled as palpably fraudulent. Provision must be made for the withdrawal of all German troops in Russia and the Peace Conference will have a clean slate on which to write a policy for all the Russian peoples.

VII. Belgium, the whole world will agree, must be evacuated and restored, without any attempt to limit the sovereignty which she enjoys in common with all other free nations. No other single act will serve as this will serve to restore confidence among the nations in the laws which they have themselves set and determined for the government of their relations with one another. Without this healing act the whole structure and validity of international law is forever impaired.

The only problem raised here is in the word 'restored.' Whether restoration is to be in kind, or how the amount of the indemnity is to be determined is a matter of detail, not of principle. The principle that should be established is that in the case of Belgium there exists no distinction between 'legitimate' and 'illegitimate' destruction. The initial act of invasion was illegitimate and therefore all the consequences of that act are of the same character. Among the consequences may be put the war debt of Belgium. The recognition of this principle would constitute 'the healing act' of which the President speaks.

VIII. All French territory should be freed and the invaded portions restored, and the wrong done to France by Prussia in 1871 in the matter of Alsace-Lorraine, which has unsettled the peace of the world for nearly fifty years, should be righted, in order that peace may once more be made secure in the interest of all.

In regard to the restoration of French territory it might well be argued that the invasion of Northern France, being the result of the illegal act as regards Belgium, was in itself illegal. But the case is not perfect. As the world stood in 1914, war between France and Germany was not in itself a violation of international law, and great insistence should be put upon keeping the Belgian case distinct and symbolic. Thus Belgium might well (as indicated above) claim reimbursement not only for destruction but for the cost of carrying on the war. France could not claim payment, it would seem, for more than the damage done to her northeastern departments.

The status of Alsace-Lorraine was settled by the official statement issued a few days ago. It is to be restored completely to French sovereignty.

Attention is called to the strong current of French opinion which claims 'the boundaries of 1814' rather than of 1871. The territory claimed is the Valley of the Saar with its coal fields. No claim on grounds of nationality can be established, but the argument leans on the possibility of taking this territory in lieu of indemnity. It would seem to be a clear violation of the President's proposal.

Attention is called also to the fact that no reference is made to the status of Luxembourg. The best solution would seem to be a free choice by the people of Luxembourg themselves.

IX. *A readjustment of the frontiers of Italy should be effected along clearly recognizable lines of nationality.*

This proposal is less than the Italian claim, less of course, than the territory allotted by the Treaty of London, less than the arrangement made between the Italian Government and the Jugo-Slav State.

In the region of Trent the Italians claim a strategic rather than an ethnic frontier. It should be noted in this connection that Italy and Germany will become neighbors if German Austria joins the German Empire. And if Italy obtains the best geographical frontier she will assume sovereignty over a large number of Germans. This is a violation of principle. But, it may be argued that by drawing a sharp line along the crest of the Alps, Italy's security will be enormously enhanced and the necessity of heavy armaments reduced. It might, therefore, be provided that Italy should have her claim in the Trentino, but that the northern part, inhabited by Germans, should be completely autonomous, and that the population should not be liable to military service in the Italian army. Italy could thus occupy the uninhabited Alpine peaks for military purposes, but would not govern the cultural life of the alien population to the south of her frontier.

The other problems of the frontier are questions between Italy and Jugo-Slavia, Italy and the Balkans, Italy and Greece.

The agreement reached with Jugo-Slavs may well be allowed to stand, although it should be insisted for the protection of the hinterland that both Trieste and Fiume be free ports. This is essential to Bohemia, German Austria, Hungary as well as to the prosperity of the cities themselves.

Italy appears in Balkan politics through her claim to a protectorate over Albania and the possession of Valona. There is no serious objection raised to this, although the terms of the protectorate need to be vigorously controlled. If Italy is protector of Albania, the local life of Albania should be guaranteed by the League of Nations.

A conflict with Greece appears through the Greek claim to Northern Epirus (or what is now Southern Albania). This would bring Greece closer to Valona than Italy desires. A second conflict with Greece occurs over the Aegean Islands of the Dodecanese, but it is understood that a solution favorable to Greece is being worked out.

(Italy's claims in Turkey belong to the problem of the Turkish Empire.)

X. The peoples of Austria-Hungary, whose place among the nations we wish to see safeguarded and assured, should be accorded the freest opportunity of autonomous development.

This proposition no longer holds. Instead we have today the following elements:

1. CZECHO-SLOVAKIA. Its territories include at least a million Germans, for whom some provision must be made.

The independence of Slovakia means the dismemberment of the northwestern counties of Hungary.

2. GALICIA. Western Galicia is clearly Polish. Eastern Galicia is in large measure Ukrainian, (or Ruthenian,) and does not of right belong to Poland.

There also are several hundred thousand Ukrainians along the north and northeastern borders of Hungary, and in parts of Bukowina (which belonged to Austria).

3. GERMAN AUSTRIA. This territory should of right be permitted to join Germany, but there is strong objection in France because of the increase of population involved.

4. JUGO-SLAVIA. It faces the following problems:

a. Frontier questions with Italy in Istria and the Dalmatian Coast; with Romania in the Banat.

b. An internal problem arises out of the refusal of the Croats to accept the domination of the Serbs of the Serbian Kingdom.

c. A problem of the Mohammedan Serbs of Bosnia who are said to be loyal to the Hapsburgs. They constitute a little less than one third of the population.

5. TRANSYLVANIA. Will undoubtedly join Romania, but provision must be made for the protection of the Magyars, Szeklers and Germans who constitute a large minority.

6. HUNGARY. Now independent, and very democratic in form, but governed by Magyars whose aim is to prevent the detachment of the territory of the nationalities on the fringe.

The United States is clearly committed to the program of national unity and independence. It must stipulate, however, for the protection of national minorities, for freedom of access to the Adriatic and the Black Sea, and it supports a program aiming at a Confederation of Southeastern Europe.

XI. Romania, Serbia, and Montenegro should be evacuated; occupied territories restored; Serbia accorded free and secure access to the sea; and the relations of the several Balkan states to one another determined by friendly counsel along historically established lines of allegiance and nationality; and international guarantees of the political and economic independence and territorial integrity of the several Balkan states should be entered into.

This proposal is also altered by events. Serbia will appear as Jugo-Slavia with access to the Adriatic. Romania will have acquired the Dobrudja, Bessarabia, and probably Transylvania. These two states will have 11 or 12 million inhabitants and will be far greater and stronger than Bulgaria.

Bulgaria should clearly have her frontier in the Southern Dobrudja as it stood before the Second Balkan War. She should also have Thrace up to the Enos-Midia line, and perhaps even to the Midia-Rodosto line.

Macedonia should be allotted after an impartial investigation. The line which might be taken as a basis of investigation is the southern line of the 'contested zone' agreed upon by Serbia and Bulgaria before the First Balkan War.

Albania could be under a protectorate, no doubt of Italy, and its frontiers in the north might be essentially those of the London Conference.

XII. The Turkish portions of the present Ottoman Empire should be assured a secure sovereignty, but the other nationalities which are now under Turkish rule should be assured an undoubted security of life and an absolutely unmolested opportunity of autonomous development, and the Dardanelles should be permanently opened as a free passage to the ships and commerce of all nations under international guarantees.

The same difficulty arises here, as in the case of Austria-Hungary, concerning the word 'autonomous.'

It is clear that the Straits and Constantinople, while they may remain nominally Turkish, should be under international control. This control may be collective or be in the hands of one Power as mandatory of the League.

Anatolia should be reserved for the Turks. The coast lands, where Greeks predominate, should be under special international control, perhaps with Greece as mandatory.

Armenia must be given a port on the Mediterranean, and a protecting power established. France may claim it, but the Armenians would prefer Great Britain.

Syria has already been allotted to France by agreement with Great Britain.

Britain is clearly the best mandatory for Palestine, Mesopotamia and Arabia.

A general code of guarantees binding on all mandatories in Asia Minor should be written into the Treaty of Peace.

This should contain provisions for minorities and the open door. The trunk railroad lines should be internationalized.

XIII. An independent Polish state should be erected which should include the territories inhabited by indisputably Polish populations, which should be assured a free and secure access to the sea, and whose political and economic independence and territorial integrity should be guaranteed by international covenant.

The chief problem is whether Poland is to obtain territory west of the Vistula which would cut off the Germans of East Prussia from the Empire, or whether Danzig can be made a free port and the Vistula internationalized.

On the east, Poland should receive no territory in which Lithuanians or Ukrainians predominate.

If Posen and Silesia go to Poland rigid protection must be afforded the minorities of Germans and Jews living there, as well as in other parts of the Polish state.

The principle on which frontiers will be delimited is contained in the President's words 'indisputably.' This may imply the taking of an impartial census before frontiers are marked.

XIV. A general association of nations must be formed under specific covenants for the purpose of affording mutual guarantees of political independence and territorial integrity to great and small states alike.

The question of a League of Nations as the primary essential of a permanent peace has been so clearly presented by President Wilson in his speech of September 27, 1918, that no further elucidation is required. It is the foundation of the whole diplomatic structure of a permanent peace.

1. The italicized material constituted Wilson's Fourteen Points. Lippmann wrote all of the explanation except for the text pertaining to Point XIV (which was written by Frank Cobb of the *New York World*). The text following each point provided an interpretation that Colonel House requested and Wilson approved as the basis for House's negotiations leading to the armistice. Involved as he was in the drafting of the interpretations, and aware that the Fourteen Points, so interpreted, were part of the official armistice agreement, Lippmann later took strong exception to the many ways in which the Treaty of Versailles departed from that agreement. The treaty reflected, of course, a long process of bargaining among the victorious powers which Wilson could influence but not direct. The Lippmann Collection in the Yale library includes a handwritten manuscript of the interpretations of Points VI and VIII through XIII. The manuscript for Points I–V and VII is missing. For the missing sections, there is here substituted the text as reprinted in Charles Seymour, *The Intimate Papers of Colonel House*, v. 4 (Boston, 1928), pp. 152–200. Seymour followed the text in the House Collection at the Yale University Library.

To Edward M. House

[c. November 1918]
MEMORANDUM ON PRESS CORRESPONDENTS

Whatever plan is worked out should be adopted after consultation with the representatives of the press associations and the leading newspapers. This is a matter of prime importance. The newspapers must feel that the system adopted is not imposed upon them, and that they themselves are responsible for the working of the system.[1]

Some preliminary statement should be made to them by Colonel House explaining the government's point of view. This would probably include:

a. That no political or diplomatic censorship will be exercised. But that in view of the size of the issues involved accuracy is of supreme importance, and that the government would appreciate it if carbon copies of all correspondence were filed with it; that in cases where there are doubtful points involving matters of policy or the prestige of the American negotiators or the sensibilities of the Allies are involved, dispatches should be sent off only after frank conference with some authorized official of the American delegation. The point should be made that the government does not ask more than the right to be heard before, so as to have to avoid the disagreeable necessity of issuing official denials.

b. Emphasis should be put upon the fact that since this peace conference is the most difficult task of reporting which has ever been attempted, and since no one man can be a specialist on all questions, and since the difficulty of reaching the essential points at issue is very great, the government wishes to put at the disposal of the correspondents the whole mass of scientific information which it has accumulated for its own uses. In addition it is ready to arrange conferences with the specialists who will be present to advise the negotiators themselves.

c. Suggestions should be asked as to ways and means of facilitating the work of the correspondents, in regard to cable and telegraph transmission, in regard to the furnishing of official copies of documents, meetings with prominent people, transportation, accommodations, office space, etc.

In order to guide the discussion the following points might be discussed.

I. Should an official communiqué be issued? What kind of information should it contain?

II. Should confidential circulars be issued to the American press explaining somewhat more informally and fully the point of view of the government?

III. Should a central press headquarters be set up, containing workrooms, telegraph instruments, and a central map room and reference library with men attached who can explain the questions at issue?

RECOMMENDATIONS

If the general scheme is adopted the skeleton of it, at least, should be set up now in Paris, so that the personnel and organization may be assembled.

Those in charge of the organization must have access to the information available and must be in the closest confidential relationship with those who are conducting the negotiations. This is a fundamental point. If they are to make any impression on the correspondents, and if they are to avoid the mistakes which result from leading questions, they must have a correct knowledge of what is going on, together with a real understanding of the desires and intentions of the government. Moreover they must be in a position to give the correspondents news which they would not obtain elsewhere, if the correspondents are to feel that it is worth their while to remain in close touch with the official press organization. The policy adopted should be one of confidence rather than suspicion; the newspapermen should be told many things which they are asked not to publish. So far as possible they should be made to feel that they are actually taking part in one of the most important phases of the conference, that they are regarded as insiders and that their curiosity is legitimate.

1. That objective did not materialize under the conditions that George Creel, with Wilson's support, imposed for press relations during the Paris Conference.

To Felix Frankfurter

November 3, 1918

Dear Felix,

. . . I have been a kind of high intensive sponge these last months, and sponges you know are above all inarticulate. They may have been what Herbert would call most 'fruitful' months and luckily I have been quite free to spend all my time gathering in. The propaganda business got shipwrecked very early, so I was turned loose for the Inquiry.

Of course I started off with large ideas about all sorts of places, but it soon became perfectly evident that Paris was the real center of everything in my line, at least, and the complications of it are without end. It was pretty clear that there was no use going further until I knew my way around Paris, and that was, even for the most superficial kind of thing, a job of several months. I was all booked, however, to go to Switzerland a few weeks ago, when the Colonel started over, and so here I am working, and incidentally feeling hideously inadequate. Oh, Lord God, why weren't some of us educated?

Of course everything over here has been moving much more rapidly than anyone expected. This is particularly true in regard to the problems of demobilization and reconstruction. Already they are beginning to overshadow the war, and even the peace settlement itself. It's quite clear that the settlement is going to be affected profoundly by the demobilization problems in each country. . . . I think we can take it as an axiom that the stability and prestige, and the effectiveness of the gov'ts which make the settlement depends above all on their skills in demobilizing. If the AEF is not gotten home promptly when it is time to come home, if when it gets there it is set adrift, our whole body of ideas will tend towards being discredited. Reconstruction at home will be the rod by which our international program is judged. . . .

To Edward M. House

November 7, 1918

My dear Colonel House,

I must write you this morning because I couldn't possibly tell you to your face how great a thing you have achieved.[1] Frankly I did not believe it was humanly feasible under conditions as they seemed to be in Europe to win so glorious a victory. This is a climax of a course that has been as wise as it was brilliant, and as shrewd as it was prophetic. The President and you have more than justified the faith of those who insisted that your leadership was a turning point in modern history. No one can ever thank you adequately.

1. The settlement of the armistice terms with France and Great Britain, terms that Wilson used in his negotiation of the armistice with Germany, effective on November 11. Lippmann's enthusiasm proved premature, for the peace conference moved in directions often at variance with those of the armistice agreements.

To Newton D. Baker

November 12, 1918

Dear N.D.B.:

I was never quite sure under the rules whether Captains are permitted to write to the Secretary of War, but I can't let these days go by without sending you an affectionate greeting and a word of congratulation. You have made the most humane army that ever decided a great war. For somehow or other the President and you have succeeded in making it express most of the best and little of the worst of the temper with which our country fought the war.

I have been working for the Colonel since he arrived, and I've marveled every day at his kindly skill in the midst of formidable difficulties. But the most difficult period of war lies ahead, and we shall not really be able to call the war won until we know whether Europe can produce sufficient statesmanship to reconstruct itself. Already the war looks like a thing of extraordinary moral simplicity compared with the intricacy of this transition.

If only we were sure that the US were clear about the matter. . . .

To Dorothy Straight

December 1, 1918

Dear Dorothy,

I am sending you by pouch a letter of Willard's and his diary[1] and a cable which he tried to send Herbert. With them goes my heart's deepest sympathy to you, and the hope that you will let me do some little part of whatever you want done.

In the last eight weeks I was closer to Willard than ever before. Up at the First Army we talked far into the night, hoping, planning, sometimes doubting, but in the end renewed. In that personal loneliness which is the background of so many of us over here, there was mixed also a fear that what we had meant, and what alone could justify it all, was not the meaning and the justification to those who will decide.

Willard came to the work of the Peace Mission with that thought in his mind, and went at the work with the grim sense that it would not fail because boys who had died were of the faith. Willard was passionately interested in the technique of war; never did he lose his sense that the substance of the war was a host of boys who had to go and were told to believe.

He was as quick and fine and true as a man could be, and in his young maturity. I not only admired him, but loved him dearly, Dorothy, and he is quite irreplaceable. . . .

1. Willard Straight had died in Paris of influenza.

To Newton D. Baker

February 7, 1919

Dear Mr. Baker:

I landed Sunday and was discharged Monday.[1] You can well imagine that I am eager to come to see you. Mrs. Lippmann and I are hoping to go South next week for a vacation, but if it is convenient to you we could stop off in Washington for a few hours, say on Wednesday or Thursday of next week. What I would like to do, and what I know is almost impossible, is to see you away from your office when you have a little real leisure.

I saw Ralph[2] in Paris a great deal in the last month and there are many things I would like to tell you about him in case you should be going over there soon. I hope you will go because, apart from anything there may be to do in Paris, the state of mind which prevails in the Army is one that very much needs your personal attention. Just before I came away Ralph and I made a very good trip in the American area and got certain very definite impressions about the feeling of the men. The biggest difficulty, I am convinced, arises from the thing which most of us felt was the most harassing aspect of Army life, — the utter uncertainty as to where you are going and what is to happen to you. The desire to get home is of course unanimous and intense, but that desire would not develop the amount of irritation and suspicion which it does develop if each unit felt that it was on some definite schedule to move at a definite date and in a definite direction. No amount of Y.M.C.A. work or educational work can compensate for the feeling of irrationality from on high which pervades the men. I wrote to General Nolan[3] just before I left about this and suggested that if it was humanly possible to get out a schedule for the whole American Expeditionary Forces, showing definitely when each unit might expect to move from its present place to the embarkation center and from there home, the men would settle down much more readily to waiting and might be willing to put their minds upon educational work. But when no man knows whether he is to be in France six weeks or six months each man lives from day to day, snatches up every bit of gossip and spends practically his whole time speculating on the chances of getting home. I realize that if such a schedule were drawn up many changes would have to be made in it from time to time but if the changes were definitely announced in the *Stars and Stripes*[4] and the reasons for the changes explained the danger of reaction from unfulfilled promises could, I think, be avoided.

I see in today's papers that the conditions at Brest are again being exposed. I came through Brest and spent two days there, one of them in going over the camp with General Helmick and General Butler.[5] I had been in the camp for a day last July coming the other way. That that camp is in a terrible condition is undeniable, and while General Helmick said that at the moment the health rate was extraordinarily good the danger of an epidemic must be very great. The physical conditions of mud and rain are enough to drive anyone to melancholy and the congestion at the camp is undoubtedly too great for the housing facilities. Since July the progress in building barracks and laying boardwalks is substantial and food conditions have undoubtedly improved, but much as I like General Helmick and the spirit of his staff in the 8th Division and much as I should hate to say anything which would hurt him, I can not feel that he is adequate for the really immense job which he has to handle. He did not strike me as a big organizer and he did not seem to me to have the ability of delegating his work. I also gathered quite definitely that his relations with the Admiral were rather strained. The greatest difficulty I suppose though is due to the fact that too many divisions have been rushed to Brest with the result that facilities are always inadequate. He told me that there were nearly 100,000 men there of whom only 25,000 were permanently attached to the base, the rest were awaiting transportation. It seems a little difficult to see why so many should be waiting there at any one time.

I am glad of the whole experience and glad it is over.

1. In Paris, House could not establish control over the American planning for the peace, which Wilson kept in his own hands with the assistance of his own associates. The Inquiry staff there was under the direction of Bowman, who wanted no part of Lippmann. Aware that he was without any significant assignment or responsibility, and disturbed by the confusion among the Americans, Lippmann had requested and received transfer home. Soon thereafter he rejoined *The New Republic.* **2.** Ralph Hayes, Baker's secretary, earlier his aide in Cleveland. **3.** Brigadier General Dennis E. Nolan, chief of the Intelligence Service, A.E.F. **4.** The *Stars and Stripes* was the newspaper of the American army troops in Europe during World War I. It was revived during World War II. **5.** Brigadier General Eli Alva Helmick, in command of Base Section Five, Service of Supplies, at Brest; and Brigadier General Smedley D. Butler, commander of the Thirteenth Regiment of U.S. Marines, then at Brest.

To Bernard Berenson[1]

March 18, 1919

Dear Berenson:

. . . Parsifal's visit[2] to this country did not help him much, and he left a lot of carefully minded people with the impression that he was not quite sure what his own product meant. Frankly, people are very much annoyed at being neglected and the Republicans are in ecstasies of unhappiness over his prestige abroad. A large number of the professional friends of France, the kind of people who during the war were offering her all the last drops of everybody else's blood, have turned into a band of "little Americans" shouting that by no means must America be contaminated by Europeans. As usual since the days of Thomas Jefferson, the Democratic party starts out by announcing its isolation and its neutrality, and ends by increasing the territory and the influence of the country. By some fatality the Republicans talk about world power and the Democrats manage to get it.

The main interest here, however, is not what's going on in Paris at all, — The people are shivering in their boots over Bolshevism,[3] and they are far more scared of Lenin than they ever were of the Kaiser. We seem to be the most frightened lot of victors that the world ever saw. . . .

1. Bernard Berenson, connoisseur extraordinary of Renaissance painting, had first met Lippmann in Paris. They were to become close friends and Lippmann a frequent guest at I Tatti, Berenson's villa outside of Florence. **2.** "Parsifal" (the Lippmann-Berenson code name for Wilson) had left Paris in a state of pique over various controversies concerning the peace terms and returned briefly to the United States. There he found a group of Republican senators demanding changes in the Covenant of the League of Nations he had persuaded the peace conference to adopt, and increasing opposition to the proceedings of the conference, especially from militant Irish-Americans who were demanding an end to British rule in Ireland and expected Wilson to arrange it. **3.** Lippmann continued to stress the relationship between a proper international order and the defeat of bolshevism in Europe. That theme provided one emphasis in his articles in the March 1919 *New Republic*, which appeared later in book form as *The Political Scene* (New York, 1919). At that time scurrilous about Senator Henry Cabot Lodge, who was leading the opposition to the treaty and the League, Lippmann also had doubts about what Wilson had accomplished but remained in favor of approval of the treaty after revision. He shared Lodge's view about the need to change Article X of the Covenant and to find some way that Congress could speak more directly than the Covenant allowed to the debates within the League. Again somewhat like Lodge, he saw Anglo-American control of the seas as an essential foundation for the League. And like Lodge he objected, as his letters reveal, to various territorial settlements in the Treaty of Versailles.

To Paul D. Cravath[1]

April 3, 1919

Dear Mr. Cravath,

. . . I don't believe in dealing with the Bolshevik gov't. What I do believe in is, first, setting up an international control of the ports of entry and then trading with any group of Russians irrespective of their political faith, who can meet the terms of a straight bargain.

I believe that by keeping a control of these ports we can more effectively than any other way combat and restrain the most dangerous feature of Bolshevism, namely its international propaganda. Of course I don't feel at all dogmatic about the matter, but I do think some definite action in regard to Russia is essential, and I do not believe the condition of the world would permit of successful military conquest of Bolshevik Russia.[2]

1. Paul D. Cravath, distinguished New York lawyer, was at this time a member of the House mission in Paris and had been counsel to and a member of the U.S. Treasury mission to the Inter-Allied Council on War Purchases and Finance in London and Paris. **2.** The Bolsheviks were waging a civil war against various antirevolutionary factions, which were assisted in different places by troops of the Allied nations. Fighting against the Cossacks had begun in 1918. By April 1919, General Anton I. Denikin was in command of Cossack forces in the south. At this time, the Bolsheviks were gaining control of the Ukraine, where the French had been aiding the White resistance. In June 1918, the British had landed troops in Murmansk, to which France and later the United States added contingents — the Americans in the spring of 1919 in response especially to French pressure. In Siberia the Japanese had an army moving westward from Vladivostok to try to join Czech forces moving eastward. Admiral Aleksandr V. Kolchak led the Russian White Army in the region until his capture and execution. American troops also participated in the Siberian campaign.

To Ellery Sedgwick [1]

April 7, 1919

Dear Sedgwick:

. . . I have started to write a longish article around the general idea that freedom of thought and speech present themselves in a new light and raise new problems because of the discovery that opinion can be manufactured. The idea has come to me gradually as a result of certain experiences with the official propaganda machines, and my hope is to attempt a restatement of the problem of freedom of thought as it presents itself in modern society under modern conditions of government and with a modern knowledge of how to manipulate the human mind. Could you say whether you might be interested in such a discussion? I don't believe it could be done well under ten to fifteen thousand words, though the discussion might fall into two or three parts.[2] It will probably take me about a month to finish it. . . .

1. Ellery Sedgwick, then editor of the *Atlantic Monthly*. **2.** In the end, two articles appeared that the *Atlantic* published in November and December. They formed the text of Lippmann's *Liberty and the News* (New York, 1920), a significant precursor to his *Public Opinion* (New York, 1922).

To Hugh Gibson [1]

April 16, 1919

Dear Hugh:

I am delighted beyond measure at your appointment. You are just the man for the job for many reasons which I shall express in the next issue of *The New Republic*.

What particularly pleases me is that the administration should have rewarded so deserving a democrat as yourself, a man whose intense activity in the sixth ward and whose large contributions to the last campaign fund, cou-

pled with his total inability to speak any known language, and his entire ignorance of European affairs, has marked him out as just the right man for a
delicate and responsible position. I am glad that a man has been selected who
has no previous diplomatic training, a man who can thoroughly impress these
foreigners with our rough and ready dislike of all their ways. It is certainly
fine that no attempt has been made to recognize long and useful service.

In spite of these things I'm glad for the Poles, I'm glad for the U.S., and
I'm pleased to pieces.

Now if you want a military attaché with a long and splendid record in the
matter of paper balloons, I'd offer you a suggestion if Warsaw weren't so
damn far away. . . .

1. Hugh Gibson had been appointed American minister to Poland.

To the editor, Democratic Chronicle, *Rochester, New York*

April 26, 1919

My dear Sir:

My attention has just been called to a short editorial which appeared in your
paper on April 16th, which accuses me of the absurd notion that government
ought to be turned over to so-called experts. God save us from any such plan.
What I did suggest was the establishment of a central statistical and records
office for the State of New York with legislative drafting experts for purely
consultive purposes. I don't expect you to make any correction, as the matter
is of no particular importance. Being an editor myself, I know how easy it is
to jump to conclusions on inaccurate information.

As for the Constitution of the United States, I respect it deeply, and I regard
Alexander Hamilton as the greatest constructive statesman that this country
has produced. I hope it is no disrespect to the Constitution or to him to wish
that in these days we had statesmen of equal caliber.

To Edward S. Allen[1]

May 6, 1919

Dear Allen:

. . . Of course I do not agree with you because I feel that you completely
fail to imagine the consequences of a German victory in this war. There are
many things in Allied diplomacy and in American diplomacy that I should
have liked to have seen handled differently, but if the alternatives are limited
to a choice between German victory and the kind of victory we got there isn't
the slightest doubt in my mind that our decision was correct. . . .

1. Edward S. Allen of Ann Arbor, Michigan, an acquaintance who had recently written to Lippmann.

To Bernard Berenson   HANDWRITTEN

May 6, 1919

Dear BB,

Your letter and the clippings too are a great help and comfort. This morning I have two written just at the time WW let loose on the Italian matter.[1] As usual the technic seems to have been faulty, but it was time something was done.

The treaty will be published before you receive this. I expect a compromise all along the line. Life will have considerably stained the white radiance of the 14 pts. You know what we should have had without them though. We here shall grumble and accept the result for two reasons — no peace means Bolshevism everywhere in Europe, and we don't want that; and the League is enough to build on if parties get control in France and Britain that wish to use it.

The President is just about at the lowest point of his popularity here. If I were prophesying I'd say that he will not go much lower, but that there will be a steady rise beginning in about two months. At the moment everyone is disgruntled — the jingoes of course, the Liberals because he hasn't won out at Paris and because he has tolerated creatures like Burleson at home.

The first Presidential boom is launched — General Leonard Wood[2] — favorite son of New Hampshire, says the L of N is twaddle and good for molly coddles. . . .

1. Wilson opposed Italian claims to Fiume on the Yugoslav side of the Adriatic Sea. When Italy, supported by its secret agreement with England, persisted in its objective, Wilson appealed to the Italian people. They stood by their government, which resented his interference. In the end, Italy grudgingly yielded Fiume but held Wilson to its claim to the Austrian South Tyrol. 2. An intimate of Theodore Roosevelt, who had recently died, Wood hoped to pick up Roosevelt's support within the Republican party. Besides opposing the League and the treaty, he called for harsh treatment of all radicals and had never associated himself with any significant domestic reform. After a spurt in 1919, largely among conservative Republicans, Wood's candidacy faltered.

To Ray Stannard Baker[1]

May 15, 1919

My dear Baker:

. . . The situation created by the treaty is . . . profoundly discouraging to those who cared most for what the President has been talking about. For the life of me I can't see peace in this document, and as the President has so frequently said, statesmen who cannot hear the voice of mankind are sure to be broken. Over here though there is general approval of the treaty as an instrument of punishment, there are few left who even pretend that the President has not been beaten by the diplomacy of the European Governments.

No doubt the difficulties were enormous, but I don't see how anyone can argue that they have not proved to be insuperable.

1. Ray Stannard Baker was then director of Wilson's press bureau in Paris. A progressive journalist of exposure whom Lippmann had seen frequently during the early weeks of the peace conference, he was a strong Wilson partisan and later Wilson's official biographer.

To Hugh Gibson

June 2, 1919

Dear Hugh:

. . . First I must pass along to you the best joke current in this part of the world. I assume that no censor will read these words. It comes from Dean Pound[1] of the Harvard Law School who says that a republic of which Paderewski is Prime Minister is a republic pianissimo.[2] I hope it's not true.

We, of course, get no information about Poland that doesn't come from one of the propaganda bureaus either French, Polish, or Jewish, so I haven't any definite opinions. And any tips from you as to what to read either in French or boche or preferably English would be a real help.

The country here doesn't care twopence about the peace treaty. A few of us who make a business of being terribly far sighted think it's another Brest Litovsk which will never be executed in its present form. The Great White Hope's stock is now selling on the curb market, and the American appetite for guaranteeing the frontiers of your domain is, I am afraid, rapidly diminishing. The Covenant will have hard going in the Senate. The Shantung business[3] has aroused all the Pacific Coast Senators, the Irish are almost at the exploding point and evidently the Catholic Church is more or less with them, the Italians are very sore, and of course the liberals and radicals. If Clemenceau[4] should fall in the next three months I doubt whether the treaty would pass without a big amendment as to American obligation under it. But all this is speculation because we don't know whether there is going to be bargaining at Versailles nor just what line W.W. will take on his return. . . .

1. Roscoe Pound. 2. Ignace Jan Paderewski, the provisional president of Poland and a concert pianist of considerable reputation. The Polish government at that time wanted to regain the frontiers of 1772, an ambition that led them to war against Lithuania and the Soviet Union. 3. Wilson had conceded to Japan control over former German commercial and political concessions in the Shantung peninsula of China, an objective which Japan's secret agreement with Great Britain had promised. The Japanese were able to obtain that concession partly because Wilson, involved as he was in the dispute over Fiume, could not face another major struggle among the great powers without the possibility of the breakup of the conference. 4. French Premier Georges Clemenceau.

To C. P. Scott[1]

June 4, 1919

Dear Mr. Scott:

. . . There never was a time when prophesying about American politics was so difficult. But I give you for what it is worth the estimate of one of the shrewdest political correspondents from Washington with whom I talked this afternoon. He says that for the first few weeks the Senate will talk all around the subject avoiding the German issue and striking out wildly against alleged violations of the Monroe Doctrine, American sovereignty, etc., etc. Then the thing will begin to crystallize. The Senators affected by the Japanese question, of whom there are about sixteen, will grow angrier and angrier about Shantung. The growing distrust of England which, by the way, has never been greater since the war began, will gradually focus on what one prominent middle western editor who is still supporting the Covenant calls "this British job." If there should be bloodshed in Ireland the Irish opposition will become acute, and combined with the Jewish feeling about Poland and Romania will become another point of opposition. There is at the present time a great deal of bitterness among the Italians against Mr. Wilson, and if he should yield on Silesia, as I suppose he may, he will have very little support among the Poles.[2]

After several weeks of talk about Shantung, Fiume, Poland, and so forth, and if Clemenceau should fall and the British labour party make itself felt still more, and if there should be revolution in Germany, Senators will gradually screw up their courage to the point of discussing the essential unworkableness of the economic terms imposed on Germany. Then anything may happen. I should guess that Mr. Wilson's only chance of having the treaty ratified as it stands would be to force a vote on it immediately. In a protracted debate his abandonment of principle would be mercilessly revealed.

I hear from Paris today that General Bliss[3] who is one of the solidest and most liberal members of the American Mission was kept from resigning on the question of Shantung only by the greatest effort. Of course the thing which gave Shantung to Japan was the terror aroused in Mr. Wilson's breast by the Italian outburst over Fiume.

He is the victim I am afraid of his own popularity, and he has failed in all his greatest purposes because he overestimated his popularity and miscalculated his own ability to deal with shrewder and more realistic men. The first evidence of that was his surrender in the matter of Russian intervention last July. You will remember that when we talked in London I had just come from America and was totally unable to explain to you what had happened. I had seen the Secretary of War on July 2nd and Colonel House on July 5th and both had said categorically that there would be no intervention. The turnabout was sudden and was probably due to an ultimatum from Clemenceau. . . .

---

1. C. P. Scott, editor of the *Manchester Guardian*, had signed Lippmann as American correspondent for that paper. 2. Poland, with support from France, wanted Upper Silesia, previously

German, included within her borders. In the end, Wilson agreed to temporary Polish control to be followed by a plebiscite to determine the area's future. **3.** General Tasker Bliss, the only military man on Wilson's official delegation to the conference.

To Newton D. Baker

June 9, 1919

Dear Chief:

For several weeks I've wanted to write to you and always I've hesitated because I could not quite find the words to express my disappointment at the outcome in Paris.

One can look at the matter either from the moral point of view and compare the result with our legal obligations contracted in the armistice and the pledges of honor given to the world by the President in our name; or one can look at the matter coldly from the point of view of its probable workableness in the kind of world left by the war.

I know that to you the promises made by the President were the major reality which underlay the whole conflict. How in our consciences are we to square the results with the promises? We said we would restore the French boundaries of 1871, we have gone far beyond those boundaries to the Saar[1] and have set up a regime over a population of Germans which is humanly intolerable. You know enough of modern industrialism to know that a plebiscite in a coal valley where the employer is a government vitally interested in the result of the plebiscite is bound to lead to the profoundest disorders and resentment. And this occurs in a territory which was expressly excluded under the armistice from being considered open to political transfer. You know that I had something to do with the preparation of the memoranda on which the fourteen points were based, and I know that we expressly selected the formula "the wrong done to France in 1871" in order to exclude France's claims to the Saar Valley which had already been revealed at that time in certain of the secret documents published by the Bolsheviki.

We said that we would give to Poland territory inhabited by "indisputably" Polish populations. We have put at least two million Germans directly under Polish rule,[2] and in the case of Danzig we have put them not under neutral rule but indirectly under Polish though the city is indisputably German. And as a result we have severed from the main body of the German Republic the people of East Prussia.

In the matter of Schleswig-Holstein[3] we have overreached ourselves in the desire to diminish German territory so much that we are confronted with the biting irony of the Danish people who decline a substantial part of the aggrandizement offered to them.

Upon German Austria we have forced separatism, denying to that people the essential of independence that is their right to voluntary union with people of the same language and nationality. We have done this for purely military and political reasons.

In Bohemia we have denied to probably two million Germans any right to be consulted about their allegiance. In the Tyrol for purely strategic reasons we have placed under Italian sovereignty several thousand more Germans.

All this we have done at the conclusion of a war which had its origin at least partially in the violation of national principles. In the places of Germany, Austria, and Russia as the empires based on the subjugation of a league of peoples we have set up France, Poland, Czechoslovakia,[4] and Italy at least partially on that basis. Whereas in 1914 Italy, France and Poland were agitated by irredentism, they now become the nations against whom the irredentist feeling of Europe converges. We have done this after the solemnest kind of assurances that we would not do it.

We have made a League of Nations and from it we have excluded the German Republic though we have disarmed it and left it without any means of defense. Nothing is clearer to me from reading the President's speeches than that he intended that Germany democratized should become a member of the League. I remember in August in London Sir William Tyrrell, head of the Political Intelligence, saying that the League should be formed by the Allies before the conclusion of the war. This view was proposed to the President and in the last speech he made before the armistice, the great speech of September 27th, he expressly stated that a League formed then would be no League because it was merely an alliance of belligerent powers. The exclusion of Germany from the League not only denies her the securities which the League may give to its members, but it also denies her as long as she is excluded that economic equality which was promised in all the President's speeches and explicitly in the Fourteen Points.

The method of fixing the reparations without specifying an amount,[5] and permitting the most drastic kind of interference in the internal life of Germany is surely one of the most dangerous engines of intrigue that could have been devised. So far as I can see no expert economist even pretends that the practical result can be the payment of very substantial sums, and it is difficult to avoid the conclusion that while the ostensible purpose was to satisfy vague and exaggerated popular demands in England and France for indemnities, the real purpose was to put into the hands of France and England the ultimate control of all phases of German life. Whether this was the purpose or not we already begin to see the consequences. The separatist movement in the Rhineland is an intrigue, hardly denied, which derives all its vitality from the fact that the French generals and politicians promised escape from the reparations in payment for secession.[6]

I presume that you hardly believe that this is either a just or workable peace, and I suppose that you keep your faith in the future by hoping that the League of Nations can modify the terms and work out a genuine settlement. I can't share that belief. From what I know of American diplomacy even when inspired by the best of motives, I cannot believe that it will be effective in the myriad details of European diplomacy as they result from this Treaty. Why should anyone believe that where Wilson has failed General Wood or Senator Harding or whoever it is that follows him will succeed? It seems to me to stand the world on its head to assume that a timid legal document can master and control the appetites and the national wills before which this Treaty puts such immense prizes.

Of course even with all these doubts I should be willing to try the experiment, provided we abandon all idea of a special French alliance and remove from the Covenant all those guarantees which in any way bind us in advance to support the status quo. For these agreements simply insure a willful policy against the consequences of its acts. Their effect is to quiet the apprehensions of that body of public opinion in France and England which might be depended upon to resist an aggressive policy. France, so far as her diplomacy and her militarism go, is dreaming once again her old dream of Louis XIV and Napoleon, and we shall simply encourage that dream by guaranteeing France and her satellite states in Eastern Europe.

I've run on at great length, but I feel that I must say this to you so that you may understand why it is that *The New Republic* has become so critical of the President's foreign policy. I can find no excuses in the fact that he had a difficult task in Paris. No one supposed that he would have an easy one. A good deal of the difficulty he owes to his own neglect in failing during the war to secure an abrogation of the Secret Treaties and specific acceptance of his program. Some of the difficulty he owes to his failure to surround himself with men to whom he could really delegate part of the task. Some of it he owes to the lack of popular support here. The absence of that support is traceable to the intolerance and suppression of criticism in which he so weakly acquiesced.

It's a very dark moment, and the prospect of war and revolution throughout Europe is appalling. The responsibility resting upon the men who commit the American people to detailed participation is simply enormous.

My affection for you has never been greater than it is at this moment.

1. The treaty placed the Saar area under international control for fifteen years, during which time France could exploit the coal mines. A plebiscite was then to be held under League auspices to determine the area's future.   **2.** The treaty took from Germany and gave to Poland the larger part of Posen and West Prussia; it also made Danzig a free state within the Polish customs union. The resulting "Polish corridor" gave Poland access to the Baltic but placed millions of Germans under Polish rule.   **3.** Northern and central Schleswig were to divide their allegiance to Denmark or Germany by plebiscite.   **4.** The new State of Czechoslovakia included the Sudetenland, inhabited largely by German-speaking people.   **5.** The treaty required Germany to pay for all civilian damages suffered by the Allies during the war. That sum was to be calculated by May 1, 1921. Meanwhile Germany was to pay five billion dollars, with the balance due in thirty years. That level of reparations, demanded by the British and French, ran counter to Wilson's assurances to Germany at the time of the armistice, as well as to common sense.   **6.** The French had wanted to set up a buffer state along the Rhine. Instead the treaty provided for Allied occupation of the Rhineland for fifteen years, and for a demilitarized belt thirty miles wide along the right (the

German) bank of the river. Further, as one condition for that arrangement, France obtained Wilson's agreement and that of British Prime Minister David Lloyd George to a tripartite treaty guaranteeing France's security. Clemenceau realized the U.S. Senate would probably reject the treaty, but in that event, France had the authority to extend its occupation of the Rhineland.

To Learned Hand[1]

July 10, 1919

Dear B:

They changed Article One in the second draft possibly with the Senate's attitude in mind. I'm no lawyer of course, as you no doubt know, but can't one argue that there is no League until it is ratified, and that any reservations we may care to make are part of the process of constituting the League?[2] I am quite prepared to admit that if the other powers reject our reservations then no League is constituted, at least so far as we are concerned. But if they do accept the reservations then they are valid. It looks to me not so much a legal question as a political one, and as I am absolutely sure that Europe needs us in the League more than we need the League Europe will agree.

Certainly there is no bad faith in this. Because morally nothing Wilson has done is binding until it is ratified, and the world had due notice that the Senate must be consulted. . . .

1. Learned Hand — since 1909 a United States judge for the Southern District of New York, in 1924 appointed to the Court of Appeals for the Second Circuit — was a decoration on the federal bench, one of the great jurists of his time.   2. Senator Lodge had proposed various reservations, really amendments, to the treaty and Covenant as a condition for the Senate's approval. Wilson persistently opposed them. The president argued that the adoption of reservations could force renegotiation of the treaty, a contention with which the British disagreed.

To Bernard Berenson

HANDWRITTEN

July 16, 1919

Dear B. B.

Yours of June 23 leaves me with a sense that I must have written nonsense to you early in May. I was the typical fool determined to hope till the bitter end. Well it's bitter, and we've had the pleasure of fighting the treaty here practically single-handed.[1] . . . The Republicans, for bad reasons mainly, have followed along, and we shall avoid the stultification of signing on the dotted line.

You can hardly conceive the bewilderment of mind over here. It is exploited in the interests of the blackest reaction our generation has known. The core of it is the Kolchak propaganda[2] which has now assumed a virulent form. My crowd is distinctly unpopular — parlor "Bolsheviks" etc. But it's a good fight, and if I didn't long for quiet and a chance to do my book, I'd be blissfully content to enjoy the attack on us. Popularity would be a little bit discreditable when the world is so mad.

Living in the country redeems much. One gets so good a sense of the things that do not matter, and a decent relief from the feverish factionalisms of the city. But I'm afraid it's a long pull before any considerable number of us can cultivate our gardens. Sometimes I think we are a damned generation. I suppose we are in comparison with the late Victorians.

W.W. has gained flesh and complacency and pride in his sophistication at Paris. Finis there. You can use a man whose integrity has collapsed. He's had no fight in him so far, and the Republicans are gaining every day both in strength and in sense. For the first time in their lives they are genuinely not insiders and the experience is liberalizing. . . .

1. Led by Herbert Croly, the editors of *The New Republic* had decided in May 1919 to oppose the treaty.   **2.** Anti-Bolshevik propaganda that fed American antiradicalism, then virulent.

To Newton D. Baker

July 19, 1919

Dear N.D.B.:

Your letter of June 13th impressed me a good deal and I fully appreciate the force of the argument that almost anything is preferable to more starvation in Europe. But nevertheless the argument comes down to this doesn't it? That by maintaining the blockade for the purpose of enforcing our peace terms we have created a situation under which we are prevented from insisting on good peace terms. After all we cannot escape the responsibility for the blockade and if babies are dying in Budapest hospitals for lack of food, who is it who has kept the food from them in the last few months?

I sincerely hope that for the sake of his own integrity and as a matter of frankness to the American people that the President will not pretend that the situation is more auspicious than it really is. A frank avowal that he has had to compromise, that he has had to accept situations which are highly dangerous to the peace of the world will be far more useful to everybody concerned than any attempt to show that he has accomplished what he started out to accomplish. Any such policy on his part while it may give him the temporary applause of the reactionary forces in the world will make European liberalism and labor cynical. They know what kind of peace this is and confidence can be maintained only by candor.

I can't help hoping too that the President will disentangle himself from the interventionists intrigues in regard to Russia. Our behavior at Archangel and in Siberia is one of the least gratifying episodes in our history.[1] I don't know what information you have had as to the devastations committed in Northern Russia but I have received some from a source entirely trustworthy, and passionately friendly to the administration. I realize that we have been acting in the whole Russian matter not on our own traditions and instincts but under compulsions which may have seemed irresistible. Nevertheless I am afraid that when the expedition is back home there will be revelations of a most serious character. Then on top of it all we should be so guileless as to be tempted by a man like Kolchak makes me wonder whether there is not a deep truth in the instinctive dread of the plain American at too much association with European diplomats. We've got no business taking part in unauthorized civil war in Russia. We've got no business either in law or morals or humanity trying to starve European Russia in the interests of Kolchak, Denikin,[2] and the White Finns. We've got no business suppressing documents and carrying on negotiations with various factions under cover of a censorship. Why is it that we've never had all the documents in the Prinkipo affair?[3] Why are the communications to Kolchak concealed? Why do we permit the military news in Siberia to be withheld until after we have given a kind of recognition to a dictatorship that hasn't even the virtue of success?

I can understand these things happening in a reactionary administration. I can't understand them happening where Woodrow Wilson is President. . . .[4]

1. The president had ordered American forces to join White Russians and others combating Bolshevik armies in Archangel and Siberia. The British were particularly active in the former sector; the Japanese, in the latter.   2. Admiral Aleksandr Kolchak was at this time retreating to the east after almost reaching the Volga from Siberia; General Anton Denikin, in charge of a large White Army, was in contrast advancing from the Ukraine toward Moscow.   3. At the suggestion of Lloyd George, Wilson had invited the opposing sides in Russia to a conference of Allied powers on the island of Prinkipo near Constantinople. The Bolsheviks accepted the invitation, but the White Russians rejected it, and the conference, therefore, did not occur.   4. On the same day, Lippmann wrote a similar letter to Colonel House.

To Norman Hapgood[1]

July 28, 1919

Dear Norman:

. . . I see the force of what Baker says about the treaty and the argument for ratification is a real one. I should be inclined to accept it; in fact I do accept it, subject to reservations which release us from any automatic commitment to the present arrangement of power in Europe. I am convinced that the Treaty of Versailles can never be imposed on Europe and that the attempt to impose it will produce just exactly those consequences which Baker fears. I do not believe that a real attempt will be made to impose it if France and Poland are not reinsured against the consequences by an American guarantee. I think that the net effect of our participation in the Peace Conference has been to make the European foreign officers more reckless than they would have been had they been faced with the problem of arranging the Europe in which they must live on their own strength and position.

The President's negotiations seem to me to have been based upon a fundamental miscalculation; namely, on the idea that he must purchase assent to the League by accepting the program of Imperialism. His real politics should have been to purchase the renunciation of the Imperial program with the American guarantee. He saw all that clearly enough before we entered the war and he said many times that we could only guarantee the kind of peace that had not the elements of a real equilibrium. When he got to Paris, he seemed to forget that the character of the League is not something independent of the terms of peace but a direct product of those terms and that the League at present is fundamentally diseased because it is designed to administer an impossible settlement. . . .

1. Hapgood was American minister to Denmark, February to December 1919.

To Felix Frankfurter

July 28, 1919

Dear Felix:

. . . I wrote "The Political Scene" at a stage in the proceedings when I was still determined to hope against hope. You are quite right in saying that the bottom fact of the whole failure was a failure of technique. The intentions were good enough. What Paris has demonstrated is, that you cannot in ignorance improvise a structure of good will. In the historical series the matter goes back to the early months of 1917, and the failure to secure a general agreement as to war aims before we entered the war. This omission vitiated everything else, but it was compounded by the fact that we had no diplomatic service capable of diagnosing Europe, that we never negotiated but simply enunciated, that what diplomatic service we had was insulated from the President, who worked by intimation from Colonel House, who had his own irresponsible diplomatic service. That is a long and confused sentence, but perfectly obvious to you.

Here things are in great confusion, and all of the President's powers are now being used to maintain the atmosphere of unreality which surrounds the whole American diplomatic effort. We are reactionary of course, and the so-called liberals have most of them entered a monastery where they contemplate ecstatically the beatitudes of the League of Nations. . . .

To Ralph Pulitzer[1]

July 30, 1919

My dear Pulitzer:

. . . It has been a real pain to me to find myself separated temporarily from men like yourself and from papers like the *World* on the issue raised by the treaty. We all hoped to the very last minute that we would be able to support it, but the more we study the treaty and the French alliance which accompanies it, the more convinced we become that Mr. Wilson has entangled himself in an intrigue which will have very serious consequences both for Europe and for us. This peace, if any attempt is made to enforce it, as the French government would like to enforce it, will, I am certain, provoke a class war throughout Europe, and class war is something, of course, that we must avoid, if it is humanly possible to avoid it. The French Government will not dare to enforce that treaty in its virulent form without American guarantees. But if the guarantees are given freely and fully, she will attempt it and you know as well as I that our diplomatic service abroad is totally incapable of putting up any resistance or of exercising any moderating influence. If Clemenceau could ride over Wilson, what will he do to the amiable gentlemen who act as ambassadors for us in Europe? The *World* has admitted that the treaty is not satisfactory and that only a revision of the treaty by the league can make a real peace in Europe. To that I agree, but I say that the league has neither the power nor the will to revise that treaty, if American guarantees to France are put in such a form as to make us virtually the reserve behind any policy which the French politicians may care to pursue. . . .

1. Ralph Pulitzer, publisher of the *New York World,* a leading Democratic newspaper then advocating approval of the Treaty of Versailles.

To George D. Herron[1]

August 2, 1919

Dear Dr. Herron:

Your letter interests me. *The New Republic* does not advise the rejection of the Treaty in *a legal sense.*[2] It advocates ratification with reservations which will remove America as an influence to uphold the present system of power (chiefly through the defeat of Article Ten). But it does advise the moral rejection of the Treaty as preliminary to its drastic revision by the League.[3]

Your own position must indeed be painful. But I cannot refrain from reminding you that you as much as any other man have helped to create the state of mind which made impossible a good peace. Instead of keeping the discussion at the level of objective facts, you have lent your influence to a view of the war which was fanatical and untrue in its implications. The German menace I realized as firmly as you did — I was never neutral in thought and among the first to urge American intervention. But I knew that German imperialism was a malignant phase of imperialism and not of the German peoples, and I never participated as you did in the attempt to give moral excuses for the hate campaign. . . .

1. George D. Herron — eminent American Christian Socialist who wrote extensively about Christianity, socialism, and war — had been living in Geneva since 1901. In 1919 he was designated to serve as one of three American delegates to Prinkipo. **2.** Emphasis Lippmann's. **3.** Article X of the Covenant pledged signatories to uphold the political and territorial integrity of member states. Wilson considered it the heart of the Covenant, a moral though not a legal pledge. Lippmann viewed it as an objectionable guarantee of the rigid status quo imposed by the treaty's territorial settlements; see *The Political Scene* (New York, 1919). Lodge and the Republican reservationists also demanded modification of the article, which in their opinion deprived the Senate of its constitutional role in American foreign policy.

To C. P. Scott

August 6, 1919

Dear Mr. Scott:

I sent you today a long cable on the very extraordinary situation which has arisen on the railroads.[1] I wasn't quite certain whether I was justified in devoting so much attention to a domestic issue, but for the moment the issue has overclouded all others. The President has virtually stopped all his negotiations with the Senate on the Treaty in order to deal with the problems revolving about the cost of living and the new and extremely radical demands of labor.[2] I felt that the matter would be of interest to your readers, not only because they may want to know what everybody over here is talking about, but because the situation bears comparison with your problem in the mines. It is important to remember that owing to the vast extent of American territory and its complete dependence on railroad transport the railroad question has always been the key problem in domestic, political, and social conflicts.

I touched upon the recent race riots in one of my cables.[3] It may perhaps be worthwhile to sketch the main factors of the situation for you so that you may be prepared in case new outbreaks occur if you wish to comment on them.

The war caused a large migration of Negroes from the South to the North, and this migration has caused complementary race problems in the North and South. The Negroes flowed into industrial centers like Chicago, hired there by great corporations like the railroads and the packers. Nothing had been prepared for them. They aggravated the housing problem, for, as you know, the influx of Negroes into any district depreciates real estate values, and causes immediate agitation by the landlords who are adversely affected. Being unorganized workers they earned the hostility of the white working men. They were exploited by the local politicians. In Chicago, for example, the notorious Mayor Thompson owes his election to a bargain with the Negro vote. This is the explosive material which unscrupulous newspaper agitation sets off into a race riot. In the South, on the other hand, the scarcity of Negro labor, accompanied by increased self-consciousness due to the militarization of several hundred thousand colored men, has tended to raise the status of the Negro. This the whites are determined to resist at all costs, and there has been a kind of reciprocal incitement to Negro baiting between the North and the South.

It is a very dangerous state of affairs. It is smoldering all the time, and will flame up again and again. Sober friends of the Negro would like, of course, to secure a Federal handling of the problem, but this is politically impossible during a Democratic administration, and there are rumors that the Republican politicians intend to abandon their old alliance with the Southern Negro and contest Southern elections as a white man's party. All Negro leaders now are extremely revolutionary in temper, and if they ever swing loose from the Republicans they will go to the outer Left. . . .

1. The railroad brotherhoods had supported, railroad management opposed, the Plumb plan for the nationalization of the railways, a plan Congress rejected in the Esch-Cummins Transportation Act of 1920. That legislation also created a Railroad Labor Board to adjust wage disputes.   2. The rising cost of living and the determined effort of management to roll back the gains made by labor unions during the war provoked a number of costly strikes in 1919, in some of which radical leaders played a role, though not an exclusive one, and in all of which traditional standards restricting labor militancy were challenged. Of these strikes, the most celebrated included the Seattle general strike of February, the Boston police strike in September, the steel strike in the same month, and the bituminous coal strike in November.   3. The Chicago race riot of late July 1919 was the worst of some twenty-five postwar race riots.

To Raymond B. Fosdick [1]

August 15, 1919

My dear Raymond:

. . . In my opinion the Treaty is not only illiberal and in bad faith, it is in the highest degree imprudent. It is a far worse job, I think, than the Treaty of Vienna a hundred years ago, because the men who gathered at Vienna did honestly take into account the balance of forces in Europe. The men at Paris ignored these forces. They have tried to make a world settlement on the basis of what seem to me three overwhelming fallacies. First, that the movement towards industrial democracy can be crushed. Second, that French diplomacy can be trusted with the mastery of the continent. Third, that the power of America can be employed to maintain in status quo the impossible relationships created by the first two fallacies.

The reason that our group on *The New Republic* has urged the refusal of all material guarantees as to Europe is that we see at present no other way of restoring a decent perspective by Europeans on European affairs.

Let me illustrate. It looks now as if the bloody and immoral policy of counter revolution in Russia has collapsed. Why has it collapsed? Fundamentally for two reasons. First, because there is no popular Russian support for Kolchak.

Second, because the United States was unwilling to furnish the troops necessary for a successful conquest of Russia. The withdrawal of our aid has knocked the bottom out of the whole miserable plot and as a result we shall probably see within the next few months the conclusion of peace with Russia on terms that could have been obtained last February. This means simply that the true balance of forces reasserts itself.

Now I believe that France under this treaty is pursuing a policy in Central Europe and Western Germany which is not only immoral but impossible without the American guarantee, and I am convinced that once we serve notice that we are not a pawn in M. Pinchon's[2] game France's common sense will begin to reassert itself.

So much in explanation. You ask how can the League humanize the treaty. A month ago I was still trying to believe that it might. I don't think I believe it any longer. So far as the League is concerned on the Continent it is today a bureau of the French Foreign Office, acting as a somewhat vague alliance of the Great Powers against the influence and the liberty of the people who live between the Rhine and the Pacific Ocean. Owing to the unanimity clause and particularly owing to the constitution of the Council and the new triple alliance within it, the League will be what the French Government and the British Government make it. They were able at the Peace Conference to defeat the President at every vital point. Under these covenants they will be far more effective than they were at the Conference, and while something may be accomplished by putting good men on various commissions we have to remember that in the business of preventing future war there is small credit in almost having prevented it.

We have to wait for a complete change in attitude within England and France. When this occurs we have to insist on the inclusion of Russia and Germany in the Council of the League, and only then shall we be able to say that a League of Nations is possible. Whether such a League will be the evolution of this one or something created after this one has collapsed, I don't know, but I am certain that the present League is in structure and function and ideal the enemy of a real League of Nations, and the greatest danger is that its failure, like that of the Holy Alliance before it, will disillusionize a whole generation.

You ask for my suggestions and I give them to you in the spirit you ask them. The first necessity is that the President, and if not he then Colonel House, should permit the whole world to know just what the dangers of this settlement are.[3] An American should have done and should still do what General Smuts did. Until that primary act of honesty is committed we shall be living a lie and committing one immorality to cover another. The plain fact is that nobody can get away with this Treaty, and the sooner that is confessed so that all the world knows it, the better for the world. There is no mystical power whatever in this covenant. It consists of a group of governments, and the error which it seems to me affects certain liberals today is their enormous desire to believe that the covenant is greater than the Great Powers. It would be if there were any popular representation in it, but that has been rigorously excluded. I think if I were in your position I should make publicity my whole aim. I should try to arrange the procedure so that no matter what the immediate cost the world can understand the real forces at work.

1. Raymond B. Fosdick, New York lawyer, recently a civilian aide to General Pershing, had become undersecretary general of the League of Nations and was soon to return to the United States to attempt to rally support for the League. **2.** Stéphen J. M. Pichon, then French foreign minister. **3.** As had General Smuts, who nevertheless favored the League.

To Hiram W. Johnson[1]

August 17, 1919

My dear Senator Johnson:

In accordance with your suggestion, I am suggesting a number of questions, the answers to which should be available to the public before final action is taken on the pending treaty.

1. Was the United States Government officially informed, at any time between the rupture of diplomatic relations with Germany and the signing of the armistice, of agreements made by the Allied governments in regard to the settlement of the war?

2. Was it unofficially informed?

3. If it was not officially informed why was no request for information submitted to the Allied governments?

4. If, as the President stated on July 10th, we entered the war, not because 'our material interests were directly threatened' but 'as the disinterested champions of right' was it not our duty to inform ourselves of all agreements bearing upon the ultimate settlement?

5. Specifically, was the United States Government informed of

(a) The Treaty of London, on the basis of which Italy entered the war in 1915.

(b) The agreement with Romania in August 1916.

(c) The various agreements in respect to Asia Minor.

(d) The agreements consummated in the winter of 1917 between France and Russia relative to the frontiers of Germany, and particularly in relation to the Saar Valley and the Left Bank of the Rhine.

(e) The agreements with Japan relative to the Pacific Islands and to German rights in China.

(f) The resolutions of the Paris Economic Conference.

(g) All agreements made by any of the Allied governments with the Czechoslovak National Council, the Polish National Committee, and the Jugoslav National Committee.

(h) The Swiss mission of General Smuts to confer with Count Mensdorff.

(i) The exchanges between France and Austria revolving about the letter of Prince Sixtus.

6. Was the address of January 8, 1918, containing the Fourteen Points based on a knowledge of the existence of the secret agreements?

7. Was it not deliberately intended as a program of aims to supplant the aims contained in the Secret Treaties?

8. Did the United States Government at any time subsequent to this address and previous to the armistice discuss with any of the Allied governments the terms laid down in the Fourteen Points?

9. Since the Fourteen Points "and the principles enunciated in his subsequent addresses" constituted the legal basis of the armistice, would any departure from these terms and principles constitute a breach of faith on the part of the United States?

10. In view of the fact that the armistice is subsequent to the Secret Treaties, does it not in law and in morals abrogate those treaties wherever they are inconsistent with its terms?

11. (a) Specifically, what authority is to be found in the armistice for opening a dispute as to the sovereignty of the Saar valley?

(b) Is the annexation of the Southern Tyrol, against which Lord Bryce has protested, consistent with Point IX which promises a readjustment "along clearly recognizable lines of nationality"?

(c) By what authority is the right of the Republic of Austria to join the German Republic made subject of approval by other powers?

(d) How many Germans are put under Polish Sovereignty? And how many Germans in East Prussia are separated from the body of the German nation? Are all the territories ceded to Poland "inhabited by indisputably Polish populations"?

(e) Is not the Third Principle laid down in the address of September 27 a part of the legal and moral basis of the armistice, and is it not in contradiction of the proposed Treaty of Alliance with France — to wit: "there can be no leagues or alliances or special covenants and understandings within the general and common family of the League of Nations"?

(f) Why is a special alliance offered to France and not to Belgium or Italy?

(g) Do the terms of this alliance or the terms of the Treaty of Versailles forbid the German Republic to put down separatist intrigues in the Rhineland aiming to establish a buffer state on the Left Bank of the Rhine? Would the United States be committed to use its armed forces to prevent the German government from suppressing a secessionist movement in the Rhineland? Would the use of German troops to suppress such a movement be construed as "unprovoked aggression" against France?

(h) Has France special military agreements with Poland and Czechoslovakia?

(i) If France were involved in war because of such agreements, would the United States be involved as the Ally of France?

(j) Under the terms of this alliance, who is the judge as to what constitutes an "unprovoked aggression"?

12. Did China enter the war on the advice of the United States?

13. Was the United States aware at the time this advice was given of secret
agreements affecting Chinese territory?

14. Was the United States not morally bound to protect Chinese interests
against any such agreement?

15. Did the American Commission at Paris urge that a definite sum of
reparations be fixed in the Treaty?

16. Why did this view not prevail?

17. In case the Reparation Commission fixes a sum beyond that which is
just or possible to collect within a reasonable time, is the United States
morally bound to enforce its decision?

1. Senator Hiram W. Johnson, California Republican, in 1912 Roosevelt's running mate on the
Progressive ticket, in 1919 an aspirant to the Republican presidential nomination, was also a
leading "irreconcilable," one of the group of senators opposed to the treaty no matter what res-
ervations the Senate might add. Lippmann at this time was cooperating with Johnson and his
Republican "irreconcilable" associate Senator William Borah of Idaho. Johnson used the questions
Lippmann posed in this letter to Wilson's embarrassment and to the advantage of William C.
Bullitt, who later appeared as a witness hostile to the treaty before the Senate Foreign Relations
Committee. Bullitt's testimony — with its intimate references, especially to Wilson's attitudes
toward the Bolsheviks — created a sensation. He testified partly because Lippmann, declining to
appear before the committee, recommended him in his place. Bullitt in 1919 had been Wilson's
special emissary to Russia, but Wilson had rejected his advice.

To Hiram W. Johnson

August 25, 1919

My dear Senator:
    I was staggered by the President's statement[1] that he had not known of the
secret treaties, and in the next issue of *The New Republic* we shall comment
on the matter. The puzzle is why he should have pretended ignorance when
the fact of ignorance is in itself so discreditable. . . .

1. To the Senate Foreign Relations Committee.

To Hiram W. Johnson

September 9, 1919

My dear Senator Johnson:
    Your letter of August 26 found me lost in the wilds of Cape Cod for a few
days' vacation, and I hope you will forgive the delay in answering it. It seems
to me that the time has passed when anything can be accomplished by anything I might say to the committee, though I appreciate your invitation.
    I believe that the fight is won and that Mr. Wilson, in losing his temper,

has lost his battle. It has been a gallant fight against enormous odds and no man deserves more honor for it than you.

I was for you in 1912 and I am for you now, though I guess you will not have any difficulty in understanding why I cannot be a Republican. I do not know why I should wander off into that, but it is pleasant to be candid with you.

To Thomas L. Chadbourne[1]

September 30, 1919

Dear Mr. Chadbourne:

The idea we discussed last night might be phrased as follows:

"The Conference,[2] recognizing that the conduct of modern industry is beset with unsolved difficulties, especially in the relation of the wage earner to management and capital, hereby renews its faith in the efficacy of American institutions. Consequently it declares that there is no problem of industry which is insoluble by candid negotiation on the basis of facts, impartially and scientifically ascertained. It condemns without reservation any who may decline to submit their theories to the test of conference and investigation. It repudiates class warfare and the action of any one whether he pretends to speak for labor or for capital who endeavors to obtain or to retain advantages by the mere exercise of physical or economic force. It declares that the general public has an equity in every dispute which threatens the peace of the community or the orderly continuance of productive processes, and notes that this equity cannot be protected unless every serious dispute is publicly examined and its issues determined by some process of negotiation, conciliation, or arbitration.

To this end, the Conference appoints a committee of seven which shall after public hearings, report back to it plans for the establishment of the proper agencies of investigation and negotiation. For the guidance of this committee it lays down the following considerations:

A

1. The agency of investigation shall be non-partisan and expert and unrepresentative of either capital or labor.

2. The chief officials shall be selected by the President of the United States from a list of nominations drawn up with recommendations by certain scientific associations, devoted to such professions as engineering, statistics, medicine, and economic research. All minor officials such as field investigators, shall be selected in accordance with the standards agreed upon by these scientific associations.

3. The agency shall be forbidden to pass judgment on the merits of any controversy. Its role is purely the investigation and publication of relevant facts. This shall be understood to include the contentions of the disputants.

4. The President, or someone designated to act for him, shall initiate investigations.

B

1. There shall be a central commission of adjustment.

2. In industries where no machinery of adjustment exists, it shall with the consent of the wage earners and employers establish wherever possible agencies of adjustment.

3. In any dispute, where no machinery of adjustment exists or is effective, the central commission shall establish ad hoc adjustment boards before which all parties concerned shall be invited to appear.

4. Unless otherwise agreed, all adjustment agencies shall accept as final the investigation of a fact as described under A. Their role is primarily adjustment after the facts have been ascertained and the area of dispute defined.

C

1. The Committee shall consider after public hearing the advisability of establishing a permanent national industrial conference composed of delegates from all the principal industries and technical professions where the large problems can be debated, from which recommendations to industries and to public authorities can be made.

2. In all its recommendations the Committee will proceed on the principle that the sanctions to be employed are mainly those of an informed public opinion.

I have gone into more detail than we covered last night, but some of it may be suggestive.

1. Thomas L. Chadbourne, a New York lawyer, had been counselor during the war to the War Trade Board.   2. The White House had called an industrial conference to which both business and labor leaders were invited. It convened October 6, but labor, sensing the hostility of government as well as business, withdrew on October 23. At the time of this letter, Chadbourne was working on the plans for the conference.

To Oliver Wendell Holmes, Jr.

[c. November 18, 1919]

Dear Judge Holmes,

. . . When the *Atlantic Monthly* article came out I was rather timid as to what you would think of it if you happened to see it. It is really a bit of a book on which I've been working intermittently for five years and am no where near the end of. I'm examining how 'public opinion' is made, and am deeply troubled by the effect of the tentative conclusions on our current theories of popular government. You say 'truth is the over ground, etc. etc.' But the difficulty is that in addition to men's natural limitation in apprehending truth about society, there have grown up institutions such as the press, propaganda, and censorship which block the road to truth. At best these institutions put truth second to what they think is morality or patriotism; at worst they are downright liars. How is popular government to exist when 'the ground upon which their wishes' are to be carried out is what it now is. . . .

To Newton D. Baker

January 17, 1920

Dear N.D.B.,

I feel that a letter to you is long overdue. Yet I cannot write a pleasant letter. The events of the last few months are too disturbing and the behavior of the administration too revolutionary not to put a severe strain upon men's patience. I think I can speak for a large number of your warmest and most steadfast friends; I can speak as an affectionate friend who has to the limits of his influence declined to let your name be associated with the wholesale denials of justice and the persistent reaction which has characterized Washington these last months. I believed that the motive which governs your action is a personal loyalty to the president and an unwillingness to add to his burdens while he is ill. For of course no one who knows you and loves you can believe that you approve the course of the Department of Justice and of the Post Office.[1]

You know what hopes were put in this administration, how loudly and insistently it proclaimed its loyalty to the cause of freedom. Well it was possible to fail in those hopes. It was credible that the wisdom and the strength to realize them would be lacking. But it is forever incredible that an administration announcing the most spacious ideals in our history should have done more to endanger fundamental American liberties than any group of men for a hundred years. Not since the time of John Adams has any group of office-holders made so determined and so dangerous an attack upon the constitutional liberties of this country as are embodied in the ferocious sentences for political offenses, in the hysterical deportation without trial of friendless aliens, in the censorship still maintained by Mr. Burleson and in the so-called sedition bill advocated by the Department of Justice. These are dreadful things and they have dreadful consequences. They have instituted a reign of terror in which honest thought is impossible, in which moderation is discountenanced, in which panic supplants reason. It was the solemn duty of this administration to allay fear and restore sanity. It has instead done everything humanly possible to add fresh excitement to an overexcited community.

The most important thing in America today is to quiet this panic and return to government by discussion, and I ask you as your devoted friend what you are doing to assist. I plead with you not to fail us at this time, not by your silence to seem a party to an hysteria which a few years hence will make us ashamed. I know that the panic will pass; already it is clear that people all over America are aware of its brutalities and its absurdities. There will be a reaction against this reaction. I fear it will not be moderate if this madness continues much longer. I am not speaking of revolution. The soil of revolution does not exist in America today. What I am speaking of is a hurricane of demagogy out of a people finally awakened to the meaning of what is now occurring. Only by resolute public opposition to lawlessness masquerading as law on the part of men like yourself can a reckoning be averted.

1. Attorney General A. Mitchell Palmer and Postmaster General Burleson were presiding over some of the most discreditable persecutions in American history. Without semblance of due process, the Justice Department had been raiding the offices of allegedly radical organizations and arresting supposed radicals and aliens guilty often only of strange-sounding surnames. In December 1919, the department arbitrarily deported, on the transport *Buford*, a contingent of radicals including the famous anarchists Alexander Berkman and Emma Goldman. On January 2, 1920, Justice Department agents executed more than thirty raids and took into custody, usually without proper warrants or cause, some 2700 persons, many of them confined to open-air bullpens. Palmer was also asking Congress to make even more stringent the already oppressive Sedition Act of 1918. For his part, Burleson had continued to exercise his wartime authority of censorship through the control of the mails and to resist the not unreasonable demands of workers in the telephone and telegraph industry, of which he temporarily had charge. He then used arbitrary tactics to break their strike.

To Felix Frankfurter

April 7, 1920

Dear Felix:

Very much between ourselves, yesterday I had a telephone call from Hoover to come and see him. I found him in a bewildered state of mind at the political snarl in which he finds himself.[1] He really wants to take only a liberal line, but he does not know how to take hold. He knows that the liberal people and the Progressives generally are slipping away from him and that his statements so far have done nothing to hold them. The only method he knows of stating a Liberal program is in such detail as to be almost useless for campaign purposes. Yet he wants to make a fight that will rally the Progressives. I am going to try to draft a short statement for him, but I think it is very likely that he will call on you pretty soon and I just wanted to give you this warning in case he does so that you would know what was on foot.

I am more and more convinced myself that Hoover is now pocketed because the Republicans have nothing further to fear from him and the Democrats nothing to hope. His only chance, it seems to me, is to be nominated as the alternative to Hiram Johnson and I do not suppose his chances there are particularly good.

House was here last night for dinner. He says Hoover's one chance now is to bolt the Republican party, if they nominate a reactionary, in such a way as to make himself the inevitable choice of the Democrats three weeks later. What do you think of that?

Please keep this entirely under your own hat.

1. Hoover had had considerable support as a presidential candidate among progressive members of both major parties. For months he had dallied, unable to decide on a course of action and unwilling to declare his affiliation, until shortly before the date of this letter when he said he was a Republican. By that time, other candidates — Leonard Wood, Johnson, Governor Frank O. Lowden of Illinois, and Senator Warren G. Harding of Ohio — had among them almost all of the delegates.

To C. P. Scott

June 30, 1920

Dear Mr. Scott:

. . . I won't attempt to say anything in this letter about the Presidential campaign because we are still in doubt as to who is to be nominated by the Democrats.[1] But I am strongly of the opinion that if McAdoo is nominated he has better than an even chance to be elected. I should expect also to see very interesting developments of differences between the Democrats and the Republicans in the course of the summer on the subject of foreign policy and possibly also on the subject of foreign trade policy.

You can believe me when I say that McAdoo is the most interesting of all the personalities in the field — brilliant in genius, liberal but without a sound intellectual equipment and with a slight untrustworthiness. He is by all odds the keenest politician in America today.

1. The Republicans, during a convention marked by the most renowned of "smoke-filled rooms," had nominated Warren G. Harding and, for vice president, Governor Calvin Coolidge of Massachusetts. The Democrats faced a controversial convention in which the delegates were too divided to provide the necessary two-thirds' vote to either of the leading candidates, William G. McAdoo or A. Mitchell Palmer. They settled in the end on Governor James M. Cox of Ohio, a "wet," a moderate, and a man wholly without affiliation with the Wilson administration. As his running mate, they selected a young acquaintance of Lippmann's, Assistant Secretary of the Navy Franklin D. Roosevelt of New York. Harding won by a landslide.

To Albert G. Dieffenbach [1]

July 12, 1920

Dear Dr. Dieffenbach:

. . . I am fully in agreement with your statement that society has the right to intervene and compel the settlement of differences when there is a failure to agree in vital industries, but I should like to suggest two important additions, which seem to me necessary before that idea can be accepted as a working principle. The first is that the intervention of Government in so far as it limits the right to strike must carry with it a control of property. You are familiar with the argument that a soldier has no right to strike because he is not working for a private employer. That distinction is fundamental and should be put at the head of any proposal to limit the right to strike. In other words, society has the right to prevent strikes when the business is the business of society but when it is not, when it is a private business that merely serves society incidentally it is neither feasible nor just to limit the collective power of the workers. . . .

It is my own private hobby that the most fundamental thing in making a government democratic is the purification of the news. That is a task eminently suited to the work of the churches. We suffer today more than anything else from the inability of the public to secure the necessary information on which to act in great affairs. The newspapers require criticism and assistance from outside organizations if they are to reform and improve their practice and there is no greater work that a church could undertake than to become again a witness to the truth. . . .

1. Albert G. Dieffenbach, contributor to the *Christian Register*; one-time pastor of the First Unitarian Church in Hartford, Connecticut; celebrant of the YMCA and its work during the war; popular public lecturer.

To Newton D. Baker

July 14, 1920

Dear N.D.B.:

. . . I do not seem to be able to focus the political alignment at all. The situation of the Democrats seems to me more puzzling than any I have known, but one thing seems to me fairly certain in the matter, namely, that a defensive campaign by the Democrats cannot be a successful one. In spite of the fact that the Republicans are in opposition, they have a head start which can be cut down only by aggressive political tactics. I have never met Cox, but what I have seen of his speeches leaves me with the impression that he is effervescent rather than a man of disciplined ideas. I hope this is wrong because of course I can't vote Republican and I don't want to vote pure protest. . . .

To S. K. Ratcliffe

August 10, 1920

Dear S. K.:

. . . This is the dullest political campaign on record. Two provincial, ignorant politicians entirely surrounded by special interest, operating in a political vacuum. Nobody cares who is elected. Nobody believes in anything. Nobody wants anything very badly that he thinks he can get out of politics. If the thing keeps on, *The New Republic* will have to transform itself into a fashion journal. I sometimes think that the terrific morale we developed during the war exhausted the public spirit of this country for a generation and that no-body will be enthusiastic about anything until a generation grows up that has forgotten how violent we were and how unreasonable. But I don't promise to think that a week from now. . . .

To Graham Wallas   HANDWRITTEN

August 31, 1920

Dear G. W.:

. . . The period of hysteria which you saw last winter is definitely over. It has been followed by a profound apathy. I can remember no time when the level of political discussion was so low. If it is possible to speak of "the mind of the people" then it is fair to say the American mind has temporarily lost all interest in public questions. . . .

To Graham Wallas

November 4, 1920

Dear G. W.:

. . . I am glad to say the election is over. It has been a peculiarly negative thing and Harding is elected not because anybody likes him particularly, or because the Republican party is particularly popular, but because the Demo-crats are inconceivably unpopular. They are swept out of office by general irritation, irritation at what's good in their record. The immense women's vote emphasized the result but did not affect it.[1] Unless one is prepared to regard the election as the final twitch of the war mind (that is the way I regard it), there would be cause for profound discouragement with universal suffrage. No real issue ever obtruded itself into the campaign except to be distorted beyond recognition. . . .

1. Following the ratification of the Nineteenth Amendment in August, American women in No-vember for the first time had the right in all states to vote in a presidential election.

II

Voice of the World

1921–1929

To C. P. Scott

March 2, 1921

Dear Mr. Scott:

. . . You know, of course, that when Harding was nominated, it meant that the politicians and the special interests against whom Roosevelt's and Wilson's careers had been a protest, came back into power. The men who selected Harding are the same individuals who controlled the Republican organization at the end of the 19th century. In domestic affairs they are high protectionists, anti-union and favor the unregulated exploitation of natural resources. In foreign affairs they are somewhat aggressively imperialistic towards the Caribbean nations and instinctively adverse towards any policy which would submit what they call a vital interest to international judgment. However, for a time after election, in view of the amazing plurality which Harding had (a plurality which was, as you know, negatively against Wilson, and not positively for him) there were many indications that the needs and the ideas of modern life were making some impression upon him. But the Cabinet, which he has selected, pretty effectively dispels that hope.

To be sure, Mr. Hoover and Mr. Hughes are in it,[1] but it would probably be more accurate to say that they are on the fringes of it. The real cabinet, the men who are close to Harding, are Fall, Secretary of the Interior, Daugherty, Attorney General, Will Hays, Postmaster General. And there is no conflict at all between them and Mellon, Secretary of the Treasury who is an appointee from Pennsylvania of Roosevelt's great enemy Penrose, Denby of Michigan who has a bad record, and Weeks of Massachusetts who is an extremely conservative politician banker.[2] According to the beliefs of the Harding people, foreign affairs are to play an exceedingly minor role in the next four years. Within those limits, Mr. Hughes may have a fairly free hand in the final array of American relations to Europe. But unless there is a radical change of values, he will not ask the intentions of the Harding administration. Hoover, they expect, will occupy himself with constructive projects for the development of trade and for the more economical use of commercial facilities.

1. Charles Evans Hughes was to be secretary of state, and Herbert Hoover secretary of commerce in Harding's Cabinet.   2. The balance of the Cabinet consisted of the able but rigidly conservative Andrew W. Mellon as secretary of the treasury and an otherwise mediocre, and in some cases corrupt, contingent: Albert B. Fall (Interior) and Harry M. Daugherty (Justice), both dishonest; and Will Hays (Post Office), Edwin Denby (Navy); and John W. Weeks (War Department).

To Felix Frankfurter   HANDWRITTEN

May 4, 1921

Dear Felix,

   . . . I have now heard Weizmann tell his story three times, and I've read what you sent me as well as the printed memo, the question interests me enormously, and I believe it to be a very far reaching one. The point is, I believe, a problem in loyalties. He and his crowd are all Zionist — 100% is his phrase — while you and I can never be. I never realized Jewish national-ism so acutely before. In Weizmann you get Clemenceau and Paderewski and Henry Cabot Lodge. . . . You and Brandeis . . . are to Weizmann what the NR was to the Tribune. You don't fit into his scheme of life, but damn it, you seem to have the money. And all this is compounded by the fact that any American view matches badly with continental nationalism. . . . We're me-diators, interveners, meddlers, or saviors, as the case may be, but never allies, or a 'united front'. . . . But then that's my skepticism about the whole busi-ness which has kept me from joining up wholeheartedly. . . .[1]

1. Frankfurter, a spokesman of the dominant branch of the Zionist movement in the United States, was then at odds with Chaim Weizmann, the most prominent spokesman of British and European Zionists. Lippmann, never an advocate of either position, soon became an ordinarily silent but unbudging anti-Zionist, as he remained the rest of his life.

To Felix Frankfurter   HANDWRITTEN

June 24, 1921

Dear Felix,

   I wonder whether you will be much surprised to know that I've decided to quit the NR and go on to the World January 1 next.[1] I don't think you will be . . . I see now that my effective influence on the NR is over. It has really been over for two years.

   Herbert and I no longer learn from each other, and for two years our intellectual relationship has been a good natured accomodation rather than an interesting adventure. We've done our work together, and it's just as well to recognize it . . . I am not essential to the present NR because the NR, a good 70% of it, is in tone, selection and emphasis, not the paper I want to make it. My influence is positive only in my articles, entirely negative otherwise. . . .

Among the sub reasons for going is, of course, FH.[2] One's feeling that it takes all sorts of people to make a world is allright where the density of population is two per sq. mile, but in a flat for life it breaks down. He has made the intellectual tone steadily more uncharitable, more querulous, more rasping. He has taken the department which deals with the freer life of the mind and made it more factious than the political part. I can't remember a time recently . . . when the tone of the literary criticism (which is criticism of life) has not risen above muckraking, has given anyone to feel that the pursuit of beauty, or pleasure, or truth was a genuine passion, not entirely accounted for by Veblen and Co.[3] Oh, I could say more, for I've repressed much. But I'll not need to say anything now. . . .

1. Lippmann had agreed to become assistant director of the editorial page of the *New York World* under Frank Cobb, whom he justly admired, as he also did the newspaper itself, a Democratic daily then at the peak of its reputation for the discernment and independence of its editorial page and columns. **2.** Francis Hackett, review editor since the founding of the journal. **3.** Thorstein Veblen — the notable American sociologist, economist, and social critic — and others of similar mind.

To Ray Stannard Baker

HANDWRITTEN

January 2, 1922

Dear Ray,

Arthur Sweetser[1] was at my house last night, and we were talking over the immensely important job you have in hand.[2] Naturally we got on to the subject of the secret treaties, and he said that you were taking at its face value what Mr. Wilson said at the Senatorial conference and what Mr. Lansing said in his testimony.

This seems to me a profound mistake, so great a mistake that it may cast doubt on the whole work, and I should hate to see that happen.

I know of my own knowledge that those two statements cannot be true, and I want to tell you how I know it. I'll write quite frankly, but entirely as a friend for your own information on the understanding that you will consult me before you make any inquiries that involve me. Naturally, I don't want to get into a controversy about anyone's veracity, and yet the question of the secret treaties goes to the heart of the Paris business.

1. In 1917 there existed three important secret engagements — the Italian, the Franco-Russian covering the Saar etc., the Turkish ones. Col. House attended an Inter-Allied conference in October 1917. At that time Kerensky was

on his last legs, and it was believed that a statement of war aims might save him. House tried to secure one in Paris, failed because of the secret treaties, and returned to America in December. He told me this. Shortly before Christmas he returned from Washington and asked Mezes, Miller, and me to prepare an outline of terms of peace. With the assistance of Bowman and the Inquiry staff this was done. The material included maps and memoranda of many points involved in the secret treaties. This material the President and Col. House used in preparing the 14 pts. Two of these points show unmistakably a knowledge of the secret treaties — the one on France & the one on Italy. They would never have been phrased just as they were phrased unless the terms of the treaties had been under consideration. It would have been criminal negligence not to consider them.

2. If you look at the addresses in 1918, especially that of Sept. 27, you will find frequent references to secret engagements. The Allied engagements were common talk at the time among the President's friends.

3. I know, as a matter of fact, that Lansing in the spring of 1918 (I think it was June) knew about the Japanese agreement in the Pacific, because Mezes, Miller, and I talked about it at the Inquiry office in the light of a map of the treaty which we had prepared.

4. At the end of October 1918 I prepared a memorandum for Col. House on the 14 pts. which he cabled to the President, which was approved, and used by him as the basis of his discussion with the Allied Premiers which preceded the armistice agreement. The aims of the secret treaties (except the Japanese which did not enter) are there assumed, and the divergence between them & the 14 pts. stressed. The actual words are not used, because the memorandum was intended to be read, but the intention is and was clear in the context. I still have a copy of that memorandum.

I wish you would go into the matter carefully. On the question of whether the President did or did not know about the treaties a very great deal depends. From the point of view of the historian failure to know about them will cast doubt upon his competence as a diplomat. If it should be believed that he did not know about the treaties, but became famous for a diplomatic program that could never have been constructed without that knowledge, the whole business will be absurd.

As a matter of fact I have not the slightest doubt that the President did know about them, that Mr. Lansing knew about them, that Col. House knew about them, that the whole Inquiry knew about them. — Please forgive the letter. It is prompted by warm personal regards.

1. Arthur Sweetser, journalist and war correspondent, assistant director of the press section of the American Commission to Negotiate Peace, member of the information section of the League of Nations, 1918–42, later president of the Woodrow Wilson Foundation. 2. With Wilson's authorization, Baker was writing his *Woodrow Wilson and World Settlement*, 3 v. (Garden City, 1922). He was then to go on to spend most of the rest of his life on the editing (with William E. Dodd) of *The Public Papers of Woodrow Wilson*, 6 v. (Garden City, 1925–27), and the biography *Woodrow Wilson, Life and Letters*, 8 v. (Garden City, 1927–39).

To H. L. Mencken[1]

February 8, 1922

Dear Mencken:

The letter you wrote me reached me here yesterday. I was glad to hear from you. You felt very badly on December 26th about the conference. I wonder if you still do.[2] I think it did extremely well, and I don't think Hughes surrendered anything important that he could have kept without fighting, and I doubt whether he could have kept it with fighting.[3] Until the Chinese pull themselves together Japan will have things her own way, and no one over here is going out into Asia to stop her. . . .

1. H. L. Mencken, the incomparable iconoclast of the 1920s and later a notable lexicographer of the American language, was at this time an editor of *Vanity Fair*, a monthly of the arts to which Lippmann had begun to contribute a column. 2. The Washington Conference had just adjourned. There, after a persuasive opening address by Secretary of State Hughes, the delegates of the participating nations had turned seriously to the negotiation of a set of treaties for naval disarmament and related political issues in the Pacific region. Of those treaties, one restricted submarines to the conventional rules of naval warfare; in another Japan agreed to return Kiaochow and the Shantung peninsula to China; in still another Japan gave the United States cable rights on the island of Yap, which opponents of the League of Nations and Treaty of Versailles had sought. The most important treaties, all of which the Senate later ratified, were a nine-power treaty guaranteeing China's independence and territorial integrity and restating the principle of the Open Door (equal commercial opportunity for all foreign powers there); a five-power naval disarmament treaty among the United States, Great Britain, Japan, France, and Italy, which provided for a ten-year moratorium in the building of capital ships and established a ratio among the signatories for capital ships of 5:5:3:1.67:1.67; and a four-power treaty in which the United States, Great Britain, France, and Japan agreed to respect one another's rights in the Pacific and to consult in the case of an "aggressive action" there. The five-power treaty, as Hughes had intended, led the United States, Great Britain, and Japan to scrap considerable tonnage built or being built. 3. Characteristically, Lippmann on the same day wrote Hughes a brief letter of warm congratulations.

To John M. Avent[1]

May 18, 1922

Dear Mr. Avent:

When you asked me the other day to put on paper ideas about the teaching of English in New York public schools, you were aware, of course, how great are my disqualifications. I do not know how English is actually taught today, except as I have had some chance to talk to children who were being taught. Nothing I shall say, therefore, is meant as direct criticism, and I shall have few if any practical suggestions to offer. I shall confine myself to sketching the problem as it presents itself to me.

My impression is that the canons of English teaching were formed in an environment very unlike that which now exists in New York City. They assume that the pupil studies English in order to discipline, refine, and enrich his native speech. They assume that he already possesses the idiom of the language, and that at home and at play he is in contact with the living sources of English. But, of course, for a very large part of the school children of New York such an assumption is untrue. The speech which they learn at home is a second hand and acquired English. It is a language learned by their parents rather late in life, if they have learned it at all, and it is a language learned hastily and wholly for the purpose of a quick adjustment to immigrant conditions. This urban immigrant dialect is a kind of convenient sign language rather than an expression of personality and experience. It tends to abstraction and not to imagery. Its rhythms and its idiom draw upon no folklore and no folkways, but instead upon the standardized language of newspapers and advertisements. You cannot assume in New York City, therefore, as you might still assume in the country districts or in England, that from outside of school the sap of native English flows through the pupil's mind.

Lacking the sense of language, acquiring the language learned by his parents to express their immediate wants rather than their whole sense of life, the child comes to you with a pitiably insignificant fund of words. His words are so colorless and meager that in the attempt to express himself, the modern city child uses the same words so often and in so many different meanings that at last his speech is a series of ejaculations. Everything is a "thing." "Things" are grand, swell, awful, nice, terrible, pretty, interspersed with "you know what I mean" and "do you get me." It is not a language that describes and communicates experience in a world of shapes and colors and movement, but a language of seeking and demanding and giving and refusing accompanied by exclamations of approval and disapproval.

But experience that can't be described and communicated in words cannot long be vividly remembered. For words more than any other medium prolong experience in consciousness. And then because experience can't be expressed and can't be remembered it soon ceases to be noticed. That is one reason, I think, why in a modern city like New York the enduring interests of the race seem so neglected. When you have looked at the stars once and remarked that they are grand, and then again only in order to say that the heavens are swell, why not look at the Wrigley chewing gum sign on Broadway which is equally grand and equally swell? Without words to give precision to ideas the ideas themselves soon become indistinguishable. If you go through life as so many city people do, knowing objects only by the general species to which they belong, the individuality on which all true judgment and all genuine appreciation depend is soon lost.

The Book of Genesis is wise in these matters. You will remember that the Lord's first act after the creation, even before He made Eve, was to bring every living creature to Adam "to see what he would call them." But if you ask an ordinary movie audience in New York City to tell you the names of natural objects, you know what the response would be. How many stars could they recognize and name? How many plants? How many trees, how many animals, how many parts of their own bodies? You find, I think, that the purely urban person has almost no sense of and no words for the main activities by which he is fed, clothed, housed, transported, or even amused. The whole cycle of the seasons and the weather, of ploughing and sowing and reaping, of carrying to market and distributing is a blur in his mind. Unless he happens to be in a certain trade he is shut out of the very rich and expressive language of labor, of shipbuilding, and carpentry, and plumbing, and tailoring, and cooking. The names of tools, the names of structural parts, the names of different sorts of joining and cutting and welding are mysterious to him. You search his mind in vain for the sharp aspects of real perceptions. The substances with which his imagination can work are impoverished.

Yet the business of living in what Graham Wallas calls the Great Society is an even greater tax on the imagination. For the bulk of public questions deal with matters that are out of sight, and have, therefore, to be imagined. These questions are reported to us in the thin and colorless language of the newspapers. We read this language, and unless we read it with a mind stored with concrete images, we can come to no true realization of what it all means. How can you hope, for example, to find a sound public opinion in New York City about the farmer's politics if the whole circumstance of the farmer's life is hidden and unconceived? Yet that is just the difficulty we are facing every day.

As you know I have no belief that this underlying problem of our civilization — the problem of enabling men to master an unseen environment — is soluble without a very great development of our machinery of accounting, analysis, record, and reporting. I have dealt with that elsewhere at some length. But nothing is more certain than that the teaching of English in the public schools is a critical factor in the whole affair.

On the teachers of English our society depends for the formation of habits of speech, which are in reality habits of thought, that will equip the modern citizen to give precision to experience by naming it. Our social life depends on the presence of enough people who can tell different things apart and discern identities where they exist. It depends, therefore, on people who use words without confusion as to their meaning, to whom the name of this and that is the name of this and that, and not of half a dozen vaguely related things as well. It depends on people, who in language at least, are what the Medieval schoolmen called Nominalists, on people who do not mistake general terms for objective facts, on people who can penetrate phrases like Bolshevism, socialism, democracy, liberalism, radicalism, Americanism, and can arrive at candid vivid understanding of the particular persons, acts, hopes, fears that these omnibus words are supposed to cover.

A large order, but to be a teacher in a republic is in itself a large order. An easy and inconsequential life is after all a dull one. But to teach English in a community like ours is to be dealing every day with the main instrument of civilized living. To give that instrument edge and point and temper is a sacred task.

1. John M. Avent, then the principal of Curtis High School on Staten Island, New York City.

To Arthur N. Holcombe[1]

June 14, 1922

Dear Arthur:

I was delighted with your generous review[2] and your letter. I wish we might talk political theory, because every day in doing editorial work I run into the difficulty of making the concepts one may take for granted fit.

Of course I know about the Jewish problem at Harvard only at second hand, though I've had a chance to go hastily over the statistics that the Dean's office collected for Judge Mack. Naturally I resented the way in which the proposal was made and many of the reasons that were given; and of course I felt that for Harvard to give its sanction to a policy of discrimination was an abandonment of its best tradition. And also from a national point of view the beginning of a descent into Austro-Hungarian conditions.

At the same time I recognize frankly that assimilation is a matter of proportion and that it would be bad for the immigrant Jews as well as for Harvard if there were too great a concentration. What the answer is I am not prepared to say. America has accepted a vast alien population and it cannot shirk the necessity of educating that population. It may be necessary in Massachusetts to establish a state university, and something can be done, I think, under Jewish leadership to persuade Jewish boys to scatter.

That's all I have in mind at the moment.

1. Arthur N. Holcombe, a professor in the Government Department at Harvard, had asked Lippmann for his opinion about the imposition of a quota for the admission of Jews at Harvard. President A. Lawrence Lowell, reversing his predecessor's policy, had supported such a quota, which the faculty at first accepted before reversing itself and referring the issue to a committee. 2. Of *Public Opinion* (New York, 1922).

To Lawrence J. Henderson[1]

HANDWRITTEN

October 27, 1922[2]

Dear Mr. Henderson,

As a result of our talk and of your kind suggestion that we pursue it further, I feel impelled to write for you a statement of my views on the Jewish question at Harvard. I shall be glad if you will present this letter to the investigating committee.

I am fully prepared to accept the judgment of the Harvard authorities that a concentration of Jews in excess of fifteen percent will produce a segregation of cultures rather than a fusion. Fifteen percent is, of course, an arbitrary figure, but it is, I believe, sufficiently in accord with historic experience to be acceptable as a basis for the consideration of this question. I am not disposed to invoke any general principle in order to deny what seems to me one of the distinct lessons of human experience. Nor am I disposed to translate this conclusion into any sort of moral judgment. I do not regard Jews as innocent victims. They hand on unconsciously and uncritically from one generation to another many distressing personal and social habits, which were selected by a bitter history and intensified by a Pharisaical theology.

As long as the Jew insisted with tribal mysticism upon tribal inbreeding, and as long as he lived in countries where legal disabilities confined him to a ghetto, the formation of new social habits was virtually impossible. Radically new habits could be formed only, as I conceive it, when Jewish racial mysticism rationalized by Jewish Theological exclusiveness would (in a country where there is no legal discrimination) break down under the impact of modern criticism and science. This breakdown has occurred in America for the first time on a large scale in the history of the Jewish people.

The breakdown has brought with it naturally a certain moral anarchy owing to the fact that in the break up of a tradition the good and the bad elements of the tradition are so entangled that they break down together. The consequence is to be seen in the ostentatious use of new wealth and in excessive protestantism of feeling and ideas. New traditions arise more slowly than the old ones break down. The interregnum would be shorter and easier if a satisfactory tradition existed for men to accept. But of course the older American political and religious tradition is also in flux.

When, therefore, a large number of Jews are concentrated in a university like Harvard, two groups confront each other neither of which has any very deep attachment to the ideas it professes. You get not a spiritual conflict in which there might be first argument, then understanding, and finally perhaps conversion, but a conflict of manners and appearances inspired more by irritation than by conviction. In this conflict my sympathies are with the non-Jew. His personal manners and physical habits are, I believe, distinctly superior to the prevailing manners and habits of the Jews. And I believe, also, that since the basis of Jewish exclusiveness is broken, the Jews as they become more settled will assimilate these habits and will lose their racial identity.

I believe this will happen and that no Zionism (as distinct from Palestinianism) can really prevent it. I have known too many American Zionists to have any real doubt on this point. Their Zionism, though they deny it, is hollow, is without that core of conviction which the Zionists of Eastern Europe share with any other nationalism of that unhappy region. The Zionism of the older Americans is a burden they have shouldered out of a sense of noblesse oblige, and it differs not at all in quality and very little in degree from the sympathy which most of us felt for the Armenian Christian. The East European Zionists know this perfectly well. They know that Jews who have lived here two or more generations are not themselves Zionists. They are merely, and only in some cases at that, pro-Zionist in fundamentally the same spirit as Lord Balfour and Mr. Wilson are pro-Zionist.[3] The Zionists have, therefore, rejected the leadership of these American sympathizers, and have concentrated the leadership in East European hands.

Zionism in America is, I am convinced, a romantic lost cause, a good deal like Jacobinism in England or Orleanism in France. The racial identity of the Jews in America is rapidly ceasing to have any meaning, because neither Jewish history nor Jewish theology can offer a culture that is sufficiently interesting to bind the Jews together into a spiritual community. They will not go to the rabbis for their beliefs, and therefore, in the long run they will not go to the Jewish elders for their marriage certificates.

I believe this to be the destined course of events. But there are many non-Jews and many Jews who would deny it. There will be some who say that the Jewish race is bound to remain a distinct phenomenon and some who say that it should remain distinct. I disagree with both views, both as to the fact and as to the desirability, and I should insist that the experience of the past under profoundly different social conditions is no prophecy as to the future. Only future experience will reveal whether the separatists or the fusionists are right. But, as I conceive it, we should make every effort to remove the superficial obstacles to fusion. We should not, if we can help it, allow uncouth manners to produce a forced segregation. We should favor every device which will remove these social barriers, not only because this will make life a good deal pleasanter, but because only then will there be a true test of the claim that there is some peculiar and imperishable Jewish ethos. If it exists, I myself do not know what it is, and I strongly believe that under conditions favorable to fusion it would have no binding quality.

The kind of reeducation of social attitudes which will make fusion possible can be assisted greatly by the schools and colleges. But it is outside the class room that the main process of reeducation must take place in both Jews and non-Jews, and indeed in all the newer immigrants and the older settlers. It can take place only by contact and cooperation, by working for the same specific objects and sharing the same difficulties. But much contact depends on dilution, so that the two groups shall not confront each other as corporate entities. The smaller crowd must be dispersed so that the members may mingle as individuals in the larger crowd. At worst they will only be exchanging a smaller gregariousness for a larger. At best, I believe, they will become more individualized by living in this more catholic environment.

Believing in dilution I am heartily in accord with the premise of those at Harvard who desire to effect a more even dispersion of the Jews, and of any other minority that brings with it some striking cultural peculiarity. I think this is a sound premise, not only for Harvard, but for America. There are many Americans of Jewish and non-Jewish stock who do not wish to deal with this premise, because they realize the terrible consequences which may follow from it. They realize that almost any program deduced from this premise is more likely than not to intensify the evil it sets out to cure. The very argument that fusion depends on dilution can be turned by the slightest sophistry into a policy of exclusion which would emphasize segregation, and would therefore, defeat fusion. The chance of such a corrupting sophistry are enormous. The subject is one in which objectivity of mind and purity of motive have to be fought for at every step; it is a subject which easily evokes our least civilized impulses.

Therefore, every step in deducing a step from this premise must be judged not merely as a means to the end you desire, but also as the means to ends you do not desire. You are not experimenting in your laboratory, and you cannot when you choose wipe the slate clean for a new experiment if the first experiment was a mistake. You are dealing with a cumulative process in which slight causes can produce profound effects, in which every mistake you make alters the conditions under which you make your next move.

You are not dealing with a problem which can be solved within the boundaries of the University. You are practicing with a gun whose range is so much greater than Harvard Yard that you must be careful not to drop high explosive shells throughout the land. You have already dropped a few shells in places you never meant to hit, with about the same degree of responsibility and accuracy as the young second lieutenant who the other day dropped his practice shells on Mrs. McCormick's front lawn.

I refer to the episodes of last spring, when Harvard presented the spectacle of a band of scholars who voted first and began to investigate afterwards. That first hasty vote, admittedly taken without adequate facts, and its equally hasty retraction under what may have been a twinge of the scientific conscience or fear of the newspapers and the politicians on Beacon Hill, Harvard made a mistake which in my judgment has now become a major premise in the succeeding argument. For Harvard by its panicky procedure has come very close to squandering its greatest, and for the purposes of this problem, its most useful inheritance. I mean its reputation for unprejudiced thinking towards liberal ends.

I assure you that you cannot easily exaggerate this loss of prestige, nor the importance of trying to recover it. Until Harvard has regained in public confidence the ground it has lost, the authority of almost any decision you come to will be tainted. Any formula looking towards limitation will be regarded as prejudiced. Any refusal to limit will be ascribed to fear. These feelings will persist even with people who may agree with your decisions. Something inestimable and precious, the quality of clear confidence, you cannot count upon just now.

You asked me to believe that the muddle of last spring was due, except in certain instances, not to moral corruption but to stupidity. Those were your words. I believe you. But the people of this country have never conceived the possibility of Harvard's acting stupidly. They are quite too ready to believe that Harvard might act snobbishly, but stupidity and Harvard are not associated in their minds. They think Harvard, whatever else it may be, is the beau ideal of intelligence, and they take it for granted, therefore, that any action taken by Harvard in a matter of such delicacy must be the result of the most careful inquiry.

And since it is the result of careful inquiry by the highest scholarship this country possesses, Harvard's decision is a model to them. Not only your premise, but every general principle you found upon it, and every administrative device you may elect becomes as a result of Harvard's dominant intellectual position a pattern for the country. When Harvard acts, Harvard is teaching, teaching to more consequence than in any lecture room.

You cannot escape that, and therefore your problem is how to recover confidence in your purposes without destroying confidence in your intellectual leadership. For in stating that stupidity rather than corruption was the cause of last spring's performance you posed this dilemma.

It may not be possible to extricate Harvard easily and quickly. But I think you will agree that it must be done, and I know that many Harvard men believe it must be done before any positive action can be taken by Harvard without great damage to those very Harvard traditions which are most worth preserving. I think you will agree with me at least to a certain extent, if not on the ground I have stated, then on the ground that you, as a member of the investigating committee, have not yet mustered the facts on which positive action could be based.

You have seen a great many people and collected a great many opinions. But you confessed that on certain fundamental aspects of the problem, you had only impressions. The aspects I refer to chiefly are those which would enable you to judge the concrete effect of any administrative device. You did not know what results intelligence tests honestly administered would give. You did not know what results any selective test would give. I take it, therefore, that as a man of science you are not prepared to take positive action. If you did you would simply be repeating in more aggravated form the very stupidity you yourself condemned.

But nevertheless, you will have to make some kind of report, and I am, therefore, taking the liberty of making a suggestion which in my judgment deals with every important element in the problem, except one which I shall discuss later, and deals with it in a way which will be worthy of Harvard.

I believe that the committee should declare first that among the citizens of this country it will countenance no test of admission based on race, creed, color, class, or section.

I believe it should, then, declare that it proposes to seek a test of all individuals applying to Harvard for admission which will select those who, whatever their cultural and social background, are most teachable and adaptable. I believe the committee should declare that there is at Harvard today too high a proportion of men whose attitudes and habits are so set that they do not yield to the wider educational influences which Harvard is able to exert. Finally, it should declare that it proposes to consider for two years what tests would select its classes more successfully.

In looking for such a test I believe you should choose as an hypothesis the theory which you explained to me. That theory is this: the men who seek admission to college are in themselves a selected group in their communities. The community in the midst of which Harvard is situated contains a larger proportion of newer immigrants than does the nation as a whole. Therefore, it follows, since there are no appreciable differences by race in native intelligence, that among the applicants at Harvard, the newer immigrants constitute a larger proportion of candidates than they would if immigration had not concentrated them so heavily on the Northeastern Seaboard. Among these newer immigrants, the Jews constitute a large majority of those applying.

It is probable, therefore, that Harvard receives a greater variety of Jews, with a greater admission of the less able ones, than she would if the Jews were more scattered. You believe this, and I think it is a plausible hypothesis. You agree with me that on this hypothesis, a raising of the passing work of entrance examinations would automatically cut off a larger percentage of Jews than of non-Jews.

That would be a form of selection wholly without offense to the Jewish people. Its effect would be, assuming always that your analysis is correct, to reduce the total enrollment at Harvard as well as the percentage enrollment of Jews. Assuming that your entrance examinations are good tests or that they can be made good tests, you would get a college population of higher general capacity, and more capable therefore of responding to the idea that this is a heterogeneous democracy in which tolerance and understanding are among the first of the virtues.

This is to be sure only an hypothesis, and I do not recommend its adoption now. There is, I understand no dire emergency requiring the adoption of any positive plan. I do urge you to make a study of this hypothesis with the candidates for admission who apply at the end of this college year. I suggest that you proceed somewhat in this fashion, though through ignorance of the present system of marking I am compelled to invent an illustration. Suppose the passing mark now is 50 on a scale of 100. Take all the examination papers and see what kind of freshmen class you would get by raising the passing mark to 60 and to 70. Then for two years keep really accurate personal histories of your new men, and especially of those who fall between 50 and 70. Then you might reopen the discussion if it still seems necessary to do so. In the interval, time will heal some of the bitterness which the precipitate action of last spring produced, and the Jewish leaders themselves can be induced, I hope, to establish scholarships for Jews of the Boston district which will take some part of them to western colleges.

You raised one objection to this plan. If I misstate it, I wish you would correct me. It was that a higher standard of admission would deprive many boys, destined to be business and social leaders, of a Harvard education. That is true. The whole agitation in the first instance is based on the proposal to deprive some boys of a Harvard education. The only question is whether you will deprive them of it because they are Jews or because they are less likely to make the most of what Harvard has to offer.

If you deprive them of a Harvard education because they are Jews and not because they cannot make the grade then I regret to say Harvard will have ceased to be a public institution.

I am compelled to say, too, that on this point in our discussion, you seemed to me to be suffering from a great deal of confusion as to the function of Harvard. You said that so far as you knew there was no limit to the number of students Harvard could handle, and you argued also that a Harvard education should be extended to as many as possible. I think this is a mistake. Harvard cannot directly educate the whole country, and its influence is not determined by the number of men who pass through Harvard. Its influence is determined by the strength of the influence it can exert. It cannot exert its proper influence in indefinite wholesale quantities. Its problem is to find the sort and number of men it can most fully educate, and I feel sure that number is less than the present college enrollment. Any other conception of Harvard seems to me to be infected with commercialism and the American vice of confusing bigness with excellence.

I hope you will pardon the unavoidable length of this letter. It is one of the incidental penalties inflicted upon you as a public personage.

1. Lawrence J. Henderson, a member of the Harvard committee on the admission of Jews, professor of medicine, eminent physiologist, and emerging social theorist of distinction. 2. The actual date of this letter is uncertain; I have concurred here with Ronald Steel, as I do also in his comment that there is no proof the letter was ever sent; see Introduction, pp. xv–xvi; and also see Steel, *Walter Lippmann and the American Century* (Boston, 1980), p. 613, n. 13 to ch. 15. 3. Wilson had agreed to a British mandate over Palestine, a mandate that took for granted the declaration issued for the British government by (Arthur James) Lord Balfour on November 2, 1917. That declaration stated that Great Britain favored "the establishment in Palestine of a national home for the Jewish people and will use their best endeavors to facilitate the achievement of that object, it being clearly understood that nothing shall be done which may prejudice the civil and religious rights of existing non-Jewish communities in Palestine." The closing observation about Arab rights, as well as the mandate itself, suggested that the Zionist objective of a fully independent Jewish State lay well in the future.

To Alfred E. Zimmern

November 8, 1922

Dear Alfred:

. . . Yesterday's election is, of course, no sign of enthusiasm for the Democratic Party.[1] But it is a sign of an inarticulate but violent reaction against the extreme conservatism of Harding. It is fair to interpret it as a liberal omen in domestic affairs but I don't believe it has any particular international significance. Foreign politics, so far as I can learn, played no part in the result. . . .

1. The Democrats gained seats in both houses of Congress, notably in the West, where farmers were discontented and commodity prices remained low, as they had been for several years.

To Thomas W. Lamont[1]

July 20, 1923

My dear Lamont:

Thank you for your letter. The only point at which I should differ at all would be in the feeling that a signatory of the Treaty was morally bound not to invoke the League in order to amend the Treaty against the wishes of the other signatories. It has always seemed to me that Great Britain, after she had come to disbelieve in parts of the Treaty,[2] was in an extremely awkward moral position when it came to suggesting revision. But, of course, the League is now more than ever the one real ultimate hope of improvement.

1. Thomas W. Lamont, a senior partner in the house of Morgan, was one of Lippmann's several friends in that rich and powerful group, and more and more often a social companion. 2. In 1922 the British and the French had been at odds over the question of a moratorium on German reparations, which Britain favored but France opposed except on conditions including appropriation of much of the capital of the German dyestuffs industry in the Rhineland, which Britain in turn opposed. In January 1923, the British refused to take part in a Franco-Belgian occupation of the Ruhr, an occupation made with the claim that Germany had failed to sustain reparations payments. England declared that the occupation was not sanctioned by the Versailles Treaty. Germans in the Ruhr commenced the practice of passive resistance, which damaged Belgian and French economic objectives, though probably less than did the soaring inflation in Germany — inflation already calamitous at the time of this letter.

To Graham Wallas

October 30, 1923

Dear G. W.:

. . . I am fundamentally hopeful about the Hughes-Curzon plan[1] because I am pretty thoroughly convinced that Poincaré[2] intends to wreck Germany and conduct the next French elections on the basis of a fait accompli. American opinion, however, is pretty solidly behind Hughes, and if he has the courage to go ahead with your Government we may at least get out of it all a clarification of the issues. . . .

1. British Prime Minister Stanley Baldwin, recognizing that the spread of inflation from Germany into France threatened the financial stability of all of Europe, had solicited American cooperation to fashion an international agreement on reparations and war debts. Though the United States continued to insist the two questions were unrelated, Secretary of State Hughes and British Foreign Secretary Lord Curzon had worked out plans for the organization of committees to explore the question of German reparations. In spite of Lippmann's doubts, those beginnings were to lead to the reduction of both war debts and reparations under the Dawes plan of 1924. **2.** Raymond Poincaré, the incumbent French premier, a conservative whose government had initiated the occupation of the Ruhr.

To S. K. Ratcliffe

November 3, 1923

Dear S. K.:

. . . The Administration managed to screw up its courage in the matter of the expert inquiry.[1] I really think Coolidge has a good deal more courage than Harding[2] and is better advised. At any rate, the thing has been a success here. While there isn't any wild enthusiasm for it, because people mistrust Poincaré, still we can at least say that there is no important opposition at home. Hiram Johnson broke loose, but he is the only one of the irreconcilables regarded against the idea. Borah is supporting it, and I guess is not supporting Johnson for President.

On the presidential business, Coolidge looks to me an absolute certainty to the Republicans. Not only has he all the strategic advantages which come from control of the Federal patronage, but he has proved himself a very shrewd politician.

On the Democratic side there is great confusion. McAdoo is leading, but in a Democratic convention, where it takes a two-third vote to nominate, it's a disadvantage to be prominent too early in the campaign. It tends to unite the field against the leader. McAdoo also has other serious handicaps. He is bone dry, which is all right out West but not all right on the seaboard where the strategic votes are to be found. The real weakness of McAdoo in the Democratic campaign is that he is strong in the South and in the West, whereas most of us figure that a Democrat this year has to be elected on the combination of the South and East. The West is farmer-labor in sentiment, but in the electoral college that means Republican votes.

The Ford campaign[3] is not, in my opinion, to be taken seriously. He will have some strength in the convention if he doesn't withdraw before the convention meets, but I feel certain that he has passed the crest of his popularity and that his boom will weaken. It really has no solid political backing of any kind, and consists of a sentiment even weaker than that which got behind Hoover in 1920. You remember that Hoover got all the newspaper notices and five votes in the Republican convention. If I were betting, and not hoping, I should say that the Democratic candidate will be some nondescript and that he will be defeated by Coolidge. This is for you alone, of course. I don't expect that the League will play an important part in this campaign. All Democratic candidates are determined to avoid it, which may be just as well, seeing that sentiment, while somewhat more favorable to the League, is still overwhelmingly opposed. . . .

1. On the reparations issue. **2.** Harding had died on August 2, 1923. **3.** Henry Ford at this time was enjoying a brief and fortunately transient boom as a possible Republican candidate in 1924.

To Newton D. Baker

November 27, 1923

Dear N.D.B.:

. . . I don't like the idea of fighting the bonus by means of tax reduction. The bonus ought to be fought on the merits, and the tax reduction favored on the merits, but apparently no politician is willing to do either.[1]

You asked me in a recent letter what people were thinking about John W. Davis[2] and Houston.[3] Around here they are not thinking about Houston at all, and about Davis there is some very mild talk, but almost no enthusiasm. The few times he has appeared in public, the impression has been rather flat. Personally, I like him a great deal. But he is what I should call socially absorbed by his environment, and it is a rather narrow environment.

1. Secretary of the Treasury Mellon opposed payment of a bonus to American veterans of the world war. A strong supporter of reducing all federal expenditures, he wanted also to cut federal taxes, especially taxes on the income of the wealthy. **2.** John W. Davis, a West Virginia Democrat, had been solicitor general in the Justice Department under Wilson and later ambassador to the Court of St. James's. At this time, he had become a New Yorker and a talented partner in Davis, Polk, a major law firm with a considerable corporate practice. **3.** David F. Houston of Texas, formerly Wilson's secretary of agriculture and, briefly, secretary of the treasury.

To the Editor, the Japan Times

December 18, 1923

Dear Sir:

You were kind enough to ask my opinion concerning the future interest of Japan in relation to the United States.

Briefly and frankly, I should like to say that the Washington treaties have rendered military conflict virtually impossible and therefore neither country is in a position to adopt a policy towards the other which requires the sanction of military force. So far as good feeling and development of friendship are concerned — all these depend almost entirely upon the relation between the

Japanese and the Asiatic mainland, that is to say, China and Siberia. The American people recognize the need for Japanese industrial expansion abroad in order to support the Japanese population at home. They believe that this industrial expansion can take place under a policy of liberalism towards China and Russia, and that it cannot take place under military pressure. They believe that this policy of pacific liberalism in the Far East is not only economically to Japan's advantage, but would be a final guarantee to peace with the western world.

To Julian L. Street[1]

December 26, 1923

Dear Mr. Street:

. . . I hasten to disclaim an instinctive aversion to the Roosevelt type. On the contrary, I confess to an almost irresistible hero-worship. In fact, until almost the very end of Roosevelt's life, I had a great personal affection for him and used to see him rather often, though naturally I disliked a good deal of what he said about Wilson in 1918. Of course I recognized the sincerity of his position. I cannot help thinking that on the question of a settlement after the war he would, in a position of responsibility, have taken an attitude quite different from that which he took as an officially irresponsible man. I think that he would have made the same quick and instinctive recovery which British policy has made, just because he was such a good fighter. The last years seemed to me a tragedy precisely because they revealed a Roosevelt who was much less memorable than he was capable of being under the pressure of responsibility. . . .

1. Julian L. Street, prolific author of magazine articles, short stories, and popular books, among them several works on wines and gastronomy; admirer of Theodore Roosevelt.

To Bernard Berenson

January 1, 1924

Dear B. B.:

. . . The intelligence test series[1] . . . has aroused the fury of the sacerdotal progressives. . . .

Our professors have been caught in their wave of biological preservation. The results of the intelligence tests have been used to support Houston Stewart Chamberlainism.[2] It is interesting that Lothrop Stoddard,[3] the most popular exponent of this theory is a member of the Ku Klux Klan. Norman Hapgood has just proved this charge. McDougall[4] who sits in William James' place is the most respectable sponsor of this vicious nonsense.

The report you heard about the Jews of Eastern Galicia is typical of the abuse of the best material.

The report is based on the following facts all published in the official memoirs of the National Academy of Sciences.

94,000 men were picked out as a statistical "sample" of the white draft. Of these 13,200 were foreign born. Their nationality was classified not by race but by the political unit they belonged to. "Eastern Galicia" was not distinguished, nor were "Jews." The classification was "Poland" and "Austria" and "Russia" etc.

On this classification the percentage of men showing "0" or worse gave the following countries at the bottom of the list in the following order: Austria, Ireland, Turkey, Greece, Russia, Italy, Poland.

No one knows or can know whether "Poland" means Jews or not. But in the minds of those with a will to believe "Poland" has been headed as "Polish Jews." . . .

1. Lippmann had written a series of six articles, "The Mental Age of Americans," that *The New Republic* published in October and November 1922, with a supplementary exchange of related letters in January 1923. The articles criticized the then relatively new Stanford-Binet tests, which allegedly measured the innate intelligence of children. As Lippmann observed, that claim overlooked the significance of social, cultural, and other factors affecting the results of the tests. 2. Houston Stewart Chamberlain, a British-born German citizen and husband of the daughter of Richard Wagner, had published *The Foundations of the Nineteenth Century*, 2 v. (New York, 1911), earlier published in German in 1899. A racist tract, it glorified the Teuton people, to whom it attributed all significant advances in civilization. Viciously anti-Semitic, the work provided ideas that Adolf Hitler used at this time and thereafter. 3. Lothrop Stoddard, New England–born historian, lawyer, anti-Semite, and racist author of, among other works, *The Rising Tide of Color Against White Supremacy* (New York, 1920) and *Racial Realities in Europe* (New York, 1924). 4. William McDougall, British-trained psychologist, was a professor of psychology at Harvard from 1920 through 1927.

To John L. Balderston[1]

April 17, 1924

Dear John:

. . . It's quite apparent, from your letter, that English people, like Americans, were fooled by the propagandized forecasts of the Dawes report and thought that the whole thing was going to be a triumph for Poincaré in substance as well as in form.[2] As it seems to have turned out, the experts sucked the eggs and handed Poincaré the shells. That devilishly ingenious scheme of having the Germans pay in marks only was carefully concealed from everybody's understanding until the full text was published.

The paper is getting along fine and we're keeping people guessing as to who our candidate is. The real truth is we have no candidate and though we continue to say it, nobody believes us. My own private belief is that the nominee

will not be any one of the men who shows up strongly on the first ballot. If I
were betting, I'd take the field against any of the favorites. . . .

1. John L. Balderston, the *World's* British correspondent.   2. By no means a victory for Poincaré,
the Dawes plan reported on April 9, 1924, provided for reorganization of the German Reichsbank
under supervision of the Allies. It also called for a revision in the timing of reparation payments,
with less demanded of Germany during the coming five years. Further to help Germany, that
nation was to receive a foreign loan, in which the United States would participate. The Germans
accepted the plan April 16; a conference of the Allied powers did so several months later.

To Felix Frankfurter

April 18, 1924

Dear Felix:

You know how strong the feeling is about the character of some of the
testimony brought out by the investigating committees. I am enclosing a copy
of a memorandum which we are circulating confidentially to half a dozen people — to L.D.B.,[1] to Hughes, to John W. Davis, to Pound and yourself. The
memorandum more or less explains itself, but I want very much to get as
frank and detailed a comment both from Pound and you as possible on it,
including your opinion, first, as to how far the criticisms of the investigations
are justified — meaning the criticisms that come from people who really appreciate the value of the work that Walsh and Wheeler[2] have done; second,
what remedy, if any, could be proposed for the future which would not seem
to accept the assumption of the Republican National Committee that all investigations are bad.

While all this is quite confidential, there is no objection to your getting any
other judgments which you respect. We are approaching L.D.B. directly.

1. Louis D. Brandeis.   2. Burton K. Wheeler, Democratic senator from Montana, later in 1924
ran for vice president on the ticket of the Progressive party. He was a member of the committee
chaired by Democratic Senator Thomas J. Walsh of Montana which uncovered the Teapot Dome
scandal; see p. 162.

To Ima Waterfield[1]

April 28, 1924

Dear Mrs. Waterfield:

. . . Mussolini continues to be the hero of the itinerant American bankers,[2] though I think no one here took his election victory seriously as a free
expression of Italian opinion. The thing that really damaged Mussolini in
America was Corfu.[3] But for the showing that he was an international distur-
ber, he would have been entirely satisfactory in our present extremely reactionary temper here. . . .

1. Ima (Mrs. A.) Waterfield, a resident of Florence, acquaintance of the Lippmanns', and friend of Bernard Berenson's. 2. Including Lippmann's friend Thomas Lamont. 3. Benito Mussolini had completed the coup d'état by which the Fascists, under his leadership, took over the Italian government in October–November 1922. The following August, the Italians bombarded and occupied the Greek island of Corfu, but under pressure from Great Britain they evacuated the island the next month. During 1924 Mussolini strengthened his dictatorship with increasingly repressive measures, one of which rigged the elections of April to produce a large parliamentary majority for him.

To Samuel Spewack[1]

May 19, 1924

Dear Sam:

. . . As soon as I had a chance to see the whole report, I was convinced that it had finally put France in a position where she had to make the fatal choice between a Germany too weak to pay and a Germany so strong that in the end it would not have to pay. But after all, what happens to the scheme five or ten years from now is of small consequence. Certainly I never expect to see any reparation scheme in operation ten years from now. So long as France gets some immediate help, and Germany gets her breath, the important thing would have been accomplished. All our plans will look very strange to us ten years from now. Just think how ridiculous some of the things now seem that we believed in at the time of the Armistice. . . .

1. Samuel Spewack, the *World*'s correspondent in Germany.

To Charlton Ogburn[1]

June 12, 1924

Dear Mr. Ogburn:

. . . I am certain of only one thing — that the nomination of McAdoo would be a tragic mistake, because it would naturally confuse the issue of corruption in the campaign.

I do not think that McAdoo is dishonest or in the same class with Fall, Daugherty or Forbes,[2] but I do think that the nature of his legal practice has been such as to put him on the defensive throughout the campaign. The tax refund case, which you regard as serious is, I fear, only one of a number of cases in which he committed a serious breach of taste in using political influence to assist his legal work. I don't say that each case couldn't be defended before a committee of the bar, but I feel very certain that all of them couldn't be defended before an excited electorate. The Democratic candidate this year must be a man against whose personal record no charge can be made.

What you say about the Klan strikes a very sympathetic chord in me.[3] I think it will die out, but men may very well differ as to whether it will die out quickest by being ignored or by being fought. It is necessary to remember, however, that even if the method of ignoring it would be wiser, the groups in our population under attack from the Klan will probably not take so olympic an attitude as that would imply. I am not sure that our militancy couldn't be justified to a man taking your view of the matter on the ground that if opposition to the Klan were not expressed in the way we do it, it would be expressed in a much more violent and provocative way by some one else.

1. Charlton Ogburn, Georgia-born New York lawyer, expert on electric railways, later general counsel to the American Federation of Labor and to the National Planning Association. **2.** Of the perpetrators of the major scandals of the Harding years, Charles R. Forbes had gone to jail for defrauding the government while he was head of the Veterans Administration; Attorney General Daugherty had surrendered the Justice Department to bribery (though he escaped conviction); and Secretary of the Interior Fall had accepted a bribe to permit the leasing of federal oil reserves in the Teapot Dome of Wyoming by Harry F. Sinclair, and those at Elk Hills, California, by Edward L. Doheny. Later convicted, Fall became the first Cabinet officer to go to prison. **3.** The Ku Klux Klan, spreading its propaganda of hatred against blacks, Jews, and Catholics, was at this time reaching the zenith of its pernicious influence on American opinion and politics.

To Manuel Levy [1]

June 19, 1924

Dear Mr. Levy:

I have just seen the clipping of an editorial in which the *Courier-Journal* disagrees with our interpretation of the taxation plank in the Republican platform.

I am sorry to find myself in disagreement with the *Courier-Journal* on this point, but I see no way by which a sentence like "Progressive reform" is to be identified as the Mellon plan. The essence of the Mellon plan as I understand it is that reduction of the surtax, especially in the higher brackets, will produce larger revenues. That may or may not be correct, but certainly the phrase "tax reform" does not necessarily mean reducing the surtaxes in the higher brackets. The phrase "tax reform" may mean anything. It might mean changes of definition in the law that would stop tax evasion or tax avoidance. I am convinced that it was put into the platform because it can mean anything and I think the proof will be that on the stump most Republican Congressmen will not advocate the specific Mellon plan. The Republican plank does take a few sentences out of the President's message, given out at the time he signed the present tax law, but surely we are not going to be confused in mistaking a few sentences, in my opinion largely meaningless, for the actual endorsement of a very definite theory of taxation. As for the statement that tax reform "should not be confined to less than 4,000,000 of our citizens who pay direct taxes, but is the right of more than 100,000,000 who are daily paying their taxes through living expenses," I can only say that this not only has nothing to do with the

Mellon plan, but is, in a platform upholding the present tariff, something approaching hypocrisy.

I don't know whether I have been able to convince you by this argument, but I hope you will at least believe that what I wrote was not inspired by mere partisanship.

1. Manuel Levy, an editor of the *Louisville Courier-Journal*.

To Franklin D. Roosevelt

June 27, 1924

Dear Frank:

Your speech yesterday, nominating the Governor,[1] was a moving and distinguished thing. I am utterly hard-boiled about speeches, but yours seemed to me perfect in temper and manner and most eloquent in its effect.

We are all proud of you.

1. Franklin D. Roosevelt, incapacitated by poliomyelitis during the previous several years, had nominated Al Smith — then governor of New York — at the Democratic Convention in Madison Square Garden in his celebrated "Happy Warrior" speech.

To James L. Garvin[1]

July 10, 1924

Dear Mr. Garvin:

. . . The result is creditable to the Democratic Party.[2] I wouldn't pretend to think that the chances of Mr. Davis's election are better than doubtful, but the convention became so involved in factional dispute that after a while it ceased to be a question of choosing a man who, by personal dignity and intellectual eminence, would save the party from confusion and disgrace. Davis will do that. He will prevent the domination of the party by a combination of evil and foolish forces, such as were behind the candidacy of McAdoo.

1. James L. Garvin of the *Observer* of London.   2. After a prolonged stand-off between McAdoo and Smith, the Democrats on the 103rd ballot had settled on John W. Davis as their compromise candidate.

To Edward M. House

July 10, 1924

Dear E.M.H.

I am writing to you the day after the convention finished. From the point of view of the integrity of the Party and its standing in the country, the Davis nomination was the only possible result. You will remember our discussion on the subject. Everything, however, was changed by the extraordinary bitterness of the convention. Davis was the only man to pull the whole thing out of the mud.

He will need advice most awfully. I think he really wishes to conduct an honestly liberal campaign, and I am satisfied, from several talks I have had with him, that he is a man of real intellectual distinction and decision of character. He is a little bit in the same situation that Wilson was in before you got your hands on him, and he needs more than anything else exactly the kind of thing that you gave to Wilson. I am afraid that his antennae are not very sensitive and that he doesn't instinctively know the progressive temper. I think you ought to consider seriously getting back here early enough in the campaign to help stamp it properly. Frank Polk[1] is, I suppose, his closest adviser, and is a very good one, but it's going to be a very hard uphill pull at best.

There are real difficulties in New York. Smith has been perfectly loyal and will do everything, I am certain, but the local Tammany organization is not so reliable, especially as Hearst opened up on Davis with all his guns.

I should be extremely grateful to you for any advice as to how to shape our part of the campaign.

1. Frank L. Polk, Davis's law partner, friend of Colonel House, formerly assistant secretary of state under Wilson.

To Bernard Berenson   HANDWRITTEN

July 16, 1924

Dear B. B.:

 . . . The Republican convention was cut and dried. Coolidge abandoned all the agrarian West and is to run frankly as an Easterner and representative of large property. Thus the Democratic convention was a wonder of excitement. McAdoo came in with a bloc of about 500 delegates out of 1,098. He had most of the South and the West, the backing of the anti-Saloon league (which is extreme prohibition) and the Ku Klux Klan. They were a psalm-singing fanatical lot. His weakness was his shady record as a lawyer.

The World led the fight against him and it was the hardest, bitterest but most wonderful political battle I've ever seen. We exposed his record, rallied the whole bloc of Northern and Eastern delegates against him, and after 103 ballots he broke down entirely, and we were able to force the nomination of John W. Davis. In the course of the fight, the religious issue — Protestant vs. Catholic — was raised fiercely — and between the Ku Klux Klan on one side and the Clan-Na Gael on the other, it was a triumph to come out with a man of Davis' integrity, reasonableness and vitality.

I don't know whether Davis can be elected. But he's worth campaigning for.

He has far more sheer ability than Wilson, a much wider experience in both industrial and diplomatic affairs, and is a man of finer grain. He lacks Wilson's flair for warming up people he doesn't know, and he has less dramatic sense. But he is a sounder man, I think, more dependable, and fundamentally more intelligent.

We shall be in the throes of it till November. . . .

To Newton D. Baker

July 17, 1924

My dear N.D.B.:

. . . I am particularly impressed with what you say about the tendency of liberals to scatter. Apparently their first impulse now is to scatter all over the lot, and to attack each other more fiercely than they attack their common enemy.[1]

However, I feel a good deal of confidence. If, out of all that mad convention, we could secure the nomination of Davis, this country isn't so sick as some people imagine it is. . . .

1. Most well-known liberal intellectuals were moving to support the presidential candidacy of Senator Robert La Follette of Wisconsin, who had been nominated by a new third party, the Progressive party, on a platform stressing antitrust policy, antiwar sentiment, and distrust of the Supreme Court. Lippmann and the *World* from the first considered La Follette's candidacy futile except as a threat to the Democratic party and Davis's campaign. In the end, La Follette did indeed draw many votes from Davis, though he carried only Wisconsin. During the campaign, the Republicans attacked La Follette for his alleged socialism while more or less ignoring Davis. Whatever the political liabilities that La Follette posed for the Democrats, he was a dedicated and genuine reformer, as Davis emphatically was not.

To Robert Littell[1]

July 18, 1924

Dear Bob:

The New Republic has repeatedly said one thing about the Democratic Convention which is both untrue and misleading, and I think in all fairness a serious effort should be made to correct it. I am referring to the assertion that the Klan issue was injected into the Democratic convention by supporters of Governor Smith as a device to beat McAdoo.[2] That simply isn't true.

The men who were most interested in the nomination of Governor Smith knew perfectly well that once the Klan issue was raised on the floor of the convention, the nomination of Governor Smith was out of the question. Far from trying to bring it on to the floor, they made every effort to keep it off.

The issue in the particular form in which it was raised, namely, as to whether the Klan should be named, was brought in by Democratic politicians from Illinois and Missouri and Ohio, who had no particular interest in the nomination of Smith. They were interested partly, I think, in principle, partly they were actuated in Illinois and Ohio by desire to capture the Negro vote. When the issue of naming the Klan had been raised by these men, the question was put to Governor Smith, who said that he recognized it was the end of his candidacy, but that he couldn't and wouldn't be put in the position of trying to strangle an issue of that sort. This was also the position of the *World*. The *World* never advocated naming the Klan in the platform. But when the issue was raised in such a way that naming the Klan took on real significance, we, too, felt that we couldn't run away from it.

The ultimate responsibility for bringing the Klan bitterness into the convention goes back of all this, however. It rests squarely on McAdoo. When McAdoo's candidacy collapsed under the Doheny revelations, his political managers in Texas and Georgia went out for Klan support in order to revivify his candidacy in the contest with Underwood. McAdoo came to the convention not only opposed to naming the Klan but opposed to any denunciation of it beyond the meaningless declaration in favor of the constitution. If McAdoo was liberal as *The New Republic* continues to assert that he was, he would have advocated openly a denunciation of the principles and purposes of the Klan without naming it, and there would have been no Klan debate on the floor of the convention. He refused to do this. His managers made every effort to protect the Klan, and their stubbornness invited the reprisal by the non-Smith anti-McAdoo leaders of the middle west. Your correspondent, John Owens, never really got at the inside of the matter. It seems to me rather extraordinary that Herbert should venture to write so dogmatically about this extremely important matter without at least taking the trouble to talk to me about it.

I am putting this down on paper because I think you may wish to show it to the other editors, and not for the pleasure of repeating on paper what I have said to you in talk.

1. Robert Littell, then associate editor of *The New Republic*. 2. The *World*, like Smith, had called for condemning the Klan by name, but by a tiny majority the convention declined to do so.

To Frank L. Polk

July 25, 1924

Dear Frank:

I know that you want candid opinions. So I am writing to you to tell you my impression of the way John Davis is projecting himself through the correspondents in Maine.

The impression here is worse than unsatisfactory. The thing given out today on the Klan will hurt him. The objection to it is not so much that he proposes to stand pat on the platform. No one could quarrel with him for that. The objection is that he seems to be taking advantage of a technicality to dodge a troublesome political issue. The statement sounds technical and artful and in my judgment he can't afford at any time in this campaign to seem indecisive, technical, lawyerly or clever. There is no use fooling ourselves as to the immense popular prejudice which he has still to overcome. Our letters here show that beyond a doubt. The only way that he can overcome the prejudice against him is to seem always bold, utterly frank and decisive. He's got to take enormous chances, in my opinion, if he's to project his personality beyond the circle of those Republicans and upper class Democrats who admire him for his intrinsic qualities.

I don't think he need, or ought to, denounce the Klan by name, but I believe that when he was asked about the thing he should either have refused all comment on the ground that he had nothing to say until his speech of acceptance, or he should have said, in some very human fashion, "I have no patience whatever with religious prejudice." That sort of statement would have accomplished the same result and would have satisfied many more people. The way this thing actually comes out today it's bound to alienate any Klan sentiment without helping him in the least with the Klan. It just sounds like political straddling and John Davis can't afford to sound like that. . . .

To Felix Frankfurter

August 11, 1924

Dear Felix:

Your letter[1] . . . reached me . . . and I have given it the careful consideration which you asked for it.

You're not asking me really to print the letter. You are asking me to engage in a running debate with you. It's my judgment that such a debate on the terms you propose serves no good purpose and I must decline it.

You appear to think that there is some mystery about the *World's* attitude towards Mr. Davis. There is no mystery, and I think need be none in your mind, if you will cease to regard the editorial of April 2nd as the *World's* only editorial before the nomination of Mr. Davis. There were, in fact, a great many other editorial references to Mr. Davis before the convention which modified the attitude expressed in the first editorial.

You ask whether the *World* has changed its views on its characterization of Mr. Davis as a conservative. It has changed its views. And the reasons for its change of views have been set forth on its editorial page. You may not agree with the evidence which has convinced us that Mr. Davis's espousal of liberal ideas is consistent with his public record and his background and training. At any rate that has been our conviction, and the change of view has come gradually and has been marked, I think, by the comment on the editorial page.

I write this all for you as a final word of personal explanation, because you ask it as a friend. I will not engage in public controversy with you about it, and I beg you to consider this phase of the matter definitely closed. . . .

1. The letter made a strong case for La Follette.

To S. K. Ratcliffe

September 10, 1924

Dear S. K.:

. . . I wonder whether you in England have any notion of the general mess stirred up by the Prince's coming.[1] I think it's important that the liberal and labor editors should know something about it, and I think the substance ought to be conveyed to MacDonald[2] himself. I will write you very frankly and rely on you to expurgate as required.

In the first place, his coming to Long Island in September of a presidential year was atrociously bad taste. He planted himself within a few miles of John W. Davis's home and put Davis in a frightful quandary. Davis, as a former Ambassador would naturally have had to show courtesies to him; as a presidential candidate he simply could not mix himself up with the Prince's dissipations. The result was that Davis's western trip had to be timed so that Davis should be west of Chicago the whole time the Prince was in this country.

In the second place, the Prince has been involved in a cloud of scandal and surrounded by a group of newly rich social climbers exploiting him in the most flagrant fashion. The intricate connection between the lady to whom he's attached and the gentleman who is her host and her husband's banker, are known to everybody and have caused a great deal of disgust.

Politically, the net effect of his visit is simply this. It's utterly impossible to persuade the mass of people in this country that the British economic situation requires sympathetic attitudes when this over-rich idle and dissipated young man is held before their eyes daily as a symbol of Great Britain.

I assume that the foreign office has some control over his movements. If it has, it seems to me it made a gross blunder in permitting him to come to this country under these circumstances. . . .

1. The visit to the United States by the Prince of Wales, later Edward VIII.   2. James Ramsay MacDonald, then head of the Labour party and British prime minister.

To Arthur W. Page[1]

October 6, 1924

Dear Arthur:

. . . My own convictions about the Philippines are controlled by two considerations: First, in view of the Washington conference, I am afraid that we have a military obligation there which we may not be able to make good. I think that's always a bad position to be in. In the second place, I think that the problem has been tactlessness in the handling of the Philippines under Wood which has stimulated the independence movement.[2]

Furthermore, agreeing with you that American rule is on the whole better for the Filipinos than rule by the Manila cliques, by what rule are we to determine that it is our business to establish good government in the Philippines? I don't think you can state a rule which requires us to govern the Filipinos well, which wouldn't involve us or any other so-called advanced nation in interminable adventures all over the world. As I look upon it, we happen to be in the Philippines, though I wish we had never gotten in. Being in, we ought to send out there governors who build up moderate sentiment rather than exceedingly extremist sentiment, and we ought to clear up very decidedly the military status of the islands.

1. Arthur W. Page, at this time editor of *World's Work,* later vice president and then president of the American Telephone and Telegraph Company. **2.** As governor general of the Philippines, General Leonard Wood had reverted to the heavy-handed colonialism that the Wilson administration had begun to dissolve as a step toward independence for the islands.

To John L. Balderston

October 30, 1924

Dear John:

. . . The interesting thing about the British election[1] to me is that MacDonald's attitude towards the liberals is exactly like La Follette's attitude towards the Democrats. There is this difference, however, in the outcome. MacDonald has probably smashed the liberals. It's out of the question to smash the Democrats. Our whole electoral machinery is such that no matter how badly the Democratic Party is beaten in the national field, it is so thoroughly entrenched in the states that it revives as soon as the smoke clears away. Of course I do think that the Democratic Party, out of economic evolution and the wide distribution of property in this country, is now a minority party. I think the Republicans have the normal majority of the population, — probably they have had this normal majority since 1896 and only their own blundering has ever prevented them from mobilizing it.

At any rate, don't over-estimate the real significance of the large popular vote that La Follette will pull. The vote has behind it no stable organization and you know as well as I the popular votes in one election that don't leave behind them office holders, patronage, and loaves to feed the fishes in the lean days never make a very permanent dent on political situations. In this respect, La Follette is even worse off than Roosevelt was in 1912. . . .

1. Ramsay MacDonald had become British prime minister in January 1924. Heavy unemployment in Great Britain had helped the Labour party win a major triumph over the Conservatives. For their part, the Liberals, continuing to lose their popular support, had become distinctly a minority third party. Both Labour and Liberals had opposed the protectionism the Conservatives advocated.

To McAlister Coleman[1]

November 3, 1924

My dear Mr. Coleman:

I don't suppose you expect a reply to your letter, because I don't imagine, from your letter, that you are prepared to admit that anyone not supporting Mr. La Follette in this campaign can be progressive or honest. At least your letter sounds as if you felt that way.

Of course I do not admit that the attacks on Senator La Follette this last week have been petty or unwarranted. I charge him with a very serious thing, namely with making a campaign to insure election of Mr. Coolidge. I am not prepared to admit with you that the La Follette campaign, which has for its immediate effect on the next four years the enthronement of reaction, is without further discussion a test of progressivism. When Mr. La Follette shows that his strategy was designed to divide the liberal opposition in the East to Mr. Coolidge, I struck at him as hard as I could. You may not like my attacking him. You may regret it. But I should thank you very much if you would not indulge in the cant about lost leaders and all the rest of it.

1. McAlister Coleman of New York City, by his own account then campaigning for La Follette and upset that Lippmann had not supported the Progressives.

To Newton D. Baker

November 26, 1924

CONFIDENTIAL

My dear N.D.B.:

. . . I saw Borah in Washington and had a most satisfactory talk with him. He said he was aware of the tension with Japan and would be very glad to have suggestions as to what he ought to do to relieve it.[1] The specific point of irritation at the moment seems to be the scheduled battle fleet maneuvers around Hawaii. Borah thought they should certainly be postponed and the maneuvers held this year in the Caribbean. Both Tom Lamont and Dwight Morrow[2] were at Hot Springs while we were there and I saw a good deal of them. They both felt that the maneuvers are the danger point, and both are in favor of postponing them. I think Morrow will speak to the President about it.

I told Borah that the public had the impression that he was hostile to the League. He said that was not true and that he would take an opportunity in the near future to make it clear that he wishes the League well and was glad to see the European nations working out their problem of security to suit their own ends. He himself thinks we ought to keep up a steady agitation for American participation in a conference on the reduction of armaments. As to plan and method he is entirely open-minded and wishes suggestions. He is perfectly willing, he said, to participate in a conference of which the League is a part. I asked him whether he would be willing to have us join in a world association having much the structure of the League but containing none of the covenants. I asked him this because I had heard that some such notion was in the President's mind. He was rather favorable to that idea. He is also prepared to join the World Court and has only one main reservation. That has to do with the advisory opinions of the Court. He feels that they are not a legitimate part of the work of any Court and that we should adhere to the court with a reservation, saying that so far as we're concerned, such advisory opinions are not a part of international law and have no significance. He does not object to the present method of electing the judges and is perfectly willing to sit with the council and assembly for the purpose of constituting the Court.

I came away with the feeling that it would be up to us; that is to say, the group that is especially interested in world cooperation, to feed Borah definite suggestions. We can't, of course, ask him to come out for American membership in the League, nor for ratification of the protocol.[3] We must be content with a friendly neutrality. But I think we have a right to hope from him for a sincere and energetic activity along the lines of reduction of armaments and for a good deal of cooperation in international affairs, providing it doesn't involve commitments by covenant. . . .

1. The Immigration Act of 1924, totally excluding Japanese immigration, gratuitously insulted the Japanese, whose annual immigration, based on the terms of the act, would have been insignificant. The resulting tensions in Japanese-American relations undid the promising détente of the Washington Conference.   **2.** Dwight W. Morrow — another partner in the house of Morgan and the father of Anne Morrow Lindbergh — was a statesman and public figure whom Lippmann admired and came to know as an especially close friend.   **3.** The Geneva protocol of 1924, before the League of Nations at this time, provided for compulsory arbitration of all international disputes and for defining as an aggressor any nation unwilling to submit a case to arbitration. In 1925 a newly elected Conservative government in England rejected it.

To Arthur N. Holcombe

December 1, 1924

Dear Arthur:

. . . I don't believe that political strategy now should be based on the assumption of Governor Smith's candidacy in 1928. Certainly we here are not making any such assumption.

I am not sure I agree with you about the proposed Federal Child Labor Amendment. The political advantages of Governor Smith's advocating its ratification are obvious enough, but I am not in the least concerned about political advantages for him. The real question is whether the Democratic Party on the merits and in the light of its tradition ought to advocate such an extension to the federal power.

In other words, we seem to have somewhat misunderstood each other. I was asking you for suggestions not as to how to help Governor Smith's candidacy, but as to how to make the Democratic Party a fit instrument of liberalism, and I find you writing like a hard-boiled politician. Shame on you.

To William E. Borah

January 1, 1925

Dear Senator Borah:

I thank you heartily for your kind letter. Of course I am very glad to hear that you're going to discuss the disarmament conference.[1] I think it's important to keep the question of completing the naval disarmament separated from the much more intricate problem of land disarmament. It is possible, I should think, for Great Britain, Japan and the United States, with possibly France and Italy, if it's necessary to have them, to have a separate conference pretty soon to clarify the existing Washington Treaties and to extend them to auxiliary craft. These subjects do not involve the debatable question of the League Protocol, land security, etc. etc.

The question of disarmament on land is, as you say, tied up with economic problems. It is also tied up with what the Europeans call the problem of security. Now the problem of security involving a decision on the Protocol and all the related questions of membership in the League, the economic problems involving a fixation of the German debt, plus the solution of the intricate debt funding dispute, plus the subject of most favored nation arrangements in Europe, plus the whole Ruhr-Lorraine metallurgical dispute, are not likely to be settled easily. I think it would be a great mistake to enmesh the simpler problem of naval disarmaments with these other questions. Therefore I strongly urge you to come out for a simple naval conference as soon as it's feasible to get the naval powers together. Once that's under way and assured, you can then come out for a separate, broader conference to deal with economic questions and land disarmament. I feel morally certain that we won't make any headway with the naval question if we involve it with the debt question and that's what would happen if you put general economic questions on the agenda of the conference.

1. The prospect of another conference on naval disarmament materialized at Geneva in the summer of 1925.

To Malcolm M. Willey [1]

January 13, 1925

My dear Mr. Willey:

I am very glad to have your letter and to try to answer your questions.

The phrases "pseudo environment" and "pictures in our heads" [2] are interchangeable. They both refer to that representation of the world on which men act. That representation may be wholly true or wholly false or a mixture. I wished by these phrases to emphasize the fact that the responses of human beings to their environment, particularly to their social environment, are dependent upon the cognitive factor. They are not, generally, like blinking if someone passes a hand quickly before a man's eyes. In the field of public opinion there is an intervening step consisting of a kind of judgment as to whether someone has passed his hand before the man's eyes. This judgment of fact is liable to error. It is at this point that the whole process is what I have called the pseudo environment, or the pictures in our heads.

I should certainly classify scientific concepts as pseudo environment. A man working on a graph with a serious mathematical equation may at the end reach a conclusion which predicts, let us say, the eclipse of the sun on a certain day. But in that process of reasoning he has been dealing with the sun and the moon not in the direct fashion that a moth deals with a light in a lamp, but by means of an elaborate collection of mental constructs. They are all, so to speak, in his head, and his own responses are adjusted not to the sun and moon, but to his own representations of the sun and moon.

By "stereotypes," I mean certain fixed habits of the cognition. I use the word to describe part of the process by which the pseudo environment is pieced together in our heads. It is a pathological term for the kind of cognition which classifies and abstracts falsely, and generally violates the scientific canons for dealing with fact.

I think it is evident from this that it would not be correct to divide the pictures in our heads into (1) stereotypes, (2) mental images which are a valid effort to ascertain reality. That would, I think, be a confusion of terms between the resultant picture in our heads and the processes by which the pictures were created. The pictures in our heads are what they are however we have arrived at them. Their truth or falsity depends on verification in action.

The stereotypes are simply those fixed habits of cognition which usually, but not always, falsify the picture.

I don't know whether this is a satisfactory answer to your question. I might perhaps clarify it all a little bit by saying that the scheme of the theory on which my book is based is this — man acts on what he knows, not on what he is. He knows what the machinery of information puts within the realm of his knowledge, selected and distorted by his own habits of mind. . . .

1. Malcolm M. Willey, sociologist, then an assistant professor at Dartmouth College, later dean at the University of Minnesota.   2. From *Public Opinion* (New York, 1922).

To William Allen White[1]

February 21, 1925

My dear Bill White:

. . . I haven't had the chance I would like to go over your book for the actual verbal citations. If you have said or implied that big business, meaning by that the masters of big corporate capital, were responsible for the war, I should say No, but if you said, as I recall your saying that there were deep commercial and economic rivalries at the bottom of it, I should say on the whole Yes, and I think, with due allowance for the factors of nationalism and dynasties and general staffs, that Tom would probably agree with that. It seems to me important to distinguish between the fairly concrete entity which is called Wall Street here and the general push and drive of national businesses, including agriculture, etc. I don't myself believe at all in the La Follette theory of actual intelligent big business manipulation leading to war. First of all, big business men don't exercise as much control as that implies, and second, they haven't the intelligence or the consistency which it would require. I think a war of such magnitude must have had a wider base. There was undoubtedly a world-wide rivalry between the British and the German commercial systems, and this affected the political life of both countries, but Lombard Street, and whatever the equivalent is in Berlin, were not prime causes. This, I think is just exactly what you say in your letter of January 30th to Lamont, and if your book agrees with that letter in all its textual detail, I personally wouldn't have any dispute with you.

Of course Lamont is naturally and justly sensitive on this point and a good deal weary of reading that he and his partners made the war. They heard that a good deal during the last campaign, and I suppose anything that remotely suggests the same train of thought makes them jumpy.

I didn't know them at all well before the war, but I know several members of the firm pretty well now and I would be willing to testify that they have been a force for peace in the last five years. . . .

1. William Allen White, renowned editor of the *Emporia Gazette*, former Roosevelt Progressive now returned to the Republican fold, had recently published his *Woodrow Wilson* (Boston, 1924), a book that teetered, as White had, between admiration and doubt about its subject.

To Arthur Krock [1]

April 3, 1925

Dear A. K.:

Just for the sake of the record, I want you to know that I disagree with you about *Love for Love*. I will not personally be a party to the suppression of a Congreve play, even supposing that it were all you say it is. I should oppose the suppression of *Love for Love* as I should oppose the suppression of nude statuary at the Museum, of Boccaccio or of Arabian Nights or Rabelais.

You should understand, too, that support of the institution of the play jury in no way commits the *World* to any judgment it may happen to make. We have accepted the idea of the play jury as a protection against the possibility of political censorship. That possibility arises not from plays like *Love for Love* but from plays like Mr. Belasco's. It seems to me that the emphasis of your argument is entirely wrong. You assume that we support the play jury because we wish to see certain plays suppressed. On the contrary, we are supporting the play jury because, unless the tendency exhibited in *Ladies of the Evening* is stopped voluntarily, censorship will result. It's very important that this distinction should clearly be kept in mind.

1. Arthur Krock, then assistant to the president of the *New York World*, joined the Board of Editors of the *New York Times* in 1927 and later became that paper's Washington correspondent and senior syndicated columnist.

To Alfred E. Smith

April 22, 1925

Dear Governor:

I understand you are to be invited, or perhaps have already been invited . . . to attend the Governors' Conference in June. Some friends of mine have written me and urge that you go in order to give the meeting of Governors some importance. I agree with them. If the Democratic objection to centralization is to mean anything then we've got to build up not only more responsible government in the states as you have done here in New York, but we have got to find a way of practicing voluntary cooperation among the states. The Governors' Conference may help this along. Your going would focus the eyes of the whole country on it.

To Learned Hand

[c. June 8, 1925]

Dear B,

. . . I want your advice badly on the Tennessee case.[1] Powell and Morris Cohen[2] take the view, if I understand them correctly, that the constitutionality of the law ought not to be attacked. Such foolishness should be within the province of the legislature. Now I know this is progressive dogma as we all accepted it in the days when the courts were knocking out the laws we wanted. Powell and Cohen are consistent, but I wonder whether we don't have to develop some new doctrine to protect education from majorities. My own mind has been getting steadily antidemocratic: the size of the electorate, the impossibility of educating it sufficiently, the fierce ignorance of these millions of semi-literate priestridden and parsonridden people have got me to the point where I want to confine the actions of majorities. Down here on the edge of the South the danger is more evident than in New York, where Heaven knows the Hylan business[3] is enough to make anybody question the old democratic dogma. . . . At any rate we have got to fight this Tennessee business somehow. What do you think?[4]

I have another favor to ask of you. My book "The Phantom Public" is to be published in the fall. It is now being set in type and I had planned to send you a proof. You will have sailed before you can read it. I want to dedicate the book to you, and I am embarrassed because I feel you ought to have a chance to say no, and I am afraid you won't say no whatever your feeling about it. I'm quite prepared to believe you will think it crude and even unsound, because I have taken a flyer into a rather strange field of theory. Please be frank enough to say just what you would like best.

1. Defying a Tennessee statute forbidding the teaching of biological evolution, John Scopes, a schoolteacher, had been discharged from his position. The American Civil Liberties Union became interested in his case as a test of freedom of ideas. The choice of Clarence Darrow to handle the case generated not only an able and passionate advocacy but also spectacular publicity. Fundamentalists, determined to preserve the statute, received spontaneous support from William Jennings Bryan, who volunteered his services to a cause in which he believed as deeply as he believed in the literal reading of the Bible. The trial became one of the most celebrated episodes of the decade, but in the process the private problems of John Scopes dropped from sight. Lippmann, from the first interpreting the issue primarily in constitutional terms, hoped the federal courts would nullify the Tennessee law. They did not.   2. Thomas Reed Powell, at this time an adviser to the *World* on constitutional questions, later a distinguished professor of law at Harvard and a leading interpreter of the Constitution and the Supreme Court; and Morris Cohen, eminent lawyer and philosopher, long an influential professor at the City College of New York.   3. Mayor John F. Hylan of New York City, then eager for renomination, was facing the open opposition of Governor Alfred E. Smith, who considered him corrupt and incompetent. In the Democratic primary in September, Hylan lost to James J. Walker, who won the office in November with Smith's endorsement. Walker proved to be as corrupt and incompetent as his predecessor.   4. "I have found no competent person," Hand replied on June 10, "who differs from Cohen and Powell." He went on to express his preference for democracy and his pleasure in Lippmann's intention to dedicate to him *The Phantom Public* (New York, 1925).

To Felix Frankfurter

June 10, 1925

Dear Felix:

. . . I naturally agree with you about the Tennessee case. I'm afraid the thing is in the hands of publicity seekers, and that the scenery is being set for an outcry in the South that New York is trying to run things. It was a mistake to bring Scopes to New York. He should have stayed in Paducah, Kentucky, selling automobiles. It's a mistake to surround him with a mass of people with axes to grind. The dignity of the case has been very largely lost sight of and I feel fairly certain the issue is going to be befogged by Darrow, who will be actuated by his own pleasure in using his own mental equipment. If I get a chance I shall certainly say this to Richard Baldwin.[1] Life is like that. The friends are often more of a difficulty than the enemies. However, I have a hope that after this circus at Dayton is over, and both sides are morally bankrupt, the more intelligent crowd can take care of the case when the constitutional issue comes up. . . .

1. Lippmann meant Roger Baldwin, founder and head of the ACLU.

To Graham Wallas

June 11, 1925

My dear G. W.:

. . . The Tennessee case presents some extremely interesting issues in American constitutional law. We all assume that Scopes, the young biology teacher who has been indicted for violating the anti-evolution statute, will be convicted by the jury. And all plans are shaping up towards an effort to have the courts declare the statute unconstitutional. Here arises a very serious and important division of opinion, among the people opposed to such laws. Men like Hand take the position that bad as the statute is, it's even worse to go to the courts for an annulment of the statute, and worse even to go to the Federal Supreme Court. Others, like Felix, who object to the Fourteenth Amendment in principle, say that as long as we have it, we might as well use it to fight such legislation as this. Bryan has, as you know, based his case on the right of the majority of a legislature to determine the character of teaching in the schools for which it votes the money. This is a difficult principle to controvert. Personally, I am pretty well persuaded that it's necessary to controvert it. But in doing so, it will be necessary to invent some sort of constitutional theory under which public education is rendered rather more independent of the legislature than it is at present. I should like your advice in this matter. You have some notion, I imagine, of the dangerous condition of the State universities in America. However much complaint there may be about the influence of business men on the private universities, there can be no doubt that the influence of the legislatures is far more harassing and dangerous to freedom of thought. It seems to me that majority rule is after all only a limited political device and that where some great interest like education comes into conflict with it, we are justified in trying to set up defenses against the majority.

To S. K. Ratcliffe

October 9, 1925

My dear S. K.,

. . . What you have to say about the state of mind in England depresses me, but does not surprise me. The returning travelers have been bringing much the same kind of reports.[1] I have hesitated to comment on conditions in England because I knew they were serious and I feel very much out of touch with them. Our own conditions, on the contrary, are for the present very simple. The economic position is as easy as it's ever been in this generation, and we have even achieved a high level of prosperity without a boom. The most hopeful thing is that the old hard complacency which Coolidge represented seems to be melting and with it has come not only a better feeling of tolerance at home but a less arrogant one toward the rest of the world. I look around and wonder whether such an amazing distribution of wealth can be real, but I confess I see no serious difficulties in the industrial situation. Labor is protected by the immigration law, the western wheat farmers, and even the cattle men are making a remarkable recovery, and the industrial sections are busy without being speculative and frenzied. Lord knows I don't know what we've done as a nation to deserve these things. . . .

1. Continuing unemployment and labor unrest, as well as the rigidity and insularity of Stanley Baldwin's restored Conservative government, depressed England's American friends and forbode the general strike of the following year.

To C. P. Scott

December 11, 1925

Dear Mr. Scott:

. . . The latest reports I hear from Washington are fairly hopeful about our adherence to the Court.[1] The real issue, of course, is not the Court itself but whether we shall take a small but decisive step toward organic cooperation with Europe. I strongly hope that the English papers will hold down their comment on the forthcoming battle in the Senate to a minimum because every remark in the British press written from the pro-League point of view will be misused by the opponents of the Court. While the outlook is favorable I am not at all certain that we shall win. The trouble is that Borah, who is sincere and resourceful and able is leading the fight on the other side, and Coolidge, who is the nominal leader on our side has never yet fought for anything. It will be a battle of courage and determination against numbers and inertia. I think it is of historic importance in American foreign policy. If we join the Court, no matter on what terms, the morale of the isolationists will be badly broken. They are unnaturally strong and influential now because of their victory in 1920. I think you would find that once it is demonstrated they can be beaten on an issue of this kind, that Mr. Coolidge would follow his natural inclination and the advice of his best friends and go a long way in cooperation in Europe.

1. As he had twice before, President Coolidge, in his annual message to Congress in January 1925, had proposed American membership in the World Court, though with the understanding that that would not create any legal relationship to the League of Nations. In March 1925, the House of Representatives, by a decisive vote, passed a resolution favoring membership. The Senate did not act until January 1926, when its approval of adherence to the Court carried several reservations, one of which — dear to Borah — exempted the United States from the Court's advisory opinions. The Court refused to accept that exception, and the United States remained apart.

To Frank B. Kellogg[1]

December 18, 1925

Dear Mr. Secretary:

I should like to let you know what I have done following our talk on Tuesday at this office in regard to the Tacna Arica matter.[2]

The problem was to make contact with Peru with a view to re-opening diplomatic negotiations. After investigation and consultation with a number of people acquainted with the matter, I have done two things, one private and one which will be public.

1. Privately I have suggested to an American, Mr. Samuel A. Maginnis, formerly our Minister to Bolivia, that he suggest to the Bolivian Government that they approach you with an inquiry as to whether the time would be opportune for them to suggest a negotiation in regard to the Tacna Arica territory. I have not told Mr. Maginnis, therefore he cannot tell the Bolivians, of any talk I had with you. But I have told him that our investigations as a newspaper had persuaded me that our Government might not regard such an approach unfavorably. At any rate Mr. Maginnis has gone to Washington today to see the Bolivian Minister. Of course if Bolivia approaches you in this fashion it will then be possible for you to call in the Chilean Ambassador and Peruvian Minister and tell them that you have this interesting offer and wouldn't they like to discuss it. That would create the contact which I understood you desired. This plan, except in certain details, as to how to approach the Bolivians, was worked out by Mr. Morrow, with whom I have discussed the matter at considerable length. He thought, and I agreed with him, that this is a better method of approach than to suggest to American interests in Peru that they put pressure on the Peruvian Government. He is in touch with the American Smelting and Refining Company, Grace and Company and the Cerro de Pasco Company, which are the three largest American interests in Peru. Mr. Mor-

row asked me to tell you that he didn't think these interests could, or should, be used to initiate these negotiations, but that once the faintest beginnings of a negotiation had been made, they could be used to back it up in Peru. His information also confirms the understanding that Chile would probably be favorable to a negotiation.

2. Our information is that the Peruvians at the moment, especially their officials here, feel that they are going to win the plebiscite and they are openly saying that the President of the United States will have to back them up if they win and guarantee their victory. It is necessary, therefore, to break down this assurance on their part. I am proposing, therefore, after making arrangements to have the material transmitted to South America and especially to Peru, to begin, sometime next week, an editorial campaign saying that under no circumstances can the United States be committed to the enforcement of the results of the plebiscite, and that unless this is clearly understood on all sides, our Commission ought to be withdrawn. I think it will probably help a good deal if the Peruvians see that American sentiment is crystallizing against the plebiscite. . . .

1. Frank B. Kellogg, then secretary of state, a conventional intelligence and conservative Republican for whom Lippmann had little respect.   2. The Tacna-Arica question, a dispute over the border between Chile and Peru, had long troubled relations between those two nations. The United States was attempting to mediate the issue, in part through a supervised plebiscite. Secretary of State Kellogg was in the last stages of that effort, which produced no immediate results but helped ultimately to lead to direct negotiations between the principals. In 1929 Chile received Arica. Bolivia, from which Chile had taken the territory in 1884, obtained only a rail outlet to the Pacific.

To Adolph S. Ochs [1]

December 30, 1925

Dear Mr. Ochs:

I hope I did not give a wrong impression last night as to my attitude toward the Associated Press and its work. For that work and the spirit of it I have the greatest respect. When I used the phrase "the tyranny of the Associated Press," or the "benevolent despotism" of the Associated Press, the thought I meant to convey was that by reason of the obligation under which the Associated Press labors to supply to its members all the routine news, that the very mechanics of distribution made it extremely difficult for an accidental story to get adequate showing, or even due consideration by the papers of the country. This is not the fault of the Associated Press. It is the fault of conditions, the remedy for which I do not pretend to know.

Of course I realize that the Associated Press does cover all important news outside the regular routine. But first among such important news, other than routine, always come stories of accidents, crimes, or events of unusual interest.

What I was trying to draw attention to is the fact that there is a twilight zone of news, of considerable importance in itself and even of greater importance to editorial writers, to enable them to comment intelligently, which the Associated Press is utterly unable to cover. This inability is created by the limitation of time and mechanical facilities, and also by the fact that the subscribers to the Associated Press would be unwilling to pay telegraph tolls upon much of the material I have in mind which they would be unable to print in their news columns and yet which is valuable for purposes of editorial comment.

The "tyranny" of the situation grows out of the fact that what the Associated Press does or does not do is controlling. Papers depend upon the Associated Press. If they get something from the Associated Press they use it because it is from the Associated Press. If the same information comes from outside the Associated Press they will not use it — at least as a rule. One of the reasons for this is that the Associated Press does the editing and the rewriting of the news, thus saving the local paper that additional editorial effort and expense. But the net of it is that the Associated Press virtually controls the situation — and the limitations of the Associated Press thereby become a subject of appropriate question.

I don't know whether you see the papers of the country at large or not. I am compelled to give a great deal of attention to them and I am constantly both impressed and oppressed with the inadequacy of treatment given by the press generally throughout the country to matters of real consequence.

With reference to the Associated Press there is another factor of considerable importance. One may supply the Associated Press with an item of information of much importance, an item which a great many of the papers throughout the country would like to have, even if they don't have room to print it. Yet, if the one man of the Associated Press who happens to be in charge of receiving that particular item considers that it is not of sufficient importance or news value to send out, the entire Associated Press membership, and thereby the country, is deprived of that information unless it is obtained from some other source. I have myself often seen news items of real significance turned down by the Associated Press at one point, and this same material, having been supplied directly to the newspapers at some other point, get on the Associated Press wires from that point and thus reach the country. If one had depended upon only one contact with the Associated Press, the item would never have reached the country.

Please do not understand me as criticizing the Associated Press. I think its work is done with great competence, ability and conscientiousness. I should be very much surprised if the officers of the Associated Press would not concede the validity of these observations of mine. If I was running the Associated Press myself, I would not know how to remedy the situation insofar as the activities of the Associated Press itself are concerned. . . .

---

1. Adolph S. Ochs, publisher of the *New York Times*.

To William Watts Ball[1]

January 14, 1926

My dear Dean Ball:

I am very glad to have your letter and to find, after reading it, that we are not in any essential disagreement. You understand, of course, that in making that reference to the South I did not have in mind any moral judgment. I was attempting purely to state, perhaps a little too briefly, an objective fact. That fact, I think, is that the disfranchisement of the negro rests *ultimately*[2] upon the superior force of the whites. I think you would agree, from a scientific point of view, that the disfranchisement would be impossible if the negro were stronger (using the word in all senses: intellectually, morally, physically, etc.) than the whites. I might add that I have studied the problems of the reconstruction period in the South sufficiently to prevent me from making an easy judgment upon your political problem.

1. William Watts Ball, lawyer, journalist, at this time dean of the School of Journalism at the University of South Carolina.   **2.** Emphasis Lippmann's.

To Leonard P. Ayres[1]

January 26, 1926

Dear Leonard:

I wonder whether you have read Ripley's article in the *Atlantic* called "From Wall Street to Main Street,"[2] and whether you have seen what we've been doing about it editorially. At any rate, if you haven't, we've been urging the stock exchange to make a declaration of public policy on the new fashion in finance typified by the Dodge deal[3] of giving investors no control of the property and of keeping the control in the hands of a private banking house which has no investment. If this is a thing that has interested you and about which you have any opinions, we'd rather have comment from you than from anybody I can think of. . . .

1. Leonard P. Ayres, Cleveland banker, friend of Newton D. Baker's, and a frequent correspondent whose views Lippmann much respected.   **2.** William Z. Ripley, an outstanding institutional economist and professor at Harvard, had written his article as part of his forthcoming book, *Main Street and Wall Street* (Boston, 1927), an early criticism of the unchecked speculation and disturbing corporate practices then increasingly obvious on Wall Street. The *Atlantic* article focused on the growing separation between corporate ownership and control.   **3.** An issue of nonvoting common stock of the Dodge Motor Company.

To Frank B. Kellogg

February 2, 1926

Dear Mr. Secretary:

Thank you for your letter of February 1st. I understand from Mr. Maginnis that he saw the Bolivian Minister, but for some reason which Mr. Maginnis could not explain, the Minister was afraid to act. Apparently there was a change of administration in Bolivia which caused the Bolivian Minister in Washington to feel rather uncertain himself. I understand further that Mr. Maginnis wrote directly to influential friends in Bolivia quoting the *World's* editorials and giving it as his personal opinion that the time was ripe for them to act. In all of this I have assumed, of course, that what you told me was confidential and Mr. Maginnis does not know what you told me about your attitude.

I need hardly say that we stand ready to help you in any way we can because we feel that American interests and American prestige are very much at stake and that it is most desirable to extricate ourselves from what appears to be an embarrassing and insoluble difficulty.

To Archibald Cary Coolidge

February 9, 1926

Dear Coolidge:

Here is the review of the House memoirs. I hope you will like it for I am afraid that our mutual friend Seymour[1] won't. All I can say is that I have exercised great self-restraint under what I regard as extreme provocation. Personally, I think the editing is horrible in that it makes the Colonel look ridiculous by endowing him with omniscience and omnipotence. I don't know what the impressions you hear are, but around here the comment is both bitter and contemptuous. I think the whole thing will hurt House very much, and I am very sorry about that because I am extremely fond of him. I cannot imagine how he could have approved a job done in such bad taste.

All this is to prepare you for the shock of finding that I have taken rather sharp issue with Seymour in his interpretation of the principal event in the memoirs, namely the House-Grey negotiations of 1916. . . .

1. Charles S. Seymour, professor of history at Yale University and formerly a member of the Inquiry, later president of Yale, had just published the first two volumes of his book *The Intimate Papers of Colonel House* (Boston, 1926). Uncritically laudatory, as Lippmann observed, the work was also marred, beyond what anyone could then have known, by serious but undesignated omissions and deletions. Lippmann's review appeared in the April number of *Foreign Affairs*.

To Newton D. Baker

February 9, 1926

Dear Newton:

I am going to take the liberty of sending you in a few days the manuscript of the House memoirs. There are, I suppose, as many opinions of Wilson as there are people to write them, and I won't expect you to agree entirely with what I have written. I should, however, like very much to know not only what you think of the article in general, but whether at any point I have said anything that is clearly wrong, or anything that it would be better taste not to say. I want to call your attention particularly to my interpretation of the so-called House-Grey negotiations early in 1916. I've made a sharp issue here with Seymour and perhaps with House himself, and I should like very much to know what you think of it. The essence of the matter is that House claims Wilson authorized him to secretly promise that we would enter the war on the side of the Allies on certain conditions. My argument is that Wilson did not make any such promise, and the implication is that Wilson had too great a sense of responsibility as President to make a promise of that sort, even for the most presumably benevolent purpose.

Since you told me that you read what the papers printed about the offer to you of the Secretaryship of the Interior perhaps you'll be relieved to know that according to my present recollection there are no important references to you after that. You will, however, be simply astounded at the prescience which the editor attributes to his hero as the story progresses.

To Newton D. Baker

February 15, 1926

Dear Newton:

I am very much pleased to have your letter because it reassures me so completely on the main point, namely, as to the real purpose of President Wilson.[1] It seems to me of the utmost importance that this, which after all is the promise of everything that follows by way of historical interpretation, should be thoroughly established and clearly understood. For the moment, of course, we are still sufficiently under the spell of the war psychology so that even his friends feel themselves under the necessity of vindicating this attitude of Wilson instead of proclaiming it as a sign of his greatness and his prophetic sense.

I think you're right in saying that House will have to bear the responsibility for not having had full knowledge of the secret treaties, but I doubt whether, if I were writing as a historian, I would place the full responsibility upon him. It seems to me the President himself erred in thinking that a matter so great as the European war with such tremendous complications could be accurately mapped for him by one unofficial observer. I can't believe that there is any sufficient explanation for his long patience with Page and Sharp in Paris.[2] Surely whatever his confidence in House, those two posts should have been filled by men in whom he had complete confidence.

1. "Wilson," Baker wrote, ". . . seemed to have, as the dominant passion of his life, the desire to keep America out of the European war . . . after we went into the war his only interest was that it should issue in a rational and stable peace." **2.** Walter Hines Page, during Wilson's presidency the United States ambassador to the Court of St. James's; and William G. Sharp, his counterpart in Paris.

To Louis McHenry Howe[1]

March 8, 1926

Dear Mr. Howe:

In response to your inquiry as to my attitude on the Italian debt question, I should like to say that I am in favor of ratification of the terms approved by the House.[2]

The cash value of these debts has never seemed to me sufficiently large to weigh against the imponderable elements in the problem. I am in favor of any settlement that is a settlement. I am not in favor of attaching to the settlement any provision which will tend to reopen the question and cause a renewal of political agitation in both countries. I think that the cost of such agitation far outweighs the money involved in the debt.

I believe the present administration is censurable for failure to place the whole settlement of the debts on a high and disinterested level. The Administration has persistently led the American people to believe that the whole of these debts could be collected. The result of this mis-education has been that the United States Government is made to appear in the role of a harsh creditor, when, as a matter of fact, the terms accepted by the Debt Funding Commission are extremely generous. The Administration has got neither the money nor the moral credit, and personally I believe that its whole handling of this question has been a very serious failure.

1. Louis McHenry Howe, Franklin Roosevelt's dedicated and effective personal assistant and political adviser. **2.** With Europe in grave financial trouble, the United States in November 1925 reduced Italy's interest on its war debt and canceled 80.2 percent of that debt. In April 1926, the French interest rate was also reduced, and 60.3 percent of the debt canceled. The United States continued to demand annual payment on the balances.

To Felix Frankfurter

March 18, 1926

Dear Felix:

I have re-read your paper and it raises this question in my mind. If you agree to limit federal action to international and inter-state action, do you mean to imply that each state may decide for itself what liquor shall be manufactured within its borders and sold within its borders? I suppose you realize that such a policy means nullification in states like New York.

I myself believe that wet sentiment, finding the repeal or even amendment of the Volstead Act[1] impossible, will devote itself to limiting the appropriations available for enforcement. The objective, however, will be that nullification which you deplore. For myself I realize all the difficulties and dangers of a policy of selective law obedience, but I regard the preaching of law obedience here as perfectly futile and meaningless. A very large minority of the American people is for all practical purposes in open rebellion against the Eighteenth Amendment, and the real lesson is not to enforce the Eighteenth Amendment, but not to pass amendments of this character.

1. Following the ratification of the Eighteenth Amendment (the prohibition amendment), the Volstead Act (the National Prohibition Enforcement Act) of 1919 defined as intoxicating liquor any beverage containing more than one half of one percent of alcohol. It designated the Bureau of Internal Revenue as the enforcement agency. From the first, enforcement proved impossible. The *World* was a leading advocate of modification of the act, which was especially resented in cities with large immigrant populations, such as New York. The issue deeply divided the Democratic party, with the "dry" rural South opposing the "wet" Northeast and its articulate spokesman, Alfred E. Smith.

To Sidney E. Mezes

March 19, 1926

Dear Mezes:

I am very much pleased with your letter, for while I knew that you are always objective in these matters, I was honestly a little worried as to how a member of the Colonel's family would feel about the review. Of course your testimony about the attitude of the two men towards getting into the war is invaluable.

Since you mention the question of the secret treaties, I might say that I have been wondering why they did not play any part in House's calculations during 1916. Seymour implies that they were unknown in our government until April 30, 1917, but from Page's letters it is evident that he, at least, had got wind of them. That seemed to me the missing link in both Wilson's and House's calculations about the war. I am inclined to think that a practical historian will regard the failure to know about them and to take them into account as a great defect of the statesmanship of that period.

Since you have written me so kindly and personally, may I reciprocate by saying something to you which comes out of great affection for, and loyalty to, the Colonel? This is something that I don't feel free to say to him directly unless he asks me. But perhaps you will think it over and act on it, if you think wise. I think the editing by Seymour, and the connecting narrative, has hurt the Colonel unnecessarily. There is an undertone of hero-worship which destroys the sense of historical objectivity, and there is an overtone of a case to be proved on behalf of the Colonel's wisdom and foresight and statesmanship which ought not to be there. I very much hope that in the succeeding volumes Seymour will detach himself from his partisanship to the Colonel and present the matter not as part of an autobiography of a hero but as the record of a great series of events. The Colonel's ultimate reputation is going to be profoundly affected by the frankness and the selflessness with which the story of his break with Wilson is presented in the succeeding volumes, and speaking candidly, I am very much worried as to how Seymour is going to do it. . . .[1]

1. Seymour did not alter his ways in his second two volumes, published in 1928.

To Felix Frankfurter

April 13, 1926

Dear Felix:

At least, inexpert as I am at meeting you in court, we narrow the range of disagreement.

"My central point," you say, "is that it's high time we were stopped being fed on falsities on the theory that we cannot face the truth." Agreed.

Now what is "the truth"?

That nobody knows what Italy will be able to pay thirty years from now, or how much the United States will wish to collect? Well, we both call *that* "the truth."

That the larger payments scheduled for years some distance in the future are necessarily speculative? Well, we both call *that* "the truth."

That these larger sums were written into the agreement solely for the purpose of helping float a Morgan loan? There we differ. There it is at least pertinent to note that the Morgan loan is specifically for the purpose of exchange stabilization and not for general governmental purposes. There it is at least pertinent to note that the loan absorbs a credit of $50,000,000 advanced last spring. There it is at least pertinent to note that the loan is made on a balanced budget (following the removal of the "unofficial" administration embargo, as a result of a debt compact being reached) and that other loans to other governments have been made in the past and simply on the basis of a balanced budget. There, once more, I submit that the burden of proof rests with you, not me. And there, finally — stupid though I may be — you have yet to persuade me with your evidence upon the specific point at issue.

To Felix Frankfurter

June 14, 1926

Dear Felix:

. . . As to Sacco Vanzetti,[1] I'll wait to hear from you further. In thinking about it, bear in mind the great difficulty of discussing the details of the evidence for a newspaper audience that has no background of the case. . . . I should rather despair of being able to educate any considerable number of our readers about the testimony taken in the trial. But usually in a matter of this sort, it's possible to pick out some sample of the behavior of the court on which the argument can be made that there has been a denial of justice.

1. During the height of the Red Scare, two Italian anarchists — Nicola Sacco and Bartolomeo Vanzetti — were arrested, convicted, and sentenced to death for a payroll robbery and murder of which they claimed innocence. The complicated evidence in the case, while it by no means demonstrated their innocence, also by no means demonstrated their guilt. Further, the trial by a prejudiced jury in Norfolk County, Massachusetts, instructed by a biased judge, was grossly unfair. Protests against the conviction and for commutation of the sentence grew in force and persuasiveness as the date of execution approached. Frankfurter, who played a major role in that protest, wrote influential and relevant articles for the *Atlantic Monthly* and an important book, *The Case of Sacco and Vanzetti* (Boston, 1927). Lippmann, in charge of the *World's* editorial page since Cobb's fatal illness and death in 1923, recognized the injustice of the trial but struck a characteristically temperate posture that contrasted with the stridency, born of outrage, of Frankfurter and others in the protest movement.

To William E. Borah

July 1, 1926

Dear Senator Borah:

When I was in London in the Spring, I learned of a situation which may prove to be . . . embarrassing to the American government. . . . Professor G. Salvemini was, until a year or two ago, Professor of History in the University of Florence. He was an old-fashioned Italian liberal, never in any way associated with the Communist movement, or even, I think, with the mildest forms of Socialism. He was always, however, an anti-Imperialist and opposed the Imperialistic aims of Italy during the war in the Fiume episode. Later he became an anti-Fascist on precisely the grounds, I think, that you would become an anti-Fascist, if you lived in Italy.[1]

For that reason he has been driven into exile and is now living in London and was threatened, when I was there, with the loss of his Italian citizenship. I am not sure whether the action has actually been taken which deprives him of that or not. However, a number of people desire to have him visit the United States next year to lecture at the universities and talk before public audiences. There is every reason to think that the Italian government would oppose his entry into the United States and on the advice of American friends he has thus far refrained from applying for permission to come. The ordinary application for a visa would probably not obtain in his case in any event because he has no passport from the Italian Government and could obtain none. Testimonials as to his character and position are easily had. I am sure that Professor Archibald Coolidge at Harvard and many other Americans would go on record as to the entire mildness of the man.

He has just written me to ask me whether I would ask you to use your good offices with the State Department to obtain permission for him to come here in the Fall. If the application went through regular channels, it is to be supposed that the Italian Ambassador would be consulted and that he would object. Personally, I should feel that the barring of a man like Salvemini was the climax and the most disgraceful of all the episodes of this kind which have occurred recently.

Won't you take up the matter with the Department? No move will be made, at any rate, until I hear from you, and any information you may desire to have before making the request I can obtain for you.

1. Berenson had alerted Lippmann to the problems of Gaetano Salvemini, an Italian historian, a liberal, and a fervent opponent of Mussolini. This letter to Borah was one of many Lippmann wrote on Salvemini's behalf. After Salvemini reached the United States, partly because of Borah's intercession, Lippmann urged the publication of the exile's *The Fascist Dictatorship in Italy* (New York, 1927). Later Lippmann helped Salvemini find academic employment as a lecturer in Harvard's History Department.

To H. L. Mencken

July 29, 1926

Dear Mencken:

. . . It must be obvious to you that even assuming that the *World* agreed with your estimate of Reed[1] it could hardly throw over Al Smith at a time when he will be either running again for Governor or trying to elect his own candidate for Governor. What is more, while I pretty well agree with you that the Smith candidacy may lead to disaster, I haven't yet gotten up as much admiration for Reed as you have. Perhaps I have an initial prejudice to overcome. Certainly I admire him at least twice as much as I did two years ago, but there are certain sides to him that I cannot quite stomach just yet. I mean particularly the violence and the frequent untruthfulness of what he has to say about foreign affairs. At any rate, you'll agree that for these different reasons the best thing to do is to print your letter but not attempt to discuss it. . . .

1. Democratic Senator James A. Reed of Missouri, then an undeclared but available candidate for the party's presidential nomination in 1928 (a prospect both curious and unappealing in the retrospect of time), had the support of H. L. Mencken, who had written a letter to the *World* putting Reed's name forward. Mencken agreed with Lippmann's decision to postpone publication of the letter until September, when it appeared without editorial comment.

To William E. Borah

August 3, 1926

My dear Senator Borah:

I have not hurried to answer your letter of July 23rd because I felt that the issues raised by it should be carefully investigated. The point in dispute between us turns on the analogy between the attitude of the South toward the Fifteenth Amendment and the attitude of New York toward the Eighteenth. For the purposes of our argument I assume that we may admit that both amendments were a mistake. You have asserted that in regard to the Fifteenth and I agree. I assert it in regard to the Eighteenth. We are now arguing the wisdom of prohibition, and therefore I assume you will grant me the premise that the Eighteenth Amendment looked at from the point of view of New York was as great a mistake as the Fifteenth Amendment looked at from the point of view of the South.

We come then immediately to your fifth point, . . . you say that . . . you studied the laws and conditions of the South and came to the conclusion that you "do not know of any State in the South at the present time whose election laws are in conflict with the Fifteenth Amendment." Here is the crux of our argument. For I maintain that the South today is nullifying the whole intent of the Fifteenth Amendment, but is doing it by methods which have passed the Supreme Court. I maintain that if the precedent is a sound one, then New York could, with your approval, nullify the intent of the Eighteenth Amendment, provided it did so under a formula which would pass the Supreme Court.

The situation in regard to the South's nullification of the Fifteenth Amendment is, in brief, as follows:

1. At the close of reconstruction, the South was saddled with the Fifteenth Amendment and a set of reconstruction State Constitutions which gave to the negro broad voting privileges.

2. The South found this intolerable. For twenty years it excluded negroes from the polls by illegal or extralegal methods. The simplest and most common method was to use physical violence or intimidation. In employing this method, however, it was assisted by the Federal Courts. These courts decided (1881: U.S. vs. Amsden) that "it is not an offense against the laws of the United States to prevent a citizen, white or black, from voting at a State Election, by violence or otherwise." To make it a Federal offense the violence must have been offered on account of "race or color." But the offenders could easily allege some other motive for the attack and so avoid Federal penalties.

This period corresponds roughly to the period we are now in in respect to the Eighteenth Amendment, the period of criminal bootlegging.

3. As time passed, the South wished to employ less offensive methods. It also wished to draw up new State Constitutions which made it more

certain that the negro could not vote. The result was that between 1890 and 1905 a series of Southern State Constitutional conventions effected the disfranchisement of the negro in new ways.

4. Mississippi led off in 1890. She legally disfranchised the negro by requiring that every voter show a receipt for a $2 poll tax, and requiring that he read the Constitution, or understand it when read, or be able to give a reasonable interpretation of passages on which he was questioned. It was easy to ask a negro what part of the Constitution was derived from Magna Carta and send him home without a vote.

5. South Carolina in 1895 went further. It made the negro show evidence that he had paid *all*[1] taxes; it also imposed a property test. But from the new and stringent requirements it exempted all war veterans and their descendants. This was the first "grandfather clause"; such clauses have been held unconstitutional by the Supreme Court. But the Supreme Court ruling was not handed down till 1914 (Guinn vs. U.S., 233 U.S. 347), and by that time the work had been done. That is, the clause had put all the white persons unable to pass the stringent tests upon the voting lists. All that was necessary was to provide that once any man's name went on the list, it should stay there.

6. Other Southern States in rapid succession followed and improved upon the measures of Mississippi and South Carolina. Virginia, for example, has a poll tax provision, a property test, etc.; but she places chief reliance simply upon the requirement that a voter shall be able to interpret the Constitution if part of it is read to him. This lets the illiterate white man in; it keeps even the literate negro out. The election official is final arbiter.

In the Constitutional Convention the chairman of the committee which drew up this clause said: "I expect the examination with which the black man will be confronted to be inspired by the same spirit that inspires every man upon this floor and in this convention. I do not expect an impartial administration of this clause."

I cannot believe that you will really publicly take the position that the Fifteenth Amendment has not been nullified, because nominally negroes are prevented from voting for some reason other than their color. I do not believe you can publicly take the position that the educational qualification is in harmony with the Fifteenth Amendment, when you know that it is not enforced against the white man at all, and is enforced unreasonably and excessively against the black man. For if you do take this position, you will simply be inviting New York to be as ingenious as the South and to obtain legal nullification by some ingenious subterfuge just as the South has done.

I am perfectly willing to admit that the policy proposed in the New York State referendum[2] represents a certain nullification of the Eighteenth Amendment. But I should certainly maintain with perfectly good conscience that it is more constitutional in its spirit and less nullifying in fact than the program adopted by the South to which you have publicly given your approval.

I strongly urge upon you before you come to New York,[3] to face this dilemma, which I think is a dilemma for you, fully and with great consideration. I should add, however, that I would not join you even if you proposed it in a movement designed to enforce both the Fifteenth and the Eighteenth Amendments. I think I am loyal to the Constitution, but I think I care even more about the peace and tranquillity of the United States. For a "Constitutional revival," such as you describe, if seriously enforced in the South would breed disorders greater by far than those which now exist as a result to enforce the Eighteenth Amendment in large urban areas.

In conclusion, I want to make it perfectly clear to you why I used the analogy of the Fifteenth Amendment. In your campaign you have started from the premise not that prohibition is a desirable social policy, but that all parts of the Constitution must be literally enforced. This premise, in my opinion, is based on an historical untruth and an implied falsification of the history of American constitutional practice. It involves a charge of disloyalty against the State of New York which, if it is to be made, must also be made against the Southern States and against many other States as well. It permits the prohibitionist to wrap around himself a mantle of righteousness to which he has no title whatsoever.

The position in which New York, like other large cities, finds itself, is a very difficult and delicate one. We know that the Volstead Act cannot be honestly enforced in a city like New York. We can honestly claim to know that better than citizens of small rural states. We pay, in the disorder of our own political and social life, the price of criminal activities which are nourished by an ineffective, corrupt and necessarily futile attempt to enforce this law. We are deeply conscious of the hypocrisy which this law has produced throughout America. We know that the Constitutional Amendment cannot be repealed so long as even a very insignificant minority chooses to block the repeal. We know that any revision of the Volstead Act which would legalize sufficient alcoholic beverage to make the rest of prohibition conceivably enforceable is contrary to the literal wording of the Eighteenth Amendment, and therefore, in your sense of the word, an act of nullification. We are therefore caught in an intolerable deadlock, and somehow we must find a way out of it. The way we have chosen is open, public, constitutional in its spirit, and, I think, consonant with the deeper principles of the American political system. It may be contrary to the strict letter of the Eighteenth Amendment. But if the letter killeth, what else can we do? I assure you, you will not enforce the Eighteenth Amendment in New York. I don't believe any enforcement official . . . deceives himself on that point. Is it not, then, the part of wisdom and statesmanship, when a community is caught between a rigid law and a set of unbending facts, to seek, as we are seeking, some kind of compromise and adjustment?

With your long record of adherence to the principle of home rule, with your profound distrust of centralization and too much government, I had really hoped to see in you the leader out of this profoundly difficult situation. You, far better than an out-and-out wet from a great city could be the man to lead opinion in this country to a workable solution on which we could restore our moral harmony.

1. Lippmann's emphasis. 2. New York was to have a referendum at the time of the November election on the Volstead Act. Lippmann favored the measure, which called for permitting the sale of light wines and beer. Borah had publicly opposed the referendum as a form of nullification of the Constitution. In November New York voters heavily favored it, to no legal avail. 3. Borah was beginning his predictably futile campaign for the 1928 Republican presidential nomination.

To Robert F. Wagner[1]

September 30, 1926

Dear Judge Wagner:

1. As you requested, I am enclosing, for a start, a complete set of the *World's* editorials covering the attack we made on Mellon and the Aluminum Company.[2]

2. I think I shall be able to give you, in a day or two, an analysis of the tariff as it affects an ordinary man's daily life, beginning with the things he eats for breakfast and following him through the day.

3. I think I can also give you, in a day or two, a memorandum on the manufacturing interests responsible for particular schedules in the Fordney-McCumber Tariff Law, including, of course, the glove schedule, which figured so largely in the defeat of Calder by Copeland. Senator Wadsworth, I think, had a good deal to do with that schedule, and the *World*, during that campaign, used it very effectively.[3]

4. After thinking over the whole matter of foreign policy, I believe it would be best if you could manage to come to the office here some afternoon and spend two hours. I think that with the matter here I could help you better than by dictating a new memorandum. I have very accurate files, but they are so voluminous that I really need to talk with you and show you them in order to know what would be most useful. . . .

1. Robert F. Wagner — a justice on the New York Supreme Court, 1919–26 — was elected as a Democrat in 1926 to the United States Senate, where he served, as he had earlier in the state legislature, as a vigorous proponent of social reform. 2. The Mellon family had a controlling interest in the Aluminum Company of America, the aluminum monopoly, which profited from the high schedules in the protectionist Fordney-McCumber Tariff of 1922. Secretary of the Treasury Andrew Mellon, oblivious as usual to conflicts of interest in his own case, avidly supported that tariff. 3. Republican Senator James W. Wadsworth of New York had championed the prohibitive duties on gloves, an important product of his state, incorporated in the 1922 tariff. The *World* made an issue of that schedule in its efforts to assist the successful candidacy of Royal S. Copeland, a Democrat, for the seat in the United States Senate held by William M. Calder, a Republican.

To Florence D. White[1]

October 15, 1926

Dear Mr. White:

I suggest that at the next Council we discuss a crusade against the manufacturers of guns, aim to bring them under very strict Federal regulation as to sale, to break up their very powerful lobby at Washington and in various State Legislatures. This is suggested by the hold-up in Elizabeth, N.J., and the *Evening World*'s story tonight that these automatic guns can be bought in any sporting goods store. . . .

1. Florence D. White had held managerial positions with Pulitzer newspapers since before the turn of the century. In 1926 he was financial and general manager of the *World*.

To F. W. Bowers[1]

October 22, 1926

Dear Mr. Bowers:

I am very grateful indeed for "Winnie-The-Pooh." You are quite right in calling it irresistible. I have enjoyed it more than anything of its kind since Milne's book of verse. I hope you have a gigantic sale.

1. F. W. Bowers of E. P. Dutton and Company, publishers.

To Herbert Bayard Swope[1]

January 25, 1927

Dear Herbert:

These comments in "America" and "The Tablet" are grossly false and they betray a state of mind with which it is impossible to reason. Any paper that would accuse us, as "America" does, of trying to produce war with Mexico has no intention of being fair and can't be answered.

The only question we need to consider in our own minds is the justification of the attitude we have taken in refraining from denouncing the anti-clerical policy of the Calles Government.[2] This has been a matter of extreme difficulty and delicacy for us ever since last summer, when the Knights of Columbus made their appeal to President Coolidge asking, by implication, for a rupture of diplomatic relations with Mexico. If that demand had come from a Methodist organization we should have denounced them in unmeasured terms. Coming from a Catholic organization we said as little as it was possible to say and still keep our own record of disapproval of such action clear. It was necessary for the *World* to dissociate itself from the Knights of Columbus propaganda or admit the charge of the whole country that we were not an independent newspaper.

Once this Knights of Columbus propaganda was on foot, with its million dollar fund for agitation against Mexico, there was no way that I could see by which we could do what Mr. White suggests, namely, offer discriminating criticism of the measures taken by the Calles government. If we had taken the line that certain acts in relation to the Church were bad, we should, by implication, have approved the whole anti-clerical policy. And my judgment was, and is, that once we got in that morass, we should have been gotten into even more trouble than we are in now. We never could have satisfied the Knights of Columbus, and I believe that it is not true that they would have been satisfied . . . if we had merely denounced a few of the acts against individual priests and a few of the regulations which are unquestionably unjust and too severe. The religious controversy of Mexico is a head-on collision and anybody to take a middle-of-the-road line on it would be worse off than if he had simply stood on the side entirely.

We shall get no credit for it, but the fact is that our resistance to a break in Mexico and to intervention in Mexico is in the highest interests of the Catholic Church in America. Nothing would so certainly revive the Ku Klux Klan and general anti-Catholic feeling as a war with Mexico, which would certainly be blamed equally upon the oil interests and the Knights of Columbus. The truth of the matter is that the Knights of Columbus played with fire and they have been burnt by it. They have done more in their action in regard to Mexico to make moderate, tolerant and liberal people worry about the effect of making Al Smith President than all the propaganda for years in the past. I should go so far as to say that if intervention with Mexico comes, Al Smith's chances are absolutely finished. This country is against war, and nothing could hurt him or the church more than to be associated with the war party.

As for ourselves, we can afford to ignore these attacks. The time will certainly come when we shall be in a position to demonstrate the genuineness of our sympathy with American Catholics. In the meantime, I have no doubt that the rank and file of Catholics are as opposed to war as the Protestants. Our own enormous correspondence on Mexico and Nicaragua[3] shows that. It is full of letters containing the most exaggerated praise by men with Irish names. . . .

1. Herbert Bayard Swope, then executive editor of the *New York World*. **2.** President Plutarco Calles of Mexico had revived the reforming spirit of the revolutionary years. His social and agrarian program brought him into conflict with the Catholic Church, which in February 1927 repudiated the Constitution of 1917. The government, undeterred, ordered nationalization of church property and began closing Catholic schools. Earlier, in June 1925, Secretary Kellogg had accused the Calles administration of failing to protect American lives and property, and later he protested further the terms of the Mexican Petroleum and Alien Land Laws of December 1925. Various American Catholic groups urged intervention in Mexico, to which Kellogg at times seemed to be moving, not least because of the advice of the Mexican ambassador, a friend of the American oil companies. Lippmann led the *World* in its policy of opposition to intervention and its advocacy of negotiation leading toward a peaceful settlement of the outstanding issues. Later he became directly involved himself after President Coolidge, retreating from intervention, appointed Dwight Morrow ambassador. **3.** In September 1926, American troops imposed an armistice ending the civil war in Nicaragua between liberal and conservative forces. That war broke out again in December 1926. The Coolidge administration seemed about to intervene, and the *World* opposed intervention, until a modification of American policy in March 1927 resulted in a mission by Henry L. Stimson, who brought the two Nicaraguan sides together in a tenuous settlement.

To Ralph Pulitzer

February 3, 1927

MEMO

Article 27 of the Mexican Constitution reads in part as follows:

> The ownership of lands and waters comprised within the limits of the national territory is vested originally in the Union which has had, and has, the right to transmit title thereto to private persons, thereby constituting private property.
>
> Private property shall not be expropriated except for reasons of public means and by means of indemnification. The nation shall have, at all times, the right to impose on private property such limitations as the public interest may demand as well as the right to regulate the development of natural resources which are susceptible to appropriation in order to conserve them and equitably to distribute the public wealth. . . . In the nation is vested direct ownership of all minerals or substances. . . .

Article 14 of the Mexican Constitution says:

> No law shall be given retroactive effect to the prejudice of any person whatsoever.
>
> No person shall be deprived of life, liberty, possessions or rights without due process of law instituted before a duly created court in which the essential elements of procedure are observed and in accordance with previously existing laws.

The State Department claims that the Petroleum Law passed to carry out Article 27 is retroactive and confiscatory because, as Mr. Kellogg said in his note of July 31, 1926:

> American nationals who have made investments in Mexico in reliance on unqualified titles would be obliged to file applications virtually surrendering these vested rights and to accept in lieu thereof concessions of manifestly lesser scope and value. The use of the word "confirmation" in this relation is, to say the least, misleading. The operation would be nothing but a forced exchange of a greater for a lesser estate. That a statute so construed and enforced is retroactive and confiscatory because it converts exclusive ownership under positive Mexican Law into a mere authorization to exercise rights for a limited period of time is, in the opinion of my Government, not open to any doubt whatever.

Mexican reply is perhaps best stated in the following extract from a note from the Mexican Minister of Foreign Affairs, dated October 7, 1926:

The Government concession in exchange for the right acquired by title of private ownership seems to be a lessening of that right, but is not so in practice. For with regard to the strength of the new title the Mexican mining laws show that a system independent of the ownership of the sub-soil founded on a concession is as strong and more secure than the system of private ownership, — (All mining done in Mexico is done under concession. No private title to the sub-soil can be gotten by anyone. The statement that a concession is stronger than private ownership means that it's not subject to attack in the law courts by other private claimants. — W.L.) — and as for the life of the concession fifty years appeared to the lawmaker more than enough to protect the working of any petroleum property among those that have been discovered up to date. If it be taken into account that the most ancient investments of petroleum or the first operation works in Mexico do not antedate 1905, it will be seen that the greater part of the confirmations that may be applied for will be extended to at least the year 1955. It is a fact, however, that the greater part of the investments of consequence made in the oil business in Mexico only date from 1909 to 1919. Therefore, the application of the law to those acquired rights would have to extend up from 1959 or 1960, that is to say, thirty-three years from the year 1926 when the applications for confirmations would have to be made. It is, therefore, seen that the danger of encroaching upon rights by limiting the life of a concession is so remote that it is not worth taking into account as a paramount point in the diplomatic discussion of the petroleum laws. And even if there should be left any petroleum rights of this nature of any commercial value in the years from 1959 to 1960 they would still be of such small consequence as compared with the future development of the petroleum industry under the new principles that they would assume the character of exceptions and as such exceptions, the conflict that would arise between the Mexican Government on the assumption that it would refuse to grant an extension of those rights and the person in interest who should deem that his interests had been injured could be deferred to the courts who would pass upon the concrete circumstances of the case and decide it in justice by avoiding any injury that might be caused thereby. But under the laws a concession may be extended or a new one may be given which finally removes any danger of injury to the parties in interest.

I have cited all this to show that neither the Mexican Constitution nor the Calles Government claims the right to confiscate property. That on the contrary, both the Constitution and the Administration in power disclaim a desire or right to confiscate.

That being the case the dispute comes down to whether or not the petroleum laws as administered are confiscatory. This is a question which cannot be settled on the authority of the State Department. The meaning of the word "confiscatory" has been the subject of as much litigation as any word in American jurisprudence, and its meaning is settled in each concrete case that arises either by the application of an old rule laid down by the courts or by the creation of a new rule. All our litigation about the valuation of public utilities, about rate-making, about zoning, about welfare laws, turns on the meaning of the word confiscation. The word is an exceedingly complex one, and a very difficult word to define. In a dispute between two governments over the meaning of the word the question of who is right should be referred to an impartial judicial tribune.

The duty to protect the property of nationals abroad includes the duty to see that all the rights of property guaranteed under international law are observed. But it does not include the duty to impose a particular interpretation upon another government. Our Government will be perfectly justified, in fact it will be its duty, to see that the claims of the oil companies get an unbiased judicial determination. But it is not my conception of its duty to insist with the threat of force that the case must be decided in their favor.

The *World*'s position in this controversy is very simple. We do not take the Mexican interpretation, and we do not take the oil companies' interpretation. We say that there is a dispute which is essentially justiciable — that this is precisely the kind of dispute which can be settled by peaceable methods, that until these methods have been tried, and having been tried, the award is in our favor, and the award being in our favor, the Mexican Government refuses to accept it, we are not justified in exercising any kind of force, military or diplomatic. The fact that we are dealing with a weaker power makes it all the more incumbent upon us not to use our power in order to make our view prevail.

To F. E. Hyslop[1]

March 3, 1927

Dear Sir:

I think you have somewhat misunderstood me. I pointed out . . . that while the 18th Amendment was undoubtedly passed in the regular manner and the necessary majorities, the repeal of the 18th Amendment can be vetoed by an insignificant minority. A majority of a quorum in thirteen states' Senates is all that is required to prevent the repeal of the 18th Amendment no matter how great a popular majority might be in favor of its repeal. This is the fact which makes our present dilemma so difficult. It's not a new dilemma, however. It is one which has occurred several times before in American history due, I think, to a very serious defect in the amending clause of the Constitution.

What I pointed out further was that the historic American remedy for such a defect is to nullify, by the use of legal fictions, and I am prepared to go further and argue . . . that one of the most important methods by which our Anglo-American law has grown is by the use of just such fictions. The whole position of royalty in England, for example, has been changed by a series of nullification fictions, and of course, in our own country, the 15th Amendment has been nullified in exactly the same way. There is no reason for being horrified at an idea which has served the English-speaking peoples so well for so long a time. There is nothing in my suggestion which isn't a commonplace to any serious student of British or American institutions.

1. F. E. Hyslop of Philadelphia had written to protest Lippmann's views about prohibition.

To Frederic R. Kellogg[1]

March 4, 1927

Dear Mr. Kellogg:

. . . As to Mr. Obregón's[2] statements, I hope I made it perfectly clear that I vouched neither for their truth nor for the character of his motives, but that I was quoting him as evidence of what I believed to be an important aspect of the Mexican state of mind. That he did not represent an isolated case of grievance and malice is shown, I think, by the statement of other deputies in the same debate and by the fact that apparently no member of the Mexican Congress arose to contradict or qualify any of his statements, and that Secretary Morones,[3] in a statement to which I also alluded, singled out your companies for special condemnation. I have no way, of course, of showing how far the past record of the Huasteca Company in Mexico justifies this animosity. I imagine it could hardly be disputed that the animosity exists.

Some day, perhaps, when this controversy becomes less acute, I should like to sit down with you and discuss not the intricate legal questions which are now being debated, nor any of the other immediate phases of this regrettable affair, but the much larger question of the wisdom and statesmanship of the course we are pursuing, especially in its bearing upon the future of our relations with the countries to the south of us. I sometimes wonder, if you won a victory in this dispute and saved your present titles intact, whether the victory would not in the end be a pyrrhic victory. As I see it, the thing which is moving in Mexico is nationalism of the same kind which in recent years has so radically changed the situation for Great Britain in Egypt, in Turkey, in China, and to some degree, in India. It seems to me that this nationalistic spirit is bound, in the nature of things, to appear sooner or later in all the countries of Latin America, and I wonder whether men like you, who are charged with vast responsibilities, not only to their own stockholders, but to the American people of whom you are in a sense a representative in those countries are not making a great mistake in setting yourselves so inflexibly against this nationalist spirit. I wonder if you wouldn't gain more by attempting to work with this growing nationalist movement, by winning the confidence of its leaders and by striving to persuade them that you are not their enemies. After all, they may need you fully as much as you need their oil, and I am wondering, therefore, whether at the root of all this trouble there isn't just the old mistake made so often before in human history: a group of men so firmly convinced that they are in the right that they cannot adjust their minds to a new phenomenon and a new situation.

I write in this vein to you because I have felt in our personal contacts that I might do so, and also because I should like you to believe that strongly as I oppose the present policy which I think is arbitrary and destructive, I have not given up hope that a basis for a reasonable adjustment may still be found.

1. Frederic R. Kellogg, New York lawyer.   2. General Álvaro Obregón, at this time a member of the Mexican parliament and sponsor of Calles, earlier a leading constitutionalist reformer, had split with his revolutionary ally Venustiano Carranza in 1920, joined the revolt against him, been elected president of Mexico that year, and while in office agreed to respect American titles to land acquired before 1917.   3. Luis Morones, Mexican secretary of industry.

To Felix Frankfurter

March 4, 1927

Dear Felix:

I am printing a short and inadequate editorial on your book in tomorrow's paper. I wanted to be sure and have something in at once to call people's attention to the book and so Nevins[1] and I collaborated.

I also want to say to you that the evening at your house with Whitehead[2] was one of those occasions when the facts go beyond even very high expectations. I loved that man and felt later a curious exaltation about his being in the department where I, as a student, found all that was best at Harvard. It has depressed me very much in recent years to find that in places where I used to see James and Santayana, there was now to be seen McDougall. Whitehead's being there makes it all seem right again.

1. Allan Nevins, then on the editorial staff of the World, left the paper to become a professor of history at Cornell and later at Columbia. An accomplished journalist, he was to be a prolific and distinguished historian of the United States.   2. Alfred North Whitehead, the eminent British philosopher, had recently joined the Harvard faculty.

To Bernard M. Baruch[1]

March 7, 1927

Dear Bernie:

. . . We here are in a rather queer position. We don't like the McNary-Haugen bill and we don't like the present tariff, and yet we see perfectly clearly that if the present tariff policy is to be maintained there is no reason why the McNary-Haugen policy shouldn't also be established. Yet if we line up for the McNary-Haugen policy, which we don't like in principle, and if the thing were finally enacted into law, my own impression is that the protectionist system would be fastened on this country more firmly than ever. . . .[2]

1. Bernard M. Baruch, wealthy speculator, generous contributor to Democratic campaign funds, head of the War Industries Board during World War I, self-styled adviser to all presidents, and genius at public relations on his own behalf. 2. The McNary-Haugen bill, first considered by Congress in 1924, had evolved by 1927 to a measure that both houses passed but Coolidge vetoed. It established a two-price system, one domestic, one international, for six major agricultural commodities. To hold domestic prices at parity (the ratio between commodity and industrial prices that had prevailed during 1910–14, a golden era for farmers), the federal government was to buy surplus crops through a Federal Farm Board. The government was then to sell those surpluses abroad for the best available price, a scheme for "dumping" by any other name. An "equilization fee" on marketing transactions was supposed to cover the costs of the plan. As many of its sponsors saw it, the bill gave to farmers the kind of protection that the tariff provided to manufacturers. Passed by Congress again in 1928, it fell again to Coolidge's veto.

To Alfred E. Smith

March 21, 1927

PERSONAL AND CONFIDENTIAL

Dear Governor:

I think I should tell you about a very long talk I had with Borah on Saturday afternoon. The circumstances of the talk were such that he told me, I am sure, what he really thinks. He has no idea, I think, that I am passing on to you what he said. I am sure, however, that he would not object.

He thinks that the opposition to your nomination has collapsed and that the Reed boom is being used by a number of Democrats in the southwest and west as a bridge to cross over to support of you. He instanced as a particularly good example, Caraway.[1]

He said, further, that as soon as it became perfectly evident that you were going to be nominated, the opposition to Coolidge would break down, too. The old time politicians in the Republican Party who don't like Coolidge much and who are very much afraid of the third term argument would feel that with you as the opponent the religious issue would blanket all the other sentimental issues. Borah himself thinks that in spite of the decline of the organized power of the Klan, especially in the South, that there has been a very strong development in the last few months, of fear, on the part of progressive and on the whole tolerant-minded people about the political power of the Catholic Church. He ascribes this new fear, or the revival of the old fear, to the activities of the Knights of Columbus at Washington for a rupture of diplomatic relations and for a lifting of the arms embargo; this activity has been so great and is so well mobilized in the south and west that it would be very hard, and, he thinks, impossible to persuade those sections of the country that organized Catholics would not, under certain circumstances, use their political power to affect our foreign relations for religious ends.

I told him that you would not be influenced by such considerations and that you would, if you were President, deal with the Mexican relations purely on their merits and purely in relation to American interests. He agreed, and said that he felt just as sure of that personally, but that he felt equally sure that the argument would be unanswerable after a political campaign had opened, and that this difficulty would exist if Coolidge intervenes in Mexico or if he does not intervene in Mexico. If he intervenes, the country as a whole will believe that he has done so under pressure from the oil interests and from the Knights of Columbus. If he does not intervene the fact that this pressure has been exerted will be remembered and the belief still persist that with a Catholic in the White House intervention would have taken place.

I report all this to you for what it's worth and because I think it comes from a source which entitles it to earnest consideration. I am not offering you any advice, but I am inclined to agree with Borah's conclusion which was that if there is any way in which you can properly and consistently put yourself publicly on record now in favor of a solution of the Mexican problem by friendly negotiation and arbitration, that it will constitute a smashing and perhaps decisive answer next year to those who will make the usual anti-Catholic argument. You know your own business much better than I know it, but I can't help believing that a statement from you now, unequivocally in favor of peace with Mexico would not only be a patriotic service, but in your own best interest. I need not tell you how much I have that interest personally at heart.

1. Democratic Senator Thaddeus H. Caraway of Arkansas.

To Alfred E. Smith

April 4, 1927

Dear Governor:

. . . The *Atlantic Monthly* article[1] offers you a tremendous opportunity and I realized, as soon as I read it, that you would seize it with both hands. The case of the objectors cannot be stated more strongly than it is stated in the *Atlantic Monthly* article, I think, and therefore this is an opportunity not only for yourself but for this whole generation in a way that would be final and conclusive. I know you will do a great service to us all by the boldness and completeness of your reply. . . .

1. Charles C. Marshall, "An Open Letter to the Honorable Alfred E. Smith," *Atlantic Monthly,* April 1927, argued that a Roman Catholic could not remain faithful to his church and at the same time serve without crippling bias as president of the United States. Smith wrote a moving and persuasive reply, "Catholic and Patriot: Governor Smith Replies," for the May issue. He was, he said, free from any restraints, and he condemned the injection of religion as an issue in American politics. His eloquence was lost on those who needed to be convinced.

To Alfred E. Smith

April 11, 1927

Dear Governor:

I want to tell you that I have seen your reply to the Marshall letter, and I think it's one hundred percent. It can do you nothing but good. What's more, it will prove, I think, to be a landmark in the history of toleration in this country. It is a great document of genuine historic importance, and it completely fulfills all the expectations of those who, like myself, are your devoted friends.

The completeness with which you deal with the subject, the absolute candor and courage of the argument reminded me of a bit of advice that Justice Holmes once gave me when I was trying to attack some kind of public abuse, (I forget what it was). He said: "When you strike at a king you must kill him." You've killed the king, which in this case was the issue of divided loyalty.

To Tiffany Blake[1]

July 5, 1927

Dear Mr. Blake:

. . . Naturally, I agree with you that it's no business of ours to underwrite British enterprises in all parts of the world. We had a good test of that this winter when the British propaganda from Shanghai was in full swing for a forcible intervention.[2] The *World,* of course, supported Coolidge, who did a very excellent job there in resisting the British propaganda.

Perhaps the phrase "a policy of indifference" was a little too strong, but the overstatement is based on my own firm belief that when we have attained naval parity with Great Britain we shall be more deeply involved in the politics of the balance of powers in Europe than we have wanted to these last eight or ten months. . . .

1. Tiffany Blake, since 1908 chief editorial writer for the *Chicago Tribune.* **2.** In March 1927, Britain and other European nations, but not the United States, sent an international force to protect Shanghai from the Chinese Communists who had seized Nanking.

To Felix Frankfurter

July 21, 1927

Dear Felix:

If it were possible to persuade them to do so, I think it would be an admirable thing if Sacco and Vanzetti would make a statement urging their sympathizers throughout the world to refrain from all acts of violence which might injure innocent people. Such a statement would be entirely consonant with Vanzetti's philosophy as expressed in his speech, and I think it would do a world of good if he'd make it.[1]

---

1. Governor Alvan Fuller had refused to commute the death sentence for Sacco and Vanzetti. Earlier he had appointed a three-man commission to review their case and decide whether a new trial was necessary. Chaired by Harvard President A. Lawrence Lowell, that committee reached the extraordinary and implausible conclusion that confirmed the jury's verdict and recommended no further proceedings. When the execution of the two Italians occurred, anti-American protests throughout Europe echoed the protests of dismayed Americans at home.

To Franklin P. Adams[1]

August 16, 1927

Dear Frank:

This is strictly personal in regard to the Broun business.

Our policy all along was that the evidence in the Sacco-Vanzetti case had never been reviewed by any judge except Thayer and that Judge Thayer had shown prejudice. We therefore conducted a campaign last April urging the Governor to review the evidence himself, with the help of a committee. We fought hard for this because at the time there was strong sentiment in Massachusetts against any further review of the case. When the Governor appointed the Committee and decided to investigate the case himself as well, it was regarded by everybody, including the Sacco-Vanzetti Committee as a great victory.

The Committee had no standing under the law, therefore had no power to compel witnesses to appear before it. For that reason it had to conduct its hearings in secret, because witnesses were not willing to testify voluntarily if what they said was to be published the next day. They were afraid. For that reason we felt we could not criticize the Committee for holding its hearings in secret. That's the way the matter stood at midnight on August 3rd when the Governor published his verdict.

The verdict was a great surprise to everyone because everybody following the case in Boston had confidently expected that he would not decide on sentence of death. Thursday, August 4th, I had to make up my mind what line we would then take in regard to the affair. We were in a very tight place because we had no ground whatever for challenging either the fairness or the intelligence of the Committee's verdict. We had advocated this Committee and it was a very difficult question to decide how, having appealed to it we could reject its conclusions. I decided, however, that no matter what we had said about the Committee, we could not accept or approve the sentence of death — that it would be a terrible mistake and that we must do everything we could to prevent the execution. The doubtful point in my mind was the ground on which we should oppose the carrying out of the sentence. When I came to the office on Thursday, I asked R. P.[2] to call an informal conference — it was not a council meeting — and see whether we could work out a satisfactory line of policy. At the conference were R. P., Mr. White, Heaton and Merz.[3] Only one man present wanted to accept the finding of the Governor and do no more. The rest of us discussed at great length just what we could do that would be most effective, first to stop the execution, and second ultimately, to get a rehearing of the case. We were agreed that the Governor's statement would not convince people beyond a reasonable doubt that the men were guilty. There was some difference of opinion as to whether the first editorial commenting on the Governor's message should attempt, by concrete cases, to show why the reasonable doubt remained, or whether we should simply assert that there was still reasonable doubt and plead for mercy and for commutation of sentence. We finally came to the conclusion that in view of the almost pathological condition of mind in Massachusetts and the revulsion of feeling produced here by threats of violence, no one would listen to the argument from us about the evidence because that would all be dismissed on the ground that the Committee must have dealt with that point and knew more about it than we knew. We decided, therefore, that it was better to make a simple plea for mercy and to argue for commutation of sentence on the ground that it was bad public policy to execute two men about whose guilt a large part of the public had such serious doubts. We recognized that this policy would seem tepid to a great many people whose feelings were very strong, but I myself believed that their feelings were of no importance and that what counted was the impression we might be able to make upon the moderate conservative opinion in newspaper offices in Massachusetts. I feel sure that from the point of view of effectiveness, this was the wise decision, and I can prove it by the response which followed from quarters in Massachusetts which still have some power to influence the Governor. So much for our editorial policy.

Heywood's columns on Friday and Saturday were violently contrary to what we decided to do. They contained the statement that Governor Fuller "never had any intention in all his investigation but to put a new and higher polish upon the proceedings. The justice of the business was not his concern. He hoped to make it respectable." This statement of Heywood's may or may not be true, but if there was one statement calculated to close the minds of people in Massachusetts to anything we might say or do in that case, it was that statement. With things in the condition that they were in then, with the Sacco-Vanzetti Committee marching about Boston with Heywood's column on placards, it was absurd to suppose that people in Massachusetts would distinguish between Heywood's opinions and those of the paper. Those sentences in Heywood's column should have been edited out before publication. The News Department made a grave mistake in not doing so and Heywood admitted to me in conversation a few days later that he would not have objected if they had taken out these sentences. The result of the failure to take them out was, as is usually the case, an overcompensated action. Having failed to edit Heywood when he needed to be edited, we suppressed two columns — one of which at least I read — that were harmless and dull.

The day after he struck he came up to see me at my hotel and he said quite frankly that he had wanted to quit for a long time, that he was sick of doing the column, that he wanted to write novels and that he was delighted that the *World* had provided him with such a fine excuse for quitting. I told him all that I've just told you and he said that he had made a compact with himself and with Ruth that having made the gesture he wouldn't go back on it. He did not, however, make any attempt, after our talk, to correct the misstatements in interviews he had given out, saying that the *World* had changed its policy on the Sacco-Vanzetti case, although he said to me that he understood what we had done and couldn't quite see why he wasn't allowed to say something of the same thing in a different tone of voice. The whole thing, as I told R. P. was not an issue of principle in the beginning, but the result of absentee editing. If Heywood had been in the office, if there had been an opportunity for any member of the conference to sit down and talk with him before the episode instead of after it would have been the simplest thing in the world to persuade him to cut out those things in his columns which were perfectly disastrous to the policy we had adopted. Through bad administration we blundered into a thing which was then transformed into an issue of principle.

The principle now is whether or not the *World* has the right of ultimate decision as to what shall appear in its columns. Heywood has stated that he recognizes that right to this extent at least, and this is his own example: that if the *World* were campaigning for Al Smith for President he ought not to devote his column every day to denouncing Al Smith. Well, if you admit that then you have to admit that in a matter which is really more important than a presidential election, and in a matter where there is no disagreement as to the ultimate objective, the editors have a right to keep out of the columns opinions which, in their judgment will wholly destroy the effect of what they are trying to do. Personally, I don't care much for such arguments about principle. I always think that men talk about principles when they've made a general mess of practical things, but if there is a principle, that's the one involved in this case.

As to the future, I can't predict. The *World* is standing on its rights under the contract and Heywood can write for the *World* whenever he wishes to. . . .

1. Franklin P. Adams, one of the ablest of the *World's* staff, a friend of Lippmann's and also of Heywood Broun's, their common colleague who had broken with Lippmann over editorial policy

on the Sacco and Vanzetti case, as this letter explains. For an account less favorable to Lippmann, whom Learned Hand applauded, see Ronald Steel, *Walter Lippmann and the American Century* (Boston, 1980), pp. 230–34. **2.** Ralph Pulitzer. **3.** Florence D. White, John L. Heaton, and Charles Merz.

To Florence D. White

August 26, 1927

To: Mr. F. D. White

You asked for suggestions about terms of peace with Broun.[1] Here are my personal notions.

1. The principle that any piece of copy submitted by any man may be omitted from the paper in the discretion of the editor in charge should not be surrendered or confused.

2. Broun should be made to promise, and his promise enforced by appropriate means, that his copy will be in the office not later than, say, 4:30 P.M. Unless this rule is enforced, in my opinion, hasty judgments are likely to be made and the possibility of arguing with him ruled out.

3. He should be given to understand that where he disagrees with the policy of the paper and wishes to put himself on record he is to do so in a letter to the editor published on the editorial page and not in his column. I believe that this arrangement is not only fair to Broun, but fair to the paper. For there is no way in which the paper can answer Broun if, as has happened in the past, he attacks our policy and even misrepresents it. Here he appears merely as the writer of a letter, and we can, if we wish, append an editorial note making our position clear.

4. Whenever he wishes to write on a controversial public question, it would do no harm if he called up the man in charge of the editorial page, and even came in to the office to see him, and argued out whatever differences there might be.

5. In my judgment it's impossible for Broun to resume his column now without some kind of explanation to the public. Therefore, I strongly advise that resumption be delayed until R. P.'s return, so that he may have an opportunity, if he cares to, to make a statement.

1. Heywood Broun, who had gone on "strike," returned briefly to the *World* but left the paper permanently in 1928.

To Felix Frankfurter

September 27, 1927

Dear Felix:

I just got back today. I have a letter from Graham Wallas, of which the following paragraph will interest you.

"Lowell sent me the report of the Governor's Sacco-Vanzetti Committee with a letter saying that when he got at the actual record of the case he found the evidence very different and much more convincing from what he expected. I answered sympathetically, but pointed out how valueless evidence of identification is after even a few months or weeks of discussion, and saying that I thought that some future specialist a hundred years hence would come to the conclusion that there was not sufficient evidence to convict. I am sorry for Lowell, whom I believe that I know rather well. He is public-spirited, with a vast amount of administrative drive, but if one goes for a long walk with him one finds him a little stupid. He will suffer horribly over the S. V. business."

To Dwight W. Morrow[1]

November 3, 1927

Dear Dwight:

I have a letter from T. Arnold Robinson[2] inviting Mrs. Lippmann and me to come to Mexico at the end of November and join the President and you on a trip of inspection. He says in his letter that you had told him that you wish me to come.

I have decided that on the whole I had better not come to Mexico City under such official auspices. I should be charged, when I came back, if I wrote about things in Mexico, with having heard only the government's side of various matters in dispute, and I should be in the position in which every newspaper man finds himself if he goes to Italy or to Russia today. I think it's best when I come, for me to come independently and stay at a hotel and be free to talk to everybody. I haven't written all this to Robinson, but I wanted you to know exactly what was in my mind. I have told him simply that I couldn't come in November but that I was planning to come shortly after the first of the year at a time when I was certain you would be in Mexico City. I told him also that Ralph Pulitzer would probably come with me and that we might make it a party by bringing Mr. and Mrs. Laurence Stallings.[3] I assume that you will be attending the Pan-American conference sometime in January. I wonder if you could let me know when you're pretty certain to be in Mexico City. Of course there's plenty of time about that.

The impression you are making down there is admirable. You couldn't ask for better treatment by correspondents. I am sure the friendliness you have displayed to Mexico is popular in this country, though I have heard a few remarks that there was some grumbling from men who can't see that it's possible to respect property and protect its rights and at the same time deal imaginatively with people of a different culture. . . .

1. Dwight W. Morrow had been appointed but not yet confirmed as United States ambassador to Mexico. 2. Thomas Arnold Robinson was then acting as a kind of personal assistant to Mor-

row. **3.** Laurence Stallings — one of the *World's* editorial staff and a successful playwright *(What Price Glory?)* — and his wife were friends of the Lippmanns'.

To Newton D. Baker

November 16, 1927

Dear Newton:

I am inclined to agree with you that Dawes[1] is the most likely man for the Republican nomination. He seems to suit more different factions of that party than anyone else, although I am told that the President himself dislikes him and distrusts him. Whether he dislikes him and distrusts him enough to use his influence to defeat him I don't know. However, we've always got to remember that there is still a very real possibility that Coolidge himself will run. The present strategy of the Republican bosses is to get a great central mass of uninstructed delegates on a sort of "draft Coolidge" platform. This is being done with Coolidge's connivance, and I am not in the least persuaded that when the time comes he won't let himself be "drafted." Coolidge of course, would in my opinion be much the hardest Republican to beat.

I had not heard the rumor about Morrow, although I heard him toasted a few times at dinners here in New York as a possible candidate. My own impression is that he has given the matter no thought whatever, but that he would like to do a big job in Mexico, a job which would give a new turn to all our relations with Latin America. And that after that he wants to stay in public life, possibly by becoming a candidate for Senator from New Jersey. If he once passed through an election he would be purged of the Morgan taint. . . .

I agree with what you say about disarmament. From our point of view the only aspect of disarmament at the moment is the necessity of preventing naval competition with Great Britain. After the Geneva experience I am not sure that it isn't a mistake to attempt to prevent competition by formal agreement.[2] It may be that a better way to avoid competitive building is by a gentlemanly understanding between the sane elements of public opinion in both countries that each will fight at home against an armament program directed against the other.

1. Charles G. Dawes was at this time vice president of the United States. **2.** The Geneva Conference of 1927 had adjourned in August, a total failure. Called to extend the Washington Conference agreement to cover cruisers, destroyers, and submarines, the conference faltered from the outset because of the refusal of Italy and France, then engaged in a naval building competition, to attend. The Americans, Britons, and Japanese could reach no agreement. Japan demanded a larger quota than the others would yield, and the United States delegation was obsessed with a misplaced fear of British naval power.

To Herbert R. Mayes[1]

November 22, 1927

My dear Mr. Mayes:

I read one or two of the Alger books[2] as a boy only because I was told that they were vulgar tripe and that I ought not to read them. I don't remember being the least amused or edified by them.

1. Herbert R. Mayes, editor at this time of *American Druggist*.   2. The books of Horatio Alger, Jr., which always depicted the rise to wealth and fame of poor but hard-working and decent boys — books that helped to create the mythological American success story.

To Seymour Ransom[1]

November 29, 1927

My dear Mr. Ransom:

I had already read your very eloquent leader on Owen D. Young.[2] You have not, I think, exaggerated his qualities, and I can tell you that for years, that is, since 1924, I have wondered whether there might not be some hope of nominating him. He would make an extraordinarily good president.

But of course you know as well as I that personal ability is not the only qualification for a candidate, and I am pretty well persuaded that in view of the psychological situation which now exists among northern Democrats, the nomination in 1928, if it fails to go to Governor Smith, is not worth a bad nickel to anyone. Young is too good a man to sacrifice in 1928 as John Davis was sacrificed in 1924.

I am glad the *News* is out for Young because the discussion of a name like his will tend to elevate the whole tone of party discussion. But to be perfectly frank with you, in speaking as a warm personal friend of Young's, I should urge him not to consider the nomination this year. In 1932 it will be a different story.

1. Seymour Ransom of the *Birmingham News* in Alabama.   2. Owen D. Young, industrialist, diplomatist, middle-of-the-road Democrat, at this time chairman of the board of the General Electric Company, in 1929 would be chief negotiator of the Young plan, further to ease German reparation payments. He was close to the Morgan group and a friend of Lippmann's.

To Dwight W. Morrow

December 2, 1927

Dear Dwight:

Thank you for your letter of November 22nd and for George Rublee's telephone call.[1] I wish I could come down before Christmas but there are personal reasons which will keep me here as well as the fact that there is always so much happening at the opening of Congress.

However, I certainly would not leave until your confirmation is settled. Everything indicates that it will go through all right, but there will be some attack on you, I guess. I saw today a copy of young Bob La Follette's editorial in which he has nothing to say against you personally, but argues that the Morgan interest in Mexico is a bond-holder interest, that it is a mere accident that the bond-holder interest might coincide with the oil interest. If you believe in the materialistic interpretation of history in its most rigid and orthodox form, and if you disregard all the actual facts, young Bob's formula is fairly effective. . . . Young Bob means to express himself along that line, but . . . he is not getting ready for a stiff fight. Borah, on the other hand, seems to have become one of your warmest supporters, and I am told also that both Norris and Nye[2] are favorable. The man I am most concerned about is Reed of Missouri, from whom nothing has yet been heard, I think.

Our present plans are to go to Mexico City in January by way of the Pan American Conference, providing you plan to return to Mexico City directly from the Conference. I don't suppose your plans are definite about that, but if they are, I'd greatly like to know them. . . .

1. George Rublee was with Morrow in Mexico.　**2.** Senators George W. Norris of Nebraska and Gerald P. Nye of North Dakota, progressive Republicans and leading isolationists.

To Joseph P. Chamberlain[1]

January 16, 1928

Dear Mr. Chamberlain:

. . . I think the point you raise about "war as an instrument of policy" as against "war of aggression" is well taken. But of course the difference between the European view and the Washington view is that Europe definitely regards war as a righteous instrument of policy whenever it is a war against an enemy of the League. I do not see how any treaty to outlaw war[2] can be made consistent with this fundamental premise of the whole structure of international relations in Europe. It seems to me that the real question we have got to decide is what we will do about our neutrality in the event of a war declared by the League against an aggressor. I don't really know what to think about that myself.

1. Joseph P. Chamberlain, professor of law at Columbia University, specialist on international questions.　**2.** Anglo-French negotiations, as well as private American initiatives, were moving Secretary of State Kellogg toward his proposal of April 1928 for an international renunciation of war. French President Aristide Briand, for his part, put forward a plan for a Franco-American treaty to outlaw war. Supported by Borah, Kellogg then proposed a multilateral pact. The resulting treaty, signed in Paris in August by all major powers except the Soviet Union, which was not invited, did renounce war but provided no mechanism of enforcement. It also carried reservations by several nations, each of which undercut the declared purpose of the document. Lippmann was a skeptic from the first.

To Alice Hamilton[1]

January 18, 1928

Dear Miss Hamilton:

I need hardly tell you how much anxiety the question of capital punishment must raise in the mind of anyone who is under obligation, as we are, to take a position in regard to it. If I believed, as you do, that to take human life was invariably a crime, the problem would be simple. But I do not believe that. I not only believe that there are circumstances under which a nation may wage war and circumstances under which a people may resort to force during a revolution, but also that there is no fundamental moral difference between the punishment of death and punishment by imprisonment. If the State has the right to deprive me of all that makes life worth living, including, perhaps, my sanity, I do not see why it can't also kill me.

Since I do not have, therefore, any absolute principle which compels me to reject the death penalty, I am compelled to reach my opinion about it on the weight of evidence as to its effectiveness in fulfilling the purpose for which it is theoretically established. The effectiveness of the death penalty is open to the gravest doubt. But as I said in the editorial to which you refer, I still think that the arguments in its favor are preponderant. You mention the Sacco Vanzetti case as an instance of the fallibility of human judgment and you argue that since human judgment is fallible, human beings have no right to exact an irrevocable penalty. You know what I thought about the Sacco Vanzetti case and where my sympathies lay. Their case illustrates not the fallibility of human judgment, but a certain kind of stubbornness and pride. Had there been no capital punishment in Massachusetts, Sacco and Vanzetti would have been just as certainly convicted, and nothing remotely resembling the protest in their behalf could have been organized. They would not have died in the chair, but they would have had a living death. In other words, without capital punishment, the fallibility of human judgment would have been just as great, and the results just as tragic. I can't expect you to agree with this because, if I understand your view correctly, you make an absolute distinction between death and every other form of punishment. What I believe follows because I can't make that distinction.

I would like you to feel, however, that the *World* is not dogmatically or irrevocably committed to the maintenance of capital punishment. We are prepared to change our attitude the moment we become convinced that it is ineffective. Our present position is that we should like to see it rationalized as much as it has been rationalized in England, and then, on the basis of that experience, reach a judgment as to whether it's worth retaining.

1. Dr. Alice Hamilton, bacteriologist, pathologist, specialist in occupational diseases, member of the faculty of the Harvard Medical School.

To Felix Frankfurter

January 26, 1928

Dear Felix:

I have been having a correspondence with Miss Hamilton about capital punishment, and if you're interested, you might ask her to let you see it. I didn't
cover the ground fully there, but I did cover more fully my own state of mind
about the thing. It is, in brief, hesitant, with a feeling that the burden of proof
for the moment rests with abolitionists. Your letter implies that the burden
of proof rests with those who favor retaining capital punishment. That may
be so. Of course the question of the deterrent effect of it, which I regard as
the fundamental question, is almost impossible to settle by exact data. I am
very much impressed by the opinion of a few men I know who have had a
good deal of experience with criminals, among them a psychiatrist of considerable experience with the criminally insane, who believes that the fear of
death acts in a way that no other form of punishment does. I must confess I
am at a loss to know by what method of investigation one could really settle
this question. The comparative statistical method . . . does not persuade
me. . . .

To Dwight W. Morrow

April 11, 1928

Dear Dwight:

. . . Public feeling everywhere that I go is tremendously enthusiastic about
this settlement.[1] There is a disposition in some quarters to ascribe it to some
kind of private magic which you have at your disposal, and not to realize the
enormous amount of brain work and careful negotiation which it has involved.
But of course the actual subject is a difficult one and few people understand
what the issue was about originally, or how it was settled. They simply know
that it was a very nasty affair and that it's now over, and they are delighted
with you and with the result.

I am unable to reach any opinion which seems to me worthwhile as to the
real strength of Hoover or of Smith. But I do think it has become pretty
evident that Hoover is the man the Smith people are hoping for. They believe
he is really weak in States like Wisconsin, Missouri, Nebraska, the Dakotas,
Montana.[2] They think he'd be particularly vulnerable in the kind of campaign
that Smith knows how to wage. They think that the real antagonism to Hoover in the West would cement the Democratic Party. . . .

1. Morrow's negotiations had produced a settlement of the oil issue in Mexico. The Mexicans
confirmed the concessions made to foreign firms before the 1917 constitution; the United States
accepted the principle that in theory all mineral rights belonged to Mexico. 2. That assessment
of Hoover's weakness arose from his opposition to the McNary-Haugen bill. It was a miscalcu-

lation in 1928, partly because Alfred E. Smith was not persuasive to American farmers in his campaign statements about agricultural policy, and largely because rural America rejected Smith's Catholicism, urban background, and social views.

To Thomas W. Lamont

April 19, 1928

Dear Tom:

There are two things I want to say as a result of our talk with the Italian Ambassador.

The first is that I'd greatly appreciate it if you'd informally drop me a line personally when you see something in the *World* that's not true.

The other thing is that while I didn't want to dispute with the Ambassador, it's plain that he is not informed about the character of the censorship in Italy. The day after I saw you I had lunch with an old friend of mine who for five years until just recently was the correspondent of the *Chicago Daily News* in Rome. He tells me that while there is no formal censorship, there is a much more effective kind of censorship than a merely formal one. Dispatches which are not pleasing to the authorities are delayed in transmission until the official case of the government has got a good head start. Sometimes the dispatches are not transmitted at all. Moreover, the correspondent works with the knowledge that everything he sends comes under the eye of an official, and therefore it becomes highly dangerous for any Italian who is critical of the Government to give a correspondent information, much less to be quoted. And the rigidity of the internal censorship makes it virtually impossible for a correspondent in Rome to know what's really going on in the rest of Italy. Under these circumstances, it is inevitable that newspapers should pick up rumors on the frontiers. And on news of this character it is almost impossible to check up effectively. It's a very difficult and curious situation. It's impossible for a newspaper to ignore Italy. It's impossible for a self-respecting newspaper to print only official pronouncements and the official view. And it is almost impossible to obtain authentically any information which isn't official.

As long as the censorship lasts, I shall remain persuaded that the Mussolini Government is not certain of its hold on the Italian people. If the opposition to it inside of Italy were as negligible as Fascists like the Ambassador make out, there would be no occasion for a censorship of this character. If there existed that unity of the Italian people which the Fascists talk about, why is it that they are so desperately careful to check off all news and opinion which isn't official?

I didn't mean to write you a whole editorial, but I want to get this off my mind.

To Charles P. Howland[1]

April 23, 1928

Dear Charles:

. . . In regard to Newton Baker, I don't know what to say exactly about the criticism of your friend. Possibly there is something in what he says. Certainly his finger is pointing at the spot in Baker's character on which those who are least enthusiastic would build their argument. My impression is that the criticism was truer in the earlier part of his administration in the War Department than in the latter part; and that it was true because he is the kind of man who cannot be bold in action until he has mastered the situation intellectually. For a long time in the War Department he felt that he didn't know enough, and there was a certain hesitancy in action as a result. Toward the end of his administration he had a very remarkable grasp of the whole problem, including technical military matters, and as his grasp grew stronger, his will and his decision grew firmer. I am not sure but that this very defect in a politician called upon, unprepared, to deal with a national crisis, would not be a virtue in a college president.

All that you say about him is true and I should add to it what I think is perhaps his most remarkable trait: an exceptional disinterestedness, a disinterestedness so complete that it amounts to selflessness. I have never known less ego, less selfish ambition, less desire for personal advertisement and aggrandizement in any public man. Nor have I ever known an able man who was so gentle as he. It's his gentleness which has created the impression that he lacks virility. As a matter of fact, he doesn't. He just has no cruelty or bluster in him.

1. Charles P. Howland, New York lawyer.

To Raymond L. Buell[1]

April 24, 1928

Dear Buell:

. . . In reply to your question about career men, I'd say that without any doubt, Mr. Olds[2] is better than the corresponding type of career man. In fact, I have become persuaded that Olds is a pretty good man, and that he got into his trouble fifteen or eighteen months ago largely because he took the advice of the career men in the Department. There is very little question that they are wholly responsible for what happened up to the Stimson mission.[3] I am equally certain, though I wish you would regard this as confidential, that it was the career men, much more even than Sheffield[4] himself, who were responsible for the mess with Mexico. I am morally certain that MacMurray,[5] a career man, would have led us into intervention in China. Personally, I'd much rather take my chances with a politician or a successful lawyer, or even a rough-neck like Alec Moore[6] than with a swell young gentleman who belonged to the inner clique of career men. . . .

1. Raymond L. Buell, research director and later president of the Foreign Policy Association. 2. Robert E. Olds, undersecretary of state, 1927–28.   3. The settlement Stimson negotiated left American troops in Nicaragua and, while temporarily halting civil strife there, left in power the conservative regime friendly to American business interests.   4. James R. Sheffield had preceded Morrow as United States ambassador to Mexico, where he served from 1924 to 1927.   5. John V. MacMurray, career foreign officer, specialist on Asia, United States minister to China, 1925–29.   6. Alexander P. Moore, then American ambassador to Peru.

To Bruce Bliven[1]

April 30, 1928

Dear Bruce:

For your own information, I want to quote you a paragraph from a letter from Dwight Morrow, about *The New Republic*'s editorial of April 11 which implied that Mexico had accepted the oil regulations as a lesser of two evils, in order to get a loan, and that somehow or other Mexico has surrendered her social program. Mr. Morrow says:

"During the time I have been down here I have never talked loan with the Administration. In fact, I have told President Calles several times that I thoroughly agreed with him that he did not need a foreign loan. He is more firmly wedded to the pay-as-you-go policy than any of that school in the United States who criticizes borrowing for social programs." . . .

1. Bruce Bliven, at this time managing editor of *The New Republic*.

To Roy W. Howard[1]

April 30, 1928

My dear Roy:

. . . It does seem to me preposterous that a man should claim nomination for President of the United States without ever having declared himself on national issues, and without ever having had a record in national affairs. I am a great admirer of Smith and I shall support him, but I'll be darned if I can see on what basis he has a right to ask the Democratic Party to assume that because he was a good Governor of New York he is the right man for President of the United States.

1. Roy W. Howard, chairman of the board of the Scripps-Howard chain of newspapers.

To Bruce Bliven

May 3, 1928

Dear Bruce:

. . . I think there's a vast difference between new borrowing and a continuation of the moratorium. For one thing, new borrowing adds to the total of Mexico's obligation whereas the moratorium doesn't. For another, on new borrowing the bankers can lend or not lend, as they see fit. But on a moratorium they really haven't any choice. They've got to grant it, when the government can't pay, unless that government happens to be so small that they can seize the custom houses. Mexico, of course, isn't in that class.

On the matter of the social program, I think your implication was wrong. Even as to oil, the revolutionary program is intact, except on pre-1917 lands. And even on them, under the new regulations, the right to exercise police power is specifically reserved. If Mexico modifies her revolutionary program on oil, it will not be due to fear of our diplomatic pressure but because of desire to encourage capitalistic production. The land program, which is the essential fundamental thing in the revolution, is absolutely untouched by Morrow. All the American claims in regard to land have to do with the administration of admitted principles, not with a revision of the principles themselves. Moreover, all the American land claims affect only about 8 percent of the agrarian reform. Morrow will undoubtedly make some effort to get the labor laws amended. They are in many respects absolutely unworkable, as the government itself has demonstrated by suspending them in very important respects on its new irrigation works. In advising Mexico to make such changes, Morrow's whole case will rest not upon the rights of American business men, but upon Mexico's own desire for an industrial revival.

Of course you will find the Mexican government is becoming more conservative. If the church question is settled, it will become very much more conservative. But that is a normal historical evolution after a victorious revolution. Mexico has, so to speak, had her 1776. She is just at the end of her critical period, and she will soon pass over into the 1789 period. As she does that, the agitators of the revolution will tend to pass out of the picture.

To Alfred E. Smith

May 9, 1928

Dear Governor:

I want to be sure that a few things about my own personal attitude are clear after last night's discussion. As I told you, I would have liked to have had you declare yourself before the primaries began. I accept the fact that you didn't do so as water over the dam. The reason I kept harping on the subject was that I was led to believe that you did not intend to declare yourself until after the conventions, and that possibly you would not then take a strong stand on prohibition. I am quite satisfied with the stand you intend to take as you outlined it last night.[1] I think it's wise, courageous and fine. I am deeply convinced, however, that you must at least outline this position before the Democratic convention meets. The more I think about it the more certain I am that to do anything else is to take even greater risks than are involved by stating your views before the convention votes. I think that good faith requires you to serve notice on the convention as to the line you intend to take on a matter of such importance. . . .

1. See Lippmann to Joseph Pulitzer, May 11, 1928, inf.

To Joseph Pulitzer[1]

May 11, 1928

Dear Joe:

. . . As you know, the *World* has taken the position that Smith must declare himself on prohibition before the nomination at Houston. We did this on two grounds:

(1) as a matter of good faith.

(2) because we believe the Governor can win only by running as a wet.

He agreed with us that he must run as a wet: and the argument, therefore, has come down to the question of whether he shall declare himself as a wet before the Republican Convention, or after the Republican Convention but before the Democratic Convention, or in his speech of acceptance.[2] He makes a very strong case for not declaring himself before the Republican Convention, saying if the Republicans know how radically wet he was going to be, they would put in a moderate wet plank, which is what he doesn't want them to do. He wants them to take a dry position so that he can have the advantage of being wet. We are conceding that these are justifiable tactics, but we are insisting that since he intends to campaign as a wet he must put himself on record to that effect before the Houston convention is adjourned. We did not obtain a promise that he would do this, but he left us believing that he would almost certainly do it.

His outline of what his wet position will be has three parts:

First: an attack on law enforcement as practiced under Mellon, with a demonstration of what moderately effective enforcement would cost in the way of money, spies, abolition of trial by jury, a system of federal police courts, etc.

Second: a proposal to amend the Volstead Act in accordance with the New York referendum of 1926.

Third: a proposal to amend the Eighteenth Amendment exempting a sovereign state from the prohibition against manufacturing or transporting liquor. The object of such an amendment would be to permit any state to adopt the Quebec system. The prohibition in the Eighteenth Amendment would thereafter apply only to interstate commerce.

This, in brief outline, is all that I know.

1. Joseph Pulitzer, publisher of the *St. Louis Post-Dispatch* and a younger brother of Ralph Pulitzer.   **2.** Smith did so only after his nomination. It was probably a mistake. He could be sure of the wet vote anyhow, and the statement he issued offended the drys, including some Democrats, particularly in the South, who might otherwise have voted for him.

To Ellery Sedgwick

May 16, 1928

Dear Sedgwick:

. . . There can be little doubt that you are right in thinking that if Smith is to be elected, the campaign cannot be fought on the ordinary issues, and that prohibition offers him the only chance. I can tell you in confidence that he wholly agrees with this view. I had dinner with him on Tuesday of last week, and he expressed himself forcibly and unequivocally along that line. It is plain to him that in order to be elected he must carry, in addition to the solid south, enough large industrial states to give him about 140 electoral votes. There is very little to be gained west of the Mississippi, even supposing that he could carry a number of states, for west of the Mississippi does not count sufficiently in the electoral college. His campaign will therefore be based on an attempt to carry New York (45), New Jersey (14), Massachusetts (18), Maryland (8), Rhode Island (5), Connecticut (7), Wisconsin (13), Missouri (18). This will give him 128 votes. There are, I believe, 114 votes in the solid south, leaving out the border states, which brings him a total of 242. He will then need 25 more votes to win, and he has a good fighting chance in Illinois, Indiana, Ohio, Michigan, Montana, Colorado, Minnesota, Arizona, New Mexico, not to mention Kentucky and Oklahoma. The whole theory of his campaign must rest on just some such geologic shift in the normally Republican industrial states, and obviously the one issue on which any considerable Republican vote can be moved is prohibition. In these states, the Democrats are practically all militant wets, so he has nothing to lose by being a wet and he has everything to gain. He has worked out what I think is an honest and intelligent program which begins with a rigorous attempt to clarify the whole question of "enforcement," goes on to certain modifications of the Volstead Act which are consistent with the Eighteenth Amendment, and then proceeds to a proposal to amend the Eighteenth Amendment so as to empower a state to adopt some such system as prevails in Quebec and Ontario. All this is in strictest confidence, of course, since he is still hesitant as to whether he should announce the program before the convention, or in his speech of acceptance. I thought you'd like to know personally how matters stand.

To Gerald W. Johnson[1]

May 18, 1928

Dear Mr. Johnson:

Now I feel pretty certain that I didn't make myself clear, because you seem to think that my book is an argument for the omnicompetence of the scientific spirit.[2] That's just what it isn't. It is the most convincing demonstration I could make of the inadequacy of the scientific spirit, and for proof of that I refer you again to the dialogues between the Fundamentalist and the Modernist, and between the Scholar and the Americanist. In fact, the chief emphasis of the book is directed against the dry, thin rationalist.

1. Gerald W. Johnson, editorial writer for the *Baltimore Evening Sun* and author of many books on history and on current affairs. 2. Lippmann had given a series of lectures at the University of Virginia in 1928, later published under the title *American Inquisitors* (New York, 1928). The book looked at the Scopes case as an example of the conflict between religious convictions and the method of science. It also expressed Lippmann's growing doubts about the wisdom of majorities, in Tennessee or elsewhere.

To Orestes Ferrara[1]

June 18, 1928

Dear Mr. Ambassador:

I thank you for your letter of June 14th, and I assure you that in writing the article for *Foreign Affairs,* I had no desire to make inaccurate assertions or arbitrary deductions. I feel, after reading your letter, that while there is room for honest difference of opinion in the interpretation of the facts, there is nothing in the article to which you have called my attention which meets your descriptions.

You speak, first, of the question of dictatorship. That, to be sure, is a matter of definition, but in my opinion the character of your election laws, the absence of opposition parties and the denial of freedom of the press, constitute dictatorship.

Second, as to the spending of public money, that is a matter of judgment which, however, is confirmed by the opinion of Americans wholly friendly to Cuba and well acquainted with its history.

Third, the question as to whether or not there is ground for revolution. My statement meant that since open political opposition and free elections are not tolerated in Cuba, a revolution would sooner or later be inevitable as the only feasible way of changing the government, but that the Platt amendment[2] stands in the way.

On your fourth point, in regard to the tariff, I am in agreement with you. I see no ground for dispute. The fact that the modification of the sugar tariff would be of benefit to the United States does not alter the fact that such modification is greatly desired by the Machado[3] administration.

As to the question of loans, I think you have not quite understood me. It is true that the question of loans does not fall within the scope of the Platt amendment. But it does fall within the discretion of the State Department.

I see nothing in my statements which casts any reflection upon the conduct of the Cuban delegation at Havana.[4] It acted as any official delegation is bound to act, in accordance with its conception of the national self-interest. By all prevailing standards you are justified in describing it as just, honorable and true. All I did was to state rather bluntly certain of the concrete elements which were bound to enter into the Cuban Government's conception of its own interest. I appreciate your remark as to my own motives and good will in the matter. I can assure you that I have the utmost good will towards Cuba and a great admiration for her people and for their achievements.

1. Orestes Ferrara, Cuban ambassador to the United States. 2. The Platt Amendment of 1901, which Cuba had accepted as one condition for its independence, authorized the United States to intervene to preserve Cuban independence and maintain law and order. 3. Gerardo Machado, Cuban president and later dictator. 4. At the Havana Conference of Inter-American States in 1928, the United States delegation blocked a resolution, supported by Cuba, that declared "no state has the right to intervene in the internal affairs of another."

To Herbert C. Hoover

June 19, 1928

My dear Mr. Secretary:

. . . I can assure you that it is my intention to continue seeking to act with the most scrupulous fairness to you personally, and with the minimum partisanship in dealing with you as a candidate. I wish you the best of health and cheerfulness for the ordeal of the next few months.

To Ralph Pulitzer

June 21, 1928

Dear Ralph:

I think you should know the following:

You will remember that at our dinner with the Governor, it was understood that after the Republicans had taken their position on prohibition, he would earnestly consider and probably decide to make some sort of statement affirming his own wetness. You will recall that in our minds, apart from any question of strategy, there was a point of honor, namely that the Governor's position must be so clearly re-affirmed before he is nominated, that no one would be able to say later that he took the nomination under false pretenses.

On Monday, June 18, after the Republican Convention was over, I wrote a leader reviving our argument, which had been suspended ever since our dinner

with the Governor. . . . On Tuesday, the day it was published, I got a telephone call from the Governor asking me to come to see him that evening.
. . . I went and spent two hours with him. Proskauer[1] was present for part
of the time, and they told me that they had a new plan, which was to wait
until the nomination had been made and then, in reply to the telegram from
the Chairman of the Convention, the Governor was to send a telegram to be
read at the opening of the session to nominate the Vice President, in which he
would fully and frankly state his position. They showed me the text of the
proposed telegram which I thought was quite satisfactory from our own point
of view, but I said that I would reserve my own opinion as to the propriety of
waiting until the nomination had been made in order to express the views. On
Wednesday I put the whole matter to our editorial staff . . . and we were all
agreed that to wait until the nomination was in the bag was not altogether
honorable. I was then in the difficult position of having either to hammer the
Governor on a thing that he wasn't going to do or to abandon our own position
rather ignominiously, or to do what I dislike to do, namely, offer direct suggestions. I decided that, all things considered, I had better make a direct suggestion, so on Wednesday afternoon I telephoned Proskauer and told him that
the men here who were going to have to do most of the fighting for the
Governor were deeply dissatisfied with the plan and that they feel unanimously that they would not be satisfied unless he had taken the risk of declaring himself before the delegates voted. He asked me in reply to make a suggestion and I suggested that the Governor make a definite reply to a question
put to him by a reporter from the *World*. This morning at 11:30, I went to
the Biltmore to see the Governor and found him with Proskauer. They handed
me a slip of paper and said that if the *World* reporter this afternoon would put
the question on that slip of paper to the Governor he would answer emphatically, and that they were very grateful that we had pushed them into a position of this kind. You will have seen the result in Friday morning's paper. . . .

The consensus of opinion in the office is that the position we took this week
has straightened out the Governor's record and our own. I hope you will like
it.

By the time this reaches you, you will know as well as I do what the intentions of the Smith people are in regard to the prohibition plank in the platform. They are ready to accept a non-committal one, which permits the Governor himself to write his own plank after his nomination. I don't think there's
any objection to that under the circumstances.

So far as I can see the only other question remaining unsettled, in which
we are interested is the Vice Presidency, about which I had a fairly long discussion today with the Governor and Proskauer. The Governor is clear in his
mind that the Vice President should not be a Southerner. That is, that he
should not come from any state which debars negroes from voting. That rules
out Robinson.[2] He is also clear that it should not be Hull,[3] that it should not

be a man from the far west, nor a man from the Atlantic seaboard, but that the candidate should be picked preferably from Missouri, Wisconsin, Illinois, Indiana, Ohio and Michigan. There was some talk about Donahey,[4] but I told them I thought that was an impossible nomination. Donahey is an illiterate man who will add nothing to the ticket. My own belief is that Newton Baker would be the best choice. He comes from the largest doubtful State which the Governor has a chance to carry. He will weld together the Smith democracy with the Wilson democracy. He is a powerful campaigner, a man who would greatly help Smith to formulate his ideas on national questions, and he has an immense following among women and among Protestant churches, — in just those sections of the population where Smith is weakest. On the other hand there is nothing in his record which makes it inconsistent from the prohibition point of view to nominate him. . . .

1. Joseph H. Proskauer, New York State judge, a close adviser of Al Smith's.   2. Senator Joseph T. Robinson of Arkansas, a dry, was in fact nominated as Smith's running mate.   3. Cordell Hull, then a Democratic congressman from Tennessee.   4. Vic Donahey, then Democratic governor of Ohio, later United States senator from that state.

To Herbert Bayard Swope   TELEGRAM

June 27, 1928

In the light of Robinson's speech endorsing the McNary-Haugen Bill and the character of his statement on prohibition his nomination plus an evasive platform is conceding too much.[1] An evasive platform could be interpreted as a blank check to Smith but Robinson will turn it all into a straddle. For how can Smith speak boldly when other man on ticket is so definitely aligned on other side. The Smith people should not sacrifice everything to harmony.[2]

1. The platform pledged the Democrats to make an honest effort to enforce the Eighteenth Amendment, a position suitable to Robinson but at variance with Smith's obvious preference for repeal.   2. This telegram was directed through Swope (the *World*'s executive editor), who was in Houston, to Belle (Mrs. Henry) Moskowitz, Smith's closest political adviser and director of his personal campaign for the presidency.

To Herbert Bayard Swope   TELEGRAM

June 28, 1928

. . . It's going to take some bold work to offset the effect of platform and Robinson. . . . Smith people at Houston can easily sacrifice too much by failing to look beyond their immediate difficulties in dealing with the die-hards at Houston. Those die-hards are of no importance once the convention adjourns. They represent no strength in debatable territory which Smith has any chance of getting. . . .

To Felix Frankfurter

July 3, 1928

Dear Felix:

I wholly agree with your letter. And I intend to deal with just that phase of Hoover's responsibility at considerable length.[1]

The thing that annoyed me about Bowers's speech[2] and about most of the talk at Houston was that it really neglected just the point you made. And there was an underlying implication that men like Hoover and Coolidge were themselves part of the "plunder bund." That kind of talk is so irresponsible that it can't but injure anyone who indulges in it. Bowers's speech as a matter of fact while it was called the keynote, was really the swan song of the Bryan democracy, the anti-Smith democracy, which had hoped to prevent Smith's nomination by centering the issue on corruption and making it impossible for Smith to run because of Tammany. The corruption issue is one which has to be handled with great intelligence and shrewdness in the campaign. And I considered it necessary to dissociate ourselves brutally from the Houston oratory. The issue has got to be made, but it can't be made that way. It's got to be made in the way you make it, and to do that requires a carefully planned educational campaign.

I've had quite a long talk with Smith himself about the question of leadership. That will be the major theme of his campaign if he adheres to his present ideas. His general plan is not to make a campaign of promises to enact this bit of legislation to please that group, but to argue that the business of the President is to be a leader through whom carefully formulated programs are actually put into execution. I don't know whether I make his idea quite clear, but I think you probably catch the sense of it.

I am coming to believe that by early Autumn we shall have had a big smash on the stock market and a much more evident industrial depression. I don't know just what the political effects of that will be, but they may be very great. . . .

1. Hoover, a member of the Harding Cabinet, had been uninformed, perhaps because of his own preoccupations, about the scandals that surrounded him and had not spoken out against them.
2. Claude G. Bowers's keynote speech. Bowers was a political journalist and dedicated Democrat, as well as a historian of the Jefferson and Jackson eras and the period of Reconstruction.

To Newton D. Baker

July 3, 1928

Dear Newton:

I always have a feeling that a letter as personal as yours ought not to be answered in typewritten form, but I am just off for a few days' holiday, and I don't want to leave without a word to you.

I am very happy about your letter, and I am particularly happy because of the clarity with which you see your own position. I appreciated that, and I want you to know that in what I did about urging your name for the Vice Presidency I was not moved by friendship or even by the knowledge of how superlatively happy your nomination would have made Ralph. I argued on these grounds:

(1) You were the only man mentioned fitted in his own right to be President, and that the Democrats ought to start a new tradition in the matter of Vice Presidents by at last nominating a man who was fit to be President,

(2) That Smith needed your brain and your convictions and your knowledge of national affairs,

(3) That your nomination would mean the building of a bridge between Smith and Wilson,

(4) That you would bring to the ticket the good will of very important sections of the population who are hostile to Smith, particularly the women's organizations and the Protestant churches, and

(5) That Ohio was more important than the South.

I agree with you about the platform, though I am prepared to accept the abandonment of the tariff as a party issue.[1] The country is protectionist and will be so unless its position is modified by the necessities of its position as creditor of the world. The old Democratic tariff argument no longer appeals even to the Democrats, and it's become not so much a conviction as a political liability. That doesn't mean approval of the Fordney Tariff, of course. But it does mean an end to the rather futile argument about the theory of protection.

I understand what you mean about the Governor's spokesmen at Houston. I don't think there is any danger that they will be his trusted advisers in the White House. I'd count on you, and Owen Young, and Franklin Roosevelt, and John Davis, as the men to whom he would turn, and I consider it a very real obligation on your part to take a conspicuous enough position in this campaign, followed by what I know would be a great sacrifice of returning to the Cabinet.

---

1. The platform, breaking with the party's tradition, accepted the concept of a protective tariff but promised some reductions as well as modifications of schedules providing special favors to particular corporations.

To Dwight W. Morrow

July 11, 1928

Dear Dwight:

Yesterday I had a visit from a young Italian journalist representing the *Corriere della Sera* of Milan, who is here to write about the election. His name was Count Leone Fumasoni Biandi. I recognized it at once and asked him if he was related to the Apostolic Delegate. He said that he was his nephew. After a good deal of talk about Smith and his chances, in which I discovered that he had a great deal of enthusiasm for Smith, perhaps not wholly disinterested, I asked him what the Vatican's attitude toward Smith was. He said that of course they were very favorable, but afraid to indicate how they felt. I told him that was very wise, but there was one thing they could do that would help Smith, and indirectly help everybody, and that was to hurry up and settle the church question in Mexico.[1] He asked me whether he could talk to his uncle along that line quoting me, and I said I wished he would, and that I thought that as a supporter of Smith it was wholly desirable that the Vatican should promptly approve the proposed settlement which is before it, and that the Apostolic Delegate ought to use his influence at Rome to that effect. Nothing will probably come of it, but at least he has gone to Washington to see his uncle who, I am told, is a rather timid man, and try to stir him up.

The political situation is still inchoate, and I don't believe that anyone can really guess just what the drift is going to be, but that the country is due for the biggest political shake-up in a long time, I feel certain.

1. Lippmann had been playing an important, but at the time undisclosed, role in the settlement between Mexico and the Catholic Church; see Ronald Steel, *Walter Lippmann and the American Century* (Boston, 1980), pp. 242–43. Though a number of issues involving church property remained unsolved, an accord that Lippmann and Morrow had drafted had proved acceptable to Mexico and, in June 1929, to the Vatican. Under that agreement, the priests in Mexico called off their strike and the Mexican government asserted that it had no intention to "destroy the identity" of the church.

To Joseph P. Chamberlain

July 19, 1928

My dear Mr. Chamberlain:

I am very much interested in your letter. I am not quite certain that I wholly understand it. I realize, of course, that if France started a war with Germany and could not prove that the war was a war of self-defense, she would have broken her treaty with us. But as I understand it, Mr. Kellogg has agreed that each nation is its own judge as to whether a war is a war of self-defense. You say that the United States would have a right to inquire into the cause of the war and report upon it and that such action would not be an unfriendly act. Nevertheless, I take it that the United States would have to accept as final France's dictum that the war was a war of self-defense.

I can see that the whole matter would be vastly different if it were agreed that the judgment as to whether a war was defensive was to be made not by each signatory but by some tribunal or other. Then, of course, the treaties would make a vast difference.

I am prepared to admit, of course, that that may make a considerable difference nevertheless as a practical and psychological matter. But what I wish you'd explain to me is how just that one point, namely how, juridically, the existing situation is greatly altered as long as each nation remains the sole judge of its own wars.[1]

1. Lippmann wrote a similar letter to Secretary of State Kellogg.

To S. K. Ratcliffe

July 25, 1928

Dear S. K.:

I haven't time to write you more than just a word in reply to your query of July 12th. Raskob[1] is significant. His appointment is a definite move to dissociate the Democratic Party from the old Bryan antagonism to large corporate business. The fact that Raskob is a Catholic, a wet and an intimate personal friend of Smith's made the appointment possible, but the main political objective in the appointment was what I said first.

1. John J. Raskob, in addition to what Lippmann went on to say about him, was also a lawyer for General Motors and Du Pont. As Smith's preferred candidate, he had become chairman of the Democratic National Committee. His appointment to that post cast further doubt upon Smith's liberalism and further alienated Democrats in the South and West.

To Dwight W. Morrow

August 9, 1928

Dear Dwight:

The other day I wrote to the Governor and suggested that in his speech of acceptance he should single out several things that the Republicans have done, for praise, particularly your work in Mexico. I suggested that he make a special point about Mexico, and that he say flatly that he approved of the policy you were pursuing, and that he would ask you to continue it in Mexico City. I pointed out to him that it was particularly important to him to set definitely at rest the notion that because he was a Catholic he would reverse the present policy.

I have a letter from him today saying that he is going carefully over the suggestion, and adds: "I know that you are right, but I am not sure that your way of handling it is entirely right. However, I will handle it."

I felt I couldn't urge this thing editorially in the *World*, but I got *The New Republic* to do it last week. I think it's of real importance, and of course has no bearing upon whether you personally wish or do not wish to stay in Mexico City after March 4th. I know you'd want to feel, whether you stay or not, that in the event of Smith's election there'd be no change of fundamental policy.

I cannot get any sense yet as to how the election is going. I have Hoover's speech, which he delivers Saturday night, and I have read some of the important parts of it, though I haven't gone over it carefully. It's a badly written document and not at all inspired. It seems to be based on the notion that Hoover has a majority now and that his business is to sit tight in the hope that it will stay with him. . . .

To Newton D. Baker

August 27, 1928

Dear Newton:

. . . Governor Smith's speech made me feel pretty good — not very good. Of course it's miles ahead of the Houston platform but the deficiencies of his knowledge of national and international affairs are very serious, and I am amazed that no Republican editor has as yet pointed them out in detail. I think Smith could learn and will learn rapidly. But it took him ten years of service as an Assemblyman to comprehend the business of the State of New York, and I am afraid it's going to take him more than three or four months as a candidate to comprehend the business of the United States. Personally, I urged him and begged him and even shouted at him as much as a year and a half ago that he must seriously begin to form convictions about national questions and express them. The plain truth is he did practically nothing except on prohibition, and in a somewhat amateurish way on farm relief until he'd been nominated. His heart is all right, his character is all right, his head is all right, but his equipment is deplorable.

To Charles C. Marshall[1]

September 6, 1928

Dear Mr. Marshall:

Of course I understand that your letter of September 5th was intended to be personal and confidential. This letter is also personal and confidential.

It may be that I do not sufficiently understand your point of view, but it seems to me that the conclusion of your letter puts you in a rather curious position. You state that you accept the sincerity of Governor Smith's personal declaration and believe that he "has repudiated the supremacy of his church in theory and in practice at all vital moral points over the State." You then go on to say that the issue at this moment is not between the American people and Governor Smith but between the American people and the Roman Catholic Church. I fail to follow the reasoning. The Roman Catholic Church has made no proposals of any kind to the American people. There may be a conflict between the official position of the Roman Catholic Church and the American Constitutional System. But if Governor Smith has repudiated all those points in the doctrine of his Church out of which a conflict could arise, then the issue you have in mind is not relevant to his candidacy.

For that reason I fail to see why you persist in public prints in calling attention to the conflict between the Roman Catholic polity and the American polity when you have admitted that that conflict cannot arise if Governor Smith's personal declaration is to be taken, as you take it, as sincere. I suggested that you write the article on Quakerism because the parallel is a genuine one. It will not be denied, I think, that the Society of Friends holds the belief against bearing arms and fighting. It is true that Mr. Hoover has disclaimed all religious convictions which would prevent his acting in good conscience as commander-in-chief of the Army and Navy. His declaration is to be accepted at face value exactly as Governor Smith's declaration is to be accepted. In both instances we have a man personally disclaiming doctrines held by the religious communions to which he belonged, doctrines which might conflict with the loyal discharge of his duties as President.

Your statement that the Society of Friends exists within the State and is ruled by the principle of the consent of the governed is, in my opinion, theoretically irrelevant to the point at issue. The fact is that Mr. Hoover has disclaimed an important item in the teaching of his church and Governor Smith has disclaimed important items in the teaching of his church. The only way you can draw a distinction between the positions of these two men is to impugn the sincerity of the one or the other. This I understand you do not do.

Unless you can show that the Roman Catholic Church has power over Governor Smith's action which the Society of Friends cannot exercise over the action of Mr. Hoover, it's a wholly irrelevant question as to whether the Roman Catholic Church or the Society of Friends is the more inconsistent with the American theory of the State.

In the case of both men there is a theoretical conflict. In the case of both men there has been an absolute repudiation of those tenets of their faith which are in conflict with Americanism. An article to prove that the papal claims of the Roman Catholic Church are more deeply conflicting with Americanism than the pacifist teaching of the Quakers would constitute an interesting discussion for a student of political theory, but would be not only irrelevant to the issue now before the American people but misleading. . . .

1. Charles C. Marshall had written the letter to the *Atlantic Monthly* to which Smith had replied so eloquently; see Lippmann to Alfred E. Smith, April 4, 1927, sup.

To Felix Frankfurter

September 13, 1928

Dear Felix:

. . . I am very much afraid that Smith has wholly miscalculated the strategy in starting the campaign at this date. But for over a year he's been stubbornly convinced that his political judgment is infallible. The only way he should have dealt with the whispering campaign[1] which everybody foresaw was to have identified himself a year ago with issues of such importance that people would have had something else to think about. He wouldn't do it because he couldn't get it out of his head that he'd always turned the trick in New York in the last three weeks of campaigning. A real case of provincial-mindedness.

1. Directed against Smith's Catholicism and in lesser measure his Irish origins, his opposition to prohibition, and his connections with Tammany Hall.

To Alfred E. Smith   TELEGRAM

September 17, 1928

Suggest that National Women's Party endorsement of Republicans because of Curtis espousal of so-called equal rights amendment[1] and Hoover's equivocal support provides admirable opportunity for statement of your views of protection of women and children (stop) In today's statement you are attacked as enemy of equal opportunity (stop) Probably average woman does not realize that what is meant by equal opportunity is the destruction not only of laws unfavorable to women but laws specially designed to protect them (stop) Curtis's espousal of this statement is either sheer ignorance and willingness to gain support of noisy minority or reactionary attitude towards all welfare legislation.

1. The Republican platform endorsed the equal rights amendment, as in a recent speech had vice presidential candidate Charles Curtis, Republican senator from Kansas and at one time a leader of the farm bloc.

To Alfred E. Smith   TELEGRAM

September 20, 1928

Big attempt made here to claim your Omaha speech was vague because of failure to mention equalization fee[1] (stop) I have interpreted your position to be that equalization fee is part of the mechanics for assessing upon the crop benefitted the cost of lifting the surplus (stop) I have said further that your position is that you wish an impartial commission to examine the mechanics of the bill open-mindedly to see whether the equalization fee is the only or the best piece of machinery for carrying out purpose and principle of the McNary-Haugen bill (stop) Further that you are committed to a piece of machinery which will carry out that purpose and that if the impartial commission can find no other or better machinery you are committed to the equalization fee (stop) Further that in any event you have pledged the farmers a bill carrying out the purposes of the McNary-Haugen bill approved by an impartial commission having administration support which will be ready for a vote by Congress in time to establish a control of the surplus for nineteen twenty-nine harvest (stop) I hope I have read nothing into your speech that wasn't there (stop) I regard this position as impregnable. . . .

1. At Omaha Smith had endorsed the McNary-Haugen program and even the equalization fee if no better means of financing the plan could be found. Lippmann's interpretation of Smith's position, as explained in this telegram, was correct.

To Charles C. Marshall

September 26, 1928

Dear Mr. Marshall:

Your book came yesterday and I read it last night.[1] I want to say in the first place that in style, temper and lucidity, I know of no polemic written in America to equal it. It's a model of all that that kind of prose should be.

With the substance of your argument I think I agree entirely. It is perfectly plain, and you prove it beyond dispute, that Governor Smith's personal declaration is in conflict with the doctrines of his church. I do not, of course, know, and should be enormously interested to know, what the real attitude of the Vatican is.

To my mind your analysis suggests a deduction on which I should be very much interested to know your own opinion. It is that the election of Governor Smith would constitute a much more real menace to the Papal claims than to the American constitution. I am utterly satisfied, from my own personal knowledge of Governor Smith that if he had to make a choice in any of the dilemmas which might arise, he would decide unhesitatingly against the Vatican. In fact, if I did not believe this I could not support him. For I have long been greatly interested in Mexico, and last winter was living for a number of weeks with Mr. Morrow during a very interesting phase of the conflict between the Mexican Government and the Catholic Church. I have no doubts in my own mind that the pretensions of the Vatican are not academic but perfectly real in a country like Mexico. I believe, however, that the inevitable tendency of American Catholicism is away from Rome, and that the naive and wholly sincere declaration of Governor Smith truly expresses the average mind of American Catholic laymen. In view of the immense relative importance of the American Catholics, owing to their economic power, I should, if I were the Pope in Rome, be greatly disturbed at anything which tended to draw Catholics away from their isolation as a special class and to absorb them into the spiritual community of American life. I think that the one thing which would give Romanism new life among American Catholics would be a sense that they were proscribed. The Roman Church has been intolerant in fact and in theory towards others, but tolerance for others where its communicants are in the minority would be more dangerous to its pretensions than proscription.

1. Marshall published two books in 1928, both of the same unfortunate spirit: *The Roman Catholic Church in the Modern State* (New York, 1928) and *Governor Smith's American Catholicism* (New York, 1928). This letter refers to the latter.

To John Milton Moore[1]

September 28, 1928

Dear Mr. Moore:

I don't think you quite understand the point of view of the *World* in regard to Mrs. Willebrandt's[2] campaign. You seem to think we charge her with attacking Governor Smith as a Catholic. She has never attacked him as a Catholic and we have never charged or implied that she attacked him on those grounds. What we regard as bad in her conduct, because it constitutes a very sinister precedent, is the fact that as a high official of the Government, and an authorized speaker for the Republican Party, she has officially invited churches to engage in partisan politics. If that precedent were followed by all political parties, it would, in our opinion, nullify the whole spirit of the separation of church and state. So far as I know, this is the first time that a great political party has ever officially asked churches as a body to organize politically for the defeat of an opposition candidate. The long history of clericalism in Europe shows the incalculable dangers of this sort of thing.

I quite appreciate the fact that there will be many like yourself who imagine that we are turning our guns on a "lone woman." As a matter of fact we are turning our guns on the Republican Party for its cowardly refusal to disown Mrs. Willebrandt's campaign. They will probably be able to escape the full public condemnation which they deserve for this because Mrs. Willebrandt happens to be a woman. Were she a man of course her conduct would have aroused a bitterness far more intense than it has already aroused, and will undoubtedly continue to arouse. . . .

1. John Milton Moore, Baptist clergyman, formerly pastor of a church in Brooklyn, at this time head of Churches of Christ in America.   2. Mabel Walker Willebrandt, Republican, dry, since

1921 assistant attorney general of the United States in charge of all cases arising out of prohibition.

To Calvert Magruder[1]

October 9, 1928

Dear Mr. Magruder:

I had only one brief talk with Governor Smith on the subject of immigration. That was one evening in New York City during the Houston convention. We discussed a great many things, and finally I said to him: "Governor, you've got to make up your mind about immigration because they're going after you on that." I could see at once that he had never studied the question and that he really didn't know what was meant by the 1890 census, the national origins provisions, etc. He said to me: "I have lived among these people all my life. I can't shut the door in their face." His position was purely sentimental. I pointed out to him that whether he liked it or not, his party had shut the door, and that restricted immigration was now the settled policy of the country and that it was no business of his to try and change that policy. He agreed, though with obvious reluctance. That's the personal background of the matter.

I had no part in the writing of the acceptance speech, and I do not know how the rather curious passage got into that speech. I don't think he himself understood what he meant. At any rate I took it to mean that the 1910 census was to be substituted for the 1890 census,[2] and on the basis of that I wrote an editorial in the *World* telling him to leave the immigration question alone during the campaign. He left it alone until the St. Paul speech and interview, which I interpreted exactly as you do.

On the merits of the matter, I don't think there is any reason to fear that he as President would attempt any change in the law, except in the detail affecting the separated families.[3] On the other hand, politically the thing is rather a mess because of the little-considered statement in the acceptance speech which cannot really be adjusted to the St. Paul speech and interview. I shall advise him, if the question is raised again in such a way that he must deal with it, to say that he stands by the St. Paul speech.

I think it's undoubtedly true that the Tammany congressmen have pretty consistently fought the introduction and the maintenance of the present immigration restriction policy. So, I believe, have the Republican congressmen for New York. So, I should imagine, have the congressmen for the foreign-born districts of Boston, — although I have never checked it up. It's absurd to argue that Governor Smith as President is subject to the same considerations that a group of Tammany congressmen are. As for the alien radical agitators, I have no doubt he was opposed to the deportations during the red hysteria of 1919–20. That's immensely to his credit, and I believe there exists a very valuable document signed by a considerable number of the faculty of the Harvard Law School which takes the same position. The Governor's record in all these matters of pardons dealing with radicals and aliens is, I am certain, liberal, just and praise-worthy. There are few things he does better than the handling of just such human causes. . . .

1. Calvert Magruder, Harvard law professor.   2. Compared to the 1890 census, the 1910 census of course recorded a much larger number of recent immigrants, especially from southern and eastern Europe. If future quotas for immigration had been based upon the latter date, the 1924 Immigration Restriction Act would have been less stringent.   3. Permitting spouses and children of immigrants to enter the United States outside of the quotas established by the act of 1924.

To Nancy Astor[1]

October 23, 1928

My dear Lady Astor:

As you are now leaving the United States, I would like to send you just a word to tell you that the effects on American opinion and American politics of the Anglo-French naval and military agreement have been much more serious than the public discussion would have indicated.[2] The truth of the matter is that the responsible newspapers have deliberately discouraged public discussion of the matter. It was tacitly recognized, I think, by American editors, Republican and Democratic alike, that if the agreement were thoroughly discussed in the American press, even in such terms as have been used by conservative organs in England, the effect would have been to inflame American opinion and to set irresponsible politicians in both parties competing with each other in exploiting the issue for campaign purposes. People in England ought not to be deceived by the moderateness of American comment and the lack of attention given to the matter into thinking that the incident has not made a profound impression in this country, and that it has not deeply discouraged those who are most active workers for international understanding.

It is my own personal opinion that unless the British Government makes a more thorough explanation of all the circumstances and of all the motives than it has yet made, and unless satisfactory assurances are given that the understanding in no way constitutes an entente, that the affair may endanger the ratification of the peace pact, and will certainly enormously strengthen the case of the big navy advocates in Congress. They are silent for the moment, because in the campaign neither party wishes to commit itself to an expensive building program. I am very much afraid, however, that next winter when Congress assembles, they will be able to argue with some plausibility, and to make a very great impression on the American mind, that if an entente exists between England and France, parity on a single-power standard is not sufficient, and that for genuine parity, it will be necessary for the United States to build a two-power standard. I don't say that the big navy people could succeed either with Hoover or Smith as President in obtaining authorization for a navy built to a two-power standard, but I do believe that if they make a good case for a two-power standard, they'll get a very much larger program than they were able to obtain last winter.

I am sorry to send you this depressing news just when you're leaving, but it's my firm conviction that it's true and that in two or three months, unless the matter is really cleared up, we shall have a very serious situation on our hands. . . .

1. Lady Nancy Astor, Virginia-born naturalized British socialite, the first woman to hold a seat in the House of Commons.   **2.** Americans generally had reacted with needless anxiety and hostility to the Anglo-French agreement of 1928, which they interpreted erroneously as directed against the United States, a view shared by the General Board of the Navy, the *New York Times* and the Hearst press — an unlikely trio. The French had approached the British with a proposal designed as a basis for further international disarmament discussions. To redeem the failures of the Geneva Conference, that proposal reduced the number of categories of warships subject to later negotiations and ensuing limitations. Excluded from those negotiations were to be ships carrying guns of six inches (muzzle diameter) or less. Suitable entirely to the British, who considered small (or light) cruisers key to the defense of the routes to the empire, the proposal dismayed the American navy, which had placed a larger reliance on heavier cruisers carrying eight-inch guns. On precisely that difference with the British, the Geneva Conference had foundered.

Though the episode marked a nadir of a kind in Anglo-American interwar relations, it soon passed. In November British Ambassador Sir Esme W. H. Howard had a long conversation with President Coolidge, who lamented the dominance of technical experts in negotiations for naval disarmament. "The basis of all their arguments," Coolidge said, according to Howard's report, "is the possibility of war between us. What we need in these discussions is men who . . . will start from the point of view that war between us shall not take place." Hoover was to hold to that same assumption.

To Dwight W. Morrow

October 24, 1928

Dear Dwight:

. . . I think Hoover made an extraordinary blunder in his New York speech. He had every conservative vote guaranteed that it was possible for him to get, and it was foolish of him to try and attack Smith as a Socialist. The only effect of that has been to help Smith with the La Follette voters. And of course his defense of federal prohibition in the name of Jeffersonian democracy was amusing. . . .

To Esther Everett Lape[1]

November 21, 1928

Dear Miss Lape:

Thank you for your letter. Of course on its merits it's preposterous to ratify the Kellogg Treaty and fail to join the Court. And I find myself holding on to myself to restrain myself from uttering a few blunt truths about this Treaty. It appears now that we're going to be asked to buy a vague and probably empty Treaty at the price of a large naval program and an abandonment of the World Court. If that isn't trading the substance for the shadow, I am greatly mistaken.

The only reason I hold on to myself is that I can't face the thought of our failing once more to ratify something which we propose. That, to my mind, is the one compelling reason for ratification of the Kellogg Treaty.

1. Miss Esther Everett Lape, one of Lippmann's readers, had written him about the issues this letter discusses.

To Herbert D. Croly

November 21, 1928

Dear Herbert:
    . . . I went out to Kansas City to make a speech, and I spent a day with William Allen White and Senator Capper.[1] I found the experience intensely depressing. White surely is about the best thing that the Middle West and the small town in the Buick-radio age has produced. And judged by any standard of civilized liberalism it's a pretty weedy flower. He made me feel as if defeating Al Smith had in it an enterprise about equivalent to heaving a stray cat out of the parlor. Intellectually he's able to comprehend, of course, that Smith is a real person, representing real things, but emotionally he's no more able to comprehend the kind of thing you and I feel than he would be if he suddenly announced that he'd embraced Buddhism.

One thing was clear to me, however, that his kind — and I think there was a very large number who were wholly and absolutely concerned with defeating Smith — have no positive affection whatever for Hoover. I asked him what he expected Hoover to do for him and the other drys, and he said that he expected Hoover to begin by making Andrew Mellon go on the water wagon. That was as far as he'd considered the matter. . . .

1. Republican Senator Arthur Capper of Kansas.

To Philip H. Kerr[1]

December 4, 1928

My dear Kerr:
    . . . There is no doubt that Anglo-American relations are in a good deal of a snarl. I have great confidence that this country, if it ever believed that the Administration was really moving in the direction which led to war, would

rise with ten times the fury which it displayed when it finally made up its mind that the Coolidge Mexican policy was leading to war. I have been in something of a quandary as to whether to beat the drum now or wait until the Kellogg Treaty is ratified and then do it.

I agree with you that the difficulty arises out of a different conception which prevails in the two countries as to how to organize peace. Roughly speaking, it's the difference between enforcing peace and renouncing war. And of course until that's settled, there can't really be an agreement about maritime law.

A good deal of the immediate future depends on what happens in England after Congress passes the cruiser bill.[2] I assume it will pass it. And from the American point of view, I think that will end the agitation for armaments here for a good while to come if the British Government doesn't feel it necessary to go in for a new program of its own. I don't know whether the new cruisers will give us "parity" or not. But I'm sure that the public will think they do, and that's all that matters. Do you suppose it would be feasible and desirable for the British Government to say to the American, after the cruiser bill has passed, "Well and good. You've now got the program which Mr. Coolidge says world standards of defense require. We've got the cruisers which our imperial defense requires. Let's call those two fleets equal and let's enter into an agreement not to increase either one of them." . . .

1. Philip H. Kerr, later Lord Lothian, already one of Lippmann's English friends. 2. The bill, passed in February 1929, authorized construction of fifteen light cruisers and one aircraft carrier, but also permitted the president to suspend construction in the event of an international agreement limiting naval armament. Congressional recognition of that possibility helped to prepare the way for the London Naval Conference of 1930.

To Philip H. Kerr

January 2, 1929

My dear Kerr:

. . . I agree thoroughly with your position. . . . I agree about "parity." I particularly like your idea of treating the British and American programs after Congress passes the cruiser bill as "parity," and deriving a mathematical formula from what would then be the status quo. That's the idea I proposed to our Council of Foreign Relations group the other night, and I thought that there was some likelihood that they would accept it. I also agree with you about Borah's resolution on sea law.[1] I think as a matter of fact that's a positively dangerous proposal for the reasons you have stated. And finally, I agree that the solution of the problem is essentially political. I've put it in a memorandum . . . that we must find a basis of co-ordinating the policies of the two countries so that they shall both be neutral or both be belligerent at the same time. Of course, stated in this way the proposal would be looked upon as an alliance, but it need not be if the two countries, instead of giving pledges to one another, each gave the same pledges to a common principle for the maintenance of peace.

My own view is that the next step in the United States after the ratification of the Peace Pact is to persuade the President to make a speech, say on the anniversary of the ratification, saying in substance that whenever in the opinion of the United States, the Peace Pact has been broken, the United States will regard this breach as affecting its own interest. I don't know just what the formula ought to be, but the idea would be to have the President make a declaration not unlike the original Monroe Doctrine in its constitutional form which would emphasize not merely what the Treaty renounces, but what it prohibits. . . . If the President made such a declaration, the British Government might then conceivably make a declaration of its own, saying in substance that it would insist on the full belligerent rights at sea only where its Navy was doing what you call police work. . . .

1. Borah believed that only a codification of neutral rights would prevent a naval race between the United States and Great Britain. That codification, he also held, as did several of his colleagues in the Senate, would necessarily modify the "traditional practices," including detention and seizure of neutral vessels, that had characterized British policy in the years 1914–17. Borah's amendment to the cruiser bill favored treaties with other maritime powers to define the rights of neutrals, including the inviolability of private property, in time of war. The cruiser bill also called for a building program that would provide American equality in that category of ships with Great Britain. The mood of rivalry that the debate over the bill revealed began quickly to subside with the inauguration of Herbert Hoover in March 1929, and with his determined pursuit of Anglo-American amity.

To Robert F. Wagner

January 9, 1929

Dear Bob:

I think you have reached a fairer estimate of the Kellogg Treaty than anyone else who has spoken in the Senate.[1] You have expressed its profound weakness and recognized its intangible possibilities. I myself have supported it, though if I had a choice in the matter I never would have proceeded along this line, and I have no real confidence in it. I do not believe that the peace of the world can be or will be advanced by renunciation but only by common action whenever the peace of the world is threatened. If I didn't think that in spite of what has been said in the Senate this nation would be bound to consult with other powers in the event of a breach of a treaty, I should regard it as wholly useless. . . .

1. Robert F. Wagner, then a close associate of Al Smith's, was serving the first term of his distinguished career as a Democratic senator from New York. He endorsed the purpose of the Kellogg pact and, in other speeches, arms reduction and American membership in the World Court. Liberal and vocal also on domestic issues, he won from the *World* an editorial accolade in

July 1930: "By sheer hard work, by an extraordinary singlemindedness, by a sure sense of the difference between the trivial and the important, Wagner has in a very short space of time become a national figure. . . ."

To Laura Puffer Morgan[1]

January 30, 1929

Dear Mrs. Morgan:

Mr. Krock, who is now with the *New York Times* sent me your letter of January 25th.

I should be inclined to question the statement that the *World* has made a surprising change of policy in regard to the Cruiser Bill. The *World* did oppose the large Wilbur[2] program of last winter, but it has not opposed the smaller program. The question of consistency, however, is a small matter. Since there are no absolute principles which determine one's convictions about a matter of this kind, it is our present opinion here that a naval agreement with Great Britain is more likely when there is a substantial equality between the two fleets. And our best information is that if the British do not increase their present program there will be substantial equality by 1931. I am satisfied in my own mind that the agitation on both sides of the water will not subside while there is an obvious disparity. I am satisfied also, from the careful study of the proceedings of the Washington conference, the Geneva conference, and the League of Nations work on disarmament, that the only practicable basis for an agreement on arms is the status quo at the time the agreement is negotiated. Therefore, I am in favor of the present cruiser bill, because it will establish a substantial parity on the basis of which agreement will be feasible. I see no other possibility except unending agitation in both countries. This agitation is in itself more harmful to good relations than anything else.

One item in your letter I must, however, call your attention to, and that is your assumption that if the liberal forces in England win the election in May, that will alter the naval policy of the British Government. I can see no ground for such a belief.

1. Laura Puffer Morgan of the National Council for Prevention of War. 2. Curtis D. Wilbur, Coolidge's secretary of the navy.

To Dwight W. Morrow

May 3, 1929

Dear Dwight:

I returned from Italy this week, and I want to write you about one or two things that I saw there which I didn't feel like writing in Italy because of the censorship of the mails.

In Rome I saw Father Tacchi-Venturi, the Jesuit priest who negotiated the treaty and concordat between the Vatican and the Government, and I also saw Cardinal Gasparri.[1] I spoke with both of them about the church in Mexico, naturally only as a newspaper man and with no reference whatever to my having talked with you about it. I found, to my amazement, that while both of them were passionately interested, they apparently believed all the most extreme anti-Calles propaganda. Tacchi-Venturi rode a very high horse, saying that the church would consider any overtures made to it by the Mexican Government, and flatly denied that the church had had any relations within the last year with the Mexican Government. I wasn't, of course, in a position to argue about that with him. I simply expressed my surprise in view of what had already been published about Archbishop Ruiz's visit to Europe. Tacchi-Venturi, however, insisted that Ruiz had submitted nothing to the Vatican but had merely been called there to report on the attitude of the Mexican bishops. I asked him how, even if it wished to do so, the Mexican Government could make overtures to the Vatican. He replied that there was an apostolic delegate in Washington. When I asked him whether the apostolic delegate had not received informally but reliably a statement of the basis of a possible settlement, he said that the apostolic delegate had heard nothing whatever from Mexico. I report this to you without pretending to know how to interpret it.

With Cardinal Gasparri I got no further than being compelled to listen to a long and bitter harangue, in bad French, against our Government for its favoritism to the enemies of the church. When I asked him what, specifically, he had in mind, he said that it was our embargo on arms to the rebels.[2] When I asked him whether the church had an interest in arming the rebels in order to prolong the civil war in Mexico, he evaded the question. But everything else he said, in manner and in substance, amounted to saying that he wanted to see the rebels armed and to have them overthrow the present government. This talk took place about the third week in March when, so far as I could see from the news in the Italian papers, the rebellion had already been crushed. . . .

1. Cardinal Pietro Gasparri, the papal secretary of state, who in June 1929 accepted the agreement that Lippmann and Morrow had arranged between the Vatican and Mexico. 2. The embargo applied during a brief rebellion in Mexico. Obregón, elected president in July 1928, was assassinated a few weeks later. During the provisional presidency of Emilio Portes Gil that followed, Calles remained the dominant figure in the government. In March-April 1929, he subdued the minor, right-wing rebellion.

To Newton D. Baker

May 15, 1929

Dear Newton:

I'd wait a good deal longer for such a letter, and I am proud to think that the book[1] has been of some use to you.

I remember reading President Wilson's statement about how political speculations are colored by the prevailing current view of the physical universe. He must have written that before 1912, and perhaps he said it in one of his speeches during the campaign. I have used it again and again. It is one of the most illuminating ideas to an understanding of political theories. It is obvious now that just as Darwinism supplanted the Newtonian physics as the prevailing intellectual fashion, so today Darwinism is itself out-moded. The difficulty, however, is that the prevailing physics as set forth, I won't say by Einstein for none of us understands him correctly, but by the disciples of Einstein . . . simply does not lend itself to myth-making. The result is that our political thinking today has no intellectual foundations and it's my guess that we shall not find them as the Eighteenth Century liberals or the Nineteenth Century devotees of progress found theirs, in analogies from the physical sciences. In a sense we have become too self-conscious about science to use it as analogy. We know that human beings do not really behave either like wild animals in a jungle or like a collection of molecules. The foundations for us must lie, it seems to me, therefore, really not in nature as our immediate forefathers believed, nor in super-nature as their forefathers believed, but in human nature. That is to say, in an objective understanding of what we really are. I didn't try, of course, to develop this idea in the book, having bitten off quite sufficient for my capacity to chew. But it's a thing which I think could be developed. . . .

1. Lippmann's *A Preface to Morals* (New York, 1929).

To Felix Frankfurter

June 11, 1929

Dear Felix:

I've waited to answer your letter on the Schwimmer case in order to let my irritation wear off.[1] I think I ought to tell you why I was irritated now that the feeling has passed off. I was irritated at the tone of your letter and its assumption that a failure to agree immediately and whole-heartedly with Holmes, Brandeis and Cardozo[2] was a weird and strange procedure. I have a deep and affectionate admiration for all three men, and all humility for the authority with which they speak. But I am compelled to retain a belief in the possibility that one or all of them may conceivably be wrong on a particular question, and that in any event when they speak the issue is not necessarily closed.

You may be wholly right about this case. I may be seeing difficulties where there are none, but I don't want in correspondence with you to be made to feel that honestly to see difficulties is discreditable.

1. In the controversial case of Rosetta Schwimmer, the Supreme Court took away the citizenship of a naturalized pacifist on the ground that her refusal to bear arms demonstrated an insufficient

loyalty to the Constitution. In approving that decision, Lippmann put a heavier premium on patriotism than did the many critics who instead stressed the deprivation of the woman's civil liberties.   **2.** Benjamin N. Cardozo, distinguished jurist, then chief judge of the New York Court of Appeals, was appointed to the Supreme Court in 1932 as the successor to Holmes.

To Esme W. H. Howard

June 28, 1929

My dear Sir Esme:

   . . . The point on which your opinion differs from our own appears to be that of the actual sacrifice incurred by the British Treasury as a result of the announcement of the Balfour principle. It is quite true that a substantial sacrifice can be shown on paper. Several of our readers besides yourself have been reminding us of this fact. Some tabulations which I recently had prepared for the use of our staff show that under the Dawes plan and the debt settlements with France and Italy, Great Britain was scheduled to receive annually from twenty-six to fifty million dollars in excess of her debt payments to the United States. Under the Young plan[1] this excess is reduced, but a small surplus is still provided. By the Balfour note all claim to this is renounced.

   As the debt pact with France is still unratified, this surplus, of course, exists only on paper; but its sacrifice for that reason is also on paper.

   When you say, "Our reparation receipts have in the past not nearly sufficed to cover the difference between our aggregate outgoings and aggregate receipts . . . and under the new experts' scheme they never will," I think that you really admit the point which we were trying to make, but which we may have expressed rather crudely. That is to say, there never was any real prospect of your receiving from your allies and from Germany more than you had agreed to pay the United States. The surrender of a claim to more than this amount, which legally you were entitled to collect, has therefore cost nothing, but it has carried with it the advantage, on your side, of making the United States rather than Great Britain appear as the real collector of your Allied debts. . . .

1. The Young plan, proffered by a committee of which Owen D. Young was chairman and adopted on June 7, 1929, made further changes in reparations payments. It created the Bank of International Settlements at Basel, Switzerland, on the board of which all central banks of the powers involved were represented. Through that new bank, Germany was to assume responsibility for converting marks into foreign currencies for annual reparations payments. Those payments were reduced below the Dawes plan level and placed on a rising schedule. An unconditional annual minimum payment was secured by a mortgage on German state railways. The plan also provided for still further reductions if the United States scaled down war debts. On July 21, the French Chamber of Deputies resolved that France's annual payments to the United States would not exceed receipts from German reparations. Though the Young plan was intended as a permanent settlement of the reparations problem, the coming of the Great Depression and other related complications in international exchange led in 1932 to cancellation of 90 percent of the payments the plan had required.

To Gardner Jackson[1]

July 5, 1929

Dear Mr. Jackson:

I am touched that you should have had more faith in me than your friends. But even to justify you to them I am afraid I cannot come to the meeting. I am deeply interested in the Sacco-Vanzetti case, and firmly convinced that it is not closed. I think it's important that the agitation should continue. But personally I am not interested in that game and don't know how to play it. So your friends are probably right.

I had thought that possibly I might write something which you could use at the meeting, but I am not sure that you want it or that when the time came I'd have anything I would care to say.

1. Gardner Jackson, humane champion of many good causes, was an early organizer of the defense efforts for Sacco and Vanzetti, whose case he continued to promote even after their executions.

To Felix Frankfurter

July 29, 1929

Dear Felix:

. . . You will also have noticed, perhaps, from today's paper, that we're very much on guard about Gastonia.[1] I should appreciate suggestions about that from you, and some advice as to whose statements about the trial are to be trusted. I don't know whether this is another Sacco-Vanzetti case or not, but at least this time we can start howling at the beginning and not wait until most of the damage is done.

1. In Gastonia, North Carolina, one of the most celebrated of strikes had begun in April 1929. The National Textile Workers Union had walked out after management at the Loray mill had refused a series of reasonable demands designed to reduce the long hours of work, to eliminate the stretch-out, to improve living conditions in company-owned residences, and to achieve rec-ognition of the union. The rejection of those characteristic trade-union demands pushed the union, dominated by Communists, to political issues. The American Federation of Labor denounced the strike. The governor sent in the National Guard. Those developments abetted the political activ-ities of the Communist party, which used the strikers to raise money, allegedly for relief, in Northern cities. The Communist party also tried to make the strike appear to involve a racial issue, even though textile workers throughout the southern Piedmont were at that time almost exclusively white. Strikebreakers demolished union headquarters in mid-April, the strike having officially ended. But the mill evicted more than sixty families from homes it owned, and political agitation continued — as in the ballads of Ella May Wiggins, the union's minstrel. With the continuing tension, gunfire on June 7 wounded several policemen and killed one, the chief of police. There followed the arrest of two men accused of firing the fatal shots, and of fourteen other people on charges of conspiracy leading to murder. Their trial began on July 29, the date of this letter. It resulted in a mistrial, a new trial in September, and a verdict of guilty — though the issue had by then become one of heresy rather than murder, and most of the indictments had been dropped. Meanwhile vigilantes had shot and killed Ella May Wiggins, still a martyr in the pantheon of radical victims of antilabor violence.

To William E. Borah

July 29, 1929

My dear Senator Borah:

I am, of course, delighted with your letter, and happy that we had any part whatever in so good a cause.

I am glad you spoke about Russia. So far as our policy goes we have for a long time been of entire agreement with you about the recognition of Russia,[1] and I have long wished that a good opportunity would present itself for an effective campaign. It occurs to me now that the opportunity may come in the next two or three weeks. It is just possible, in fact it is possible, that a pacific solution of the Manchurian question[2] may be found just before, or just about when the Senate reconvenes. It seems to me that that might be the moment to launch a campaign, for then we should have a demonstrated case of American reliance upon the good faith of Russia's word, and of Russia's justification of that reliance.

I do not know, of course, what the views of the President are on this subject, but if a newspaper campaign, and a campaign in the Senate led by you were properly timed, we might get somewhere. . . .

1. Borah, like Lippmann, favored American recognition of the Soviet Union, so long delayed. Their efforts and those of others to that end failed until 1933 because of Hoover's opposition. 2. Russian and Chinese forces were fighting in Manchuria. The skirmishes there ended as the Nationalist government of China consolidated its authority over the area.

To Bernard Berenson

November 4, 1929

Dear B. B.:

. . . We are just finishing an extraordinarily dull Mayoralty campaign in which Mayor Walker is running for re-election on the Tammany ticket, and Congressman La Guardia is the Republican nominee.[1] There were certain aspects of the campaign which it is not safe to discuss which would have interested you, as they interested me. La Guardia is the first Italian to receive a nomination for a high elective office in America and he has made a very sorry showing. The ordinary American has been bewildered by his rhetoric and his recklessness, but I who witnessed the elections in Italy last Spring feel very much at home. In a very real sense, in a much more real sense than most people here realize, La Guardia has run counter to the American pattern. It has made people vaguely uncomfortable, not so much for what he said which was ninety-nine percent rubbish, but for the manner in which he said it, and because of the state of mind which lay behind it all. It was a remarkable exhibition of the real gap which lies between the Italian and the Anglo-American political tradition. But of course it would be definite destruction to say anything on that.

You ask about my private report on the Fascists. I started to write it on the steamer coming home, but was too lazy to finish it and when I got home I was too busy. As a matter of fact I had nothing new to say. I had found out nothing that you don't know and everything I'd found out seemed to me to confirm your own opinions.

I had dinner the other night in New York with a group of Italians, Prezzolini[2] was the guest of honor, and there were present two Italians who are teaching at Columbia. . . . They were all contemptuously anti-Fascist, and they expressed themselves with a freedom which I think they would not have employed even in the United States three years ago. I didn't have a real talk with Prezzolini. He refused to try out even his French and told me that he wanted to wait two or three months and then would like very much to have a real talk. He was curiously shy.

I saw a good deal of MacDonald while he was here.[3] Faye and I went down to Washington for the week that he was there and ran into him at a number of different functions. We also came up on the train from Washington to New York with him and saw a good deal of him and his daughter and the members of his party. They make, I think, a universally good impression, and in the two weeks following the visit, the Senate would, in my opinion, have ratified any agreement which Hoover submitted to them. I do not believe, however, that the impression made has any real depth or that it necessarily will last or that it has changed the American state of mind about England. Those things which are being said in the English press are obvious exaggerations. The future depends not upon the impression that MacDonald made, but upon the position which Hoover occupies in relation to Congress and to American opinion when the agreement is to be submitted to the Senate. I do not know what that position will be. People that you and I know here — most of us who voted against Hoover — think he has done brilliantly, but he has had a very hard time with Congress and he is facing something like a catastrophe over the tariff.[4] If things go very badly in his relations with Congress over the tariff, he will rouse hidden enmities which may have very serious consequences on his foreign policy. . . .

1. James J. Walker, Tammany's "dandy little" mayor, won re-election over his Republican opponent, the progressive congressman Fiorello La Guardia. Walker proved to be corrupt; La Guardia, while flamboyant, to be in later years a creative, reform mayor of the city.   2. Giuseppe Prezzolini, Italian anti-Fascist intellectual and émigré, author of many works on Italian culture, including studies of Machiavelli and Croce.   3. Ramsay MacDonald, back in office as British prime minister, had come to the United States for conversations with Hoover. Their meeting

eased Anglo-American tensions and prepared the ground for the London Naval Conference of 1930.   **4.** The special session Hoover had called to address farm relief and limited tariff revision had fought over the former issue, as had the regular session of the new Congress, until June. By that time logrolling threatened to produce, as ultimately it did, a considerable overall increase in tariff duties. Democrats in the Senate, assisted by Borah, were also able to attach two amendments Hoover opposed, one to provide subsidies for certain agricultural exports, another to give Congress (rather than the president) authority to pass upon modifications in schedules that were proposed by the Tariff Commission. Hoover's intercession with the conference committee later helped the House delete those changes before the enactment of the Hawley-Smoot Tariff of 1930, the highest in American history.

To Felix Frankfurter

December 23, 1929

Dear Felix:

. . . I am afraid I don't agree with you about the Wickersham Commission.[1] Of course the terms of reference are the root of the trouble, but I have small sympathy with the Commission if it gets into trouble because it accepted a reference which you must know is intellectually insincere and politically somewhat devious. The more I have heard about what they were doing . . . the more convinced I have become that they are trying to accomplish incidental good things on an unreal basis.

I do not believe for a minute that what you call a change of the mental climate can come from the work of a Commission operating under the conditions this one is operating under. I do not propose to attack them now, but I certainly shall feel that the burden of proving their usefulness is entirely on them, and it will take a lot of proving to make me believe that they haven't been used by the President as a device to divert public attention. The fact that there are a lot of hard-working and sincere men connected with the Commission does not alter this fundamental fact.

1. In May 1929, Hoover had appointed a Law Observance and Enforcement Commission with George W. Wickersham, attorney general of the United States during the administration of President Taft, as chairman. It was to conduct a survey to provide a basis for policy on the Eighteenth Amendment. Lippmann sensed that Hoover expected the survey to result in recommendations for effective enforcement of the law. The committee's report in the end stated the obvious, that profits from illicit traffic in liquor hindered enforcement of prohibition, as did public apathy or hostility, and that effective enforcement would depend on federal efforts rather than joint federal-state responsibility. Though the report opposed repeal, as Lippmann had foreseen it would, a majority of the commission favored revision. For his part, Hoover, when he submitted the report in January 1930, also opposed repeal.

To Francis B. Sayre[1]

December 26, 1929

Dear Mr. Sayre:

I am very glad to hear from you. I have been very much interested in the proposal to abolish battleships, and have been studying it as closely as I could for some time. . . . I haven't quite reached a conclusion in my own mind about the desirability of concentrating on the abolition of the battleship as a way of insuring some kind of tangible success in London. The argument for economy is, of course, obvious. The argument about the obsolescence of the battleship presents certain difficulties to my mind. If we succeeded in abolishing the battleship without reaching an agreement on cruisers, which is substantially what the French want, the effect would be, I fear, to intensify the competition in cruisers.

Now as I see it, our main objective must be not economy, and not even the reduction of the actual quantity of armaments in the world, but the stopping of international competition. I'm afraid of the battleship argument because it tends to divert attention from this fundamental matter to the quite subsidiary question of economy and reduction. . . .

1. Francis B. Sayre, son-in-law of Woodrow Wilson, at this time a professor at the Harvard Law School.

III

Of Aims and Methods

1930–1945

To John L. Balderston [1]

Dear John:

I am afraid you must feel that I'm extremely wooden and unresponsive to the battleship business. As a matter of fact I am not tremendously interested in it. I have no interest in making the Conference *appear* [2] to be a success when in fact it's a failure, and in my view the test of success or failure is not the amount of money saved, not whether there is more or less ship building, but whether all categories of naval vessels are subjected to international agreement for a definite term of years, with a provision for a conference for another agreement at the end of it. Since battleships are not subject to international agreement, I am very little interested in them for the purposes of this Conference. They are to my mind a bargaining point in relation to the crucial matter of an agreement about cruisers, destroyers and submarines. [3]

I can very well understand why British opinion should be interested in the battleships; the naive liberals, because a reduction there would *look* like disarmament, conservatives like the London *Times* because reduction in battleships without agreement in other categories would strengthen their relative naval position.

In my opinion the reduction of battleships is one of the aces that the Americans hold, and they ought to make the Europeans buy the reduction in battleships at as heavy a price as possible. By price I mean, of course, agreement in other categories. It would have been a great mistake, therefore to come out and advocate the abolition of the battleship or its reduction to ten thousand tons or anything else of the sort. We should have made the same mistake that Woodrow Wilson made at Paris when he bought the League from Lloyd George and Clemenceau at the expense of the Fourteen Points, instead of selling the

League to Lloyd George and Clemenceau in return for the fulfillment of the Fourteen Points.

I don't know that you will agree with this, but at least I hope it makes clear to you my own motives for not being moved by your arguments about the battleships.

I hope you will get into close relationship, as soon as possible, with George Rublee, who is with Morrow, and I hope you will not feel that anyone here in this office expects you to make sensational revelations, or pull off any stunts. What we shall need most of all is clear exposition of the points of view of the other delegations, and I would lean over backwards, if I were you, in avoiding any suggestion of prejudice or of suspicion against the Italian or the French. I would assume in both cases that their fundamental position is every bit as respectable as the British or the American, and I would try to make their point of view persuasive even when it runs most against American or British policy.

Good luck to you. Don't let the job wear you down too much. The main points, the main positions, will be relatively simple, and I wouldn't let myself get tangled in the detail.

1. John L. Balderston, then the *World*'s correspondent in London.   2. Both emphases in this letter are Lippmann's.   3. The London Naval Conference was about to convene, as it did on January 21, 1930, to continue until April 22. Like many other informed Americans, Lippmann had expectations for the conference that seem, in retrospect, fancifully high. The Franco-Italian rivalry and the Anglo-American disagreements about cruisers that had so crippled the conference at Geneva three years earlier continued, though less severely, to divide the participating powers, as did also Japanese ambitions. Yet the American delegation, headed by Secretary of State Henry Stimson and including, among others, Dwight Morrow and Hugh Gibson, was now free of the anglophobia of Admiral Hilary P. Jones, who had damaged prospects at Geneva. The growing worldwide depression, for its part, had fostered strong sentiments for economy in naval construction, especially in Washington and London. Still, the conference achieved only a small success. After France refused Italy's demand for parity, neither nation would sign the most important provision of the final treaty. In it, the United States, Great Britain, and Japan adopted a plan to limit the construction of cruisers, both "light" and "heavy," but an escalator clause allowed Great Britain to build up to the combined equivalent of any two continental powers. In the face of the French and Italian rivalry, that clause permitted British, and then Japanese and American, building programs. The 10:6 ratio for capital ships, established at the Washington Conference in 1922, was extended to cruisers, but Japan, restless with that figure, received a 10:7 ratio for other auxiliary vessels except submarines. For those ships, parity was based upon an upper limit of total tonnage. The continued ratio of 10:6 for capital ships, supplemented by a building holiday for them until 1936, entailed the scrapping of five British, three American, and one Japanese warship. The treaty contained no political guarantees, though the French had tried to obtain one. In the large, the conference revealed a growing rapprochement between the English-speaking powers. Its strategic significance paled partly because the United States during Hoover's presidency had no intention of building up to treaty strength, whereas Japan did.

To John L. Balderston

January 23, 1930

Your stuff excellent in substance and manner (stop) Hope you will not share impatience expressed by some correspondents with refusal to define issues sharply or make public commitments at early stages (stop) This is deliberate American policy and wise object to prevent opinion from solidifying irreconcilably (stop) Would discount and ignore rumors Anglo-American disagreement (stop) Have strong reason believe this for French consumption to overcome suspicion of Anglo-American entente

To George Rublee

February 12, 1930

Dear George:

This letter is not about the Naval Conference, except to say that so far everything is going well over here, with every disposition so far as I can see, to trust the delegation and to support it. In view of the lack of definite news, I think the American press is behaving well.

What I really want to write you about is the question of Dwight's position on prohibition in the New Jersey primaries.[1] As you probably know, there is already a great deal of talk about it in private, and some in the newspapers, and a great disposition to wonder whether he intends to straddle or evade the issue. I have been thinking about it a good deal, trying to see as fairly as I can the argument against the position I would naturally want him to take, but I am satisfied that from the point of view of political expediency, from the point of view of his usefulness as a Senator, and from the point of view of his personal reputation, the only course for him to take is an unequivocal stand in favor of modification of the present prohibition system.

Unless I am wholly incapable of judging the currents of public opinion, there is a more radical change of feeling in the last three months than in the whole previous ten years of prohibition. The wets in the East are organizing politically, and they are making great inroads in all the doubtful sections. Just yesterday the second Massachusetts district, where Calvin Coolidge lives, and which for forty years has been Republican by a large majority, was turned over and elected a wet Democrat by a large majority. There is no doubt that discontent with economic conditions plays some part in this result, and that there was a certain amount of factional fighting inside the Republican Party, but it is nevertheless a fact that this rock-ribbed Republican district which if any district, ought to represent administration Republicanism, has gone Democratic and wet. It is no less significant, I think, that the chief proposal of the Wickersham Commission, the one proposal which would have speeded up penal enforcement, the proposal to reduce trial by jury, is hopelessly lost in Congress, in spite of the overwhelmingly theoretical dry strength in that body. But more important than any of these things is the change in temper of the wets. They are no longer hopelessly resigned and cynical. They are in a fighting mood. And I have heard men who loved and admired Dwight say that they would not vote for him if he failed to take a forthright position. The editor of an important Republican paper in New York City, a great admirer of Dwight's, told me that his paper would smoke Dwight out if he tried to straddle. And I know that I should find it impossible to give him effective support in the *World* if his position is not clear on prohibition. I would not know how to persuade our readers to share my own admiration for him in the face of what I know would be a storm of protest.

I think it is fair to urge these considerations of expediency because I take it that the only conceivable ground on which Dwight would consider supporting the Hoover position would be the ground of expediency. I believe it is highly inexpedient for him to take that position. And I should go as far as to say that I think New Jersey is wet enough, and by November will be so much wetter that a dry ex-Morgan partner would not be elected. . . .

I don't believe, however, that these considerations of expediency will determine him. The real fact is that whether we like it or not, prohibition is the paramount political issue in this country today, and no man ought to try to enter American political life who isn't willing to face it. This doesn't mean that Dwight has to announce a program in detail. It does mean that he has to accept the premise that the present system is unsatisfactory and that a substitute has to be found. I realize that this in a sense means a break with the present administration, but as a matter of fact the administration needs Dwight more than he needs the administration.

I don't think I exaggerate in saying that what he does about this is likely to be decisive not only as affecting his election but as affecting his future influence in politics. The time has gone by when the attitude that Coolidge took is politically feasible. Hoover has been forced to a more positive attitude — as it happens on the dry side — but still a more positive attitude. Yet in taking that attitude he is suffering his heaviest punishment. You will find when you return that the wet movement in the east is far more formidable than you imagined it to be when you sailed for London. And you will find, I venture to prophesy, that the New Jersey primary will attract national attention and will become a national test of the wet-dry issue. Nothing else really matters in American politics except the wholly irrational factor of business depression. I believe Dwight's only course is a clear, bold and decisive one, which would put him instantly in the position of leadership.

Anyway that's what I feel today, and wanted to get it off my chest. Think it over when you get your mind off the cruisers.

1. In a primary election in October to fill an unexpired term in the United States Senate, Morrow ran for the Republican nomination. As a wet, he called for repeal of the Eighteenth Amendment. He defeated his dry opponent, as he did also his Democratic rival early in 1931.

To Ernest Gruening [1]

February 20, 1930

Dear Ernest:

The opportunity which you say the *New York World* has muffed was failing to advocate the abolition of battleships. Isn't that begging the question? Or doesn't it assume that the abolition of the battleship would in itself have brought us any nearer to disarmament? I quite agree that many people would have been enormously impressed if the Conference had declared for the abolition of the battleship, but as the proposal came from England, it meant that the Conference should deal with battleships and not try to deal with cruisers. I think there's no question about that. Now the competition in cruisers is the heart of naval competition today. Battleships, while they are expensive, are not on a competitive basis. They are, therefore, a relatively unimportant factor in the field of international politics. The proposal as it came from England was essentially a Tory and Admiralty move which some Labour men played in with to avoid dealing with the crucial question of cruisers and to sugar-coat the failure by a fictitious success on battleships.

Our delegation quite properly squelched this maneuver, for they see clearly what I think is the essence of the matter. The greatest single step towards disarmament which can be taken now is to get every kind of war vessel off the competitive and on to an agreed treaty basis. As a matter of fact, however, though the delegation refused to take up battleships first, what they are actually proposing between now and the termination of the proposed treaty, namely 1936, involves a reduction of battleships to the amount of 300 million dollars. This is a very substantial reduction, and you can figure out for yourself on the table of Washington Treaty replacements how very near it comes to a decision not to replace battleships at all.

I don't for one minute think that the British Admiralty would have agreed to the abolition of battleships, and I don't for one minute think that Mac-Donald proposed the abolition of battleships. What MacDonald had in mind was a proposal not to replace the existing battleships when they became obsolete by ships of the present size, a wholly different and much less dramatic proposal. That proposal has been, to a very large degree, accepted already.

Moreover, I don't for a minute think that the French would abandon the submarine if the United States and Great Britain dramatically or otherwise declared that they would never build another battleship. You wholly misunderstand the French political mind, I think, if you imagine that they would sentimentally throw away their own desire for, and possibility of having, a navy strong enough to threaten the British lines of communication.

I quite agree with you that the Conference has been undramatic and that people have lost interest and don't understand it, . . . and that something very much needs doing to revive the emotion with which the Conference began. But it's very hard to know what to suggest which would do that and at the same time have the slightest chance of being accepted and not run the risk of defeating what the Conference will almost certainly achieve, which is to bring the war vessels for the first time in history under international regulation.

1. Ernest Gruening, Harvard '07, a dedicated progressive who was at this time editor of the *Portland Evening News* in Maine and much later a courageous and articulate Democratic senator from Alaska.

To Carl Tivel[1]

February 26, 1930

Dear Sir:

The question which you have chosen for debate is one which will arise in practice only in the case of those foreign investments which are made in countries with weak governments. It seems to me that when American nationals make investments in regions where the protection of property and the payment of debts is not assured they have no right to expect their own government to come to their aid in time of trouble. They have voluntarily assumed a great risk and there is no obligation on the part of the American government to see that they do not suffer loss therefrom.

If these investments, however, are to be under the sole protection of the government of the territory in which they are made, and that government should be practically non-operative in a period of revolution or civil war, our own government could not well avoid the obligation of protecting both American lives and American property in the disturbed areas. It could not therefore leave complete jurisdiction under all conditions to the government of the territory where its nationals have made investments.

Where the foreign government is strong and stable, there is no question that it should have the sole jurisdiction over investments made within its own territory. Where the government is not strong and stable, the procedure should vary according to the circumstances in each particular case. In some instances, courts of arbitration formed by all creditor countries holding property interests in the debtor country would be desirable, as you suggest. There are conceivable conditions, however, under which this mode of procedure would not be practicable. I should not advocate it as a universal rule.

1. Carl Tivel, whose letter to Lippmann has been lost, had obviously written with the proposal about courts of arbitration to which Lippmann replied.

To Marc Connelly [1]

March 4, 1930

Dear Marc:

We saw *The Green Pastures* last night and I wish I could make still louder the general enthusiasm. It is not only a beautiful and entrancing play. It is a religious vision greatly conceived.

In one respect I was misled by some of the reviews. I had thought that this was a highly successful attempt to reproduce a primitive Negro religion. What it actually is, it seems to me, is a universal fable of the growth of human wisdom, and its dramatic theme is the education of God. What makes it a universal, rather than a quaint and exotic thing, is that the path which God travels from omnipotence to mercy is the path which everyone travels who travels at all. That is why, I think, people are so deeply moved.

That, at least, is what the play gave me, and if you say you didn't mean all this I shall believe it none the less. For when men are inspired they lose control of their work.

1. Marc Connelly, a friend of the Lippmanns', sometime member of the staff of the *World*, distinguished playwright and author of *The Green Pastures*, then playing to applauding audiences on Broadway.

To James G. McDonald [1]

March 8, 1930

Dear Mr. McDonald:

As I was saying to you on the telephone, I believe we are in general agreement that the hope of substantial reduction below what would be called for by the principle of parity and the British two-power standard, and the present French program, lies in making Washington concede a political treaty for consultation. There are some differences between us as to the best form of argument.

The one that I think most effective is to shock the country into a realization that it faces enormous costs unless it rouses itself out of its opposition to political concessions. I don't think that parity and reduction are consistent except by political concessions, and it is this dilemma which needs to be forced upon the attention of Congress and the people generally. The failure to make this dilemma real is the criticism I should make of Buell's calculations as they appear in this morning's papers. The reductions he proposes as consistent with parity are entirely contingent upon a political agreement with the French. Yet I am afraid that they will give the impressions that they are obtainable by mere negotiation over naval matters in London. They are not obtainable by negotiations on naval matters. They are obtainable only by political negotiations and the delegation in London is helpless to enter into political negotiations until the state of mind in Congress and the country generally has been radically altered.

1. James G. McDonald, then chairman of the board of the Foreign Policy Association.

To William Allen White

March 17, 1930

Dear Will:

I have your letter of March 11th from Haiti, and since then, of course, we have had the dispatches of your really triumphant success. . . .[1]

It was plain to me that it was you who created the atmosphere which made the success possible, and as I learned in Mexico, atmosphere is nine-tenths of diplomacy in Central America, perhaps everywhere.

I have been giving a good deal of thought to the question you put in your letter, namely, whether we couldn't establish a fairly regular procedure where these interventions seem to be required. I think the general principle is clear enough. The difficulty is in applying it. The principle is to make these interventions something more than an arbitrary act of our own national sovereignty. At the time of the Havana Conference, which I attended, Nicaragua was the subject of discussion, and I urged through the *World* that we ask the Pan American Union to set up a machinery which could pass upon the necessity for an intervention and would then authorize us to act. I discovered, however, that the divisions among Latin American states were so great and the domestic political reasons so strong against theoretically approving an intervention which their governments would approve, that I concluded the scheme was not workable in that form. I have now come around to a modified notion of the scheme which at the moment seems to me worth considering. It is, that we establish it as our own national policy that we will never intervene without submitting the reasons for our intervention to the members of the Pan American Union, and without making a formal report to them of our actions during the intervention. This procedure does not involve their issuing an approval of the intervention. On the other hand, it does put our policy on the basis of a decent respect for the opinion of mankind, and gives it in fact an international quality even without any formal international consent.[2]

If I'm right in thinking that this is a good principle of action, then the policy might be inaugurated immediately in respect to Haiti by the simple device of submitting a report on the American occupation and a statement of the policy which your Commission is recommending after the President has approved it. We could send the report to all the members of the Pan American Union with an announcement that we submit it because we recognize we are acting as trustees of civilization and not in our own right alone.

There will be many who will object to this, but I don't see any serious objection to it. I am going to try it out by advocating it in the *World* during the next few days so that if you should decide for something like this you will have had some test of public opinion in advance.

In the meantime let me repeat that I think you've done the neatest and most brilliant diplomatic job done by anyone since Morrow revolutionized the Mexican question. I am proud of you.

1. White was a member, W. Cameron Forbes the head, of the president's investigative commission on Haiti. Disorder there had prompted Coolidge in 1929 to send in more American forces, which Haitian mobs had attacked. Hoover appointed the commission to find terms for a settlement of the internal politics that had produced the disorder. The commission recommended various administrative reforms, the appointment of a civilian to replace the military American high commissioner, and a continuation until 1936 of the treaty between Haiti and the United States, a treaty that gave the United States a protectorate. The commission also persuaded Haiti's controversial president to resign. His successor, assisted by American money and advice, restored order and worked out a treaty calling for eventual American withdrawal. But the Haitian assembly demanded immediate withdrawal, which the United States executed only after the end of Hoover's term.   2. Lippmann's proposal built upon the recent publication of a memorandum prepared two years earlier by Reuben Clark, then undersecretary of state. Repudiating the corollary to the Monroe Doctrine announced by Theodore Roosevelt, the memorandum, now official policy, declared that the doctrine did not concern purely inter-American relations. Intercession by the United States in the affairs of any other American State, Clark wrote, was intended only to protect that State from aggression by a European power.

To Franklin D. Roosevelt[1]

March 19, 1930

PERSONAL

Dear Frank:

I think you ought to know that there is a great deal of perturbation among some of your best friends here over the question of appointing a successor to Proskauer.[2] The opinion seems to be unanimous that all the names on the Tammany list are very poor, and the commonest comment I hear is that you don't seem to realize that your position is so strong that you can afford, apart from the intrinsic desirability of the thing, to make appointments independently and courageously. I don't want to press you in the paper on this matter but I know we should feel very badly indeed if, for example, you took any of the names on the present Tammany list and passed over a man of the quality of Shientag.

I don't want you to regard this as a letter urging you to appoint Shientag. Any man of his capacity and independence would do quite well from our point of view. But what we are very much opposed to is a poor appointment as a concession to Tammany even if that appointment has the conventional endorsements.

You've been making great progress at Albany which of course delights us here very much.

1. Franklin D. Roosevelt, then in his first term as governor of New York. 2. Proskauer had resigned from the New York Supreme Court. Roosevelt appointed to succeed him Bernard L. Shientag, a friend of Al Smith's and also a vigorous social reformer who won election to the seat in his own right when the unexpired term came to its end.

To Herbert D. Croly

March 24, 1930

Dear Herbert:

I'm very much ashamed at not having written you sooner, but for nearly three months Faye and I have been planning on a visit to California sometime this winter, and our intention was to come and see Louise and you first of all.[1] Now I find that it's impossible for us to get away, which distresses me greatly because I had counted very much on a talk with you about a number of matters that have puzzled, and still do puzzle me very much.

I would particularly like to know how, in the light of our old interest in an Anglo-American agreement, you now look upon the prospect of a three-power naval treaty as the only probable salvage from the wreckage of the London Conference. I am very much afraid, myself, that the manner in which the whole negotiation has been handled may give us something like an Anglo-American agreement under the worst possible auspices. My own inclination is to take it even then, in spite of all my misgivings about its effects in accentuating British isolation from the Continent and the Nationalist policy of France.

The management of the Conference by Hoover and MacDonald has been incredibly amateurish. It seems to be a fact, though it's hard to believe it, that no preliminary understanding of any kind was reached with either France or Italy, and that MacDonald and Hoover went ahead on the assumption that they could somehow bluff the French out of their announced policy. Early in January, I saw the President and most of the members of the delegation in Washington. They all said that they were perfectly satisfied that they had an agreement with the French. As the thing has worked out I cannot believe that they really knew what they were talking about.[2]

Hoover's had a wretched first year. Everything he touches seems to go sour on him. And yet I cannot quite bring myself to condemn him completely. For underneath all his failures, there is a disposition in this Adminstration to rely on intelligence to a greater degree than at any time, I suppose, since Roosevelt. Hoover seems to be the victim partly of bad luck, partly of a temperamental weakness in dealing with irrational political matters, and partly of bad advice in matters where he has no personal experience. But you have probably seen these things in a better perspective than we do here. . . .

1. Croly was then living in Santa Barbara, California.   **2.** They had had an operable agreement with the British but not with the French or the Italians.

To John L. Balderston

March 25, 1930

Dear John:

. . . Your general sizing up of the situation has been correct from the start and I have the greatest admiration for the way in which you've kept your perspective under extremely difficult circumstances. There's no use my trying to write you at this late date about the situation here for there's really nothing I could tell you that you don't know. Hoover's alibi for refusing to discuss political matters at London will be that the French demanded a guarantee and would take nothing less. My own view is that if we'd agreed to a consultative pact and had shown the British that such a pact would mean at least a benevolent neutrality in case they had to apply sanctions, that the British would then have been able to go much further than they have in meeting Briand.[1] I wonder whether I'm wrong in assuming that the value of the consultative pact is not that it would have satisfied the French but that it would have enabled the British to satisfy the French.

1. Briand was then French foreign minister and a delegate to the conference.

To Seward Collins[1]

March 25, 1930

Dear Mr. Collins:

I thank you for your generous letter, and I should like to return the compliment by saying that I have greatly enjoyed the vigor and intelligence with which you have championed your views in the *Bookman*.

I must, however, dissent from your assumption that I am "opposed" to Babbitt and More.[2] I am opposed to a certain sectarianism in Babbitt. But I am not opposed to the central insight of the new humanism. On the contrary, I am in sympathy with it. I can't help it if Mr. Babbitt and Mr. More insist upon excommunicating me on the basis of what I believe to be a misreading of a few isolated passages in my book. It is my own belief that my position is at least as consistent with theirs as, for example, is Mr. T. S. Eliot's, that while I do not qualify, nor desire to qualify, as one of the strictly orthodox members of the inner cult, that I am at least on the main points in substantial agreement.

I am somewhat confirmed in this belief by the fact that Mr. Foerster strongly urged me, last summer, to become one of the contributors to the symposium.

I declined the invitation, partly because I was busy with other things, partly because I don't care for symposia, and partly because I knew I could not feel comfortable with the harsh doctrinaire spirit of Mr. Babbitt. All of this does not in the least affect my own belief in the wisdom of Mr. More's main intuitions, though I wish they could be purged of a certain temperamental blindness to some aspects of modern life, liberated from their bondage to a rather crude metaphysic, and dissociated from the temptation of sectarianism.

I have no desire to be counted among what you call the "head-on" opponents, for I am not one of them. I have, however, had enough experience in controversies to realize that invariably the propagandist is more interested in the small divergences of those nearest to him than in the larger contradictions offered by the main body of his opponents.

1. Seward Collins, then editor of the *Bookman*.   **2.** Paul Elmer More and Irving Babbitt, distinguished conservative humanists, had criticized Lippmann's *Preface to Morals* in contributions to a published symposium, *Humanism in America* (New York, 1930), edited by the prolific critic and anthologist Norman Foerster, a professor of English at the University of Iowa.

To John L. Balderston

April 28, 1930

Dear John:

. . . If you do go,[1] I wish you'd make a point of seeing Croce,[2] who lives in Naples. Croce is by all odds the most important figure in the intellectual life of Italy today, and the way he has stood up against the dictatorship is genuinely heroic. I don't dare to write to him very much, but you could see him and tell him that we are his friends and if there's ever anything we can do we'd like to help. . . . Of course if you see Croce you'll be careful afterwards, in writing about Italy, to protect him from seeming to be the source of any unfavorable criticism you make.

In my opinion, the great unwritten story in Italy today is the relationship between the Vatican and Fascism. I don't suppose that in a short time you can really get the inside of that, but if you could I think it would be extremely interesting. . . .

1. To Italy on vacation.   **2.** Benedetto Croce, eminent Italian philosopher and liberal statesman.

To Felix Frankfurter

May 23, 1930

Dear Felix:

I am very grateful to you for your letter. Not only for what you say about my article[1] but particularly for your supplementing analysis. I think it may be that I continue to look at his past glories through the glasses of the Hoover legend. I think the men whose judgment I most respect and who knew him best in those days would agree with you. I do not have the materials for correcting my own view. And so, with some hesitation I continue to give him the benefit of the doubt. After all, I was not pretending to do anything like a rounded analysis of the whole man. What you say would belong in such an analysis. But I might put it in a little different perspective at the point where you use the word "promoter." I have used that word myself about him in the political campaign, but it has a somewhat disparaging implication which I shouldn't want to make without qualifications. Hoover, in spite of everything, is a very considerable fellow.

This letter would be more coherent if it hadn't been interrupted by a twenty-five minute telephone call from Dwight Morrow. It's pretty hard to defend Hoover when you think of Morrow.

1. Lippmann's "The Peculiar Weakness of Mr. Hoover" appeared in the June 1930 issue of *Harper's.*

To Henry L. Stimson

May 29, 1930

My dear Mr. Secretary:

Naturally, I am greatly pleased with your letter, though it is characteristically over-generous. I thank you for it and would like to take this opportunity to bring up a matter which has been troubling me for some weeks.

It is in regard to the attitude of the admirals who are opposing the Treaty.[1] Apart from the obvious embarrassment which many of their acts must cause abroad, I think the nature of their testimony raises a fundamental question in the relationship between the military and the civilian power. It is a matter which you, in your own experience as Secretary of War, must have thought about a great deal. I wonder whether you have recalled in recent days the regulations issued by Mr. Root as Secretary of War on the position of the General Staff. In Mr. Root's report for 1903 he says that the tenth article of these regulations "states explicitly the new theory of control inaugurated by the General Staff Act." The tenth article of the regulations ends as follows:

> The successful performance of the duties of the position requires what the title denotes — a relation of absolute confidence and personal accord and sympathy between the Chief of Staff and the President, and necessarily also between the Chief of Staff and the Secretary of War . . . and if at any time the Chief of Staff considers that he can no longer sustain toward the President the relations above described, it will be his duty to apply to be relieved.

It seems to me that this is the soundest and most authoritative statement of the matter that could be had and that it applies essentially to the relationship of the General Board to the President.

I wonder whether in the interest of maintaining sound precedents in vital matters of this sort the President can afford to let the conduct of the General Board pass by uncriticized. I cannot help believing that the matter must have been troubling you a great deal in recent weeks.

1. Led by Hilary P. Jones, many senior American admirals opposed the London treaty, though Admiral William V. Pratt, chief of naval operations, supported it. The Senate approved it.

To Gerard Swope[1]

June 22, 1930

Dear Gerard:

I have had a few letters about the Hoover article, most of them complaining that I was too tender. As a matter of fact, what I am now beginning to think is that Hoover, in the dark spaces of the night is telling himself that his main job now is to make certain of his renomination. And that then, in his second term, he could do all the great things which he wants to do. He probably tells himself that if he started those great things now and risked failure of renomination, he would jeopardize great ideas, great causes, etc. etc. The capacity of ambition to delude people is endless. I imagine it is out of some such self-delusion that he gets his comfort now.

1. Gerard Swope, brother of Herbert Bayard Swope and president of General Electric.

To Graham Wallas

June 24, 1930

Dear G. W.:

I was happy to get your letter, written just after my radio speech. I thought of you while I was making it, and wondered whether by any good luck you'd be listening. Of course the mere fact of being able to go into an office building at 55th Street and Fifth Avenue, in New York City, on a rainy Monday afternoon, and be heard in your room in London, is so exciting and important that anything one says on an occasion like that seems utterly trivial. However, it's no substitute for a visit. And I wish I could see a prospect of our coming over. There is none at the present. . . .

There is an extreme mood of depression prevailing in this country, probably as exaggerated as the elation last year over the boom. I imagine it will do us good. There are already very plain evidences that American opinion has learned a great deal in the last four or five months that it didn't know before about the fact that our economic system is not invulnerable and does not operate in isolation. Poor Hoover is the victim, although his own political clumsiness has made things very much worse for himself. He is certainly in the worst political position in his own party than any Republican president since Taft in 1912, and unless there is a dramatic economic recovery it's a fair guess that his administration will collapse, and he will not be renominated. I think, however, that there is likely to be a recovery before 1932, or at least the beginnings of one, and that, plus the hopeless division of the Democrats on prohibition, should save the Republicans.

The most encouraging thing that has happened here in a long time was Dwight Morrow's overwhelming victory in the New Jersey Republican primaries. We all thought at the end of the campaign that he would win, but no one had any idea that he would take something like 70 percent of the total vote in a field of three candidates. His victory is in part the revolt against prohibition. He stood for the outright repeal of the Eighteenth Amendment. But it is also the most encouraging recognition by the electorate of his own great qualities. There is no one, I think, in our public life, who has anything like his equipment. . . .

To Ruth Hanna McCormick[1]

July 9, 1930

My dear Mrs. McCormick:

I have your letter of July 7th from Byron, Illinois, and I have had an opportunity since I first wrote you to read your letter again carefully. I think I understand your point of view, and I may say that I am not personally disposed to quarrel about the amount of money spent. I think I was away at the time when the first news came out. If I had been here I should have emphasized not the total amount spent, but the proportion of the total amount contributed by yourself. I cannot help believing that there is something inherently bad in the expenditure of so large a sum of money by any one person for his own election to a public office. I realize the danger of going to interested parties for contributions; still, it seems to me fundamentally better to raise the necessary campaign funds among a large number of individuals rather than from the candidate himself.

The unfavorable note which you have undoubtedly detected in the *World* in regard to your candidacy is due, not to the question of money, however, but to the intellectual character of your campaign. I do not object to your being opposed to American adherence to the World Court, if that is, in fact, your sincere conviction, but I cannot believe that a person of your education and intelligence and friendships can sincerely believe the arguments which you used and which you countenanced. I am also deeply out of sympathy with the manner in which you deal with prohibition. I believe you are deliberately, and as a matter of expediency, equivocal. While I have not the slightest doubt that you are ever so much better qualified to sit in the United States Senate than either Deneen or Lewis,[2] or than most of the men now in the Senate, and that, for several personal reasons I should like nothing better than to have you there, I cannot stomach the idea that the first woman to be elected to such a high office should reach it by debasing the intellectual character of her political argument. I feel so sure that you know better and that you deliberately stooped to conquer, that I must tell you in all honesty, that I'd like to see you defeated. I hated to write this way to you but I have said this to your friends, and as long as you have written to me I feel I must say it to you. There is no personal animosity in what I say. On the contrary, my personal feelings run entirely the other way. If I followed my feelings I should want to see you elected on any terms. But I honestly don't think you deserve it. . . .

1. Ruth Hanna McCormick — daughter of Marcus A. Hanna, the late celebrated Republican leader, and widow of Medill McCormick, until his recent death a Republican senator from Illinois — had long been active in politics, at one time as a Theodore Roosevelt Progressive, thereafter as a Republican. She had also worked to improve the working conditions of women and to make child labor illegal. The Republican national committeewoman from Illinois, 1924–28, she served in the House of Representatives, 1926–31, and in 1930 ran for nomination as a Republican for the Senate.   2. Charles S. Deneen, Republican senator from Illinois, 1925–31, lost the primary to Ruth McCormick, who in turn lost the election to her Democratic opponent, James Hamilton Lewis, Democratic senator from Illinois, 1913–19, 1931–39.

To Felix Frankfurter

October 20, 1930

Dear Felix:
   Your letter reaches me at a moment when I am genuinely distressed about the issues raised by corruption in New York City and their relation to the present election. I fully recognize, and have been aware for some time, of the force of the criticisms you make of Tuttle and of Todd. In fact, it is these things, plus a general distrust of the man which has alone prevented us from coming out for the election of Tuttle.[1]
   The different values in the whole situation are extremely subtle and difficult to weigh. On the one hand we have the conduct of Tuttle which you describe. I would add to it my own extreme distrust at the use of the Federal Income tax law and other laws of that sort to investigate local political scandals. I think on principle the instruments which Tuttle employed to produce his revelations are indefensible.
   On the other hand we are in a situation here in New York City where all the proper agencies of investigation are closed because of the Tammany monopoly. I don't need to spell out these assertions in detail for you, but I think

I could justify it in detail. Tuttle's unprincipled conduct has been the first and only means in a great many years for penetrating the Tammany defenses. There is no doubt that in the Ewald case he genuinely penetrated them.

On the other hand we have Roosevelt's conduct which seems to me wholly and consistently dictated by a desire to make the public think he really meant to investigate these scandals while seeing to it that the chances of prosecution and investigation should never get so out of hand as to cause a genuine fear in the ranks of Tammany. I think I could spell that out for you in detail.

It seems to me, therefore, that Roosevelt today occupies a position almost identical to that occupied by Coolidge and Hoover in 1924 in the face of the Harding scandals. I am not sure but that an attitude based on the reasoning of your letter would not lead to the position very much like that occupied eight years ago by papers like the *Times* which were more concerned with the improprieties of investigators like Walsh or Wheeler than they were with the crimes which were exposed.

I am trying in a very brief and summary way to tell you the balance of considerations in my own mind. I have not been able to come to any conclusion as to where finally to throw our support in this election, and I am acting for the present on the principle that it's an obligation of honor, assumed by all of us who denounced the Republicans in 1924, to hold Roosevelt to the same standards to which we then held Coolidge. Beyond that I do not see any light and I should be very grateful to you for your advice.

1. The issues that Lippmann addressed here explained, better than did any other, his growing doubts about Franklin Roosevelt and his conviction, at this time and for some months to come, that Roosevelt was an amiable but weak man. Like his colleagues on the *World*, Lippmann had almost an obsession about the corruption then endemic in Tammany Hall. Though Governor Roosevelt had ordered two investigations of that condition, Republicans accused him, as did anti-Tammany independents, of moving too slowly to bring the power of the state to bear upon matters within the city. Charles H. Tuttle, United States attorney for the Southern District of New York, had exposed much of the rascality in the city, including a payment of ten thousand dollars by the wife of George F. Ewald to a Tammany district leader shortly before her husband was named a city magistrate. Tuttle, an aggressive but not always a meticulous prosecutor, became the Republican candidate for governor in 1930 and made the question of corruption his central issue in campaigning against Roosevelt. He also ran as a wet, a rather disingenuous tactic since his running mate was a dry and the G.O.P. had obviously taken a wet stand only for the sake of expediency. It proved costly, for many Republican drys swung their support to the Prohibitionist candidate, and Roosevelt was wet enough to hold genuine anti-Prohibition votes. Further, Roosevelt had a strong record as governor and exploited the issue of the depression and the resulting unemployment for which Democrats throughout the country gladly blamed Hoover and the Republicans.

Further still, the investigations Roosevelt had commissioned were going forward during the time of the campaign, one of them under Judge Samuel Seabury, an independent Democrat, whose efforts were to continue to reverberate in New York politics for another year; the other under New York Attorney General Hamilton Ward, whose special assistant, Hiram C. Todd, was pursuing the Ewald case. Ward had tried but failed to win the nomination that went to Tuttle.

To Herbert Bayard Swope

October 23, 1930

Dear Herbert:

Thanks for your letter. The Roosevelt editorials have been a thankless thing to write,[1] but it had to be done. I agree with you entirely about his having tossed away a great opportunity, and I very much hope that you are right in thinking that he has destroyed his chances of a presidential nomination. He never was big enough for that, but he would have looked big enough if these events hadn't taken place.

1. In the spirit of Lippmann's letter to Felix Frankfurter of October 20, 1930, sup.

To Felix Frankfurter

November 8, 1930

Dear Felix:

. . . I am genuinely concerned about Hoover in a human way. I felt, since before he was nominated, that he had a very bad temperament for high public office. Ambition and anxiety both gnaw at him constantly. He has no resiliency. And if things continue to break badly for him I think the chances are against his being able to avoid a breakdown. When men of his temperament get to his age without ever having had real opposition, and then meet it in its most drastic form, it's quite dangerous. . . .

To Felix Frankfurter

December 17, 1930

Dear Felix:

I agree with your letter in general and in detail, and I assume I am right in thinking you have not misunderstood my editorials as meant to subscribe to the Fascist doctrine of getting rid of parliaments. I have employed the particular form of presentation which you have seen as, in my judgment, the most effective way at this moment, given the state of mind here in the city, to accomplish two things: first, of making people realize that there are constructive measures which it would be desirable to have Congress take; and second, of trying to shame people into a realization of what it means to believe the machinery of our government is impotent and not to be trusted.

I believe that a special session is inevitable, and my next task is going to be to try to get people to see that a special session of Congress need not be regarded as the last and worst of all bearish news. But on the contrary, given some kind of coherent public opinion and leadership of thought, a great many things could be done, both of lasting and immediate benefit.

The underlying state of mind here is much worse than I think the country realizes. While of course the big banks are sound, there have been many more runs than the newspapers have dared to tell about. There are a number of interesting problems in newpaper ethics which have come to my attention in the last month in this connection. I wish I had a chance to talk them over with you.

To Robert P. Ludlum [1]

January 7, 1931

My dear Mr. Ludlum:

. . . Of course you're right in saying that we advocate many things that we cannot believe will soon come to pass. I do not find that so discouraging, principally because I have learned to realize that what really matters in the long run is not the fate of particular notions that we may have, but the development of the habit and tradition of trying to speak truthfully about public affairs. Our real contribution as individuals must inevitably be trifling in its effect upon the world. The daily effort to speak realistically, without prejudice and with the fullest possible information is a comparatively new thing in human experience, and every man who seriously engages in it is contributing to precedents on which I think in the long run the salvation of men depends. It is impossible to work with the expectation of immediate rewards. They are not available in the kind of world we live in. . . .

1. Robert P. Ludlum, a young man who had written Lippmann for advice about a career in journalism.

To William Allen White

January 31, 1931

Dear Will:

. . . The substance of your letter surprises me. I did not realize you felt that way about the Eighteenth Amendment. And I am delighted, for it means that as a matter of national principle, we are really in agreement. The Eighteenth Amendment is a supreme political blunder from the point of view of anyone interested in social progress. The curse of it is its inflexibility, its complete rejection of the principle that the regulation of a social evil must be accomplished by trial and error. In foreclosing all experiment by the states, in attempting to foreclose all debate as to ways and means of achieving temperance, the Eighteenth Amendment has got us into the trouble we are in.

I am not prepared, however, to share your belief that the Eighteenth Amendment can neither be repealed or modified. It was ratified in less than two years by states of which only thirteen were bone-dry on the day we entered the war, and less than twenty were bone-dry when the ratification was completed. What could be done under those conditions, can, I believe, be undone. I used to think that a quarter of the states could stand out indefinitely. I don't believe that's the fact any more, for I think public opinion in America has a much greater underlying uniformity than that assumes. I think the time will come when men like yourself and Norris and Borah will come forward prepared for a political solution of this utterly intolerable business, and I don't think the solution will be delayed more than five or six years after that. My belief that we shall really get a solution rests on the fact that this is not a problem which can disappear because the public loses interest in it. It is not a problem which can be solved as the problem of the Civil War amendments were solved. For the truth is this as I see it: that the Eighteenth Amendment, though it is not enforced in the wet centers, does prevent all the wet communities from dealing with the underworld which prohibition finances. Cities like Chicago and New York, Philadelphia and many others must recover the right to deal with the problem, and that right is denied to them as long as the Eighteenth Amendment stands. We can get all the liquor we need while the Eighteenth Amendment lasts, and the quality of the liquor is improving and the price is coming down. There is no possibility of depriving the wet centers of their liquor. But we cannot get law and order while the Eighteenth Amendment stands. It is on that ground fundamentally that the repeal or drastic modification of the Eighteenth Amendment is necessary, and, I think, in the end inevitable. . . .

To Newton D. Baker

February 26, 1931

Dear Newton:

. . . We are sailing the end of March for Greece, and now that I am about to be free of all responsibilities, I don't know exactly when I shall come back.[1] I know it would be impossible for me to be in Europe without spending two or three weeks in Florence, which, to my mind, is the loveliest joint product of providence and man that I know of. I am glad you saw it when you could feel the quality of the place.

As I write this, we are waiting for the decision of the Surrogate, so I don't know just when this chapter will be completed. As you probably know, it ended for me about the time that Ralph's experiment here demonstrated conclusively the hopelessness of any reconstruction under the present management. I have stayed on the last eight or nine months only to fulfill what was presented to me as my duty to the members of the staff and to the institution. Of all the possible solutions the sale to Scripps-Howard seems to me the most desirable. For the purchase of the paper by any of the other potential bidders would have been fatal to its spirit, however much it might have preserved its outward appearance. There were no bidders in the field except groups of rich men who were not interested in publishing independent newspapers but in acquiring an instrument of power. I much prefer to have the *World* die a clean death than to have it become a newspaper kept by ambitious politicians and financiers.

I don't expect to see much of the *World* survive in the Scripps-Howard merger. But there is sufficient community of purpose to justify the belief that the *World-Telegram* will carry on as ably as the *World* ever did militant campaigns for honest government and the championing of those who have no friends at court. The extinction of the *World* and the increased power and prestige of the *World-Telegram* will not deprive New York City of a fighting newspaper.

I have made no personal plans. And I have told two or three people who have approached me that I would like to hear what they had to say but that I would like not to have to make any decision until I'd been away from this desk for quite a little while. . . .

1. The Pulitzers had sold the *World* to the Scripps-Howard chain, which merged it with their New York evening paper as the *World-Telegram*. While the sale was pending, Lippmann had entertained several offers or near-offers of new positions but deferred decision. After his return from Europe and after further reflection, he agreed to write a column for the Republican *New York Herald Tribune*. For decades thereafter, that column, "Today and Tomorrow," remained a major syndicated feature in American newspapers. For a full account of the sale of the *World* as it affected Lippmann, see Ronald Steel, *Walter Lippmann and the American Century* (Boston, 1980), ch. 22.

To Lynn Weldon [1]

March 23, 1931

Dear Mr. Weldon:

. . . It is not the intention of "A Preface to Morals" to tear down anything that people believe in. The first part of the book is a description of the causes and results of the process of tearing down beliefs which has been going on in the history of the world during the last four or five centuries. If you will look at the opening paragraph of the book you will find stated there my own attitude towards this destruction of beliefs. The latter part of the book is an attempt to find some slight thing that remains in spite of all this destruction but the book has no pretension to being more than a preface, and that part is not worked out in any detail. . . .

It is very hard to say who the greatest living man is, but I suppose the man who is most likely to affect men's view of the whole world is the man whose influence will longest be felt, and presumably that man is Albert Einstein. As for the greatest man I have personally ever known apart from Einstein himself, who I have met only once for a short time, I should perhaps say Mr. Justice Holmes. . . .

1. Lynn Weldon, the "Wheelchair Reporter" of Wetumpka, Alabama.

To Bernard Berenson   HANDWRITTEN

June 28, 1931

Dear B. B.

We are now on our way from Bremen to Cherbourg: I hardly know whether I can come anywhere near digesting all the talks I had in Berlin during this last week. To speak German six or seven hours a day, especially financial and economic German is exhausting work — I found myself at the end muttering German in my sleep.[1]

Except Communists and Nazis I saw the principal leader of all groups from the German Nationalists to the top Social Democrats. I had a brief talk with Bruening, who is of course the busiest man in the whole world at the moment, not exactly a dictator but the person who for the moment holds the political parties together. He has the face and bearing of a priest. If one did not know how devout a Catholic he is, and how intimately related to the church, one could still hardly miss his clerical exterior. His training, they tell me, was that of a perfect bureaucrat and leader of the Catholic trade unions, and his specialty has been the budget. His strength today is partly his technical competence and partly his extreme indifference to personal property and the superficial movements of public opinion. Apparently he has no money, few personal wants, no strong family or personal attachments, and a kind of imperturbable conviction of his own mission — not a man people would love, but something they elect to hold on to in a hurricane. The Germans are lucky to have him — I should take his present case as that of Poincaré when he took over in France in 1924.

With Curtius I had a rather long & frank talk — He seemed to me a more facile and a much less strongly founded person. His position internally is a weak one and he seems to realize it. Von Bülow,[2] the permanent head of the Foreign Office (nephew, I believe, of the Chancellor) is a man of much greater intuition and of subtler insights. He puzzled me — He seemed to me the only German official who had the detachment to understand the French state of mind. . . . The finance minister . . . doesn't count; the Under Secretary . . . was an honest but rather mediocre bureaucrat. But, of course, the real finance minister is Bruening. Stegerwald,[3] the Minister of Labor, who administers the dole, seemed to me a very able person — Curiously enough Bruening was a clerk in his department ten years ago.

Löbe,[4] the President of the Reichstag, is a Social Democrat . . . and a good example of the thorough universalism — or rather moderateness, of German socialism. The most striking personal figure I saw was Otto Braun,[5] Prime

Minister of Prussia for ten years; the man who next to Hindenburg and Bruening has the greatest popular authority in Germany. The Prussian elections next spring will be very critical — for it is around Prussia rather than the Reich that the fight of the Communists & Nazis for control of the police power rages. A victory of either in Prussia might be decisive; as long as the socialists control Prussia there is no danger that Hitlerism or Bolshevism will control Germany.

I had also a dozen long talks with leading bankers. . . . We arrived in Berlin the day Hoover made his proposals. The Germans acted like a man reprieved an hour before his execution — For on the previous Friday the gold cover at the Reichsbank fell to 40.8% and the legal limit is 40%. This ———[6] up the edge of another inflation or of a literal bankruptcy. Even the savings banks were threatened — Hoover turned the tide: there is no doubt of that, and it was a matter of hours, not even of days.

Before this reaches you you will know how the negotiations with France work out — I am terribly interested to hear when I get back just what happened in Washington between June 10 and June 22 to bring about a revolution in our foreign policy. . . .

1. Lippmann had been in Germany at a singularly tense time. Following the collapse of the Austrian Credit Anstalt in May, a financial panic gripped Europe as owners of capital moved their money rapidly and erratically to find stable havens. The Bank of England tried to ease the flight by advancing a large credit to the Austrian National Bank, but the Bank of France did not help Austria because France was trying to force an end to the customs union between Austria and Germany. Meanwhile a flight of capital from Germany had begun. The German chancellor, Heinrich Bruening, had realized even earlier that he would have to request some alleviation of Germany's reparation payments to prevent national bankruptcy. Early in June he and Julius Curtius, his foreign minister, discussed their plight with the British, who, while sympathetic, believed that any action to delay or reduce reparations required an American initiative on the closely connected problem of war debts. On June 20, President Hoover took that initiative by proposing a one-year moratorium on interallied debts and reparations. The French, however, opposed that proposal until July 6, and while they delayed, conditions worsened — in central Europe especially.

In Germany the continuing crisis encouraged further agitation by the extremist political parties, the Communists on the left and the Nazis on the right. They threatened the stability of the Bruening government, already ruling by emergency decree, and beholden to the centrist right parties but not the Social Democrats, the largest party. It was under those circumstances that Lippmann held the discussions this letter reported. **2.** Bernhard Von Bülow. **3.** Adam Stegerwald, leader of the Christian trade unions, for which Bruening had earlier served as executive secretary. **4.** Paul Löbe. **5.** Otto Braun, a Social Democrat whom Bruening had deliberately excluded from his cabinet. **6.** Handwritten word illegible, perhaps "conjured."

To Hamilton Fish Armstrong

July 8, 1931

Dear Hamilton:

. . . I came back on the Fourth of July, to find almost no one over here who had any sympathy with or understanding of the French point of view.[1]

Everybody seemed blandly to assume that the French ought to have the same over-night conversion that we had. And everybody was extremely impatient and irritable because the French weren't ready to sign on the dotted line, scrapping the principles which we had been upholding as fixed dogma four weeks earlier. I don't know how much damage Hoover's method has done in stiffening and irritating the French, probably a great deal. But there is this to be said for it: it was one of those steps that had to be taken rather suddenly or not at all in order to overwhelm the opposition here and in France. The necessity for this rather abrupt action arises, of course, out of the fact that for ten years the American government has mis-educated the world and mis-educated American opinion above all, and when the time came for a radical reversal, the only way to effect the change was to do it without giving anyone a chance to think or argue. . . .

1. See note 1 to Lippmann to Bernard Berenson, June 28, 1931, sup.

To John L. Balderston

July 30, 1931

Dear John:

   . . . Since I got here on July 4th, I have been working on the story of American foreign relations during the depression[1] and have found it very amusing to see in detail how fixed dogma gradually yield to invincible fact. There is no doubt that American opinion has moved very rapidly indeed in the last two or three months. Cancellation of debts, which was utterly un-thinkable on the first of May now is a practical political question, and I should not be surprised at all to see Hoover in the next two or three months attempt the lead for revision of reparations and debts.

   People have at last learned here that this depression is no mere technical setback on the stock exchange, and they have almost stopped expecting the trend upward to start the day after tomorrow.

   The British theory that we ought to inflate has a certain amount of support over here. As a matter of fact the Federal Reserve Bank has been making money so cheap that it couldn't be made any cheaper and still pay the salaries of clerks in the banks, but cheap money won't start things going. There are definite surpluses which have got to be swallowed somehow before there can be a real movement upward.

   I think myself that the next winter in America is going to be the most agitated that we have witnessed in this generation. We shall probably have about seven to eight million unemployed by January in the cities and in the western and southern farm lands at least a quarter of the farmers are bank-rupt. It's a time when another William Jennings Bryan may easily arise and in addition we have something like the Pullman strikes of '93. Wage reductions which have been going on steadily under cover will be made in the open beginning in about two months under the leadership of the steel corporation. All in all it will be quite fascinating to a journalist and quite distressing to a human being. . . .

1. Lippmann was serving temporarily as editor of *The United States in World Affairs*, a review of that subject published by the Council on Foreign Relations.

To Henry L. Stimson

October 1, 1931

Dear Mr. Secretary:

I am much obliged to you for your letter. I am interested in what you tell me about Manchuria,[1] and particularly in the reception of your act by Shide-hara. The more I consider the matter the more persuaded I am that your policy has been the wise one in view of all circumstances. But it appears that we are by no means at the end of our difficulties in the Far East.

Since you were kind enough to say that you would welcome suggestions, I might say that the thing most on my mind is concern as to whether the Administration has made preparations which might enable it to achieve some substantial result from Laval's visit.[2] I feel certain that it is dangerous, and that it may be a disastrous mistake, to wait until the next congress be organized before taking serious action in regard to debts, reparations and the political stabilization of Europe. Events are running away from us anyhow, and a resumption of payments on the first of July is, in my opinion, psychologically impossible, even if it were economically possible. What I fear is that we shall wait so long to decide what is to happen that when we decide it the advantages of our position will have been lost. It seems to me that if an understanding between France and ourselves isn't reached during Laval's visit or soon thereafter as a direct result of it, we shall get default in bankruptcy, instead of an orderly extension of the moratorium and revision of the obligations. The problem has become so grave and so acute that time is the essence of it, and I do not believe that the cataclysmic progress of events in the world can be arrested to suit the artificial fact that congress meets on the first of December.

1. In mid-September Japanese military officers in Manchuria had seized upon the excuse of an explosion along the South Manchurian Railroad, an explosion that may or may not have occurred, to provoke a confrontation with the Chinese in Mukden. Foreign Minister Baron Kijuro Shidehara protested to the war minister, but other civilian leaders in Tokyo yielded to the military and Japanese forces began what was to become their conquest and occupation of Manchuria. Distracted by the depression at home and the financial crisis in Europe, the Hoover administration recognized the emergency in the Far East but hoped to avoid major responsibility for its resolution. Secretary of State Stimson, who was later to mark the episode as the start of the Fascist aggression that culminated in World War II, decided at first on a measured course, as he put it, "to let the Japanese know we are watching them and at the same time do it in a way which will help Shidehara, who is on the right side, and not play into the hands of any Nationalist agitation." During the next several months, Stimson in diplomatic notes expressed American concern and regret, but he also drew back from joining discussions of the Council of the League of Nations, partly in order to avoid having the problem of Manchuria "dumped" on Washington, partly because he believed Shidehara and other moderates in Japan were "sincerely trying to settle" the matter.   **2.** French Premier Pierre Laval was to visit the United States late in October to discuss the question of war debts and reparations. At the end of his stay, the two powers stated that when the moratorium ended, some further agreement on interallied debts might be necessary. But when the time came, congressional opposition still prevented the United States from pursuing effectively any such course.

The joint statement was in any case a weak response to the continuing financial crisis. A flight from the pound sterling had forced Great Britain to abandon the gold standard in mid-September. Flagging confidence in the British government contributed to the onset of serious strikes there. And in Germany, both financial and political conditions were deteriorating. Yet no nation stepped forward to lead the Western world out of the financial morass.

To Newton D. Baker

October 14, 1931

Dear Newton:

. . . The thing that's most on my mind these days is the necessity of getting a real tariff plank for the next Democratic platform. . . . As I see it, the debt problem may actually be settled before a new administration takes office. It is likely to be settled for some considerable period of time at least, but the tariff policy, the effort to revise the fundamental national economic policy of this country in the light of our being a creditor, is something that would take several years, and I should think would be in the field of larger politics the major task of a Democratic administration. I don't think we can get anywhere by taking particular schedules as extortionate. More and more I am convinced that a bold and far-reaching policy of, not free trade, but much freer trade, is what we ought to advocate. We stand historically in the position of the Liberal Party in England at the middle of the Nineteenth Century, and we ought to rise to that opportunity.

To Ralph Hayes

October 20, 1931

Dear Ralph:

I should have written to you sooner to tell you how things are going. I now report that they are not going a bit well for Mr. Franklin D. Roosevelt. I don't refer to Smith's attack on him, though that has some importance. . . .[1] I refer to the much more impressive fact that if the Democrats win the coming election, as they are certain to do, he will be forced to a show-down over the

Seabury investigation.[2] Seabury will carry the inquiry right to the Mayor himself, and the evidence already existing is tremendous and devastating. Roosevelt cannot continue to carry water on both shoulders, and the situation which he has created for himself by the attempt, and by which he has tried to justify his trimming will rise up to damn him in the next few months. I never felt so confident as I do now that the weakness of the man will become revealed to the general public well in advance of the conventions. . . .

1. Al Smith, who was opposed to Roosevelt's unannounced candidacy for the Democratic nomination for the presidency, still hoped for the nomination himself. He and his close allies, including John J. Raskob, were supporting various favorite sons in an effort to block Roosevelt. They were also attempting to push the Democratic National Committee to a strong wet stance, which Roosevelt, eager to straddle the liquor issue and to court the South, opposed. Smith in 1930 openly attacked Roosevelt, however, on only one question — a proposed amendment to the New York constitution, subject to referendum that November, to empower the state to buy submarginal lands for reforestation and to issue nineteen million dollars' worth of bonds for that purpose. This was a favorite project of Roosevelt's which Smith denounced in a number of speeches and press releases. On Election Day, the amendment passed. 2. Judge Seabury was investigating corruption in New York City. Republicans had proposed that investigation, to which Roosevelt had agreed. Roosevelt had cooperated with Seabury, contrary to the implications in Lippmann's letter, but their relationship had become strained, perhaps because Seabury had presidential aspirations of his own. Seabury also appeared determined to make a strong case against Mayor Walker, at a time early in 1932 when Roosevelt would have to face the difficult choice of supporting the judge or further alienating Tammany.

To Felix Frankfurter

October 22, 1931

Dear Felix:

 . . . There is . . . a much deeper question raised which I take it you have in mind, namely, whether a capitalistic industrial society is workable; if its elasticity is diminished by the imposition of social standards on the one side and a growing burden of fixed charges on the other. That seems to me the real question raised by the British crisis, and it raises the most fundamental kind of question about capitalism as we know it today, and also about progressivism as we have known it. I have only in the last few months begun dimly to see even the outlines of the problem, but I think it really is the problem.

To Louis Domeratzky[1]

October 22, 1931

My dear Mr. Domeratzky:

 . . . I did not wish to suggest that the present development of Soviet Russia is an exact parallel of the early industrial development of the United States and England. What I meant to imply simply was that Russia was going through a transformation which we had already passed through, and that it was unfair to judge the problems of our maturer development with the success of Russia's much more immature development.

On the other hand, as to Russia's immunity from a depression, I can only say that that remains to be proved. It is quite true, as you point out, that her present capital investments in water power, iron and steel, etc. may be workable in any time up to capacity, but what I was asking was whether, when Russia's capital investment had been greatly increased, it would turn out that these capital investments had been correctly planned.

It seems to me that there is something confusing about the notion that the Russian economy is all planned, and that ours is all unplanned. In both countries those who control capital have to judge the future, and that's the science of planning. It seems that our bankers misjudged our future badly in the four or five years preceding the depression. But I do not know of any reason why we should be certain that the men who control Russian capital will judge their future so much more wisely than we have judged ours. . . .

1. Louis Domeratzky, Russian-born civil servant, had served in the Department of Commerce since 1911 and was at this time chief of that department's division of regional information. He also wrote about world economics and had published *International Cartel Movement* (Washington, D.C., 1928).

To Russell C. Leffingwell[1]

October 22, 1931

Dear Russell:

I have no doubt . . . that the Chinese are morally guilty of the original provocation, assuming you start from the premise, which I guess we have to start from, that Japanese treaty rights in Manchuria are legitimate. The thing was phrased very well the other day by someone who said that a man can die just as well from a thousand pin pricks as from one thrust of a dagger.

However, I do not follow . . . that our cooperating with the League may provoke a more dangerous enmity between Japan and the United States. It seems to me that unless we are surrendering all rights under the Kellogg Pact and the Nine-Power Treaty, cooperation with the League is the least dangerous way in which we can deal with the situation. That is to say, least dangerous from the point of view of drawing Japanese fire upon ourselves. Any way is dangerous, but that simply proves what we have known all along, that peacemaking in this world is a difficult and dangerous job, and should not be undertaken by nations which want to avoid risks.

I am greatly convinced in my own mind that if the League on its part and we for ours had failed to act in the Manchurian crisis, it would have been an absolute disaster from the point of view of any hope of restoring confidence in Europe for a good long time to come.[2] Everything I hear from Europe confirms the view that Manchuria has become a test case in Europe of whether there is any organized security in the world, and I'd be willing to take enormous risks in order to meet that test successfully.

1. Russell C. Leffingwell — a partner in J. P. Morgan and Company, an eminent financier, assistant secretary of the treasury, 1917–20 — was a friend of Lippmann's with whom he frequently corresponded.   **2.** In mid-October President Hoover gave Stimson the permission the secretary had requested for an American representative, Prentiss Gilbert, to take part in sessions of the Council of the League that discussed the Kellogg-Briand Pact. Gilbert attended such a session on October 16, and the next day the French, British, and Italian governments cabled Japan and China to invoke the pact. The United States sent a similar note on October 20. But on October 19, Stimson had instructed Gilbert to cease attending meetings except as an observer. In the absence of any contribution from either Gilbert or Stimson, the council on October 24 passed a resolution calling upon China and Japan to work out their differences, and on Japan to evacuate occupied areas.

To Henry L. Stimson

November 12, 1931

Dear Mr. Secretary:

I hope you feel that you are getting the proper kind of support in the brave and enlightened policy which you are pursuing in regard to Manchuria. I don't see how the policy can fail in the long run, provided you are in a position to convince the Japanese that we are in earnest. This seems to me a time when Roosevelt's philosophy, as expressed in his criticism of Wilson in the days of our neutrality needs to be taken very much to heart. . . .

To Amos Pinchot[1]

November 23, 1931

Dear Amos:

. . . The relief business is a discouraging thing either way you take it. I don't like these private drives any better than you do. On the other hand, our experience with the G.A.R., the American Legion, and, on the other hand, with Tammany, gives me the willies when I think of government relief to private individuals. The thing has been pretty bad in England and Germany, but their administrative standards are very much higher than ours, and political corruption is much less deep and much less prevalent. I hesitate to start a system which, from the point of view of legislatures, would inevitably become a method of purchasing votes.

As for the higher bracket income tax payers, nothing can save them anyway. They are going to be taxed, and I believe they should be taxed, as heavily as it's productive to tax them. I don't think much money can be gotten out of them this year, but they'll have to be the first victims before any other taxation can be imposed. Therefore, it doesn't seem to me that the relief question has much bearing upon them.

1. Amos Pinchot, whose brother Gifford was at this time governor of Pennsylvania, remained the fiery reformer he had long been. He was deeply concerned, as were so many liberal Americans, about the plight of the unemployed. With charitable sources exhausted and the states near bankruptcy, only the federal government had the tax base and credit to provide the necessary relief; but Hoover was still resisting Democratic efforts on the Hill to establish a relief program.

To Newton D. Baker

November 24, 1931

Dear Newton:

. . . I hear from a good source that your views on the present Governor of New York are rather more favorable than some of us here think the facts justify. I was an enthusiastic Roosevelt man up to the week of his first inauguration as Governor. In that first week I had a terrific shock when I discovered that though he had run on a platform advocating public ownership of the St. Lawrence water power site, he was in fact actively working on a plan to lease the site. It was only as a result of a storm of criticism the *New York World* stirred up the first ten days or so of his administration that he was prevented from abandoning the whole water-power policy which he has since exploited so much politically.[1] In those days I was hearing from him pretty constantly, and I was satisfied that he had never understood the problem which he had made so many speeches about. I am now satisfied, from a good many other experiences, that he just doesn't happen to have a very good mind, that he never really comes to grips with a problem which has any large dimensions, and that above all the controlling element in almost every case is political advantage. His record of relationship with Tammany has been calculating and ambiguous in the highest degree. It was due to his distribution of patronage to Curry[2] that the better Tammany element represented by Smith and Wagner has lost all control of the municipal situation. His record in the Seabury business has been timid and equivocal, and his recent triumph in the so-called reforestation matter was solely due to the fact that Tammany, partly out of considerations of patronage, decided to support it. He has never by one phrase expressed disapproval of the gross corruption and even greater squalor of half of the party of which he is a titular leader, and he has maintained through all of these revelations, a political and social working arrangement with the present regime in Tammany. On the other hand, he has done everything that he could, from the day that he took office to destroy the political power of Smith, and I am told that until their luncheon the other day he never consulted Smith on one single problem of the State government. When you consider that Roosevelt had been out of state politics for fifteen years before he was elected

Governor, and that Smith is the greatest expert on New York State government living, I think it's an ominous performance, and certainly would cause
me to distrust Roosevelt's willingness, if elected President, to sink his personal
jealousies and select the ablest man.

I am convinced that he has never thought much, or understood much, about
the great subjects which must concern the next president, about such matters
as the tariff, foreign policy, taxation, currency and banking. He is best on
certain questions of social welfare, old age pensions, and that kind of remedial
legislation, but on the real problems of statesmanship, my impression, from
many long talks in the last few years, is that he is a kind of amiable boy scout.
I consider it extremely important that he shouldn't be the Democratic candidate for president.

1. This statement was less than fair to Roosevelt, who had proposed the establishment of a distinguished body as trustees of the Water Power Resources on the St. Lawrence River to plan, subject
to legislative approval, the construction of a dam and generating plant on the river. Private companies would then have distributed the electrical power, but under state regulation. He did not
propose public distribution, as some advocates of water-power development would have preferred.   2. John F. Curry, head of Tammany Hall.

To Bernard Berenson   HANDWRITTEN

November 25, 1931

Dear B. B.

. . . In Vienna we saw lots of people in the gov't and out of it. The
Chancellor[1] is a pleasant old bureaucrat, an old police official, who has suddenly had to extemporize a knowledge of finance. . . . He tried to explain
the idiotic finances of Austria. It was a great deal as if I should volunteer to
lecture on early Christian art.

There is no doubt about the peril in Austria. . . .

On the surface, as you know, Vienna is thriving, but it's a dangerous sort
of prosperity, based on foreigners, on speculation, and on the fact that the
whole Austrian people (money changers and men with foreign capital ex-
cepted) is spending all it earns on food, nothing on clothes, houses, or capital.
The luxury of Vienna is that of a bankrupt selling his heirlooms, and spending
what he gets for them as fast as he gets it.

The saddest part of this business is the steady destruction of self-respect,
habits of work, which is the inevitable result of living in a world where no
possession, no labor is measurable in any fixed terms. It is impossible for a
private person in Austria to think ahead one month.

But nothing is more obvious to me than that the problems of all these little
states are incidental, and sympathetic to, the principal business between France
and Germany. . . .

1. Karl Buresch.

To Newton D. Baker

December 18, 1931

Dear Newton:

May I make a suggestion inspired by pure affection which you mustn't feel any obligation to reply to? I have had fairly close contact with the last two Democratic presidential candidates, with John W. Davis and with Al Smith, at the time of their nomination and in the early days of their campaigns. In both instances they had been so pre-occupied before their nomination that they had not had leisure to prepare themselves for the issues they were called upon to discuss. I believe more and more firmly that you're destined to be nominated, and I am writing to say that I hope you can find a way to reduce the amount of your activity in your law practice so as to have ample time for reading and reflection, and perhaps even to have careful studies made, under your direction, of matters that will be discussed in the campaign. I think this is the time to face this aspect of the matter, and I take the liberty of urging it upon you.

To Russell C. Leffingwell

December 21, 1931

Dear Russell:

. . . I am perfectly prepared to support the President in every possible way, but I do not believe that anything is to be gained by avoiding considered criticism of his actions. For example, I have certainly tried my best to support his moratorium. . . . As to the budget . . . I believe that the failure to aim at a balanced budget next year is one of Hoover's major strategic errors, not because I regard it as of prime importance that the debt retirement be covered next year, but that a truly balanced budget presented now would produce the most effective possible check on Congressional expenditures this session. I think that he has made the kind of mistake here which he made on the tariff and on the moratorium. He has misjudged the real political forces with which he has to deal. I believe that a resounding appeal to the country to balance its own budget would have got him an amount of support of an amazing kind. . . .

I do not know, from your letter, whether you think I have been urging further deflation. I certainly have not meant to, but have simply meant to state the case practically as you state it, namely, that costs and other matters have to come down somewhere near the present wholesale level. Certainly I haven't meant to give the impression that I wanted deflation for its own sake, and more and more of it. . . .

To Henry L. Stimson

December 22, 1931

Dear Mr. Secretary:

. . . I have been giving a good deal of thought to possible action on our part in regard to Manchuria, and it seems to me from information which I have, that the most effective practical thing that can be done, assuming the Japanese carry out the movement against Chinchow,[1] is to publish the correspondence, attempt to persuade the other signatories of the Nine-Power Treaties to join in the declarations that the Nine-Power Treaty has been violated, that Article Two of the Kellogg Pact has been violated, and that, therefore, the powers cannot recognize as legal any agreements which may result from Japanese action since September 18th. I think then we could afford to sit and wait, leaving Japan indicted and on the defensive. Time would work against her, and so would economic circumstance, and it would be fair to hope that the military party would eventually be overthrown. This policy seems to me the most effective we can look to, in view of the fact that all resort to force is barred to us. Since all resort to force is barred to us, any measure short of it but in that direction should be avoided, such as withdrawing ambassadors, for gestures of that kind are effective only if the nation making them is prepared to go the limit if necessary. . . .

1. The Japanese were moving into South Manchuria, toward the city of Chinchow, an operation Shidehara had assured Stimson would not take place. Stimson on November 27 asked Hoover to consider economic sanctions against Japan, but Hoover declined for the time being. At the League, Charles G. Dawes was now acting as American observer. On December 10, the council, acting on an earlier Japanese suggestion, decided to send a commission of investigation, the Lytton Commission, to the Far East to examine the facts and prepare a solution. But the Japanese army in Manchuria marched on. In Stimson's view, if Japanese troops took Chinchow, it would constitute an act of aggression in violation of Chinese sovereignty, and it would violate the Kellogg-Briand Pact and the Nine-Power Treaty of Washington. On December 23, the Chinese retreated from the defense line protecting Chinchow; on January 2, 1932, that city fell. President Hoover had earlier, on November 9, suggested the nonrecognition of any conquest of Manchuria, as did Lippmann in this letter. Secretary of State Bryan had pursued a similar course in 1905. Stimson, who had been thinking about that possibility, turned to it after the fall of Chinchow, drafted an appropriate note based on Bryan's action, and, with Hoover's approval, sent it to Tokyo on January 7, 1932. It stated that the United States "cannot admit the legality of any situation *de facto* nor does it intend to recognize any treaty or agreement entered into between [China and Japan] which may impair the treaty rights of the United States or its citizens in China, including those . . . which relate to the sovereignty, the independence, or the territorial and administrative integrity of the Republic of China, nor to . . . the open door policy; and . . . it does not intend to recognize any situation . . . which may be brought about by means contrary to . . . the Pact of Paris," that is, the Kellogg pact. Whatever its legal and diplomatic merit, the note violated one dictum of Theodore Roosevelt's, that hero of both Stimson and Lippmann, to "speak softly but carry a big stick," for the United States then lacked both the will and the means to go beyond words.

To Arthur A. Ballantine[1]

December 22, 1931

Dear Arthur:

. . . My belief is that if the President had proposed the extra taxes and economies necessary to balance the budget (and in view of the rates of taxation in England, I can hardly believe such a program would not have been practical), he would, in my opinion, have been in an infinitely stronger position. In the first place, it would have given him an almost impregnable front-line defense against increased expenditures by Congress. It would have shocked the country into realizing the seriousness of our present expenditures, and, in case your estimates of the yield of revenues for next year proved to be optimistic, you would have a cushion to fall upon. Although I have not said so, and would not, I wonder whether you feel really confident that the 1933 budget will work out as you say.

I cannot accept your argument that since the budget cannot be balanced this year, it is not necessary to balance it next year. This year is half done, and the Administration, mistakenly, I believe, has allowed this enormous deficit to accumulate. It would be impossible, I take it, now to balance the 1933 budget. I don't like taxation any better than the next man. But when you say that you have proposed very drastic increases in taxes for next year I cannot agree with you. Measured by the size of the emergency and the importance of sound government finance, the taxes seem to me timid. I'd like to add, too, that it doesn't seem to me a wise proceeding to offer Congress and the country a program based on the present judgment of what there is a practical likelihood of Congress adopting. It would be much better to ask for more, so as at least to get as much as you are asking for. . . .

1. Arthur A. Ballantine, then assistant secretary of the treasury, became undersecretary in February 1932 and served in that post through March of 1933.

To Russell C. Leffingwell

December 28, 1931

Dear Russell:

. . . On the subject of inflation and deflation, I'd like to put this to you. Assuming that the present crisis of confidence is overcome by the Hoover program, and assuming that some tolerable arrangement is made in Europe about reparations, it would still remain a fact that the wholesale price level is so low that it is almost impossible to deflate down to it. Therefore, the whole structure must remain imperiled and unemployment continue. Is it not necessary to consider again positive action to raise the price level? . . .[1]

1. Lippmann held to that position for several years and on that account ordinarily later supported the New Deal's monetary policies.

To Felix Frankfurter

January 15, 1932

Dear Felix:

. . . You say that you do not know what the emergency is which causes the President and others to demand prompt action. The emergency, as I understand it, is the danger of tremendous bank failures, not in New York but on the west coast and in the central part of the country, failures on such a scale as probably to precipitate a nation-wide closing of all the banks. I do not think we can under-estimate the reality of the emergency, and I think the whole matter would have been better handled if Congress had been willing to give the Corporation very large powers without attempting to write too many details into the bill. I do not believe it is possible to draft legislation of that sort with appropriate safeguards against all contingencies. If the emergency is as real and great as it is believed to be, the best thing to do is to give the Corporation adequate power and resources and rely upon wise administration.[1]

Of course everything will depend upon how the Corporation is administered. And in that general field of consideration we come to the other question which you raise, namely, the problem of recognizing losses and writing them off. It will be a difficult problem to determine at what point the general interest makes it desirable to save a bank which, on the merits, probably oughtn't to be saved, in order to prevent general panic in a community.

I personally believe that the crisis will, in the end, be cured only by the deflationary method. But I think the Administration is justified in attempting to avert an excessive and hysterical deflation arising from spectacular bank failures. I hope the thing will work. I think it should be supported, and while I do not expect from it any miracles, I do think it may, probably can, save the country from the very real agony of a general suspension. The whole matter raises troublesome issues which it is difficult to clarify at this time, how far, for example, it is justifiable to tell the country how great the danger is, and if telling it would not multiply the danger enormously. I think if you inquire in the proper quarters you will find the danger which this thing is designed to deal with is much greater than your letter indicates.

---

1. On the day this letter was written, the House of Representatives followed the lead of the Senate and passed the bill, recommended by Hoover, to establish the Reconstruction Finance Corporation (RFC). That corporation, capitalized at five hundred million dollars, was authorized to borrow another two billion dollars in order to provide emergency loans to banks, life insurance companies, farm mortgage associations, and railroads. Hoover set up the new body under Charles G. Dawes on February 2.

To Learned Hand

February 25, 1932

Dear B:

. . . I have had a busy and interesting, but not a good time, since I reached Europe. Not since the war has there been such a malignant suspicion of each against all as now. Everybody is obsessed with a sense of conspiracy. All of Europe sees in France a sinister power plotting for power and for gold; all of France sees the outer world as hostile and dangerous. The degree of misunderstanding is tragic. Yet it is so easy to see that muddle rather than evil purpose is at the bottom of it all. . . .

Geneva is full of deep confusion owing to the fact that the small powers and the League's partisans want to act like a League to Enforce Peace against Japan, while the great powers — Britain, France and ourselves — quite plainly don't. They will try to make us the scapegoats for the League's impotence. . . .[1]

There are many belligerent pacifists at Geneva wanting another war to end war and another war to make Asia safe for democracy. I don't believe in them, and much as I hate to see the impotence of the League demonstrated so spectacularly, I can see no other course which doesn't involve terrific bloodshed and economic exhaustion. . . .

---

1. The crisis in the Far East had been growing. In September 1931, the Japanese occupied several big Manchurian towns and by January 1932 had moved on to control much of the rest of the province. On February 18, they set up the puppet state of Manchukuo, their new name for Manchuria. Meanwhile on January 8, retaliating against a Chinese economic boycott, the Japanese had landed some seventy thousand troops at Shanghai, China, and shocked the world by bombing the unprotected city. The League of Nations was then still awaiting the report of the Lytton Commission, which remained unfinished until September 1932. It then found the Japanese attacks of September 1931 to have been unprovoked and the creation of Manchukuo to have been unrepresentative of any spontaneous local movement for independence. The League later adopted that report and subscribed to Stimson's nonrecognition policy. But in February, when Lippmann wrote the letter, delay in Geneva left Washington with the question of whether or not to act unilaterally. Hoover opposed a boycott but agreed to permit Stimson to address a letter of February 24, 1932, to Senator Borah which was intended particularly for China, Japan, Great Britain, the League, and American public opinion. In that letter, Stimson observed that the Washington treaties were related; Japan's violation of the Nine-Power Treaty on China raised the possibility of American modification of the naval limitation treaty and the treaty inhibiting the fortification of the island of Guam. The implicit warning in the letter to Borah rested on empty threats, for neither Hoover, nor the Congress, nor the American people had any intention of proceeding along the lines Stimson suggested. Consequently it did not serve to deter Japan.

To Felix Frankfurter

April 5, 1932

Dear Felix:

I did not mean to suggest that "the unwisdom of excessive immunity from taxation in the lower ranges of income" mitigates the objections to the sales tax. How did you ever come to think that I did? Obviously the sales tax is a wretched tax and nothing would justify imposing it except inability to raise the money in other ways. As a practical matter the choice, as the House bill shows, narrowed itself down to imposing a fairly general sales tax or a selected sales tax. The insurgents were never within sight of balancing the budget under any income and inheritance taxes that they proposed. I do not think that the difference between a general sales tax which exempted the sheer necessities of life and the sales tax actually imposed is sufficiently great to justify much moral heat.[1]

What I should like is a fiscal system like the British in which 60 percent of the revenue is obtained through income and inheritance taxation; a larger amount through a revenue tariff than we now get, and then excise taxes on things like beer and tobacco. But Congress will not establish a productive income tax system because it won't stop the tax exemptions, it won't tax the medium incomes enough, and it won't tax the small incomes at all. . . .

Why do you ask whether I think the distribution of incomes in the United States today is socially desirable? Have I ever written anything or said anything that implied it? I regard the present distribution of income in the United States as wholly undesirable and I greatly desire to see it leveled down. But so far as I know the only tax which can do it is the inheritance tax. For that alone reaches the tax exempt fortunes. The income tax, when the rates are sufficiently high to cause a redistribution of wealth, are sufficient to drive the larger fortunes into the tax exempts. You are, of course, quite right in saying that there are limits to the extent to which tax exempts can be or will be sought, but I should think that these limits were not such as to destroy the argument that the existence of tax exempts prevents our income tax from operating as effectively as the British. . . .

1. The House of Representatives had been considering new taxes for several months. Progressives in both parties opposed the Treasury's recommendation for a sales tax and a broadening of the income tax base by reducing personal exemptions. Those taxes would have borne most heavily on the poor and the middle class. Instead, the progressives argued for raising revenue by increasing surtaxes on large personal incomes. On April 1, 1932, the House passed a compromise measure that included selective new excise taxes and raised personal income taxes. After further debate in the Senate, the Revenue Act of 1932 was passed in June. It tried to balance the budget by imposing one of the largest tax increases in American history. The tax changes included many new excise taxes, a new gift tax, higher estate taxes, higher personal and corporate income taxes, and some higher tariff schedules.

To Felix Frankfurter

April 8, 1932

Dear Felix:

. . . I quite agree that in writing about fiscal matters since my return from Europe I have not tried to deal with the wider considerations involved in a long range policy of taxation. I quite admit that I have been dealing with the balance of the budget as an ad hoc piece of public business. I did this because my observations in Europe convinced me profoundly that the balancing of the budget was an extremely urgent necessity. You might say, if you like that I am too much concerned with the immediate, but I think the immediate is, at this moment, so important that I would not personally take the responsibility of failing to concentrate on it in the effort to get a solution. My attitude here is not confined to taxation. It applies also to the reform of the banking structure, to future control of investment which I regard as central in any effective reconstruction, and to such extremely important matters as the extension of public control over public services. It may be that I misjudge the situation, but what I learned in Europe gave me a sense that the world was suffering from a fever which had to be assuaged before an orderly reform of its public habits could be undertaken. The necessity of stopping the decay does seem to me supremely urgent, and since that involves a concentration of attention, I am prepared for it. I don't ask you to agree with this, but I feel sure that you will not fail to understand it. . . .

To William Allen White

April 22, 1932

Dear Will,

   . . . I've been trying very hard to think about a better tomorrow, and of course it would be easy enough to adopt the Socialist view and assume that that would be better, but that raises as many questions as it solves. The great difficulty in seeing into the future, to my mind, lies in trying to decide whether or not the die is cast for a world of more or less self-sufficient, or at least isolated economic empires, or for a truly international world with international markets. All our conclusions depend upon which premise we adopt and I don't know that any one of us is yet able to decide that fundamental question. . . .

To Arthur C. Salter[1]

April 28, 1932

My dear Salter:

   . . . Your book has made a great impression in this country. I see it everywhere and on all best seller lists, and portions of it have even been read into the Congressional Record by Senator Borah.

We shall not, however, follow the advice contained in your book. I think the die is cast here for a policy of national isolation even at the sacrifice of export trades and a large part of foreign investment. This means a period of important social change and also, I should imagine, a revaluation of debts. But there is nothing in the atmosphere which suggests even a tendency in the direction of an international solution of the crisis.

The failure of the European powers to make any progress . . . plus the example of Great Britain in cutting herself loose from the international gold standard and from free trade, have about settled the issue over here I think. . . .

1. Sir Arthur C. Salter had recently published *Recovery: The Second Effort* (London, 1932).

To Russell C. Leffingwell

May 5, 1932

Dear Russell:

I find in your letter evidences of one misapprehension and of one misinterpretation.

The misapprehension I take to be a fear that I am about to jump off the Brooklyn Bridge and advocate abandonment of the gold standard. I judge this from the way you have underlined references to the gold standard in your letter. Have no fear. I don't count it outside the realm of the possible that for several of many reasons we may be driven off the gold standard, but I shall not advocate it or wish it. I think it important, however, that the possibility be not wholly discounted, so that if things took that turn we should not find ourselves unprepared.

Now as to the misunderstanding, — you assume that I have taken up what you call the Owen Young suggestion of a two-billion dollar bond issue for public works. I did not know that Owen Young was advocating such an issue. And even if he is, I am not. I do raise the question, and I think all of us ought to consider it open-mindedly, as to whether the present Federal Reserve policy may not have to be supplemented by some kind of direct stimulation of productive processes. I take it that you cannot feel any absolute certainty that the amount of credit which the Federal Reserve banks will create will, within a reasonable time, translate itself into a resumption of activity. And I think it not at all unreasonable, but on the contrary merely a matter of profound foresight that we should think carefully now what next step may be necessary in case the credit made available lies unused. . . .

If direct stimulation is necessary, it should, if possible, be applied in such a way as not to add additional burdens to federal, state, or local budgets. That would mean that we ought probably to consider loans to railroads and public utilities for desirable capital improvements, when those loans appear to be fairly well secured; that we ought to consider loans for public works of a self-supporting character, such as toll bridges, toll tunnels, toll roads, and possibly even slum clearance. I don't want to build any more free highways or put up a lot of Washington monuments or get into debt for other pleasant but expensive projects. But I don't think it's entirely to be ruled out of consideration that there are projects in hand, both in the realm of private industry and in public activity, which could profitably be undertaken provided the initial hesitation were overcome by some kind of government backing.

I have no idea that such projects would in themselves provide any unemployment relief that would make any difference to our problem. I look upon it entirely from the point of view of overcoming the initial hesitation of banks and of borrowers. For it may be that depression has been so deep and the fright so harrowing that confidence will not return except by artificial stimulation. I have no objection in principle to applying such artificial stimulation, for if it is proper for the government to support the banks, as it is doing, it is equally proper for it to intervene to prime the engine so that it can turn past the dead center.

I'd like to see the problem explored from the point of view of seeing what can be done without issuing any government bonds but simply by giving government backing to approve bonds of public agencies and even of private companies. If any money is needed I personally should like to examine the possibility of raising it by a sales tax which would, I think, conceivably pass Congress if a part of the proceeds were to be used affirmatively to stimulate employment. But I would not rule out entirely as an arch heresy the possibility even of a bond issue, for as I conceive the situation very much more drastic remedies than that will be applied if the present Federal Reserve policy is allowed to fail. You say that such a federal bond issue would destroy the hope of reviving the bond market. My answer is that if the bond market revives it will be unnecessary to adopt the measures I am discussing. If it doesn't revive by itself then it will mean that the Federal Reserve policy is not working and that extra stimulation is required. As I conceive the whole matter we ought to consider these proposals and study them now. They cannot be put into effect for some months even if there were agreement on them. Within these months we shall know whether these measures are needed and we shall at least be ready to take them if we have to.

I hope this is fairly clear. I don't always succeed in expressing myself very clearly when I dictate a letter but your preternatural insight will see through my clumsiness of expression.

On the subject of public confidence at the moment great emphasis is properly being put on the state of affairs in Washington. But I think there is little doubt that confidence is also greatly disturbed by revelations such as those that are coming out of the Kreuger and Toll affair.[1] To me what is being shown there is really quite appalling. In its indication of lack of public responsibility it would seem to match a good deal what we so loudly deplored in Washington. . . .

---

1. The scandalous failure of the firm of Kreuger and Toll had implicated American brokerages that held its now worthless securities in various of their investment trusts and provoked the suicide of the larcenous Ivar Kreuger on March 12, 1932.

To Newton D. Baker

May 11, 1932

Dear Newton:

. . . I . . . agree entirely with what you say about the sales tax both as to objections to it in theory and the need for it in practice at the moment. I cannot persuade myself that the taxes proposed will come anywhere near balancing the budget. Ogden Mills[1] himself told me that they were based on the assumption of a decided improvement in business, whereas for the first half of this year we have certainly had a decided decline in business. From the point of view of the national credit, I feel convinced that a sales tax would do a world of good in that it would assure ample revenues. And it is that assurance that the whole world is looking for.

1. Ogden L. Mills, New York Republican, for five years undersecretary of the treasury, had become secretary in February 1932, after Andrew Mellon resigned at Hoover's instigation and accepted appointment as ambassador to the Court of St. James's.

To Owen D. Young

May 18, 1932

My dear Owen:

Had I known the other day when we lunched together what the afternoon papers would carry, I should not have been able to proceed quite so impersonally.[1] However, I probably wouldn't have been able to say as clearly then as I can now what I feel: that deeply as I regret the reasons which must have led to your decision, the real effect of it, in my opinion, will be greatly to enhance your own power in the present crisis. It's my honest belief that you can contribute more to the determination of fundamental policies in this country than any other man. And there is no one whom I would rather see exercise this great power. The circumstances which have made it impossible for you to have an active political career enable you to have a much more influential one. For in the present state of popular government the man in office is inevitably hopelessly compromised, and our ultimate salvation must lie in the influence of men who are listened to and are, at the same time, disinterested.

1. On May 16, Young had announced unequivocally that he was not a candidate for the Democratic presidential nomination.

To Elizabeth Bibesco[1]

May 23, 1932

My dear Elizabeth:

Your letter is appalling in its insight into American conditions. You're so right about everything in it, that I am worried at disagreeing with you about

Baker. I feel as if I were disputing with a sybil. However, Morley[2] said politics is a science of the second best, or something to that effect. And I maintain that of those who are conceivable for the Democratic nomination, he is the most intelligent and the most courageous. I make that statement in a wholly relative world, and with a real feeling at the bottom of my mind that there isn't a man in America over forty who hasn't been ruined by his past, and who is a fit man to govern the country in the times that lie ahead. The whole system of education, pre-war and post-war period, has mis-educated men over forty so that they have to unlearn so much that they haven't time to learn things. In a country like England, where you have firm traditions, you can get along in crises without big men. That's really what I take it is carrying England along now. But America has no traditions in that sense, and unluckily it hasn't any men who at all measure up to what's demanded of them. They all have to play by ear and improvise, having no reliable old tunes they can fall back upon. . . .

1. Princess Elizabeth Bibesco — daughter of Lord Herbert Henry Asquith, the former British prime minister — was the wife of a former Romanian envoy to the United States. **2.** John Morley, the late English statesman and author.

To William Allen White

May 24, 1932

Dear Bill:

. . . My chief objection to the Goldsborough Bill[1] . . . is political. I don't like to have Congress passing laws as to what the price levels should be. If it were possible to fix the price level at the point Congress says it shall be fixed at, we should spend the rest of our natural lives debating the question of where the price level should be moved next. It is inconceivable that Congress, having once exercised its power, would ever cease to meddle with it, and I don't think we dare to entrust to Congress the power which can redistribute the national income in a few months.

Of course I am in entire sympathy with you in believing that the world cannot get out of its present jam unless prices do rise. I know of no informed person who questions that. . . .

1. Never enacted, the bill amended the Federal Reserve Act by declaring it national policy that the average purchasing power of the dollar in the wholesale commodity markets should be restored to the average of the years 1921–29 and "maintained by the control of the volume of credit and currency."

To Ogden L. Mills

June 3, 1932

My dear Mills:

. . . At this particular moment, as I see it, a balanced budget means a situation in which Congress is really retrenching and really raising taxes on as broad a base as possible. An actually balanced budget is not in sight. I should prefer the Wagner Bill without the non-self-liquidating bonds, but it's my opinion, though I quite readily admit I may be wrong, that the Wagner Bill represents about as harmless a form of the public works idea as you can expect Congress to agree to.[1] Rightly or wrongly I should guess that seven people out of ten, apart from bankers, believe in the public works theory, and it seems to me that if you resist it too absolutely you will be overwhelmed by a really dangerous performance of it such as the Garner Bill.[2]

Your letter lays stress upon the dangers which might result from the sale of $500,000,000 of long-term bonds under the Wagner proposal. Personally, I am getting more and more alarmed at the size of the Treasury's floating debt. And I have come to wonder whether the way in which the Government is financing itself at the moment by means of artificially cheap bank credit is not itself a dangerous form of inflation. Certainly this method of Government financing was a prelude to trouble in France, and I wonder whether the time hasn't come when you will be compelled to finance yourself by longer issues, and then face the problem of interest rates. . . .

1. Senator Wagner of New York had proposed in May that the federal government issue long-term bonds to finance a $500 million public works program. That bill represented an effort to meet Hoover partway. Earlier the president had attacked a similar bill of Wagner's that contemplated the expenditure of $1.1 billion. The May compromise won the endorsement of many national organizations (among others the American Legion, the NAACP, and the National League of Women Voters) and of many economists, social workers, and businessmen. **2.** Speaker of the House John N. Garner of Texas, a candidate for the Democratic presidential nomination, had introduced a bill authorizing the RFC to make loans to "any person," as well as to states, for both relief and public works. Later modified and merged with the Wagner bill, the Garner bill passed in Congress, but Hoover vetoed it. A revised measure, more to the president's taste, won his acceptance. It enlarged the lending authority of the RFC by $300 million for loans to states for relief and also empowered the agency to make loans for self-liquidating public works. The sum for relief, wholly inadequate, was barely used during the next year, in which federal relief loans totaled only about $30 million.

To Newton D. Baker

July 18, 1932

Dear Newton:

. . . The choice, as it appears to me at this moment is an exceedingly unpleasant one. I cannot bear the thought of casting a vote which would signify the forgiveness of the Republican record. On the other hand I have no confidence in Roosevelt, and I have a tremendous aversion for the whole Garner-Hearst-McAdoo association.[1] There remains Norman Thomas[2] of course, but my feeling is that unless a man believes that Thomas's ideas are at least theoretically right, however impractical they may be at the moment, he ought not to vote for Thomas. It does the Socialists no good to get non-Socialist votes, in fact to be treated as a kind of trash basket by people who do not know how to cast their votes, and it is a shirking of responsibility for non-Socialists, for after all we do have to decide who is to govern this country in the next four years. So I rule out Thomas and plead for advice from you.

My own position is a little different from yours in that I have never been a member of the Democratic Party in good standing and I have no real party association. What I really want you to do is to try and persuade me to vote for Roosevelt.

That may be a bigger chore for you to undertake than it sounds, for I strongly suspect that your own preference gives you very little exhilaration. . . .

1. William Randolph Hearst, the publisher, and Senator William G. McAdoo of California, Hearst's ally, had supported Garner for the Democratic nomination. In the end, they swung their voters at the Democratic Convention to Roosevelt, partly because of McAdoo's hatred of Al Smith, partly because Roosevelt's managers agreed to accept Garner as the vice presidential nominee.
2. In 1932 Norman Thomas ran as Socialist candidate for the presidency for the second of many times.

To Newton D. Baker

July 29, 1932

Dear Newton:

. . . My own view is that while a certain amount of improvement is probably in prospect we must count on three things at least. The first is that in any event the really serious social consequences of the depression still lie ahead of us. The second is that a false and temporary recovery is a distinct possibility. The third is that no satisfactory recovery is conceivable unless there are far-reaching changes in international economic policies. I think we have greatly to fear the restoration not of confidence but of complacency.

On the campaign I am in entire agreement with you and I am going to exercise the privileges of an independent Democrat by waiting as long as possible to see whether the fryingpan or the fire appears to be the more uncomfortable. Did you notice Franklin's message to the National Economy League?[1] What a weaseling mind he has; how much he would like to have everybody vote for him! . . .

1. Roosevelt's telegram, besides repeating the pledges in the Democratic platform, stressed the need for economy in government and promised he would strive to reduce federal expenditures by

one-quarter. He also said he favored limiting relief to war veterans to those who had been disabled in service.

To Audrey Wallas[1]

HANDWRITTEN

August 16, 1932

Dear Audrey

The news about Graham reached us here in the woods and we tried to send May and you a cable of affectionate greeting. I hope it reached you so that you knew we were with you in those hours.

I have been trying to think of it all as he would have wished us to think of it, and for me at least I know he would have wished that the grief at not being able to see him and hear him should be merged in remembrance of his teaching. He was the greatest teacher I have ever known, and already I believe he has altered decisively the course of Anglo-American political thinking. There is no student of politics under fifty today but must think in the terms he originated, and as time goes on the radical nature of his influence will be increasingly appreciated.

For myself I owe everything to him that enables me to understand at all the human problems of the Great Society and I have for him a loving gratitude which is boundless. I should also rather be known as a pupil of Graham Wallas than in any other way and no one can ever take that title away. But he was more than teacher to me, the kindest, richest human being of my life. . . .

1. Audrey Wallas, the wife of Graham Wallas, who had died on August 9.

To Felix Frankfurter

September 14, 1932

Dear Felix:

. . . Naturally, since I am supporting Roosevelt I hope you are right in thinking that he will do better in the White House than I have been fearing. The two things about him that worry me are that he plays politics well and likes the game for its own sake and is likely to be ultra-political almost to show his own virtuosity. The other fear I have is that he is such an amiable and impressionable man, so eager to please and I think so little grounded in his own convictions that almost everything depends upon the character of his advisers. I have been fully re-assured about that in recent weeks, particularly as to the Hearst-McAdoo connection. The things that are generally objected to about him, his willingness to make changes and his general sense that re-valuations are necessary naturally appeal to me. But I am only slowly convalescing from the shell-shock of his earlier performance with Tammany and his pre-convention campaign. . . .

To Felix Frankfurter

September 26, 1932

Dear Felix:

. . . I have read only the first part of Berle's book,[1] and of course the material is fascinating. I haven't yet got to his generalizations except as I begin to see them appear in the part that I have read. . . .

I feel exactly as you do about Al Smith. I spent quite a long time with him on Thursday and was really greatly distressed at his state of mind. I don't think that it's merely that some of the people around him are giving him bad advice. I think his hatred and resentment and personal frustration are almost overwhelming. . . .

I am afraid that he has developed what almost amounts to a persecution complex, and that his whole attitude is now governed by fierce resentment at the idea that he, a Catholic, couldn't be elected in 1928 and couldn't be nominated in 1932. Something is needed to lift him out of this bog in which he is floundering, and I have been casting about in my mind, wondering how it could be done. To my mind the effect on the campaign is the smallest part of it, and even the injury he is doing to his fellow Catholics is secondary to the awful human spectacle which I fear is gradually presenting itself to the people generally. If you have any ideas as to how he might be pulled to, I wish you'd let me know. . . .[2]

1. Adolf A. Berle and Gardiner C. Means had recently published their seminal book, *The Modern Corporation and Private Property* (New York, 1932). An economist, lawyer, and professor of law at Columbia University, Berle was a member of Roosevelt's "brain trust" and later an influential New Dealer.   2. With a visible lack of enthusiasm, Smith, in a speech at Tammany Hall on October 20, did come out in favor of Roosevelt's election.

To F. Meredith Blagden[1]

September 30, 1932

Dear Mr. Blagden:

. . . I'd like quite briefly to say a few things about the three points you raise. As to the first, about the analogy between Roosevelt's action up to the time of the Walker hearing and Hoover's action during the Harding scandals, I am afraid I disagree with you wholly. My real view, which I didn't express because it did not seem necessary to me to press the point that far was that a far better case can be made for Roosevelt's conduct than for Hoover's. Roosevelt's explanation of his aloofness was that since he had to be the final judge of Walker's tenure of office he could not take an unjudicial position and lead a fight against him.[2] I happen to think that this view of the matter suited his political convenience, but I think it must be admitted that a case can be made for it. Hoover's conduct, on the other hand, must be considered in the light of the facts which I think you overlooked. The truth is, and the record will show it, that the exposure of the Fall, Forbes and Daugherty scandals was carried on by the Senate not only without the encouragement, but against the obstruction of Administration centers and government departments. At that stage of the proceedings Hoover knew as well as Roosevelt knew last winter that there was something rotten in the State of Denmark. And he not only sat quiet through the whole proceedings but went through the campaign of 1924 without ever once putting himself on record as denouncing what was the worst corruption in the history of American government. I do not agree that his first duty was a loyalty to his chief. His first duty was loyalty to the truth. And if that had involved resignation, as it did, that was his duty. We have a very bad tradition in this country in matters of this sort. Men never seem to resign on principle. They resign only to take lucrative jobs. I believe myself that the silence of Hughes, Hoover and Coolidge on the Harding scandals deeply injured the morale of the American people.

Your second point I can deal with briefly by saying that if you assume, as I do, that Hoover's record up to last spring was one of concession and expediency, not at all unlike Roosevelt's, you have no right to infer from Roosevelt's concessions that he is intrinsically any less capable of standing firm in an absolute emergency than Hoover more or less proved to be. What I was dealing with there was what seemed to me a non sequitur in the *Herald Tribune* editorial. Of course that has no bearing upon your own personal belief arising from your acquaintance with Roosevelt that he would flinch and run, but that testimony is, I think, uncertain.

On your third point, — Hoover's lack of courage in anticipating and preventing, I could, I am afraid, write a treatise, but I will simply name one, his failure to hold Congress to the original purpose of farm relief legislation and his signature to the Hawley-Smoot bill;[3] two, his promises up to within a few months of the assembling of the last Congress that no increase of taxes would be necessary and that the Government deficit was not serious. It is this point upon which I myself lay greatest stress. And as I happen to know, it was only by the exercise of the greatest possible pressure that Mr. Hoover was finally persuaded, about November, 1931, that it was necessary to try and balance the budget. His record on economy seems to me extraordinarily weak and timid. It must not be forgotten that the worst piece of Veterans legislation, the one which wrecked the distinction between disabilities incurred in the war and apart from it, was an Administration measure, signed by the President, and put through without the approval of the Legion itself. It is that piece of legislation which will cause us more trouble than any other single thing affecting the budget. . . .

1. F. Meredith Blagden, New York City investment counselor.   2. Roosevelt had acted on Seabury's charges against Mayor Walker by presiding at hearings that forced Walker's resignation on September 1, 1932.   3. The Agriculture Marketing Act of 1929 had failed to fulfill Hoover's

promise of legislation that would place agriculture "on an economic equality with other industries," and the Hawley-Smoot Tariff of 1930, the highest in American history, had contributed to the economic plight of European nations that needed to export to the United States in order to earn dollars to pay their debts.

To Arthur A. Ballantine

November 2, 1932

Dear Arthur:

I was very glad to hear from you again and I am glad you expressed your feelings so candidly. . . .

. . . You say "I have not seen any statement by Mr. Roosevelt that he was against the greenbacks." You have seen a perfectly clear statement from him that he was against the consideration of any new expenditures until the budget was actually in balance. Will you tell me in the name of sanity what else he must say to assure you and Ogden Mills that he doesn't propose to start the printing presses? Does he have to use the same language that you choose to put into his mouth, or is he at liberty to state his position in language of his own, which is perfectly plain to anybody who chooses to read it? To my mind, Governor Roosevelt's statement in regard to balancing the budget is far more impressive, far more unequivocal, and far more reassuring than if he said, "I am opposed to the issue of greenbacks." For nobody admits that he is proposing to issue greenbacks, and there are many ways of inflating the currency which do not involve the issue of greenbacks. I do not, therefore, admit that you are right in saying that he has "merely adumbrated" his views on this point. I believe he has stated them decisively.

I agree with you entirely as to the weight of the pressure behind some program of inflation which will make its appearance in the next Congress. That, as you may have gathered from my articles, is one of the reasons why I think it so important to put in office a man who commands the confidence of the debtor classes of the nation. They will accept a leadership from him that they will not accept from Mr. Hoover. They will accept it because for the present at least they trust him. And I, for my part, holding all the reservations I do about Roosevelt believe that there is one clear gain to be had from his election and that is the restoration of popular confidence in the federal government. . . .

To Theodore Roosevelt, Jr.[1]

November 22, 1932

Dear Ted:

. . . In my opinion there was never the slightest doubt of Hoover's defeat after his Acceptance speech. The only question was the size of it. The Republican campaign blew up before it started, and any Democrat could have been elected, but probably no other Democrat could have obtained as large a vote as Franklin did. I finally voted for him and wrote some articles in favor of him when I realized that no human power could prevent a large Democratic majority in both houses of Congress. It then seemed to me that a Republican president facing a hostile Congress for the next two years was just too horrible to contemplate and that unity in the government was the immediate need.

The last ten days of Hoover's campaign were pretty desperate and lost him thousands of votes among conservative Republicans who would not stand for his tariff speeches and his appeals to fear. At the end about thirty percent, as I figure it, of the Republican Party, swung over to Franklin, causing a split almost as great as that in 1912.

Now is the time when the Republicans of your generation had better take the party in hand, for the Old Guard is hopelessly beaten and discredited, and your chance has come. You can be very pleased that you were as far away as Manila during this campaign. You would have been taking rhubarb and soda in the effort to be loyal and partisan.

As to what Franklin will do, I venture no prophesies. All I feel reasonably sure of is that he is a good politician. He stands a better chance of keeping his crowd together than Hoover did. And when the story finally is written I think the verdict will be that Hoover, in spite of real abilities was one of the worst-equipped men for the presidency by temperament and political ideas that we have had in this generation. . . .

1. Theodore Roosevelt, Jr., was then governor general of the Philippines.

To Bernard Berenson   HANDWRITTEN

November 27, 1932

Dear B. B.

. . . The people here are repeating the French performance in reparations exactly. They cannot understand why they should not be paid when Britain has a navy, France a hoard of gold, and Italy such luxuries as the Rex.[1] The politicians are all obscurantist, partly through ignorance, largely through cowardice. We shall probably become reasonable when we have paid the price of being unreasonable. These democracies cannot learn from hypotheses.

From the European side the debt business was as usual bungled. The British note was written without consulting Stimson (who is enlightened) and delivered before Hoover could return to Washington from California. The note said the wrong things in the wrong way & Stimson has had to tell MacDonald to start over again & try again.[2]

It looks as if it would require another six months of deep depression to change opinion here. . . . Hoover can do nothing with Congress or the public.

The election here was a foregone conclusion from the start. Perhaps the most interesting result was that the Socialists in this year of discontent, polled the lowest proportion of the total vote in thirty years barring only their vote in 1928. As for the Communists, they got .0006 of the total vote. So if American capitalism is threatened it will not be by the conscious action of the people just now. . . .

1. The Italian ocean liner.   2. Hoover had rejected a British proposal, which they had expected him to accept, for deferring the payment of the installment on their war debt due in December. The president also asked Roosevelt to confer with him about the matter. Mutually suspicious, they met on November 22 to no effect. Hoover thought Roosevelt had agreed to his plan to demand payment before further negotiations to reduce the debt, but Roosevelt held that the issue was the responsibility of the incumbent administration. Hoover then wrote the British a tough note. They did pay the December installment, but the French did not. Hoover also proposed the establishment of a commission to consider the related questions of the debts, disarmament, and the depression. He requested Roosevelt's support, but the president-elect would not accept a plan about which he had not been consulted. He also doubted the utility of the linkage of issues Hoover had defined, considered the debts relatively unimportant, and continued to believe Hoover was trying to impose his policies on the new administration. The whole matter remained unresolved during the difficult period before the inauguration in March.

To Newton D. Baker

January 11, 1933

Dear Newton:

I am moved to write you because I have become more than a little anxious about the appearances of things in the Roosevelt camp. I think the thing that disturbs me most is an apparent disposition to pay no attention to the highest and most seasoned Democratic leaders. I don't notice that you have been in consultation with the President-elect. I don't believe Al Smith has been. I think Owen Young saw him once since election. John Davis appears to be on the black list. And night before last I heard that the Governor had been too busy to see Frank Polk this week. He has, however, seen Father Coughlin[1] of Detroit. The one man he has talked with who has direct experience of the biggest affairs is Norman Davis,[2] and there are very ugly attacks upon Davis emanating from the inner circle of the Kitchen Cabinet and the Brain Trust.

It may be all right for Frank not to use many or any of the men I have named in his Cabinet, but I cannot believe he can afford to do without their advice. I cannot feel that Moley[3] is altogether of the size which his influence would seem to call for, and the other Columbia professors whom I know better than I know Moley would rate, even in the academic world, as not much better than B plus. . . .

1. Father Charles E. Coughlin, Canadian-born Detroit priest, a master of the radio and in 1932–33 both a Roosevelt supporter and an ardent inflationist.   2. Norman H. Davis was a delegate to

the 1932 Disarmament Conference in Geneva. In 1933 Roosevelt made Davis chairman of the American delegation to that conference and in 1935 head of the American delegation to the London Naval Conference. **3.** Raymond Moley, a Columbia law professor, was at this time probably the most influential of the brain trust that Roosevelt had recruited. The Columbia group also included Rexford G. Tugwell and Adolf A. Berle. It never had exclusive possession of the president's ear.

To Henry A. Wallace[1]

January 18, 1933

Dear Mr. Wallace:

I am very glad indeed to have your letter, and more than pleased to have you confirm what I assumed must be the truth, that the Jones Bill doesn't suit you.

There are two points in your letter which I'd like to talk about briefly. In the first place, the criticism about including dairying and peanuts was not in my article. That must have appeared somewhere else. However, I look upon the inclusion of dairying and peanuts as an example of the dangers which the principle of the bill involves, namely, the log-rolling of special interests. That was exemplified rather viciously, I thought, in the way the bill finally dealt with tobacco.

What you say about the sales tax interests me. I suppose there would be no question whatever that the bill does lay a sales tax in almost exactly the same way, but in enormously larger amounts, as the manufacturers' sales tax which the Democrats are opposing. If this isn't a sales tax, neither is the tax proposal a sales tax. Both are laid upon the manufacturer, and no one knows exactly how much of the tax will be passed on to the consumer. However, if it is true that a hundred percent tax on wheat would only advance the price of bread 15 percent, then what becomes of the argument that a 2¼ percent tax would be an intolerable burden on the consumer? It seems to me that the agricultural politicians are trying to have their cake and eat it too. If it is justifiable to lay a sales tax of such enormous size upon necessities of life such as wheat and cotton then how can they justify their opposition to the very moderate general sales tax which exempts food and clothing? . . .

1. Henry A. Wallace — son of Harding's secretary of agriculture and grandson of the influential Henry Wallace who had been editor and publisher of *Wallace's Farmer*, a prominent agricultural journal — had succeeded to his grandfather's role and was about to become FDR's secretary of agriculture and later, in 1940, running mate. A specialist on agricultural economics, Wallace had grave reservations about the bill that Marvin Jones, chairman of the House Committee on Agriculture, was advancing in Congress. Much altered, largely according to Wallace's preferences, that bill became part of the Agricultural Adjustment Act of 1933, a major achievement of the early New Deal. The act established the Agricultural Adjustment Administration to manage a system of allotments for the production of commodities. It also provided for compensatory federal payments for farmers, which Wallace had advocated. In writing Lippmann on January 16, Wallace opposed the inclusion of dairying and peanuts within the developing legislation. He also corrected Lippmann's calculation of the burden on consumers that would result from the rising prices of wheat and of bread because of the provisions of the plan.

To Russell C. Leffingwell

[February 1933]

Dear Russell:

. . . I had hoped it might be Glass[1] and you in the Treasury, but today it does not seem probable. However, if Glass is administration spokesman in the Senate, as he is entitled to be now that F.D.R. has begged him to join the Cabinet, he may be almost as influential. But I would so like to see you in the thick of things with all due respect to your present activities and to J.P.M. & Co. . . .

What strikes me, having been in this typical small town two years ago, is how little the depression has changed the standard of life or the habits of the middle class. They are all theoretically poorer but they live in the same houses, play golf, drink corn, drive cars, play bridge, and dress up for parties. The cars are a little shabbier, the clothes a little less brand new, the golf balls are now "seconds" and the caddies don't receive tips. But superficially there is no other change. Yet the place is a commercial center of the citrus industry in which local prices have fallen 85 per cent in three years. The rest of the people are small rentiers. Damn it, Russell, they don't even seem worried. Are we boobs or are they?

1. Senator Carter Glass of Virginia, in folklore the father of the Federal Reserve Act, had declined Roosevelt's offer of appointment as secretary of the treasury. He had held that post briefly toward the end of the Wilson administration, when Leffingwell had served under him. Roosevelt turned instead to William H. Woodin, a capable financier, who as it later developed had enjoyed the favor of J. P. Morgan and Company — by Leffingwell's standard, and Lippmann's, a positive attribute.

To Felix Frankfurter

March 3, 1933

Dear Felix:

. . . Your diagnosis seems to me half the truth, but not the whole of it. I feel that you are vividly and properly aware of the influence of wealth and vested interests in government policy, but that you do not give sufficient weight to the effect on government by the pressure of organized minorities like the Veterans, the prohibitionists, in some of their attitudes the farmers, etc. The government is subject to distorting influence from a relatively small class of wealthy people and from the distorting influence of a very large class of people who are not wealthy but equally selfish and dangerous. Thus I thoroughly agree that we must have heavy taxation of incomes and inheritances for financial and social reasons, but I believe that we shall do no good with that taxation if we do not resist just as firmly the minorities like the Veterans, who would absorb the proceeds.

With this as a premise I cannot agree that it is the whole truth to say that our difficulty has been the lack of executive leadership. We have lacked executive leadership, I fully realize. But I also am very confident that executive leadership will not be as easy as you imply if we do not subdue those electoral minorities which rule so large a part of Congress.

I am afraid I have not expressed myself very clearly, but your own mind will have made allowances for the awkwardness of my language.

Let me just say that my plea for concentration of authority for Roosevelt[1] was not made until I had been satisfied as to the essential wisdom with which he would use such authority. I have not agitated for any such thing to be given to Hoover because I distrust his purposes. But in the case of Roosevelt, especially in view of the Cabinet he has chosen,[2] I think there is no reason to be concerned that the policy of the Executive will be abused by selfish interest. The chances are that its purposes will be obstructed by the selfish interest of those minorities I have talked about. . . .[3]

1. Lippmann had seen Roosevelt earlier in February at Warm Springs, Georgia, while the president-elect received treatment for his crippled legs. "The situation is critical, Franklin," he said, according to his biographer. "You may have no alternative but to assume dictatorial powers," a theme he had reiterated thereafter in "Today and Tomorrow"; see Ronald Steel, *Walter Lippmann and the American Century* (Boston, 1980), p. 300. The crisis of the winter of 1932–33, a winter of despair, especially involved the collapsing American banking system, which suffered alike from the illiquidity of many banks and from the accompanying distrust of their depositors and the resulting runs on their cash. With Roosevelt and Hoover unable to cooperate on the terms that Hoover demanded, terms that Roosevelt thought would seriously impair his own freedom of action, the crisis worsened until his inauguration on March 4. He then did request emergency powers and at once ordered the banks closed to stop the runs. Roosevelt also ordered the immediate preparation of measures to restore liquidity to the banking system. On March 8, the Congress by acclamations passed the first emergency banking act.   2. The Cabinet included, besides Wallace and Woodin, Cordell Hull as secretary of state, George H. Dern as secretary of war, Claude A. Swanson as secretary of the navy, James A. Farley as postmaster general, Homer S. Cummings as attorney general, Harold L. Ickes as secretary of the interior, Daniel C. Roper as secretary of commerce, and Frances Perkins as secretary of labor. Except for Wallace, Ickes, and Perkins, they were largely conservative in their orientation, though not reactionary; and except for those same three and perhaps Hull, they proved to be rather undistinguished in their performance.   3. That forecast proved largely incorrect. As Lippmann had hoped he would, Roosevelt did enjoy special emergency authority after the inauguration on March 4, but his influence helped to persuade the Congress, in spite of the opposition of veterans and prohibitionists, quickly to pass the legislation reducing appropriations for the Veterans Administration and permitting the manufacture and transportation of light wines and beer, a first step toward repeal of the prohibition amendment. Farmers, in contrast, at least those farmers with large commercial holdings, subscribed to the new policies of the Agricultural Adjustment Act.

To Felix Frankfurter

March 8, 1933

Dear Felix:

. . . The doctrine of powers that I have been preaching in the last few weeks does not arise from any doubt as to the value of discussion, reflection, criticism and persuasion as conditions for wise action, but out of a conviction that the character of this crisis requires extraordinary methods. That extraordinary methods are very dangerous and can become a habit I vividly realize, but I think we must not be afraid to resort to them if we realize the dangers and are clear about the necessities.

In regard to the point about the selfish rich and the selfish poor, I would agree that the rich strike the pitch for the poor. Nevertheless, the dangers to the commonwealth from the bribing of great masses of voters are present and real and I do not think we dare to be unconscious of them to the extent of concentrating our whole animus upon the Mitchells.[1] If you would see my mail on the subject of the veterans, you would see that there are elements of corruption down deep in the electorate which were not put there by the Mitchells, but are part of the old Adam in every man, part of those same qualities which keep the Mitchells from being unique among human beings. It seems to me that you seem to imply that the wickedness and selfishness that pervade society come entirely through bad example from the top. I do not subscribe to that doctrine one hundred percent. The evil works down from the top, but it also works up from the bottom.

1. Charles A. Mitchell had been chairman of the board of the National City Bank and a director of the Federal Reserve Bank of New York. To reduce his large liability for income taxes for 1928, he had, as he later admitted, fudged a number of transactions on the stock market, for which he was indicted as a criminal but acquitted. He did have to pay the government's civil claim for taxes and penalties, in all $1,100,000. Roosevelt in his inaugural address had promised to drive the moneychangers from the temple; Mitchell had already become a symbol of that breed.

To Felix Frankfurter

March 14, 1933

Dear Felix:

. . . I fully appreciate your own experience in government and I know it's been much greater than my own. But I have some acquaintance with the way public opinion works, and relying upon that, the only comment I would make upon what you say in your letter is that it leaves me with a feeling that you are a little bit hesitant about breaking the eggs to make the omelet. I take it from your letter that you approve of what's been done during the past ten days, but that you deplore the arousing of the public which has accompanied it. Aren't you a little bit in the position of desiring the end but being hesitant to will the means?

Of course the means are rough and, to a degree, irrational. But the process of reason in public affairs is necessarily a very slow process, and in an acute emergency you have either the choice of means that will procure the end or forgo attaining it.

I recognize fully the *potential*[1] danger of too hasty, too ill-considered reorganization, but what would you have done in the circumstances of the last two or three weeks? Do you really think, for example, that I should have urged Congress to consider carefully and attempt to understand thoroughly the provisions of the banking bill before passing it,[2] or was it right to call upon Congress to take the thing on faith, suspending debate, suspending the process of education, suspending the deliberative method? I faced that choice honestly in my own mind, and I am prepared to risk the potential dangers which you point out for the sake of averting the much more actual dangers which were right upon us.

I agree with you that the public needs education in the factors relevant to wise decisions. But I do not frankly believe it's possible to educate the people on all the factors that are relevant to all the wise decisions that have got to be made in the next few weeks. It is utterly impossible to perform such a feat of education. The matters are too intricate, prejudices are too deep and complex, the necessary technical knowledge is too lacking.

1. Emphasis Lippmann's. **2.** The Emergency Banking Relief Act had been drafted in the Treasury Department by some New Dealers and some of the staff Ogden Mills had earlier assembled. It permitted the Federal Reserve Board to issue currency for various kinds of bank assets not previously approved for that purpose. Consequently the board could supply more than enough currency and credits to compensate for the gold flowing to Europe and out of the American banking system, as European investors withdrew from the depressed and uncertain American market. The act also gave the secretary of the treasury power to prevent the hoarding of gold and to take over gold in exchange for paper money; to review and reopen sound banks under license; and to appoint "conservators" — receivers by another name — to manage shaky banks until they were ready to open and had re-established their solvency. Along with the legalization of beer and the reduction of appropriations for the Veterans Administration, the Emergency Banking Relief Act provoked Lippmann to write in his column: "In one week, the nation, which had lost confidence in everything and everybody, has regained confidence in the government and in itself."

To Philip J. Roosevelt[1]

April 28, 1933

Dear Phil:

Apparently I give the wrong impression because I am considerably puzzled by a great many things. However, I'll try to answer your questions if I can.

(1) The complaints about the high cost of living are the characteristic complaints of a period of rising prices and the movement against the cost of living became politically active somewhere around 1910 and culminated somewhere around 1921. Complaints that prices are too low are characteristic of

periods of deflation and falling prices. The desirable thing would be stable prices. But in view of the fact that prices have fallen to the point where the whole debt structure is endangered, it is necessary to raise prices before attempting to stabilize them.

(2) The purpose of the embargo on gold[2] is not to depreciate the dollar and create a tariff, but to give this country freedom to act on its own price level divorced from the effects of the appreciation of gold.

(3) It would be nice to have a trade revival. And credit does depend upon the sanctity of contracts, but contracts are threatened with destruction by the fall in prices and the destruction of incomes. However, I agree with the implication of your remark, if you imply that the powers of the Thomas Bill are to be used arbitrarily to reduce the gold content.[3] I do not see that intention. What I see is an effort by credit inflation to raise our prices, which may or may not mean the depreciation of the dollar in terms of gold. When the time for stabilization comes that point will give the gold content of the dollar, and I read the bill as meaning that the President then has power to stabilize at that point. If the operation is conducted in any other way, your objections certainly apply to it. . . .

1. Philip J. Roosevelt, New York investment banker, a rather distant cousin of Eleanor Roosevelt's.   2. To the applause of Lippmann and of the Morgan partners alike, as well as that of many rural inflationists and others, the president on April 19 had ordered an embargo, except under license from the Treasury, on shipments of gold outside of the United States, including shipments to cover exchanges of the dollar for other currencies. He had also ordered the nationalization of all gold and of all gold coins except for those in numismatic use. That required exchange of gold for paper currency upset the conventional belief, endemic in financial circles, that only gold and the automatic gold standard (which Roosevelt's order abandoned) afforded a safe basis for currency. Men of that belief also objected that holders of federal bonds, which contained clauses promising payment in gold, could instead receive paper currency, a condition they equated with breach of contract.   3. The Thomas bill — the brain child of Senator Elmer Thomas, Oklahoma Democrat — required the president to inflate the currency in any of several ways, of which one called for increasing the price of gold, which would of course decrease the gold content or gold value of the dollar. In altered form, the bill became an amendment to the Agricultural Adjustment Act of 1933, but that measure gave the president permission to inflate the currency rather than requiring him to do so. It took a major effort on Roosevelt's part to effect that change.

To Lewis W. Douglas[1]

May 2, 1933

Dear Lew:

I am writing to you to suggest that an enormous advantage would be gained immediately on the passage of the Thomas amendment if someone authorized to speak for the Administration would really make the editors of newspapers understand the policy as you outlined it the other day, and would ask them for their help on the ground that this is a national emergency. The disposition is to help, but the policy is not understood and Mills and Carter Glass have done a great deal of damage in the way of shaking people's confidence.

The other thing on my mind is the gold clause. . . . That seems to me very misleading. On the question of whether interest on long-term bonds should be paid in gold I should think that the policy of the Administration would be perfectly clear. There is no more reason why the long-term debtors of the United States should be favored over those who hold United States notes. Since it's impossible to redeem all the obligations in gold, none should be redeemed at the present time. If this decision is taken, it should also be explained carefully so that we don't get thrown into a destructive controversy on the theme of repudiation.

1. Lewis W. Douglas had resigned as a Democratic congressman from Arizona to accept appointment as Roosevelt's first director of the budget. Unhappy about the president's monetary policies, he resigned as budget director in August 1934 because of his still greater gloom about the growing federal deficit. He was later to serve as President Truman's ambassador to the Court of St. James's.

To George W. Davison[1]

May 8, 1933

Dear Mr. Davison:

I am very much obliged to you for sending me this extraordinarily useful memoranda on guaranteeing bank deposits.

In writing the article of May 4th, I was particularly careful not to favor the principle of a guaranty of bank deposits and in fact I am opposed to it under our present banking system or under any system that we're likely to have in the near future. What I do believe is that the Federal Government has assumed a moral obligation to prevent banks which have opened from closing during the present crisis, or until permanent banking legislation has been enacted. I do not see on what other ground the government can ask people to return their gold and to re-deposit their funds. But it doesn't follow that this moral obligation must take the form of a legal guaranty of deposits. . . .[2]

1. George W. Davison, at this time president and chairman of the board of the Central Hanover Bank and Trust Company of New York City and a director of the Federal Reserve Bank of New York. 2. The Glass-Steagall Banking Act of June 1933 did provide that legal obligation by creating the Federal Deposit Insurance Corporation to guarantee bank deposits. The same act divorced commercial from investment banking.

To Raymond Moley

June 16, 1933

Dear Ray:

. . . I still have it on my mind that I promised to write you a letter putting in words what we talked about the other day in regard to the Administration having reached a point where it now has to consolidate the tremendous advance over new territory which it has made.[1] As I think the matter over, the point seems so obvious that it hardly calls for elaboration. The fact is, I suppose, that in the administration of those laws, things which are successful will tend to become permanent and to be worked out further. Things which are unsuccessful will tend to be eliminated.

There are, however, certain additional reforms which I think it would be well to begin planning now, although the time for their adoption might not come even next winter:

(1) There should be made, without any preliminary publicity, a really expert and searching study of the income tax law.[2] It is obvious that the law works badly, and yet it is equally obvious that it must not only be preserved as the chief source of revenue but must be used also for the social purpose of altering the distribution of wealth. If this is to be done, the law itself has to be made simpler to administer, simpler to observe and simpler to understand. My notion is that two or three men should very quietly be put to work upon the income tax returns themselves, studying them individually by samples and statistically, with a view to working out a comprehensive reform. I don't think Congress and spectacular public investigations can do more than uncover isolated evils and arouse a certain general public sentiment. The administration, I think, should prepare itself for a really thorough house-cleaning and reconstruction of the tax laws.

(2) I think we have to get ready for a system of control of the flow of capital. I have a few ideas as to how this might be begun, but I won't try to specify here. The idea will be obvious to you. It seems to me necessary to get ready for it and logical to do so after the banking bill and the securities bill.[3]

(3) I think somebody ought to be at work making plans for a more far-reaching federal coordination of, and perhaps assistance to, the states in the general field of social insurance.[4] One of the real reasons we have the Veterans racket is that it is a partial substitute for unemployment, illness and old age insurance. Its vice is, of course, that it sets up a privileged class. The only fundamental remedy for that is to absorb the veterans who are old, ill, or unemployed, and have no direct injuries from the war in the mass of the citizens who are entitled to the benefits of social insurance. I don't want to see the Federal Government go very deeply into this, but I think it ought to go far enough to stimulate adequate systems in the states.

(4) I would suggest that somebody be assigned in each office concerned with the administration of some one of these new laws to the task of being the

historian of the law, keeping a detailed historical record of what happens, day by day, collating the documents, digesting them, etc. Such a record would be invaluable some months hence, first as indicating where amendments and improvements are desirable, and second as a defense against criticism and attack. The need of this is borne in upon me by the fact that I have had the greatest difficulty, for example, getting a clear conception of what's been going on in the Bureau of the Budget and the Veterans Bureau under the Economy Law. The difficulty in following the Industrial Bill is even greater. What attempt I have made to follow the Farm Bill convinces me that the ordinary hand-outs are not illuminating enough. I'd put a professor who has no administrative responsibility and no axe to grind at work on each one of these important projects just to keep the record complete and straight. . . .

1. Besides measures already described in preceding notes, the New Deal had by executive decree or congressional action also by this time established the Civilian Conservation Corps; passed the Federal Emergency Relief Act and the National Industrial Recovery Act, which created the National Recovery Administration and provided funds for the Public Works Administration; passed the Farm Mortgage Refinancing Act and the Home Owners' Refinancing Act to refinance farm and home mortgages; created the Tennessee Valley Authority; and passed the Federal Securities Act, the Farm Credit Act, and the Emergency Railroad Transportation Act — a remarkable record for the first Hundred Days of the Roosevelt administration. On those Hundred Days, Lippmann wrote in his column, "We became again an organized nation confident of our power to provide for our own security and to control our own destiny." **2.** Such a study began within the Treasury Department in 1934 and produced the administration's revenue bill of 1935. **3.** The system of control Lippmann had in mind was already contemplated and would emerge in the Securities Exchange Act of 1934. The Securities Act of 1933 took a first step in that direction by requiring full disclosure in the issue of new securities. **4.** A committee of which Frances Perkins was chair studied the problems of social insurance and made the proposals that resulted in the Social Security Act of 1935. In this, as in the other questions (except the fourth) raised in this letter, the administration moved along paths Lippmann commended but did so on the basis of its own decisions, not because of his advice.

To Victor A. Cazalet[1]

July 24, 1933

Dear Victor:

. . . The day I arrived was the top of the speculative market. The next day, I hope not merely appropriately, the crack-up began, and all the speculative advances made since the first mess over stabilization at London have been erased in three days.[2] We are an incredibly ticker-minded people. And as a result great masses of people who believed implicitly in the Roosevelt program are now skeptical and pessimistic about it. The truth of the matter, I think, is that in the last week of May and the first two weeks of June Roosevelt was so deeply engaged in getting his legislation through Congress, in fighting off the veterans, and in getting by the June 15th debt payment without an explosion, that his mind simply did not work at all upon the monetary problem. Unfortunately, as you know, the Treasury is very weak, the present secretary being a feeble and largely discredited man. The Federal Reserve Board has been demoralized for a year and the bankers dare not show their faces in Washington. The result is that literally nobody had either authority or knowledge to devise a monetary policy, and the result was that the delegates in London had no instructions and tried to improvise one. Roosevelt was away on his vacation when this happened and lacking advisers and lacking knowledge of the subject himself, he disowned the improvisations of his representatives in London without having any policy of his own. This produced the whole speculation of the past thirty-five days. And only at the end of it, after a number of people had issued warnings, did they begin to see that the thing was really dangerous. But then it was too late. The bubble had burst. So far as the bubble goes, of course, it's good riddance, but the stock market has such an influence on American enterprise that I am really somewhat alarmed as to the future. It is clear that we cannot, for all kinds of reasons, return to the orthodox path. That led us to such threats of disaster that it's unthinkable we should take that road. But I do hope that in the very near future the Administration will develop a positive policy about the dollar. Until it does, I see no prospect of any substantial progress.

The mood of the people here is as nationalistic as it has been reported to be, but my impression is that this nationalism is much more the result of an inability to think out an international policy than any willful desire to abandon the benefits of an increase of international trade. This means that the real answer to the mood of self-containment is to develop specific projects for international cooperation. These projects must not be publicly announced before they are privately discussed, however, or we shall go through the same blunders that led to the debacle of the World Economic Conference. . . .

As I look back on my stay in London, the three men from whom I learned the most were Neville Chamberlain, Walter Runciman and McKenna.[3] Chamberlain, as you know, has an anti-American reputation here. Personally, I was completely disarmed and liked him very much indeed. He seemed to me the kind of man I'd want to negotiate with if I had anything to say in Washington. But I think one has to meet him rather than to read his speeches to feel that. McKenna is a real darling. I don't think there's a man in your public life who would get on as well with the people now in authority here as he would. In London Moley promised me to try to arrange a quiet invitation to have him come over here and talk about things. I do hope that will be arranged. . . .

1. Victor A. Cazalet, Conservative member of Parliament, four times English amateur squash champion, and friend of Lippmann's.   2. After Roosevelt's "bombshell" message to the London Economic Conference, in which the president had rejected the agreement Raymond Moley had negotiated looking to an eventual stabilization of currency values, Keynes had declared Roosevelt "magnificently right." The president was determined to let no international pact tie his hands at home, where he intended to alter the value of the dollar so as to ease interest rates and maximize the chances for recovery — a policy Keynes endorsed, as did Lippmann. Nevertheless both men

had joined Moley and others in discussions, ultimately futile, to ascertain whether any saving declaration might carry the support of both Roosevelt and the British; see especially Herbert Feis, *1933: Characters in Crisis* (Boston, 1966), pp. 242–43; Raymond Moley, *After Seven Years* (revised, Lincoln, Nebraska, 1971), pp. 264–65. **3.** Neville Chamberlain, then chancellor of the exchequer; Walter Runciman, later Viscount Runciman, then president of the British Board of Trade; and Reginald McKenna, former chancellor of the exchequer, at this time chairman of the Midland Bank. Chamberlain had indicated briefly a willingness to adjust to Roosevelt's position on stabilization.

To Robert E. Wood[1]

August 1, 1933

Dear Mr. Wood:

. . . There are four philosophies at work in Washington. First we had the internationalist versus the nationalist view, then the nationalists split up into the planners and the monetary people. Personally, being by temperament a skeptic and having very little faith in the power of any formula to encompass the enormous variety of real things I am an incurable eclectic. That is to say, I believe in all four philosophies at the same time and think the contractions between them are much less important than the positive contributions which each can make. Therefore, whenever the emphasis swings to nationalism I am inclined to emphasize the importance of the internationalist view, and when the inflationists get the upper hand I like to encourage the planners. And vice versa.

At the present moment there is strong evidence that the zeal of the Administration for the N.R.A. has diverted its mind from the problem of monetary management. There is also a strong pressure from financial centers for a policy which would, in the end, lift the dollar back to its own parity. My own view is that the more the dollar appreciates the more drastic will have to be the measures taken under the N.R.A. and the Farm Bill. And that the wise policy now would be an approximate de facto stabilization within wide limits of the dollar at something around thirty to thirty-three percent of gold, and a more moderate use of the N.R.A. in basic industries rather than in all industries. . . .[2]

1. Robert E. Wood, president of Sears, Roebuck and Company, had reached the rank of brigadier general during his prior Army service. While on duty in Panama, he had concluded that the future of Sears, Roebuck and similar mail-order houses lay in their establishment of a network of retail stores, a policy he later furthered to the benefit of Sears. Wood was also a senior officer of the Committee for the Nation, an organization composed in large part of businessmen who favored deliberate inflation and federal management of money and credit as the keys to the return of prosperity. **2.** The National Recovery Administration (NRA), the centerpiece of the administration's recovery policy at this time, had been created by the National Industrial Recovery Act of the previous spring. That act empowered the agency to supervise the making of industry-wide codes to govern output, prices, wages, and hours of firms subscribing to them. Representatives of management, labor, and consumer groups were to participate in the code making. Though the

NRA had coercive authority under the enabling legislation, its chief, Hugh S. Johnson, relied on volunteerism — in his case a mixture of exhortation and propaganda, both tempered with public scoldings when he so indulged himself. He also had the agency produce a general code for industries that were small, disorganized, or otherwise slow or incapable of developing a code of their own. Though codes for several industries seemed on the whole to be working at this date, the details of administration disrupted the operations of codes for industries characterized by small firms or functioning under the general code. Lippmann was only one of many observers to remark upon that early problem of the NRA.

Lippmann had not ceased his advocacy of a monetary policy that would, in the word of the day, "reflate" prices to their level of the mid-twenties by reducing the gold content of the dollar, a step toward which the president had moved in his rejection of the proposal of the London Economic Conference for a stabilization of the values of currencies in international exchange. Stabilization of the dollar in terms of the pound or franc would have cost FDR the free hand he sought in dealing with the future of the dollar at home. He was soon to commence his temporary venture in buying gold in order to increase its value and decrease the gold content of the dollar, that is, to inflate the dollar in terms of gold, a venture which by its completion reached the target that Lippmann and others were advocating at this time. The resulting low interest rates (the product of easier money), while a condition for renewed investment did not in themselves occasion that investment — so the gold buying had little effect on recovery or, in the immediately ensuing years, on prices. Indeed the NRA, by dividing markets and restricting production, discouraged investment in new capital plant and machinery and, therefore, tended to offset any contrary impact of New Deal monetary policy.

To Claude G. Bowers[1]

October 12, 1933

Dear Bowers:

. . . I am sending you in this mail a series of three articles which I have written this week which can tell you more than I can tell you in a letter what I think are the central difficulties of the Administration at the present time. Besides these interior difficulties of trying to combine a business recovery with a fundamental social reform, there are difficulties arising out of personalities and temperaments. About this I don't like to write publicly because it's hard to prove these things, but they are real factors. As I see it, one of the great difficulties is that the Cabinet as a Cabinet seems to have no real existence. There is, therefore, no continuing collective judgment operating to make the decisions. They seem to be personal decisions of the President. It's my notion that the problems he has to deal with are much too complex for personal decision. He cannot possibly extend his mind to cover the infinite variety of the problems that he's dealing with, and I am afraid he's trying to do too much himself. It's a tragedy, for example, that he has no real responsible Secretary of the Treasury and no effective head of the Federal Reserve Board.[2] The financial statesmanship required to manage an inflation is a whole-time job, and cannot be done as effectively as it should be done by a man doing a hundred other things at the same time. An example of the difficulty, I think, is found in the Cuban situation, where, as I see it, we have allowed perfectly sound moral disgust with Machado to run us into a moral intervention in Cuba's internal affairs, with the result that we have got a bear by the tail.[3] I have no doubt that Machado's regime was as detestable as any there has been recently in a Latin American country. But no matter how detestable, I cannot say that it was our business even informally to encourage its overthrow, because once you start that you get pulled along by inevitable steps into the complicated business of trying to build up a substitute. The State Department may have learned the lesson of the Huerta business in Mexico, but apparently Mr. Roosevelt hasn't. Yet, if he'd had the real time, to think steadily about that question, instead of sandwiching it in between so many others, he'd probably have realized the implications of our intervention.

Another difficulty is a lack of adequate personnel in the Administration of much of this very complicated domestic program. The fact is, I suppose, that we Democrats have been in power too little in the last half century to have drawn to ourselves our due proportion of the ablest younger men, and as we're attempting more, in the way of government, than has ever been attempted before in times of peace, we suffer the disadvantage.

However, I feel reasonably confident about the outcome. The President's popularity is not a hundred percent what it was in May or June, but it's ninety-five percent. He still has an overwhelming prestige. He is, moreover, a truly inspired political leader, and he's genuinely open-minded and willing to learn. . . .

1. Claude G. Bowers had received his political reward in 1933 when he was appointed United States ambassador to Spain. **2.** The incumbents were ill, but in November Roosevelt appointed Henry Morgenthau, Jr., acting secretary of the treasury and in January, secretary. Morgenthau had by then been Roosevelt's chief agent in the gold-buying venture. Though Lippmann never thought well of Morgenthau, he came to admire Marriner S. Eccles, the Utah banker whom Roosevelt appointed in 1934 as head of the Federal Reserve Board. **3.** Gerardo Machado, the president of Cuba, had been exercising dictatorial powers that, along with the island's continuing deep depression, provoked a revolt by the Army, which threw him out of office. Cárlos Manuel de Céspedes then became president, but when disorder continued, the United States in August sent warships to Cuba and blinked at another Army coup led by Fulgencio Batista. Still another coup soon followed. The American intervention temporarily damaged relations between the United States and the Latin American nations, but in May 1934, a conservative Cuban regime negotiated with the United States an agreement that abrogated the Platt Amendment.

To Alice Roosevelt Longworth[1]

November 9, 1933

Dear Alice:

I have just finished reading "Crowded Hours." Kermit[2] tells me that you don't think much of the book yourself, but I think you're wrong there. It really is a fascinating story, a kind of American fairy tale which fascinated me from beginning to end. Of course after being so magnificently frank up to about 1921 you did turn out to be a bit of a coward about the last twelve years. You really must write that part of the thing in another volume. But the book is gay, malicious, witty and romantic. And every professor of history for a hundred years will have to read it. Don't have any slightest doubt about your ability to say what you want to say in print.

1. Alice Roosevelt Longworth, Theodore Roosevelt's only daughter by his first marriage to Alice Lee, who had died after bearing her child. Alice Longworth was for many years the premier hostess in Washington, especially but not exclusively for eminent Republicans. She had sent Lippmann an early copy of *Crowded Hours* (New York, 1934), her memoir. 2. Kermit Roosevelt, the second son of T. R.

To Hugh S. Johnson

November 10, 1933

Dear Hugh:

It was extremely thoughtful of you to sit down and take the trouble to write me that personal note about my article. I should have acknowledged it much sooner if I hadn't been away from my desk and from all my mail. I won't burden you now with an attempt to argue the point you raise beyond saying that I did not for a moment question the legal powers of the President. I have no doubt he had the power to do everything that he has done. The question I was raising was as to the general spirit and intent of the Act as read by a man who is not a lawyer. And I still think that the Blanket Code and the pressure to codify so many industries in such a short time is a mistake. However . . .
I am with you one hundred percent and for you whole-heartedly in the deeper objectives of N.R.A. And when the whole story is written, it will be realized that those mistakes, if they are mistakes, are relatively minor, and that the achievement is conveying this new idea, and the whole notion is really a stupendous one. So I don't want to be among those throwing synthetic dead cats at you.

To Carter Glass

December 29, 1933

Dear Senator Glass:

. . . The question of what to do with the gold profit in case of devaluation is, of course, a difficult one, but I am not sure that I could agree with you in characterizing its seizure by the government as legislative theft. That profit will have been created solely by act of government in the exercises of its sovereign power to regulate the value of currency, and I do not see that the banks have any claims on that profit.[1] The moral principle seems to me not essentially different from that of taxing the enhanced value of a piece of land which has gone up because of public improvement. Or, to take your own example, that of the bank buildings. The government would clearly have no right to seize the bank buildings, but if the city, let us say, built a subway line past the bank building and increased its value, I should see nothing immoral in putting an assessment on the bank building. . . .

1. Glass objected to the provision of the Gold Reserve Act of early 1934, then pending, which took as seigniorage the profit the United States government had made by increasing the price of gold to thirty-five dollars an ounce, some 40 percent above the pre-1933 price. Since April, of course, the government had owned that gold. The act removed the gold from the Federal Reserve System to the Treasury, and the government then issued equivalent gold certificates to the Federal Reserve. The seigniorage profit also went to the Treasury, which under the act was enabled to use much of it for a stabilization fund. The Treasury employed that fund to buy and sell currency in order to stabilize the exchange value of the dollar in international markets and had the authority also to use the fund to buy and sell federal securities, or in other words, to sustain the par value of government bonds and notes. The threat of the latter use gave the Treasury the means to hold the Federal Reserve to the easy money policy the New Deal pursued.

To Norman H. Davis

December 29, 1933

Dear Norman:

Put in the briefest form I think I'd like to discuss with you the following:

The offer which you made at Geneva last spring required that under certain circumstances the United States would abandon the obligations of a neutral.[1] Almost immediately after the offer was made the resolution which passed the House and which would have empowered the President to carry out the offer was amended in the Senate Committee, flatly denying the President any such power. The action of the Senate Committee, in my opinion, clearly represents the will of Congress and of the people and the Administration made no effort to get the Senate Committee to change its mind. After that episode the Geneva offer was in effect withdrawn. And what is more, there was an implied decision that our policy would continue to be that of neutrality in the old sense. That being the case . . . the Administration, it seems to me, is under a mandate to prepare itself for a neutral position in the event of war. I do not see that preparations of that sort are being made and I believe that they must be made without loss of time. . . .

1. If the Geneva Conference in 1933 could reach an agreement on a substantial reduction of armaments, Roosevelt had proposed, the United States would be prepared to consult with the other nations in the event of a threat to the peace. Should the other states identify an aggressor and take measures against it (the president had Nazi Germany much in mind), then the United States, he went on, would, if it concurred, "refrain from any action tending to defeat such collective effort" — in other words, the United States would not insist on its traditional neutral rights, including freedom of the seas. But when the administration asked Congress to pass a resolution permitting the president to embargo the shipment of arms to an aggressor, the Senate Foreign

Relations Committee amended it to compel the president to embargo shipments to all nations, victims as well as aggressors. The administration managed to have the amended resolution defeated, but the Senate committee had destroyed Roosevelt's original proposal to the disarmament conference. Since the effort at disarmament failed, as Hitler doubtless would have arranged in any case, the obvious American alternative was, as Lippmann here argued, to fall back on neutrality, the policy the Congress designed in the next several years.

To Leonard P. Ayres

December 29, 1933

Dear Leonard:

. . . My view is that we cannot possibly develop a sound policy for the future until we come to some understanding as to why the monetary reconstruction of the 1920s broke down. If we can agree on the diagnosis, we have some hope of finding a cure. For then we'll know what we're trying to do. It's precisely because the so-called sound money people have no intelligible explanation of the monetary phenomena of the last ten years that I distrust intensely their demands that we return immediately to the gold standard. There was something radically wrong the last time the world returned to the gold standard. Within a year of the time the process was completed, the world price level collapsed. I cannot believe that there is no connection between the two things. For that reason I think we have got to make up our minds first of all why it collapsed, and when we have done that we're in some position to argue about the practical value of the various remedies. . . .

To Irving Fisher[1]

January 2, 1934

Dear Mr. Fisher:

. . . I'd like to take this occasion to raise a question which troubles me a good deal, and it might be described as the issue between the gold revaluationists and the silver advocates. I can see clearly enough, I think, that gold revaluation will enable us to alter the dollar price level and probably to stabilize it. But such a policy does nothing that I can see to raise or to stabilize the world gold price level. There seem to me to be plausible arguments in favor of using silver to depreciate gold and to stabilize gold, and I am wondering whether you have come to any conclusion in your own mind as to whether these two policies are mutually exclusive or whether a combination of the two might not be desirable. Presumably with the combination we could get some rise of prices from the depreciation of gold and the rest of the rise through the revaluation of the dollar, and after that we could attempt to maintain stability both by using silver and by varying the gold content. . . .[2]

1. Irving Fisher, professor of economics at Yale University and one of the eminent economists of his generation, had a deserved reputation as an expert on the changing purchasing power of money, a subject to which he had long given his attention, for example in his *The Making of Index Numbers* (Boston, 1922); *Stamp Scrip* (Adelphi, N.Y., 1932); and *After Reflation, What?* (Adelphi, N.Y., 1933). **2.** The silver lobby, still powerful in the Senate, was determined to have the government lift the price of silver, an objective accomplished by the Silver Purchase Act of 1934. Though that legislation forced heavy purchases of silver at home and abroad, it did not require bimetalism of any kind. Further, in executing the terms of the act, the Treasury retired National Bank notes to offset increases to currency arising from the monetization of silver.

To John Maynard Keynes [1]

April 17, 1934

My dear Keynes:

I have been on the point of writing you for sometime to urge you to write another article, following up your letter to the President of December last. I don't know whether you realize how great an effect that letter had, but I am told that it was chiefly responsible for the policy which the Treasury is now quietly but effectively pursuing of purchasing long-term government bonds with a view to making a strong bond market and to reducing the long-term rate of interest.

Our greatest difficulty now lies in the President's emotional and moral commitments to the N.R.A. and to the various other measures which he regards as the framework of a better economic order. As they are being administered, they are a very serious check to our recovery, for the obvious reason that they have raised costs faster than production has increased.

Nobody could make so great an impression upon the President as you could if you undertook to show him the meaning of that part of his policy.

1. John Maynard Keynes, the great British economist, had published an article in the form of an open letter to President Roosevelt in the *New York Times* of December 31, 1933. The letter praised the "reasoned experiment" of Roosevelt's program to that date, though Keynes believed that the task of recovery took precedence over the task of reform. On that account, he had more confidence in the possibilities of an expansionist monetary policy than he had in the NRA. His expressed belief in the utility of an interest rate on long-term government bonds of 2.5 percent — a rate that would ensure cheap credit in the United States — became the objective of the Treasury Department in its use of the Stabilization Fund, as Lippmann recognized.

To Lewis W. Douglas

May 25, 1934

Dear Lew:

. . . The thing I'd like to get and don't seem to be able to work out of the figures, is the amount of money spent month by month since November, say, which is not (a) the ordinary expenditure of the government, or (b) the substitution of government obligations for old private obligations.

I have been seeing something of Keynes[1] in the last week and he lays great stress upon the volume of excess expenditure which does not fall under either of the two categories above. His estimate is that the amount of this directly inflationary expenditure has been somewhere around 400 millions a month since January, but that it has fallen off in the month of May. . . . I think the point is of sufficient importance to justify trying to put the figures together in order to see whether and to what extent there is a relationship between this type of expenditure and the increase of production throughout the country.

1. Keynes was in the United States to receive an honorary degree from Columbia University. He was then close to completing a first draft of his celebrated *The General Theory of Employment, Interest and Money* (London, 1936) and accordingly was concerned with deliberate countercyclical spending as the key to economic recovery. While in the United States, he had an interview with President Roosevelt, who wrote that he liked Keynes "immensely." Yet there is no evidence to suggest Keynes exerted any particular influence on Roosevelt. He certainly did on Lippmann, as was clearly revealed in Lippmann's *The Method of Freedom* (New York, 1934), a book based upon the Godkin Lectures that Lippmann gave at Harvard in May 1934.

To Charles Warren[1]

June 12, 1934

Dear Mr. Warren:

Thank you for your letter which I am just now answering because I have been away and did not see it until a day or so ago. I fully understand that your own judgment is that we cannot remain neutral in a war where an important naval power is involved, I presume, specifically, Great Britain or Japan.

I agree with this view, to the extent at least of believing that it would be incredibly difficult to remain neutral. However, if there is such a thing as the will of the people by which we must be governed, the will of the American people to remain neutral in a European or an Asiatic war is as articulate and absolute as it could be on any public question. Therefore I count it a very high service to explain to them what the minimum preparation is that they must make to have any hope of remaining neutral, and no one has done so much as you have in this direction.

You must be very much closer in touch with these things than I am and I am wondering whether you have any reason to believe that the Administration contemplates legislation. I know that some sort of study of the problem of neutrality is being conducted in the State Department. But that's all I know.

One of the difficulties in legislating would be to find a way of doing it which wasn't tantamount to an official judgment on our part that war in Europe and Asia was inevitable. For while it seems to me probable, it is not inevitable, and

I'd well understand why the Administration would hesitate to make a move which would be taken by the opinion of the world as expressing a belief in the inevitability of war.

Have you thought of the possibility of legislation attached somewhat inconspicuously to some measure dealing with arms traffic, for example, giving the President extraordinary powers in the event of a declaration of war to draft regulations to preserve neutrality subject to ratification by Congress within a reasonable period of time? This is an offhand suggestion, but you will see the problems meant.

1. Charles Warren, lawyer, periodically a professor of law, a Harvard alumnus and benefactor, outstanding authority on the Constitution and the Supreme Court, and on jurisprudence and international law, author of — among many other works — the Pulitzer Prize-winning study *The Supreme Court in United States History*, 3 v. (Boston, 1922).

To George W. Davison

July 26, 1934

Dear Mr. Davison:

. . . I appreciate the point you make about uncertainty in regard to money, but I am impressed with the fact that the British, who are wise in these matters, have never made a definite commitment as to where they would stabilize the pound. I assume that they believe the world situation is too uncertain to make a definite commitment which may later prove to be a wrong one.

My belief is, therefore, that while the President ought to reassure the country, he ought not to make a commitment now which might be very embarrassing later. It seems to me that the best way for him to reassure the country is for him to take into his confidence the leaders of finance[1] and count upon them to create a sense of confidence elsewhere. After all, the reason why the British people are not worried, even though the pound is not stabilized, is that the City of London has personal confidence in the men who are managing the British currency. Something like that seems to me the effective thing to aim at now.

1. Which was not Roosevelt's intention.

To Franklin D. Roosevelt

December 7, 1934

My dear Mr. President:

I have started to work after quite a long absence, and I just wanted to tell you, in the hope that you would admire it, of my restraint in not asking you to let me come and see you. I haven't the heart to ask you to take on anything more, and I haven't anything in my mind that you can't afford not to hear.

At the same time I shouldn't like this consideration on my side to look as if I didn't really very much want to come and see you sometime. Please don't think this is an indirect request for an appointment.

I was very happy about the election. The vote of confidence which you got was as magnificent as it was well earned.[1]

1. The vote in November 1934 returned increased Democratic majorities in both houses of Congress, the only such result obtained by a party in power in the White House in an off-year election in the twentieth century before 1934 or since (as of 1985).

To William Phillips[1]

December 18, 1934

Dear Mr. Phillips:

. . . I am very much troubled by the proposal to give the President power to determine the rules of neutrality after a war has begun. It seems to me that this is open to objection on two grounds: first, it would force the President to determine whether Article XVI of the Covenant was to be applied, and whichever way he decided our moral position as a neutral would be gravely impaired. Second, he would at once become the target of exporting interests in the United States and of sympathizers with the various belligerents, all urging him to use his discretion one way rather than another.

I am inclined to think that a nation like ours, which declines to take part in the collective maintenance of peace and which wishes in fact to be neutral in a war, cannot make the rules of the game after the fighting has begun. To do that would be in fact to cease to be neutral, for every decision taken would weight the scales in favor of one side or the other and would be so interpreted.

It seems to me that the theory of discretionary powers is almost certainly a fallacy if, as I take it it must be, our major premise is that we wish to be neutral. The alternative would seem to be to revise our neutrality laws and make declarations of policy before these new rules become applicable to a specific conflict.

For my part, for example, I would be willing to forbid the export of munitions of war, as defined in the draft, to all belligerents once war is declared. And I should consider whether our trade in commodities outside this relatively narrow field might not be effectively protected by a law or a declaration that we will not export to one belligerent any commodity which he forbids us to export to his enemy. This might prove to be an effective way of maintaining a considerable degree of freedom of the seas if that is our national purpose. Thus, for example, under this rule if England stops shipment of wheat to Germany we should stop shipments of wheat to England. If Germany torpedoes ships carrying food to England we should embargo food shipments to

Germany or to countries which would re-export to Germany. I am not wholly satisfied that this is a sound principle but I'd like to throw it into the ring for consideration. Its purpose is to set the rules before a specific war begins and to preserve as much of our export trade as we can preserve without going to war to protect it.

A final and, it seems to me, conclusive reason for abandoning the discretionary principle and seeking to set the rules in advance is that I strongly suspect that Congress and public opinion will not grant such powers to the President. It would be necessary for an honest commentator to point out that this discretionary power would force the President to take a position which in fact is to the advantage of one side or the other. I believe that once the country grasped this it would refuse to sanction such a program.

The point must, of course, be made that it's extremely difficult to determine in the abstract and a priori what the best neutral policy would be in any specific war. I think the answer to that is that in case the rules of neutrality that we now set forth appear to be impracticable in a specific war it will still be possible to call Congress together and revise the rules or give the President discretionary power. That would not involve greater risks of becoming un-neutral than would be inherent in granting the powers in advance. In other words, we could still fall back on the principle that your committee has adopted if we had to. . . .

1. William Phillips, career diplomat, undersecretary of state, 1933–36, had asked Lippmann to comment upon the pending neutrality legislation. Deferring to increasing isolationist pressure, the administration agreed that the president should have the authority to prohibit neutral ships from carrying guns and munitions, to withdraw protection from Americans traveling on the ships of belligerents, and to place an embargo on arms and loans — a stipulation that reflected congressional disenchantment with Wilson's policies between 1914 and 1917. The administration wanted the new law to give the president discretion about those matters. The Senate voted to make it mandatory that he use his powers against all belligerents, victims of aggression as well as aggressors. The House passed a bill permitting discretionary use. In the end, the Neutrality Act of 1935 set a mandatory arms embargo until March 1936, but in other matters did give the president discretion.

To Alice Hamilton

December 27, 1934

Dear Miss Hamilton:

. . . We must proceed to build up to treaty strength,[1] which can hardly be defined as competitive building in view of the fact that the treaty limitations exist for the very purpose of preventing an armament race. The question of a race of armaments will arise only in case there is no new treaty after 1936 and in case Japan begins to build substantially beyond the treaty strength.

However, I realize that what you're concerned with is not the technical question of a race of armaments but with the general attitude towards armaments which my letter to you implied. Of course I must admit frankly that I have never believed in the philosophy which your letter implies, namely, that of non-resistant pacifism. And unless you feel that it is impossible to work effectively for peace without accepting that philosophy, I don't really see why my letter should have dismayed you.

As to the specific policy we ought to adopt in regard to the Japanese navy, I am not clear as yet in my own mind, beyond the belief that when the present treaty expires two years hence, the chances of another agreement will be better if our navy is of treaty strength than if it is far below it. What I should want to do in the event Japan starts to build on a large scale beyond the treaty ratios, I don't now know.

1. The United States Navy had at this date fewer capital and auxiliary ships than the nation was allowed by the naval limitations treaties of 1922 and 1930.

To John Maynard Keynes

January 9, 1935

My dear Keynes:

. . . Have you been following our affairs here? My view is that the President's policy today is far more in accord with what you advised last spring than it was then. N.R.A., at least in those aspects which involved monopolistic prices, rigid wage rates, and deliberate raising of wage costs, is completely discredited, I think, in the President's mind and certainly in the minds of his closest advisers. The new policy consists essentially of deliberately running deficits large enough to give work on public projects to the able-bodied unemployed now on relief, and the plan calls for deficit expenditures of about 350 million a month, which is right in line with the figure you named.[1] The startling thing to me, about the announcement of the program, has been that Wall Street, which was supposed to be terrified of deficits and inflation, greeted the budget with a strong bond market.

The new policy of having a deliberate deficit large enough to provide employment for the destitute but able-bodied unemployed is intended to become a permanent policy in this sense: we shall set up a scheme of unemployment insurance more or less on the British model, but we shall supplement by providing that when an unemployed man has exhausted the fifteen or twenty-six weeks benefit (the exact amount is not yet settled) to which he is entitled, he will then go off the insurance, but will acquire the right to a job on a public works project at a wage considerably below that which he could earn in private industry, but still sufficient to keep him going.

If the President succeeds in devising a method by which public work can be made extremely elastic, so that it can be started quickly and stopped quickly,

I think we shall be making an extremely interesting experiment in this country. . . .

1. Lippmann was writing here about a change of direction that resulted, in the view of many observers at the time, in a second, or at the least a different, New Deal. Though the president did not say that he had given up on NRA, administrative difficulties within the agency provoked him to replace Hugh Johnson, and a congressional investigation conducted by Clarence Darrow soon revealed the monopolistic aspects of NRA, to which many congressmen objected. It was the Supreme Court that finally ended NRA later in 1935, in its decision in the Schechter case when all nine justices found the enabling legislation unconstitutional, "delegation run riot." By that time some of the president's advisers were beginning to embrace Keynesian theory, though Roosevelt himself did not. Rather he supported the concept of work relief, which animated the legislation of 1935 authorizing $4.8 billion, largely for that purpose. He also advocated the social security legislation, enacted later that year, to which Lippmann turned in the next paragraph of this letter. As it developed, however, Congress never appropriated sufficient funds to permit the employment on work relief projects of all those who needed that assistance. As the year wore on, the president also sponsored other important legislation, including among others, the Wealth Tax Act, increasing income and inheritance taxes; the Banking Act of 1935; the Wagner Labor Relations Act, establishing the National Labor Relations Board; and the Public Utility Holding Company Act, limiting the number and kinds of public utilities holding companies. The 1935 Revenue Act and the taxes supplied by the Social Security Act much reduced the federal deficit from the level it would otherwise have reached and revealed the administration's continuing resistance to the kind of deliberate countercyclical deficits Keynes had recommended.

To Mark Sullivan[1]

February 7, 1935

Dear Mark:

    . . . I am not so sure I agree with your . . . point, namely that FDR is a contemporary Bryan. If I had a little more time I'd set out to prove to you that he may be a somewhat shrewder Grover Cleveland, who may succeed in avoiding precisely that split which Cleveland, with all his excellent but insufficient virtues, was unable to avoid. Seriously, though, there's a vast difference between a Roosevelt adopting progressive and even populist measures, and a populist himself carrying them out.

1. Mark Sullivan contributed, as Lippmann did, several columns a week to the *New York Herald Tribune*, columns that Sullivan infused with a stalwart Republican voice.

To William Hard[1]

February 8, 1935

Dear Bill:

    . . . I have been yelling about the N.R.A. and small business since the first few weeks of it, and I have become boring on the subject of price restriction and monopoly under it. So when you end by summoning me to consider whether there is not a distinction between journalists and other people I say that so far as the general question of monopoly goes I have never made the distinction, and in fact attacked monopoly in business before I attacked the newspaper code.

However, I do say this: that while it's a debatable question as to whether industry should become collectivized, through the N.R.A., through cartels, or any other way, it is not a debatable question as to whether journalists should become cartelized. There is a distinction between the press and other industries, and that distinction is not because we are superior people but because we perform a function which the Constitution itself recognized as distinctive and therefore specifically guarantees. . . .

1. William Hard, journalist, broadcaster, later (in 1937) chairman of the Republican National Committee.

To Russell C. Leffingwell

February 17, 1935

Dear Russell:

. . . On the point about the terrors of business, I agree, though I do think that business men tend to be terrorized about a good many things that more enlightened men would not be terrorized by. However, I have serious doubts as to whether you have put your finger on the basic trouble.[1] . . . The British Government is not attacking business men, yet apparently their capital market is also virtually closed. . . .

1. Roosevelt's "attacks" on men of business and wealth.

To Peter Molyneaux[1]

February 27, 1935

Dear Mr. Molyneaux:

. . . You are, of course, quite right on the literal question of whether two-thirds of the senators means two-thirds of the people. But I feel now, and have always felt, that the provision requiring a two-thirds' vote, however much I dislike its results, rests on a sound conception of foreign policy, — which is that an international commitment must represent not a bare majority but an overwhelming majority of the people. Unless that overwhelming majority exists it will cause uncertainty in international relations and deep division at home. . . .

I am not an isolationist and have never been one, but I have always recognized that there are times when political cooperation with Europe is possible and there are times when it is not. The present moment is one when it is not, in my opinion. But the judgment of what is possible and what is not possible should not be identified with the feeling of what one might like to see. . . .

1. Peter Molyneaux of the *Dallas Weekly*.

To George K. Livermore[1]

March 21, 1935

Dear Mr. Livermore:

I am replying to your letter of March 14th. Neither in the President's message, nor in the text of Section 10 of the Bill, nor in the statement given out by Mr. Rayburn[2] do I find ground for your belief that the Bill seeks to destroy all holding companies. It does not, as I read these texts, seek to destroy holding companies in the gas and electric field, but only those holding companies which control scattered operating companies. I wonder if you won't look at the texts again to see whether or not I am wrong in this interpretation.

On the other point you raise about investment trusts, the President, at least was very clear in his message. As I recall his words, not having the text before me, he said that the essential difference between investment trusts and holding companies was that the managers of the investment trusts passed independent judgment upon the soundness of the management of the companies in which they invested, whereas in the holding companies the functions of management and of independent judgment as to investment were confused. Of course, I don't think that holding companies like the Union Pacific should be destroyed. I don't even think that all electric utility holding companies should be destroyed, but I do think that, while it is probably not wise to raise the issue at this moment, it is true that a holding company of widely scattered properties which attempts to manage them is undesirable.

1. George K. Livermore, an affluent New Yorker, had written Lippmann criticizing the pending public utilities holding company bill.   2. Sam Rayburn, Democratic congressman from Texas since 1913, chairman of the House committee handling the holding company bill, became majority leader in 1937 and Speaker of the House in 1940. In 1935 he was already a power within his party, as he continued to be thereafter.

To Norman H. Davis

March 22, 1935

Dear Norman:

It seems to me that a hopeful point at which we can take a hand in the European crisis is to suggest to the British and the French that this is the moment to stabilize currencies, settle the War debts, and lift the financial blockade under the Johnson Act. If such an agreement could be made it would, without any political entanglement on our part, be an impressive demonstration of common action, and would have a quieting effect on all of Europe. From the French point of view stabilization is an internal necessity, and from the point of view of her defense in case of war the lifting of the Johnson Act, a vital matter. It is positively idiotic of France not to make a very substantial offer on the debts to placate American opinion, and, above all, to protect an indispensable source of supplies in case of war. It seems to me that the British, in spite of their desire to manage sterling independently, ought to feel that the crisis is grave enough to make it worthwhile for them, too, to demonstrate some moral unity with us to remove the stigma of the default, and to open up our capital market in case they become involved in a life and death struggle. All these things can't be said publicly, but if there is any wisdom in Washington, London and Paris it seems to me they ought to be said privately and quickly. The real difficulty, of course, is American public opinion and Congress on the war debts, but I wonder whether the President couldn't persuade even Hiram Johnson and Borah that a concession on the war debts would be a small price to pay for arresting the deflation of gold prices which is now again actively under way throughout the world, and which, if it continues, will set us back more than anything that can happen internally. . . .[1]

1. The tensions in Europe, which had been growing since the Nazis gained control of the German government in 1933, had reached larger proportions in 1935. In January a plebiscite in the Saar, conducted by the League of Nations according to the terms of the Treaty of Versailles, resulted in an overwhelming vote to rejoin that area to Germany rather than France. In March Hitler denounced the clauses of the Versailles Treaty that provided for German disarmament. Though France, Great Britain, and Italy protested that statement, Germany began to rearm. Hitler soon agreed to limit his naval program, a move that placated the British but not the French. For its part, France in May concluded an alliance with the Soviet Union designed to preserve the status quo. But from March onward, Hitler seemed to profit from the Johnson Debt Default Act, which Congress had passed in 1934. It forbade loans to nations that had not paid their war debts, a crippling provision for France and England. Neither could afford to pay those debts; both were going to have to rearm, but Congress was in no mood to alter the legislation, nor was Roosevelt prepared to make an issue of that controversial question. Only in 1936, when Germany had moved troops into the previously demilitarized Rhineland, did the president permit the Treasury Department to negotiate the tripartite stabilization agreement with France and Great Britain. It permitted France a necessary devaluation of the franc without fear of monetary or economic reprisals.

To Bernard Berenson

March 23, 1935

Dear B. B.:

. . . I have spent a lot of time on Toynbee's first three volumes.[1] They are very impressive to me. While they are not brilliantly written, they are so just and so liberal in spirit that they create enormous confidence in his incredible erudition. They are not as much fun to read as Spengler, but they seem infinitely more reliable. Have you looked at them, and if you have, what do you think about them?

I need hardly say that the crisis in Europe seems even more hopeless now than it was when I was there in the autumn. The economic crisis is quite evidently getting worse, and, of course, the military crisis is accentuated by the economic crisis, and, in turn, accentuates it. There is nothing, of course, that the United States can do on the political side, but on the economic side we might do a good deal, and I am very much hoping that in the course of the next six or eight months we shall get currency stabilized and the debt settled. But on the political side I have never felt so gloomy about the future of Europe.

In spite of all that you probably hear from your friends in the United States, we are making fairly good progress, and were it not for the fact that we are under pressure from the European crisis, the prospect would be still better. We are in a serious situation at home where business is very much better than the state of mind of the business men, and it would be ludicrous, if it weren't so sad, to read the financial pages and see production increasing and profits rising while business men declare that the end of the world is at hand. Sometimes I think that American business men, particularly in the big centers, are so shell-shocked by the 1929 crisis that they have lost their self-confidence, and their composure, and if that is true, it is the most dangerous factor in our economy. Apart from this factor the readjustments necessary to recovery are proceeding as rapidly as anyone could have expected.

The President has not lost nearly so much ground as many people think. He has just performed a feat of leadership which in any other period would have been regarded as a political miracle. He has induced Congress to appropriate nearly five billion dollars,[2] without ear-marking any of it for specific expenditure in the congressional districts, and he has persuaded the whole Congress to reject the plea of the American Federation of Labor for an artificially high wage scale. No other American president has ever done a thing like that with the American Congress. My only real fear as regards his leadership is that he has undertaken too many things at this session and that there will be a dangerous congestion of business in about sixty days, but he is amazingly confident, and his political insight has so far proved to be uncanny. . . .

---

1. Arnold J. Toynbee, the celebrated British historian, published his *A Study of History* (London) in twelve volumes that came out in the years 1934–54. A humanist and idealist, Toynbee stood in marked contrast to Oswald Spengler and his prediction of the eclipse of Western civilization in *The Decline of the West*, 2 v. (London, 1918–22), an earlier influential work. **2.** In the $4.8 billion relief act.

To W. Randolph Burgess[1]

March 23, 1935

Dear Randolph:

. . . I thoroughly agree . . . about an all around reduction of 25% in the costs of construction. . . . Such a move is politically impossible unless the initiative is taken by the business men. Do you think there is any possibility that the steel, cement, lumber, et cetera, industries would come forward with such a proposal? I think if they would they would not only do a great thing for recovery, but an even greater thing for their own moral standing in the country. It is very evident that the interest in "planning" has practically disappeared entirely in Washington, and that interest is now centered upon the old-fashioned American attack on monopoly. I don't know what will come out of the N.R.A. hearings, but it looks as if Congress would seek not only to restore the anti-trust laws, but to put new teeth in them. A proposal by the industries supplying construction materials to reduce their prices would be not only a sound move at this time, but a very shrewd one. . . .

1. W. Randolph Burgess, vice president of the Federal Reserve Bank of New York.

To Milton Handler[1]

March 26, 1935

Dear Mr. Handler:

. . . I was not, of course, as you recognized, analyzing the Wagner Bill, but I mean to do that shortly, and when I do I shall dwell upon Section 9-A, which, in my opinion, is totally unworkable, and will cause a great deal of trouble. This section says that the representatives selected for the purpose of collective bargaining by the majority of the employees shall be the exclusive representatives of all the employees. If you will read again the Opinion of the National Labor Relations Board in the Houde Case you will see that the Board recognized the difficulty here which this Bill does not recognize, namely, that representatives may be chosen by a "mere plurality of the votes cast, or by a majority of the votes cast, but by less than a majority of all employees entitled to vote." The elections in the automobile industry show that this is precisely the situation that is likely to develop in the big unorganized industries, and the Bill, it seems to me, is extremely unrealistic in assuming that elections will produce representatives of a clear majority. The Section is not thought out, and yet it is the vital one of the whole Bill. It will lead Labor to believe that the choice in an election must be limited to the Union ticket and some one other ticket, whereas, if the elections are really fair, there may be many tickets, and no majority. The result will be either another long dispute such as we have now over Section 7-A, or a vast disillusionment on the part of Labor because it is not getting what it thought it was going to get.[2]

I have one other serious objection to the Bill, and that is that it confers only rights and recognizes no duties. The Houde Opinion is far more realistic and honest. It recognizes that there are . . . abuses of privileges by Unions. . . .

1. Professor Milton Handler of the Columbia Law School, a leading arbitrator in labor disputes.   **2.** As finally enacted, Section 9-A of the Wagner Labor Relations Act of 1935 stipulated that "representatives designated or selected for the purposes of collective bargaining by the majority of all the employees . . . shall be the exclusive representatives of all the employees. . . ." That phraseology conformed to Lippmann's argument in this letter, took into account the opinion he cited, and eliminated the ambiguity inherent in Section 7-A of the National Industrial Recovery Act, to which he referred. The act of 1935 did not address itself to the issue Lippmann raised in the next paragraph of this letter.

To Stevens Werner[1]

March 29, 1935

Dear Sir:

. . . I do not accept your statement of the justification of free speech. I do not believe that "under free speech truth is supposed to automatically conquer falsehood." History shows clearly, it seems to me, that falsehoods often conquer truth. The reason for free speech is not that truth is automatically victorious under it but that there is a chance to correct error.

Of course I admit that free speech won't always work. It won't work if the other fellow draws a gun and says he will kill me if I don't agree with him and, therefore, my argument is that free speech can be extended only to men who won't draw guns. . . . Free speech in actual life depends upon certain rules of the game and the most important of them is a willingness to continue free speech. When men appear who say that they will argue with you once and then never permit you to argue with them again they render the rules of the game unworkable and their force has to be met with equivalent force.

1. Stevens Werner of Ithaca, New York.

To Hamilton Fish Armstrong

March 30, 1935

Dear Hamilton:

. . . A system of collective security having no real legislative powers can not in any expansive sense hope to alter the status quo. It must in its very essence freeze the status quo in all its essentials. And it must, therefore, expect every so often to be faced with what amounts to a revolution by the dissatisfied backers. Some of these revolutions it will suppress; some of them will be successful, and when they are successful a new system of collective security will be imposed for a time. The only hope of preventing these revolutions lies in the formula which Wilson aimed at but couldn't carry through, namely, the reduction of national frontiers to a level where they mark cultural rather than economic boundaries. In short the ideal of permanent peace through collective securities would require essentially free trade.

To say all this is to be obviously very pessimistic and, frankly, I am. I have ceased hoping for permanent peace and now have reduced my hopes to the idea of long periods of tranquillity such as the world knew in the Victorian Age. It is possible that we might have such an era once the central European issue is decided by war or by revolution.

Isn't this horrible? . . .

To Cordell Hull

April 2, 1935

Dear Mr. Secretary:

I have been thinking about the contribution which the United States might make towards the preservation of peace in Europe and I am writing to tell you the tentative conclusions which I have come to. I assume that a direct intervention in Europe is impossible, would be ineffective and is undesirable. I assume, too, that for the time being the preservation of peace depends upon the political and moral unity of the allied coalition. No permanent peace, of course, can rest upon such a foundation but in order to avert immediate dangers and create a sufficient sense of security to put the people of Europe in a state of mind to consider more permanent solutions, the reconstruction of the coalition is the only practicable method. At least in what follows I use this as a premise.

One of the most serious weaknesses of the coalition is that Russia is engaged on two fronts. This not only weakens Russia's position in Europe but carries with it the threat that if war broke out in Europe it would extend to Asia, thus involving us doubly in all the dangers of neutrality. It seems to me, therefore, that our greatest political contribution must lie in trying to find a solution of the Far East problem good enough to last a few years at least. This would involve a willingness to reconsider our Manchurian policy, a willingness, in fact, to accept the accomplished fact if it can be made the basis of a general stabilization of relations between Japan, Russia, China and ourselves. It seems to me just possible, and perhaps even probable, that Japan would, after a settlement of the Manchurian question and after a naval agreement, do what Italy has done within the past year, namely, turn from being an agitator in the family of nations to a defender of the existing international order. If that should happen, it would not only strengthen the forces of peace in Europe but it would greatly reduce our own risks in case of war. I think we ought to consider with the utmost seriousness and without too much fear of changing our minds, the desirability of exploring directly with the Japanese full settlement of the outstanding issues. . . .

To Russell C. Leffingwell

April 2, 1935

Dear Russell:

I read your testimony before the Senate Committee at least two weeks before you sent it to me which proves that I am a good and faithful student of your teachings. I don't admit that I have abandoned the cause or even that it is lost. Where I think we do differ is as to the political conditions necessary to freer trade. The abstract argument is unanswerable to me but I have convinced myself that the reduction of tariffs is a political possibility only when a period of rising prices has made the high cost of living a dominant issue. I think that one can roughly demonstrate from our own tariff history that tariffs rise during periods of falling prices and fall during periods of rising prices. If you will take our significant tariff acts since 1819, I think they bear out pretty well this generalization. To go back no further than our lifetime, we had the McKinley tariffs at the end of the deflation of the 70's, 80's, and 90's. We had the Underwood tariff after 15 years of rising prices. We had the Fordney tariff after the first post war deflation and the Smoot tariff in the midst of the second. Britain almost went to protection under Chamberlain at the end of the nineteenth century. Then the issue died. It revived in the midst of the present deflation. Moreover the consistently rising barriers to trade all over the world are clearly due more than to anything else to deflation and the attempt to protect domestic industry and domestic currency against the deflation. It seems to me that until we reverse the deflationary process, not merely at home but in the whole world, we can not make a turnabout in the present process of economic nationalism. That is why I continue to harp upon the desirability of stabilization plus devaluation in the gold block. I believe that enormous enhancement of the gold stocks due to devaluation and the end of gold hoarding due to stabilization must inevitably produce a very great rise in gold prices and that it is this rise in gold prices which alone can end the era of economic nationalism. The reason is very simple. Today in Congress and in every other parliament the producer is dominant and is given protection. If prices rose, profits would go with them. The producer would be no longer an object of pity and then it would become the consumer's turn to cry out against the high cost of living. It is in that atmosphere that tariffs could be reduced.

In other words if you look at the problem not as one in economics alone but in political economy, you will come, I think, to the conclusion that reduction of tariffs is a hopeless ideal until the prices have risen.

To Joseph P. Kennedy[1]

April 29, 1935

Dear Joe:

. . . You can well imagine that I liked the President's speech last night. For it came close enough to doing what I hoped he would do — namely, to name the whole program for the rest of the session. I liked also the approach to the Work Relief Bill. I think he is dead right in assuming that the way to get that money spent honestly and with a minimum of trouble is to perform the whole operation as publicly as possible in every community, inviting criticism, demanding criticism, from start to finish. The thing to do is to make the country feel that it is spending that money. That, I take it, is the spirit of the enterprise. And I suppose it will be somebody's business in the whole organization to be looking for trouble all the time and exposing it before anyone else can expose it.

I think, also, the President is quite right in wanting to get both the utility and the banking bill settled and out of the way now. Neither bill is anywhere nearly so important as the advocates and the critics say it is. And it would be ridiculous to quarrel over how the i's are to be dotted and the t's crossed. The important thing is to put both bills behind us as effectively and in much the same way as we have put the Securities Act and the Stock Exchange Act behind us.

It seems to me that the only serious thing to worry about is foreign exchange and its effect upon our price level and the security markets. It is startling how closely the movement of industrial securities and of the sensitive commodities correspond with the movement of sterling. It seems pretty evident that the bad slump which we had from Washington's birthday to the third week in March was primarily due to the fall of sterling. And that the revival since then has corresponded with the return of sterling to somewhere near its own parity after Belgium went off the gold standard and capital began to seek refuge among them. Incidentally, that same slump in the markets coincided with the general impression throughout the country that the President's prestige was lost and his leadership impaired.

To my mind the most important thing about that slump was that the fall in sterling occurred at a season in the year when, by all precedence, sterling ought to be very strong. That makes it look very much like something that has been engineered. It also suggests that we may come into a very dangerous period from June to the autumn, for that is when sterling is normally weak. If, in that period, the British, who apparently want to put down sterling, have the assistance of its natural weakness, we may run into another depression here which would, to some important degree, neutralize the stimulating effect of the Works program when that gets under way in the autumn. It seems to me, therefore, that the most important thing of all in the future is to make up our minds that we won't let the dollar and sterling get far away from their old parity and that to do that we ought to be prepared to take any one of a number of measures, such as embargoing gold and pegging the dollar to sterling, or sterling to the dollar, or selling gold. I wish I felt more certain that this whole problem of currencies and exchanges was thoroughly understood in the Treasury. I'd feel very confident of the outlook if I felt sure of them.

1. Joseph P. Kennedy, at this time chairman of the Securities and Exchange Commission, resigned from that position in September 1935 and became chairman of the United States Maritime Commission in 1937 and ambassador to Great Britain later that year. He was the father of nine children, among them President John F. Kennedy, Senator Robert F. Kennedy, and Senator Edward Kennedy.

To Lewis W. Douglas[1]

May 8, 1935

Dear Lew:

. . . Your reference to the per capita tax here and in England was just as misleading as the usual reference to the per capita debt in Great Britain and here. Surely the true estimate of the weight of the debt or of the tax payment is the proportion it bears to the national income, which is the fund out of which it has to be paid. Now in accordance with the figures I have: in 1933 the interest and amortization charges on our national debt amounted to about 2½ percent of our national income while in England they amounted to between 8 and 9 percent of the national income. Moreover, in 1932, the debt of all our public bodies was about 88 percent of our annual national income while the debt of all public bodies in England was about 237 percent. I understand that the debt of the Australian commonwealth and the Australian state governments is almost three times the national income. . . .

1. After resigning in August 1934 as budget director, Lewis Douglas had become a vocal opponent of New Deal policy, especially of the pending revenue bill of 1935.

To Corliss Lamont[1]

May 16, 1935

Dear Corliss:

Thanks for sending me your pamphlet on *Socialist Planning in Soviet Russia.* I have read not only the passages in which you dispose of me but the whole pamphlet as well.

Perhaps the only point at which I was a little startled was to find on page 29 that I am disqualified because I have, as you put it, "never bothered to go to Soviet Russia." The implication is, I take it, that if I had gone to Russia as you have that I would be as well qualified to discuss Russia as you are. I don't profess to be a specialist about Soviet Russia but I do know something about the reporting of affairs in a foreign country, and I have learned that a few weeks' trip such as you have taken to Russia is no qualification whatever. I'd like to go to Russia and sometime I hope to do so. But when I go, and if I spend no more time there than you have spent there, and if I speak no more Russian than you speak when I get there, I shall not come home imagining that because I was a tourist in Russia I am an expert on Russia.

I know that you would like me to be frank about this pamphlet and so I shall be. I have read as many good accounts as I could lay my hands on in English of the system of planning in Russia and your account seems to me one of the least satisfactory. I cannot find out from it how any of the vital economic decisions are made, particularly at the most crucial point of all, which is the investment of new capital. You assure the reader that "the Soviet system insures a balanced and even flow of capital into the channels most useful and important." But what I'd like to know is who decides what is most useful and important and by what standards is the flow balanced and kept even. There must be some system, though I imagine it's not a very good system, since Soviet production appears to develop shortages at so many different points in the system. But you don't even approach the question, and yet that's a vital question in all planning.

Nor can I find in your pamphlet any discussion of the very vital decision which was apparently taken to increase production of certain kinds of capital goods at the expense of consumers' goods. What's the good of pretending to write about planning unless you tell the reader how the planning is done and what the planning is? It's all very well to describe the meetings of the workers in the factories and all that, but surely you can't imagine that you've said anything real when you say that there is a "collective brain of the entire country." As a writer of Soviet pamphlets you may believe that but as a philosopher you know that those are empty words. . . .

1. Corliss Lamont, the wealthy and articulate publicist, champion of civil liberties, and in the 1930s, consistent apologist for the Soviet Union.

To Joseph P. Kennedy

May 22, 1935

Dear Joe:

I thought the bonus message was a hundred percent.[1]

It seems to me the next big job of public speaking that needs to be done is a message or a speech after Congress has finished its program in which there are three themes:

(1) That the New Deal is now on the statute books; that in its scope it is the largest body of progressive legislation ever brought together in this coun-

try in so short a time; that it covers every major promise made in the campaign, and that now the job is to administer the laws wisely, and to digest them.

(2) That barring unforeseen emergencies, the government has now set in motion all the measures that can wisely and prudently be taken to promote a recovery; that these measures involve a net deficit of x amount; that this deficit is well within the means and credit of the country, but that no addition to it would serve any useful purpose, and that the deficits already approved represent the maximum deficit of this Administration; that it is the intention of the President next winter to propose a program designed to bring the budget into balance.

(3) That the combination of the reform program and the recovery program has made more secure free institutions and private enterprise, and that no believer in either has any ground for fear.

A message of this sort at the end of the session would, I think, prove enormously stimulating and reassuring, and would be politically very effective. It wouldn't be a question of giving up reform for recovery, but of pointing out the immense reforms that have been achieved and at the same time making people feel that they had a pretty good idea as to what the new rules of the game are.

1. Roosevelt had vetoed a bill to pay at once the bonus certificates earlier awarded to American veterans of World War I.

To Franklin D. Roosevelt

June 4, 1935

Dear Mr. President:

I'd like to make this suggestion: that you have the New Deal legislation examined at once for doubtful points and delegated power and interstate commerce and that if necessary amendments be drafted and introduced at this session.

What I have in mind is not merely to protect the legislation against judicial destruction, but principally to seize the opportunity of putting Congress on record once again to reaffirm these measures. It seems to me that the moral, political, and psychological effect of a series of big votes reaffirming the major policies would impress the country and the Court, would completely answer the people who are saying that the whole New Deal has been shattered, would put an end to all the talk that you are trying to upset the Constitution by indirection and would put the reactionary Republicans and reactionary Democrats clearly on record once again as to where they stand on the agricultural bill, the securities act, etc. etc. It would be equivalent to asking and obtaining a new vote of confidence from Congress.[1]

1. Lippmann was writing about the series of decisions of the Supreme Court in 1935 which had found unconstitutional much early New Deal legislation, including the National Industrial Recovery Act, the Railway Pension Act and the Bituminous Coal Act. In those and other decisions, the court had rendered a narrow reading of the federal commerce clause and of the permissible delegation of executive and of rule-making authority. Taken together the decisions called into possible question the constitutionality of the legislative achievements of 1935. Though the president did not undertake the exercise Lippmann here recommended, he did later attack the court, as he had already questioned some of its rulings. For its part, the court in 1937 and thereafter, partly influenced by Roosevelt's new appointees, underwent a major change in its opinions, which sustained the later legislation.

To Hamilton Fish Armstrong

June 25, 1935

Dear Hamilton:

Your letter of June 10 just reached me, and I share your apprehensions. However, in my opinion the fundamental danger in Europe is the internal weakness of France, arising from what looks to me like suicidal devotion to the gold standard. If the internal tension in France could be overcome as it has been in Belgium, and France could feel vigorous and strong, the Stresa combination would have a wholly different prospect.[1] France is the keystone, and if the keystone is internally weakened, the arch won't stand. The reason France has to plead is that her government is weak, and her government is weak because it is attempting the impossible.

Now for the six words about Roosevelt and N.R.A. You know what I think about N.R.A. and I won't go into that but I'll give you my view of the political consequences of the Court's decision. Thanks to Johnson's ballyhoo, thanks to the accident that the codes were called the National Recovery Administration, the public as a whole identifies the New Deal with N.R.A. To my infinite dismay, Roosevelt himself apparently does that, which is by far the most discouraging thing about him that I have learned since he came into office. The result was that when N.R.A. was knocked out, both Roosevelt and the country took the view that the New Deal had been 80 percent knocked out. This involved a tremendous psychological temporary set-back for Roosevelt's prestige.

On the other hand, my view is that not only intrinsically but politically the destruction of N.R.A. was Roosevelt's greatest stroke of luck since 1933. First, it has relieved him of the embarrassment of trying to enforce codes that were breaking down of their own inherent foolishness. In this respect he is in the position that Hoover would have been in if the Supreme Court had knocked out the Eighteenth Amendment in 1929. Second, the destruction of N.R.A.

will, I think, accelerate the recovery which was strongly under way anyhow. Third, both businessmen and labor will now remember the benefits that they had under N.R.A. and forget the defects and Roosevelt will become the inevitable beneficiary of this feeling. The Republicans over-played their hand, exulted so loudly that Roosevelt drifted easily into the position of champion of the common man against unreconstructed and unregenerated wealth. He was quick to take advantage of that by pushing through his other reform measures, capped by the taxation measure. Unless another fit of mid-summer madness strikes him, and I don't guarantee that it won't, he is now in the incredibly strong position where in about a month he will have completed the most comprehensive program of reform ever achieved in this country in any Administration, and at the same time he is well set for a very substantial business recovery. If he wants to play the cards that are now in his hand, I believe that he can come to the election next autumn with reform and recovery both achieved, with the currency stabilization in sight, and with a budget balanced definitely in sight. What the Republicans would have left to complain about under these conditions I can't imagine. The thing that will prevent Roosevelt from achieving that result, I think, is that he is restless and would get bored with his job if he didn't have something big under way, and the idea merely of administering what he has achieved doesn't appeal to him. So instead of digging in for a year, which would be the sensible thing to do, he will probably start a new putsch just when the Republicans badly need an issue. . . .

1. France had called the conference that met in Stresa in April 1935 to respond to German rearmament and potential threats to Austria. There Italy joined France and England in protesting Germany's course, but Italian intentions to annex Ethiopia had become patent by late June, so that the Stresa accord had effectively collapsed even before Italy actually invaded Ethiopia in October.

To John W. Davis

July 1, 1935

Dear John:

. . . I should agree that the similarity in the policies of Hoover and Roosevelt is in no sense conclusive evidence. But when I note that the essentials of the policy have been adopted in practically all countries, I am personally persuaded that, whether we like it or not, responsibility for the successful operation of a nation's economy is now just as much a function of government as is the national defense. Personally, I wish it were not the case, for I can see the enormous and perhaps insuperable difficulties, but the tendency seems to me world-wide, cumulative and irresistible. Nor are the reasons for the tendency hard to discover. When, on the one hand, you have large populations dependent for their living upon an intricate economic mechanism, and, on the other hand, you have those populations conscious of their political power, there is nothing, I think, that can withstand their insistence that somehow or other the economic machine must work pretty well. This may be, as you say, beyond the capacity and power of governments, but I do not think that will prevent the mass of the people from insisting that governments attempt it.

Personally, I should much prefer a world in which governments did not have to attempt so tremendous a task. But I don't think we live in that kind of world any longer.

To Hugh R. Wilson[1]

July 30, 1935

Dear Hugh:

. . . In so far as I have "positive thoughts," they are that it would be a mistake to proceed on the assumptions of the Wilson era at a time when those assumptions have no reality. I should frankly therefore favor a system of alliances in Europe to maintain the peace. Through the League, if possible, but maintained as alliances unequivocally. For ourselves, the thing I am most interested in is a political understanding with Japan which I think may be possible, and if possible, would be extremely desirable. I think we have got to swallow the Stimson doctrine,[2] which I favored at the time, which hasn't worked. I think we have got to give up the idea that we're the guardians of China, and I think that we have got to limit and redefine the area of our interests in the Pacific. In other words, it seems to me that it is better to do a good job under the methods of the old diplomacy than a bad one on the assumption of a new one. . . .

1. Hugh R. Wilson, then American minister to Switzerland. 2. Of nonrecognition of Japanese domination of Manchuria.

To Marriner S. Eccles

August 6, 1935

Dear Governor Eccles:

. . . Of course I do not think you have been stubborn. What I think about the political strategy of the battle is, in essence, that the Banking Bill is much the most important piece of legislation before Congress, that it deserves to be given a central place in the President's legislative program, and that the whole public sponsorship of the Bill should not have been left to fall on you alone. Had the President given the Bill the support it deserves, he, rather than you, could have accepted amendments that it would be obviously impossible for you to approve publicly, such as the withdrawal of the Secretary of the Treasury from the Board. . . .[1]

1. Eccles, as head of the Federal Reserve Board, approved that amendment, though he had fought hard, and largely succeeded, to defend the banking bill of 1935 — an amendment to the original Federal Reserve Act — from attacks by conservative Democrats, especially Senator Carter Glass, and Republicans. The act as finally passed accomplished its major original purposes, including the location of authority over open market operations under the Federal Reserve Board, but Eccles was nevertheless disappointed, as he revealed in his memoir, *Beckoning Frontiers* (New York, 1951), Part III. For his part, Lippmann did not regularly endow the legislation with the importance he attributed to it here; compare his letter to Joseph P. Kennedy, April 29, 1935, sup.

To Edward B. Sheldon[1]

September 19, 1935

Dear Sheldon:

Your letter came just after I had returned from a visit to Hyde Park where I spent about four hours with the President.

In so far as he was explicit about his intentions I felt reasonably satisfied about the immediate future. He does seem to have made up his mind that he has gone as far as he should go with the reforms that require important mental readjustments by the people of the country. But I was rather disturbed to find him so very tired. I thought he was dangerously tired, and that if he were confronted with very difficult decisions at this moment, his judgment couldn't be depended upon and that it might lead to a severe nervous breakdown. He is, of course, planning a vacation on a cruiser, and that may restore him. But what I am afraid of is that he is suffering not so much from physical weariness as from a moral depression which reflects itself in his physical condition. He will be put to a very severe test in the next few months because the attack on him will be relentless. And I don't know whether his inner resources are sufficient to meet it. His good humor up to the present time has gone along with success and popularity. Whether he can retain the buoyancy that the public thinks he has naturally when he isn't succeeding and isn't very popular I am a little doubtful. I thought, while I was with him on Monday, of Buchan's interesting comments on Cromwell's nervous and physical condition before he made great decisions and his good health after he had made them. . . .[2]

1. Edward B. Sheldon, prolific playwright and Harvard contemporary of Lippmann's. 2. Lippmann was referring to Sir John Buchan (Baron Tweedsmuir), Scottish statesman, novelist, and biographer of Sir Walter Scott and Oliver Cromwell, among others. In 1935 Buchan became governor general of Canada. But Lippmann made, perhaps, too much of his psychological theorizing about Roosevelt. The president was genuinely tired, as he himself knew. "I was so tired," he later told Henry Morgenthau, Jr., "that I would have enjoyed seeing you cry or . . . sticking pins into people and hurting them"; see John M. Blum, *From the Morgenthau Diaries*, v. 1 (Boston, 1959), p. 257.

To Arthur Sweetser

October 8, 1935

Dear Arthur:

. . . I am writing today after hearing that the Council has actually decided that Italy has broken the Covenant, and I feel that the event is of such significance that it is impossible for anyone to measure its consequences at this time. Personally, I confess that the League has gone further in this matter than I thought it would go in the light of the Manchurian affair. If it actually goes through to the end and succeeds not only in stopping the war but in achieving an acceptable solution, it will probably have revolutionized the whole outlook for international affairs. But it is foolish to write of these things when this letter will be read after so many other things have happened. . . .[1]

1. On October 3, Italian forces invaded Ethiopia. On October 7, the Council of the League declared Italy the aggressor and began to prepare sanctions. On November 18, the League voted to apply sanctions against Italy, which therefore terminated economic relations with the sanctioning powers and, undeterred, proceeded with its conquest of Ethiopia, completed in May 1936.

To Ogden L. Mills

October 17, 1935

Dear Ogden:

. . . I wish you would consider turning your attention sometime to a speech answering this question: What did we do wrong in the 1920s and what have we learned from our experience? It seems to me that some such speech from you would greatly clarify public opinion and strengthen your present position. After all, the most pungent public answer to your criticisms is "Well, all this may be true, but look what we got into before 1929. Are we to go back and do over again the things which landed us in this disaster?" It seems to me that the Republican Party must somehow purge itself and get itself into a position where it is not advocating a return to the status quo ante. I know perfectly well that you feel the country made serious mistakes which contributed to the severity of the depression, and it would be easier to agree with your criticism of the New Deal, as I, in fact, do agree substantially, if with it there went some kind of assurance that the Republicans had learned something they didn't know before. It seems to me you occupy a position of peculiar influence at this moment, and I am making this suggestion because I'd like it to be even greater — in fact, as great as possible.

To Hamilton Fish Armstrong

November 9, 1935

Dear Hamilton:

Yesterday I emerged from the dark caverns where I have been writing a book.[1] . . . This has been the first opportunity I have had in nearly five years to concentrate uninterruptedly on something not in the immediate day's news — and it was high time that I did it.

The product is in an extremely raw condition, and is nothing better than an elaborate scenario for a book which remains to be written. But at least I am satisfied that I have cleared up my own mind on several fundamental questions about which I have been confused and uneasy, and for me at least this book, if it's ever finished, will be something in the nature of a positive statement of what I really think about government. I am extremely anxious to show it to you and to talk to you about it. The thing that interests me most in it and will, I think, interest you most is that I have (I think) succeeded in relating domestic and foreign policy organically one to the other. . . .

I have been giving a good deal of thought more or less in connection with this book to the Ethiopian business, and I have some extremely radical doubts as to whether the British are pursuing a far-sighted policy and whether the President and Hull are looking far enough ahead. The thing that troubles me most is the effort to have us "cooperate" in the sanctions by preventing or discouraging the sale of raw materials to Italy.[2] Assuming that we did that in one way or other, either by moral force or by new legislation empowering the President to embargo raw materials. The precedent seems to me extremely dangerous. For we have to assume that Congress will insist that whatever embargoes are placed shall be placed against all belligerents alike. Now suppose that Britain and France became involved in a really first class war with Germany. The precedent we now establish would then become a vital handicap to them and would nullify their sea-power. If what we are after in the long run is to promote peace by supporting the democratic countries, then we must base our policy on the assumption that they will use their sea-power. That means allowing them to cut off their enemy from our supplies while retaining access to them themselves. Under this Ethiopian precedent, if it's carried very far, our embargoes would be a terrible handicap to them. On the other hand, once the precedent is established we cannot, without becoming un-neutral, alter it to remove these disadvantages.

The whole situation would not have arisen if they had closed the Suez Canal or had declared a pacific blockade on Italy. Within the terms of the Congressional mandate we could have acquiesced in that without setting a dangerous precedent for the future. . . .

1. Ultimately *The Good Society* (Boston, 1937).   **2.** In January 1936, Roosevelt condemned Italy, issued a proclamation of neutrality, and imposed a mandatory arms embargo. He believed that embargo would hurt Italy, which had dollars, more than Ethiopia, which did not. But existing neutrality legislation did not cover raw materials, the Italians' main import from the United States, and Roosevelt's request for voluntary restrictions of those materials — a "moral embargo" — had little effect, especially on American oil companies, which increased their shipments to Italy.

To Bernard Berenson

HANDWRITTEN

November 15, 1935

Dear B. B.:

. . . I found Paris infinitely depressed and depressing. There we have crises — one, economic — that awful but usual deflation of a country trying to maintain an excessively high currency; the other the international danger arising from the German re-armament.

The economic crisis seems to be soluble. The other — looking at the parts and their logic — appears insoluble. The Germans will be re-armed in the spring. From the French point of view the question is whether they can hold the Little Entente[1] & make an entente with Italy at the same time, and then, of course, whether they can count on England to stand by the alliances of the status quo. . . .

1. Czechoslovakia, Yugoslavia, and Romania.

To Herbert C. Hoover

January 16, 1936

Dear Mr. Hoover:

. . . I have no other desire than to state your own position not only accurately but sympathetically. In the past year or two I have not only read all your utterances of which the text was available but have studied them with reasonable care. It is probably my fault, but I have been under the honest feeling that they conveyed the distinct impression that the present Administration has been wrong in all important matters from start to finish.[1] I can't remember a passage in which, on an important matter of policy, you distinctly and definitely stated your agreement. Of course I must be mistaken, since you now assure me that that is absolutely untrue. But I would be ever so grateful if you or one of your secretaries would send me a note indicating the passages in your speeches in which you supported measures of the present Administration, or, failing that, a note on the measures which you do, in fact, support. If I had that information, I should want to make public amends. . . .

1. In a letter to Lippmann, Hoover had said he had been sympathetic to some New Deal programs.

To Newton D. Baker

January 22, 1936

Dear Newton:

. . . I am becoming increasingly troubled about the Roosevelt administration.[1] And increasingly, since last spring, I have begun to feel that a situation might develop as a result of a kind of loss of balance where it would be absolutely necessary not to re-elect Mr. Roosevelt. This feeling doesn't rest merely on disagreement with certain of his policies, but with anxiety that the strain of the office, particularly as he has administered it, has produced effects which raise serious doubts as to whether he can remain master of the situation which he is creating.

Whether these anxieties are justified or not I wouldn't attempt to say for certain. But they are sufficiently real to make me feel that I'd like to know what alternatives there are to supporting Mr. Roosevelt for re-election. I should suppose that the same problem confronts you in one form or another, and that you have as strong a distaste as I have for the present leadership of the Republican Party. Of course it is not necessary, nor would it be desirable, to come to a decision now, but I should very much like some advice from you as to how the question ought to be approached.

1. So was Baker. He condemned the New Deal for its "frightful extravagance" and for "wickedness" in the distribution of favor. "Our present government," Baker continued in a letter he wrote a friend in May 1936, "is a government by propaganda and terrorism . . . against the continuance of which I protest with all the vehemence I am capable of"; quoted in Arthur M. Schlesinger, Jr., *The Age of Roosevelt: The Politics of Upheaval* (Boston, 1960), p. 517.

To Arthur N. Holcombe

January 27, 1936

Dear Arthur:

I have been longing for a talk with you in the past forty-eight hours about the political situation which is developing so rapidly.[1] Apparently Roosevelt has determined to burn his bridges so far as the conservative Democrats go and to stake his chances for reelection on an appeal to sectional and class feeling. I put it baldly but that seems to me what it comes to. For if he were bidding for the support of people like Smith, Byrd,[2] and the like he would, of course, have to make a very different popular appeal. The effect of that, it seems to me, is to create an immense and, I think, increasing opposition which is entirely inchoate, without principle and without common conviction. It would contain all ranges of opinion from the Borah type of agrarian Progressives on the one side to the blackest type of reactionary Republicans on the other. The fact that they have no common principles will mean, I fear, that they will appeal to passion and primitive emotions and if they win, which I think not at all unlikely, we may very well face a period of severe reaction.

Have you any ideas as to the course which a sober and critical friend of the New Deal can take under these circumstances? I fear that the time has gone by when the actual course of the Roosevelt Administration can be effectively influenced. . . .

1. On January 25, 1936, at the Mayflower Hotel in Washington, an audience of some two thousand anti-New Deal Democrats attended a dinner that Al Smith addressed. In a shocking speech, Smith identified the New Deal with Marx and Lenin. "Let me give this solemn warning," he concluded, "there can be only one capital, Washington or Moscow. There can be only one atmosphere of government, the clean, pure, fresh air of free America, or the foul breath of communistic Russia." Pierre Du Pont, chairman of the board of the Du Pont corporation, considered the speech "perfect." It was so, in one sense, for Roosevelt, for the hyperbole of Smith and the similar temper of his audience — largely men of great wealth — provided a timely tonic for the president's reputation among Americans less well-to-do and a vulnerable target for the president's attack. **2.** Senator Harry F. Byrd, a conservative Democrat from Virginia, Episcopalian, Mason, Elk, and successful apple farmer.

To Bernard Berenson

February 7, 1936

Dear B. B.:

. . . Here at home there is a great deal of political excitement but since actual conditions are considerably better and continue to improve the issues do not have that acute character which belongs to a period of crisis. The people are far less excited than the politicians. It seems to be much too early to have any confident opinion as to whether Roosevelt will be reelected. The astonishing thing is that there should be any doubt about it. But there is some doubt. There has been ever since last summer when, as I see it, he lost control of himself and of the situation and put an intolerable strain upon the patience and good nature of the country. Nevertheless he is still very strong and if the election were held today I should have no doubt whatever about his reelection. The doubt arises from the fact that he has been losing support and that there is a certain tendency for the losses to come at an accelerating rate which if continued for six or eight months would be enough to defeat him.

It looks now as if the Republicans would nominate Governor Landon of Kansas.[1] They could do far worse and there isn't any sign that they could do any better. . . .

1. The Republicans did later nominate Governor Alfred M. Landon of Kansas as their presidential candidate.

To John Cudahy[1]

February 21, 1936

Dear Cudahy:

I am very much interested in your letter of January 30th about neutrality. I am afraid, however, that one point I failed to make clear. I have no objections to — in fact I am in favor of — renouncing the freedom of the seas and the protection of American traders during a great war and I believe that by renouncing it we can avoid the entanglements which drew us into the Napoleonic War and the World War. My quarrel with the neutrality legislation (now tabled incidentally) was not over this point but over the second step which was not merely to refuse protection to American traders but to forbid them to do much trading.[2] This seems to me unnecessary and unwise, positively dangerous and likely actually to provoke wars in the world for if we who are the greatest source of supplies in the world announce that we will refuse to sell supplies to those who can come and get them and can pay for them, we have put a premium upon heavy armament in time of peace and an extreme penalty upon disarmament. Moreover we shall have greatly undermined the authority of the League which depends upon sea power for such an embargo policy would strike at the root of British and French security and would compel those countries either to build up enormous armaments immediately, much greater than they contemplate, or to form military alliances with other countries to supply them or to become powerless to resist if and when an aggression takes place. Moreover, once we had adopted that policy we should be powerless to resist insult and injury from any quarter of the globe because no nation would have anything to fear or hope from us. . . .

1. John Cudahy, Harvard classmate of Lippmann's, since 1933 United States ambassador to Poland.   2. The mandatory arms embargo imposed by the Neutrality Act of 1935, passed in August of that year, was to expire the end of February 1936. The bill then pending in Congress, once removed from the table, in its final form extended the other provisions of the 1935 legislation until May 1, 1937, and also banned credits to belligerents. The 1936 act left it to the president to decide that a war existed before the measure could be invoked.

To Mabel Dodge Luhan[1]

March 1, 1936

Dear Mabel:

You will have to give me a few days more before I send you the letters that you may publish. It is obvious that all of them can't be published for I would never consent to publishing private and immature attacks on or expressions of contempt for living persons. In other words I have to go over the letters with some care and do considerable selecting and editing and that will take me a little time as I am myself writing a book. However, I will get off something to you within a week.

I might as well tell you that I don't really like the idea of reprinting the private letters of a living person or of publishing private conversations and if it weren't you who is doing the thing I should just say a blank "no" but as it is I am going to do my best to give you enough letters to be of whatever use to you that you think they may be.

1. Mabel Dodge Luhan had asked to quote some of Lippmann's letters to her, as she did according to his terms, in her book *Movers and Shakers* (New York, 1936), the third volume of her memoirs. She had married Antonio Luhan, her fourth husband, in 1923.

To Arthur W. Page[1]

March 4, 1936

Dear Arthur:

I agree entirely and I have felt that way for many years about the party system in America. It has always seemed to me strange that men like Nicholas Murray Butler[2] should so completely miss the point and talk about the desirability of dividing the country into two parties with sharply differentiated principles. It is utterly incompatible with a federal form of government and would be the most dangerous development that could occur. Our present system forces us to fight out our vital differences in small areas and insures that necessary compromise on national lines which a great country under a federal system absolutely has to have.

1. Arthur W. Page was then vice president of the American Telephone and Telegraph Company.   2. President Nicholas Murray Butler of Columbia University, for many years a regular apologist for the conservative wing of the Republican party.

To Victor A. Cazalet

March 5, 1936

My dear Victor:

. . . I am glad you saw Vandenberg.[1] While he is a much less likely candidate than he was a month ago he will grow in influence though as you easily detected he is a pretty third rate fellow. The best of the Republican prospects is Landon whom I have never met but who has something I think of the Baldwin[2] quality — a kind of instinctive niceness of mind and decency of manner. Also he has his intellectual and emotional roots in the Mississippi Valley that is near the real center of gravity so that while he would be a conservative his conservatism would be authentic and popular rather than the kind of thing which passes for conservatism in Wall Street or on Long Island or at Palm Beach.

I am following affairs in Europe as best as I can and with intense interest. The one most reassuring fact in the whole outlook to me is your rearmament. It seems so obvious that I don't see how anyone can dispute it that the only hope of Europe lies in having Britain preponderantly strong, so strong that no one can question her strength. . . .

1. Arthur H. Vandenberg, Republican senator from Michigan since 1928, in 1936 a conservative isolationist but a fading candidate for his party's presidential nomination, later — during and after World War II — a leading Republican internationalist. 2. Prime Minister Stanley Baldwin of Great Britain.

To Lewis W. Douglas

March 16, 1936

Dear Lew:

. . . I wonder how the project for a statement of principles is coming along.[1] My impression is that it is more important than ever that liberal Democrats should make themselves felt for it begins to look to me more and more as if the Republicans were too demoralized to organize an effective opposition. What with prosperity coming on and with Roosevelt shrewdly cutting his losses and the Republicans without a candidate who appeals to the popular imagination and with no program whatever we are in great danger of getting into a situation where no effective opposition to the collectivist side of the New Deal will be made. I have a strong feeling that the Liberty League[2] and Old Guard Republican attack on the New Deal has overplayed its hand and that there is a wide and strong reaction against it on the part of people who simply won't believe that with things getting better everything that Roosevelt has done is as bad as those critics say it is. The danger now is that the country for lack of an effective opposition won't be made to see the things that are really bad. . . .

1. Douglas was drafting a statement of principle intended to be a creative rallying point against the New Deal. 2. The Liberty League had been founded by such conservatives as John J. Raskob, the Du Ponts, and Alfred P. Sloan of General Motors to oppose Roosevelt. Its members reflected the views of the reactionary group to whom Al Smith had spoken at the Mayflower Hotel in January 1936. The league had become a political liability, so much so that the Republicans persuaded it not to embrace Landon.

To Lewis W. Douglas

March 27, 1936

Dear Lew:

Thank you for your letter. I am delighted that the project is making headway. It is a very important one. It looks more and more as if the real fight would have to be made within the Democratic party, though I haven't closed my mind to the possibility of crossing the line but there is very little over there to invite men who think as we do and there are really more people who take our view of things still in the Democratic Party than elsewhere.

My present notion is that the best time to hold the meeting would be around about the first of June when everybody is politically minded. A declaration at that time under impressive circumstances might have some influence on both platforms and would have considerable influence if it is properly done on the campaign arguments.

The declaration should be so framed that it will cut a cleavage in the sympathies of the men now in power in Washington. It should be a declaration which men like Hull and even Wallace would genuinely subscribe to. It also should be one which would cut through the Republican alignment, engaging the sympathies of men like Ogden Mills. That isn't at all an impossible thing to do. One of the ways to do it is to avoid putting anyone in a position where his personal or party allegiances are at odds with sincere convictions. We must make it easy for those to agree with us who really do agree with us, and we must build bridges over which those who have strayed from their convictions can retreat. . . . The selection of men to occupy a prominent place in the proceeding is, of course, a vital matter. I should draw the line absolutely at the Liberty League and all associations with it. This would exclude Al Smith but not men like Joe Ely.[1] Al shouldn't be invited; first of all because he doesn't believe in the 1932 platform in any of its fundamental principles and second because his presence at such a meeting would confuse everything with his threat to "take a walk." The men I hope to see in the front would be Carter Glass, Harry Byrd, Newton Baker and, if he could face the partisan music, Ogden Mills. . . .

1. Joseph B. Ely, Democratic governor of Massachusetts, 1931–35.

To Lewis W. Douglas

April 16, 1936

Dear Lew:

Here is the draft I told you about.[1]

1. Enclosed with this note was the following draft, which Lippmann had prepared. In his public statements, Douglas adopted substantially the same reasoning, which had long been his own.

(Tentative) DRAFT OF DECLARATION OF PRINCIPLES

Since the time is at hand when political parties and their candidates must once again declare their principles and their purposes, we venture to submit to our fellow-citizens a statement of our views. Although the signers of this declaration are normally and traditionally members of the Democratic Party, we are not an organized political faction seeking by force of members to impose our views upon either political party. Nor are we seeking to organize such a faction. We are stating our views in the hope that they will find favor and that they will have some influence upon the party platforms and the declarations of the candidates.

It is our conviction that in certain fundamental respects the course of national policy in the whole post-war period is jeopardizing the highest interests of the American people, that it has marked a departure from the enduring principles of American society, that it is profoundly reactionary, however much its sponsors may imagine it to be enlightened and progressive. We believe that the time has come to challenge the policies which, under the twelve years of Republican rule, fostered the growth of private monopoly subsidized by exclusive privilege of tariff protection, which then, under three years of Democratic rule, has sought to check, balance, and supplement these private monopolies by state-created monopolies based on more legal privileges and more subsidies. We see perfectly well that if certain favored industrial interests are to enjoy privileges and immunities which enable them to exercise monopolistic or quasi-monopolistic control in the markets for goods and for labor, then as a matter of simple justice, similar privileges and immunities must be extended to farmers, to wage-earners, and to other groups. But we hold that this course of policy, begun under the Republicans and continued under the Democrats can lead only to the progressive impoverishment of the people and the destruction of their liberties.

It must lead to their impoverishment, we believe, because the whole array of privileges is in the last analysis a system for restricting the production of wealth in order to provide monopolistic profits for favored groups. By means of exclusive tariffs, by means of devices for reducing production and raising prices, a premium is put upon the less efficient use of the nation's capital and its labor, a penalty is laid upon the free exchange of the most efficient work. However much particular interests may argue that they have benefited by these privileges, the nation as a whole is injured and its progress towards a higher material standard of life arrested.

This course of policy must lead to the destruction of the liberties of the people because these powerful private monopolies, in business, agriculture, and in labor, can be restrained and regulated only by an excessively powerful government. The evidence is already at hand which demonstrates, we believe, that in order to have a government strong enough to cope with the great privileged interests which it has fostered, it becomes necessary to delegate powers to a bureaucracy, — powers to legislate, to tax, and to spend, — over which neither Congress nor the voters can exercise an effective check. The record shows, too, we are convinced, that this enormous concentration of power in the hands of appointed officials cannot be exercised wisely, that it is beyond the capacities of men to use that much power successfully, that it can lead only to waste, confusion, bureaucratic rigidity, and the loss of personal liberty.

Holding these views, we cannot subscribe to the view that the monopolistic tendencies, which had official sanction from 1920 to 1932, were conducive to material efficiency, and we cannot subscribe to the view of those New Dealers who claim that their experiments in monopoly, restriction, and centralized political power are in the interests of the abundant life. We believe that the New Era and the New Deal are two streams from the same source. The one fostered private monopoly in the name of national prosperity. The other has fostered state controlled monopolies in the name of the national welfare. We believe that both are an aberration from the basic principles upon which this nation has grown great and has remained free.

We believe, therefore, that if a political party is to be worthy of the confidence of the people, it should declare itself in favor of these principles:

1. The withdrawal, step by step, of the immunities and privileges on which monopolistic practices depend with a view to the regulation of the economic order, not by the fist of government, but by genuinely free bargains in the open market.

2. The withdrawal from appointed officials and the restoration to Congress of the power to make national laws governing the rights and duties of individuals.

3. The withdrawal from the central government and the return to the states and to local communities of responsibility for the regulation and the relief of individuals, the federal government intervening to assist the states only when there is exceptional need.

4. The restoration of responsible government finance in the nation and in the states by substituting for taxes that are now largely indirect and regressive, direct, visible, and progressive income taxes, levied as generally as possible.

5. The unqualified reiteration of the belief that all officials, and the government as a whole, are under and not above the law, and that the lawfulness of any act of government may be tested by individuals before independent tribunals.

We regard these five principles not merely as basic but as indivisible. Thus we suggest to those who may be disposed to agree with our desire to stop the delegation of power, the centralization of power, and the irresponsible spending, that none of these things can in practice or as a matter of justice be stopped, unless accompanied by a withdrawal of the privileges and immunities, the exclusive tariff subsidies and the tolerated monopolies, enjoyed by big business. The evils of bureaucracy, centralization, and extravagant expenditure are a popular reaction to the evils of private privilege. They are defensive and complementary. They are fire used to fight fire, and only those who are prepared to deal with the causes can deal with the consequences.

We believe that these principles are no more than a reaffirmation of the great tradition which comes down to us from the foundation of this Republic and that in them are to be found the guaranties of our security and the promises of our national life.

To James B. Conant[1]

May 13, 1936

Dear Mr. Conant:

I had some time on the train yesterday to think about your suggestion concerning newspaper training. It seems to be an excellent and feasible idea. It occurs to me that there ought to be certain controlling principles in the experiment.

The first is that the opportunity should be open to men who have already proved that they are competent enough newspaper men to have a career as newspaper men. In other words, it should be open to men who already have good jobs with promise of advancement.

As a corollary of this, there should be scholarships sufficient to enable these men who are already earning a living to quit for a year. It may be taken as an almost universal rule that practically none of the men eligible would be able to take a year off at his own expense.

The opportunity, then, should be offered to them not as a chance to learn anything more about journalism, but as an opportunity to improve their general education and to specialize in the fields where they are already working. Thus, I can well imagine that a young assistant financial editor might want to come to Harvard for a year to study banking and corporate finance, that an assistant dramatic critic might want to study the drama, that an assistant working in the book section might want to study literature, that other men would want to come to study politics, etc. etc. These men ought to come with the attitude of newspaper men trying to learn more about a subject already assigned to them. Thus their own demonstrated interest and competence would become the guiding principle of the work they undertake at Harvard, and no special organization would be required. It seems to me that all that would be needed would be the money for the scholarships plus two or three men willing to spend a good deal of time with them advising them on their courses.

I think it ought, also, to be taken for granted that they all have a college degree and are doing graduate work.

On this basis, the experiment could be made without any real commitments in case it didn't work. But I think it would work, and I think you have really found a solution to the problem. . . .

1. President James B. Conant of Harvard was corresponding with Lippmann about the gift the university had received from the Nieman family for the advancement of journalism. The establishment of the Nieman fellowships and the plan that governed their use reflected the weight of Lippmann's counsel.

To Frank Knox [1]

July 17, 1936

My dear Frank:

. . . I think I'll take this opportunity to say that what worries me most about the Republican ticket is what I regard as the extremely reactionary commitments in the platform against the reciprocal tariff policy, and generally in favor of economic nationalism. They are inconsistent with the excellent speech you made last winter in New York, and from all I hear they are inconsistent with Governor Landon's real views. If I could feel certain that no resumption of the Hawley-Smoot business is contemplated or threatened, my own personal decision would be vastly simplified. For I feel certain that a policy of economic nationalism can have no result except to force the country towards a policy of domestic regimentation. The two things are two sides of the same shield, and of course the wisest Republicans will understand it. But the party platform doesn't. . . . [2]

1. Frank Knox, one-time Rough Rider, publisher of the *Chicago Daily News,* in 1936 Landon's running mate, in 1940 appointed secretary of the navy.   2. Knox's reply probably helped to ease Lippmann's later decision to support Landon. That reply is quoted in the letter that follows.

To Lewis W. Douglas

July 30, 1936

Dear Lew:

We were so happy to hear from Peggy that you have got to the point on the up side where you can be visited, and I am going to take advantage of that very soon, as soon as I dare to leave a job I am doing which, at the moment, is a good deal like a man trying to cross the Hippodrome on a tight rope juggling two or three chairs as he goes. If I stop suddenly I'll drop the whole darn thing and have to start over again. But some day in the next week or two, I'll either drop it all anyway or get over to the other side, and then I'll rush into town, hoping to see you. In the meantime your secretary has been a perfect brick about answering questions, and I am most grateful to him.

I wasn't too badly disappointed by Landon's speech, though I do feel his inexperience and a certain lack of sureness even about his own convictions. Why, for example, holding the philosophy that he professes, did he have to announce a formula about trade unions? Would it not have been far truer to the implications of his principles as well as shrewder, and very refreshing, if he had said in effect: "People come asking me what my policy towards trade unions will be if I am elected president. In my opinion it is not the function of the president to get himself entangled in labor disputes, and my policy is to insist that these questions be settled by those concerned with them and not dragged to the door of the White House."

I wrote the other day to Frank Knox telling him that I was having an awful time about their attitude on the tariff, and I have the following from him in a personal letter, which I am sure he would be glad to have me quote to you:

"As to your concern about the Republican program on tariff, please accept from me for the present, in confidence, a positive assurance that there will be no reversion to the Smoot-Hawley position in the coming administration if the Republican party is successful. You are entirely sound in your assertion that economic nationalism would certainly ultimately force us into some form of domestic regimentation. The trouble with the platform was that it tried to harmonize divergent views and as usual, failed. I don't suppose we will ever arrive at a point where party programs will become forthright and definite. I did my best, as you know, at Cleveland to get the best possible platform. The platform adopted has a number of inconsistencies and contradictions in it." . . .

I am going to wait until about the middle of September before saying anything, though I am pretty clear in my mind that I am going where you're going. . . .

To William Allen White

August 11, 1936

Dear Will:

. . . In September I am going to make every effort to see the Governor if he has a free moment.

I want to vote for him and I am almost surely going to do so. But I must tell you that some of Hamilton's[1] speeches, particularly on the tariff, are pretty hard pills for people like me to swallow. They seem to me both ignorant and reactionary and, worst of all, to appeal to parochial prejudice. When you come to think of it, is it such a good idea for the Chairman of the National Committee to present himself to the country as the interpreter and even the spokesman of the Governor's policies? Somebody is bound to get up and say that since the Chairman is going to control the patronage and run the machine and collect the contributions, it becomes a very dubious business for him to be talking about matters of policy as well. The suspicious will begin to ask whether instead of being Governor Landon's manager he is not setting up as the boss, and I do not need to say how little relish most people would have for the idea that the man who collects the contributions also names the policies.

I do not think I have exaggerated the dangerous possibilities of this unusual relationship, and I think the Governor would be well advised to tell Hamilton to stop making speeches on matters of high policy. . . .

1. John D. M. Hamilton, in 1936 chairman of the Republican National Committee.

To Arthur N. Holcombe

September 22, 1936

Dear Arthur:

. . . I . . . have a rather strong opinion on the use of the word "planning" in the sense that you are using it. I think that is very misleading. "Planning" now has definite significance, almost a technical significance, as denoting a centrally directed economy, whereas you use the word, I take it, loosely to mean foresight and coordinated action and prudent anticipation. Of course I am in favor of the latter and therefore I shall be interested in your proposals.

My own thought, such as it is, has been that the military general staff provided a false analogy for what you have in mind, for the general staff administers only one arm of the military force and is comparable with the staff that might exist in any one of the many departments of the government which have to do with fiscal policy. What you are after, I take it, is something more like the war cabinet created in Great Britain which tried to make the whole war effort coherent. The problem in Washington is to make coherent the credit and monetary policy of the Federal Reserve Board, . . . the tax policy and the expenditures, etc., etc. It is clear that the coordinator of all that has to be the president himself, but that he is not equipped for the task and that his cabinet is not truly representative for the purpose. I have toyed with the idea of building up a presidential secretariat. It is just possible, however, that the same thing could be done by your proposal to build up the office of the director of the budget.

To Arthur N. Holcombe

October 7, 1936

Dear Arthur:

. . . I cannot resist commenting, even now, though I still do not know enough to comment. The point I should like to raise is that a presidential secretariat should be more than an agency of supervision and coordination of administrative policy. It should sift, analyze, and prepare for the President's judgment all the questions that come up to him for decision. We treat the President as a man in our government, when as a matter of fact he is an institution, like the Crown. The presidential form of government will be workable in the long run only if the presidency operates as an institution and not merely as a one man show.

To Malcolm W. Bingay [1]

October 14, 1936

Dear Bing:

That was the pleasantest chastisement I ever received, and I hope I shall always be spanked in that fashion. May I show my ungrateful nature by saying that my complaint against the campaign is not that Roosevelt and Landon are not talking like gentlemen and scholars, but that they are not talking about real issues — the issues which you state so well and which you and I both have so much at heart.

I thought Landon made a very good speech in Portland[2] but that speech needed to be hammered in with the broad sword and battle axe if the country was to understand it. Instead, he began to deliver a series of amateur orations on half a dozen subjects of no vital consequence which he does not understand very well anyway, and the net effect is to leave a blurred impression on the public mind. It seems to me positively childish to think that he is called upon to deliver analytical criticisms one after the other of all the major measures of the New Deal — social security, reciprocal tariffs, farm benefits, etc., etc. I do not call that practical politics. That is academic in the worst sense of the word; and it comes, as you well know, from the professors in his brain trust.

In the kind of fight that Landon is making, the whole art is to concentrate on one single fundamental idea and hammer it home until at least the public understands it. And that idea, of course, ought to be the idea which you talk about and which he talked about at Portland, and which he has never talked about since. Here it is the 13th of October and so far as I can remember he has made one speech on the main issue, with some additional reference to it in his acceptance speech.

No wonder he is not registering. And the more the campaign goes on, the more I am reminded of John W. Davis in 1924 — who was also a first rate man with admirable principles and a broken-down party behind him.

Forgive me for blowing off to you privately this way, but I have been feeling a little sick about the campaign. It seems to me that you and I and some others have been trying to tell the public that our candidate stands for some things which our candidate is unnecessarily vague about.

1. Malcolm W. Bingay, editorial director of the *Detroit Free Press*. 2. That speech attacked the NRA and AAA as products of a planned economy. A "planned economy," Landon said, "is incompatible with the democratic form of government." The United States, he warned, had to have either a "system of free competitive enterprises" or "a system under which the minutest doings of every citizen are scrutinized and regulated . . ."; there was "no half-way house." The Republicans carried Maine, which in 1936 still held its national election earlier than did the other states.

To Franklin D. Roosevelt

January 6, 1937

Dear Mr. President:

I listened to your message to Congress today, and I was delighted by its manner and I rejoiced in its substance.[1] You have taken the wise approach, I feel sure, to the Constitutional question. For myself, I should be prepared to go a very long way in extending the federal power to make uniform laws for industry provided those laws do not undertake to fix by statute or administrative decision the main body of prices and wages throughout industry and agriculture. Price fixing is a morass which we ought to stay out of, but there seems to me to be very good ground for more uniform legislation covering the powers of corporations.

1. Still distressed by the Supreme Court's nullification of much New Deal legislation, particularly the National Industrial Recovery Act, which Lippmann attacked in *The Good Society*, Roosevelt in his State of the Union message to Congress struck several themes Lippmann was sympathetic with. "Sober second thought confirms," the president said, "most of us in the belief that the broad objectives of the NRA were sound." He went on to call for new federal legislation providing adequate pay for labor, curbs on monopoly and unfair trade practices, and the intelligent development of the social security system.

To Thomas W. Lamont

January 8, 1937

Dear Tom:

I am very much interested in those comments, but I do not say that Mr. Sloan's statement to his employees was an "ultimatum."[1] I said it was couched in the language of authority. Nor can I agree that it was "simply a statement of fact." The statement does not say that General Motors' standard work week is 40 hours. It says that the General Motors standard work week will continue to be 40 hours. In fact all five points made in the statement deal with the future and not merely with the present, and there is no suggestion at any point, that they are subject to negotiation at any time. They are prefaced with the statement "the employees are entitled to know what General Motors' position is." If Mr. Sloan recognized the principle of collective bargaining he would not be informing his employees what the position of General Motors is and will continue to be.

I am very much disturbed by the attitude of the company and I feel that no good can come of it. I am more disturbed by what I believe to be a lack of understanding of the position it has taken than by any specific policy which the company insists on. The substance of . . . Mr. Sloan's statement seems to me eminently reasonable, but the manner of presenting these points to the public and the manner of arriving at them places the company in a very vulnerable position before the public and before Congress.

1. Alfred P. Sloan, Jr., president of General Motors, a dedicated conservative and adamant foe of labor unions, had warned General Motors workers on strike at company plants in Flint, Michigan, that GM would not recognize any union as an agency for collective bargaining. The strike was making national headlines because the United Automobile Workers were "sitting in" several plants as a technique to bring the company to negotiate.

To Lewis W. Douglas

February 8, 1937

Dear Lew:

I think you misunderstood me. I did not say that the strike was something for Mr. Roosevelt to settle. I said that Mr. Lewis' ambitions and the movement he leads and the tactics he employs are Mr. Roosevelt's baby, not Mr. Sloan's. Roosevelt made Lewis a national figure and should be held strictly accountable for the consequences. Mr. Sloan should not and cannot jeopardize General Motors and incur the risks of violence and political reprisal[1] resulting from an attempt to use the General Motors strike as the occasion for dealing with Lewis. That, I think, is common sense. . . .

1. Lippmann, like most commentators on the GM strike, was here misinterpreting a remark of John L. Lewis, the head of the Committee for Industrial Organization, which had in effect founded the UAW and was directing labor tactics in the GM strike. On January 21, Lewis had said the union was willing to confer with management, but not to relinquish the buildings in which its members sat until the strike was brought "to a successful conclusion." He also then rejected any "half-baked compromise" and remarked on the importance of labor in the Democratic victory in 1936. "The workers," he concluded, "expect the Administration in every reasonable and legal way to support the auto workers in their fight. . . ." Overlooking Lewis's words "reasonable and legal," most commentators read his statement as a demand for a quid pro quo for political favors rendered. Sloan used the statement as an excuse for declining to attend any further conferences with Roosevelt, whom he had reluctantly agreed to see. On the day Lippmann wrote this letter, Secretary of Labor Frances Perkins and Michigan's Governor Frank Murphy were helping to work out the agreement that settled the strike on February 11. A preliminary to collective bargaining, the agreement called on the union to evacuate the plants, and on GM to recognize the union as representative of its members only and not to discriminate or retaliate against those members.

To Lionel C. Robbins[1]

March 24, 1937

Dear Mr. Robbins:

. . . I have studied von Mises' book with great care as well as the books on planning edited by von Hayek.[2] In the published book I am attempting to make full acknowledgment of my indebtedness. While I had grasped the logical incompatibility of planning with a democratic system, as any one must, I think, who considers the problem at all, I have been enormously helped by von Mises' work and the Hayek symposium.

However, their work is critical and they do not, it seems to me, arrive at a positive theory of liberalism which gives a method of social control consistent with the exchange economy. It is this that I have tried to develop in the much longer and unpublished part of the book. That book will be published at the end of the summer under the title, "The Good Society," and I shall take the liberty of sending you a copy as soon as one is available.

1. Lionel C. Robbins, professor of economics at the London School of Economics, published his first book, *Economic Theory and International Order* (London, 1936), at about this time. **2.** Ludwig von Mises, *Socialism: An Economic and Sociological Analysis* (London, 1936) — the first English translation of the book; and Friedrich A. von Hayek, ed., *Collective Economic Planning* (London, 1935). Both Mises and Hayek became major cult figures in the folklore of American conservatism.

To James B. Conant

April 19, 1937

Dear Mr. Conant:

After our talk on Friday morning I canvassed the matter rather thoroughly with Judge Learned Hand at lunch, and then in the afternoon with Alvin Johnson.[1] I felt I could be perfectly frank with Hand, and with Johnson I could be frank too except that I was careful to make clear to him that the matters I was discussing were not your suggestions, but my own, and that I wanted his advice to me in making suggestions to you.

I found that both men were in entire agreement with the principles on which you acted in the Walsh and Sweezy cases, namely, that the judgment of academic work must be made by the department and governing boards.[2] Both of them were very clear that on no other basis could academic freedom be sustained. With Hand I raised the question as to whether in a case where the department's judgment was seriously disputed by a minority in the department or by members of some closely related department, there could not be some form of appeal and review. Hand felt that if there were to be appeal and review, it should be to some committee consisting of men in the same field of learning. He rejected absolutely the idea of an appeal to a committee consisting of members of other departments, for example, or to a committee of supposedly disinterested laymen, and said that only a committee of economists could sit in judgment on the decision of a department of economics. Therefore he was willing to consider as a speculative possibility a procedure of review and appeal by a committee consisting of eminent scholars belonging to other colleges but working in the same field of knowledge. I report this to you as a suggestive possibility and as nothing more. I should add that Hand is available if you want him for any investigation. I think if there is to be any committee, he would be of particular value. He is greatly respected by the liberal lawyers and he has, of course, been Overseer, and president of the Alumni Association. Apart from those qualifications the real point is that he has great qualities of mind for dealing with a problem of this kind, and nothing he put his name to would look foolish.

I found Johnson not only unreservedly certain of your own attitude on academic freedom, but positive in his conviction that your own attitude in this particular case has been correct. His Graduate Faculty, the University in Exile, operates under a constitution embodied in the deed of trust, which places appointments, promotions and dismissals entirely in the hands of the faculty. It may interest you to know, by the way, that in drawing up that constitution, especially devoted to the principles of academic liberty, it was provided that any professor may be dismissed for cause and after a hearing, by a vote of two-thirds of the faculty; and that any professor may be dismissed without a hearing and for no specified cause, by a vote of three-fourths of the faculty. When I looked a bit astonished at hearing that members of this faculty did not possess permanent tenure, Johnson said that they had made up their mind that they would not turn the principle of academic freedom into a property right. So you can see how far this school has carried the principle of self-determination by the faculties.

Johnson is prepared to cooperate in any way that you wish him to. He said he was busy, of course, but that the importance of having Harvard give the right lead to schools in this country was so great that he would make any sacrifice necessary to help in working out this difficult problem. . . .

You suggested on the telephone that I might organize the committee in order to dissociate it from your office. I have thought about that, and while of course I am perfectly willing to do anything you think desirable, I doubt very much whether I have any authority to appoint a committee, since all the Visiting Committees are appointed by the Executive Committee of the Board of Overseers. I am a little bit afraid that the Board might feel I had gone too far in taking the initiative. . . .

1. Lippmann had been a member since 1933 of the Board of Overseers, the senior governing board of Harvard University. He was also the head of the committee to visit, essentially to advise, the Department of Economics. His talk with President James B. Conant of Harvard related to problems of that department (see note 2 below), which he had then discussed with Judge Learned Hand, long an active and involved Harvard alumnus, and Alvin S. Johnson, the economist who served also as a director of the New School for Social Research and chairman of its graduate faculty in political science. The New School contained the University in Exile, a faculty of émigré Europeans that had the authority to grant graduate degrees. **2.** President Conant, confronted with a limited budget, had moved to force departments to terminate the contracts of nontenured faculty who had been at Harvard for many years and had no prospect of permanent appointment there. The Department of Economics decided to shorten from three to two years the remaining time of appointment of two of its most effective undergraduate teachers, instructors Alan R. Sweezy and J. Raymond Walsh. Both had also been active in organizing a teachers' union at Harvard, of which Walsh was president, and both subscribed to a realist economics at variance with conventional theory. Their discharge at once stirred serious protests among undergraduates, interested alumni, and many faculty who attributed the decision to the political views of the senior members of the department.

The issue absorbed energies and inflamed tempers at Harvard during much of 1937 and 1938. There was indeed a budgetary problem, and Conant was wisely trying to establish a sound financial basis for the size of the faculty, but the faculty protests, especially, persuaded Conant in August 1937 to accept a committee of nine faculty members to investigate the reasons for the action of the Economics Department. That committee included seven of the most distinguished and respected professors of the faculty of arts and science and two similar representatives of the Law School. Their report of June 1938 blamed Conant for a lack of clarity in his directions to the department (he had not stated categorically that the five nontenured members not to be promoted would have to leave) but concluded that politics had not influenced the decision about Walsh and Sweezy. The committee also recommended their reinstatement, for both men had resigned; but Conant, supported by the governing boards, refused. Throughout the episode, Lippmann often served as an adviser to Conant.

To James B. Conant

May 5, 1937

Dear Mr. Conant:

I had a talk today with one of the retired professors of the Department of Economics under whom I studied at college. He sought me out and . . . made some observations which I think throw a real light on the underlying problem in the department. I shall not mention his name in this letter but I shall tell you who he is when I see you. . . .[1]

My talk with this retired professor strengthened a conviction which has been growing upon me recently but which is not new, namely, that the present chairman of the department[2] does not have the qualities for dealing with the very peculiar situation which exists in that department. He is, I think it fair to say, a man of no professional standing among economists. So far as I have been able to see in extended conversations with him, he is not interested in the new developments of thought in his field, nor in the men who are making those new developments. The plain fact of the matter is that he is an extreme reactionary. It also seems to be true that he dominates personally all questions of personnel in his department and that therefore the judgments which you receive from him are much more likely to be personal than to be collective. After all, John Williams[3] has many outside interests and apparently does not take much of a part in the management of the department. The same is true of Professor Black.[4] Professor Schumpeter[5] is a specialist pursuing his own line of inquiry, and there are no others, I think, of equal seniority. The result is a kind of one-man organization.

Now if we are to apply the general principles contained in the Report to the Overseers, it is of the utmost importance that the department itself should make its recommendations without bias, with a broad sense of intellectual responsibility, and with imagination about the development of economic science. I am afraid that under the present chairman the quality of the department does not meet those requirements, and I am inclined to think that that may be the basic cause of this whole trouble; that the trouble will be repeated until there is a new chairman and a change in the center of authority within the department itself. After all, while there is little doubt that the principles of the report are the right principles for maintaining academic freedom, you do have the responsibility of seeing to it that there is a healthy intellectual atmosphere in these autonomous departments. Three years' contact with it has convinced me that the atmosphere is not healthy, and when I see you this is one of the phases of the matter I should like to talk over with you.

1. He was probably Frank W. Taussig. **2.** Professor Harold H. Burbank, the chairman, was then engaged, in the view of his junior colleague J. K. Galbraith, "in a failing struggle to protect Harvard from alien intellectual influences," not the least being the ideas of the Fabian Socialists and of Keynes; see John Kenneth Galbraith, *A Life in Our Times* (Boston, 1981), p. 46. **3.** John H. Williams in 1937, apart from his teaching at Harvard, served as an adviser to the Federal Reserve Bank of New York and as that bank's vice president. **4.** John D. Black, an outstanding economist of agriculture and a benign teacher, served often outside of Harvard as a consultant on population and food problems. **5.** Joseph A. Schumpeter, Austrian minister of finance, 1919–20, and professor of economics at Bonn, 1925–32, had then moved to Harvard, where he continued to pursue his celebrated studies of entrepreneurship. "No economist of this century," in Galbraith's assessment, "so effectively articulated the case for capitalism." But Schumpeter also praised Marx and doubted that capitalism could survive. Alan Sweezy's older brother Paul was one of Schumpeter's most admiring students; see J. K. Galbraith, *A Life in Our Times* (Boston, 1981), pp. 49–50.

To Wendell L. Willkie[1]

May 28, 1937

Dear Mr. Willkie:

Of course terrorism is as objectionable as packing, but whether the Court is in fact terrorized seems to me an open question. It looks that way, but actually I think the decisions this year would have been about what they have been without the Judiciary Bill. I think the President has been hammering on a door that was already open.[2]

1. Wendell L. Willkie — corporation lawyer, since 1933 president of Commonwealth and Southern Corporation — had successfully challenged certain chapters of the legislation establishing the Tennessee Valley Authority. Though no one in 1937 could have forecast his imminent future, he became the Republican candidate in 1940 for president of the United States. In that role and thereafter, until his death in 1944, Willkie served as an eloquent spokesman for American internationalism. **2.** Lippmann was referring to the series of decisions by the Supreme Court which were either directly or in effect overruling the positions the court had taken in 1935–36 that nullified much New Deal legislation as unconstitutional. The new rulings, as he implied, reflected modification of views, especially on the parts of Associate Justice Owen Roberts and Chief Justice Charles Evans Hughes. Willkie had attributed the changes to Roosevelt's unsuccessful effort to enlarge the Supreme Court, as provided in the Judiciary Reorganization bill of 1937, which the Senate in the end tabled.

To Murry Nelson[1]

June 17, 1937

Dear Murry:

I . . . realize that I am more tender-minded about the Constitution and the courts than you are, or than B. Hand is, or the best of the men of that group. And I guess the reason for the difference is that you have been dealing with the legal stuffed shirts whereas I have been dealing with the post-war lunatics produced in large part by the legal stuffed shirts. When I see some of the most eminent members of the Bar, I feel as you write. When I see their enemies in Washington, as I did yesterday, for example, I begin to feel there is a horrid choice between the stuffed shirts and the mob. . . .

1. Murry Nelson, Chicago lawyer.

To William Allen White

June 28, 1937

Dear Will:

. . . I am glad you think well of my book.[1] I have no idea that a solution of the current problems of the world is possible. The best we can hope for is to outlive and outgrow them. The idea which I had in my mind in writing that book was that our present troubles originated in a wrong turn taken by human thought about the middle of the last century, just as the best of the pre-war world is owing to a good turn which you have talked of in the seventeenth and eighteenth centuries. We might hope, perhaps, to change the direction of the current a little in our time but no one can hope to see the results in his day, for according to my calculations it takes about sixty or seventy years for a change in fundamental ideas to express itself in public life. Our generation is hopelessly entangled in the errors of the later Victorians. . . .

1. *The Good Society* (Boston, 1937).

To Burton K. Wheeler

July 23, 1937

Dear Burt:

You must be tired and I shall not trouble you with a long letter of congratulations,[1] but I must write a line, at least, to tell you that no one else could have led that fight as you led it. Your name is now fixed in the history books. Moreover, above the obvious victory which has been won, in my opinion you have saved not only the Court and the conception of constitutional government, but the soul of American progressivism itself. On the line that Roosevelt began to travel last February, the end could only have been the blackest kind of reaction.

1. Democratic Senator Burton K. Wheeler of Montana, long-time progressive and isolationist, had led the opposition to the judiciary bill.

To Carl Snyder[1]

December 3, 1937

Dear Carl:

. . . I feel sure from all I hear that Roosevelt will not and cannot reverse his policies sufficiently to make any important effect on the behavior of business, that therefore the depression will grow worse in the next few months and that is inevitably bound to result in a change of political trend.[2] I rather dread to think how far to the right the pendulum may swing. But if some imp of the perverse had set out to make progressivism unpopular and to insure a reactionary demonstration in 1940, he would be doing just about what Roosevelt has done in the past twelve months. . . .

1. Carl Snyder, economist and statistician. **2.** The recession of 1937–38 had become acute by December. A deliberate reduction in federal spending for relief and public works and a premature tightening of money rates had brought the economy down from its apparent improvement in late 1936. Business had also contributed to the recession, partly by a too rapid build-up of inventories, partly by the attitude of executives who took excessive alarm at New Deal labor and revenue policies and at Roosevelt's antibusiness rhetoric. They were bothered too by his movement in 1937 toward opposition to the increasing concentration of American industry. Those attitudes perhaps adversely affected the stock market, though they probably had little effect on the actual level of business investment. During 1938 the president did alter his economic policies, particularly by accepting the counsel of those of his advisers convinced of the relevance of Keynesian economics, but Lippmann in that year was preoccupied, almost to the exclusion of other public issues, with problems of American foreign policy.

To Lewis W. Douglas[1]

January 25, 1938

Dear Lew:

. . . The most interesting thing I have learned is that there is a genuine struggle going on inside the palace between the people who want to break up monopoly and the people who want to revive the N.R.A. The leader, or at least the figurehead, or both, of the anti-monopoly faction is R. H. Jackson, backed by Corcoran, Cohen, Leon Henderson.[2] Garner is generally understood to be sympathetic with the philosophy but not the manners of this faction, and there is little doubt that it could find overwhelming support in Congress. The other faction seems to consist of people like Richberg, Roper, and above all, the President himself, although of course the President has not any firm convictions on this subject and plays with both sides. But I am convinced that temperamentally he likes big business and big government, but that in practice he will do a little for each side. . . .

1. On January 1, 1938, Lewis Douglas had become principal and vice chancellor of McGill University in Montreal, a position he held for two years. **2.** That "anti-monopoly" faction included those Lippmann listed, though Robert H. Jackson, then assistant attorney general, was not their leader, if they had any leader at all. They were also advocates of Keynesian theory, and they won the president's favor by the end of March 1938. The others Lippmann mentioned were Thomas G. Corcoran, "Tommy the Cork," and Benjamin V. Cohen — two of the brightest and most influential of New Deal lawyers — and the liberal economist Leon Henderson, at this time officially consultant to Harry Hopkins's Works Progress Administration. In 1938 the group far surpassed in its access to the president such then receding figures as Secretary of Commerce Daniel C. Roper and Donald R. Richberg, who was practicing law in Washington; see Arthur M. Schlesinger, Jr., *The Politics of Upheaval* (Boston, 1960), especially chs. 21–22.

To the publisher of Fortune magazine[1]

February 1938

In response to your invitation am sending following statement quote *Fortune*'s advice is, I believe, that of a discerning and candid friend of the system of free enterprise and of the liberties which are indissolubly connected with it. The development of combinations in business which are able to dominate the markets in which they sell their goods and in which they buy their labor and their materials must lead irresistibly to some form of state collectivism. So much power will never for long be allowed to rest in private hands, and those who do not wish to take the road to the politically administered economy of socialism must be prepared to take the steps back towards the restoration of the market economy of private competitive enterprise.

Fortune states the argument with admirable clarity, and it will have, one may hope, a sympathetic reception followed by an exhaustive study of the ways and means.

1. *Fortune* had solicited this response to its article of February 1938, "New Deal: Second Time Around."

To Harold G. Nicolson[1]

February 28, 1938

My dear Nicolson:

Thank you for your letter. It reached me just as Eden was resigning. Here in America a rather tragic view is taken of his resignation but I am inclined to think myself that until Eden has a better mandate from the people to take the risks involved in his principles it is just as well that he should not be put in the ambiguous position where he must proclaim his principles without being able to enforce them.

I think you should not take too seriously the reports you probably are receiving in England about American feelings towards Great Britain. These outcries represent the views of a minority and they have been expressed very emphatically recently as a means of opposing the President's bill to increase the navy. But the opposition to that bill will be quite ineffective I think.[2] There has been a very radical change in American opinion during the past three or four months. The turning point was the *Panay* incident, which changed opinion so much that there is an overwhelming majority in favor of building up American armaments.[3] Perhaps this may not seem to you much of a contribution to the solution of the world's troubles, but my own feeling is that as this country grows stronger and becomes more conscious of its strength, its influence in the Orient and possibly in Europe will necessarily increase. Although no American politician is able openly to avow his sympathy with Great Britain and France, that sympathy is almost universal, and I cannot help feeling that at a critical moment it will be translated into effective action.

The paradox of the situation is that the weaker British policy is, the stronger is American isolationist feeling. The more Great Britain dares to exert herself in Europe, the more disposed will this country become to help. I think we had a very crucial test of that during the Ethiopian sanctions. I have no doubt, myself, that really effective sanctions would have brought not only general enthusiasm in the United States but action designed to make the sanctions succeed.

It seems to me that the problem of American cooperation turns upon your willingness to take the lead in Europe and our willingness to take it in the Pacific, and though neither of us can count upon the other fully as yet I think that as we feel ourselves to be better armed and stronger, that our hesitation will diminish.

Of course, being democracies we move slowly and we are faced with adversaries who strike swiftly. It is that that may undo us.

---

1. Harold G. Nicolson — a Conservative member of Parliament, biographer of Dwight Morrow and others, and incomparable diarist of the time — had long known Lippmann. Nicolson was a member also of the "Eden Group," sometimes known as the "Glamour Boys," a group of about thirty Conservative members of Parliament who met informally to discuss their growing concern about the international dangers posed by Hitler and Mussolini. The group formed on February 28, 1938, on the occasion of Anthony Eden's resignation as foreign secretary in the cabinet of Prime Minister Neville Chamberlain. Eden resigned in protest against Chamberlain's effort to seek agreement with Italy, while the problems of Spain, where Mussolini had assisted the Fascists, remained unresolved; and in protest, too, over Chamberlain's efforts to negotiate with Hitler about German demands for territory. The prime minister's agent in that task, Lord Halifax, succeeded Eden; see Anthony Eden, *The Reckoning* (Boston, 1965), ch. 1.   **2.** Lippmann erred. The opposition, composed of most Republicans and some Democrats averse to any armament program, seriously crippled the bill.   **3.** In December 1937, Japanese bombers, which had been attacking Chinese cities in Japan's undeclared war against China, hit British and American ships near Nanking and sank the American gunboat *Panay*. Japan evaded official American protests over this unprovoked action but did issue an apology, which Roosevelt accepted. Early in the crisis, he had contemplated retaliatory economic measures, but with American opinion much opposed to risking war he abandoned those secret plans. He did send a confidential envoy, Captain Royal E. Ingersoll, U.S.N., to London for informal talks with the British Admiralty.

To Bruce Bliven[1]

March 11, 1938

Dear Bruce:

. . . I agree that the policy I am advocating is based upon a general knowledge of the purposes of the fascist powers. You contend, if I understood your testimony correctly, that this policy ought to be defined more specifically. My reply is that until we have a more particular knowledge of the fascist policy, it is impossible and it would be unwise to define our own policy more specifically. You say that you did not suggest that the United States is aggressive in the same sense that Japan is aggressive in China. I maintain that the United States is not aggressive in any fair sense of the word. I should agree that we have been aggressive in Latin America and even in the Far East, but there is no sign of aggressiveness today that I can detect. As for the Americans in China, there is undoubtedly a case to be made for withdrawing them, but that case must rest on the grounds of proofs, and leaving them there should not be confused with aggression. That confusion which I think you were guilty of concedes to the Japanese propaganda more than one should concede.

As for the 20 to 7 naval ratio, I honestly think that is fantastic. As long as Britain is unable to put her fleet into the Pacific, the fact that the Suez and Panama Canals exist has no bearing on the matter. The fact is, of course, that the British fleet is pinned in Europe. There is no British fleet in the Pacific. There can be no British fleet in the Pacific unless a bargain can be struck with Italy and Germany and if that happens, the utmost the British hope for is, as you know, the release of six capital ships. While I did not report the Washington Naval Conference from day to day, I have talked at length and repeatedly with the Japanese ambassadors since that time, with the Japanese correspondents in this country and with Japanese officials here and abroad. I never heard one maintain that there was an Anglo-American ratio of 20 to 7. As for our proposal to create a navy which is 2 to 1 as against Japan, I wonder whether the fact is not that Japan's expansion is ahead of ours and that with difficulty we shall maintain the 5–3 ratio. Moreover it is not true that such a navy can be used effectively in the Far East against a Japanese navy. No American naval man that I have talked to thinks that the American navy, even expanded, can operate west of the line from Alaska to Hawaii.

I know that the Japanese have been disturbed over our actions in China, and I myself am opposed to the old policy of maintaining the integrity of China. But that policy was scrapped in fact at the Washington Conference when we agreed not to build naval bases west of Hawaii, and the Manchurian affair proved up to the hilt that we would not intervene by force in Asia.

I am sorry that I misunderstood your remark about "foreign policy being settled in the dark by a little handful of officials." But that is your own fault. Those words are melodramatic words and carry the innuendo of something sinister. Taken in conjunction with the charges made that we had secret agreements with Great Britain, I assumed that that is what you had in mind. Your letter itself, which talks about fighting for Hong Kong, confirmed my interpretation. If all you mean, however, is that the American people do not know what our foreign policy is, then we are back again at the original point of controversy, namely, whether it is possible, in view of the uncertainties of the world, to define our foreign policy more exactly.

In regard to your final paragraph, I am of course on the whole in agreement, except at one vital point I feel convinced that in so far as the fascist states believe that we will use only measures that are "short of the application of force," they will be undeterred by our wishes. I see no way of putting any stop to their aggrandizement except by convincing them in advance that at some point they will meet overwhelmingly superior force.

1. Bruce Bliven, editor of *The New Republic,* was calling in 1938 for American self-insulation from the troubles of east Asia, especially the war between Japan and China. That issue had naturally received attention in the American press after the *Panay* incident.

To Joseph P. Kennedy [1]

April 7, 1938

Dear Joe:

. . . Your general feelings about the prospect of war and about British policy seem to me quite probably true, but there was something in your second letter which disturbed me and which I feel, as a friend, I must tell you about. As you know, I have specialized a good deal on foreign affairs since the war time and I have been particularly interested in the American ambassador to Great Britain because obviously he holds the key post in our diplomatic service. Don't take it amiss if I say that your letter shows some of the same symptoms which have appeared in every American ambassador that I have known since Walter Hines Page, namely the tendency to be over-enthusiastic about the government of the day. When you tell me that Chamberlain's speech impressed you as a combination of high morals and politics such as you had never witnessed, I am frankly a little worried for you. British parliamentary oratory is most seductive to Americans after the awful ranting which they are used to in Congress and the excellent manners and the impressive literary style of the House of Commons manner can very easily affect our judgment as to the substance. I happen, for example in the present thing to believe that Chamberlain is doing the most sensible thing in a bad situation but that his policy represents "high morals" I do not for one minute believe. He is yielding to superior force and trying to buy off one, at least, of his potential enemies.[2] This is an expedient thing to do but it hasn't much to do with morals, and I cannot feel that to accept a speech like Chamberlain's at its pretended value is consistent with . . . independence of judgment. . . .

1. Joseph P. Kennedy had been appointed ambassador to Great Britain in December 1937.
2. The British government had not protested Hitler's invasion and annexation of Austria in March, a step toward German demands for Czech territory.

To James B. Conant

May 25, 1938

My dear Conant:

I have had a chance to give the report of the Committee of Nine one reading. If the main thesis of the report that there was a misunderstanding between the department and the President as to the meaning of the President's ruling is correct and cannot be contradicted by any important evidence, then it has been proved, it seems to me, that Messrs. Walsh and Sweezy were not fairly judged.

Correction of this injustice and the removal of any feeling in the University that an injustice has been committed, or that having been committed, it would be persisted in, should, I believe, be the paramount consideration. In this affair nothing else is so important as to demonstrate convincingly to the University community that the University authorities mean to do justice.

I therefore recommend that you accept the report, note with approval its recognition that no political prejudice was involved, acknowledge that there was misunderstanding of the administrative ruling, and re-open the case by asking the department to vote once more on their resolution of January 26, 1937. If they vote in the affirmative, I recommend that you submit the vote to the Governing Boards with your approval.[1] The effect of such an action, if ratified by the Governing Boards, would be to give either or both of the men, as the case may be, three years more in which to demonstrate their fitness for promotion to permanent tenure in the University. If they are unfitted, that will be demonstrated in three years. If they are fitted, if they are as good men as the Committee of Nine seems to think they are, the University will be the gainer. In either event, the fairness and disinterestedness and magnanimity of the University authorities will have been demonstrated beyond possibility of dispute.

1. Conant did not take Lippmann's advice; see Lippmann to James B. Conant, April 19, 1937, note 2, sup.

To Bernard Berenson   HANDWRITTEN

September 17, 1938

Dear B. B.

. . . My own view of the Czech question is that finally everything depends upon the Germans themselves.[1] If they can maintain their authority *inside*[2] their frontiers and if they are prepared to resist invasion, Hitler will either not attack, or if he attacks, the Austrians and French must come to the help of the Czechs. They would like not to. But to stand aside *if* the Czechs are perishing is almost inconceivable. To attempt it would, I think, be such a humiliation that the governing classes in Britain and France would lose all moral authority vis-à-vis their own people. I should suspect a naked aggression which was connived at by London and Paris to inaugurate a period of civil disorder all over Europe. But this reasoning depends wholly on the assumption that there is not another Schuschnigg and that the Czechs are not Austrians.[3] If they are, then we shall see the triumph of pan-Germanism and decades of war and revolutions as the consequence.

It is difficult for me to see how a compromise can be reached after Nuremberg & Chamberlain's visit to Berchtesgaden. Can Hitler retreat? Can Chamberlain, who has now staked everything on peace *with honor*, advise the world to buy peace at any price? These two men have very nearly burned their bridges — for until a fortnight ago Hitler was not finally committed personally. . . . But now, if the Czechs stand firm, there is an impasse in which Hitler must either attack or retreat, in which Chamberlain must either resist aggression or confess that he must submit to it. . . .

1. The European crisis over Czechoslovakia was approaching its climax. On September 12, Hitler in a speech at Nürnberg had first demanded the right of self-determination for the Sudeten Germans — the German-speaking people of the Sudetenland, an area included within Czechoslovakia by the Treaty of Versailles. Nazi-fomented disorder in that area led the Czech government to declare martial law on September 13. Two days later, British Prime Minister Neville Chamberlain met Hitler in Berchtesgaden. There Hitler, now demanding German annexation of the Sudetenland, threatened war as his alternative. On September 18, in London, Chamberlain and the French leaders, Premier Édouard Daladier and Foreign Minister Georges Bonnet, decided to urge the Czech government to give in to Hitler. Continuing pressure from Britain and France led the Czechs to do so on September 21.

Not yet satisfied, Hitler, again in conference with Chamberlain on September 22–23, insisted further on immediate surrender of the area without removal of its economic and military assets, and on plebiscites to determine the future of other Czech regions with heavy German populations. Chamberlain balked. The ensuing crisis was resolved on September 29 at the Munich Conference of the heads of government of Germany, her ally Italy, Great Britain, and France (but not Czechoslovakia or the Soviet Union). The Munich agreement forced the Czechs to evacuate the Sudetenland by October 10, called for an international committee to determine plebiscite areas, and provided British and French guarantees for the new, reduced Czech border. The agreement became the enduring symbol of Chamberlain's appeasement of Hitler. **2.** The emphases in this letter were all Lippmann's. **3.** Kurt von Schuschnigg, Austrian chancellor, had made concessions to Hitler in 1936 but became more independent in 1937 until the open alliance of Germany and Italy further weakened his nation's already tenuous position. In 1938 he accepted Hitler's demand for an amnesty for Austrian Nazis, though he also reasserted the independence of Austria. When Hitler invaded Austria, he had Schuschnigg arrested and imprisoned without trial. Though Lippmann obviously considered Schuschnigg and the Austrian people pusillanimous, they had in 1938 no available means successfully to resist the Nazis. Anthony Eden believed Schuschnigg's response to Hitler had been "robust" and the Austrians "hapless." As he put it: "For having understood the true Nazi menace . . . Dr. Schuschnigg was to undergo seven years of imprisonment"; Anthony Eden, *The Reckoning* (Boston, 1965), p. 9.

To Herbert Bayard Swope

October 12, 1938

Dear Herbert:

   . . . I am afraid . . . that in the near future we shall have to modify somewhat our traditional conception of freedom of speech in order to meet the
totalitarian attack. I have given some indication of that in an article. . . .[1]

1. Lippmann wrote in "Today and Tomorrow" that American laws "antedate, and therefore
ignore, the whole postwar phenomenon of the totalitarian revolution under which democratic
institutions are used to destroy democracy." For a similar statement, see Lippmann to Louis
Rougier, October 28, 1938, inf.

To Lee Simonson[1]

October 12, 1938

Dear Lee:

   . . . For the moment I'll just say that while the fear of the Soviets undoubtedly played a part in the outcome,[2] especially in the refusal of the French to
turn the Franco-Soviet pact into a genuine military alliance, the deciding thing
about Russia this summer was Russia's weakness. Had Russia been a genuine
military power, nobody could have excluded her from Munich, and if the
French politicians of the Front Populaire had not believed Russia was weak
they would have felt differently about their obligations to Czechoslovakia. In
other words, I think it is true that Chamberlain was influenced somewhat by
anti-Soviet feeling, but I think a much more important factor of the situation
was Russia's own inability to make herself felt as a European power. If Russia
had been strong it would have been as impossible to keep her out of Europe as
it is impossible to keep Hitler out of Europe. Russia had a greater interest in
the maintenance of Czechoslovakia conditional upon French military action.

1. Lee Simonson, the celebrated scenic designer, was a Harvard contemporary and old friend of
Lippmann's. 2. At the Munich Conference, to which Great Britain and France had declined to
invite the Soviet Union.

To Jerome N. Frank[1]

October 25, 1938

My dear Frank:

   I don't think you are a simple-minded person, but I will try briefly to say
what I think about a few of the many points you raise in your letter.

   1. What I mean by the balance of power is exactly what you say . . .
namely that when a balance of power existed in Europe and Asia the nations

of the Old World were too busy watching one another to consider any extension of empire into this hemisphere. No one of them had a free hand, and of course the power of each was checked by the power of the others. So far as the maintenance of the Monroe Doctrine goes as against Europe, it has depended, it seems to me, since the time of Canning, on the fact that no military power of the Continent could get through the British navy and the British navy could not extend the British power in this hemisphere because it was too preoccupied in Europe.

In the Far East the balance of power was maintained as between Russia, Japan, Great Britain, and the United States. . . . In 1931 this balance of power had been disturbed in the Far East because Russia was incapable of offensive warfare and because Britain was pinned down in Europe. That is what opened the way for Japan's conquest of China.

The exceptions you cite are in my opinion debating points, and not real ones. The Venezuela incident, for example, was a technical violation of the Monroe Doctrine but not a serious threat to its substance. The Civil War incidents are more serious, and conceivably if the South had won, the British imperialism would have advanced in this hemisphere. But except for that important occasion, which is hypothetical, it is impossible, I believe, to explain the closing of this hemisphere to colonization when the United States had no naval power to speak of, except on the theory that there was a balance of power in Europe which prevented any power from moving into this hemisphere.

My point about the Munich peace is that the power to intimidate Great Britain by the aerial threat to London has immobilized the British Navy, and that there no longer is in Europe an effective balance of power, as there is no longer one in the Far East. How soon we shall feel the practical consequences in this hemisphere I don't know, but that there has been a radical change in the conditions of our security I feel certain.

What you say about the evil effects on Europe of the British doctrine of the balance of power may be true, but it is beside the point of this argument. A policy of political unification of Europe might have been more desirable but it isn't the policy under which this country has lived for a hundred years.

2. My remarks on the Hull trade program you have misunderstood. My argument is that Great Britain and France will not make themselves dependent upon our exports in time of peace if they know that those exports will be cut off in time of war. The Neutrality Law may be a good thing for us but it is fundamentally inconsistent with the Hull program, and that is all I was trying to say. I am not now arguing for a revision of the Neutrality Law but only for a recognition of its consequences.

3. The reason why I regard our exports to Europe as undependable now in a sense that they were not undependable before the Munich peace is that I think the British and French have lost control of the seas. That is a new fact which I should not have anticipated two years ago. . . .

1. Jerome N. Frank, at this time a member of the Securities and Exchange Commission, had been an early exponent of legal realism in his controversial book *Law and the Modern Mind* (New York, 1930). Like many others of the New Deal's left flank, he was also then an isolationist in foreign policy for reasons he set forth in his *Save America First* (New York, 1938).

To Louis Rougier[1]

October 28, 1938

My dear Rougier:

I won't even attempt to say in a letter how I feel about the disaster which has overtaken the free nations of the world. . . . In many ways I feel that the immediate problem in Europe is no longer how to save liberty but how to save the national independence of the peoples who would like to preserve their liberty. It may be that to preserve their independence they may have to sacrifice for the time being much of their liberty. . . .

1. Louis Rougier, eminent French historian, philosopher, and economist.

To John L. Balderston

October 31, 1938

Dear John:

I have no doubt that our interpretation is fundamentally correct. I have talked with correspondents who were at that luncheon and there can be no doubt that Chamberlain never regarded the integrity of Czechoslovakia as a casus belli. He regarded it as an entanglement which might become a casus belli because of the French-Czech alliance in the first instance and the British dependence upon France in the second. His major problem throughout the summer was to avert a situation in which the Czechs resisted and the French were compelled to support them. This was clearly the purpose of the Runciman mission.[1] In the absence of proof to the contrary I have felt it necessary to assume, however, that Runciman went to Prague with the hope of trying to find a solution that did not involve dismemberment. The fact, however, that Hitler knew that neither Chamberlain nor Bonnet were willing to go to war to prevent dismemberment caused him to move quickly from the Carlsbad program of autonomy within the existing boundaries to the Berchtesgaden demands. The situation which Chamberlain and Bonnet were trying to avoid at all costs could have existed only if the Czechs had determined to resist, and their powers of resistance were undermined during the summer.

My own belief is that Runciman gave up all hope of a settlement without dismemberment after the third week in August and that he made no real secret of his conviction, and that he directly inspired the famous *Times* editorial[2] before Nürnberg, and that after that Hitler never ran any real risks of war. . . .

The only "moral" judgment I am disposed to make is that the Czechs were misled by the French and the British into thinking that they could afford to resist the Carlsbad demands. France and England were bluffing all summer, but their bluff worked only with the Czechs and with opinion in the democratic countries.

1. Lord Walter Runciman had been Chamberlain's special representative and mediator in Prague during the early stages of the Czech crisis. **2.** The *Times* of London, then ordinarily an unofficial voice of the Conservative government, on September 7 had carried a leading editorial that foreshadowed appeasement. It said in part: "It might be worthwhile for the Czechoslovak Government to consider whether they should exclude altogether the project, which has found favor in some quarters, of making Czechoslovakia a more homogeneous state by the secession of that fringe of alien populations who are contiguous to the nation with which they are united by race."

To Lewis W. Douglas

November 7, 1938

Dear Lew:

. . . Until our own position in foreign affairs is more clarified than it is, I am disinclined to do any talking outside of the United States on the subject of foreign policy. I don't believe we have yet begun to adjust our minds to the consequences and all our relations with the outer world have to be thought out from the new premises. I am afraid that Mr. Hull, much as I love him, is disinclined to do that, as one can see by his Far Eastern policy for example. What I dread is the growing divergence of policy between the British Empire and ourselves. That might in the end become a nightmare to both peoples.

I am writing this on the day before Election, so it is useless to speak about that. But I shall be very much surprised if the Republicans don't gain 75 seats in Congress. . . .[1]

1. The Republicans gained eighty seats in the House and eight in the Senate.

To Harold G. Nicolson

November 15, 1938

My dear Nicolson:

. . . I am wondering whether responsible people in Great Britain have begun to appreciate as yet how radically Munich has changed responsible American opinion about international affairs. I think it would be no exaggeration to say that almost every one now thinks that the British Empire is in mortal danger, not as a speculative matter for the far future, but in the very near future, and that Britain may not be permitted, even if her people develop the will, to make herself strong enough to defend her really vital interests.

Our own feeling about ourselves is that we cannot begin to have a foreign policy for the outer world until we have made ourselves so impressively strong in this hemisphere that what we say will really be heard everywhere. I think that civilization must have an invulnerable center around which the forces of law and order can rally. The British Isles were that center for a long time but now that they are no longer invulnerable, it seems to most of us here that Britain can no longer be depended upon to do for the world in general what it did in the Nineteenth Century. We are still an invulnerable great power, and the only one left, and for the next few months I think we shall put plans in operation which will really make us extremely formidable.[1] We watch with a kind of dread what looks to us like the failure of Great Britain to arouse herself to the danger she is in. . . .

1. Though instead, as Lippmann was later to comment, the United States for another several years continued to rely on the "unearned security" to which the country was long accustomed.

To Harold G. Nicolson

December 6, 1938

My dear Nicolson:

Your letter of November 25 came on Saturday.[1] . . . The more I watch France, where the elements of the thing seem to me clearer and nearer the surface, the more I am convinced that it is necessary to make armaments the paramount purpose not only in order to be able to withstand the attack, but also to prevent disintegration from within. I don't see how Great Britain and France are going to hold their possessions or even preserve their independence if they go on living in peace when they are under the constant threat of three nations that are on a war footing all the time.

My feeling is that another crisis fully as acute as that which led up to Munich is in the making and will be upon us within a few weeks or a few months at the most. But this crisis will differ from the previous one in one vital respect: last summer it was the territory and the national independence of others that were at stake — Czechoslovakia, the succession states of Central Europe, China, Spain. In the next crisis, the one now impending, the actual possessions of France and Great Britain, in one important matter the United States, will be directly threatened, — your position in the Mediterranean, and ours in the buffer states around the Panama Canal. And that, it seems to me, is bound to make this a much more acute crisis than the one in September. For while it was possible to surrender Czech territory, how is it going to be possible to surrender French territory? If it isn't possible to surrender it, isn't it going to be necessary to say no to these people, and at long last with an emphasis that really carries conviction? So it seems to me, and, therefore, when I hear people talk about appeasement, I feel as if they were talking about a wholly imaginary and wholly incredible state of affairs. . . .

1. Nicolson had written, in part: "The situation here is extremely fluid. Public opinion was not prepared for the Munich crisis and we were physically frightened by the handing out of gas-masks and the digging of trenches in our familiar parks. The thought that within a few hours the night would be shattered by the howl of high explosives and the crash of familiar buildings created widespread physical alarm. When therefore Mr. Chamberlain went off to Munich and gave us peace a tidal wave of relief and gratitude passed over the country. This wave . . . has rapidly receded leaving England rather shamefaced and rather battered.

"Had the Germans behaved with average consideration I think in our usual optimistic and complacent way we might have settled down to the pretense that Munich was the first step in a real settlement with Germany and the prelude to a prosperous peace. Hitler's . . . speeches, the continued vituperation of the German press and above all the persecution of the Jews has rendered impossible, even for the British public, to ignore the fact that Munich was a vast strategical surrender and that the Germans have become much more impossible since Munich even than they were before."

To Thomas W. Lamont

January 6, 1939

Dear Tom:

. . . I am sorry I gave you the impression that I think we ought to assist China in resisting Japan. What I tried to express were the alternatives, and I am far from being clear in my own mind as to which I think the wiser. I agree, of course, that $25,000,000 is nothing at all[1] and that a little encouragement, but not enough assistance, would give us the worst of both alternatives and the benefits of neither. The real question is whether to give sufficient assistance to those who are resisting aggression, or to give none whatever. It is no doubt too late to decide whether we shall give sufficient assistance to the British and the French, or whether we shall apply the principle of the Neutrality Act. The Chinese example illustrates the fact, I think, that the policy of neutrality and isolation involves the risk which nobody had foreseen until recently, that the victim of the aggression will not only be overcome, but in being overcome will be the ally of the aggressor. The danger in the Far East is not that Japan will conquer China and thus deprive us of certain rights and interests that we may have in China. The danger is that the conquered part of China will become the effective ally of Japan in the much larger plan of aggression in the Pacific which I have no doubt is contemplated. The question is not whether something we care about is destroyed, though that is bad enough, but that a power which was on our side of the scale will be transferred to the other side. This is what has happened in miniature as regards Czechoslovakia. It is what may happen in regard to Spain and Portugal. And if the great catastrophe happens to France and Great Britain, it might happen with regard to them. That is the sense, I think, in which the issue becomes clearer to us by recent events, that is to say, the alternatives are much more dangerous than even those of us who opposed the Neutrality Act realized at the time. . . .

1. Largely because the Treasury Department pushed so hard, the Export-Import Bank in December had provided a twenty-five-million-dollar credit to China for the purchase of American agricultural and industrial goods. In the view of Secretary of the Treasury Morgenthau, that step helped to sustain Chinese resistance to Japan in the face of the disheartening implications of the Munich agreement.

To Arthur N. Holcombe

January 13, 1939

Dear Arthur:

. . . After six years visiting these departments,[1] I am left with the feeling that the problem of adequate instruction is becoming more and more insoluble. All the teaching staff seem to be overburdened, and there never is enough money. So I have begun to wonder whether we don't have to look for a solution not in an enlarged budget, which is improbable, and not in administrative changes, which I think would be ineffective, but in a radical revision of the curriculum for undergraduates. There are too many overlapping courses. There is undue specialization and insufficient synthesis and coherence. Just to provoke speculation, and not because I would know how to carry it out in practice, I asked Professor Burbank whether it would not be possible to offer one course in the social sciences for sophomores, one for juniors, and one for seniors, and to combine in these courses a progressive education in economics, government and history, confining all specialized courses to the Graduate School. I am wondering whether undergraduate instruction could not be organized around a study of the classical texts in political science with the appropriate history accompanying them, so that at the end of an undergraduate course the student would have a pretty good acquaintance with what the greatest thinkers have had to say, from Plato and Aristotle to Adam Smith, the authors of the Federalist, Mill, Marx, Justice Holmes . . . etc.

I suppose this will sound like an amateur's dream, but having seen something like this actually being attempted at St. John's,[2] I have come to think that it is not impossible and that it might be not only very desirable as education, but also a remedy for the budgetary problem.

I hope you won't misunderstand me and think that I place more value on these suggestions than I really do. But I think we ought to speculate boldly, for it does seem to me that the problem in the university is much more fundamental than we have yet admitted to ourselves.

1. The Harvard Economics Department and Government Department. 2. St. John's College in Annapolis based its unique undergraduate program entirely on great books, a scheme Lippmann had heard much about from his friend Stringfellow Barr, the president of the college.

To Louis Rougier

January 19, 1939

My dear Rougier:

. . . I shall not attempt to say anything particular about the European situation. You can judge it better than I can. It may interest you to know, however, that here we feel that the moral recovery of France after Munich has been much more genuine than the British recovery. I myself felt certain that this would happen even in the darkest days of September, because it seems to me that the social constitution of France is intrinsically the best of any great power in the world, and that it is this constitution which will in the end cause France to survive all the ordeals through which she has still to pass.

The British position I look on without optimism, and that, I think, is the prevailing view in the United States, and this view will control American policy. It will cause us to base our policy and our armaments on the assumption that the British control of the seas is no longer to be depended upon. . . .

To Russell C. Leffingwell

January 27, 1939

Dear Russell:

. . . I am afraid there is not much chance of getting back to the pre-Nye neutrality and I have been trying to think out in my own mind what the consequences of our present neutrality laws are likely to be in case there is a European war. My present notion is that since we are not going to sell arms to France and Great Britain, and are therefore going to take a chance on their being defeated, we ought to use our facilities to make arms for ourselves. . . .

To the Marquis of Lothian[1]

April 5, 1939

My dear Philip:

. . . Things have changed a great deal since we talked. It seems to me that the British government is started on a line from which there is no retreat that would not involve general disaster. Our main concern at the moment is that the impending hearings and debate on the American neutrality law will cause great confusion in world opinion,[2] both in discouraging your government and in encouraging Hitler to take great risks. I am unable to guess how the issue will be decided in Congress but of one thing I am certain, — the more it appears that the coalition which you are organizing depends on American support, the stronger will be the isolationist forces in this country. You will understand because you know America that if it is made to appear that the coalition is depending ultimately upon America, people here will turn away from it, whereas if it appears that the coalition is strong and determined in its own right, the chances of our helping by measures short of war could be greatly improved.

From every point of view it seems to me important that the British and French should take the attitude that they are doing what they are doing for their own reasons, and will do it whether or not they obtain more or less assistance from the United States. . . .

1. Lippmann's friend Philip Kerr had become the marquis of Lothian. Late in April, he was appointed British ambassador to the United States, "the obvious man" for that post, as Lippmann then wrote him.   **2.** The administration's effort to persuade Congress to amend the Neutrality Act of 1937 failed that spring. The act imposed an arms embargo that would militate to the disadvantage of Britain and France in the likely event of a war with Germany. Operating confidentially and outside of the range of the act, for war had yet to be declared, Roosevelt used the Treasury as his agent for arranging British and French purchases of American military aircraft, a development that brought the funds of those nations into the building up of the undernurtured aircraft industry. Only after war began in Europe later in the year did Congress pass the Neutrality Act of 1939, which repealed the arms embargo and allowed the export of arms to belligerent powers on a "cash and carry" basis — a provision advantageous to the British and French, for they were maritime powers as Germany, boxed in by the British Navy, was not.

To Murry Nelson

April 26, 1939

Dear Murry:

For once I don't agree with you. The charge that Roosevelt is manufacturing a war scare for his personal political advantage is a matter of deadly seriousness at this particular time in the world's affairs, when the charge is made by a man like Senator Taft,[1] who is a probable Republican nominee to succeed Mr. Roosevelt. It passes beyond the limits of any form of domestic political controversy.

I am surprised that you should think I criticized Taft because I wish to stop criticism of the President. That would be ridiculous, as I live by criticizing the President. My contention is that there is a limit to criticism, and that that limit has been passed when, during a crisis neighboring on a world war, the leading member of the opposition strikes at the President's influence in this fashion.

I know this sounds serious, but I feel serious about it.

It may amuse you to know that we ran into the Tafts last night at dinner and everything was very cordial, so I have to go on record that he is, whatever his defects are — and they are many — a good sport.

1. Robert A. Taft of Ohio, a son of former President William Howard Taft, was elected in 1938 to the United States Senate and had already become a leading opponent of Roosevelt's domestic and foreign policies, as well as a strong candidate for the 1940 Republican presidential nomination.

To Gerald P. Nye

May 6, 1939

Dear Senator Nye:

. . . I cannot forget that the embargo applied in Jefferson's day was followed by American entanglement in the Napoleonic wars. And my own belief is that the misery and dislocation produced by the kind of non-intercourse which you advocate[1] would breed a far more insistent war party in this country than would the export of munitions according to established principles of international law, subject to the control of the Munitions Board, limited by the inhibitions of the Johnson Act, and supplemented by the withdrawal of diplomatic protection of all trade through the war zones. . . .

1. In the debate over neutrality legislation in 1939, as in previous debates about the same issue.

To the Marquis of Lothian

September 9, 1939

Dear Philip:

. . . There have not been many real surprises for you, I imagine, in the past few weeks; not even the Russian affair, I suppose.[1] For the immediate future the most puzzling thing to me is Italy.[2] I should think that what to do about Italian neutrality would be the most difficult problem the British and French governments have to deal with, and I should suppose that the whole character of the struggle will be determined by what they decide on this question.

So far as historical analogies hold at all, it seems to me more and more that we must study not 1914 but the series of coalitions that followed the Napoleonic wars. In this connection I recommend to you reading, if you haven't it in mind, the concluding chapter of Mahan's book on the French revolution.[3] There is, it seems to me, a striking resemblance between the policy of Chamberlain and of Pitt, and an even more striking resemblance between the policy of Russia then and now. Alexander, like Stalin, first wanted an all-embracing agreement against Napoleon, whereas the British held out for more specific and limited agreements. Then, having been totally against Napoleon, he turned around and made peace with Napoleon. In the Napoleonic analogy, I shouldn't be surprised now to see a series of wars with intervals of armistice and truce and shifting of the subordinate partners in the two coalitions. I hope, however, that the analogy won't apply to this country, which managed to be first on the one side and then on the other. . . .

1. On August 27, 1939, in Moscow, the Soviet Union had signed an agreement with Germany that provided that neither party would attack the other or join any other power or powers in such an attack. With communism and Nazism in that startling embrace, the way was open for both Hitler and Stalin to invade and divide Poland. Hitler had been making demands on that country,

which he invaded September 1, 1939, in the face of British and French commitments to the Poles. After Hitler refused to withdraw, on September 3 Britain and France declared war on Germany. **2.** Italy remained officially and surprisingly neutral in spite of its political and military alliance with Germany of the previous May. **3.** Alfred T. Mahan, *The Influence of Sea Power upon the French Revolution and Empire* (Boston, 1892).

To Arthur H. Vandenberg

October 2, 1939

Dear Arthur:

Thank you for your letter. I am in favor of the neutrality embargoes on shipping and finance. I believe in the shipping embargo because I believe it to be the one thoroughly effective way of preventing a collision between Americans and the German submarines, and, therefore, as the one effective way of preventing our being drawn into the war as a by-product and incident of the struggle for the control of the seas. And I am in favor of the embargo on finance because I regard it as the most promising method of protection there is against the development of an inflation which would dislocate our own economy unnecessarily and would make the subsequent reconstruction after the war very much more difficult. It is the application of the principle of paying as you go rather than paying by credit inflation, and that is a sound principle.

I regard the cash and carry system[1] applied to all war trade as not only being far better designed to keep this country out of the war but as far better suited to our national interests than the law as it is, or the arms embargo plus the shipping or financial embargo. As I see it, the two things most likely to involve us in a European war are (a) incidents arising out of the destruction of ships, since we have no common land frontier with Germany; and (b) a military disaster on the western front which gave or threatened to give Germany naval power in the Atlantic. The shipping embargo prevents our being entangled due to incidents; the repeal of the arms embargo is the only method available to us of enabling the Allies to strengthen their defenses so that they will not be brought to a surrender of the British fleet and of their naval position in the Atlantic.

I regard it as of crucial importance that we should avoid getting into a situation where intervention in the European war is even to be considered as a practical possibility. My reason for saying that is that with the situation what it is in the Pacific ocean we cannot and must not consider military intervention in the other ocean. In my judgment, our fleet must remain in the Pacific and only a lunatic would contemplate military intervention overseas in the Atlantic with no navy to assure the return of the American forces. The only question this leaves open, it seems to me, is what this country would do in case of a collapse of the Allies. Since I am convinced that it could not, would not, and should not send an army overseas, we should probably have to take some extraordinarily bold measures in the Atlantic ocean to hold strategic outposts while we expanded our navy to a two-ocean standard. . . .

1. The Neutrality Act of 1939, with its cash and carry provision, passed in the Senate on October 27 and in the House on November 2. Vandenberg, in 1939 a leading isolationist, opposed the measure.

To John L. Balderston

October 2, 1939

Dear John:

. . . In my opinion, it would have been lunacy for the British and French to send a force to Poland[1] where it could be annihilated, or to attempt to break through on the western front at a cost which would have decimated the French army. It is wholly right, in my judgment, to regard this as a siege and not as a war of movement, and above all to keep the military force intact. Nobody in his senses has ever thought the guarantee to Poland has meant that Poland could be saved from invasion conquest. It meant that Poland will be freed after the war is won.

I don't agree at all either that the Allies have chucked the cause for which they went to war by not declaring war against Russia. That accepts the German propagandist view that the issue in this war is the Versailles boundaries of Poland. That would be an idiotic thing to fight for, and I am sure the British and French are not fighting for the Versailles boundaries, nor for the question as to whether Poland is to be reconstituted as she was. So far as Poland is concerned, the war will have been won if an independent Poland exists after the war. The boundaries don't matter — it is the independence which does matter.

But the larger issue of the war is, of course, whether anybody can preserve his independence in Europe, and Poland is obviously only incident to that issue. . . .

1. The British and French had sent no forces to Poland, which Russia invaded on September 17th. On September 27th, the Polish government surrendered to the Germans and Russians. The victorious nations divided Poland between themselves two days later. Until April 1940, during the period of "the phony war," the British and the French did not engage and were not engaged by the Germans, nor did they in that period and for over a year thereafter suspend relations with the Soviet Union.

To Fred G. Stickel, Jr.[1]

October 12, 1939

Dear Mr. Stickel:

. . . For at least a fortnight at the time of the outbreak of the war, I devoted practically every article I wrote to insisting on the establishment of a thorough-going non-partisan working arrangement between Congress and the President which would do away with unlimited personal discretion on the President's part.[2] I think no one else writing in the press argued this oftener than I did. And in the very article to which you take exception you will find, I am sure, on rereading it I made precisely the point you insist on — namely, that the members of Congress must use their own judgment, both as against the executive and as against the clamor of pressure groups.

I should be the last one wanting to discourage the people from interesting themselves in their government, but I do most seriously think it important to protect Congress against the kind of organized intimidation which has been only too evident in the past month.

1. Fred G Stickel, Jr., a lawyer in Newark, New Jersey, had been in the New Jersey Assembly, 1911–13, and later a judge of common pleas, 1919–24. **2.** The president, though he did not make an issue of it, would have preferred a revision in the neutrality law that gave him more discretion than he received, particularly in designating an aggressor nation, which would be barred from acquiring American-made arms on any basis. As the 1939 act read, his only discretion lay in designating or not designating the existence of belligerency in the case of an undeclared war, such as that between Japan and China, which he did not officially declare a war. In the heavy lobbying on both sides of the neutrality issue, the isolationists had been particularly opposed to any expansion, real or cosmetic, of executive authority.

To Hugh S. Johnson   TELEGRAM

October 23, 1939

Dear Hugh:

You are quoted in the World Telegram as saying that I have described Colonel Lindbergh as pro-Nazi. I never said this or implied it and am no more responsible for what Mrs. Roosevelt or Miss Thompson write than you are.[1] You also describe me as pro-war. This is flatly untrue. I am a convinced believer that neutrality is necessary and is possible, and have argued for this conviction with pontifical ponderosity. Please do not misrepresent me. I take care not to misrepresent you. Personal regards.

1. Charles Lindbergh was already a leading opponent of American aid, even on the cash and carry basis, to France and Great Britain. He and his articulate wife expected Germany to win the war. He had been the object of attacks in the newspaper columns of Eleanor Roosevelt and Dorothy Thompson, against whom Hugh Johnson had defended him in his column. Lippmann in "Today and Tomorrow" on October 17 had criticized both Lindbergh and Herbert Hoover for calling for a continued embargo on offensive weapons. That position, Lippmann then wrote, advocated a "double standard of morals"; see Lippmann to Ernest E. Wheeler, November 3, 1939, inf.

To Ernest E. Wheeler[1]

November 3, 1939

Dear Mr. Wheeler:

The *Herald Tribune* has just sent me your letter of October 18th, in which you reply to my article on "The Double Standard of Morality." You will remember that I was writing, not about a general embargo, but on Mr. Hoover's specific proposals that certain types of weapons be embargoed on the specific ground that they are offensive weapons and barbarous. My point was that if Congress branded these weapons as, per se, offensive and barbarous, then the possession of such weapons by the United States government would have been confirmation that we had offensive purposes. For if these weapons are, by their very nature, offensive, how could we ever claim that when we possess them they are defensive?

The question of a general embargo on arms does not raise this moral issue. An arms embargo can be justified on the ground of national policy; for example, to keep out of war, or to help one side rather than another. A general embargo on arms involves no declaration that arms are immoral, but to single out particular weapons on the ground that they are specifically offensive is to turn from the level of national policy to a question of morals.

I don't want to bore you with the argument, but I note you say that the true analogy would be that of "the man who, although possessing and using liquor, prefers not to engage in the liquor traffic or even give it away." In my opinion, a man who possessed and used liquor and then declared that liquor dealers were immoral would himself be more self-righteous than righteous.

1. Ernest E. Wheeler, Harvard alumnus and New York City lawyer.

To Jacques Maritain[1]

November 14, 1939

Dear M. Maritain:

. . . Your article[2] in the *Commonweal*, written when the war began . . . seemed to me profoundly right and I myself have no doubt that, in your meaning of the words, western European civilization has already been saved.

One can see this even here. For however much the Hitler-Stalin agreement may have complicated the diplomatic and military problem of the world, it has enormously simplified and clarified the spiritual problem. The Allies are lucky that their negotiations with Russia failed and of course the reasons for the failure, the refusal to betray the Polish and Baltic peoples, do them great credit. In the United States this has had a very important practical result as well. I doubt seriously whether the arms embargo would have been repealed had Russia been signed as an ally of France and Great Britain; for then those of us who favored repeal would have found it almost impossible to convince the people of this country that there was any deep moral difference between the warring powers. . . .

1. Jacques Maritain, the celebrated French philosopher, a founder of the neo-Thomist school in France and, especially after 1940, in the United States. He believed, as he often wrote, in the essential foundation of Christian faith and morality, the principles of natural law as he saw it, in democratic thought. Lippmann, who in 1939 was already at work on the book that became *The Public Philosophy* (Boston, 1953), which advanced a somewhat similar case for natural law, found Maritain a sympathetic as well as a persuasive intellectual. **2.** "To My American Friends."

To Roland C. Hood[1]

November 20, 1939

Dear Mr. Hood:

. . . I believe . . . that even if a decisive military victory could be obtained by the sacrifice of, let us say, another million men, the Allied statesmen would not seek such a decision as a matter of high political policy. For a victory at such a cost would be a pyrrhic victory that in the case of France particularly might reduce her permanently to the rank of a second or third rate power.

I had a long talk in June with General Gamelin[2] and I know that the problem of the French birth rate as affected by two great wars in one generation is a controlling element in his whole philosophy of war. The Allies have to win the war by methods that do not cost that many lives.

Moreover, I believe that a similar calculation must be in the minds of many Germans, though not in Hitler's mind — namely, that their only hope of a negotiated peace is to end the war with their army substantially intact. . . .

1. Roland C. Hood, an acquaintance of Lippmann's, had been city editor of the *Birmingham Age-Herald* in Alabama before joining an advertising firm in Atlanta, Georgia. **2.** General Maurice G. Gamelin, then commander in chief of the French Army, had an outsize faith in the Maginot Line, the nation's eastern fortifications. It was his strategy, after war began, to await a German attack while building up the numbers of French troops and increasing their materiel.

To Jerome D. Greene[1]

November 29, 1939

Dear Jerome:

. . . I have been giving a little thought to the Browder affair,[2] but only one thing is clear to me about it. That is, that the reason given by the University for refusing, namely, that he is under indictment for a felony, is not a sound reason, because it violates the principle that a man is not guilty until he is proved guilty. On the other hand, the critics are wrong, it seems to me, who argue as if it would have been all right to exclude him after a conviction. If

Harvard University is subject to the same principles of the Bill of Rights as, let us say, the City of Boston in issuing permits to speak, then a man who has been convicted of a felony has not lost his other civil rights.

It follows, it seems to me, that the fundamental question is whether Harvard must apply in its own buildings the same principles that govern freedom of speech in the country at large. I think not. I think Harvard is entitled to make a judgment on the concrete question, just as the editor of a newspaper reserves the right to decide who is to be invited to contribute to his columns. If the University has decided that Browder's change of line after the Nazi-Soviet pact was evidence that he is a disguised foreign agent, then it would have been justified in refusing to let him speak in the University Hall. I admit that such judgments are difficult and delicate and perhaps inexpedient, but I do not see how a university can, in theory at least, relinquish the right to make judgments of that character. . . .

1. Jerome D. Greene, assistant secretary to the Harvard Board of Overseers. 2. Harvard had denied a platform to Earl Browder, then head of the Communist party of the United States, on the ground that he was under indictment for passport fraud, for which he was later convicted.

To Harold G. Nicolson

January 2, 1940

My dear Nicolson:

. . . I have . . . received from your American publishers your book, *Why Britain Is at War*,[1] which seems to me much the best statement of the Allied case that anyone has done.

Our own public opinion, as you know, is in a most curiously paradoxical state. Actually, at least 70 or 80 percent of the articulate people of this country accept completely the case as you state it. The rest object to it on grounds that are a curious mixture of pacifist, Nazi, and Communist contentions. But though a great majority believe in the Allied case, they shrink from having it openly supported because in their hearts they fear they would feel a moral obligation to back up their beliefs. Therefore, because of the decision not to enter the war, there is a general determination to arrange the convictions of the American people so that they fit the decision. The American state of mind can best be explained, I think, by this conflict between the practical decision not to intervene, (for which I myself think there are sound reasons), and the sympathies of the people, which have no relation to the decision. As a result, the whole psychological structure is very unstable, and is easily unsettled by the outbreak of active warfare; as, for example, in Finland,[2] or in the naval battle of Montevideo.[3]

I wish your public men would state your case oftener than they do. They take too much for granted when they act on the assumption that having said a few times why they are at war, it is not necessary to reiterate. But, of course, the talking should be done in London and not in the United States, and the speeches should be addressed to the Allied peoples and merely overheard by the Americans.

1. Harold G. Nicolson, *Why Britain Is at War* (Harmondsworth, Middlesex, 1935), distributed in the United States by Penguin.   2. The Soviet Union had invaded Finland on November 30, 1939. In spite of the stalwart resistance of the Finns, Soviet forces breached their crucial defensive position, the Mannerheim Line, in March. On March 12, Finland accepted Soviet terms, including the cession to the Soviet Union of the Karelian Isthmus and the city of Viborg.   3. British cruisers in mid-December 1939 attacked the German pocket battleship *Graf Spee* off the coast of Uruguay and forced it to put into the harbor at Montevideo. There, in accordance with international law, Uruguay refused the ship a long stay. After consultation with Hitler, the ship's captain scuttled his vessel and committed suicide. The battle off the Uruguayan coast had violated the inter-American declaration of Panama, which called on the belligerents to stay clear of the "waters adjacent to the American Continent," a statement Britain and France had rejected. Nevertheless the United States on December 15, 1939, organized a joint statement of protest to Britain and Germany.

To John Maynard Keynes

January 31, 1940

My dear Keynes:

. . . You cannot pick any bones with me about the American reaction to the war, because I shall be agreeing with you, I am sure. I don't know whether anything I have written has given you the impression that I think there is moral beauty in the attitude of the neutrals. I can think of one or two things said in the very trying days of the struggle to repeal the arms embargo which may have sounded like that to you. All I can say in self-defense is that there were times during that bitter struggle when it seemed to me that almost any kind of self-respect and self-confidence would have been better than none at all. I don't know whether people in England understand how extraordinarily difficult it was to repeal the arms embargo after war started, and what a price had to be paid for it. . . .

To Arthur H. Vandenberg

January 31, 1940

My dear Senator Vandenberg:

Thank you for your letter of January 30th. I appreciate the trouble you have taken to make clear your own position. The situation which confronts us all now is so grave that I feel justified in imposing on your time by making some observations about your letter.

First, as to whether it is historically correct to say that your resolution "precipitated the situation in which we now find ourselves." You say that the committee rejected your resolution and that the State Department acted immediately upon the heels of this rejection. Am I wrong in thinking that the State Department acted because it knew that it had the support of the committee? Though I cannot put my hands on the clipping at this moment, I think I am right in recalling that you publicly applauded the action of the State Department. I did not say it was "controlled" by your initiative but I think I am right in supposing that it would not have acted so promptly if it had not known that you and the committee favored serving notice on Japan. However, as you say, all of this is of no particular moment as regards the problem itself, since it is agreed that notice of the termination of the treaty was served with your approval and without, so far as I can remember, any objection by your associates on the committee.[1]

Second, in discussing the consequences of this momentous event, I discuss not your attitudes and purposes, but the terms of the resolution itself. You are well aware that in matters of this sort the intention is not what counts. You say that the author of the resolution did not intend that its "automatic purpose" was to "free us to apply a one-sided embargo." I was careful to note in my article that you yourself do not accept that interpretation, but I do not see how you can escape the responsibility for the interpretation that was universally placed upon it.

Third, I am unable to agree with your statement that the resolution is not concerned with opposition to the Japanese conquest of China. The second part of the resolution, dealing with the Nine Power Treaty, can have no other meaning, it seems to me, for the language employed is the language always employed to express such a meaning.

Fourth, your letter of August 7th to Mr. Hull expresses a hope which I am sure is shared by every sensible man, but there is some ambiguity in it. You say that your purpose is to enact "a new treaty with Japan in the light of 1939 realities." Were you referring to the commercial treaty or to the Nine Power Treaty? If you were referring only to the commercial treaty, what was the matter with it? If you were referring to the Nine Power Treaty of 1922, is it not evident that the only purpose in abrogating the commercial treaty of 1911 was to put pressure on Japan to negotiate with us about the matters dealt with in the Nine Power Treaty? The matters dealt with in the Nine Power Treaty, as you well know, concern not our limited rights, but the constitution of China.

Fifth, in referring to your request that the Brussels conference be called together[2] in order to decide whether Japan had violated the Nine Power Treaty, and to recommend the course to be pursued, you must have recognized, it seems to me, that this was collective action and that the effectiveness of the collective action would depend upon our associates in that action. I do not understand the reasoning by which you could at the same time take the risk of grave entanglement in the Far East and the risk of denying to the nations whose assistance we should need if it ever came to war there, the right to purchase arms.

I do not raise this question in order to rake over the embers of an old controversy, but because I am seriously concerned with the extremely dangerous
position we have gotten into in the Far East, a position which, in my opinion,
may become catastrophic.

I do not feel that I have assigned to you a place of undue prominence in our
Far Eastern policy. I regard you as a very prominent man who may in a very
short time have the highest responsibility in this country, and what you do
and what you think, I therefore take very seriously. But always I take it with
great good will towards you personally.

1. In July 1939, Senator Vandenberg had submitted to the Senate Foreign Relations Committee a
resolution calling for the abrogation of the United States' commercial treaty with Japan. He
intended that resolution, among other things, to balance the British recognition of the responsibilities of the Japanese military in China. While Democrats on the committee hesitated to support
a Republican's resolution, Roosevelt and Hull acted. The resolution suited their intention of re-
straining the Japanese, but they feared it would not receive an impressive majority in the Senate.
Accordingly on July 26, Roosevelt on his own announced that the required six months' notice for
termination of the treaty was being sent to Japan. That step, designed to hearten the Chinese in
their resistance to Japan and to strengthen British resolve to oppose the Japanese conquest of
China, troubled Japanese moderates but provoked Japanese militants to urge an alliance with
Germany.

In January 1940, the commercial treaty expired. The following September, Japan joined Germany and Italy in a military and economic alliance, while in the interim, relations between Japan
and the United States had deteriorated. Whatever the merits of the termination of the commercial
treaty, that deterioration arose essentially from Japan's determination to expand its power in east
Asia, the equal determination of the United States to oppose that expansion, and the preoccupation of the European powers — which left the United States alone as the counterpoise to Japan in
the area. Before the end of 1940, Lippmann had come to the view of the administration about
preventing further Japanese expansion.   2. The Brussels Conference of 1937, a meeting of the
powers that had failed to settle the Sino-Japanese war.

To Alfred M. Landon

February 13, 1940

My dear Governor Landon:

It was very kind of you to write me, and I am much reassured to find that
you do not think I have taken an unduly alarmist view of the situation in the
Far East. As a matter of fact, I consider it far more serious than I dared to say,
or thought it wise to say, or could have proved was true if I had said it. But I
think there are very strong reasons for believing that any serious reverses to
the Allies in Europe during the coming months will cause the Japanese to
move in the Pacific in such a way as either to inflict upon us a humiliation as
great as Munich or to precipitate war. The pressure of both Germany and
Russia in Tokyo is in that direction, and among the Japanese here, even those
who have been most opposed to the military party, there has been a sudden
and disconcerting appearance of a strongly anti-American feeling.

The European position and the Far Eastern are closely related and any radical change in the balance of military power on either side will precipitate something very serious on the other side. I think you are entirely right in feeling that our relations with Europe are much less dangerous than our relations in the Far East. For in Europe we can be involved only indirectly, and not again in the sense that we were involved in 1917; whereas in the Far East we can be involved directly in a war that would probably last several years, and a war in which for the first two years we might well look as if we were being beaten.

To George H. Moses[1]

May 5, 1940

Dear George:

. . . I am not prepared to say just exactly what concrete proposals ought to be made at this time. I am sure that if the Republican Party were worth its salt and regardless of whether it wants to take a 100 percent or an 85 percent isolationist position, the fundamental thing that needs to be done is to increase this country's military power; that is a matter of building up war industries that are now in such feeble condition that, according to information that I think cannot be doubted, the Japanese are out-building and will within a year — if they haven't already done it — have a superior navy. The rest of our war industries, apart from the airplane factories which are being subsidized by the Allies, are in such a low state of preparedness that we probably could not equip and supply three divisions of troops. We could not be ready to fight a first class war within a period of two years.[2] The country is being deluded into thinking that because Congress makes large appropriations for the navy the country is getting the navy it is authorizing. It isn't. And why in thunder the Republican Party, which has always stood for preparedness and nationalism, isn't howling about that I don't understand. It seems to me incredible that the Republican Party should have its mind made up for it by Gerald Nye. . . .

1. George H. Moses had been a Republican senator from New Hampshire, 1918–33. 2. An accurate estimate, as senior American military officers then knew.

To Henry A. Wallace

May 23, 1940

Dear Mr. Secretary:

. . . When I spoke of the likelihood of a great famine next winter, I was, of course, referring to the Scandinavian countries, Holland, Belgium, and France. I imagine you would also have to add Switzerland if Italy intervenes in the war; and, perhaps more seriously, England if the war goes badly for them.

I have no suggestions to offer about the financial and political problems involved in getting supplies to the needy people of Europe. But I am certain that no private effort can hope to cope with the problem and that the government must not only finance it but take it in hand, according to a plan conceived on a very great scale. While public opinion in this country has not yet realized the incredible dimensions of the problem, it is bound to realize them, and one of the urgent things, it seems to me, is to prepare a great plan.[1]

In preparing it, we must have in mind at least two alternatives: the one more hopeful alternative is that we shall provide food in order to sustain the resistance of the Allies; the other is that we may be trying to save them in the midst of a total wreck of their institutions, their systems of transportation, and their critical means of production. We can make no mistake by conceiving the problem at its worst and on the greatest scale. The big risk in this matter, as in all others, is to follow a policy of too late and too little.

It is a great comfort to know, as I should never have doubted of course, that you are taking this matter in hand.

1. Wallace was as much concerned as was Lippmann with the problem of food in Europe, but the German victories of 1940 made any official plan of relief impossible and temporarily unnecessary. The provisioning of Europe would in effect have assisted the Nazi effort to defeat Britain. Further, German dominance permitted agriculture throughout most of the western half of the continent to function much as it had before the war.

To Arthur A. Ballantine[1]

June 8, 1940

Dear Arthur:
    . . . There is no particular point, I think, in arguing the theoretical question about the internal debt. However, I have no doubt — and the experience not merely of Germany but of France and England confirms it — that a nation in a war economy, having unlimited power to tax, to conscript life and labor, and to raise consumption, is limited only by the actual physical goods inside the country and by its capacity to work. Don't forget that the British internal debt was larger at the outbreak of this war, per capita, than ours is. That has no bearing upon the British rearmament program.

As to your second point about our not being any longer in a civilian economy, my reply is that we cannot afford to be. As a matter of expediency we may decide to adhere for a time to the voluntary system of enlistment, industrial production, taxation and lending, but only as a matter of expediency. A nation which seriously means to prepare itself for war in a world of totalitarian states must in principle prepare totally for war. To fail to accept this principle is to make the fatal mistake of Neville Chamberlain and of the British Labour Party. They, too, refused to accept this principle until the disaster was at hand.

I was not proposing that the nation should take over all of the property of the people. Here you are erecting a straw man. I am proposing that the nation assert an absolutely prior claim upon the services and the property of the people. This means the principle of universal service both for the armed forces and for industrial production. It means the power to tax to the limit of what is practicable. It means to direct the savings of the people into investments which serve the national defense. It means the power to restrict consumption, to ration materials, and to shut off all forms of purchasing power and invest- ment which compete with the needs of the national defense. Any other prin- ciple of rearmament is, as I said before, the fatally erroneous principle of the Chamberlain government.

I do not agree that the adoption of this principle is an abandonment of our way of life. Our way of life is determined by its ends, not by the means that are required to defend it; and it seems to me as illogical to say that we have become like the Nazis because we have adopted universal service and are pre- paring totally for war as it is to say that the Frenchman flying a bomber is indistinguishable from the Nazi flying a bomber. There is all of the difference in the world, because the two bombers have different purposes and ideals.

I hope this doesn't startle you, but this is what I think, and this I am satis- fied is what the country will be compelled to come to, and quickly at that.[2] I do wish I could have a chance to talk these things over with you.

1. Ballantine at this time was a partner in the New York law firm of Root, Clark, Buckner and Ballantine. **2.** Lippmann's letters curiously reflect little of his deep concern with developments in Europe during the spring of 1940. The Germans in that season successively invaded and con- quered Denmark, Norway, the Netherlands, Belgium, Luxembourg, and France. On June 4, the British evacuated 200,000 of their own and 140,000 French troops from Dunkirk, but without their equipment. On June 10, Italy entered the war against France. France asked Germany and Italy for an armistice on June 17. On the day of this letter, it was already clear that Britain, now standing alone, would be Hitler's next target; that a German victory would leave control of the eastern Atlantic in Hitler's hands; and that that control could seriously threaten the United States and the rest of the Western Hemisphere. Consequently Lippmann was urging a program of na- tional mobilization and American aid for England. The priority he gave to those objectives ac- counted for his insistent arguments at that time for avoiding hostility in the Pacific and Far East.

To John F. O'Ryan[1]

June 10, 1940

Dear General O'Ryan:

. . . I am enclosing a few articles which I have written on the subject of Japan during the past year. Not every word in them fits the present situation, but the general point of view is fairly consistent, and it might be of some use to you to be able to point out to some of the Japanese that there is a school of American opinion which has sought to avoid irreconcilable conflict.

That such a conflict must be avoided at all cost seems to me evident on the face of things, since by no stretch of the imagination can our interests in the Far East be considered as anything but secondary to our interests in this hemisphere and in the Atlantic. Japan cannot threaten the independence of any state in this hemisphere, either politically or economically, whereas a victorious Germany can and will. For that reason, it seems to me self-evident that we must find a basis of compromise with the Japanese which will permit us, if necessary, to take the fleet out of the Pacific. This will be a truism to you, I am sure.

I might add, for your information, that I know on the best of authority that both the State Department and even some members of the high command of the navy are misinformed as to the relative strength of the two navies. The real ratio, I am told, is not 5 to 3, but on an optimistic estimate 5 to 4¾, and on a conservative estimate 5 to 6. What is more, for the next year the Japanese will be out-building us. I learned to my dismay that the men who formulate the discussions in the State Department are not really aware of the real military position in the Pacific, and I am sure, from personal contact, that your mission has the heartfelt approval of the wisest men in the navy. They have told me so in the past two or three days. . . .

1. John F. O'Ryan, New York City lawyer, much-decorated major general in the National Guard, and outspoken advocate of American aid for England, was about to go to Japan and China on a retainer fee from the Japanese Economic Federation to attempt to spur Japanese-American commercial and diplomatic relations.

To Joseph Warner[1]

June 11, 1940

Dear Mr. Warner:

Thank you for your letter. I have much the same reservations about Mr. Roosevelt that you have, but I will say frankly to you that with all of his limitations he is far better qualified to be President than Dewey,[2] Taft or Vandenberg. Dewey is inexperienced and unstable. Taft is an excellent human being and would make a good cabinet officer or a good judge, but, for the world we live in, he would be a lesser Neville Chamberlain. He simply does not grasp the realities. The same holds true of Vandenberg.

As far as I can see, the Republicans have only two men, Hoover and Willkie. Hoover has well-known limitations, but I believe he would be a better President the second time than he was the first time. Willkie has the makings of a first-class statesman, and for my own part I hope the Republicans will nominate him. If they do, the country will have a real choice and a real alternative to Roosevelt. If the Republicans nominate Dewey, Taft, or Vandenberg, I don't think there will be a real choice.

1. Joseph Warner of Goshen, Massachusetts, a rather frequent commentator, in letters to Lippmann, about "Today and Tomorrow." **2.** Thomas E. Dewey, celebrated as special prosecutor in a New York investigation of organized crime, 1935–37, ran a strong but losing race as Republican gubernatorial nominee in 1938. A leading candidate for the G.O.P. presidential nomination in 1940, he achieved that position in 1944 (and again in 1948) after election in 1942 as governor of New York. In 1940 he was identified with the Republican noninterventionists in his foreign policy.

To Bryan Rust[1]

July 1, 1940

Dear Mr. Rust:

How very, very true everything you say is, both as to Mr. Roosevelt and about the nature of leadership in political democracies. Mr. Roosevelt, in my opinion, lost his chance to lead the country in foreign policy in the winter of 1939 when he subordinated foreign policy to a whole mess of New Deal reforms.[2] That split his party, made the opposition intransigent, and compelled him to compromise on foreign policy. From then on, the position has been lost.

1. Professor Bryan Rust, a member of the Department of Government at Wayne University in Detroit. **2.** Roosevelt had then endeavored to get Congress to accept his lending program, which it rejected, and to prevent congressional limitations on New Deal administrative agencies, in which he succeeded. Still, Lippmann's comment was rather wide of the mark. The president had already begun to focus primarily on foreign policy, but he faced a hostile Congress in which a coalition of Republicans and conservative Democrats could block reform and, unless he could appease the Democrats, also impede his foreign policy programs.

To Wendell Willkie

July 30, 1940

Dear Wendell:

If I understood correctly what you said yesterday on the telephone, I feel all the more that I shall not be imposing on you by setting down some ideas which I have reached since the Philadelphia convention.[1] They are concerned with the basic theme of your campaign.

This is obviously a matter of the utmost importance and my own belief is, speaking frankly, that the momentum behind you has slowed down since you were nominated because you have not shown the road you intend to take, and your well-wishers have been moving in several different directions at once. That is why I am rather disturbed at the prospect of your waiting until August 17 before you really assume the leadership of the Willkie Movement. In the highly unstable state of opinion these days, and with *the initiative in action*[2] in FDR's hands, it is a great risk to leave a popular movement without leadership.

Let me cite two important examples of "issues" which are, I believe, not being handled to your ultimate advantage: (1) anti-third term, (2) anti-New Deal.

As to the third term, it is all very well for conservative Democrats and regular Republicans to use this as a talking point. But there is a kickback in it for your real supporters. It is that many of them would have supported Roosevelt for a third term if you had not been nominated. Moreover, I believe, you would never have been nominated had Roosevelt withdrawn before Philadelphia and left the Republicans with no one to defeat but Hull, Jackson, etc., etc. The spearpoint of the Willkie movement was composed of people who were so concerned about American security (external and internal) that no other political consideration seemed important. People of this sort will not vote against Roosevelt because of the third term principle but they will vote for you if they believe you will do better than he in making the country strong. These people are a minority of the voters but they supply the driving energy of the Willkie movement. The only way to state the third term issue to them is to say that with you in the field, Roosevelt is not indispensable. If Taft were the candidate, these people would, however reluctantly, go to Roosevelt.

As to anti-New Deal: Many of your supporters are, I believe, making the mistake of suggesting that by electing you the country will go back to the old system of private enterprise. This is utterly impossible (a) because the social gains will not be repudiated, (b) because total defense requires government planning and regimentation, (c) because if Hitler wins, or if the war is a long stalemate, or even if he is defeated, economic life cannot for years to come be left to the free play of economic forces; it will have to be directed to national ends. The real reason for voting for you is, in my opinion, that you can organize the economy better than Roosevelt can. But many of your friends, who have a 1936 mentality, are presenting you as the opponent of organization. Such a presentation will not stand up against the events of the next three months. You must, in my opinion, appear as the organizer of security[3] and not as the champion of laissez-faire.

For this, I submit, is the only line on which the class issue can be transcended. In a slugging match about W.P.A., S.E.C., spending, etc., Roosevelt can, I think, win in what will be a disastrous campaign. There is no doubt that his great strength, and it is a very great strength, is that the poor regard him as their friend. For that reason, bitter anti-New Dealism will help him, and you will be maneuvered into the position of a supposed reactionary.

Your opportunity arises out of the fact that people feel insecure and want the assurance of a strong competent man. Roosevelt is not a strong, competent man, and that is where you can beat him if you take "the hard line" and summon the people rather than vaguely try to please them all. You have nothing to lose, in my opinion, by being the Churchill rather than the Chamberlain of the crisis, and by charging Roosevelt with being the Daladier, the weak man who means well feebly and timidly. You must not let him be the Churchill, for he is not a Churchill. But he will try to seem like one, and if you do not seize the initiative, he may succeed.

You will know the spirit in which this is written. My very best wishes to you.

1. Where the Republicans had nominated Willkie and, as his running mate, Senator Charles L. McNary of Oregon. **2.** The emphasis is Lippmann's. **3.** While engaging increasingly in what he later called "campaign oratory" of an anti-New Deal nature, Willkie was also contributing to the organization of national security. He was doing so out of conviction and also at the behest of William Allen White, urged on by Lippmann. By keeping out of the campaign the issue of American aid to England and Roosevelt's part in it, Willkie made politically possible the late summer agreement by which the United States transferred to Britain fifty overage destroyers, essential for British use in the Atlantic, and Britain gave to the United States long leases on various of its naval bases in the Western Hemisphere — bases important for hemispheric defense and beyond Britain's power any longer to protect. On Lippmann's role in that episode, see Ronald Steel, *Walter Lippmann and the American Century* (Boston, 1980), pp. 384–86.

To Edmond E. Lincoln[1]

August 6, 1940

Dear Mr. Lincoln:

I hope you will permit me to write a word of reply to your letter of August 5th, or, rather, to restate my own view. It is that given command of the seas, the landing of troops in this hemisphere is a perfectly conceivable operation.

The misunderstanding seems to have arisen because of your assumption that I thought it would be easy or possible to land troops in continental United States. I do not think that. But I do think that the landing of troops or the establishment of air bases in South America within striking distance of the Canal, or perhaps even in Canada, would be entirely possible for a power which had an absolute naval superiority.

You ask me whether I honestly believe that our navy, plus our airships and our coast defenses, would be able to prevent the landing of German troops operating three thousand miles from their home base. My answer is that if our navy is bottled up by superior navies in both oceans, it would be no more difficult for Germany to land troops in Venezuela, Colombia or Brazil than it has been for Great Britain to land Australian troops in Egypt. Distance as such is no barrier if the seas are under control.

1. Edmond E. Lincoln, former faculty member at the Harvard Business School, since 1931 economist for the E. I. Du Pont Company.

To Henry R. Luce [1]

September 30, 1940

Dear Harry:

. . . I do not think we disagree really about the Far East. I have been in favor of a Fabian policy of avoiding a direct and open and irrevocable conflict with Japan as long as it was uncertain whether Great Britain could stand up until next year, and while it was uncertain whether the United States would give serious and decisive help to the British and would seriously arm itself. Both of these things have been in doubt during the summer. And for that reason alone I have thought it desirable to play for time and not to force the issue. I have never been for appeasement with Japan, in the sense of surrendering China to her, and I know at first hand, because I went into the matter personally with Japanese officials over here, that no agreement with Japan would be conceivable in which we did not surrender China; but I have thought it prudent to protest and procrastinate during the period when so many of our own experts were predicting that Great Britain would be overwhelmed by September.

As for Willkie, I feel very badly indeed. I hoped and believed he would be the man this country needs, but I think he set his campaign on a fundamentally wrong line back in July and has lost ground ever since. . . .

1. Henry R. Luce — the founder, oracular editor, and publisher of *Time* and the head of the Time-Life magazine empire — had been born in China, a country about which he considered himself a leading authority.

To Alfred P. Sloan, Jr.

October 18, 1940

Dear Mr. Sloan:

. . . I should like to make my own position a little clearer. I did not have it in mind, and certainly did not intend to imply, that General Motors should shut down its plants and confine its operations entirely to defense projects. When I spoke of speeding up, I had in mind speeding up plants already in operation, producing airplanes, etc. Surely something can be done there by longer work and more intensive work. There are certainly plants where the groundwork has been laid and there we should speed up. That is a problem not so much for the industries, however, as for the government and the labor leaders. [1]

The matter of enlarging the scope of the program is another thing. I do believe that the scope of the program should be enlarged, but that again is not a criticism of the industries but of the government. I might add, however, that I think the word "superimposed" an unfortunate word in that it conveys the impression to the ordinary reader, as it did to me, of a point of view like that of Chamberlain's, which did not give priority of intention to re-armament over all other considerations.

1. American mobilization was proceeding very slowly, with the industrial sector under the weak guidance of the National Defense Advisory Commission, which had no authority over either business or labor. In the defense industries, especially the automobile industry, the United Automobile Workers were still struggling to obtain concessions long overdue from management. Management for its part was persisting in the manufacture of automobiles, as it did in spite of the country's defense needs, for another year and more.

To Alexander Woollcott[1]

October 25, 1940

My dear Alec:

Not only are you entitled to an answer to your letter, but I am glad of the chance to explain to you personally why, unless something develops which I do not now foresee, I am taking no part in this campaign. I am making this explanation to you personally as an old friend but I do not think I shall make any public statement during the campaign. For while I want my friends to understand what I do, I have an almost fanatical conviction that columnists who undertake to interpret events should not regard themselves as public personages with a constituency to which they are responsible.

It seems to me that once the columnist thinks of himself as a public somebody over and above the intrinsic value and integrity of what is published under his name, he ceases to think as clearly and as disinterestedly as his readers have a right to expect him to think. Like a politician, he acquires a public character, which he comes to admire and to worry about preserving and improving; his personal life, his self-esteem, his allegiances, his interests and ambitions become indistinguishable from his judgment of events. In thirty years of journalism I think I have learned to know the pitfalls of the profession and, leaving aside the gross forms of corruption, such as profiting by inside knowledge and currying favor with those who have favors to give, and following the fashions, the most insidious of all the temptations is to think of oneself as engaged in a public career on the stage of the world rather than as an observant writer of newspaper articles about some of the things that are happening in the world.

So I take the view that I write of matters about which I think I have something to say but that as a person I am nobody of any public importance, that I am not adviser-at-large to mankind or even to those who read occasionally or often what I write. This is the code which I follow. I learned it from Frank Cobb who practiced it, and abjured me again and again during the long year when he was dying that more newspaper men had been ruined by self-importance than by liquor. You will remember that he had had opportunity to observe the effects of both kinds of intoxication.

So I do not feel called upon to make a public explanation why I do not take a position in this campaign. Now I wish to tell you why I am not taking a position. For reasons which seem to me good, I have not wanted to take a position ever since Willkie was nominated and Roosevelt was re-nominated. By accident I do not have to take a position, even privately, because being a resident of the District of Columbia I have no vote. If I had a vote, I should have to choose, and having chosen I should not wish to take a political position privately which I did not explain publicly. But since I cannot vote, I have felt free not to choose and, therefore, to devote all my attention to what I feel are the transcendent problems posed by the calamitous fact that we are compelled to have an election during what may be the culminating crisis of modern history.

The first problem was how the campaign could be conducted so that it would not irreparably divide the nation on the issue of foreign policy, paralyze the action of the government, prevent rearmament, demoralize the free peoples abroad, and cause the American democracy to destroy men's faith in democracy. The second problem was how, once the election was over, to reunite the nation promptly because, obviously without unity, we shall go to a disaster.

Having written so much about the war and the national defense, I made up my mind before the conventions that if there was any way of keeping these questions detached from the party struggle and from candidates, it was my duty to do so. When Willkie was nominated, and after I had satisfied myself personally of the sincerity of his convictions, I felt that foreign policy could be kept out of the campaign, and that second only to the successful defense of Britain, this was the most important and fortunate event that had happened in the midst of an unbroken series of horrors and catastrophes. So I decided that if Willkie stood fast on his commitments and convictions, the best thing I could do in this campaign was to stand aside, try to deflate the foolish and embittering arguments of both sides, and to keep reminding people that they were going to have to live after November fifth with the consequences of the stupid things they do before November fifth.

Though the campaign is very bitter, it might have been infinitely more bitter if the two candidates had not been Willkie and Roosevelt. The bitterness which exists is class bitterness, a most dangerous thing, but it would have been a thousand times worse if in addition the country had been torn by a struggle between "appeasers" and "warmongers." We have escaped that, thanks to the nomination of Willkie and his fairly firm resistance to the isolationist politicians in his own party. But the ominous class conflict remains and, whoever is elected, the liquidation of that conflict is our immediate and our paramount task.

If Roosevelt is re-elected, a very large part of the most energetic part of the population will be disaffected, and it will require a supreme effort, I think, to produce in Roosevelt and in the defeated opposition a genuine spirit of conciliation and unity. If Willkie is elected, he will have a divided and incoherent party and there will be profound distrust among millions of people. To overcome this he will need from Roosevelt and the Democrats a kind of magnanimity and patriotism which is rare in politics.

There are in both camps men close to Willkie and to Roosevelt who see this and they are the men we must count upon to bridge the chasm which has been opened up. A few journalists who have kept themselves detached from the charges and counter-charges may, then, come in handy.

You asked me how I was going to vote. You have gotten back a little treatise. But I wanted to answer your question because it was you who asked it, and if I have been long-winded it is because I haven't the time to be more concise. . . .[2]

1. Alexander Woollcott, popular critic of the arts, renowned wit, friend of Lippmann's for many years. 2. Lippmann used much of this letter in "Today and Tomorrow." On his increasing disenchantment with Willkie's campaign and his neutrality in the election of 1940, see Ronald Steel, *Walter Lippmann and the American Century* (Boston, 1980), pp. 386–89.

To Lowell R. Burch[1]

November 16, 1940

Dear Mr. Burch:

I shall try to answer your letter, but first I want to make it clear to you that I was not in favor of Mr. Roosevelt's running for a third term, and I said so in an article published after the Republican convention and before the Democratic convention.

What my recent article said was that the voters have always reserved the right to decide whether to continue a president in office, and it is a fact that although innumerable proposals have been made to amend the Constitution in order to make a president ineligible for reelection, not only has no such amendment ever been adopted, but none has even been submitted to the people. Moreover, it is not true that the rule against the third term is so ingrained in the American tradition that no legislation would be needed if it were the intent of the people to prevent a third term under any conditions. For example, in the Republican convention of 1880, Grant had 306 votes for a third nomination for thirty-six ballots, and was within sixty-five votes of a nomination. In 1927 when Coolidge was seriously being considered for a third term, a vote was taken on the La Follette Resolution condemning a third term. Twenty-six Senators, including practically all of the conservative Senators — among them Senator McNary — voted against the La Follette Resolution. Grover Cleveland was nominated three times in succession, and each time received a plurality of a popular vote. He failed the second time to receive a majority in the electoral college.

These and many other facts which I could cite seem to me to support the view of my article that the rejection of the third term, while a very strong tradition, is not an absolute rule in American politics, and never has been. The only president known to have declined a third term on principle was Jefferson, and even he said that under certain circumstances he would accept a third term.

1. Lowell R. Burch, president of the New York Air Brake Company.

To Eric Hodgins [1]

November 19, 1940

Dear Mr. Hodgins:

I have read once the Fortune Forum of Executive Opinion which you have just sent to me, and I would agree with you that it is a document of real national significance. It proves what most of us have believed from our own personal experience, that there is no irreconcilable conflict between business executives and the New Deal, but that there is on both sides an irreconcilable temper among a sufficient number of important people to create a general atmosphere of irreconcilable conflict. Such an analytical study as yours is a good deal like dynamiting a log jam in a river and is extraordinarily useful. Now if only it would be possible to take in the order of importance the measures listed on page 169 which business men feel are preventing recovery, and if one could find out what changes in these measures would change their opinion of them, we should have the foundation of a practical program.

In reply to your specific question, my view is that you ought to make a broad distribution of this report, accompanied by a request to make as specific as possible the specific objections to specific measures.

The more I see the New Dealers here in Washington and their opponents here and elsewhere, the more persuaded I am that the greatest thing we have to do is to bring the level of argument down from high-sounding generalities to specific, practical questions. I realize that there is involved a general attitude which is perhaps controlling in the feeling of people on both sides, but the only way to melt this feeling is by the discussion of practical questions. That is very evident here in the Defense Commission where we have in practice a much higher degree of national unity, with debate, criticism and differences of opinion, than there is in any other place.

1. Eric Hodgins, publisher of *Fortune* and a vice president of Time Inc.

To John Crosby Brown[1]

December 19, 1940

Dear Mr. Brown:

. . . My view on the question of diplomatic relations with the Vatican is that diplomatic relations do not involve moral questions and that the whole discussion is based upon a mistaken view of the meaning of diplomatic representation. My view is that the United States government can and should be represented diplomatically at any place and have relations with any organization or institution with which they have relations and where there is value in representation. The modern notion that diplomatic recognition involves anything more than the opening of communication seems to me quite erroneous. . . .

1. John Crosby Brown, president of Tamblyn and Brown in New York City, had asked Lippmann's opinion about the extent to which the United States government should cooperate with the Vatican after the war. Roosevelt had sent Myron C. Taylor, a socially prominent lawyer, to the Vatican as his unpaid personal representative on a mission of peace, with the rank of ambassador, an appointment that had stirred up some protest. Roosevelt reappointed Taylor in 1941, as did Truman on the same basis after the war ended.

To William R. Mathews[1]

December 19, 1940

Dear Mr. Mathews:

I am very much interested in your very able editorial. With its fundamental argument I am in entire agreement and I have some reason to think that a statement of war aims will be forthcoming from the British in the fairly near future. The point on which I am dubious is whether such a statement of war aims should contain specific territorial proposals. As it happens, one of my tasks for a long time in the other war was work on the preparation of Wilson's Fourteen Points, and your eleven points have a strong resemblance to them. For many reasons I have come to doubt the wisdom of stating during a war specific aims which ought properly to be the subject of negotiations after the war, and my own tentative present feeling is that the real problem is contained in your eleventh point — namely to state clearly what kind of German government it would be possible to negotiate peace with. I think, though I am not sure yet, that I would be willing to recognize the German army as the responsible government of Germany providing there are restored during the negotiations sufficient freedom of the press and radio in Germany to permit the presentation to the German people of all responsible statements and announcements from the other side.

None of these things is entirely clear in my own mind yet, but this is the

line on which I have been thinking. I do hope that you will send me anything
else of this sort that you write.

1. William R. Mathews, editor and publisher of the *Arizona Daily Star* of Tucson.

To Harold G. Nicolson

January 1, 1941

Dear Nicolson:

. . . You speak of Hitler's New Order. It has not caught the imagination
of Americans. But you should not tire in repeating what actually goes on in
the occupied countries. All news of that is useful. For people forget.

Here the position is, I believe, as follows: Since May the *intellectual*[1] conviction is general that American security is directly involved with the British
cause. But it is the courage of the British people which has won the hearts of
the people here. The effect has been immense — no one dares to be openly
anti-British and the overwhelming majority are for the first time in my lifetime really pro-British.

The passage from ideas and feelings to acts is slow because, 1, democracies
do not quickly declare war without a provocative act — which the Germans
have avoided — solely on ideological grounds and to forestall *future* dangers;
2, the lack of a specific program (now being remedied by the President); 3,
most importantly, the fear of being engaged in war before we are fully armed —
in case Britain could not hold out. This is the nub of the whole matter: the
fear of becoming engaged in both oceans at the present stage of our military
preparedness. In proportion as you convince the American people of your
determination and capacity to hold out and as our own armament program
begins to produce real results, which it will in a reasonably short time now,
the willingness to take action here will grow greater. . . .

1. The emphases in this letter are Lippmann's.

To T. B. Huff[1]

February 11, 1941

Dear Mr. Huff:

. . . The argument of those who say this bill[2] gives the President power to
go to war or to regiment American industry is false, because both of those
powers he already has if he wished, which he does not, to exercise them. What
this bill does do is not to increase his power to go to war or his power over
industry but simply what it professes to do, namely to provide the British
with some weapons out of our existing stores and to provide the authorization

for financing them. If you understand the procedure of Congress you will understand that an authorization does not give the President any power. It merely authorizes Congress later on to appropriate money if it chooses to do so. Therefore, this bill, except for the billion, three hundred millions' worth of weapons already in existence, gives the President no powers, no money, nothing, until through subsequent legislation Congress makes specific appropriations. The reason people are so opposed to the bill is that unfortunately the opponents have misrepresented it, because perhaps they did not read it carefully and understand it correctly.

1. T. B. Huff, president of the American Cooperative Serum Association of Sioux City, Iowa. 2. The lend-lease bill, H.R. 1776, provided for the defense of the United States by aid to the nations opposing Germany. It incorporated Roosevelt's innovative idea for supplying England with the arms and materiel that the British could no longer afford to buy, for they had nearly exhausted their dollar holdings. The bill also circumvented the Johnson Debt Default Act by empowering the president, when American security was at stake, to lend or lease equipment to eligible countries for return after the war ended. Debate over the bill in the Senate, echoing a national debate between isolationists and interventionists, focused largely on two questions: the implications of lend-lease for the war in the Atlantic, where British ships would be threatened by German submarines, and the effects of the bill on presidential power. Before Congress passed the bill, it added amendments demanded by Republicans and noninterventionists that specified that nothing in the bill could be construed to give the president the authority to order American convoys for British vessels, or in other ways to increase the authority of his office. Those amendments left untouched the constitutional powers of the president as commander in chief which Roosevelt later interpreted as the basis for convoying and for ordering American naval vessels to shoot German submarines on sight.

His authority was contained by the congressional decision to demand semiannual reports from the executive before appropriations for lend-lease were made. That stipulation sustained a congressional voice in lend-lease policy throughout World War II. Congress did later extend the policy to cover other nations at war with the Axis countries, including, among others, Greece, the Soviet Union, China, Australia, most of the Latin American States, and the overrun nations of Western Europe as represented by their governments-in-exile. For its part, the United States received important help through reverse lend-lease. The lend-lease program, effective beginning in April 1941, brought the United States to the edge of belligerency, a predictable consequence that had accounted for the intensity of national controversy over the bill.

To John M. Vorys[1]

February 17, 1941

Dear Mr. Vorys:

. . . Of course you cannot think that I do not believe in the function of an opposition, or that there is any implication to that effect in anything I write. But I do adhere to my view that the Republican opposition in Congress has misjudged the situation of the world, and has, therefore, had to retreat steadily from each position that it has occupied. A good opposition should see further and more clearly than the party in power, and there is nothing in the record of the Republicans, either on questions of national defense or on our relationship to the Allies to justify any belief that they have had foresight. If they had had it, they would not now be compelled to reverse themselves so completely that the only issue left between them and the Administration is one of procedure. It is not surprising that when the Republicans have been so wrong for so many years, and have admitted it by their subsequent votes, the majority of the people now take the view that the President probably understands what is the necessary procedure today better than the opposition. . . .

1. John M. Vorys, Ohio Republican, had been elected to the House of Representatives for the first time in 1938. He was a qualified pilot, had been a delegate to the Washington Conference of 1922, and had a large interest in foreign affairs.

To Richard B. Scandrett, Jr.[1]

February 18, 1941

Dear Mr. Scandrett:

I was very much interested in your letter to Anne Lindbergh. I had not read her book until very recently. It struck me as an almost desperately pathetic book, an attempt to explain her views before she had really succeeded in coming to terms with them herself. What a pity that she couldn't have clarified her mind by talking with her father.[2]

1. Richard B. Scandrett, Jr., a New York City lawyer whose mother was a member of the Morrow family, had been a defeated Republican candidate for Congress in 1938 and was the author of Divided They Fall (New York, 1941), an interventionist book. He had sent Lippmann a copy of his letter to Anne Lindbergh, in which he expressed his dismay with her statement about the war.   2. Anne Lindbergh, Dwight Morrow's daughter, had written The Wave of the Future (New York, 1940), a defeatist tract with Fascist overtones that argued against American aid to England as futile in a world moving toward authoritarianism.

To Herbert C. Hoover

April 4, 1941

My dear Mr. Hoover:

The very last thing I would ever wish to do is to misrepresent you or to attack you personally. I think you know from long experience that even when I have been on the other side of a question I have always written about you, because I have always thought about you, with great respect, tinged with much personal affection.

The statement in my article that you did implicitly advise the American people to come to terms with the New Order was not an accusation but what I believed to be a statement of fact. It is based on your address at the University of Pennsylvania on September 18th, on the subject of the post-war economic problems. In it you stated that you had the depressing conviction that for many years after any so-called peace that is likely to come from this war, we shall be confronted with grave economic dangers and that it seemed to you likely that the totalitarian domination of Germany and Italy will cover most of the continent of Europe from Russia to the Atlantic, and will also include much of the dependencies of these former European states in Africa and the East Indies, and in the East the Japanese will for a long time to come strive for a similar control of China and Asia. You then proceeded to describe the measures we ought to take in a world in which the totalitarian area would be likely to embrace about sixty percent of the world's population and about forty percent of the world's trade. I read this at the time, and on re-reading it I still read it, as meaning that the United States must find ways to come to terms with the New Order. I did not say and I did not imply and I did not think that you liked this New Order, but I did think you believed that it had conquered sixty percent of the world's population and that we must adjust ourselves to the idea of living in such a world.

I am sorry that you should do me the grave injustice of saying that I advocate sending our boys to this war. I have never advocated it. I have always advocated a policy which, in my opinion, is most likely to avoid just that result. And it is my opinion that if the policy we are now pursuing had been put into effect sooner the chances of our being involved in actual hostilities would be far less than they are. I hope that as between us neither will impute to the other "hopes" which are contrary to fact.

Finally, as regards the question of food for the occupied small countries, you may perhaps have noticed that I have not discussed the problem at all in the form in which you have presented it recently. My reason for not discussing it has been that I respected your purpose and the arguments in favor of it but felt that the arguments, if valid ought to be taken up by you personally in direct negotiations with the British government, rather than by a public discussion in this country in which a real weighing of the facts and their consequences is entirely impossible.

To Margaret Peters[1]

April 7, 1941

Dear Mrs. Peters:

. . . Of course, I cannot speak for Mr. Roosevelt. In fact, I have not had a talk with him since long before the war began and I can only judge by what I hear from those who do see him and from his actions. I believe that he is thoroughly opposed to the sending of an expeditionary force to Europe similar to that sent in the last war. What you must remember when you think of your son is that it would be equally serious if he had to spend several of the years of his life as a soldier guarding the coast of Brazil or Venezuela or Canada.

The policy of helping Great Britain to win the war by delivering weapons is the best and only chance we all have, not only of avoiding a total war in Europe but a total war in South America or somewhere else in the Western Hemisphere. No one can honestly guarantee that this country will not ever have to engage in war. All that any honest man can do is to try to find the policy most likely to preserve what has to be preserved at the very smallest risk and cost. I believe very sincerely that the President's policy is inspired by that purpose.

1. Margaret Peters of Albion, Michigan, was despondent about the prospect of Roosevelt's leading the United States into a war in which her son would have to fight, as her husband had in World War I.

To Sibyl Colefax [1]

April 26, 1941

My dear Sibyl:

Your letter mailed March 31 reached me yesterday and makes me ashamed of myself for not writing oftener and more legibly. This letter I'll have typed, sending one copy by clipper and another by ship.

This is the end of a bad week but it is ending better than we had dared to hope — what with the Germans admitting that the British forces are getting away from Greece [2] and here an increased action [3] — rather than hesitation — after the military reverses.

Perhaps there were compelling reasons why the Balkan campaign had to be advertised as the opening of a new "European front" by your newspapers and information services. But it was an error as regards the U.S.A. This campaign, and all land actions in continental Europe, should be represented as filibustering raids. . . . There are two reasons for this — one that when little is expected, the subsequent withdrawal is not a defeat; the other, and most important, it keeps the war in its true perspective as a grand struggle between land and sea power. We do not wish to fight a land war in Europe but our people have now realized that the North Atlantic must be held securely by the English-speaking nations. You can say, I believe, — in so far as Americans see the war as a struggle for freedom by means of sea power they are vitally interested and in so far as they imagine it as a repetition of 1914–1918 with the need of head-on collision with the German army on the continent they draw away.

I see that in England you speculate a lot about "American opinion." My judgment, for what it's worth, is that the controlling factors are the following: one, as I said above, that the war must be conceived as fundamentally a *naval war*,[4] and that it can be won with sea power (British and American) as the principal means.

Two, American optimism and pessimism and our morale is, and will continue to be, a reflection of yours. We exaggerate everything both ways being so far from the scene of action, but what the British people and spokesmen say and feel is critical for what we feel and say. So tell your people not to go about asking "What will be the effect on the Americans of the Balkan defeat?" because your own reactions are cause and ours are the effects.

Third, the American people will follow Roosevelt on any measure which he says is *necessary* and *feasible*. The sense of what is feasible is directly related to our own progress in war production and mobilization.

The facts about our own progress are, I believe, as follows: it will be a long time before we have a large first class army, and this fact will and must control our policy and our popular opinions. Our navy is strong and growing stronger, but most of it is immobilized by the Japanese. But we already have considerable naval power available in the Atlantic, and our production of weapons — airplanes, tanks, etc. — will come along quickly beginning about July. We are far from prepared for total war on our own account but we are in the final stage of very successful and effective preparation to help you this year. By the end of the year and before next season our mass production, which is the thing we know best how to do, will be really impressive. The preparatory period of "tooling up" and "making ready" is almost over. Here there is more optimism on the inside than the public yet realizes. . . .

1. Lady Sibyl Colefax, widow of Sir Arthur Colefax and a frequent correspondent of Lippmann's, was then active in British war relief and in strengthening Anglo-American friendships. 2. The British had begun to evacuate their expeditionary force in Greece. They succeeded in removing some forty-eight thousand of the sixty thousand men involved, but they had to abandon their equipment. Britain had first landed troops in October 1940 to assist the Greeks in their resistance to an Italian invasion; in January 1941, the Germans moved in to retrieve Italy's losses there. British forces were also on Crete, which fell to the Germans on May 31, 1941. 3. On April 9, 1941, the United States and Denmark had completed an agreement that pledged the United States to defend Greenland, a Danish territory in the Western Hemisphere, from Axis attack and granted the Americans the right to install necessary bases there. Lippmann was doubtless also heartened by the conference of late April at Singapore among American, Dutch, and British representatives to plan for combined operations against Japan in the event that that nation attacked the United States. 4. All emphases in this letter are Lippmann's.

To Karl A. Bickel[1]

July 14, 1941

Dear Mr. Bickel:

. . . I expect little of the Russian resistance,[2] so that any resistance they do put up will be clear gain. We, on our part, must act on the assumption that they can't last through the summer.

1. Karl A. Bickel, president of the United Press. 2. On June 22, 1941, German forces invaded the Soviet Union along a two-thousand-mile front. Churchill at once promised to provide all

possible aid to the Russians, a promise the United States also made in October, but during the summer most American military experts predicted a quick German victory. It was not to materialize, though the Russians had to fall back regularly during the first year and a half of fighting.

To William R. Mathews

September 23, 1941

Dear Mr. Mathews:

My own views on the subject of the army are, as I tried to make perfectly clear, extremely tentative. But what I think about the matter of the relationship of our army to our diplomatic policy I made as clear as I know how to make it, in the two articles I have written about the subject. I cannot make the matter any clearer in a letter. Whether I am right or wrong, you will, if you will be kind enough to re-read the articles, see that I don't think the use of an enormous American army is feasible, desirable or probable.

I have no information that is not available to you on this subject, and there is nothing contradictory in the recommendation. The simple fact is, as stated in my articles, that there are in Europe and Asia today, on the side opposed to the Axis powers, millions upon millions of trained troops who cannot be equipped. There is not in this war, as there was in France in 1917, a shortage of manpower. On the contrary, there is a surplus of manpower and a shortage of weapons. Therefore, I have always considered our main contribution to the war to be the production of weapons and the use of the navy to insure their delivery. I regard the army as essentially an enlarged marine corps, that is to say, as an auxiliary of our naval power, to be used for garrisoning naval outposts and, in certain obvious cases perhaps, seizing them.

It seems to me, therefore, a misunderstanding to suppose that we are engaged in training a mass army to fight in Europe or Asia, when there are already in being the vast armies of the British Empire, China and Russia.

As a matter of fact, our present army is not an enormous army and is not designed for the kind of expeditionary force which you apparently have in mind. It is, as regards combat troops, a small army, perhaps not larger than 700,000 combat troops in the whole 1,800,000. This number of troops have no relationship whatever to the kind of thing you seem to have in mind. . . .

To James M. Drought[1]

September 26, 1941

Dear Father Drought:

I have just very recently come back to Washington and only today have had an opportunity to see the mail that had accumulated during the summer. This will explain the delay in answering your letter of August seventh, in which you asked me whether I have changed my attitude in regard to the Far East since the early spring.

I have not changed in that I have not given up hope of a diplomatic settlement with Japan. But I have changed my view as to the probability of arriving at such a settlement. I am convinced by the Japanese advance into Indochina that the moderate party in Japan is unable to negotiate a settlement in the Far East, as long as the road to expansion through military conquest is still open. Therefore, I am in favor of barring all of the roads by superior force and then negotiating with the Japanese government. That is the policy the government has been pursuing during the summer and I think it is a sound policy. It has at least halted the advance of the Japanese military power and produced the most serious negotiations which we have had with Japan since 1931. But we still have a long way to go before we can really induce the Japanese to abandon their ambition for the conquest of the whole western Pacific.[2]

There is one paragraph in your letter which I do not understand at all. It is the one in which you ask whether there is any informed person who does not know that the Oriental war is continuing because of the cynical self-interest of European countries and the United States. I can't imagine what ground there is for saying that. If the reference is to the British, I can tell you that they have been far more disposed than we to help Japan.

1. The Reverend James M. Drought of Maryknoll, New York, had written Lippmann in opposition to American foreign policy in the Far East, which Lippmann had been supporting in "Today and Tomorrow." **2.** In September 1940, Japanese troops had occupied Indochina, which the French government, a puppet of the Germans, made no effort to defend. In retaliation, the United States, having warned Japan against that aggression, placed an embargo on the export of high grades of scrap iron, which Japan needed and had been importing. Later that month Japan signed its pact with Italy and Germany, an alliance supplemented in April 1941 by a Japanese neutrality agreement with the Soviet Union. Japan, now protected to its north, continued to exploit Europe's wartime preoccupations by moving farther into China and solidifying control over Indochina. In July 1941, the United States froze all Japanese credits as did Great Britain, a step that effectively stopped Japanese imports from both countries. The United States also then placed all armed forces in the Philippines under the command of General Douglas MacArthur. In August Roosevelt warned the Japanese ambassador in Washington that the Japanese policy of military domination in Asia, if it persisted, would force the United States to safeguard American interests, and Churchill announced that Great Britain in that event would support the United States. Prince Fumimaro Konoye, at that time the Japanese premier, would have reached toward an accommodation had he been able to control the dominant military influence in the government. That domination was expressed in October by the replacement of Konoye with General Hideki Tojo. Konoye's efforts at an accommodation with the United States had also been set back by Roosevelt's decision, on the advice of the State Department, not to negotiate himself. The State Department's insistence, which the president supported, on making the termination of the war against China an essential basis for any agreement with the Japanese had also impeded Konoye.

To Albert Gailord Hart[1]

September 29, 1941

Dear Mr. Hart:

. . . I have no great faith in price fixing. . . . I rely, as you do, on drying up purchasing power and ultimately upon rationing as effective means of preventing a runaway inflation.[2] It is because raw materials and industrial goods can be rationed that I wrote my article saying that this is where the real price fixing should pivot. I do not believe the general ceiling can be enforced by law but I believe the formula I suggested, namely parity for agriculture and the standard of living for wage rates, provides a political and moral ceiling to restrain the political farm bloc and the trade unions. But of course, obviously and without question, the crucial and important measure is the mopping up of the purchasing power which will expand and the rationing of essential consumer goods that are scarce.

In my view, the real difficulty of the mopping up operation is that no tax program will be great enough to do it. Therefore, I am very much interested in the Keynes plan of supplementing it by some form of compulsory saving. . . .

1. Albert Gailord Hart, an associate professor of economics and sociology at Iowa State College, had written Lippmann with various recommendations for controlling inflation. This reply touched on each of Hart's points. 2. In April 1941, the president had established the Office of Price Administration, with Leon Henderson in charge, but that agency first undertook to ration commodities in short supply only after the United States was at war. Before the end of the war, thirteen rationing programs that Congress empowered by statute in January 1942 had been imposed by the OPA. As Lippmann recognized, heavier taxation also proved necessary to control inflation, as did the Treasury's energetic bond drives, which constituted the administration's preferred alternative to the compulsory lending program that Keynes worked out for the British government.

To J. E. Schaefer[1]

October 9, 1941

Dear Mr. Schaefer:

I wish I could discuss this matter with you at length, but there are two fundamental errors in the premises of the whole discussion.

The first is as to the size of the public debt in Britain and in the United States. The true measure of a public debt is in relation to national income, and on that basis our public debt is not now nearly so large as the British public debt. The principle for this in private life is that if John Smith and John D. Rockefeller each owe a thousand dollars, John Smith may be considered to be heavily in debt whereas John D. Rockefeller isn't. Since our national income is very much greater than that of the British Isles a debt of the same size is not nearly so great.

The other serious error is to suppose that the lease-lend commitments are a sizable factor in our war economy. Out of 60 billions available for war purpose in the United States, 3 billions are British money ear-marked for contracts, 7 billions are lease-lend money appropriated by Congress, and about 50 billions are for American defense under authorizations made by Congress in the summer of 1940, months before there was any policy of aiding Great Britain. Our contribution to Great Britain is thus less than 10 percent of our war expenditure, and even under the new lease-lend bill I doubt whether the proportion will grow much greater.

1. J. E. Schaefer was vice president of Stearman Aircraft, a division of Boeing Aircraft, in Wichita, Kansas, and a supporter of Charles Lindbergh's activities in opposing American involvement in the war.

To Stringfellow Barr

December 9, 1941

Dear Winkie:

What you said the other day, referring to Hobbes, made a great impression on me but I was troubled by it, feeling that there was something wrong, though at the time I was too full of your good lunch to think what it was. This is what I think is the error.

To say that all commonwealths must either be formed by acquisition or institution is to hide the real problem, which is that, with practically no exceptions, they were formed by a blend of the two methods and that there are virtually no examples of the formation of any enduring commonwealths by either of the methods in its pure form. Precisely because Hitler's method has no admixture, it is not only intolerable but unworkable, and because the League was all covenant and institution it was unworkable. The actual problem which confronts any unifier of separate states, and particularly so today, on the world scale is lost by this form of analysis, because the problem is to decide what the blend is to be.

I don't think the analogy of our own federal union is a good one because, in that instance, the union of the states had behind it the historic fact that they had all had a common allegiance to the British crown. I think, if I remember correctly, that some of the framers of our Constitution were aware of the fact that they were establishing in a new form the central powers of the king. Similarly, in my own thinking about the future order, my first preoccupation has been not with the factor of institution (heaven forgive me for this jargonese shorthand) but with the factor of power, which must be the organizing center of institutions. While I do not think that Streit's form of union with Great Britain is a workable thing,[1] I do believe that British-American unity in world affairs is the basis of any future order that will be tolerable, and I have spent a good deal of time speculating on the forms of alliance which could make it effective. I think I am not being vaguely mystical in basing my hope on two facts: that the geography of the North Atlantic favors it and compels it, and that politically the union is a reunion.

The danger, as I see it, in the sharp distinction which you used is that people who have no faith that commonwealths can be established by institution will then helplessly regard Hitler's method as a necessary evil. . . .

1. Clarence K. Streit, formerly a correspondent in Europe for the New York Times, had advocated his plan for an Anglo-American federation in his recent books Union Now (New York, 1939) and Union Now with Britain (New York, 1941). Those books had a growing audience at this time following the Japanese attacks on December 7, 1941, against Hawaii, the Philippines, Hong Kong, and Malaya. The United States declared war on Japan December 8, as did Great Britain; and on December 11, Germany and Italy, already at war with Britain, declared war on the United States. The Anglo-American alliance formed a special and strong link in the alliance against the Axis powers which included the Soviet Union among its principal members, France and China in somewhat lesser roles, and also the other United Nations.

To H. L. Bailey[1]

December 30, 1941

Dear Mr. Bailey:

The matter is very complicated and I fully appreciate the kind of difficulties a manufacturer like you has met. But there is very little doubt that from the summer of 1940 to and into the late spring of 1941, there was resistance, reluctance and inertia to an all-out industrial effort, both in the OPM[2] and in the great mechanical industries. The effect of this was to limit the armament program and the effect of that limitation was what you ran into when you dealt with a subordinate officer in the General Quarter-master's Corps, who was concerned with a secondary defense article.

I can assure you that this statement is not a matter of mere personal opinion, and that both objective over-all proof and specific proof could be brought out if, as is of course not the question, the matter were to be treated controversially.

The error, I think, in your reasoning is in your assumption that the industrial policy of the government has been determined by army officers and Administration officials alone. This omits the critical part played by the industrialists in the OPM.

In a large sense, the matter is really indisputable when you consider two things: one, the 1941 boom in automobiles, whereas in every other country at war or preparing for war the manufacture of private passenger automobiles has been stopped; and two, the distressing attitude in 1941 by the highest official in OPM that our armament program could be "superimposed" on normal business and blank resistance in the winter of 1941 to the proposals to convert the automobile plants to war production.

1. H. L. Bailey had complained to Lippmann about confusion in government procurement of cotton textiles, about the negative effect on production of federal antitrust policy, and about the absence of a national industrial leader of mobilization.   **2.** Roosevelt had established the Office of Production Management in December 1940 to coordinate defense production for the United States. The agency also supervised production for lend-lease recipients. Ineffective from the start, the OPM suffered alike from a lack of real authority and from the conflict between its head, the automobile executive William S. Knudsen, and Knudsen's associate director, the vice president of the CIO, Sidney Hillman.

To Theodore Roosevelt, Jr.[1]

January 10, 1942

Dear Ted:

Your letter provokes me to do what I, in an amiable but ineffective way, meant to do anyhow, namely to write to congratulate you on your promotion and to say that none could be more well deserved, and to send you every good wish.

The underlying thesis, on which we agree, is much more important than any question of policy, about which we may have disagreed. We have got where we are through our own weakness and not through the strength of our enemies. And that weakness runs very deep, I am afraid, down to the roots of our educational philosophy and to the popular mores. It was as evident in the unrestrained materialism of the 20's as in its counterpart, the paternalism — or should we say the grandmotherliness? — of the New Deal. In fact, it is a dangerous disease which has all but destroyed western civilization, which probably has become incurable except by terrible suffering and mortal danger.

But it is easier to say these things this way than to write a book about them. I have a book which I have been working on for some years which does deal with this whole question,[2] but I had to lay it aside in 1939 and I have never had the leisure or the freedom of mind to go on with it. . . .

1. Theodore Roosevelt, Jr., a heroic officer during World War I, had been promoted to the rank of brigadier general. In 1944 he landed with the first wave of assault troops in the Anglo-American invasion of Normandy. During the campaign in France, he died of a heart attack.   **2.** The book became *Essays in the Public Philosophy* (Boston, 1955).

To Norman H. Davis[1]

January 31, 1942

Dear Norman:

I had another talk yesterday with Tixier, the head of the Free French in this country, and I am more than ever satisfied that Mr. Hull ought to look into the matter of their treatment by the State Department officials with special care.[2] They are in a very dangerous state of mind, not over our policy in regard to the Vichy government but in regard to our attitude towards them in their own territory and our attitude to them here in the United States. There is no reason in the world why they should be dealt with rudely and inhumanly, as in fact they have been and are being. I believe they can be made to accept our Vichy policy if in the things that directly concern them they are better treated. The matter is of urgent importance because both in Africa and in the islands of the Pacific which lie along our present communications to the Far East, Free French territory is of very great practical and strategical importance to us. If something goes wrong in this territory, the State Department will have a terrible but quite unnecessary responsibility. I regard the matter as so serious that unless something is done very quickly to improve our human and personal relations with the Free French here and with General de Gaulle in London, it will be necessary to raise the question publicly. That is very undesirable and it can be made unnecessary by a more intelligent and sympathetic treatment of the Free French than they can get from the lower State Department officials now in charge of these matters. Mr. Hull's interview with Tixier made a big difference, but of course it can't cure the matter unless it is followed up.

This business of the Free French is part of a larger question which is boiling up all over the place, namely the manner in which government departments and agencies like the Red Cross itself treat friendly aliens, particularly those engaged in fighting the Axis. A situation is gathering which will make the affair of the blood plasma seem small.[3] I know you are busy but this is really an important matter which can't be neglected any longer. If I had had a chance to see Mr. Hull last week I should have liked to say this to him then, because I feel that he personally is getting too much of his information on this very delicate business through official channels only. . . .

1. Norman H. Davis was then ambassador-at-large and also chairman of the American Red Cross. 2. Adrien Tixier, representing the Free French government in Washington, confronted the exasperating attitudes of both Roosevelt and Hull toward that government and its head, General Charles de Gaulle. French refugees under de Gaulle considered themselves the legitimate rulers and army of their nation, the engine of French resistance to Germany, and the proper representatives of French interests in the world. For those roles they had a strong claim, since the dictatorial puppet government the Germans had installed in unoccupied France — the government at Vichy headed by Marshal Henri-Philippe Pétain — bowed to German orders on all important matters. De Gaulle had found refuge in England, where Churchill provided him with a sometimes reluctant but essential support. In contrast de Gaulle met open hostility in Washington, where Roosevelt and especially Hull disliked and distrusted him. Indeed the United States, as a deliberate expedient, was at this time maintaining official relations with the government at Vichy. American relations with de Gaulle had recently reached a temporary nadir when the Free French on Christmas, 1941, took over Saint Pierre and Miquelon, two small French islands off the coast of Newfoundland which the Vichy government had previously held on terms to which the United States had agreed. In a rude statement about the issue, the State Department referred injudiciously to the "so-called Free French," a phrase that provoked much criticism from the American press and public. The episode infuriated Hull, who never overcame his resentment of de Gaulle. 3. A shortage of blood plasma had necessitated a special drive for blood by the American Red Cross.

To Francis Biddle[1]

February 20, 1942

Dear Francis:

I have just this morning got back from the West Coast and found your letter of February 19th.[2] I should, of course, like to have a talk with you about the situation, one important aspect of which is the great gap between what you knew in Washington and what was known on the Pacific Coast. The irresponsible drives of which your editor speaks were clearly in the making when I was there, due to a grievous lack of communication between Washington and the Coast. . . .

1. Francis Biddle, patrician New Dealer, served as chairman of the National Labor Relations Board, 1934–35; judge on the United States Circuit Court of Appeals, Third Circuit, 1939–40; and attorney general of the United States, 1941–45. **2.** The attorney general wished Lippmann had talked with him or with Secretary of War Stimson before writing the "Today and Tomorrow" column urging control of the Japanese-Americans on the West Coast. In the spirit of the spreading panic there, Lippmann had referred to the "imminent danger of a combined attack from within and without." Biddle knew that no such dangers then existed. Yet Lippmann, like the West Coast newspapers, also called for requiring those in the coastal area to prove their right to be there. That demand fed the anti-Japanese mood of Californians long prejudiced against Asians and the anti-Japanese bias of the commanding officer on the coast, General John L. DeWitt, whom Lippmann had consulted. DeWitt's own recommendation persuaded Stimson in turn to urge upon Roosevelt the president's executive order of February 19, 1942, which authorized the War Department to designate military areas and to exclude any or all persons from them. Biddle, uncomfortable with that order, nevertheless yielded, to his later admitted chagrin, to Stimson. The order took the first step toward the evacuation in March of all Japanese-Americans — of whom many were American citizens — from their homes on the coast. That evacuation predictably led to their internment in camps in the interior. All in all, those developments constituted the worst mass violation of civil liberties, except for chattel slavery, in American history.

To Stephen Early[1]

February 24, 1942

Dear Steve:

For future reference, may I make one or two suggestions which have occurred to me while listening to some of the President's recent speeches, including the fine speech last night:[2]

1. He often sounds hurried, even concerned whether he will finish within the radio time. That impairs the effectiveness of the delivery: makes the address sound like a reading rather than like a speech or a conversation. This is accentuated by the fact that one could hear him turn the pages of his manuscript. The remedy is not to shorten the speeches — in fact the explanatory part of the speech would have been better if it had been longer and spoken more slowly — but to take more time, so much time that there is no sense of the President of the United States being fitted in neatly into a radio program.

2. Large sections of his speeches are written in a style to be read and not to be spoken. This is a matter of sentence structure and phrasing which can be caught by reading the speech aloud while it is being prepared.

3. I think the President ought to have some audience in the room with him which he can address so as to overcome the effect of reading. Last night I did not feel he was in contact with his audience until the latter portions of the speech — that at the beginning he was just reading a manuscript to himself.

4. He should not be put on the air or taken off the air without intervals of several minutes to separate him from the commercial programs. These intervals are necessary to create the right mood of expectancy and to let the effect of the speech sink in at the end. There should be some preliminaries — music, etc. — as there was after he had finished. . . .

1. Stephen Early, former journalist, at this time the president's press secretary.   2. In a "fireside chat" on the progress of the war, which was going badly, Roosevelt had condemned "the rumormongers and the poison peddlers in our midst," admitted to losses at Pearl Harbor but noted the remaining strength of the Pacific fleet and of American productivity, stressed the importance of unity among the United Nations, and repeated the commitment of those nations to the principles of the Atlantic Charter — the Anglo-American statement on August 14, 1941, of the four freedoms: freedom of speech, of religion, from want, and from fear.

To Thomas H. Thomas[1]

March 18, 1942

Dear Mr. Thomas:

I have such a high regard for your opinions that I would always be disposed to defer to them. But in this case, permit me to say that you have misread what I have written and read into it things I did not say and did not mean to say. I have reread the only two articles that you could possibly refer to, to see whether there was any ground for the false impression which you received.

The first of these articles dealt with the bombardment of the munitions plants in the suburbs of Paris and the point of that article was that, since the decision had been taken to strike so deeply into France and at Paris, it could be justified politically only if it was the beginning of a sustained aerial bombardment of occupied France. Far from my having taken the position of pushing Churchill, I followed his own action, tried to support it against a good deal of misunderstanding in the United States, and urged that the action be reinforced. Moreover, I was so conscious of the shipping problem to which you refer that I laid particular emphasis upon the fact that the aerial offensive in Western Europe could be supported by us without drawing heavily upon the shipping. I have never advocated a landing in Europe, and if you will reread that article you will see that there is no ground for the conclusion you reached.

The other article which you must have had in mind dealt with the problem of the dispersal of our forces — a problem which I happen to know is of the deepest concern to all of our responsible military leaders. Not only did I not advocate a landing and all that implies as regards shipping and naval forces, but I was so conscious of the shipping problem that I dwelt upon the desirability of trying to concentrate forces where the lines of communication were the shortest and easiest to protect. When and how these forces were to be used I did not presume to suggest.

Your second complaint is that I have been trying to find reasons for the loss of the Indies[2] in the age level of the American officers and in other shortcomings within the Army and Navy. That simply is not a correct account of what I have said. I attribute the loss of the Indies to the dominance of political considerations before December 7th and after that date. You will find that in my article of March 10th. The age levels of American officers are another matter and I feel that here I was on the right track. That the Army itself thought it necessary to rejuvenate the command is shown by the recent reorganization of the Army, and it is almost certain that a similar rejuvenation will be carried out in the Navy. Of course I know quite well that age is not an infallible criterion. But as a practical matter it is necessary in both of the services to break up the accumulation of infirm and inadequate admirals and generals, so many of whom got where they are through the rule of seniority. . . . On this point I would not be prepared to defer to your judgment without considerable argument, because I have been to the Pacific Coast and have seen and talked with commanders, among them some from Pearl Harbor, who must, if this war is to be conducted properly, be retired quickly. It seems to me less invidious to retire them for age than for incompetence. . . .

1. Thomas H. Thomas of Cambridge, Massachusetts, a Harvard alumnus, art historian, and local man of letters.   2. The Japanese had in January captured Manila and within another five months overrun the Philippines. They had also in January taken some of the Netherlands Indies as well as the Solomon Islands. In February they captured Singapore. During February 27 to March 1, their Navy in the battle of the Java Sea defeated Allied units there and opened the way to the conquest of the rest of the East Indies. Britain evacuated Rangoon on March 7. Before the date of this letter, Japan had also conquered Java.

To John Maynard Keynes

April 2, 1942

Dear Maynard:

. . . The thing that matters most, I think, is that while our two countries are now more closely connected than they have ever been before in action, there is no corresponding union of ideas and feelings. Your people here in Washington ascribe this to the growth of anti-British sentiment. But this is, I am sure, a superficial view.

The real trouble is that since the death of Lothian[1] there has been no one here who has had any philosophy and doctrine about the changing relationships between the United States, the British Commonwealth, and the British Empire. There is almost a complete intellectual vacuum on that subject, and because of that vacuum all the irritations of any coalition are magnified, and, unguided, popular sentiment rises and falls as British military prestige goes up or down. The whole approach of your people here is ad hoc on details of this and that arising from the conduct of the war itself. There is no general conception among them which they propose to our people which provides any political philosophy into which all of the mighty changes now going on in the world might fit. They are drifting as regards America much as they have, I fear, drifted in regard to India.[2] And while I don't prophesy anything seriously bad, I am sure that things could be much better, not only now but in the future.

There is very little that any one outside the official circles can do about it under present circumstances. I imagine, for example, that other independent editors and journalists have had the same experience as I have had. Since we entered the war the only responsible Briton with whom I have had a serious talk was Beaverbrook[3] when he was here in December with the Prime Minister. I have no idea, therefore, what the British government is thinking on any major question of policy. And though I have argued for more than twenty years that our relations with Great Britain were the cornerstone of our foreign policy, I haven't written about Anglo-American relations since we entered the war. I know of no one else who has and the field is wide open to the inveterate enemies of British policy.

In lieu of any serious effort to make British policy intelligible to responsible American editors, there is apparently . . . an active speech-making campaign under way to advertise Britain directly to the American people. This, in my opinion, is stupid and if it does anything it can do only harm. As nearly as I can make it out, the Embassy has become infected with one of our worst diseases — namely the idea that good relations between two countries can be promoted by the methods of advertising men and publicity experts. Thus they send us all kinds of printed and mimeographed advertising material in the hope that we will give it publicity, but it hasn't occurred to them apparently to ask any of us what is really in the minds of the American people or to realize that Americans who understand our vital interest in the British cause can still, as they always have in the past, explain to Americans what Americans need most to know about our relations with Great Britain.

I wouldn't mind a bit if you showed this, as a private letter, to Bracken. . . .[4]

1. Lord Lothian had died suddenly on December 12, 1940. Lord Halifax succeeded him as British ambassador to the United States but never developed an equivalent rapport with senior American officials. 2. Sir Stafford Cripps, a leader of the Labour party and member of the war cabinet, was then on his mission to establish a basis for India's continued participation in the war without the immediate steps toward independence which the All-India Congress was demanding. The

mission failed, to Roosevelt's dismay, but in spite of the pacifism of most of the congress leaders, Pandit Jawaharlal Nehru and others agreed not to embarrass the British war effort against Japan. **3.** His health failing, Lord Beaverbrook — Canadian born as William Maxwell Aitken, later a successful English newspaper publisher — had resigned as British minister of war production and undertaken, in Churchill's phrase, a "vaguely defined mission to the United States. . . . I felt his loss acutely." **4.** Brendan Bracken, British minister of information.

To John Maynard Keynes

April 18, 1942

Dear Maynard:

I had a cable from Bracken yesterday (April 17), two weeks after sending you my letter. The mails are better than I feared.

I should like to develop the general complaint of my letter of April 2.

Anglo-American relations have passed through the following general phases:

1) Pre-war absolute neutrality and total isolation. This phase was approaching its end during the late winter and summer of 1939 with the first unsuccessful effort of the President to amend the neutrality act's embargo on the sale of munitions.

2) Amended neutrality — from November 1939 to May 1940 — (when the U.S. government openly declared in favor of supplying munitions out of existing stocks).

3) *The destroyer-bases transaction* (summer of 1940) *and the beginning of American rearmament.*[1] In this period was laid the foundation of lend-lease. This foundation was a demonstration by Lord Lothian and by leaders of American public opinion that the security of Britain and the Americas were vitally inter-related. The development of this thesis brought about the conversion of American opinion from isolation to participation. It led to

4) Lend-lease (December 1940 to March 1941) in which Congress accepted the doctrine of security developed in the preceding phase.

Lothian died shortly after the initiation of the lend-lease policy but before its adoption in Congress. Lord Halifax arrived some weeks before Congress acted. It was evident to me, and to others who have followed these matters closely, that with the adoption of lend-lease, a new phase would begin; that in this phase the doctrine, now generally accepted, that the defense of Britain was vital to the defense of the Americas, would be insufficient to regulate and illuminate the ever closer daily contacts between the U.K. and the U.S.A. The relationship under lend-lease was bound in practice to be extremely difficult — for example, depriving our army to supply Britain — and it seemed to me certain that the infinitely greater return we got — namely that Britain fought on — would become obscured after the people had become accustomed to the fact of British resistance and had begun to take it for granted.

I felt strongly that a British political action — on the highest level — was

necessary as soon as Congress adopted lend-lease. I urged this view on Lord
Halifax and Nevile Butler[2] several times, suggesting that in some form or
other the British government should make a formal declaration that the defense of the Americas was a vital interest of Britain, and that the facilities of
the British Empire would be made available to the U.S. if needed. I do not
insist, of course, on this or any other formula. But I do insist that some *reciprocal political action* by Britain was needed after the U.S.A. had by act of
Congress entered into a unilateral alliance with Britain. It was needed for
many reasons, chiefly, I think, to make it clear to our own people that lend-
lease was not a one-way transaction which, in addition, was likely to involve
us in a *British* war. No economic agreement to implement lend-lease now or
post-war was a sufficient substitute for a large political agreement. The controlling considerations in lend-lease were not economic but in the largest sense
political.

Nothing was ever done along these lines and I was told (a) that such a
guaranty by Britain to the U.S.A. was empty in that Britain had her back to
the wall and (b) that the Foreign Office would feel that Britain had already
made too many commitments.

Thus from lend-lease to our entrance into the war, Anglo-American relations had to subsist on the intellectual capital inherited from the Lothian era.
Nothing had been done to develop political relationships corresponding to the
ever closer material relations. In fact political relationships were neglected and
allowed to drift.

But immediately after December 7 political relations were a matter of the
greatest urgency. They revolved about two great matters.

1) One, the new relation of the U.S.A. to the dominions — most acutely
Australia — and the consequences with respect to the United Kingdom. All
of us have been caught intellectually unprepared for a situation which, if properly handled, would greatly strengthen the bonds of union throughout the
English-speaking world. In the absence of any doctrine, the net effect is centrif-
ugal — with Australia and Canada exerting a strong pull upon the U.S.A.
away from the U.K. This is, I believe, one of the fundamental causes of the
so-called anti-British sentiment in the U.S.A. and it can be corrected only by
establishing a conception of a new and better Anglo-American order of things
which fits the new facts. Since Lothian's death, there has been no one over
here who talks or, so far as I know, thinks of these matters. Yet they have
long been in the making and could readily have been anticipated.

2) Second, the new relation of the U.S.A. to the empire, as distinct from the
commonwealth. Americans believe that their war aims in Asia are radically
different from those of Great Britain. This may be naive but it is the fact that
they think that the actions of the Filipinos (who had formally been guaranteed
independence) present a sharp contrast with Malaya and Burma. There is also
the strong feeling that Britain east of Suez is quite different from Britain at
home, that the war in Europe is a war of liberation and the war in Asia is for

the defense of archaic privilege, that the defeat of Japan is made much more difficult because the United Nations are inhibited from appealing to the native populations as liberators.

The Asiatic war has revived the profound anti-imperialism of the American tradition, and this is the second of the controlling causes, I believe, of the anti-British sentiment which has appeared. Note that it did not exist when Mr. Churchill was here in December and that it developed after the fall of Singapore. Obviously the popular feeling reflects the condition of military prestige. But that does not explain the popular feeling. British stock went up, not down, after the reverses in Europe (the Balkans, Crete). It went down after Singapore because there the Americans saw that the imperialism they have always disliked was also inefficient.

I am afraid I have burdened you with a long letter which, after all, represents nothing more than my own opinions. But it will give you the reasons why I do not think it is so necessary to send us an imperial statesman who will interest himself in the mighty political changes which are in progress among the English-speaking nations. . . .

1. All emphases in this letter are Lippmann's.   2. Nevile Butler, minister at the British embassy in Washington.

To Russell C. Leffingwell

June 6, 1942

Dear Russell:

. . . On the main point, I do not agree with your historical judgment about the post-war period and I think the reason for our difference of opinion lies in the fact that you are remembering your own views and those of your enlightened friends and associates whereas I am thinking about the great mass of industrialists, among whom you were a voice crying in the wilderness. I don't know where the great mass of industrialists stood in 1919, but I do know that in the twenty years that followed, their net influence was towards a narrow, isolationist view of foreign policy. There were plenty of exceptions, but the exceptions were not able to prevail over the mass of businessmen, men who insisted upon the tariff measures; who accepted even if they did not always approve the debt policy, who right down to our own entrance into the war resisted the conversion of industry. Your views are not, and never have been typical of the great mass of American businessmen, and those who think as you do have never been able to lead them during these twenty years.

I think it would be dangerous to deceive ourselves on this very important point and misleading to treat the history of this period as if the politicians had overborne the enlightened businessmen. If the businessmen had been enlightened on international affairs and had had the full courage of their convictions they could certainly have overruled the policy of the politicians, particularly in the Republican Party. I am convinced that with the new prestige which industrialists have gained since Pearl Harbor, they hold the key to the future in this country, and because they hold the key I think it is of great importance to emphasize their responsibility. And I must tell you that I reject absolutely the suggestion that there is any trace of hate, demagoguery, or hostility to industrialists in this. I think it is saving common sense and sheer practical wisdom to tell the businessmen that if they use their influence wisely they can save themselves and the order which they belong to, and that if they don't use their influence wisely they will have missed their very last chance. . . .

To Felix Frankfurter[1]

July 13, 1942

Dear Felix:

I am just back from Maine, and I have read the manuscript of Stimson's press conference on Bataan. While I didn't attend that conference myself, I remember very clearly the newspaper reports which resulted from it, and there was nothing in them which was related to the remark I made at dinner, which apparently Colonel Stimson misunderstood. I didn't follow up in the misunderstanding at the time because it didn't seem a good occasion to argue the matter.

My point was that the defeat of Bataan was a very solemn occasion indeed in American history and that it should not have been passed over by the President without adequate public recognition of its solemnity. I was not criticizing the Secretary, whose public statements about the war have seemed to me consistently admirable in substance and tone for the Secretary of War. The text of this press interview fully confirms that feeling of mine.

But all of that has nothing to do with the fact that on an occasion like the loss of the Philippines, the President himself should have talked to the people. I don't know why Colonel Stimson thought that remark of mine applied to him. What I said was dictated by a feeling, which is growing upon me and which has been confirmed by being away from Washington for two weeks, that the people are being spiritually starved for lack of the right words from the White House, and indeed that the routine publicity that emanates from the President's White House conference is positively harmful, because the tone of it is in general destructive of the mood of high seriousness.

1. Since January 1939, Frankfurter had been an associate justice on the United States Supreme Court but no less involved on that account in his long-standing friendship with both the president and Secretary of War Stimson.

To Nicholas Murray Butler[1]

July 16, 1942

Dear Dr. Butler:

. . . I have read the passage on the single department of national defense. The plan is, of course, right, but to put such a plan through Congress now would involve debate and controversy that would take the mind of every high-ranking officer away from the conduct of the war for weeks to come. It will be necessary, I think, to reach the same end by more indirect methods: by unifying procurement through the Nelson office,[2] and probably by unifying the combat command through the appointment of something like a Chief of Staff to the President, with the right to exercise some of his powers as Commander-in-Chief in dealing with the Army and the Navy.[3]

In practice the real bone of contention now between the two services is air power. All of the serious rivalries and disagreements turn on the fact that air cannot be divided neatly between land and sea. There is, consequently, a great struggle between the services for the control of air power. That was a basic cause of the trouble at Pearl Harbor. It has been very evident in the Caribbean and there is trouble about it in Alaska. . . .[4]

1. Nicholas Murray Butler, then still president of Columbia University.   2. Donald Nelson, an executive from Sears, Roebuck, was head of the War Production Board, which Roosevelt had established in January 1942. He lacked the legal and the personal power to unify procurement, which remained in large measure under the armed services and subject to debilitating competition between the Army and the Navy. By 1943 Ferdinand Eberstadt, the ablest by far among Nelson's staff, had much improved the process of procurement with his controlled materials plan, which won the services' support, preserved much of their independence, and met their needs.   3. Admiral William D. Leahy, Chief of Staff to the president and head of the Joint Chiefs of Staff, exercised some of the authority Lippmann had in mind but never enough to contain the continuing rivalries among the services and the chiefs of each.   4. Coordination of Army and Navy air and sea forces in the battle against German submarines in the Caribbean, a battle crucial to American supply lines to the Pacific, was less than desirable, as was coordination between those services in the defense of Alaska. There on June 12, Japanese forces had taken two of the Aleutian Islands, Attu and Kiska. That loss of American territory seemed more serious than it was, for the Navy had had to leave the islands open to assault during the vital battle against much of the Japanese fleet at Midway from June 4 to 7, an American victory of decisive importance about which the government had for some time to maintain a high order of secrecy.

To Frank J. and Ellen S. Mather[1]

July 28, 1942

Dear Mr. and Mrs. Mather:

I am very sorry indeed to have made such an impression on you both, though I cannot for the life of me imagine what I said to justify Mrs. Mather in thinking that I had depicted the President "as a sort of amiable idiot." I was discussing a matter which is common knowledge in Washington, namely that

Colonel Knox is quite unable to perform the functions of the civilian head of
the Navy and that Mr. Roosevelt does attempt to perform those functions.[2]
Considering all of the duties of the President's office, it is, in my judgment,
quite impossible for the President to give to the Navy Department that continuous attention which is needed in the man who is Secretary of the Navy. His
attention is bound to be intermittent, hurried, and often casual. There isn't
time enough in a day for him to give his whole attention to naval matters.
"Tidbits of information" may be a rather sharp phrase, but it conveys the idea
that his information is not continuous and direct.

Let me say in conclusion that what I have written about the Navy is based
entirely on almost anguished concern about deficiencies in it, particularly in
regard to the planning of its programs and its conduct of the submarine war,
which arises from the lack of competent civilian direction. You have not seen
me write anything comparable about the War Department, because there the
situation is radically different and altogether better. As for Mr. Mather's suggestion that I am actuated by spite, I may say that Colonel Knox has been a
personal friend of mine for fifteen or twenty years and that criticizing the
Navy Department has been, therefore, an extremely painful personal experience.

1. Mr. and Mrs. Frank J. Mather, Jr. He had been a professor in the Art and Archeology Department at Princeton. A naval reserve officer during World War I, Mather was later, like Lippmann,
a member of the Century Association.   2. Secretary of the Navy Frank Knox, the Republican
publisher of the *Chicago Daily News* and Landon's running mate in 1936, had been recruited to
the Cabinet in 1940 at the same time as Secretary of War Henry L. Stimson. Unlike Stimson,
Knox could never command his department, always a difficult arena for its civilian head. Admiral
Ernest J. King dominated decisions about naval strategy, an appropriate function for the senior
naval officer of the time; but naval procurement and logistics throughout the war lacked the
efficiency that Stimson's staff brought to the Army. More than Lippmann appeared to realize,
Roosevelt did often intrude in naval affairs, especially those pertaining to supply — largely be-
cause the president, on the basis of his service as assistant secretary of the navy under Woodrow
Wilson, considered himself his own best expert about naval organization.

To John C. Slessor[1]

October 13, 1942

Dear Jack:

. . . The thing that strikes me most here on coming back[2] is what I think
is the unmistakable evidence that we are out of the doldrums. So much energy
has now been released in this country that it is impossible to feel properly and
prudently pessimistic. The fact of the matter is that the country begins to feel
powerful and that this feeling is exhilarating. The problems we discussed,
namely of using this energy and directing it, are far from settled. I suppose
that they are the hardest and the latest problems that any pacific nation gets
solved, but what is coming out of the mass of the nation itself is now impres-

sive and far more than I should have dared to hope for six months ago. This is no longer a war in which the Administration leads and drags the nation along. The war is now a genuine national struggle, though, as compared with England, we are still of course in an early phase of it. . . .

1. Sir John C. Slessor, British vice air marshal.   2. From London, where Lippmann had gone in August as an observer at the invitation of the British government.

To John J. McCloy [1]

October 21, 1942

Dear Jack:

The *Stars and Stripes* [2] goes a long way towards giving some news but, in my opinion, it is too low-brow and underestimates the seriousness and intelligence of a very considerable part of our men, and the most important part of them at that. This paper is sub-tabloid, and certainly a large part of the officers and many of the men are used to better journalism than that.

I think this criticism can be generalized further by saying that we always tend to set the intellectual standard too low in the morale work.

1. John J. McCloy, then assistant secretary of war and one of Stimson's ablest and most trusted subordinates.   2. The newspaper of and for the G.I.'s, with editions ultimately published in every theater of the war.

Memorandum for John J. McCloy

November 17, 1942

MEMORANDUM
ON
OUR RELATIONS WITH DARLAN [1]

The problem is how the United States is to reconcile the immediate necessities in North Africa with its permanent political ideals and interests.

1. General Eisenhower's dispatch discloses, if I understood it correctly, that upon landing in Africa he was confronted with a situation radically different from that which our political intelligence had led him to expect. It appears that he had been led to believe that the French military and civilian authorities would adhere to General Giraud and would obey his orders. The event showed that only Admiral Darlan, exercising the powers he had derived from Marshal Pétain, was in fact able to give the order to surrender in Morocco and Algiers. Moreover, reasoning from this experience, the American and British commanders on the spot judged that only Admiral Darlan possessed the authority

to bring the French in Tunisia to our side, and to obtain the voluntary sub-mission of Dakar.[2]

2. It was evident, it seemed to me, from the urgent tone of General Eisen-hower's dispatch that due to the miscalculation in the political preparations, he had had to improvise this unexpected solution of his immediate problem, which was to hold North Africa without having to fight for it and without having to immobilize his troops to occupy it and pacify it. In the circumstances he made the only possible decision. But it is of the utmost importance that the authorities in Washington deal correctly with the immense and dangerous consequences of his decision.

3. The crux of the matter, I submit, is in the estimate we now place upon our relations with Darlan. The one disturbing aspect of General Eisenhower's dispatch was, I believe, a disposition — natural enough under the circum-stances but seriously wrong — to look upon Darlan as the possessor of great benefits in the shape of collaboration with us, Tunisia, Dakar and the Toulon fleet, which give him the whiphand over us. We cannot form a sound policy towards Darlan if, even unconsciously, we accept this view of our relations with him.

4. It is probable that Darlan went to Africa, and deliberately allowed him-self to be captured, in order to maintain the Vichy regime in Africa. If he had remained in metropolitan France he would have become a prisoner of the Ger-mans and once France was liberated by the Allies, his doom would have been sealed by the French organization of resistance. By setting up a Vichy region in Africa, he provides a refuge under American protection for himself and some of his associates against French retribution when the Germans leave France. It is in the highest degree probable that he went to Africa some weeks before our landing there in order to make the arrangements by which he would sell to us in installments non-resistance and then various degrees of collabora-tion in return for the grant on our part of installments of recognition and authority. This is the way he dealt with the German occupation and there is every reason to think that he is using the same essential tactics in dealing with the American occupation.

5. In dealing with him it is, therefore, essential that we should not let a mistaken sense of gratitude on our part open the way to unending blackmail on his part. Our indebtedness to him arises out of the armistice in Morocco and Algiers, and on the prospect of tranquillity on our lines of supply to the Tunisian front, and upon collaboration in Tunisia, upon the cession of Dakar, and upon the neutralization of the Toulon fleet. We should consider, I believe, that payment in full for these favors received and favors to come is the pro-tection of Darlan's life, and his chance to live it out comfortably, against the revenge of the French people for his treason. We should be clear in our own minds and consciences that the relation between us is as follows: that he is being spared from the consequences of his treachery to France and to the Allies by making partial restitution for his crimes. He is essentially a refugee from

the France which will condemn him as a traitor. The favors he can now do for us are his by virtue of his treason, and we must accept them with the moral conviction that if he is saved from the consequences of his treason, he will have been generously repaid.

6. It follows that no commitment should be validated in Washington which recognizes him as the legitimate repository of French sovereignty, and no obligation should be assumed which gives him anything beyond his personal security, comfort, and eventual freedom. Even these benefits should be regarded not as payments for what he has already done for us but as depending upon his obeying our orders in the future. He is in our power and we must firmly insist on not letting him put us in his power. We are dealing with a man who betrayed the Allies in 1940 and then betrayed the French Republic and has now betrayed the Germans. In dealing with a man who makes a profession of treachery, the essential point is to keep him within your power until you are able to liquidate his power to blackmail or to betray you.

7. Our policy from now on should be, I submit, first, to force out of him all the favors he is capable of doing for us, and second, to make ready to liquidate his whole political authority.

The probable limit of time for the delivery of his favors is the time it will take to gain possession of Tunisia and Dakar.

In the meantime we should prepare secretly to liquidate any political authority which it becomes necessary in the emergency to concede to him. The justification for his course has been set forth in sections 5 and 6.

8. The program of liquidation, I suggest, should be based on the principle of compelling him to annul step by step the Vichy decrees which have robbed France of her constitutional liberties. We should ask a group of French and American constitutional lawyers to make a list of all the measures of Axis collaboration and of oppression which Pétain, Laval,[3] and Darlan have taken since Bordeaux. We should select those which are in force in North Africa, and in an orderly and systematic way we should confront Darlan with a series of commands to annul them and to restore the legitimate constitutional rights and the legitimate laws of France. Just as the German occupation forced Vichy to abrogate French rights, so the American occupation should force Darlan to restore French rights.

9. This will liquidate Darlan and Vichy in Africa. Either he will refuse the program and we shall then have ground for removing him and returning him to his status of a prisoner of war, or he will comply and the regime which he represents will gradually disintegrate and be replaced by a legitimate French regime in which the French opponents of Vichy will have recovered their rights.

10. This program will vindicate our war aims, and indeed clarify them and fortify them. What we do in the first territory liberated by American arms will obviously have the profoundest influence as an example and as a precedent upon all other occupied territory in Europe. It is self-evident that we must dispel any idea that we shall recognize and uphold Quisling governments. On

the other hand, we must in liberated territory establish a foundation of order, and no other foundation is conceivable, I submit, except that of the last legitimate constitution before it was subverted by Quislings or destroyed by the Nazis.

That is why it is so desirable to reestablish in North Africa the constitution and the laws of the Third Republic. Under those laws, which provide for freedom, the French nation can then when the time comes adopt any other constitution, consonant with the four freedoms, which a constituent assembly may decide upon. We shall have done the work of liberation in a substantial and practical sense when we, while the supreme authority is in our hands, have restored the legitimate laws of France. Any other regime installed under our authority would be arbitrary and illegitimate.

We shall also provide the only possible platform upon which all patriotic Frenchmen can be united. For the one common denominator of all loyal factions is in the legitimate constitutional liberties of France.

11. Finally, I should like to call attention to the fact that if we had paid attention to the intelligence service of the Fighting French, General Eisenhower need not have been surprised by the actual situation he found in North Africa. On the critical points of resistance and collaboration in North Africa, General de Gaulle's intelligence service was more accurate than our own, and it will be a grievous error to continue to ignore it.

1. Lippmann sent an identical memorandum to Secretary of State Cordell Hull. The memo expressed the disenchantment, by no means peculiar to Lippmann, in both the United States and Great Britain with the political aspects of the Anglo-American invasion of West Africa and North Africa on November 8, 1942. The commander of that operation, General Dwight D Eisenhower, had negotiated through his deputy commander, General Mark W. Clark, an agreement of November 13 with Vichy Vice Premier Admiral Jean Darlan, a notorious collaborator who was Vichy chief of state in French North Africa. The terms of that agreement left Darlan, who had called on French forces to cease firing two days earlier, in his position as chief of state and left unaltered Vichy decrees in North Africa, many of them anti-Semitic.

With Darlan's assassination on December 24, 1942, Eisenhower turned to General Henri Giraud, who had escaped from a German prison, to succeed Darlan. Eisenhower and Clark had courted Giraud before the invasion with the expectation of using him as their agent to prevent French resistance, but he lacked sufficient influence in North Africa for that role, and he had been a principal in Clark's agreement with Darlan. Throughout those developments, and contrary to British preference, the Americans had ignored General Charles de Gaulle and the Free French.

By the date of Lippmann's memo, the Germans in Europe had taken over previously unoccupied France, and German troops in North Africa had counterattacked in Tunisia, where a major battle was under way. French crews, not Darlan, had scuttled the French fleet at Toulon. By then it had become clear that the Darlan deal had gained less than Eisenhower had expected, had offended democratic sensibilities in Europe and America, and had further alienated de Gaulle. 2. The capital of French North Africa. 3. Pierre Laval was at this time Vichy vice premier.

To Frederick J. Hoffman[1]

November 18, 1942

Dear Mr. Hoffman:

I am not sure that I can, in a very short letter, answer all of your questions. But I can tell you that I first became acquainted with Freud's *Interpretation of Dreams* in the spring and summer of 1912. I had been a pupil at Harvard of William James and of Graham Wallas and was preparing to write a book on politics, which was published under the title, *A Preface to Politics*. I had a close friend who shared a cabin in the Adirondack mountains with me while I was writing that book who had been a patient of Dr. Brill[2] and who was engaged in translating the *Interpretation of Dreams* into English. His name was Alfred Booth Kutner. I read the translation as he worked on it and discussed it with him and began to see how much Freud had to contribute to the psychology which I had learned at college. If you care to examine *A Preface to Politics*, you will see the effects. It may also interest you to know that the book was reviewed by Freud in his journal, "Imago."

I may add that in those days few of us read Marx or knew anything about him, and while Bergson was well known and greatly admired, Jung had not yet become a well-known figure.

In regard to your questions . . . I can say that serious young men took Freud quite seriously, as indeed he deserved to be taken. Exploitation of Freud into a tiresome fad came later and generally from people who had not studied him and had only heard about him. . . .

1. Frederick J. Hoffman of the English Department at Ohio State University. **2.** A. A. Brill, a Freudian analyst.

To Henry L. Stimson

November 19, 1942

Dear Mr. Secretary:

In view of the close relation between the military and political action in the African campaign, there have been two disclosures since our landing which seem to me most embarrassing. The one was Mr. Hull's press conference on the day of the landing, in which we made confession to the world that we had maintained diplomatic relations with Vichy in order to prepare an invasion of territory governed from Vichy. I do not know what the Axis propaganda has done with this admission, but I should think it could be used most effectively against us, in Spain and Portugal.

The other matter falls within the province of the War Department directly. I am referring to the dispatches from North Africa which told about General Clark's secret mission and disclosed the fact that he had a very large sum of money with him.[1] Only one interpretation will be put upon this news by our enemies, which is that we are bribing French officers and officials. I do not object to bribery, if that is what it was, but I feel sure that our enemies can use this disclosure to cast suspicion on any Frenchman who joins us, by the simple device of claiming that he was bribed with General Clark's money.

This disclosure alarms me, not only in itself but as evidence of a dangerous naivete. I wonder if it does not indicate that some very shrewd person should be sent to General Eisenhower's headquarters to advise on censorship. I cannot believe that the censor should have passed a story of that kind. . . .

1. Before the invasion of North Africa, General Clark had gone secretly to Algeria by airplane and submarine to negotiate with French representatives there for their help, but his negotiations failed. Clark escaped, but not without losing a substantial sum of money he had carried to ease his purpose.

To Cordell Hull

November 24, 1942

Dear Mr. Secretary:

I have your letter of November 21st, and I feel sure that, on reconsideration, you will agree that it ought to be expunged from the record.[1]

Your letter is in answer to the memorandum which I sent you on November 17th in which I stated that since you had been "good enough to discuss the North African situation with me, and in the light of General Marshall's conference on Sunday (November 15th),"[2] I had drawn up the memorandum and that I was "sending a copy of it to the War Department."

In view of the fact that the only two copies of this memorandum were sent, one to you personally and one to the War Department, I cannot permit you to rebuke me on the ground that I "published" it.

Nor can I permit you to rebuke me for having failed to come to you and to the War Department to inform myself before writing the memorandum. The fact is that I did come to you, on Saturday, November 14th, and spent over an hour in your office, and that the following day I attended General Marshall's private press conference in the War Department.

If you wish to construe my comments on the preliminary political preparations for the North African campaign as an "attack" on "the record of the American government" that is a matter of your opinion and not mine. What my memorandum stated was that General Eisenhower "upon landing in Africa . . . was confronted with a situation radically different from that which our political intelligence had led him to expect." I do not see why you should resent my stating this fact since it is based on what you yourself told me, namely that the arrangement with Admiral Darlan had been made by General Eisenhower and you had no special knowledge of it. If you had no special knowledge of it, it is obvious that the arrangement with Admiral Darlan was not prepared in advance by our political officers. The statement is also confirmed by General Eisenhower's dispatch which General Marshall read to us. It is implicitly confirmed by the President's statement, which made it very clear that he had not anticipated the arrangement which was made with Admiral Darlan. Therefore, I repeat that the critical part of my memorandum, which you construe as an attack on the American government, consists simply of a statement of fact which came from you yourself, from General Eisenhower, General Marshall, and the President.

My purpose in dwelling on this fact, that our political intelligence had not properly anticipated the real situation in North Africa, was to call attention to two things, one the need for the future to improve our sources of information in regard to French affairs, and the other to make constructive suggestions as to how to handle the consequences of the decisions taken by General Eisenhower on the spot and not anticipated by our political intelligence.

May I say in conclusion that what I regret most in your letter is not only its complete inaccuracy but its resistance to what was an attempt on my part, made in complete good faith, to offer you privately a constructive criticism on a grave problem which is very far from being solved. . . .

1. "Today and Tomorrow" on November 19, 1942, made many of the points in Lippmann's memo of November 17 to McCloy and Hull and also referred to the "increasing prejudice against General de Gaulle" of some American officials. Angry with both memo and column, Hull in his letter condemned Lippmann for attacking the "record of the American government." In "Today and Tomorrow," Lippmann frequently returned to his criticism of American policy toward de Gaulle; see Ronald Steel, *Walter Lippmann and the American Century* (Boston, 1980), pp. 400–403.
2. General George C. Marshall, the formidable Chief of Staff of the United States Army, had explained and supported Eisenhower's political policies in North Africa.

To Henry A. Wallace

November 26, 1942

Dear Henry:

Yesterday I saw the movie of your Free World speech[1] and I just wanted to drop you a line to say that I thought it the most moving and effective thing produced by us during the war. In fact, I thought it perfect, and you need have no qualms about letting it be circulated not only all over this country but all over the world. Congratulations.

1. In May 1942, Vice President Henry A. Wallace had delivered a speech, "The Price of Free World Victory," calling for "the century of the common man" to come out of the war. He was deliberately answering Henry Luce's earlier *Life* editorial that spoke of "the American Century," a century to be shaped by American leadership. Instead of Luce's neoimperialism, Wallace urged a "people's revolution." The *Wall Street Journal* and other conservative voices criticized the speech, but the text nevertheless provided a telling document that the government broadcast at home and abroad in both a printed and a filmed version.

To Ivar Bryce[1]

December 23, 1942

Dear Ivar:

There is almost nothing in your letter to which I don't subscribe completely and, therefore, I am a little bit surprised to find that I have given you the impression I have given you.

I suppose the reason for this is that I accept the original military arrangement with Darlan by Eisenhower as necessary, and have then devoted my attention to attacking the effort to give it more than temporary military importance and to give it political significance. It is at bottom a question of fact, and, to the best of my present knowledge, the facts are as follows:

The operation was originally based upon General Giraud, and the forces which it was possible to take to Africa were not large enough to occupy all French territory. It was necessary, therefore, to rely upon a French administration during the period when our forces were building up, and the original hope was that General Giraud could do that for us. On the third day, or thereabout, after the landing, General Giraud went to General Eisenhower and told him that, while he could deliver Algiers, he was unable to control Morocco and that it was necessary to make an arrangement with Darlan. After a conference in which, as I understand it, Admiral Cunningham[2] participated, the decision to do this was taken. Darlan had been previously captured by a commando force and was held as a prisoner of war. There are details of the arrangement which are not clear, but it is apparent that Darlan assumed that he had been recognized as the permanent political chief of North Africa, an assumption which the President dealt with in his statement of November 17th.[3] Whether the judgment of Giraud, Eisenhower, and Cunningham was correct about the need to deal with Darlan may be open to question, but I think we must give them the benefit of the doubt. At any rate, I understand that in the past few days the whole situation has been placed before Stalin and that a message has been received from him saying that he agrees with what has been done (not with what some people say has been done, of course, but with what the President is actually doing). There have, of course, been direct discussions between the President and the Prime Minister on the same subject, and apparently the understanding has been good enough so that when the Prime Minister went before the House he received unanimous support.[4]

All of this does not affect your main point, which I fully share and which I firmly believe is shared by the President. Nor have I any doubt that, unless we run into a military catastrophe, Darlan will be liquidated not long after, if not before, the Germans are expelled from Africa. The moral damage is just what you describe, but I hope it is not irreparable, and many things can be done, and I think will be done, to repair the damage as best we can. In the last analysis, the damage is due to the fact that we could not go to Africa in sufficient force to attack the Germans before they got themselves firmly entrenched in Tunisia and at the same time to quell all of the trouble which the Vichy people were capable of stirring up. For, as you no doubt realize, the problem in Morocco was not merely the one of storming the beaches, but of avoiding a revolt of the tribes. That risk, plus the ever-present and, I am afraid, growing risk of trouble from Spain was, I believe, decisive.

You may have heard that General de Gaulle is coming to Washington soon. That will be, I hope, an opportunity to repair some of the damage. . . .

1. Ivar Bryce, a personal friend of Lippmann's, had written to express his distress about the Darlan deal. 2. Admiral Sir Andrew Browne Cunningham, commander in chief of the British Mediterranean fleet. 3. Saying that the arrangements with Darlan were a temporary expedient. 4. This account was well informed, though Roosevelt was more supportive of Eisenhower's decisions than the letter perhaps implied.

To George C. Marshall

January 5, 1943

Dear General Marshall:

I hope you realize how very useful is the kind of off the record press conference which you had yesterday.

There was, however, one point which puzzled me and several of the other men with whom I discussed it afterwards. In regard to North Africa you made, as I understood you, two points: one, that General Eisenhower's supreme command must be preserved jealously, and the other, that he must be enabled to concentrate his attention on Tunisia and the Straits. That left me wondering whose actual business it was to put his whole attention upon the problem of governing this vast territory. For granting, of course, that the final authority is General Eisenhower's, yet if in fact he is to concentrate on the battles, then his political and civil authority must be exercised through some one.[1]

I think I am right in saying that there is considerable anxiety as to whether adequate provision has been made for dealing with this unavoidably political situation. . . .

1. Eisenhower's chief of civil affairs was the career diplomat Robert D. Murphy, who was also Roosevelt's personal representative with the rank of minister to French North Africa. Murphy had been deeply involved in American policy toward Vichy and in Clark's political negotiations preceding the invasion of North Africa. He was often a target of Lippmann's public attack.

To John K. Jessup[1]

January 19, 1943

Dear Mr. Jessup:

I have read the study of European Resistance with the greatest of interest. It is incomparably the best thing I have seen on the subject, and I hope I am not merely prejudiced by the fact that it gives such factual and reasoned support to my own a priori reasoning.

I think the case for the exile governments is conclusive. What needs to be done, however, is to carry on the study to the exceptionally difficult problem of France. I am more and more persuaded that the European continent will be unmanageable if we cannot rely on a reasonably strong provisional French government as soon as hostilities end. For if there is no such French government, there will be no strong and reliable government in Europe west of Moscow.

1. John K. Jessup, at this time a member of the editorial board of *Fortune,* had sent Lippmann an unpublished study that the magazine had commissioned about the resistance in Europe and the governments-in-exile.

To Henry A. Wallace

January 27, 1943

Dear Henry:

Here in a nutshell is what you asked me to write out for you:

The principal cause of the disintegration of the popular support for Wilson's international policy was not, I believe, the Senate debate on the League, but the fact that Wilson did not have an effective plan, or indeed any plan, 1) for demobilizing the army, 2) re-locating the war workers, 3) reconverting the war industries, and 4) carrying the farmers through the transition from war to peace demands for their products.

The lack of plan meant that the war controls were not gradually relaxed, but suddenly scrapped. The War Industries Board dissolved immediately after the Armistice. The international controls were broken up before peace was established.

The net effect was that every soldier, war worker, business man, and farmer, had in effect to demobilize himself. The resulting anxiety made it impossible for him to consider the larger issues of international cooperation, and it was to this feeling of personal anxiety in each man that Harding appealed when he called for normalcy and the rejection of Wilson's plans to worry about foreigners.

It follows, I believe, that an international post-war program should be *preceded*[1] by a program for domestic demobilization, thus establishing the government's first concern for its own people. To this end I believe that within the next few months, Congress should be asked to enact a series of *authorizations* dealing generously with soldiers, workers, farmers, business men.[2] They should be on the statute book before authorizations are asked for any kind of post-war international relief and rehabilitation.

1. The emphases in this letter are Lippmann's.   2. Congress did not.

To Robert H. Jackson[1]

February 4, 1943

Dear Bob:

I am very grateful to you for taking so much trouble and I have no doubt that you are right when you say that our Cabinet is not constructed so as to be a policy making body. My references to the desirability of placing men like Nelson or Henderson[2] in Cabinet rank or under Cabinet members was inspired not by the belief that the Cabinet could make policy effectively, but by a different feeling. It was that the improvised agencies are naked and unprotected and would fare better politically if they were assimilated with the established departments of government where there exists the tradition and the routine of political procedure. My impression is that on the whole the old departments have done better than the new agencies and that the old departments with a big infusion of the newer men would do best of all.

On the policy making side I subscribe entirely to what you say . . . namely that we should strive for some kind of War Cabinet consisting of men without departmental responsibility. I wonder if the embryo of that doesn't exist in Leahy and Byrnes? . . .[3]

1. Since July 1941, Jackson had been an associate justice on the United States Supreme Court. 2. Donald Nelson and Leon Henderson. 3. James F. Byrnes, Democratic senator from South Carolina, 1931–41, and associate justice on the Supreme Court, 1941–42, had been appointed director of economic stabilization in October 1942. Roosevelt in May 1943 made Byrnes director of war mobilization, a powerful position many commentators interpreted as assistant president for domestic affairs.

To Glen Perry[1]

April 8, 1943

Dear Mr. Perry:

I don't think there is any mystery about the Russian-Polish boundary. It has been an unsettled boundary from the beginning, and it has always been a recognized fact that the British alliance with Poland does not guarantee the preservation of the exact frontier of 1939.

. . . I did have a good talk with General Sikorski[2] on both of his visits. . . . General Sikorski is compelled by his government in exile, and by the fact that it is a government in exile, to stand on the exact frontier, but I am certain that there are very patriotic and competent Poles who realize that there are borderlands in which the Poles are in such a minority that there can be no permanent good relations with Russia unless there is a rectification of the frontier. What General Sikorski was seeking here was our unqualified diplomatic support of his position that there must be no change in the boundaries, and it is not clear just how far our government went in promising him that support. But it was the effect of that situation which preceded Stalin's public statements about the borderlands.[3]

1. Glen Perry, Washington correspondent of the *New York Sun*.   **2.** General Wladyslaw Sikorski, head of the Polish government-in-exile in London.   **3.** Stalin opposed restoration of the prewar boundary between Poland and the Soviet Union. The Polish-Russian agreement of July 30, 1941, called for the annulment of the German-Soviet partition of Poland but did not restore Poland's eastern frontier.

To Hugh R. Wilson[1]

April 8, 1943

Dear Hugh:

I am very glad to have your letter and am most reassured by what you say. I am more and more convinced that it is just as important to define the limit beyond which we will not intervene as it is to convince our people that we cannot find security in an isolationist policy. I have a book in the press,[2] of which I shall send you a copy as soon as it is ready, in which I have attempted this definition.

In general, I find myself believing that the primary area of our responsibility is the basin of the Atlantic on both sides, and the islands of the Pacific ocean. Within this region and for its security, we must, I believe, make military and political commitments. But I do not believe that we can or should permanently and regularly participate in affairs in the interior of the European continent, or of Asia, or of Africa except on its western side. I believe that if we define our responsibilities in some such concrete fashion as this, the American people will support them on the grounds of national interest. If we go beyond that, we shall become involved in controversies for which we lack the trained personnel, the traditions, and the political interests. . . .

1. Wilson had served in many posts since that of minister to Switzerland, including ambassador to Germany, 1938–39, adviser to the secretary of state, 1940–41, and delegate to several disarmament conferences. In 1943 he was with the Office of Strategic Services, the wartime intelligence agency.   **2.** *U.S. Foreign Policy* (Boston, 1943).

To Mark Sullivan

April 12, 1943

Dear Mark:

I had heard Willkie's story about the dinner, but not the story that Churchill referred to Stalin as "that monster."[1]

My own guess, when I heard Willkie tell the story of the dinner, was that he had not made the proper allowances for Stalin's uncouth peasant humor and bluntness.

I spent an evening with Churchill in London in September and he talked a lot about Stalin. Of course the men are worlds apart, but he left me with the distinct impression that they had found common ground, in that they are both warriors. Churchill certainly did not take Stalin to his bosom, but, on the other hand, he got along with him because they are both fighting men, and I gathered he felt he could continue to get on with him on that basis and at that level. If he called him "that monster," my guess is that he had in mind respect and appreciation as well as distaste. You would have to hear a man say a thing like that to know just what he meant.

He told me one story to illustrate his mixed feelings about Stalin's ruthlessness, that is to say his appreciation of its effectiveness in waging war and his personal distaste for it. In the villa where he was staying, there was a pool with some goldfish in it and Churchill used to feed the fish every day when he was in Moscow, and he got quite attached to them. When he was leaving, he told Stalin he regretted leaving the fish and Stalin replied, "Why not take them with you?" Churchill said he could not manage a bowl of goldfish on his plane, and Stalin retorted, "Why not cook them and eat them?"

As for Stalin's opinion of Churchill, I have heard two or three times from people who have talked with him that he always ended by appreciating Churchill's quality as a military commander.

1. Wendell Willkie's dinner in London with Winston Churchill during Willkie's trip around the world had proved less than a success. The two men did not like each other. Willkie complained often thereafter about Churchill's imperialism and Churchill about Willkie's naiveté. In 1942 Willkie had asked Roosevelt to send him on the trip, which resulted in Willkie's best-seller, *One World* (New York, 1943).

To J. M. Macdonnell[1]

April 30, 1943

Dear Mr. Macdonnell:

. . . In saying that there will be no partitioning of Germany I was using the word in the exact sense, that is to say, in the division of the country into parts which are then placed under the sovereignty of the neighbors of Germany. In other words, I was using "partition" in the sense illustrated by the partitions of Poland. This is, I think, impossible to do and undesirable. For example, to whom would Prussia be given? But in saying that, I do not exclude, and in fact I favor, the use of our control to induce separatism within Germany. That is a very different process from partitioning.

You ask me why I feel it necessary to say that the period of military occupation must be short. I said it because I am firmly convinced that a long and indefinite period of occupation will not be sustained by popular sentiment in this country and I think not in England, but certainly not here. Therefore, it seems to me imperative to make plans for the control of Germany which are effective beyond the period of direct military occupation. This limitation does not exclude, of course, measures for the prompt reoccupation of Germany or even the bombing of it if the treaty imposed is violated.

The Saar occupation can illustrate both points of view. It may be said, and I would say it, that the occupation lasted so long that the public sentiment lost interest in it.

1. J. M. Macdonnell had met Lippmann at a dinner party in Toronto, as he observed in his letter to Lippmann about postwar policy for Germany.

To Thomas C. Wasson[1]

May 29, 1943

Dear Mr. Wasson:

. . . I should like to make clear to you, at least, a thing which you quite naturally misunderstand, but which the State Department officials, who have been rather resentful, have no excuse for misunderstanding. It is this: I have never criticized the Vichy policy as it existed up to the landing in North Africa. There are many who have criticized it, but I was not one of them. I have always taken the view that once the decision was taken back in the summer of 1940, it was impossible and undesirable to change the policy until we were ready to intervene with force.

My criticism of the State Department rests primarily on its failure to see that, while the Vichy policy was a diplomatic necessity, it must ultimately cultivate the forces of French resistance which have rallied to the Fighting French. It should therefore, quietly but firmly, have maintained at all times close and friendly relations with General de Gaulle, and should never have allowed itself to become irritated or provoked into an attitude of hostility.

The events in North Africa since the November landing have fully substantiated this criticism. This is shown by the fact that, though we backed General Giraud with our diplomacy and though he possesses the largest French military force, the principles for which de Gaulle has stood have had to be accepted by him. The reason they have had to be accepted is that General de Gaulle, whether we like it or not, is the focal point of the French national spirit and, therefore, he was bound to prevail. All you say about the psychology of the Pétain emotion may be true, but the resurrection of France can come only by the liquidation of this psychosis of defeat. It makes me acutely unhappy, to borrow your own words, to think that we have drifted into a position where we are morally estranged from the vital forces of the France of the future. . . .

1. Thomas C. Wasson, a foreign service officer, had been assigned in the Department of State since 1942.

To the Editors of the Nation

June 29, 1943

Dear Sirs:

In his review of my book "U.S. Foreign Policy," Mr. Albert Guerard[1] says that "from the point of view of the realistic historian, the weakness of Lippmann's book is that he ignores Europe west of the Curzon line."[2] I am genuinely puzzled by this statement. For the thesis of my book is that the American nations have always since their settlement been members of an historic community, comprising the peoples who live on the shores of the Atlantic Ocean. These nations include, besides the American republics, Canada, the United Kingdom and Eire — the following states of continental Europe: France, Spain, Portugal, Belgium, the Netherlands, Norway, Sweden, and Denmark. *All*[3] of these states constitute, I insist, a single system of security in that an aggression against any one of them will of necessity involve all of them. I call this system the Atlantic Community. The members of it in continental Europe are all of them "west of the Curzon line."

My argument is that the alliance of the Atlantic Community with Russia and with China is the necessary nucleus of a stable world order. I argue that a world order cannot be generated on the League of Nations principle of an association of more than fifty states acting by unanimous consent, and that historic experience teaches us that larger societies grow by agglomeration around a nuclear state powerful enough to provide protection and the benefit of wider intercourse. Those who take the League of Nations view frequently argue from the analogy of the American union which, they suppose, was formed by the voluntary consent of thirteen sovereign states. I argue in my book that this analogy is historically false in that the authors of our Constitution did not create a new union but, as they said, perfected a union which had in fact existed from the first settlement of North America under their common allegiance to the British crown.

Mr. Guerard is, I judge from his review and from a private letter, a partisan of a European union comprising all the nations west of Russia and including Britain. I am not. I regard such a union, if it were consummated as a military federation, as wholly undesirable if, fortunately, it were not wholly unrealizable. Such a "Europe" would inevitably be a Pan-German Europe. For there is no state west of the Curzon line large enough to resist German domination. Such a Europe would at once be mortally at odds with Russia. It would alienate Britain from Russia, and it would — if the United Kingdom followed Mr. Guerard's advice and adhered to it — cause the dissolution of the British Commonwealth and the isolation of the Americas.

---

1. Albert L. Guerard, French-born literary critic and historian, since 1935 a professor of literature at Stanford University, served with the American Office of War Information, 1942–45. His review of Lippmann's U.S. Foreign Policy (Boston, 1943) had appeared in the Nation of June 26, 1943. 2. The Curzon Line was the eastern boundary of Poland as defined by the League of Nations in December 1919. 3. The emphasis is Lippmann's.

To Jacques Maritain

July 1, 1943

Dear M. Maritain:

I thank you very much for your letter and I am most grateful for the opportunity to discuss with you, in the midst of your heavy duties, the critical points which you raise. They were, as a matter of fact, my greatest concern while I was at work on the book, and the most difficult question I had to decide was whether to develop at length and explicitly or merely by implication, the reasons why I did not propose as an "ultimate end" a "federation of peoples inspired by an heroic ideal."

This was not, as you realize, due to an oversight or to a lack of interest in such an ultimate end. It was due to a deep conviction on a matter of fundamental principle. I do not believe that this end can be approached unless military power has first been organized for security against the threat of great wars. But I believe no less that it is wrong to suppose that out of the necessary work of the police there can evolve the creative work of civilization. The policeman must not be regarded as a potential priest, teacher, and constructer of the good life. He should be confined to the limited task of preserving an order within which the priest and teacher and constructer can proceed.

After prolonged consideration of the question you raise I concluded, therefore, that if I was to propose and discuss the ultimate temporal end of society, I would have to make an historical and philosophical argument against the notion that it was the mission of the allied powers to rule the world in order to promote that end. My view, as I indicate in the book, is that security against great aggression and not the promotion of civilization is the function of the great power alliance. Such an alliance would be not only intolerable, but, as I sought to prove, altogether unworkable if the allied great powers took upon themselves more than the specific and limited function, which in this age they alone can exercise effectively, of providing security against world conquerors. My view is that by resting the case for the alliance on the limited ground of their own self-interest, I was offering the only insurance that could be depended upon against the insidious temptation of imperialism to act as if the ultimate ends of human society were entrusted to the foreign offices in London, Moscow, Chungking, and Washington. In view of the fact that power corrupts men's minds, I was very specially concerned to avoid the suggestion that the power we must exercise is an instrument for the attainment of ultimate ends. That could lead only, I believe, to a new version of Kipling and the white man's burden.

The more I pondered the problem the more clear it became to me that the problem of security must be settled conclusively *before*[1] a larger society of peoples can be organized. For I do not think that a general federation of the peoples can organize security, and I believe that if this particular task is entrusted to it, it will not only fail to organize security but will be prevented by this failure from carrying out its creative task. In 1919 I did not think Clemenceau was right when he asked for an alliance in addition to the League. But experience has taught me that he was profoundly right, and that if the alliance he demanded had come into existence, the League would then have had the freedom and security to devote itself to the promotion of intercourse and welfare. Therefore, I now most earnestly wish to settle decisively the question of security without entangling it with the problem of world organization.

It goes without saying, for you know where I stand, that I regard France as indispensable both to security and to the guidance of the western community. But the more certainly men believe that the threat of aggression has been removed for some generations to come, the greater, I believe, will be the spiritual influence of France. It is in the anarchic conflict of gigantic powers that France can least exert her influence.

You may perhaps ask why I did not make all this explicit in my book. My answer would have to be that I was writing a tract for the times, devoted to the specific end of showing how the people of the United States could unite quickly on a decision which, if it is not taken within the next twelve months, would leave us paralyzed and would render impossible an orderly solution of the war. I sought, therefore, to find the least common denominator of an agreement to act, and while my book is as sincere and as truthful as I knew how to make it, it has no pretension to being more than, let us say, the speech of a public man at a critical juncture in public affairs. . . .

1. Emphasis Lippmann's.

To Henry Cabot Lodge, Jr.[1]

July 1, 1943

Dear Cabot:

I have read your speech carefully and I feel sure you have done a great service in turning men's minds from the hackneyed phrases which have obscured the discussion of foreign affairs. But I am sure the friendliest thing I can do is to be frank. I think the influence you will be able to exert will be much less than I hope it may become if you do not correct certain defects in your reasoning — which reflect a bias.

First. You are, for example, properly insistent upon the errors of the transcendentalists. But how can you fail to recognize at the same time the costly error of those who have talked and acted as if American security were solely a matter of defending continental United States against invasion? If you do not deplore both errors equally, you will inevitably lay yourself open to the charge of partisan bias.

Second. You begin your speech with a statement which is not true. You say that Britain has a very practical national aim which is to maintain the Empire, but that we have no such practical national aim. In fact, in this respect we have exactly the same definite practical aim as Britain: we too intend to maintain our pre-war position — in Alaska, Hawaii, the Philippines, in the Caribbean, and in South America. The British aim to hold what she had is so obviously our own aim too that it is universally taken for granted and outside the bounds of discussion. It is, therefore, misleading, and will cause the British to suspect your motives for you to equate our need for something *more* than we had before the war with Britain's retention of *what* she had before the war.[2]

I am in genuine agreement with what you wish to obtain for us. However, I think that the first point in your summary — about "effective international collaboration" — is an example of that cosmic transcendentalism which you deplore. It is too late in the day for any man to use such empty phrases: the time has come to particularize and to be practical by defining the strategic positions, the commitments, the alliances which give substance to the phrase. . . .

1. Henry Cabot Lodge, Jr., grandson of the late Senator Henry Cabot Lodge, had been Republican senator from Massachusetts from 1937 until 1942, when he resigned to serve as an officer in the Army. After the war, he returned to the Senate. Conscious always of his grandfather's career, he had made a speech calling on the administration to define American postwar needs.   2. The emphases are Lippmann's.

To Jan Munzer[1]

July 7, 1943

Dear Mr. Munzer:

. . . I can well understand why you should raise the question which you do raise, namely, how to tell the difference between a local problem and a general threat of world conquest. In my view, the Sudeten question was a world question — not because frontiers must be inviolable, but because of the known purposes of Nazi Germany. It was the character of Germany that one had to make up one's mind about. Thus, a frontier dispute between Peru and Chile over Tacna-Arica is not a world problem because no world power with great aggressive purposes is involved in it.

When Chamberlain professed to believe that the German designs on Czechoslovakia were a purely local problem, he was refusing to believe the evidence which was perfectly clear to other British statesmen like Churchill and Eden. The fact that his government had signed Article I of the Covenant did not affect the matter at all. Therefore, there is no assurance in giving guarantees of that type that another Chamberlain will not use the excuse of pretending that a problem is local when he ought to know better.

My criticism of your implied conclusion would be that you are searching for automatic guarantees of the good judgment and right behavior of great states. There are no automatic guarantees, and in the last analysis, if we can't find governments capable of discerning the nature of a regime like the Nazi, no machinery we can set up will do us any good.

My own view is that with the suppression of German military power the continent of Europe should find its own equilibrium, with American power obligated only to prevent for a definite period of years the revival of the German power. I believe that that amount of American military commitment is sufficient to ensure a long peace in Europe and that at the same time it is the maximum commitment which will be likely to be made by this country. . . .

1. Jan Munzer of the Czech Information Service in the United States.

To Mark W. Clark[1]

July 8, 1943

Dear General Clark:

Thank you for your kind letter about my book. Certainly a great deal has happened since we had that delightful evening with you in London last fall and when we so discreetly didn't talk about what was so obviously coming.

It occurs to me that it might be useful if I wrote you a little bit about the political side of North African affairs, as I am under the impression from seeing people who return that there is a good deal of misunderstanding in North Africa about the views of responsible people who have criticized certain aspects of the political history.

I have been told, for example, that the impression prevails that General Eisenhower and you and Mr. Murphy are being criticized for the Darlan arrangement. There was, of course, a natural outcry in uninformed circles here and in England at an association with Darlan, but those of us who were informed as to events at the time not only did not criticize the arrangement but approved with warm admiration the decisions which were made. There has never been any doubt in my mind, and I don't see how there could be any in any responsible man's mind that the right decisions were taken.

My own criticism has turned on two aspects of our diplomacy, neither of which involved the Army. My first criticism has been that the arrangement with Darlan was a military decision and that it was a grave error on the part of the State Department to issue public statements associating itself with it. It is one thing for a commander to take a military action; it is quite another to give the world the impression that this action stems from the foreign policy of the country. I feel sure in my own mind that if the Darlan arrangement had been left to the soldiers in Africa and to the War Department here, there would have been not one-tenth the misunderstanding and confusion in England and elsewhere.

My other criticism has been that, whether we like him or not, the movement represented by General de Gaulle is an immensely real factor in the life of France and that it was an error not to treat him respectfully from the outset, to cultivate him, and to win his confidence. There was no reason that I can see why, when we associated ourselves with General Giraud, we had in our dealings in London and in Washington to dissociate ourselves so rudely and sharply from General de Gaulle. Publicly we have professed to favor all Frenchmen who resist the enemy, but in fact we have from the beginning kept the Fighting French at arm's length. I believe that this was an error, that it is having grievous consequences, and that it may even permanently impair our relations with France.

I hope that this makes it clear that neither General Eisenhower nor you has been subject to criticism, but on the contrary, that there is everywhere intense pride in your immense achievements. . . .

1. At this time Clark was commander of the United States Fifth Army, which accompanied by British forces, was about to invade Sicily on July 10.

To Quincy A. Wright[1]

July 22, 1943

Dear Quincy:

. . . What I do wonder about is whether there isn't an unexamined difference between us on the subject of collective security. I take it that you envisage an organization of the nations more or less led by the Big Four, committed to suppressing aggression, no matter by whom. That is what I mean by the Wilsonian conception. I suspect, for reasons which I don't know whether I can make clear to you in this letter except to say that such a general organization, directed against everybody in general and nobody in particular, would quickly develop a pro and anti-Russian alignment. For it is on the Russian frontiers, both east and west, that the largest number of cases are likely to arise where the strict application of League principles will bring out dangerous antagonisms.

In my view, the great object of international organization in the next generation is to hold together the alliance and to hold it together at almost any cost. I feel sure that it will hold together better if Russia and the rest of us deal generously with our own neighbors. But the alliance must be held together so as to ensure us against another great war within the next thirty years and in order to give us, as a correspondent just wrote me, a period of grace in which to do a lot of other things that need doing to make the world more peaceable. Therefore, I want to find ways of binding together the Allies which are sure to bind them, and I do not believe they will be successfully bound together by any general covenant.

You will naturally want to know how I think that can be done. This letter will get too long if I try to explain my idea, but essentially it is that we must be bound together by this common interest — in keeping Germany and Japan from reviving as military powers we will be able to improve the general association among peoples.

This would be much better in talk than it is in a letter. If what I have said isn't clear, put it down to the heat and to the fact that I am writing this letter on a railroad train. . . .

1. Quincy A. Wright, professor of international law at the University of Chicago.

To James P. Selvage[1]

August 4, 1943

Dear Mr. Selvage:

I can give you my own views quite simply in reply to your question. I am not a New Dealer; the only time I voted for Mr. Roosevelt was in 1932, when there was in my opinion no alternative, owing to the collapse of our economy.

Although I am opposed to the collectivist trend of the New Deal, I regard it as a misleading use of words to call it fascist. It is no more fascist than Henry Wallace's opponents are fascist. Fascism is a system of government by one legally authorized party, in which no opposition parties are permitted by law. It is therefore loose talk to describe our present situation as fascist.

As for the re-election of the President to a fourth term, I very sincerely hope that that can be avoided, but I am sure that it cannot be avoided just by declaiming against the fourth term. It can only be avoided if the Republican Party is able to offer the country the prospect of an administration aware of the national and international problems which we face and capable of dealing with them. The old rule that you can't beat a horse with no horse will, I think, decide the election. . . .

1. James P. Selvage, then assistant to the chairman of the Republican National Committee.

To Gerard Swope

September 7, 1943

Dear Gerard:

. . . As for the break-up of the German Empire, I'd like to see it done if I felt sure there was a way of doing it. This is the view, I believe, of the Prime Minister, the President, and even of Stalin. This week I talked at length with Cadogan,[1] the permanent head of the Foreign Office, and it was evident that they are very much puzzled as to how to accomplish the break-up so that it will stick.

. . . As for . . . the disruption of the Prussian military caste, I certainly agree in principle that that is one of the principal objectives. The problem is how to prevent them from becoming an underground movement after they are formally outlawed.

Another point, which I put great store upon, but which should not, I think, be talked about at all in public, is the seizure as part of the spoils of war of the archives of the German War Office, the Foreign Office, the Admiralty, and all other agencies connected with the making of war. I believe that if we could get possession of the archives, we would make it very much more difficult for them to rebuild the military machine. . . .

About the demobilization of the German army and using the men to rebuild, I know it is the intention of Stalin to insist upon that point. Whether the French or the Poles would be willing to have Germans in their countries at all is another question. Russia would feel strong enough to have them and use them; Poland and France might not. . . .

1. Sir Alexander Cadogan.

To Jessie Allen Page[1]

September 7, 1943

Dear Miss Page:

. . . There are no real differences between us on the Russian question. The problem is very difficult but you might remember one thing, and that is that Stalin is not immortal, and that, as I heard Mr. Churchill say privately the other day here in Washington, the Army is now much more important in Russia than the Party. As a result Stalin is in effect leaving the Party and joining the Army.

All of which goes to show that what will determine Russian policy in the future is the movement of opinion within the mass of the Russian people who are now very much waked up and very conscious of their strength. . . .

1. Jessie Allen Page of Bryn Mawr, Pennsylvania, an ardent reader of "Today and Tomorrow," which on occasion provoked her to write its author.

To Joseph W. Jones[1]

October 2, 1943

My dear Mr. Jones:

. . . Perhaps you will let me say a few words of explanation about your criticism of my book. I am vague about China, not because I do not believe the inclusion of China is necessary and desirable, but because I am frankly not sure what the future in China is to be. It seems to me that you are equally uncertain, for you confine yourself to arguing the importance of China and the dangers if China is not with us, but you do not deal with the question as to how probable it is that in the near future China will be unified and capable of playing her part. If I may say so, you rather tend to take the view that what ought to be, will be. I felt my particular job was to be vague if in fact the future is uncertain, but I would certainly proceed on the assumption that China will be an effective great power. . . .

1. Joseph W. Jones of *Fortune.*

To Robert G. Vansittart[1]

November 4, 1943

My dear Vansittart:

I was very happy to get your letter of October 2 about my book. I hoped you would think it on the whole sound and perhaps useful as a tract for the times.

Your own book has just appeared here, and I read it last week just before your letter came in. I am going to make the opportunity soon of saying that nobody here must make up his mind about the terms for Germany until he has read your book and candidly faced the argument which it raises. As you know your position has been misrepresented in this country as being in effect German racialism in reverse. That is because your articles have not been published here; what people have heard here is echoes of the controversy about them in England.

I read the outcome at Moscow as meaning a settlement with Germany more to your taste than that of your critics.[2]

I think I detected in your book the realization that it would be unwise to expect this country to participate directly and actively in administering prolonged treatment to Germany. That will have to be the work of the peoples closer to Germany, and I am very much hoping that American troops can be withdrawn from Europe and especially from enemy territory at the earliest possible moment after the fighting stops. I am sure you will appreciate the wisdom of that. . . .

1. Lord Robert G. Vansittart, a senior, permanent member of the British Foreign Office, diplomatic adviser to several foreign secretaries, and occasional poet. He advocated a Carthaginian settlement with Germany and expressed his views about that subject in two books, *Black Record: Germans Past and Present* (London, 1941) and *Lessons of My Life* (London, 1943), of which the latter was also published in the United States by Alfred A. Knopf. 2. At the Moscow Conference, just over, the foreign ministers of the Soviet Union, Great Britain, and the United States had agreed to establish a European advisory committee on terms of the German surrender and to separate Austria from Germany. They also agreed to set up a postwar international organization

for peace and security and to destroy the Fascist regime in Italy, where Anglo-American forces were meeting stiff resistance from the Germans.

To Gerard Swope

November 5, 1943

Dear Gerard:

. . . I appreciate the distinction which you have in mind, but there is another distinction which I should like to suggest to you. I don't hold the German people responsible for the acts of their leaders and masters in the sense that I feel they must be punished for those acts. But if they are to be treated as morally responsible people in the world they must accept the moral responsibility for the kind of government they have submitted to. There is danger of a good deal of confusion in the hypothesis that the Prussian military caste exists independently of the rest of the German nation. . . .

To Geoffrey Parsons [1]

December 13, 1943

Dear Geoffrey:

. . . I agree that the Republican outlook is not very good. I have just come back from Cleveland and Chicago, and it's clear there at least that Wendell's chances are diminishing. I think myself he is conducting a poor campaign, full of generalities, without ever showing that he can go to the bottom of any question.

I came back convinced that all possible influence should be exerted to prevent the breach between Willkie and Dewey from becoming irreparable and if possible to heal it. Otherwise we'll either get another Harding or Dewey will fall into the clutches of the wrong people or Willkie will get the nomination from a hopelessly divided party. . . .

1. Geoffrey Parsons, since 1924 chief editorial writer for the *New York Herald Tribune*.

To Russell C. Leffingwell

December 30, 1943

Dear Russell:

. . . One thing I would like to clear up: that's the question of whether there is a real difference between a deficit of 50 billions and of 40 billions. I agree that in these matters a difference of degree is important, but I should also argue that there are some differences of degree which don't matter. If a man gets roaring drunk on three highballs, the fourth highball doesn't make the difference between his being drunk and his being sober. My point is that a 40 billion dollar deficit may produce a great inflation; so may a 50 billion dollar deficit. Reducing the deficit from 50 billions to 40 billions may still leave you with a gigantic inflation.

The point of the whole argument is that we can't possibly tax enough to reduce the deficit to a point where it isn't potentially very inflationary. Therefore, we shall have to use other methods for controlling the effects besides taxation. . . .[1]

1. The pending revenue bill, which the House Ways and Means Committee had emasculated, provided for only about $1.5 billion in additional revenue, far below the president's request for $10.5 billion, which itself severely pared the Treasury's larger target. Even that would have left a deficit for fiscal 1945 (July 1, 1944–June 30, 1945) of some $40 billion, as this letter suggested. Lippmann, like most of Roosevelt's senior advisers, still favored a compulsory savings program to stem the inflationary potentialities of that deficit, but the president continued to support the voluntary bond program the Treasury preferred.

To Harold L. Ickes

February 24, 1944

My dear Secretary Ickes:

Thank you for your letter.[1] I don't think we are really in any disagreement.

In regard to the consultation with the State Department, I seem not to have made myself perfectly clear. When I said "seriously consulted," I meant *seriously*.[2] Serious consultation would have meant that when the project was put forward there was evidence that the strategic and political implications had been considered and had entered into the decision. That's the only reason why it is important to consult the State Department at all. Its opinion on the value of particular oil reserves or about the commercial value of a pipe line is of no importance.

I think you will have to agree that in no part of the public presentation of the project is there any reference to the real strategic and political implications of the plan.

1. Secretary of the Interior Harold Ickes had played a leading role in the negotiation of the Anglo-American oil agreement with Saudi Arabia. Responding to Lippmann's column about that pact, Ickes wrote on February 22, 1944: "There is one observation that I would like to make and that is in connection with your statement that 'the State Department would seem not to have been seriously consulted' in this Arabian oil matter. I cannot agree with this since every step was taken after full consultation with the State Department. . . . Everything was further checked fully with the President before final action. It is true that . . . the State Department held back and perhaps, if left alone, would have charted a different course . . . but surely it cannot be argued that because it was reluctant to agree to some move it was not 'seriously consulted.' "

The agreement, which Congress never approved, would have provided diplomatic but not military support for the large American interests in Arabian oil, but it met the opposition of the petroleum industry, which objected to the large role of government inherent in the pact; see Michael B. Stoff, *Oil, War, and American Security* (New Haven, 1980). **2.** Emphasis Lippmann's.

To Ernest Angell[1]

March 15, 1944

Dear Ernest:

This is purely personal, and please don't pass it around. I don't want to get into a controversy, but I'd like to talk to you privately about that statement which you and others got out the other day about Russia and Poland.

Before I saw it, Raymond Swing[2] told me how very much upset he was by it, and now that I have read it, I must say that I fully share his feelings. The first thing about it that is distressing is that it's based on a false premise, namely, that the Soviet Government has refused mediation by her allies in the Polish problem. I know about the mediation which has been going on ever since Churchill's return to England, both in London and in Moscow, and that we have been fully consulted about that mediation at all stages and were quite free to express our views if we wanted to. There is certainly no doubt that Churchill and Eden have mediated in detail in all phases of the Polish question between Stalin and Molotov[3] on the one hand and the Polish government on the other. That they have not been able to obtain an agreement is true, but it is not true to say that there has been no mediation.

I am also surprised that you should put your name to a document which says what this one says about the Curzon line. For while the Curzon Line may be close to the Hitler-Stalin line of 1939, it is not that line, and it merely arouses prejudice to say that it is. The Curzon Line is the only eastern frontier of Poland ever defined by that process of consultation which is the premise of your protest. It was drawn by British, French, and American experts in accordance with Wilson's promise in the Fourteen Points, and it represents their consensus of a just frontier; it has a wholly different moral basis than any other frontier in that part of the world. The 1939 Polish frontier east of the Curzon Line was established by a unilateral war of aggression not only against Soviet Russia but against Lithuania as well. The frontier in Eastern Galicia was established by force in defiance of the Allies' decision to give Poland a twenty-five year mandate over that territory. Finally, the Polish frontier with Czechoslovakia was established at the time of Munich in collaboration with and by the consent of Hitler. It is not advisable to have to tell this story publicly, for it is a sad story which injures the Poles and can only make matters worse, but it does astonish me that responsible people who are supposed to know about foreign relations can issue a statement at this critical time which ignores so many of the essential facts.

I note also that you say that the Curzon Line would violate the Atlantic Charter. Does it? The Atlantic Charter became a legal commitment of the

United Nations on January 1, 1942, and Russia was accepted without reservation as a signatory of it on that date. At that date the Baltic States and the former Polish territory had been legally incorporated within the Soviet Union. Therefore, the question is whether the Atlantic Charter is retroactive from the date of its signature, and if so, how far retroactive it is. You will readily see that if it is retroactive, it reopens innumerable territorial settlements in Europe and elsewhere in the world.

There has been so much moral confusion about the Atlantic Charter that I am considering making the suggestion that a commission of jurists be set up to give advisory opinions on certain questions which have already arisen under it. The first would be whether it is retroactive. The second would be whether China, for example, has the right to ask for the cession of Hong Kong if the inhabitants of Hong Kong object. The third is whether we have any right to claim, as we certainly intend to claim, the annexation of the Japanese mandated islands. The fourth would be whether if, as is probable, we intend to alter the frontiers of Germany, we ought formally to amend the United Nations declaration of January 1, 1942. . . .

1. Ernest Angell, New York City lawyer, had been a Harvard contemporary of Lippmann's and was a fellow member of the Century Association. **2.** Raymond Gram Swing, veteran reporter and analyst of foreign affairs and popular evening commentator for the Mutual Broadcasting System. **3.** Vyacheslav Molotov, then Soviet foreign minister.

To Sallie L. White[1]

April 27, 1944

Dear Sallie:

Last spring, when Will had read the proofs of my book "U.S. Foreign Policy," he telephoned me and wrote me, urging me to add another chapter at the end stating more positively and at greater length a positive program for keeping the peace after the war. I had to tell him that I couldn't write that chapter then because I hadn't worked out what he wanted me to do.

Since then I have written that last chapter, but it is now a new book. It is to be called "U.S. War Aims" and is to be published in mid-summer. I should like to dedicate it as follows: "To the Memory of William Allen White." But of course I want first to have your permission and the approval of Bill. . . .[2]

1. Sallie Lindsay White, widow of William Allen White, who had died on January 29, 1944. **2.** Both Sallie White and her son, William, agreed to the dedication Lippmann then used in *U.S. War Aims* (Boston, 1944).

To Russell C. Leffingwell

June 10, 1944

Dear Russell:

. . . As for President Roosevelt's foreign policy, the fact is that its virtues have stood out by contrast with his opposition. In itself the record, if you take the whole ten years up through Pearl Harbor, is a sorry one, but his Republican opponents were infinitely worse, and that's the only reason why the record seems so good. In fact, we were unprepared for a war that we knew was coming and never took a serious measure in advance to prepare for it.

I'm hoping I can persuade myself that there is a good alternative to him. I could be against him with fervor; being for the alternative is the difficulty.[1]

1. Two weeks before the election, Lippmann came out against Dewey, not the least because of Dewey's support in the campaign of the "reactionary Poles," then resisting any compromise with the Soviet position on Poland's eastern frontier; see Ronald Steel, *Walter Lippmann and the American Century* (Boston, 1980), pp. 412–14.

To John L. Balderston

July 27, 1944

Dear John:

. . . I don't see why my book[1] should leave you with a feeling of despair. What on earth have we the right to expect better than that which I think not only possible but distinctly probable, namely that we shall have a long peace without great war. What we do with that peace I didn't attempt to say; that's a whole series of other books. But I would certainly insist that on the lines I have suggested, which are, I think, the lines that events are actually taking, the present cycle of wars will be definitively completed. That's the utmost that can be hoped for as a result of any war. There's a great deal of confusion among our friends who think that war, which is a destructive process, can create the brave new world. The brave new world, in my view, can be created only if and when the threat of great war has disappeared for two or three generations. In other words, I think we shall get a peace as conclusive as that which followed the Napoleonic Wars and a century as free from great wars as was the Nineteenth. That's a devil of a lot when you think about it.

One other point: I didn't appeal to Russia to put her constitution into effect; I said to the Russians that they must recognize that the character of the collaboration depends upon whether or not they put it into effect. My information, from very reliable Russian sources, is that they do intend to put it into effect. Why else do you suppose they keep talking about democracy? They don't have to talk about it, but they do, and they can't be such fools as to talk about democracy in Poland and Italy and elsewhere unless they intend to have a good deal of it at home. . . .

1. *U.S. War Aims* (Boston, 1944).

To Jeremiah M. Evarts [1]

September 9, 1944

Dear Mr. Evarts:

Why should you assume from my article that I was talking politics when the article explicitly argued that the problem of employment was above parties. I don't say such things to deceive people; when I say them I really mean them.

I am as much concerned as you are to preserve republican government and to prevent the growth of bureaucracy, and I devoted nearly seven years to writing a four hundred page book on the subject.[2] But I must remind you that the developments since 1932 which you complain about and which I have criticized persistently for over ten years, were the direct consequence of the total collapse of our national economy and of the world economy in the years preceding the advent of the New Deal. In my view, unless a similar collapse after this war is resolutely prevented, we will get the same consequences in a more acute form. . . .

1. Jeremiah M. Evarts — who shared the views of many others who earned a good living, as he did, on lower Manhattan — had objected to Lippmann's "Today and Tomorrow" column of September 7, 1944, which defined employment as the paramount domestic issue of the time. Evarts believed "the most important issue . . . is to preserve our republican form of representative government and to remove the festering growth of bureaucracy." 2. *The Good Society* (Boston, 1937).

To Grenville Clark [1]

September 19, 1944

Dear Grennie:

Thank you for your letter of September 16. I should not be happy if we disagreed fundamentally, and so for the purpose of agreeing, I am going to make an attempt to say where, as I see it, we now differ.

You start with the basic assumption that the national states of the world today may be regarded as if they were the thirteen American states at the end of the Eighteenth Century. You are not sure whether the present time is 1787–1789 or whether it is 1781, but your reasoning is controlled by the idea that the political evolution in our time can and should pass through essentially the same phases to essentially the same end. . . . The alliance is to become a confederation and the confederation a federal union.

I think this reasoning is based on a radically false historical analogy. The difference between the Philadelphia Convention and the Dumbarton Oaks Conference,[2] or your proposed United Nations Convention, is so great that to overlook it is to beg the whole question at issue. The Thirteen States originated as British colonies. Except, I think, for New Amsterdam until 1664, they were settled, and from the beginning had always been governed, by men who owed allegiance to the same sovereign. They had always been united, and at no time had they been separate and independent national states. They had the same king, the same laws, the same history, the same culture, and the same language. Their unity was primordial. As early as 1774 the first Continental Congress spoke of themselves as representing "the people of America" and as "the inhabitants of the English colonies in North America" possessing certain rights "by the immutable laws of nature, the principles of the English Constitution." Founded together, they rebelled together, and in 1787–1789 they formed not a new union, but "a more perfect union."

The problem of international union today is, I submit, radically different from theirs in that we have to unite peoples who have always been separate, whereas they were framing a constitution for a people who had always been united. This difference is so crucial that to reason analogically from the American experience is an almost certain way to obscure the real issues of world peace.

It makes all the difference in the world whether you start with unity and seek to perfect it, or whether your first and greatest task is to achieve unity where none has existed. If, therefore, we are to use historical analogies to indicate the nature of our own problems, we must look to some time and some place where hitherto independent and conflicting principalities and powers have been pacified and united. All historical analogies in this field have to be treated with extreme caution and skepticism, but if we are to use any we might study how modern national states — such as Great Britain, France, Germany, Italy, Russia, were pacified and united out of the feudal system.

For the international world today does not resemble at all the little world on the Atlantic seaboard at the end of the Eighteenth Century, and to approach the world as if Britain were Massachusetts, the United States were New York, the Soviet Union were Pennsylvania, China were New Jersey, and France were Virginia, is to raise false expectations from a false premise. The political principles which may be invoked to federate an already essentially united people, are not the same principles that must be invoked to pacify and unite separate and conflicting peoples.

My view is that in our thinking we must not substitute for the world as it is an imaginary world such as Eighteenth Century America. We must begin with this world, making as just an estimate as we can of the actual and potential connections and conflicts among the nations, and then seek the principles of order which apply to it. My book was an effort to do that, and the principal conclusion which I reached was that the world could not be pacified and united by a constitution, but that it had to be pacified and united in order that a constitution could be made operative. I believe this to be the critical lesson of the Wilsonian effort.

In my view the course of events within the Dumbarton Oaks Conference is demonstrating the truth of this conclusion — that pacification must precede, because it cannot be accomplished by, a universal juridical society. The Dumbarton project has run into two major difficulties, the one centering around the Soviet Union and the other around the United States. Both difficulties originate, I believe, in the failure of the British and American delegations to grasp clearly that pacification must precede the establishment of a reign of law.

The Soviets, as you know, are refusing to accept the principle of the sovereign equality of all states. They insist first on a veto which can prevent the enforcement of peace anywhere without their consent, and second, can also prevent the enforcement of peace against them. On their second point they are opposed by China and Britain, and now also, though not originally, I think, by the United States.

The motive of the Chinese is obvious: they foresee a conflict on the Soviet-Chinese frontier, and they wish to organize the support of the world behind them and against the Soviet Union. The British position is, I am satisfied, the result of believing on the one hand in the principle of the equality of states and of a conviction that this principle would not be turned against them. For they feel almost entirely sure that even if Britain could not vote when her vital interests were at stake, the vote of the United States and of France would almost certainly be as good as if they themselves had a veto. We also can afford this principle since we know that Britain and France will never vote for a world war against us. But the Soviets are isolated among the great powers. They have no certain ally who would exercise a veto for them. Thus an ugly and at bottom an unjust dilemma has been produced in which the world is aligned in principle against the Soviet Union.

The cause of this dilemma is that the Dumbarton Delegates have sought to create a universal society to enforce peace before the world has been sufficiently pacified. The right procedure, I believe, was to put pacification ahead of law enforcement by the universal society. What has been done is to confuse the two. Our first postwar agreements, in so far as they involve force and not merely collaboration in the arts of peace, should not be a new covenant. They should be conventions among the victors to enforce the terms to be imposed on our present enemies, and conventions to perpetuate the military and political organization of the United Nations, with due regard to the realities which make Britain and America a *combined* force, the American and Chinese, the American and Soviet, *allied* forces.[3] With these conventions to pacify and unite, we should not be quarreling with Russia over the conundrum of legal equality, but should be bound together with Russia to make and keep the peace in the critical generation ahead of us.

With these conventions agreed to, and ratified by Congress, we could postpone in the covenant of the new League the problem of enforcing peace in hypothetical cases. We should have binding agreements to enforce peace in the real cases immediately ahead of us, and we should have some unity because of these agreements. We could then set up an Assembly and a Council and a Court, putting our emphasis on them as organs of consultation and of disclosure, and leaving the questions of power to be resolved as the habit of collaboration develops in a world which has been in some measure pacified.

There is no reason that I can see why in setting up the framework of the League we must also settle now all its powers in hypothetical cases. Yet that is what we are trying to do. Before we have finished with Germany and Japan, we have caused a rift in our alliance by raising the question of whether the new League may go to war with the Soviet Union.

We have also planted the seeds of a dangerous controversy in this country. We know that we can immediately, and by bi-partisan agreement, join in a convention to enforce the demilitarization of Germany and Japan. We can get also a charter setting up an international organization. What we cannot get, without a debate which would tear the country apart, is a general mandate from Congress to the President to wage war in hypothetical cases. In this debate the position of the opposition in Congress will be the complement of that of Russia at Dumbarton Oaks. For Russia is objecting to the possibility of a League war against the Soviet Union, and the American opposition will object to the President's having the power to wage such a war, or even to get entangled in it, without the specific consent of Congress. The Russian and the American objections would not have arisen if we had separated clearly the task of pacification from the establishment of a universal juridical society.

The conundrums of the veto, of sovereignty, of the American separation of powers, of large versus small states, have been produced by an unclear analysis that yielded a false major premise — namely that the Dumbarton Oaks organization can and should be a universal society to pacify the world. The truth is that only in a reasonably pacified world can there be a universal society.

Forgive the length of this letter, but the subject is, I believe, of the highest importance, and in my view the line you are taking can have very serious consequences. You have shifted your attention from the problem of pacification and unification to the formation of a constitution which cannot, I believe, solve that problem, which in failing to solve it while presuming to, will disunite the great powers and will interrupt the enforcement of the peace we win in this war.

1. Grenville Clark, eminent New York lawyer, prime organizer in 1940 of the movement for conscription; chairman of the Citizens Committee for National War Service, 1944–45; valued friend of Henry Stimson; and Fellow of Harvard College.   2. At Dumbarton Oaks in Washington, from August 21 to September 27, 1944, delegates from the United States, the British Commonwealth and the Soviet Union conferred about terms for a permanent international organization — the United Nations — to preserve world peace and security. The meeting prepared the way for the San Francisco Conference in 1945, which drafted the charter for the UN.   3. The emphases are Lippmann's.

To John Foster Dulles [1]

October 25, 1944

Dear Foster:

I am just about to take off for Europe, and so I won't attempt any long discussion of your letter, though after election I should be very glad if we could talk it over sometime. . . .

On the Polish question I can't help wondering what kind of secret negotiations the Governor indulged in as "particular precautions" before delivering a speech which was an attack on secret diplomacy. Surely you don't want me to assume that his public statements have some other meaning than that which they appear to have.

Finally I wonder if it would be profitable to argue about who is more aware of the moral issues involved in this war, for that would involve examination of the record, whereas I for one prefer to let bygones be bygones.

I am sorry we don't find ourselves on the same side. I had hoped we might, and after the election I hope we shall again.

1. John Foster Dulles, who was Dewey's adviser on foreign affairs, had objected to Lippmann's statement about Dewey's position on Poland (see note, Lippmann to Russell C. Leffingwell, June 10, 1944, sup.). Dewey, Dulles argued, was privately well informed about the issue. "The basic difference between you and the governor," Dulles continued, "is that you do not believe that the United States should have any policies at all except in relation to areas where we can make those policies good through material force."

To Karl E. Mundt [1]　　　　　　　　　　　HANDWRITTEN

[c. January 22, 1945]

Dear Mr. Mundt:

I greatly appreciate your kind invitation to discuss the policies which should be followed by the permanent House Committee on Un-American Activities. I share your concern about the absence of a suitable and working criterion, and I agree with you that, nevertheless, there are in fact revolutionary and subversive activities which must be effectively opposed.

The primary business of your committee is, it seems to me, to find the answer to the very question which you put in your letter. For under our constitutional systems the function of a legislative committee is to report to Congress on the need for legislation. It is not the function of a legislative committee to execute the laws, nor is it a tribunal before which cases are tried and judged. I venture to think that by a faithful observance of these basic principles, the problems can all be clarified.

Approaching the matter in that way, the committee would conduct its investigations and hold its hearings with a view to determining whether it would report to the House, whether legislation was required and what legislation was advisable. I venture to think that in the last analysis the difficulties of the former Dies Committee originated in its failure to remember that it was a legislative committee, and not a judicial tribunal, that its business was to propose laws and not to enforce them. When it avoided the responsibility of reporting on legislation and instead asserted in the absence of laws defining their offenses, the necessity to try men and convict them and punish them with public disgrace, it was departing from the elementary principles of the American constitution. It was violating the principles of the separation of powers and it was violating the intent and meaning of the Fifth Amendment as expounded by Daniel Webster in that Dartmouth College case that "every citizen shall have his life, liberty, property and immunities under the protection of the general rules which govern society."

The function of a committee, such as yours, is to advise the House whether "the general rules which govern society," that is to say, the laws of the land, need to be supplemented or amended in order to defend American society. If the committee will resolve that it must report on legislation, and that all its activities are for the purpose of making such a report, it will, I believe, have adopted the true criterion by its own actions. Only then can it hope to find the answer to the questions which you put in your letter. For an un-American activity would then be one which in the judgment of Congress violates the law that exists or laws that Congress deems as necessary and desirable to enact. Congress can be concerned only with activities that are un-American under the law.

In debating what activities fall within the scope of the law as it is or ought to be, my view is a free society such as ours has both the right and the duty of self-preservation. Thus there is a limit to the extent of political freedom, and that limit has been reached when the Bill of Rights and the suffrage and the misbehavior of representative government are used by men who would, if they had the power, destroy political freedom. We cannot conceive that any activity is admissible which aims to carry an election, after which elections would be abolished, which uses free speech to promote a movement which intends to abolish free speech, which uses due process of law to achieve this. . . .

1. Karl E. Mundt, South Dakota Republican, had been in the House of Representatives since 1939. He was a member of the Committee on Un-American Activities, which the House had voted to reinstate. In its earlier incarnation, the committee, with a notorious disregard for civil liberties, had engaged in witch hunts for radicals, particularly those allegedly within the administration. The revived committee was to resume precisely that role under the chairmanship of Texas Democrat Martin Dies. Mundt, a career redbaiter, on January 20, 1945, wrote Lippmann to ask his opinion about the committee's task. Lippmann neither completed nor sent this handwritten draft of January 22 but instead informed Mundt that he would think about the question. To that statement, Mundt replied on February 10, 1945, that he was glad Lippmann was "giving thought" to a "definition of un-American activities," particularly the types of "forces and influences" the committee should examine. Lippmann did not reply. This draft of an effort to reply ran counter to the procedures in which Mundt continually invested large energy.

To Robert Hale[1]

February 16, 1945

My dear Hale:

Thank you very much for your letter. I had been deeply perplexed to understand what the conscientious argument is for refusing to confirm Wallace.[2] I am very glad of the chance to examine it with you.

You say that if you were a Senator you would feel it your constitutional duty to determine whether he has the character and capacity to discharge the duties of the office. I agree. But the question is what tests of character and capacity. Surely these tests must be in some measure objective and could not be expanded to cover such criteria as whether you like him, whether you agree with him, whether he is able, whether he is wise. Now there are no charges that I know of against Wallace's character or his capacity, either as Secretary of Agriculture or as Vice President of the United States. You do, in your closing sentence, speak of diverting "the powers of his office for ulterior ends," but I cannot feel that his announcement that he will pursue a policy which, incidentally, has the same end as that proclaimed by the Republican candidate for President, can reasonably be described by the sinister word "ulterior." I think your letter itself shows pretty clearly that you wish to reject Wallace on the same ground that a member of the House of Commons might vote for a motion of no confidence in a minister, and I submit to you that this is alien to the American system of government. It might well be argued that the British system of ministerial responsibility is better than ours, but we do not have the British system, and we ought not to try to operate our system as if it were the British.

In discussing the point raised under (b) about the payment of political debt, I am sure you will not think that I didn't think the President's letter was a horror when I say that to reject a Cabinet official on the ground that he is appointed in payment of a political debt would be a revolutionary novelty in American politics. Consider for a moment any Cabinet, Republican or Democratic, in our history, and tell me, if you can, whether a very large number of the appointments in all Cabinets have not been payments of political debts. It was shockingly cynical of the President to state that as the reason for his appointment, but if you refuse to confirm on this ground, it will be to punish the cynicism and not the fact.

You disagree with my contention that if the Senate sets up confidence as the criterion of confirmation, then it is usurping the power of appointment. But I ask you just what would be the situation if, after Wallace was refused on the grounds put forward against him, the President then nominated another New Dealer who had exactly the same views as Wallace. Would you reject him too? If so, would you not be saying that you will confirm no one whose political history and whose purposes you do not approve? . . .

1. Robert Hale, Republican congressman from Maine, 1943–47.   **2.** Roosevelt had proposed Henry A. Wallace as secretary of commerce in place of Jesse Jones — long a rival of Wallace's — who had resigned. The president did so after he had connived in the dumping of Wallace as vice presidential candidate by the 1944 Democratic National Convention, which instead turned to Senator Harry S Truman, whom the Southern and the machine politicians much preferred. Wallace had nevertheless campaigned hard for Roosevelt's re-election. He had continually stressed the importance of postwar full employment and of government's obligation to bring it about, and he stood for strong labor and civil rights policies, all issues of importance to liberals. Conservative Democrats and Republicans balked at the nomination of Wallace to the Commerce Department in spite of his outspoken commitment to an expanding international trade. The battle over Wallace's confirmation by the Senate took place largely while Roosevelt was traveling by ship to and from the Yalta Conference, which had adjourned shortly before this letter was written. Roosevelt's absence from Washington probably hurt Wallace's cause. In the end, he did win confirmation, but only after the Congress had stripped the large lending agencies, including the Reconstruction Finance Corporation, from the Department of Commerce, where Jones had administered them.

To Edgar R. Smothers, S.J.[1]

March 3, 1945

Dear Father Smothers:

Under the agreement reached at Yalta, which I understand will be made public shortly after France, as one of the sponsoring powers, has been consulted, Poland will have equal juridical status with the Soviet Union and all other members. If the Polish government which comes into existence through the free elections that must be held by the new provisional government that is to be formed, believes that the frontier with the Soviets or any other feature of its relations with the Soviet Union comes under Chapter VIII, Section A, Paragraph 1, of the Charter, it can bring the question to the Security Council. The relevant section reads as follows: "1. The Security Council should be empowered to investigate *any dispute, or any situation which may lead to international friction* or give rise to a dispute, in order to determine whether its continuance is likely to endanger the maintenance of international peace and security." (Emphasis supplied.) Under the formula agreed to at Yalta neither Poland nor the Soviet Union may vote in the procedure of conciliation or arbitration. The Soviet Union could impose no veto on an international hearing of the dispute or on any settlement of it by pacific means.

I should suppose from your letter that this will not satisfy you and that what you really want is to have the international organization delimit the frontier rather than to determine whether the frontier, after it is delimited, "may lead to international friction or give rise to a dispute." That, in my judgment, would be to put upon the new international organization a burden greater than it would be able to bear. The Yalta decision about Dumbarton Oaks goes a long way toward providing Poland with the right to a full hearing before the world on whether it is the victim of injustice. You must remember that the Polish government which will exercise that right is one that will come into existence by an election which is to be supervised by the American and British governments and is not to be held, so I am informed, until the Red Army has ceased to occupy Polish territory.[2]

1. The Reverend Edgar R. Smothers, S.J., of St. Joseph's Mercy Hospital in Ann Arbor, Michigan. **2.** As it worked out, Lippmann was mistaken, but his error lay in expecting the Soviet Union, precisely as did Roosevelt and Churchill, to live up to the agreements made at Yalta. The agreements pertaining to Poland put that nation's eastern frontier close to the Curzon Line and its western frontier at the Oder-Neisse Line, which placed some former German territory within Poland. Roosevelt, Churchill, and Stalin also agreed to a tripartite commission to organize the Polish government, a task that would involve reconciling the rivalry between the Polish government-in-exile in London (the claimant preferred by Great Britain and the United States) and the Lublin government (the Soviet-dominated Communist claimant). The tripartite commission was to arrange for free elections by the Polish people. But the Soviet Army retained military control of central Europe long enough to permit Stalin, in violation of the Yalta accords, to impose a Communist puppet government on Poland as well as elsewhere. The boundaries set at Yalta did obtain after the war, but there was little freedom within them.

To the Editor, the Washington Post

March 5, 1945

Dear Sir:

With all due respect to the Polish Ambassador,[1] I am replying to his letter of March 2 charging me with a series of inaccuracies, misstatements, and untruths.

It was, I grant, inaccurate to speak of the disputed eastern territories as having been "conquered in 1922." I should have said between 1921 and 1923. For the territory ceded by the Soviet Union was conquered in 1921, the territories seized from Lithuania, and from the Principal Allies and Associated Powers, were recognized as Polish in 1923. But then, of course, the Ambassador is mistaken in saying that Poland's eastern frontier was fixed by "a freely negotiated peace treaty between Poland, Soviet Russia and the Ukrainian Soviet Republic." For the most hotly disputed parts of that frontier, namely around Vilna and Lvov, did not then belong either to Poland or to the Soviet Union, but to Lithuania and to the Allied Powers as heirs to the Austria-Hungary Empire.

And if the Ambassador means to imply that this eastern frontier was not conquered because the acquisition was recognized in part by the Treaty of Riga and in part by a decision of the Allied Powers, then no territory has ever been conquered. For after every conquest, there is a treaty.

The Ambassador challenges my statement that in 1926 Pilsudski[2] overthrew the Polish democratic regime and set up a military dictatorship which, under the new constitution of 1935, became a totalitarian state. I defined a totalitarian state, correctly I believe, as one in which there is only one legal political party. The Ambassador says that "no political party was outlawed and all of them continued to function." But not as political parties, for under the electoral laws political parties as such were not allowed to be represented in the Parliament. (Cf. Political Handbook of the World, 1935 — published by the Council on Foreign Relations.)

What happened in the elections to which the Ambassador refers has been described by Professor Halecki in his "History of Poland,"[3] and I quote from a copy of it which Mr. Ciechanowski was once kind enough to send me as a present: "The rules . . . after the passing of the new constitution . . . had given a fictitious character to the elections to the legislative bodies."

The Ambassador says it is "untrue" that Poland was in bad relations with all its neighbors. In support he says that "Poland reestablished diplomatic relations with Lithuania in 1938," failing to add that this was done by means of a forty-eight hour ultimatum backed by a mobilization against Lithuania. The Ambassador also says that the government he represents "remained in friendly relations with Czechoslovakia during the whole time of the independence of both states until the occupation of Czechoslovakia by Germany in 1939," and fails to add that then in agreement with Hitler his government occupied the Czechoslovak territory of Teschen.

Finally, the Ambassador dismisses as "flatly disproved" any reference to the existence of Polish feudal landlordism. It surprises me to hear him say that, and it will surprise many of his friends who have visited some of these great estates.

1. Jan Ciechanowski, the ambassador of the Polish government-in-exile to the United States, an unbudging and persistent advocate of Poland's cause as he interpreted it. **2.** Marshal Józef Pilsudski, a former chief of state, had led a successful military revolt in 1926 against Poland's government. After ruling through a friend, Pilsudski in 1928 assumed dictatorial authority, through which he suppressed his opposition from the left. **3.** Oskar Halecki's *History of Poland* went through many editions, among others a first in French in 1933, London editions in English in 1936 and 1942, and an American edition in 1943.

To Ross J. S. Hoffman [1]

March 15, 1945

Dear Professor Hoffman:

. . . I suppose I have decided not to spend any effort at the moment on whether I am hopeful or not. We have to do what we can with things as they are, and if we can avert a condition which makes another world war inevitable within the next thirty years, that will be a great deal. What we are fighting for above all, I think, is time to understand these things which are not understood, and I think we have a better than even chance of not setting the stage for another world war thirty years hence.

As I look back on the past year, I can't help feeling that Welles's book[2] did enormous damage in diverting the American people from an understanding of the historic realities. It was, in a sense, bad luck that I published a book at the same moment, for that stopped me from saying what I thought of Welles's book, and I might have accomplished more by a running criticism of him than I did by my own book. But that's all water over the dam.

In the meantime, the struggle goes on inside the Administration as well as in public to shape the Wilsonian ideology into something that fits the realities. I think the struggle would be won inside the government if the public and particularly the idealistic public were not so stubbornly naive.

1. Ross J. S. Hoffman, professor of history at Fordham University.   2. Sumner Welles's *The Time for Decision* (New York, 1944) carried the weight of its author's prestige as the former undersecretary of state, an office he had then just left. Welles had a much more Wilsonian view of a desirable postwar settlement than had Lippmann.

To John Maynard Keynes

March 23, 1945

Dear Maynard:

. . . I wish San Francisco had been prepared with something like the technical thoroughness that went into Bretton Woods.[1] The closer we get to it the more amateurish and second-rate the preparations seem to be. I suppose we shall improvise something that all can accept, but that will be only because those who understand the thing best agree not to expose its weaknesses. I do wish we'd had the foresight to make some kind of security pact as underpinning between Britain, France, and North America. . . .

1. At Bretton Woods, New Hampshire, in July 1944, delegates from the United Nations had negotiated the agreements that created the International Monetary Fund and the International Bank for Reconstruction and Development. Careful, confidential Anglo-American exchanges predated the Bretton Woods conference. Keynes played the major role for the British throughout those developments.

To Herbert B. Elliston[1]

April 18, 1945

Dear Herbert:

I misunderstood you the other night. You remember you brought up the matter as we were walking in to dinner.

What I have written about the land campaign in Asia has always been said with the idea in the back of my mind that we would need Russian help,[2] and my own idea has always been to avoid entangling an American army on the mainland of Asia. That's been the context of my whole argument to point out that something had to be done about the troops on the mainland and to find a way to avoid engaging a large American army to do it. . . .

1. Herbert B. Elliston, veteran journalist, at this time associate editor of the *Washington Post*.
2. That was also the opinion of Roosevelt, of his military advisers at Yalta, and of General Douglas MacArthur at that time. The Yalta agreements called for Russian involvement in the war against Japan after the end of the war against Germany. Though the successful American development of the atomic bomb later made that agreement unnecessary, there was no way, short of military force, to prevent the Soviet Union from entering the war against Japan, as it did at the eleventh hour.

To Charles D. Drayton[1]

April 19, 1945

Dear Mr. Drayton:

. . . The position you take in your first paragraph arises from an inaccurate reading of the sentence which you quote correctly. You will note that I said best fitted of all the men "available." Two sentences later, you argue as if I had said "best fitted." The word "available," as you no doubt will recall, is a thoroughly recognized term in the American political vocabulary, and everyone who knows American politics knows the difference in meaning between the man best fitted and the best fitted available man. A man, no matter how well fitted he may be, is unavailable if he cannot be nominated or if he cannot be elected. Our history is full of instances of pre-eminently fitted men who were not politically available, and I am astonished that you should have overlooked the crucial word which I chose carefully and deliberately.

Your second paragraph contains an even greater distortion of what I said. You make me say that the convention knew that Mr. Truman would "shortly succeed to the Presidency." I said nothing of the kind. What I said was that the convention knew that it was almost certainly choosing a man who would become President at some time, and that did not mean necessarily shortly, but at some time in four years. This did not mean that Mr. Roosevelt was known to be a very ill man; what was known was that his life expectancy was no longer so high that it was probable that he would fill out his term. That is why there was such intense interest in the nomination for Vice President, which ordinarily arouses very little interest in a national convention.

You make two other statements which are matters of opinion, and as it happens they contradict one another. At the beginning of your second paragraph you say that Mr. Roosevelt was nominated for a fourth term because the machine politicians thought he was the only candidate who would win; in the last sentence you say that the reason for his nomination was the maxim about not changing horses in the middle of the stream and the belief that he was the best fitted leader to win the war. These two interpretations are difficult to reconcile. As a matter of fact, the second one is the correct interpretation.

If it had not been for the war and the risks involved in changing not only the President but the whole upper level of the administration of the war, Mr. Roosevelt could not have been re-elected, he would have known that he could not be re-elected, and no matter what the machine politicians thought, he would not have accepted a nomination in order to be defeated.

I regret that you use such strong words as "perpetration of the greatest fraud on the American people." There was no element of fraud whatever in taking the view that continuity was essential and in assuming that Mr. Roosevelt's health was good enough to carry him over the period when a break in continuity would have been most disastrous. In my opinion, and of course this is purely opinion, the event has proved this judgment to be correct. For though he served only a short part of his fourth term, the continuity was not broken. If he had declined the nomination there would have been no presidential authority beginning last July. If he had been defeated in November there would have been none beginning on election day. The period from July to the present has been as crucial as any during the war, and the transition from Roosevelt to Truman is far less of a shock to the success of the war and of the coalition than would have been the transition from Roosevelt to Dewey, which would have begun last November.

1. Charles D. Drayton, an attorney in Washington, had occasionally written Lippmann admiring letters, but he had just objected to "Today and Tomorrow" of April 17, 1945. In that column, Lippmann, five days after the death of Franklin Roosevelt, had held that "there was no secret" during the 1944 campaign that the Democratic Convention, in selecting Harry S Truman as Roosevelt's running mate, was choosing the next president.

To James F. Byrnes[1]

May 10, 1945

Dear Judge Byrnes:

. . . I have been more disturbed about the conduct of our own policy than I have thought it expedient during a great conference[2] of this sort to say in print. In brief, what troubles me most is this: Though the issue here has apparently been drawn between the Soviets and ourselves, this alignment is not inherent in the nature of things but is due to inexperience and emotional instability in our own delegation. There is a far deeper conflict of interest between the British and the Soviets than between the U.S.A. and the Soviets, but we have allowed ourselves to be placed in the position where instead of being the moderating power which holds the balance, we have become the chief protagonists of the anti-Soviet position.

This should never have happened. It would never have happened, I feel sure, if President Roosevelt were still alive, and it will lead to great trouble not only over such matters as the Polish question but throughout the Middle

East if we do not recover our own sense of national interest about this fundamental relationship. . . .

1. Byrnes, to whom Truman had already turned as his chief adviser on foreign affairs, was to
become secretary of state in July 1945. So as not to undercut the incumbent in that office, Edward
R. Stettinius, Jr., the president had not announced that change, for Stettinius was chairing the
American delegation to the United Nations conference at San Francisco, which met from April 25
through June 26, 1945. **2.** The San Francisco Conference was providing an open forum for
disagreements between the United States and the Soviet Union. Among the controverted issues
were questions of procedure and of representation. In two major matters, the United States succeeded in preventing the seating of the Lublin Poles, whom the Soviet Union was championing,
and in including Argentina, which the Soviet Union had opposed because of Argentine sympathy
for and assistance to Germany during most of the war. Though public disagreements then receded, during the first week of May, the delegates learned that representatives of the anti-Soviet
Poles from London had been arrested in Moscow and would be tried for allegedly aiding Germany.
That news confirmed growing Anglo-American anxieties about Russian policy in Poland, anxieties
that persisted for good reason after the jubilation over Germany's unconditional surrender on
May 8.

To John J. McCloy

June 1, 1945

Dear Jack:

. . . I can't imagine how the conception of the policy would be improved
or how it could be stated better.[1] I really think it is admirable, and what is
more, I believe it will work if the men who conceived this policy remain in
control of the administration.

Anyone who objects to control and guidance in the transition from nazism
to some sort of democracy is really arguing, whether he realizes it or not, that
all the Germans were really good democrats all along, and that all you have
to do is to let them alone.

I am greatly impressed with this and also with what I have been learning
from General Hilldring. . . .[2]

1. Lippmann was referring to JCS 1067, the directive for American occupation policy in Germany.
McCloy had presided over the interdepartmental committee that revised and completed that document. It had evolved from a more punitive plan of Secretary of the Treasury Morgenthau, who
approved the final version largely because it contained much of what he had proposed. **2.** Major
General John Hilldring, chief of the Army's Civil Affairs Division, had been much involved in
the preparation of successive drafts of JCS 1067.

To Hans Kohn[1]

June 4, 1945

Dear Mr. Kohn:

. . . I share your view about the empires, and I have not only never subscribed to the Welles-Wallace-Willkie line, but have combated it and have got
into controversies with both Willkie and Welles about it.

You will agree, on the other hand, I think, that, granting the need to preserve the British and French Empires, the working out of a satisfactory relationship between them and the United States is an extremely difficult problem and that we shall fail if we continue to give the impression that from Malta to Singapore and Hong Kong our partnership with the British means underwriting their actions. How we are to support them fundamentally without being presented with a series of situations where we simply have to say yes I don't profess to know, but I am sure it's the most difficult problem we have to solve in our relations with Great Britain. . . .

1. Hans Kohn, professor of history at Smith College.

To Hans Kohn

June 5, 1945

Dear Mr. Kohn:

Your letter of June 2 interests me very much, and you come very close to what troubles me when you say that England, relying on the U.S.A., is refusing a close alliance with France and the Low Countries.

As you may remember, I believe in the formation of what I venture to call the Atlantic Community, a proposal which, incidentally, infuriated *Pravda*. But British policy as respects France and very probably also in the Middle East is, I think, on a dangerous course in that its tendency is to exploit American support without forming a true western community. My talk about mediation and all that is far more a matter of tactics in the immediate situation than it is the presentation of a final view of our position in the world.

I quite agree with you in the need of a firm alliance with England and France and the Western powers, but British policy at the moment will not lead to that firm alliance, and it is necessary for us somehow to influence British policy. I see no way of doing that except to warn them that they cannot make unlimited drafts upon our political support. . . .

To George Fielding Eliot[1]

June 14, 1945

Dear George:

. . . At the present time . . . we shall need some governing conception of our position within the council of the Big Five. Though all my life I have been an advocate of an Anglo-American alliance, we have not proceeded on that line, and the formation of an Anglo-American alliance would make the Big Five an unworkable thing.

Among the Big Five the most serious conflicts of vital interest and the most frequent controversies are certain to arise (1) as between the British Empire and the Russian in the region from the Baltic through the Middle East to India, (2) as between Britain and France in the Low Countries and at the mouth of the Rhine and in the Mediterranean, (3) as between Russia and China along their 4,000-mile frontier.

There are no direct conflicts of vital interest as between the Soviet Union and the United States, and in fact none as between the United States and any of the other four big powers. This seems to me to indicate clearly our role as mediator — that is, intercessor, reconciler, within the circle of the big powers. And in playing that role, which is an entirely positive one, we shall be serving our national interest pretty much as you define it. . . .

1. George Fielding Eliot, a retired major who had served in military intelligence, was the military critic of the *New York Herald Tribune* and a prolific author of books and articles about American military policy.

To Ross J. S. Hoffman

July 4, 1945

Dear Mr. Hoffman:

. . . Speaking of Castlereagh, you say that "he could not achieve a secure peace in Europe without diminishing the Russian preponderance. He could not reduce that power without coming to terms with those states which otherwise must have followed the Czar's lead. And he could not come to terms with them unless he wrote finis to the wartime crusade for the Whig political ideology." You suggest that that is what Churchill has been trying to do since D-Day. I agree. But are you sure that his practical procedure would have been workable provided, as you imply, that Roosevelt had given him unqualified support? I am inclined to think not. To "come to terms with those states which otherwise would follow the Soviet lead," Churchill has in Belgium, Spain, Italy, Greece, and the Arab world, tried to come to terms with the ultra-conservative forces.[1] Are you sure that that is the way to keep them from following the Russian lead? I should suppose this would end in their following the Russian lead, since I do not believe that the pre-war rightist elements can continue to govern in Europe. I do not think it is ideology, but realism, to argue that the support of governments somewhat left of center has the greatest promise of accomplishing the end which you set.

However, I raise the question whether a direct challenge to the Soviet power, such as Churchill has made and has tried to persuade us to underwrite, is not inexpedient. I wonder whether your historical analogy would not be more complete if you didn't identify Churchill with Castlereagh but rather with Metternich. . . .

1. Churchill knew that his influence was fading. Later in July, the Conservatives lost the British general election to Labour, and Clement Attlee succeeded Churchill as prime minister. But for

months before that election, Churchill had been increasingly worried about Soviet intentions in Europe and Asia and about British power in the postwar world. He had not become the king's "first minister," he had said, in order "to preside over the liquidation of the British Empire." Yet the exhaustion of British resources during World War II, resources already depleted by the first war and the depression, foretold the early decline of the empire. In a series of delaying actions, Churchill was supporting, as Lippmann wrote, reactionary forces in many nations, forces that had once contained the social and political strife he had hoped somehow to avoid. To that end, he favored the retention or restoration of prewar monarchies, a prospect European Socialists almost universally resisted, as they did in Belgium, Italy, and Greece. Churchill was also resisting current Egyptian demands for the end of the British occupation and was supporting through the British occupation in Greece the regency of Archbishop Papandreou Damaskinos, whom the left wing opposed.

To Bernard Berenson

July 11, 1945

Dear B. B.:

. . . As for our part in Europe, the great question, I think, is whether Truman can quickly enough pull the administrative machine of our government together so that decisions are made not only in principle but in detail and effectively carried out. Roosevelt governed by ear, and the incoherence and indiscipline during the past twelve months have been so great that we are far less effective in European affairs — for example, relief and rehabilitation — than our intentions or our means would justify. . . .

IV

Cold War Critic

1945–1969

To James F. Byrnes

August 23, 1945

Dear Mr. Secretary:

Your invitation caught me so completely unprepared that I know I did not find words to say on the telephone how much it will always mean to me. The notion that I was being considered for Assistant Secretary of State or for any other post had never crossed my mind, and so I have had to take these few days to think about it.

I can tell you now that I am ready and would be glad to serve under you for an agreed period of time on the work you outlined to me but that I think it would be a mistake for me to accept this office at this time. Please bear with me while I explain the reasons which seem to me to compel this conclusion.

There is serious doubt whether anyone can successfully administer the office from which Mr. MacLeish has resigned.[1] The office itself is a new one, and it is founded, I believe, on the misconception — quite common these days — that public relations are a kind of advertising which can be farmed out to specialists in the art of managing public opinion. At the higher levels of government this is certainly an error: the conduct of public relations is inseparable from leadership, and no qualified public official needs the intervention of a public relations expert between himself and the people. No one can state a policy or interpret it except the man responsible for formulating it and administering it.

To have a separate set of officials to do the public talking about what the government is doing is to establish a presumption of insincerity which can never be fully overcome. The instinct of the people has been sound, and it is no accident that in the free countries all ministers of information, official spokesmen, and publicity experts have been distrusted and disliked. They stand between the people and their public servants, and are, therefore, suspected of erecting stage scenery for the public to look at while the real action takes place behind the scenes.

Under your predecessor, if I may speak frankly, the Department relied excessively and naively on the supposed power of public relations experts, and laboring under this illusion this particular office of Assistant Secretary was created. I believe it would be impossible to live down the idea in the public mind that you intended, under somewhat different management to continue in the same method of dealing with the public, especially this would be true if Mr. MacLeish's successor were another professional writer. For this reason alone I would strongly urge you to abolish the office entirely, or, failing that, to appoint to it a man who comes from public life and not from any branch of the writing or talking profession.

I realize from what you said on the telephone, and I would have known it anyway, that you are concerned with the problem of how to make the new position of the United States intelligible at home and abroad. I do not pretend to know now how that can and should be done. But I am sure it can be done, and if I could help in finding the way to do it, nothing would interest and please me more. Since it is a new undertaking, for which there is no fixed pattern of action, a quiet investigation of the problem is, I believe, a necessary preliminary. It seems to me that given facilities and support in the Department, the working basis of a good start could be developed in three or four months — a month at home in Washington, two months in the capitals of our principal Allies, and another month at home to consult, and to formulate the results. . . .

1. Archibald MacLeish — eminent American poet, librarian of Congress, 1939–44, director of the Office of Facts and Figures, 1940–42 — had resigned as assistant secretary of state for public information, a position to which Roosevelt appointed him in 1944. Lippmann declined Byrnes's offer of that post, and Byrnes in turn declined Lippmann's offer to explore its responsibilities, though the two men did confer about the position; see Ronald Steel, *Walter Lippmann and the American Century* (Boston, 1980), pp. 422–23.

To James V. Forrestal[1]

September 24, 1945

Dear Jim:

. . . There is, I think, a basic, unexamined, and unconscious premise in this article which is that there can be no German settlement in which Germany does not remain the leading great nation of the European continent. That's the real reason why the *Economist* feels that the settlement is unworkable. Now in 1919 that premise was true, and I can remember writing articles about Versailles which were an almost exact duplicate of this one. In 1945 the premise is not true because in fact the Soviet Union, which was no power at all in

1919, is the strongest power in Europe. The result of this war, therefore, is to reduce Germany permanently from the rank of first power in Europe. That's a catastrophic consequence for the Germans, but it does not arise from the harshness of the terms but from the fact that she has been defeated by Russia.

The *Economist*'s argument that the terms of the settlement are unworkable because we won't have the will to enforce them is true enough if we take too seriously the details. The real settlement, however, results from the annexation of Eastern Germany by Poland and Russia. This annexation, whatever moral objections there may be raised to it, produces one tremendous result: there can never be a reconciliation between nationalist Germany and the Soviet Union. The annexation precludes that. Therefore, Poland and Russia are irrevocably committed to keeping Germany from recovering its military power, and the burden of enforcement upon us and the western countries is very much lighter than the *Economist* assumes. For since the Soviet Union must suppress a revival of German nationalism or lose the annexed provinces, the way lies open to us to come to terms eventually with a nonnationalist Germany. I consider it a virtue, not a defect, of the Potsdam settlement that the economic alteration of Germany is limited to the removal of capital equipment during a short period of time. The surgical operation which that, plus the annexation, involves, will soon make it unnecessary to dose Germany with much medicine. In fact, I believe that as soon as we have removed the capital equipment and fixed the legal status of the Rhineland and the Ruhr, we should withdraw our armies of occupation, leaving behind only a constabulary for a short time, and then proceed to govern Germany by indirect control, as in Japan.[2]

That Germany's internal position will be miserable is true, but this misery will be due only in small degree to the Potsdam terms; by all odds the greater part of it is due to the consequences of the war, which Potsdam could not have altered if it had wanted to. For that reason I deplore the tone of this article because it invites the Germans to attribute to our stupidity and malevolence the misery which is in fact the consequence of their own actions.

---

1. James V. Forrestal, former president of Dillon, Reed and Co., an investment firm, had been appointed undersecretary of the navy in 1940 and then secretary in 1944 after the death of Frank Knox. Later he became the first secretary of defense. He had written Lippmann about an article in the *Economist* of August 11, 1945, "The German Settlement." It criticized the agreement reached at the Potsdam Conference by the heads of government of the United States, Great Britain, and the Soviet Union. That agreement called for the disarmament and demilitarization of Germany; for the trial of German war criminals, which later occurred at Nürnberg; for restoration of local self-government and democratic political parties; and for freedom of speech, religion, and the press insofar as military security permitted. Germany was also prohibited from manufacturing war materiel; its production of metals and chemicals was to be controlled, as were its exports, imports, and scientific research in order to prevent remilitarization; and the German economy was to concentrate on peaceful domestic industries, particularly agriculture. Germany was, too, to compensate as far as possible for the losses it had caused the United Nations. Those agreements left for future consideration the method of enforcement that the occupying powers were to apply in their respective zones, zones earlier defined for each of the great powers and for France. As tension mounted among those nations, however, the Soviet Union went its own way in its eastern zone, and the other powers gradually eased their original intentions.   **2.** Japan had surrendered on August 14, 1945, after the United States had dropped atomic bombs on Hiroshima on August 6 and Nagasaki on August 9, and after the Soviet Union had declared war on Japan and invaded Manchuria on August 8. The formal terms of surrender of September 2 left the emperor as head of state but placed Japan under the rule of the American occupation authorities, of whom the head was Douglas MacArthur. The terms of surrender also called for disbanding the Japanese Army and Navy, and for American occupation of former Japanese-controlled islands in the Pacific.

To Glen H. Corney [1]

November 1, 1945

Dear Mr. Corney:

I don't even remember having said that conscript armies do prevent wars. That would be an absurd statement and of course it isn't true. What would be true is that without them you can't win a war, as we have proved twice in this century.

Your chief misunderstanding, however, is due to the fact that you have not grasped the difference between compulsory military training and conscription, although the President explained it clearly and correctly. [2] No one is proposing peace-time conscription in the United States. The men who would take compulsory military training would not be part of the American army and could not be used for any kind of military service either against an enemy or for strike-breaking or for anything else without a special act of Congress. This proposal, if enacted, would compel every young man to have a military education, just as every child in this country is compelled to have other kinds of education. What he does after he has received that education is a wholly separate question, though it is proper to assume that in case of war or the imminence of war Congress would pass a selective service act under which certain of the men who had had military training would be drafted into the armed forces.

1. Glen H. Corney of Cincinnati, Ohio.   **2.** On October 23, 1945, in a speech before a joint session of Congress, President Truman had proposed universal military training, a program he continued to support and Congress continued to reject. Truman and the Army considered universal military training a preferable substitute for a large standing Army. Under the proposal, all men between the ages of eighteen and twenty would be called up for a year of training. They would then and later remain civilians, subject to military service if Congress declared it necessary.

To William O. Player, Jr. [1]

December 4, 1945

Dear Bill Player:

Thanks for your column. I think the evidence you bring out confirms my criticism, which is, in substance, that our foreign relations are conducted, not by the State Department alone, but also and equally by the War Department, the Navy, the Treasury, and the White House, and that if there is to be a true foreign policy their decisions must be collective decisions.

There is nothing in the schedule which you report about any meeting, regular or otherwise, of the men who are really the key men in our foreign affairs. That is why, it seems to me, our policy in the Far East is so full of contradictions. It is made in different places by different departments of the government.[2]

1. William O. Player, Jr., Washington correspondent and columnist of the *New York Post.*
2. Patrick J. Hurley had resigned as ambassador to China on November 23, 1945. He then contended that the professional foreign service officers in China favored the Chinese Communists, who were at war with the Nationalist government of Chiang Kai-shek. At that time, the Soviet Union was removing factories from Manchuria and northern Korea as reparations in kind, which President Truman interpreted as part of a Soviet policy to keep China divided and weak. Increasingly the State Department considered the Chinese Communists to be agents of the Soviet Union, a debatable view at variance with the expert opinion of veteran China hands. To still the outcry in Congress over Hurley's charges and to inform the administration about the actual conditions and prospects in China, Truman persuaded General George C. Marshall to come out of retirement and go to China as his special representative with the rank of ambassador. Marshall departed on December 15. Meanwhile MacArthur was overseeing the American occupation in Japan and North Korea. And until the end of the war, the Treasury Department had had agents in Chungking working with Nationalist officials on American credits to China and reporting continually about the corruption and inefficiency of the government of Chiang Kai-shek.

To Lithgow Osborne[1]

December 7, 1945

My dear Osborne:

Your letter from Oslo written November 1 reached me about ten days ago, and I have put off answering it hoping to write you something more than just a note of thanks and personal greetings. I really haven't got the time even now, but I don't want to put it off any longer.

We here in Washington are dizzy, like a child at a circus, trying to watch all the different things going on at once. This week, for example, we have the British loan agreement,[2] the President's labor program,[3] the climax of the Pearl Harbor inquiry, the explosion of Pat Hurley, the Army and Navy merger,[4] not to speak of the increasingly critical problems of the German occupation, the Japanese occupation, the Chinese civil war, and the turmoil of the Middle East. In our leisure moments, you will be glad to know that we are installing democracy in Bulgaria, Romania, Yugoslavia, Greece, and Albania.[5]

If it all looks a bit confusing at a distance, which I assume it must, all I can say is that it is also confusing near to.

All that Truman and Byrnes have to do before Christmas is to hold up the British Empire, hold back the Russian Empire, and create a new China. I'll bet they wish they were with you in Norway. I certainly do.

1. Lithgow Osborne, professional diplomat, since 1944 American ambassador to Norway. **2.** The British, their reserves of dollars spent, had sent to Washington a delegation headed by J. M. Keynes, now Lord Keynes, to seek an interest-free loan of $5 billion. Truman's new secretary of the treasury, former Democratic senator from Kentucky Frederick M. Vinson, had little sympathy for the request and a personal dislike for Keynes. He persuaded Truman to hold the loan to $3.5 billion, to demand 2 percent interest, and to obtain trade concessions as a quid pro quo. That inadequate, even mean, proposal barely won congressional approval. **3.** A wave of serious postwar strikes had occurred as unions attempted to lift wages so as to keep up with the rising cost of living, and as management reverted to its prewar antagonism toward organized labor. To the dismay of the unions, Truman, who had been too hasty in lifting price controls, proposed the use of fact-finding boards to delay strikes in national industries for at least thirty days. Though Congress did not act, the president on his own prepared to use such boards anyhow, for which he was denounced by the heads of the automobile and steel unions, then on the verge of strikes. **4.** Congress was considering the president's proposal for unification of the armed services within a single Cabinet department, a development recommended by the experience of the war. **5.** Only by protesting the Soviet Union's imposition of authoritarian governments in those countries.

To John Maynard Keynes

January 2, 1946

Dear Maynard:

Yesterday evening I had my first chance to read the full text of your speech[1] in the House of Lords, though I haven't yet seen the debate which followed.

I must tell you how much I admired it and how much I was moved by it. It made me think of our conversation saying that explaining a foreign country to your own country is now the hardest and yet the most important part of diplomacy. No one has ever done that more bravely or more effectively than you did in that speech. . . .

The reception of the agreement in England as it was reported in our papers here had the general effect of chilling the enthusiasm of its supporters and weakening the criticism of its opponents. The opposition in England has now convinced most people over here that our negotiators were sufficiently tough and mean to be trusted, but for that reason they pay in the feeling here that the larger aims of the agreement do not find genuine support in England. I am disturbed myself by the action of the Conservatives in refusing to vote. I would find it hard to answer a criticism here that while of course Great Britain would honor the financial agreement under any government if it could, there is no real assurance that the Conservatives will try to make the imponderable parts of the agreement successful. . . .

1. About the British-American loan agreement.

To George H. Haines[1]

January 2, 1946

My dear Haines:

. . . What troubles me most is my doubt as to whether the Koreans can run a government which is sufficiently honest and strong to stand up. If they can, they can get protection for their gold and their fisheries through the trusteeship and the UNO. If they can't, I don't see that anything can save them from falling under the domination of the Soviet Union.[2]

1. George H. Haines of the Johnson newspapers of Flint, Michigan.   2. The terms of the Japanese surrender divided Korea, pending the establishment of a democratic government, with the southern half, below the 38th parallel, under American control and the northern under Soviet control. In December 1945, the United States, the Soviet Union, and Great Britain had agreed on a joint trusteeship with China for a five-year period, but a Soviet-American commission failed to arrive at mutually acceptable terms for that trusteeship, so Korea remained divided. At the date of this letter, the impasse had yet formally to be referred to the United Nations (known briefly then as the United Nations Organization, or UNO).

To William F. Sollman[1]

May 24, 1946

Dear Mr. Sollman:

. . . Given the fact that there was at that time no German government able or willing to surrender, and given the fact that the defeat of Germany could be brought about only by the concerted invasion of four armies meeting inside Germany, was there any alternative at that time to the division of Germany into four military zones of occupation?

In other words, was not the division of Germany, which we all deplore, the consequence of the war and not of an error in allied statesmanship? . . .

While I thoroughly agree that it must be our object to liquidate the zonal division, I see no way by which it could originally have been avoided. The point becomes clear when you contrast the situation in Japan with that in Germany, for in Japan there was a government capable of surrendering before the Japanese homeland was invaded. If the invasion had been necessary, there would have been an American army coming up from the south, probably also a British Empire army, and almost certainly, if the resistance had been prolonged, a Russian army coming from the north.

1. William F. Sollman of the division of history and the social sciences at Reed College.

To Dwight D. Eisenhower

June 4, 1946

Dear General Eisenhower:

I was very much moved by the speech you made the other day in which you spoke of how vicious it is to be thinking of another war.

Coming back from Europe, as I just have, I almost feel that the soldiers are going to have to save the peace which the diplomats and politicians will, if they don't look out, most surely wreck.

To Warren R. Austin[1]

June 10, 1946

Dear Warren:

. . . The more I think about your appointment, which was altogether unexpected so far as I was concerned, the more I see how great can be your contribution to the United Nations.

I say that not because you have been a pioneer, but for another reason, namely, that you have what is very rare these days, a thing which one might call constitutional wisdom, — an instinctive knowledge of what constitutions can do and can't do and how far they can be strained and how far they cannot be strained.

My own view is that we have strained the United Nations charter almost to the breaking point, much as the Hamiltonians threatened to do in the early days of our own Constitution, and that there is needed a Jeffersonian period in our attitude towards the charter, a period of relaxation so that this fragile thing may grow strong before too great burdens are put upon it, for it is more important that the charter should survive the inevitable difficulties of the immediate post-war years than that it should be used up before the world gets accustomed to it.

We ought to remember that the men who wrote the Bill of Rights into our own Constitution were willing to pay the price of accepting slavery and the slave trade and the Fugitive Slave Laws in order to have a constitution at all, and I think there is a moral in that for us in our dealings with Russia.

1. Warren R. Austin, Republican senator of Vermont, had been appointed the first United States ambassador to the United Nations.

To Herbert L. Spencer[1]

June 25, 1946

Dear Mr. Spencer:

. . . I might say that I don't think that the show-down on the basic question can take place. The Russians will not suddenly agree to become a free country, and we cannot take their refusal as the last and final word on the subject. For that would leave us with no alternative but to prepare as rapidly as possible for war.

I believe myself that we must be prepared to persist over a long period of time and that it would be a mistake to think that our plan can readily be accepted or quickly put into effect. It is much too complicated an idea for that. I believe, however, that we have nothing to fear, so far as atomic energy goes, from the delay. We still have the monopoly, and our head-start is so great that we can negotiate with the upper hand for some years to come.[2]

Nor do I take quite so absolute a view of the iron curtain and the capacity of the Russians to create an atomic energy industry without our knowing it. In my view, whether or not they agree to inspection, we would find out about anything as big as an atomic energy plant through the intelligence services which will be operated in Russia by at least ten or fifteen countries. It has never yet been possible in any country in the world to hide the construction of one battleship. An atomic energy plant is an immense construction and it can be put only in certain locations which are obvious, namely, near water power.

I cannot believe that, with all the Poles, Ukrainians, Yugoslavs, Czechs, who are available for employment in the secret service of Great Britain, France, and the United States, that somebody would not get some report about so big an enterprise, and all you have to know in order to raise the issue diplomatically and take whatever steps are then advisable, is that something is being done which calls for explanation.

---

1. Herbert L. Spencer of Pasadena, California.   2. International policy for atomic energy had become a major divisive issue in Soviet-American relations. As the best-informed American scientists knew, and as a few Cabinet officers realized, the explosion of the atomic bombs in Japan, by demonstrating the feasibility of the weapons, removed any doubt about the ability of the Soviet Union sooner or later to make atomic bombs of its own. The basic science necessary was no secret, and the necessary engineering could be worked out, as it had been by American and British scientists during the war. Soviet espionage at the most would reduce by a small factor the time the Russians needed. But the American public, the Congress, and many of those around the president continued to view the atomic bomb as an American monopoly based upon a dark secret. Yet Truman and others also wanted to head off an atomic arms race. Those variables contributed to the plan for international control of atomic energy that the United States took to the responsible United Nations committee — a plan presented there, and drafted in its last stages, by Bernard M. Baruch, the Wall Street financier and intimate of many presidents, though fewer than he claimed. To most Americans, the Baruch plan seemed a generous gesture, precisely as Truman intended it should. Not so to the Soviet Union, however; for according to the plan, the United States would have retained its monopoly on the bomb until the Soviet Union passed through various steps of demonstrated readiness to share the vital knowledge, steps some of which required on-site inspections, which the Russian leadership would not tolerate within Soviet borders. Inspections would have revealed both the weaknesses of the Soviet economy at that time and the authoritarian nature of Soviet society.

Soviet insistence on the retention of the veto in the Security Council, even when that body was considering questions of atomic energy, seemed to Baruch, Truman, and others of like mind to testify to Soviet obduracy and militancy. The reciprocal suspicions of the two powers marked the rhetoric of the debates about international control of atomic energy and blocked any chance of a resolution of the issue within the UN, though hopes for a solution had not evaporated at the time of this letter.

Indeed Baruch had presented the American proposal on June 14, just eleven days before the date of this letter, and it was February 1947 before the Soviet Union officially proposed its amendments, which were unacceptable to the United States. As the impasse continued, the Soviet veto prevented the UN from imposing the American plan. For a full discussion of this complex matter, see R. G. Hewlett and O. E. Anderson, Jr., *The New World* (University Park, Pa., 1962), chs. 15, 16.

To Eustace Seligman[1]

June 28, 1946

Dear Eustace:

. . . My underlying view is not what you think it is, namely, that the veto power is a good one, but only that it cannot be eliminated by any form of majority rule among governments. My view of the veto is the same as Hamilton's basic argument against the Articles of Confederation. Hamilton demonstrated clearly, I think, that in a confederation the veto power, as we now call it, is inherent and irremovable, and that only the establishment of law dealing with individuals can overcome the veto power. I think that proposition is as unanswerable as any in political science.

On the specific arguments which you discuss, I might say this:

1. The United States would refuse to sign a treaty which it disliked, even if a majority of the other members of the Security Council favored it. That is the essence of the American proposal, and there is not the slightest suggestion in it that the United States would surrender its monopoly if outvoted by a majority of the other nations. If you have any doubt on that point, I suggest that you consult any Senator.

2. I contend that in a case where a great power has violated its agreements and committed aggression, the veto cannot prohibit the other nations from taking action if they wish to take it. If you will talk to the people who worked on that section of the Charter at Dumbarton Oaks and afterwards, you will find that they thought there was no point in writing into the Charter a provision as to what was to happen if the Charter itself had been destroyed. What would happen was self-evident, and no form of words could alter it. That's why I think I am right in saying that the Charter is silent on what happens when a great power violates it just as our Constitution is silent on what happens if a state rebels or secedes from the Union. That didn't prevent Lincoln from enforcing the Constitution on the southern states, though there is no provision in the Constitution which says anything about that.

3. If the Russians decide to violate the atomic bomb treaty, the veto will not protect them for the reasons I have already stated. So far as its effect on our own action goes, which is what you seem to have in mind, you may be right, but it still remains true that the real effect of the Baruch proposal is to

obligate ourselves for a future course of action. That may be a good thing to do, but that isn't the way the matter has been presented to our own people.

1. Eustace Seligman, partner in the prestigious New York law firm Sullivan and Cromwell.

To W. D. Rowlands[1]

June 28, 1946

Dear Mr. Rowlands:

. . . I was careful not to say that the British are maintaining a large German army in their zone. I knew that they weren't. The point is that their treatment of the German army at the time of the surrender was essentially different in spirit and character from the American treatment, and this has very great political consequences in its effect on the attitude of the German corps of officers.

As a matter of fact, though I did not say so, they did maintain a very large number of German troops in military formations for quite a long period after the surrender, and the breaking up of these formations did not take place until after repeated protest not only by the Russians but by General McNarney.[2] I can tell you privately that I have seen the official records of the Allied Control Council meetings in which the protests were made.

The "Economist" in its issue of May 18, 1946, in the course of a very angry article about what I wrote in fact admitted the truth. . . .

1. The Reverend W. D. Rowlands of the Congregational Church in Manchester, New Hampshire. 2. General Joseph T. McNarney, then commander of United States forces in Europe.

To George Fielding Eliot

July 6, 1946

Dear George:

. . . I quite understand that the atomic bomb is a strategical and not a tactical weapon. But I think it important to consider its limitations as a strategical weapon. For example, I am convinced that in the event of localized trouble in Venezia Giulia — that is to say trouble in which the Great Powers were not immediately and overtly involved, and where the disorder was more like that in Spain in the 30's, it would be quite impossible for us to consider the use of the bomb against Belgrade for example. The weapon is too powerful to be used for police work which calls for a limited use of force.

In the event of a general war, I would, at least, question your thesis that the destruction of the munition centers of Soviet Russia would compel the surrender and evacuation of the Red Army in Europe. That was the argument used in the German war but the air enthusiasts found it didn't prove to be correct. The ground forces had to finish the war. In my view as against Russia, this would be even more the case, for we must not forget the munition centers of Europe in Bohemia, Austria, the Ruhr, Sweden, etc., which the Red Army could occupy. Their total capacity is greater than that of Russia itself, and I do not think you are right in saying, therefore, that the destruction of the Russian centers would mean that the Red Army had no ammunition after it had fired off its existing supply.

I do not doubt, of course, that the atomic weapon is the chief countervailing weapon to the Red Army but I was merely pointing to the inverse of that truth which is that the Red Army is a countervailing weapon to the atomic bomb.

We must not forget also that if the Red Army is used tactically as a countermeasure to the strategical use of the bomb that it will find immense support among the people of Europe. The very centers of Europe which are most necessary to support the Red Army are most favorable to the Soviet Union.

My general feeling is that the popular overestimate of the conclusiveness of the atomic bomb as a weapon is the basic reason why Congress and the public do not support a sound military policy in the United States. The people think they have a weapon which makes all other weapons unnecessary and that is a most dangerous deception, — one which you, yourself, have fought against more than anybody else.

To Joseph R. Grundy[1]

July 27, 1946

Dear Mr. Grundy:

. . . Far from wishing to disband Congress or to weaken it as a coordinate branch of the government, I fear that Congress is weakening itself in the eyes of the country, by the inordinate time it takes to reach decisions on matters of vital national interest. This is no question of whether it should be for or against any particular measure, such as the British Loan. My criticism of Congress is that it shouldn't require nearly six months for Congress to make up its mind whether it will or will not approve an agreement of this sort. . . .

May I say that it is a great mistake to identify constructive criticism of this sort with totalitarian opposition to parliamentary government. The way to meet that opposition is to make democratic government efficient and effective, intelligent in its debate and prompt in its decision.

1. Joseph R. Grundy of Bristol, Pennsylvania.

To James K. Pollock[1]

July 29, 1946

Dear Doctor Pollock:

Mrs. Reid[2] has been kind enough to show me your memorandum of June 4 about the articles I wrote early in May after my return from Germany. You raise certain questions which are of such critical importance to the formation of U.S. policy that I am venturing to burden you with this letter. I do this, as I hope you understood from my articles, as a grateful admirer of the work you have done in the American zone.

You say: "He emphasizes that the American conception of how to deal with Germany is the best one which has been suggested, but I do not quite follow him when he seems to feel that we are not promoting this principle outside our zone. There is nothing particularly inconsistent between advocating the re-establishment of a central German government and in working on a problem of decentralization in our zone. Every modern government must centralize certain functions — the important thing is *that there will be a strong regional underpinning which will anchor a decentralized system and not allow it to be captured by an efficient centralized bureaucracy.*"[3]

My contention is that, except in our own zone, we have not insisted upon "a strong regional underpinning" for a central government. We have been the advocates of a central government *before* a regional underpinning has been created in the other zones. In order to have carried out the federal principle you state we should have promoted decentralization in the other zones before proposing a central government. That was the way to prevent its being captured "by an efficient centralized bureaucracy." In practice what we have been advocating is first a central government and then decentralization in the other zones. This is not likely to produce a federal Germany. For unless the separate states exist before the central government exists, unless that government is one to which these states have delegated limited powers, the states are almost certain to be mere administrative agencies of the central government. All experience shows, I believe, that it is much more difficult to decentralize a centralized government than to federate autonomous states. In Germany, where the forces of centralism are so much stronger than those of localism, it was particularly important — so it seems to me — to do first in all the zones what we have done so well in our zone. Yet can it be denied that in our dealings with the British, the French, and the Russians, our emphasis has been predominantly, indeed well-nigh exclusively, upon a central government? When and where have we argued, as you do in your memorandum, that our allies should create "a strong regional underpinning" for the central government?[4]

What I feared would come of this when I wrote my articles has now happened. Molotov has plumped for German unity against "dismemberment" and against federalism. One had only to study the propaganda of the communist party to see that the Russian line would be for German unity, centralized in Berlin. We are now in imminent peril of getting a central German government without any of the underpinning and anchors that you consider essential. For it will be extremely difficult for us to say now that while we want a central government we do not want the kind of central government which Molotov wants. We have talked so much to the Germans and to our own people and to the world about the unity of Germany, and have so seriously neglected to make it clear we meant federal unity, that we are now, thanks to Molotov, in a dangerously awkward position. We are faced with the prospect of German unity without federalism, German unity backed by the power of the Soviets and the momentum of German nationalism.

If there was any doubt at the time I wrote my articles that there was a duel for the control of the whole of Germany, there is no longer any doubt after Molotov's statement. We have missed the bus, not the last bus I hope, but still the bus: we have failed to use our influence to get the British and the French to organize their zones for a federal Germany. We have failed to solve the problem of the Ruhr within the framework of federalism. We are now confronted with the momentous fact that the Russians are the champions of German unity in exactly that form which is most certain to defeat our main purposes in Europe.

You raise other questions but they are, I think you will agree, either of secondary importance or matters of emphasis. When I wrote of our being "back-seat drivers" I was not reflecting on General Clay, for whom I have the warmest and highest admiration: I was referring to the fact that in the economic and the political structure of Germany our zone is much less important than the British or the Russian. While we have a voice in the control of all the zones, we actually govern only in our own.

As for Washington, I have found that at the top levels there was little interest in or understanding of the crucial importance of what you call regional underpinning. It is evident that General Clay and Ambassador Murphy have thus far failed to make Secretary Byrnes see the vital connection between what has been done at Stuttgart and what is to be done with Germany as a whole. . . . The White House and the State Department and the War Department policy are concentrated on the immediate economic problem and the demand for administrative unity to relieve it. So, I think you will agree, has been all the publicity out of Berlin and Frankfort.

I hope you will forgive me for inflicting such a long letter upon you. But I am deeply concerned that the political achievements in the American zone should not be lost. In them alone is there any beginning of a constructive settlement with Germany. The achievements will be lost, I fear, unless we can produce a statesmanlike alternative to the line which Molotov has taken. . . .

1. James K. Pollock was in the Regional Government Coordinating Office of the First Military Government Battalion in Stuttgart, Germany, the headquarters of the American occupation authority under General Lucius D. Clay, the American deputy military governor.   2. Helen R.

Reid, then vice president of the *New York Herald Tribune,* of which her husband, Ogden M. Reid, was editor. **3.** The emphases here and elsewhere in this letter are Lippmann's. **4.** Occupation policy in Germany had suffered from the start from the varying administrations and purposes of the four nations involved. France seemed committed primarily to preventing any step toward German unity. The Soviet Union was determined to extract large reparations in kind and to retain control of its zone in East Germany. Britain moved more slowly than did the United States toward de-Nazification. By the spring of 1946, the American authorities, annoyed with the French and suspicious of the Russians, were also increasingly eager to restore enough of the German economy to relieve American taxpayers of the burden of relief in Germany. On April 29, 1946, Byrnes tested Russian intentions by proposing a four-power treaty guaranteeing the disarmament of Germany for the next twenty-five years. That guarantee would have relieved the Soviet Union of any fears about another attack from Germany, but Soviet Foreign Minister Vyacheslav Molotov rejected Byrnes's proposal. Less than a week later, General Clay, the major voice in the American occupation authority, suspended further reparation shipments from the American zone until the four occupying powers could agree to treat Germany as an economic unit. That step seemed threatening to the Russians.

Molotov had rejected the proposed treaty with the statement that demilitarization should not obtain until reparation deliveries had been completed. He had also renewed the Russian demand for ten billion dollars of reparations. To Lippmann's dismay, he had urged the establishment of a strong central German government, a dramatic alteration in the Soviet position, but one tied to the question of reparations and designed largely for German public opinion. In July Molotov opposed any separation of the Ruhr from Germany while also asserting that the Russian people would not obstruct the "rightful aspirations" of the German people or destroy their economy. That language again courted German opinion, whereas Soviet policy remained fixed upon further reparations and continuing domination of East Germany. So persuaded, Byrnes and Clay, as well as Robert Murphy, who was the senior State Department representative in Germany with the rank of ambassador, moved toward the economic unification of as much of Germany as possible. Convinced that the Soviet Union would never cooperate with the other occupying authorities, Byrnes was also reconciled to a divided Germany as preferable to a Germany under Soviet control.

With Truman's approval, on September 6, 1946, in a speech at Stuttgart, Byrnes repeated American support for German economic unity with the qualification, obviously addressed to the Soviet Union, that if complete unification proved impossible, the United States would do "everything in our power to secure maximum possible unification." He also called for a German provisional government. That speech marked a major change in American occupation policy, a departure in most respects from JCS 1067 and the remnants of the Morgenthau plan it contained. It also prepared the way for the December agreement for the economic fusion of the British and American zones (Bizonia) and the ensuing reconstruction of the German economy.

To Dean G. Acheson[1]

October 1, 1946

Dear Dean:

I should like to make a suggestion which I think might be useful in connection with the next meeting of the Assembly. Two important subjects will come up there, one the general problem of the veto, and the other that of a Bill of Rights, which, as I understand, the Social and Economic Council is working on.[2]

I suggest that we take the position that the verdict at Nürnberg[3] establishes organic law for the United Nations and that the Charter must henceforth be construed in the light of this verdict, just as the Constitution of the United States has been construed in the light of the important opinions of Marshall. If this is sound legal doctrine, then one of the great questions about the veto in people's minds has been resolved, namely, that the veto gives the great powers the privilege of waging aggressive war legally. I think we are entitled to take the position now that in spite of the veto aggressive war is a crime, regardless of the action of the Security Council.

In order to make this point clear and dramatic and well-understood, it might be a good idea to invite Lord Lawrence[4] to address the Assembly and to expound the legal significance of the verdict. I don't need to labor the incidental advantage of bringing back into focus the causes and meaning of the war, on which we have been able to act throughout in essential harmony with the Russians. There are so many things about which we disagree that spectacular emphasis on this great thing where we have agreed seems to me to have large political advantages in addition to its legal importance.

The object of all of this would be to consolidate the advances made at Nürnberg and to put in a better perspective the coming debate about the veto and to enable us to defend, as I assume we must, the preservation of the veto without taking the position that it is an absolute right.

It is our business, however, not only to consolidate what we have got, but to advance, and here again the Nürnberg verdict gives us an opportunity. Though I have not read the full text of the judgment, it seems clear that the court was unable to accept the whole doctrine of the prosecution on the subject of crimes against humanity. I don't doubt this was sound for the court, since that would have involved more judicial law-making than they could have justified. But it seems to me quite feasible that the Assembly itself should take up some of the points which in the opinion of the court are not yet law and move to make them law for the future. Here also the opinion of Lawrence and of the other judges would be useful in making clear to the Assembly where they found that international law was not sufficiently developed to justify them in convicting. All of this might be made to result in a directive from the Assembly to the Social and Economic Council to prepare a declaration on human rights closing the gaps in the law as found at Nürnberg, which could then be adopted by the Assembly and ratified by the United Nations. . . .

1. Dean G. Acheson had become undersecretary of state in August 1945. 2. The Social and Economic Council was working on a bill of rights, or a definition of human rights, but it was a long way from completing that task, for disagreements among the American, British, Soviet, and Chinese delegations were deep and persistent. 3. The International Tribunal at Nürnberg had announced its decisions about Nazi war crimes the previous day, September 30, 1946. The tribunal found guilty of crimes against humanity a number of Nazi organizations, including the Gestapo (or secret police) and nineteen Nazi leaders. 4. Lord Justice Sir Geoffrey Lawrence, a British jurist who had sat on the International Tribunal.

To Eustace Seligman

October 25, 1946

Dear Eustace:

. . . It seems to me that our first worry is whether unanimity within the atomic authority would destroy its effectiveness. The best course is to urge the Russians to adopt the veto principle there, as it is now used in Austria. There, as you probably know, by a most remarkable reversal unanimity in the Control Commission is required in order to prevent the Austrian Government from acting. You will readily see how different that is from requiring unanimity in order that they may act. As this reversal was agreed to by the Soviets themselves, it seems to me a most promising way to get at the problem of effective administration.

As for "the right to veto the enforcement of the treaty," I now take the view that under Article 51 of the Charter, there is reserved the right of collective self-defense in spite of the veto. It seems to me that under the Charter, as it now stands, we would have every right to consider the production of atomic weapons in violation of the treaty as an aggressive act and, veto or no veto, to take measures of collective self-defense. . . .

To Chester Bowles[1]

November 10, 1946

Dear Chet:

. . . I agree that we must find some solution for the situation that will exist if the Republicans control Congress. I don't think your suggestion would be acceptable to the people, even if Truman could be persuaded, which I think altogether impossible.[2] I think the people would say that for Truman to appoint a Republican President of the United States was an arbitrary exercise of power which nullified the '44 election. The Republicans have no right to govern the country until the people elect a Republican President.

I saw the other day a somewhat different suggestion which seems to me to come near meeting the difficulty. It is that President Truman should announce that he will under no circumstances be a candidate for re-election, and that in the remaining two years of his term he will recognize the verdict of the elections by renouncing party leadership. I think that might lay the basis for a sufficient amount of cooperation between the Executive and Legislative branches to enable us to wobble through. He would not be resigning his office; he would be resigning his party leadership.

On the question of Price Control, I feel ashamed of myself. I have been so preoccupied with foreign affairs during the past year that I never felt I knew enough about the situation to write effectively on it. I have no doubt you were right in taking the position that unless Price Control was really effective, it was worse than none. The event has certainly proved it. I am inclined to feel, however, that no Price Control could have been effective under present conditions, in view of the fact that we had abolished rationing. The fatal error was to abolish rationing. But I don't know enough about it to prove it, and am willing to believe I may be wrong.[3]

1. Chester Bowles, then director of the Office of Economic Stabilization.   2. Republican gains in the November elections gave the party control of Congress for the first time in fourteen years. That victory, along with doubts about Truman and his policies, persuaded some Democratic liberals, including Chester Bowles, that the president should resign. They would have had him first appoint a Republican as secretary of state, the office next in line for the presidency as the law then stood and in the absence of a vice president. With Truman's resignation, that Republican would then have become president.   3. Truman had vetoed an emasculated price control bill that Congress sent him in June 1946, a bill Bowles had considered impossible to administer. Price control ended, but the president restored it on his own in a weak form in July, only to terminate it in October — with the predictable result that prices soared, especially for meat, an issue of large saliency in the 1946 congressional elections. Wartime rationing had ceased in 1945 in the face of public and congressional pressure, to which Truman had yielded. As Bowles later commented to Truman in keeping with Lippmann's point, rationing was one essential part of any effective price control system.

To John J. McCloy

November 14, 1946

Dear Jack:

. . . I am getting more and more concerned at the way in which we are taking contradictory positions, owing to the fact that foreign policy is being made in separate compartments, and in bits and pieces. For example, Austin says we will go along with disarmament if we get inspection. In the same week we propose a trusteeship in the Pacific, which is based on the principle of excluding inspection in our own strategical areas. Inconsistencies of this sort are almost impossible to explain away, and put us in a very difficult position among the nations. If anybody were sitting back and trying to view our foreign policy as a whole, we wouldn't need to get into contradictions of this sort.

I feel that the way we are trying to make this peace settlement is as if during the war General Marshall had appointed himself Commander of the Third Army, in place of General Patton, leaving no one to consider the overall strategy of the war.

The situation where Byrnes is away from Washington all the time, being his own negotiator, is very bad indeed. With Truman what he is, there is simply no one to take a general view of our interests and our policy. That's why the policies we have are made in bits and pieces — now in one department, now in another; now in one bureau, now in another.

Since Truman can't conduct foreign affairs as Roosevelt did, or Wilson,

Byrnes is the only man who can perform that function, but since he is his own negotiator for the details, he just can't perform the function and there is, therefore, a terrible vacuum at the central point where policies must be made. We shall all break our hearts trying to improve details of our position on this or that question, and we shall not succeed until we overcome this fundamental trouble that there is no control of foreign policy.

To John J. McCloy

November 20, 1946

Dear Jack:

I have no doubt you are right about Byrnes but, of course, it is a case of tout comprendre tout pardonner. The vacuum in Washington is a very great danger, and Marshall's position in China is perhaps the greatest example of the result of it. Apparently the directive under which he is operating, and doing better than I should imagine he could have possibly been expected to do, represents, as I understand it, the views of the Far Eastern Division of the State Department and no doubt of Acheson. But I doubt whether it represents the views of all the high political officers of the State Department or of the War and Navy Departments.

It is only General Marshall's enormous prestige which has thus far prevented him from being attacked as an appeaser. Sometimes I wonder if Marshall couldn't be extricated from his anomalous position in China, and at the same time be enabled perhaps to achieve the purpose for which he went there, by persuading the President to bring him home and give him for a while overall authority in dealing with China. This wouldn't give him a rest, but maybe he is the kind of man who won't rest until he has achieved his end.

Marshall back in Washington as the top policy man on China, answerable only to the President, might yet be able to succeed and get the satisfaction which goes with success.[1]

I know that such a suggestion violates all the ordinary rules of organization, but they are being violated anyway by Byrnes being absent from Washington. And to bring back Marshall with overriding authority over Chinese affairs would certainly be acceptable to Congress and to the people here.

---

1. Marshall remained on his impossible mission to China through May 1947 when, at Truman's request, he agreed to become secretary of state, an office he assumed in July. As the general had ascertained, there was no feasible way to effect a reconciliation between the Nationalists and the Communists in China, or to provide sufficient political or military support to sustain Chiang Kai-shek's tottering regime.

To Robert Brand[1]

February 25, 1947

Dear Robert:

I have a strong impression that the estimates and calculations on which British, and also American, post-war policies rest have not worked out, and that in the course of the next few months drastic measures will be necessary. At the moment no one I have talked with has reached definite conclusions as to what the measures should be — certainly I have not. But one thing is clear to me, and it is that to decide the measures and to prepare official and public opinion to receive them will take time, and that we cannot wait any longer to begin.

I do not know what the Embassy here is doing about it, or what it is telling the government in London about the American attitude. The higher personages are extraordinarily elusive and unresponsive, and I know of no one who could play a part in explaining matters to our people who gets any help from them. So far as I can make out from talking to some of the junior officials, the Embassy takes a passive attitude because it believes —

1. That the Republican isolationists are in the saddle, and that nothing can be done.
2. That Britain cannot honorably re-open any of the questions which were supposed to have been settled when the loan was approved by Congress.
3. That the Labour Government cannot afford to admit that the Conservatives who objected to the terms of the loan are in any way justified by events.
4. That the prospects may not be so bad as they seem, and that courage and character will win out.

On the first point, which is crucial, my view is that appearances are deceptive. It will be enormously difficult, of course, to get any big new constructive program adopted. But I do not think it impossible — if it is well worked out and properly prepared. It is not, I think, harder to do than was the British loan and a great deal easier than was Lend-Lease. That is impossible to prove, but I have taken some soundings and I believe it is true.

It is quite clear, it seems to me, that the reactionary Republican victory of last November did not reflect correctly the political conviction of this country. It is almost certain that the Democrats are still the majority party whenever the mass of the people turn out to vote. The turnout last November was extremely small; the Republicans won, not because they had gained new votes, but because so many Democrats were temporarily disgusted with Truman and did not vote.

Ever since the election the Republican influence has been declining and Truman's has been rising. No one today would put the odds on a Republican victory in 1948 at better than even, and the underlying trend continues to favor the Democrats. Within the Republican Party the isolationist leadership of Taft is increasingly challenged. I am convinced that the country has out-grown that leadership, and that the more Taft and his associates are compelled to show their hand, the weaker their position. Moreover, Marshall's appoint-ment has made a radical difference in the balance of power between Congress and the Executive. Under Byrnes the Senate was the dominant organ of gov-ernment. Marshall is stronger than the Senate, and any policy to which he gives his full support is likely to prevail.

All this, and more that could be said, goes to show, I believe, that London will make a mistake if it adopts what seems to me the mood of the Embassy: that nothing can be done.

I wish you would come over and see for yourself. Perhaps I am mistaken in thinking that a great crisis is in the making, and that this country can be persuaded to act to prevent it. But I don't think I am so wholly mistaken that it is not worth a try.

We hear that soon Lord Halifax is coming for a visit.[2] You might perhaps like to show him this letter.

1. Robert Brand, who had just become Baron Brand, had been an influential member of the British delegation to negotiate the loan from the United States. That loan, as Lippmann recognized, had not relieved Britain's economic plight; see Ronald Steel, *Walter Lippmann and the American Century* (Boston, 1980), ch. 34, which is also useful for the other major issues of 1947. 2. "On a purely personal visit," as Halifax himself put it.

To John M. Hancock[1]

March 11, 1947

My dear Mr. Hancock:

. . . You ask me what I "call the 'so-called Baruch principles.' " . . . They are those "principles" which Mr. Baruch contributed to the American plan, upon which he focused public attention, and in his statement of Decem-ber 27th made of their acceptance the basic issue.

The issue with which his name is specifically identified is whether the veto is to be waived in the Security Council if the case before it deals with a "major breach" of the atomic energy treaty. The statement of December 17th, though the language is not precise, may even be construed as an offer of American atomic disarmament if the veto in the Security Council on punishment is waived.

I am one of many who hold that in view of Article 51 of the Charter, Mr. Baruch's preoccupation with the veto obscured the real issues.

1. John M. Hancock, the prominent industrialist, had for many years been a friend of Bernard Baruch's and was now his associate in formulating atomic policy.

To J. William Fulbright[1]

April 3, 1947

Dear Bill:

Your statement on the United States of Europe is impressive and I won't spend any time in this letter telling you how much I agree. I have, however, one criticism to make of the way it is presented.

I realize that from the point of view of the Senate and American opinion the idea is more attractive if European union is treated more or less as an anti-Soviet bloc. But as a matter of fact, in Europe this approach is hopeless. It is conceivable, I think, that a Western Federation might be started if great emphasis were placed on the fact that the Federation has an open end towards Eastern Europe. Actually, however, I believe that this idea even then cannot make progress in Europe today and that it is necessary to plump for an all-European Union, including the states in the Russian orbit. This looks harder to do, but in fact I don't believe it is.

Unless we can push and buy the Russians out of Europe, there is no hope anyway, and I for one don't think it impossible to push and buy them out. If we take that as the major premise of our action, then an all-European Union can be promoted as the thing which is to follow the evacuation of Europe by the Russians, and the advantages to Russia as well as to Europe can be brought out. . . .

1. J. William Fulbright, Arkansas Democrat, had urged American support for a federated Europe in a speech in the Senate on March 21. He also later introduced a resolution calling for a united states of Europe, essentially the federation he had advocated in the speech and, in his formulation, basically Western European.

To Dean G. Acheson

May 14, 1947

Dear Dean:

I wonder if you've had anyone call your attention to the article put out by the United Press, published in Tuesday's paper, which deals with the Italian Cabinet crisis. The article is very disturbing and I am sure it will be used as propaganda against us thoughout the world.

It begins with the statement "the Italian Cabinet fell today in a crisis generated by Premier Alcide de Gasperi's efforts to rid his government of communists, the second western European cabinet to be shaken up within two weeks in what some observers saw as spreading application of President Truman's foreign policy doctrine."[1] Farther on in the article it says that "Mr. Ramadier's coup was followed quickly by the grant of a $250,000,000 loan by the World Bank, in which U.S. influence is predominant." It also says, "Rome reports said American influence was taking a hand in the Italian situation.

American diplomats were said to have linked the elimination of communists from the government to the possibility of increased American financial aid to the hard-pressed Italian regime."

When articles of this sort are published over here and signed, as this one was by Harrison Salisbury, United Press Foreign News Editor, we can't be surprised if *Pravda* in Moscow has a Tass dispatch saying that we are inspiring the cabinet crises in Italy and in France.

I don't see how any kind of broadcasting from the State Department can undo this type of anti-American propaganda, which originates right here in America. I do think it is a very serious matter which the Department ought to take up and deal with.

1. The previous day, May 13, 1947, de Gasperi had resigned because of his rift with the left-wing members of his cabinet. At the end of the month, he formed a new government composed of Christian Democrats and Independents. In France, the coalition government of Premier Paul Ramadier had been unstable since January, with the Communists increasingly antagonistic to the non-Communists. On May 9, the latter group excluded the Communists from the cabinet, but continuing strikes and shortages of food occasioned persisting political instability, as was also true in Italy. Those developments arose largely from the deep economic crisis that afflicted the whole of Western Europe as well as Great Britain. They may also have been accelerated by American implementation of the Truman Doctrine; see Lippmann to Henry R. Luce, November 14, 1947, inf.

Truman had announced his doctrine after it became clear that Great Britain could no longer afford to play its historic role as a source of political and economic power to stabilize Greece and the eastern Mediterranean. The president then on March 12, 1947, announced the Truman Doctrine, which called for American economic and military aid to nations threatened by communism — at that date specifically Greece and Turkey; see Lippmann to Robert Waldo Ruhl, June 17, 1947, inf.

To Henry Steele Commager[1]

May 31, 1947

My dear Commager:

. . . You are quite right in saying that *The Good Society* was an attempt to resolve the dilemma of the choices between anarchy and despotism. You are right in saying that I went back to the 18th Century for foundations, because I do believe that that is when the foundations were correctly laid and most clearly understood. You are quite right also in pointing out that the main contribution of the book, as I saw it, was the attack on the perversion of classical economics which masquerade as liberalism. You are very right in pointing out that it was not the substance of the New Deal, but the method of the New Deal which I have objected to, and that my constructive purpose was to show a method by which the objects of liberalism and indeed of socialism could be obtained while preserving the essential principles of liberty. I like particularly the phrase "the reformation of the economic order through the reconstruction of the legal."

I can't quarrel with your statement that clarification was not a solution. I might perhaps venture to argue with you that the only possible solution in a social problem is the discovery of the right method of proceeding. There is no one social problem which can, so to speak, be solved. There has to be a continuing adjustment of human relations by methods that will work, and will not falsify any of the indispensable ends of human life. In so far as we can perfect the method of action, we have done all we can do towards finding a solution of the social problem. . . .

1. Henry Steele Commager, then a professor of American history at Columbia University and already a prolific and respected scholar in his field, was working on *The American Mind* (New Haven, 1950). He had checked his interpretation of Lippmann's writings in a letter to which Lippmann here replied; see *The American Mind*, pp. 221–25.

To Robert Waldo Ruhl[1]

June 17, 1947

Dear Mr. Ruhl:
  . . . The difference between us arises out of a distinction which I have made consistently in my articles, and which I think you have overlooked. It is the distinction between supporting Greece and Turkey against Soviet aggression, which I regard as necessary and of vital importance, and the so-called Truman Doctrine, which is a promise to do the same kind of thing everywhere in the world where a government may be threatened by a minority.
  I have not only been in favor of supporting Greece and Turkey but was actually the first advocate in the press of sending American warships into the Eastern Mediterranean and to the Dardanelles. I am opposed, however, to the general promises of the Truman Doctrine because I feel that there are many places in the world where it's not so vital for us to act and where, as a matter of fact, we are unable to act. We should not, therefore, promise to do anything that we can't fulfill. In Greece and Turkey we were able to act, and I was in favor of the action. . . .

1. Robert Waldo Ruhl, editor and publisher of the *Medford Mail Tribune* of Medford, Ohio.

To Lewis W. Douglas[1]

September 8, 1947

Dear Lew:
  After a few days in Washington, before leaving,[2] sounding out the general situation, I have made one observation which I think it may be useful to pass on to you.
  When the question comes before Congress for large appropriations over a

long period of time aimed at reconstruction and not merely immediate relief, I believe that the difficulty of getting approval will be enormously increased if there is a party division in Great Britain and in France about the economic use of the American help. I can't imagine a more powerful argument against the Marshall proposals,[3] whatever they may be, than the opposition party in England being able to say that the government is incompetent or that the government is unable to use the help effectively that we may give them.

It seems to me, therefore, that some way must be found by which the Marshall plan, so to speak, is raised over party issues in Great Britain and is presented to the American public as a plan which has the support of all parties in Great Britain and of all the chief interests within Great Britain, such as the Trade Union Congress, the British Federation of Industries, etc.

I don't need to labor the point; you'll see what I mean quickly enough, though how such a thing is to be done (assuming it ought to be done) is more than I would presume to say. But I have no doubt that it would be a good thing if leaders of British opinion knew privately that the chances of our succeeding here will be greatly affected by whether or not they can come to some united front on this matter.

1. Douglas had become American ambassador to Great Britain, an office he held into 1950. **2.** En route to England a few days later. **3.** Speaking at the Harvard commencement on June 5, 1947, Secretary of State Marshall had called upon the European nations to draw up a plan for European recovery. "The role of this country," he then said, "should consist of friendly aid in the drafting of European programs and of later support. . . . Our policy is directed not against any country or doctrine but against hunger, poverty, desperation, and chaos." The whole of Europe, as Marshall knew, needed a strengthened economy, for which American support was essential. His address opened the way for the participation of the Soviet Union and the Eastern European countries. The Soviet Union would reject that possibility for itself and its clients. In contrast, from the first Great Britain seized the promise Marshall had made, as did the Western European states. Meeting in Paris in July, sixteen of those European nations set up a committee of economic cooperation to draft a European Recovery Program (ERP). As Lippmann hoped, political divisions in England and France did not prevent non-Communist factions in the West from uniting in their eagerness for Marshall Plan aid and the economic revival it portended.

To Raymond Gram Swing

November 13, 1947

Dear Raymond:

. . . There is no use my trying to write you anything in detail but I might just say that my main conclusion after the whole business[1] is that either the Marshall Plan, as it is understood in Europe and expounded in the report of the Committee of Sixteen in Paris, will liquidate the political foreign policy of the State Department, or the State Department's policy will destroy the Marshall Plan. The two are irreconcilable, so incompatible that at some point there will have to be a showdown or a resolution. Not only the Department as a whole, but the chief individuals in it, and this I am afraid includes George Marshall and runs down through Lovett and Bohlen to Kennan[2] and the smaller boys, is suffering from a real case of schizophrenia. When they study the realities they come to one set of conclusions; when they construct their political ideas they come to an opposite set. The problem is to reconcile the two.

It is rather lonely here. I feel a little bit like somebody trying to swim up Niagara Falls, so come back soon.[3]

1. Lippmann's personal trip to Europe, September 11 through October 31, 1947, which took him to France, Germany, Switzerland, and Poland as well as Great Britain. **2.** Robert A. Lovett was then undersecretary; Charles E. Bohlen, counselor; and George F. Kennan, head of policy planning in the State Department. **3.** Swing was due back in Washington November 27 after a lecture tour he was then making. Like Lippmann, he considered the State Department, as he put it in his reply, "obsessed," as was the nation in their view, with maintaining a "he-man attitude toward Russia." In that atmosphere, Swing wrote, "there can be no Marshall plan, constructively speaking."

The attitude the two friends lamented had had its most celebrated expression in the summer issue of *Foreign Affairs* where an author called "X" — who was George F. Kennan — explained Soviet conduct as rooted in a messianic ideology, Marxism, and in a classically Russian and paranoid sense of insecurity. The Russians would expand at every opportunity, Kennan maintained, unless they were contained until "either the break-up or the gradual mellowing of Soviet power." Those ideas had influenced the State Department for more than a year, ever since their exposition in a secret "long telegram" Kennan had sent from his post in the Moscow embassy. Later Kennan held that his doctrine of containment had not contemplated the strongly military policy the State Department advocated, but in 1947 most observers interpreted containment as requiring a military response to Soviet ambitions.

Lippmann disagreed with Kennan's analysis. The Soviet Union, he argued, acted out of a historic Russian sense of insecurity, of fear of Western aggression, and a historic Russian effort to acquire warm-weather ports in the Mediterranean. Lippmann amplified his analysis in a series of columns of "Today and Tomorrow" that began in September and were later compiled and published in a book, *The Cold War* (New York, 1947). The columns appeared in the fall during Lippmann's absence in Europe; the book, later in the year. The trip to Europe strengthened Lippmann in his convictions that Kennan was wrong and that a revitalized Germany would fall to autocratic rule. It also confirmed his earlier recognition of the need for the Marshall Plan, which seemed to him an essentially economic venture at variance, as he said in this letter, with the spirit he saw in the containment policy. For a full discussion of Lippmann's response to the X article and of his European trip, see Ronald Steel, *Walter Lippmann and the American Century* (Boston, 1980), pp. 443–47.

To Henry R. Luce

November 14, 1947

Dear Harry:

Instead of writing you a letter for publication about the reference to me in the editorial in this week's *Life*,[1] I am writing you this personal note in order to avoid a tiresome and long-winded argument in print.

I think you will find it interesting if you had your research people make a study of the communist vote in western European countries since the end of the war. I think you will find that there has been a ceiling on the growth of that vote in all the western countries at approximately 30% of the electorate. My argument is that communism cannot gain power by accumulating enough votes to come into power legally in any country with a fairly advanced social order. The only way the communists could come into power would be with the assistance of the Red Army, which is required to suppress the national armies, the police and the other forces of the nations. I contend that experience since the end of this war confirms the pattern which was followed after the last war; that without the Red Army to install the communists in power, the effect of misery and hunger and of communist agitation is to revoke a reaction of the right and center which may take a conservative form, but in extreme disorder and misery will take a fascist form.

What has put the Russians on the defensive in western Europe is not the Marshall Plan — that wasn't even mentioned until June — whereas it's perfectly clear from the record that they were already out of the Italian and French governments before that. They were put on the defensive by the checkmate to any possibility of a military movement into western Europe, and that was accomplished, in my opinion, by the massing of American military power, in token form to be sure, but nevertheless significantly, in the eastern Mediterranean where the Red Army in Europe was outflanked. That, in my view, is how and when the Cold War was lost by the Russians though, of course, like the Germans and the Japanese after they knew they were beaten, they continued to fight on. . . .

1. A page-long editorial in Henry Luce's pictorial weekly, *Life*, asserted that Lippmann erred in seeing a stalemate between communism and its opponents in Western Europe, as he had reported in "Today and Tomorrow." For its part, *Life* contended that the Soviet Union was working to bring about "the collapse of civilization, and the communization of the European continent"; see Ronald Steel, *Walter Lippmann and the American Century* (Boston, 1980), p. 447.

To Bernard Berenson

November 19, 1947

Dear B. B.

. . . I don't really know where to begin telling you what all we saw and what I believe I learned from the trip we did take. If you have read the articles I have been writing and which probably have been published in the Paris *Herald*, you will know a bit of it anyway. One of my chief conclusions, which very few people now agree with, is that west of the military line the probable outcome of the struggle will not be communist governments, but neo-fascist governments of one kind or another. There is, in essentials, a remarkable similarity in the development underneath the surface in this war as after the First World War. Germany was a most interesting place to visit. I came away

convinced that out of the dissolution of German society and the general chaos
which exists there, the Officer Corps and the old bureaucracy will emerge as
the centers of new German political power.

Unless we act with great foresight and decision, particularly about the Ruhr
and about the schedule of events in Germany, which must be set down for the
restoration of German self-government, these German nationalists will inevitably, it seems to me, be polarized to the east — not by their communist
sympathy, but by the fact that the eastern territories annexed by Poland will
become the focus of all German political associations. . . .

The outlook here for approval of the Marshall Plan is far better than anyone
would have dared to predict five or six months ago. There seems to be little
doubt whatever that the interim aid for France and Italy will pass quickly in
the next two or three weeks, and on the longer program there is no real dispute about the principle. The main difficulty lies in deciding on the form of
the organization for administering it in this country. My real concern is about
the Council of Foreign Ministers meeting in London, for which I feel that the
British and we are not well prepared.

In our own politics here at home, everything will turn, I believe, on whether
Truman's political strength increases or diminishes during the coming session
of Congress. If Truman is weaker than he is now, I should think that the
chances were very great that the Republican nominee will be Dewey. If, on
the other hand, the Republicans in Congress make a poor showing, and if
Truman gains in strength as he has in the past six or eight months, then I
think the Republicans may decide that they must do something extraordinary
and that they will nominate Eisenhower and Stassen.[1] But that is the sheerest
guesswork; nobody knows, not even the inner high command of the Republican Party. . . .

1. Harold E. Stassen, Republican governor of Minnesota, 1938–43, in 1947 a candidate for the
G.O.P. presidential nomination, as he was again almost every four years at least through 1980.

To John Foster Dulles[1]

November 19, 1947

Dear Foster:

. . . There is an additional argument which I began to realize more clearly
after I had been in Germany this fall, one that has not been stated publicly by
anyone, but which I discussed the other day with Chip Bohlen.[2] In brief, it is
this: the ultimate power of Russia over German political life is the fact that
the eastern provinces have been lost to Poland. This great historic event is
bound to polarize German politics toward Russia. If, as seems probable, the
German heirs to the present social and political chaos in Germany are to be
the German nationalists and particularly the members of the German Officers

Corps, it is of particular importance that the western powers have some equivalent power in the west which compels the attention of the Germans. The best one is to establish a control over the Ruhr by some form of bait to the Germans, who would otherwise be inclined to turn their back on us once we had made a peace and do all their dealings on the essential subjects with the Soviet Union.

I was always in favor of some treatment of the Ruhr on the grounds that you state, but I am now coming to think that as an essential to a balance of power in Europe the considerations are even more compelling. . . .

1. Dulles, still the unofficial adviser to Governor Dewey on matters of foreign policy, had also served as chief adviser to Secretary of State Marshall at the Moscow Conference on European issues in February 1947. Throughout the year, he advocated the reindustrialization of Germany (including the Ruhr) and the integration of that nation and area into the European economy, objectives the Soviet Union opposed. In November President Truman named Dulles to the American delegation to the forthcoming conference of foreign ministers in London. Then, as earlier, the spontaneous agreement of Dulles and Marshall about European policy made bipartisanship on that issue both natural and easy. 2. Bohlen, a career foreign service officer, was an expert on European and Soviet affairs. His duties in 1947 included the role of appointed adviser to the American delegation to the London meeting of the Council of Foreign Ministers.

To John Foster Dulles

December 8, 1947

Dear Foster:

I have been giving a good deal of thought to the question of what we could do in the probable event of no substantial agreement on a German treaty at this conference in London,[1] and I am venturing to pass on to you what conclusions I have reached on that subject.

For reasons which I needn't go into, it seems to me clear that we must not set up a German government in the two or three western zones, and certainly that we must not make a separate peace with it. This does not preclude action designed to give the Germans greater autonomy and also greater responsibility for the administration of the western zones during the period of waiting for a general settlement. All this, however, would not be enough. There is need for decisive action of some kind to alter the position which will exist in the event of disagreement.

My own conclusion is that the most useful move we could make is to make an open agreement with the British and the French that in principle we shall not restore the Ruhr resources to the sovereignty of any future German government, and that if and when a general German peace treaty is to be written the Ruhr is to be in European and allied hands, not exclusively in German, so far as its juridical position and perhaps also its ultimate ownership is concerned. It would not be necessary in such an agreement to work out the details of an agreement for the control of the Ruhr — that would probably be left to negotiation later — but an agreement on principle, making it irrevocable that the Ruhr cannot be returned to German sovereignty would, I believe, have a far-reaching effect upon the Russians and the whole of Europe, and it would constitute that kind of a decisive act which I believe American opinion will demand if and when the Four Power negotiations come to nothing substantial.

The position then would be that before the Russians and the Poles can obtain what they very much want, namely, legalization and legitimization of the eastern boundary, they must agree to an alteration of the status of the Ruhr. Until they do, the Ruhr will be de facto internationalized by the western powers. . . .

1. The Council of Foreign Ministers, which met in London November 25 through December 15, 1947, again stumbled over the repeated demand of the Soviet Union for ten billion dollars in reparations from Germany. Disagreement on that matter prevented a general settlement of German problems.

MEMORANDUM UNADDRESSED[1]

December 18, 1947

The United States has three vital interests, namely that Europe, the Middle East and China shall not be absorbed into the Russian military empire. But the obverse of this does not follow, namely that Europe, China and the Middle East can be organized as an anti-Soviet coalition. This is a critical error. The U.S. has the force and the strategic position to prevent Russia directly from invading and dominating in a military sense Europe, China and the Middle East, but it does not have the means to organize the whole of those three areas as an anti-Soviet coalition.

How can it forbid them directly? In Europe by our capacity to strike at the vital centers of Russia, the Ukraine and the Caucasus, by air and sea power coming from North Africa and perhaps through the North Atlantic, Iceland, etc. In the Far East our capacity to hold the Russians in check depends not on the organization of the armies of Chiang Kai-shek, but on our ability to strike at eastern Siberia from Japan and from Okinawa and from the Philippines. In the Far East the Luce-Bullitt-Wedemeyer view is really a heritage from pre-war days, namely, from the time when Japan (a formidable sea power) was threatening to organize China as her hinterland. The destruction of Japan, the occupation of Japan by the U.S., the undisputed supremacy of the U.S. throughout the Pacific has completely altered the American interest in China. We have attained strategical domination over Russia in Asia, we have eliminated Japan as a hostile power which could organize China. Therefore, we have no rival in the Far East that could reach any vital part of the U.S. Therefore, in strict terms of power politics it is no longer of vital interest to the

U.S. that China should be unified. On the contrary, whatever danger there may be in the fears expressed by Bullitt and Wedemeyer that China could be organized. . . .

1. This incomplete memorandum was apparently a reminder to himself of Lippmann's current thoughts about American strategy, especially in light of the frenetic statements of William C. Bullitt, General Albert C. Wedemeyer — who had earlier been commander of United States forces in the China theater — and others who also attributed Communist gains in China to alleged failures of American policy there. The United States had given up on mediation in January 1947, with General Marshall wisely attributing the rejection of that effort to extremists in both the Nationalist and Communist camps. Thereafter, as Chiang's power declined, his American supporters called for immediate military aid to his forces and predicted that his fall would make the United States vulnerable in the Far East. Some of those supporters were also already finding in the Communist gains fatuous evidence of "twenty years of Democratic treason" in China.

To Robert Brand

December 20, 1947

Dear Bob:

The Marshall Plan has now gone before Congress and I thought perhaps you'd like an early estimate from me of the main difficulties which we shall have to meet in passing it. As of now, they are these, I think.

One. The reluctance of Congress to make a commitment over a four-year period. There is some doubt as to whether, in fact, it is in accord with the spirit of the Constitution for one Congress to commit another Congress, particularly when a national election must intervene so soon.[1]

Second. The inflationary condition here which threatens to become very serious in the early spring just about the time when the critical votes will have to be taken both on the authorization and on the appropriation. The crop outlook, apparently, is bad and we are almost certainly in for a third round of wage increases by the big unions, which will upset the whole price structure once more.

Third. Powerful pressure from many quarters, particularly Republican quarters, for big help to China, including military help. Some of this is based on a genuine interest in China, a good deal of it really concealed isolationism which is using the agitation about China to divert attention from Europe. As you know, all isolationists are isolationist only about Europe.

Fourth. The proposal of the Republicans to reduce taxes, using up our budgetary surplus for that purpose. The President will probably almost certainly veto a tax reduction bill, but I would think, as of now, that the chances were that Congress would override his veto and that before election there will be tax reduction.[2] If so, of course, one of the brakes on the inflation will be removed and the incentive will be all the stronger for the Appropriations Committee, which is usurping a great deal of power from the Congress, to cut the actual appropriations below the authorized figures.

Fifth. Congress really doesn't understand this recovery program and its underlying disposition is to treat it as a relief measure.

I think these are the main focal points of the difficulty which we shall have to overcome in getting this legislation through in some decent shape. It will be a hard fight. In the end I think the fight will be won, but we shall certainly need a good deal of sympathy and understanding abroad.

Still when I look back to the condition of affairs very early last winter, and think how far we have come and how fast, and how grandiose the whole plan is compared with anything that was then considered, I can feel almost cheerful. . . .

1. Congress did approve the Marshall Plan in March 1948, partly as a reaction to the Russian coup in Czechoslovakia the preceding month. 2. Just as Lippmann predicted, over Truman's veto Congress in 1948 passed a revenue act providing for a large tax reduction.

To Duncan Phillips[1]

January 16, 1948

Dear Duncan:

I am rather worried about the prospects of the Marshall Plan. The administration made a number of unnecessary mistakes in the presentation of it, particularly the failure to have come to an agreement in advance with Vandenberg and Herter[2] on the administration of the Plan. That would have been easier to do privately before the public statements than it will be now. I am also concerned about a matter which hasn't come up at all, namely, that the Plan cannot be made to work if the conflict with eastern Europe becomes more severe. I am afraid most people here think that the Plan can be worked without the economic reunion of Europe. . . .

I don't think Marshall's difficulties with Congress arise so much out of his military habits as out of the fact that he has had very little to do with the working of the Marshall Plan, that he doesn't fully understand it as he used to understand his military problems. He sounds amateurish when he tries to explain the Plan to the Congressmen, and he hasn't among his advisers at the State Department enough men of high wisdom and political understanding. There are too many experts, not enough statesmen. The old rule that experts should be on tap, but not on top has been disregarded. . . .

1. Duncan Phillips, art critic and founder and director of the Phillips Memorial Gallery in Washington, D.C. 2. Christian A. Herter, Republican congressman from Massachusetts since 1943, internationalist in foreign policy, about which he had become a leading spokesman for his party in the House of Representatives.

To Quincy A. Wright

January 23, 1948

Dear Quincy:

. . . In my own mind that is exactly the assumption that I make about Soviet intentions. They will expand the revolution, if the balance of power is such that they can; if it is such that they cannot, they will make the best settlement they can obtain for Russia and the regime in Russia.

But I hesitate to use the argument in what I write. That is because such an argument is bound to provoke a dispute among experts on Russia as to what Russia's *real*[1] intentions are. And that leads to realms of metaphysics and dialectic where I don't want to go. Thus far I have been avoiding any discussion of what the Soviets want, taking the line that our policy should be based upon our ability to withhold what we do not want them to have. I quite grant that maybe I am wrong, and that this would be an effective argument, since, in fact, it is probably a true one.

Have you ever thought about the analogy between the communist ideology which calls for the expansion of communism throughout the world with the conception of the holy war in the Mohammedan theology? I have been reading a very interesting book published by the University of Chicago Press on medieval Islam by Gustave Von Grunebaum[2] in which he says "Islam divides the world into regions under its control, the dar al-Islam and regions not subjected as yet, the dar al-Harb. Between this 'area of warfare' and the Muslim-dominated part of the world there can be no peace. Practical considerations may induce the Muslim leaders to conclude an armistice but the obligation to conquer and, if possible, convert never lapses." Yet after the first century of conquest the relation between Islam, the Greek empire and the western empire became fairly well stabilized for many centuries.

The only point of the analogy is that the doctrine of universal conquest and conversion has never been abandoned and yet no one would think of measuring the role of Islam in the world simply by its aspirations. . . .

1. Emphasis Lippmann's.   **2.** Gustave E. Von Grunebaum, *Medieval Islam* (Chicago, 1926).

To Philip B. Stockton[1]

February 3, 1948

Dear Mr. Stockton:

. . . On what you call the short range problem of whether a mutual withdrawal would tilt the balance of power in favor of the Russians, I think I'd say that it definitely would not. The forces which we now have in continental Europe are purely token forces, incapable of actual resistance to the power of the Red Army. It is not they who check the continental expansion of the

Russians, if that is what they have in their mind. What checks them is the potential of our long range air and sea power; that would continue to exist whether or not we had troops in Europe.

Your second point is a more difficult one to answer briefly, but I think that I can go to the heart of my objections to the theory by saying that I do not believe, in fact, that there are now any such things as absolute weapons. I have never met anyone who really knew about these weapons who thought they were absolute. All weapons, including the most powerful and that includes the atomic bomb or bacterial warfare, are relative. That is to say, there is some form of reply to all of them. . . .

1. Philip B. Stockton of Boston had been present on January 3, 1948, at Lippmann's address to the Harvard Club of that city and had written to ask for elaborations of several of the points the speech made.

To John Foster Dulles

February 13, 1948

Dear Foster:

I thought all that part of Governor Dewey's speech which dealt with Europe was admirable and will make a real contribution to the whole business. I don't need to tell you that I regret what he says about American responsibility for what has happened in Eastern Europe.[1] If Governor Dewey had been President, he couldn't have prevented those things from happening; they were the consequence of the military situation. It really isn't fair to imply that the United States had the power to compel the Russians to act differently in the area which was under complete domination of the Red Army. All we could do was talk about what they ought to do, and we did plenty of talking but to no effect. . . .

1. On February 12, 1947, Dewey, as he would again, had attacked Franklin Roosevelt's alleged wartime concessions to the Soviet Union.

To Francis Biddle

March 30, 1948

Dear Francis:

. . . The distinction which you make between Socialism and Communism is, of course, correct. But there is a deeper problem which you do not face, and to which I personally do not know the answer. It is the problem raised in my book, *The Good Society*, from which you quote,[1] namely, whether a planned economy can be operated with the maintenance of democratic freedom. That question has not yet been answered by the British experience since 1945. It is conceivable in my mind that the answer may be in the negative. In fact I am afraid that I think it is probable that that is the answer. It would be difficult for me to say more about that in this short letter, but if you care to discuss it, I'd love to do so. . . .

1. In the Walgreen Lectures at the University of Chicago, which were published in 1948 under the title *The World's Best Hope.*

To Forrest P. Sherman[1]

April 5, 1948

Dear Forrest:

. . . My own guess is that the present actions of the Soviet Union[2] are the result of decisions taken some time last summer after the Marshall Plan and its political consequences were reasonably clear and assured. My feeling is that the essence of the Soviet decision was that time was no longer on their side, and that whatever action they took must be taken before western Europe got the benefits of our assistance, before it became politically consolidated, and before the United States could rebuild its military power. It seems to me necessary to assume now that the Russians, though not necessarily intending to precipitate war, will take actions which they deem necessary to themselves at the risk of war now rather than at the risk of waiting for a showdown some years hence. If this is correct, the next twelve to eighteen months are probably the period of greatest danger.

It seems to me, therefore, that we must prepare for the showdown in the near future. For that we have, of course, to take military measures which are obvious and which I need not talk about to you, namely the re-establishment of selective service, the mobilization of our industries, and the building up of a balance of military power. It is the diplomatic aspects of this thing that seem to me most puzzling, but in regard to them it is evident, I think, that the showdown will come in Europe and that, therefore, we must be very careful not to become over-extended and committed in secondary regions.

Therefore, a fundamental reorientation of American Far Eastern policy is now necessary. For over forty years, from the time of John Hay to Pearl Harbor, American Far Eastern policy has been based on the assumption that our vital interests and our security in the Pacific could be maintained only by the unity and the integrity of China. This was a sound view as long as the island empire of Japan with its first-class naval power could threaten to use the manpower and resources of China as its hinterland, and to draw from them a power for expansion in the Pacific. With the conquest of Japan, the situation is radically altered and our policy should, if not openly, because that may involve much misunderstanding, then at least in our inner decisions, recognize this change.

Our Far Eastern position should now be based not on China, but upon Japan, and our main base for action in eastern Asia should be the Japanese islands. We should build up there the power to dominate Soviet Siberia, and should make Japan a subordinate ally of the United States.

If this is done, the unity of China is no longer a vital interest of the United States. From the point of view of our own national interest, the prevention of the unity of China is advantageous in view of the fact that China can be unified only as an ally of the Soviet Union or unified as an independent power which might very well itself become aggressive in southeastern Asia, the Philippines, and perhaps even in India.

Recognition that the unity of China is no longer an American vital interest is a novel thing in our history, but I am pretty nearly completely persuaded that it is now fundamentally necessary.

In the Middle East the same basic principle should, I believe, be applied. Our aim should be not to encourage the unity of the Arab world and of Islam, but to keep it divided. No dependence can be put upon the friendship and the reliability of a united Mohammedan world; a united Mohammedan world must in the end expel the western powers from all its territories, not only in the Middle East, but in North Africa. The only basis of unity in Islam is the theological and religious unity against the non-Mohammedan world.

Therefore, we should devote our first attention to Turkey, building it up as a strong ally. We should encourage Trans-Jordan to occupy the Arab part of Palestine. We should use pressure and inducements to keep Saudi Arabia from acting with the Arab League. We should aim to turn Egypt away from the Middle East and back into Africa. It will be by breaking up Arab unity, not by cultivating it, that the position of the western powers in the Middle East can best be maintained. The barrier to Soviet expansion in the Middle East must be erected not in the Arab states, but in Turkey and, above all, by the building up of powerful American striking forces capable of reaching the whole Black Sea basin and the industrial centers of the Soviet Union.

While pursuing a policy of division in the Far East and in the Middle East, in Europe we should pursue a policy of unity. For Europe is the theater where the conflict will be decided, and it is in Europe that unity can give us positive military and diplomatic advantages. The political unity of western Europe should be supported by the restoration of Lend-Lease and by the establishment somewhere in western Europe of strategical and tactical forces of our own which will put an end to the assumption that the Red Army can overrun western Europe virtually unopposed. It will no longer do for us to take the view that if war comes, we will defeat the Soviet Union itself. We have, as a result of the political developments in western Europe, to take measures of security for western Europe, not merely for victory over the Soviet Union.

This whole policy is, of course, an extremely dangerous one. It should not be undertaken unless the United States is on a virtual war footing, for it is only the possession of overwhelming power or the prospect of being able to develop it within a reasonably short time that could prevent this policy from provoking violent reactions from the Soviet Union. We must face the fact, I think, that it may nevertheless provoke them. But if we concentrate our effort instead of dispersing it all over the globe, we shall at least be in a position then to have a good chance of winning the war rather than of being paralyzed all over the world with no prospect of a decision and only the prospect of indefinite and unlimited entanglement. . . .

1. Admiral Forrest P. Sherman was then in command of American naval forces in the Mediterranean. A friend of Lippmann's, he had been the designated recipient of a letter drafted but not mailed in which Lippmann wrote with much more heat and anxiety about the developments discussed in this draft, which he did dispatch; see Ronald Steel, *Walter Lippmann and the American Century* (Boston, 1980), p. 451.   2. Those actions included the Communist coup in Czechoslovakia on February 25, 1948, which led to a purge of anti-Communist democrats in that country, to the death in March of Jan Masaryk, the democratic foreign minister, and to the transformation of the nation into a Soviet satellite. In Germany the Soviet delegates, in protest against Western policy there, walked out of the Allied Control Council in March and began on April 1, 1948, to interfere sporadically with traffic moving between the Western zones and the city of Berlin, a city jointly controlled by the occupying forces but entirely within the Soviet zone. With Finland the Russians negotiated a treaty, signed during the first week of April, directed against Germany. Earlier they had extracted other concessions from the Finns.

To Robert Brand

April 5, 1948

Dear Bob:

. . . One of the things I should like to have talked over with you is the extremely difficult question of how far Great Britain can commit itself to the European continent and how such a commitment can be reconciled with the Commonwealth and the Empire. The issues involved here are so complex that I hardly know how one begins to think about them.

I have been back a week[1] and have done a little exploring of our own political prospects. The present indications are that Dewey, who was the leading contender last autumn, is losing ground rapidly and may actually be knocked out of the competition in the coming Wisconsin primary.[2]

The disintegration of the Truman Administration and of the Democratic Party has gone more rapidly than was anticipated. As of a few months ago that should have meant the rise of Taft's strength on the theory that a normal, orthodox Republican could win the election and that Taft would be the first choice of the professional Republican politicians. But there is reason to think that it isn't working out that way, and that somewhere down among the masses of the voters there is a demand for something more promising than Taft would be. This is the explanation of the almost irrational demand for Eisenhower from both parties. This demand is not based on any judgment of his capacities as a President; it is a kind of romantic projection upon him of all the wishes of the people. They would like to think that this most engaging man possesses all the qualities they wish the President of the United States would have. As of today, however, I think that Eisenhower must still be regarded as not a probable candidate in either party.

The real beneficiaries of the present situation seem to be Vandenberg and Stassen and, again speaking as of today and subject to all the accidents and incidents that will occur before June, a Republican ticket with Vandenberg for President and Stassen for Vice President seems to me a good bet.

I would be for that ticket myself, though with a great deal of misgiving. I like and believe in Vandenberg though I have the greatest doubt whether a man of 64, who has never had any executive office in his life, could develop the necessary executive ability. However, there is no better combination now in sight.

1. From a holiday in California.   2. Dewey ran a poor third in the Republican presidential primary in Wisconsin, behind Harold Stassen, who won, and General Douglas MacArthur. That defeat did not, however, cost Dewey the Republican nomination, with Governor Earl Warren of California as his running mate.

To Charles B. Gary [1]

April 15, 1948

Dear Charles:

. . . The argument as to the untenability of the Middle East and the conclusions you draw from it about pipelines and refineries seem to me sound and of the highest importance.

I am troubled, however, by your timetable. The hypothesis that Russia would wait until we had developed the properties so that she could seize them is, to me, highly questionable in itself. Certainly I am not convinced that it would be a controlling consideration. In my view the controlling consideration would be whether in the course of four or five years the relative power of Russia, as against that of the United States and its western allies, would go up or down. Is it not just as arguable that the next two years, in which American power remains potential and in which western Europe is without any power at all, are the most critical? If Russia is willing to allow us four or five years, we may not only be able to achieve a consolidation in western Europe, but we shall have developed the massive long-range air power which could strike at the heart of Russia itself. In that event, the occupation of the Middle East would do Russia no good.

It is for these reasons that I have regarded the events in Czechoslovakia and in Finland as indicating a much faster timetable than you assume and than that of most of the military leaders here and in western Europe are assuming. . . .

1. Charles B. Gary, then head of the General Motors Overseas Corporation.

To Geoffrey Crowther[1]

May 11, 1948

Dear Mr. Crowther:

In your issue of April 24th, on page 674, there is a note called "The Form of a Military Guarantee" which is extraordinarily uninformed and misleading.

The problem of a formal guarantee arose in connection with the Brussels Pact.[2] As respects the signatories of that pact, there is nothing ingenious or theoretical in the statement that they cannot be attacked without encountering the American army in Germany, and that, therefore, they need no special formal guarantee as long as the American army remains in Germany.

Your correspondent writes that my "reasoning will hardly reassure the Scandinavians, the Turks or the Greeks for unfortunately the Russians are not bound to shape their tactics to suit Mr. Lippmann's theories."

As for the Scandinavians, no request for a guarantee has come from them, and it is highly probable that they would not accept one if it were offered. As for the Turks and the Greeks, they have an automatic guarantee resulting from the presence of American military personnel in Greece and of the military support given to Turkey. It is inconceivable that either of them could be attacked without the United States being involved at once. Your correspondent does not mention Austria and Italy, but of course the same situation exists there. There is an American army in Austria, there are American troops in Trieste. Neither Italy nor Austria could be attacked by the Russian army with the American armies remaining neutral.

Thus, of the Marshall countries which are exposed to the threat of invasion, the only ones which do not have an automatic guarantee are the Scandinavian. That is why responsible people here in Washington have wished to avoid a formal guarantee. Such a guarantee would seem to exclude the Scandinavians.

The real question of substance, which your correspondent overlooks entirely, is not whether the guarantee is to be automatic or formal or both. It is whether the guarantee means that the U.S.A. will go to war to "liberate" the continent, or whether it will and, if war comes, can defend the European countries against invasion. That is the hard question which has to be examined and settled. . . .

---

1. Geoffrey Crowther, editor of the *Economist*. **2.** Britain, France, Belgium, the Netherlands, and Luxembourg signed a fifty-year treaty of mutual assistance at Brussels on March 17, 1948. The pact provided for economic and social, as well as military, cooperation and set up a common military committee in London. President Truman immediately and explicitly endorsed the treaty, though the United States was not officially a party to it. As it worked out, the Brussels agreement established a preliminary basis for the North Atlantic Treaty Organization formed in Washington in April 1949.

To Robert Strausz-Hupé[1]

May 20, 1948

Dear Robert:

I have been reading with great interest your paper on "The Great Powers in the New World Order," in the May issue of the Annals of the American Academy of Political and Social Science. It is one of your best performances.

Besides congratulating you on it, I'd like to say a word about the three major assumptions implicit in the American postwar conception of diplomacy. Of the two mentioned by Sumner Welles and the one added by you, in my view the third is far more important than the other two. The assumption that Great Britain would be able to carry the burden of great power responsibilities was the major assumption underlying the other two. Thus the concessions that had to be made to the Soviet Union would not have proved too costly if the British position in Europe and in the Middle East and in the Far East had proved to be what Roosevelt and the rest of us assumed it would be. I am inclined to think that the verdict of history will be that it was not the unexpected aggressiveness of the Soviet Union, but the unexpected weakness and defaults of the British which caused the present postwar situation. But for the British weakness, there would have been no problem of Russian containment. Russia would have been ipso facto contained.

There ought to be a careful study made of the political consequences of the unexpected British weakness. The whole story of the meetings of the Council of Foreign Ministers dealing with the satellite states, all the meetings of the U.N. dealing with Greece, Iran and Palestine, the whole problem of Germany, the problem posed by the Marshall Plan, ought to be reviewed in relation to that great and unexpected fact. It probably explains the intellectual bankruptcy of the so-called policy makers in the State Department. . . .

1. Robert Strausz-Hupé, Austrian-born investment banker, since 1946 professor of political science at the University of Pennsylvania, author of many books and articles on foreign policy, later American ambassador successively to Ceylon, Belgium, Sweden, NATO, and Turkey.

To Bernard Berenson

June 8, 1948

Dear B. B.:

. . . I take a reasonably optimistic view about the avoidance of war. At the time of the Czechoslovak coup it seemed to me that what the Russians had done there, and what they had attempted in Finland meant that if they intended to take military action, they were certain to take it within a year. The fact that they show no evidence of a military response to our huge military rearmament in this country is a pretty good sign, I think, that they do not intend to march. For if they are going to march, they must march before our rearmament has progressed much further.

On the other hand, I do not take an optimistic view about the prospects of political reconstruction in Germany and in western Europe. I do not believe that Truman, Bevin, and Bidault[1] are capable or have the statesmanship required for political reconstruction. . . .

1. Ernest Bevin was then British foreign secretary; and Georges Bidault, French foreign secretary.

To Harold G. Nicolson

June 14, 1948

My dear Nicolson:

. . . Palestine has indeed been a sad story,[1] though now at long last I have hopes that a way will be found out of the muddle. But I do not think that Bevin and the government really understand the harm that has been done here.[2] They measure it, apparently, by the outcries of the Zionists. The real harm is much subtler and more pervasive. It consists in a kind of spectacular destruction of the moral authority of the United Nations. That is a very serious matter indeed. For all our participation in European affairs depends, I believe, in the last analysis not on fear of Russia, not on economic considerations, but on the widespread simple American hope that the United Nations can be made to work — or perhaps I should say what the Americans hope the United Nations means can be made to work.

I don't believe it can be realized abroad how enormously difficult it is to persuade a people like the Americans year after year to make large contributions to another continent, especially when those contributions are visibly at the expense of domestic improvements, such as housing, health and education.

In my view, and I think it is demonstrable, that the revival of isolationism and the very real threat to the continuity of the European Recovery Program is traceable directly to the loss of faith in the idea of the United Nations. The men who have carried along the mass of the people during the war through the whole period of UNRRA[3] and the British loan, and now into the Marshall Plan, are a relatively small group who exercise great influence. If they lose heart, there will be no one to carry forward projects of this kind, and these precisely are the people who have been the most disillusioned and disheartened by recent events. Their disillusion is not a matter of being pro-Zionist or anti-Zionist, but a feeling that the United Nations is unworkable even without the Russian veto because its two strongest supporters — Britain and America — are not faithful to it. . . .

1. In May 1948, the British mandate in Palestine had terminated. During the previous several years, the British had moved from advocating an independent Palestine with local autonomy to

proposing a division of the area between Arabs and Jews, then increasing in number as European emigrants arrived and as Zionist activities mounted. In 1947, after Britain referred the issue to the UN, the General Assembly voted for partition, a solution the Jews accepted but the Arabs rejected. With the end of the British mandate, David Ben-Gurion, the Zionist leader, proclaimed the State of Israel, which both the United States and the Soviet Union quickly recognized. The war between Israel and the Arab League now succeeded the reciprocal terrorism that had preceded it. Israeli forces were prevailing when the UN negotiated a shaky truce that lasted from July through October 1948. Count Folke Bernadotte, the UN mediator appointed on May 20, was assassinated by Zionist terrorists in September. In December 1948, the Palestine Arabs proclaimed their own king of Palestine, but the Israelis controlled the country before that gesture, held elections in January 1949, and received admission to the UN in May 1949. The development of 1948 provoked continued criticism from American Jews who, like Lippmann, were anti-Zionists, though a majority of American Jews probably applauded the creation of the State of Israel, which Truman recognized, as he admitted, in large part in order to woo the Jewish vote in New York State.   **2.** Bevin had opposed the establishment of an independent Israel, and Britain had trained the Arab Legion of Trans-Jordan which invaded Israel on May 15, 1948.   **3.** The United Nations Relief and Rehabilitation Administration, established in 1943 and dissolved in 1947.

To Lewis W. Douglas

July 9, 1948

Dear Lew:

. . . I have pretty well made up my mind that the election of the Dewey-Warren ticket is much the best thing for the country. As I am dictating this letter there is going on all over again a most extraordinary draft Eisenhower movement.[1] The people who want to draft him disagree about everything except that they would like to find a winner.

I should look upon Eisenhower's acceptance of this draft and his possible election as a very dangerous thing. In the first place, the truth of the matter is that Eisenhower is not personally qualified to be President of the United States. The public legend about him is justified on his human qualities, but it takes no account of his intellectual equipment and his real experience. I have never seen anything like it. He is not a real figure in our public life but a kind of dream boy embodying all the unsatisfied wishes of all the people who are discontented with things as they are. Moreover, no workable or stable administration could, I believe, be formed out of the contradictory factions which are behind the Eisenhower movement.

Dewey and Warren, on the other hand, have their obvious limitations and certainly the Republican Party is not an inspiring instrument of government today. But I am satisfied that they are strong men, exceedingly efficient men, exceedingly astute politically, and that with the fresh power that will be theirs in the first year or two after the election they will be able to impose discipline and order upon the Republicans.

I would count on Dewey being able to dominate Joe Martin and Taber[2] far more confidently than on the power of Eisenhower to do it. Beyond that it seems to me that the country has been wanting to have a conservative administration since 1944, and that it will have something like a nervous breakdown if it is frustrated much longer. The Republicans also have been out of power too long for their good and for the good of the country. They need the experience of responsibility.

Actually, before the convention I wanted to see a Vandenberg-Dewey ticket. That was rather a fanciful arrangement, I am afraid, because of Dewey's strength and his personal ambition, but it seemed to me that Vandenberg was a little better seasoned than Dewey, was a little bit more likely to create confidence and that Dewey would surely have succeeded him at the end of the first term, and perhaps during the first term. But it has always seemed to me essential that among the available people today Dewey should be brought into high office in the federal government.

Because I was interested in Vandenberg, I was rather close to the people who were working for his nomination, and I can pass on to you one interesting though now academic piece of information. It is that if Vandenberg had been nominated and elected, he planned to keep you on in London as the chief symbol of the continuation of the bi-partisan policy. That seemed to me a nice compliment and tribute which ought to make you feel good amidst all your troubles.

If you have seen any of my articles written recently on Germany, you will know that I am far from happy with the basic decision which guides our present policy.[3] I wish I could talk to you for several hours about it and, of course, the only thing that keeps me from feeling worse about it is the fact that you are identified with it. I had a long talk with John Foster Dulles in Philadelphia,[4] and while I don't want to seem to quote him, and I know that you will protect me in this, I can tell you that he is extremely perturbed about the development of our German policy. I, myself, feel that this policy has been made not in the State Department but in the War Department, and particularly by Draper[5] and that to my mind is, in principle, very bad. The planning people in the State Department, as you no doubt know, are also very unhappy about the development and in private say that they have had no real voice in the shaping of the policy.

What happened in Congress over the appropriation for E.C.A.[6] and in the platform committee of the Republican convention indicates to my mind quite definitely that the battle over the second installment of the appropriation will be the decisive one. That means that if the program is to go ahead well, the conditions must be prepared for it during the remainder of this year because the struggle will begin immediately after the new administration and the new Congress come into being in Washington. In my view, in addition to the utmost effort to carry out the economic purposes of the act in the form of increased production, exports, stabilization of currency, etc., it is indispensable that at least three political developments should take place to prepare a proper climate of opinion for the wholehearted support of the European Recovery Program over a long term of years.

The first is that the moral authority of the United Nations must be reestablished. In the long run the American people will not remain interested in international cooperation if the United Nations is allowed to disintegrate. The obvious and necessary means to reestablish faith in the United Nations is to achieve through it a solution in Palestine. In my view this requires a substantial acceptance of the partition line drawn by the United Nations itself though, no doubt, some exchanges of territory could advantageously be made.

In addition I believe, and I have been telling some of our people in the State Department privately, that we should insist on the other part of the United Nations plan which was the economic union of the Arab and Jewish parts of the whole of the former Palestine, including Trans-Jordan and I have urged them to take the position that so far as loans by the U.S. or by the World Bank are concerned, our position would be that these loans will not be made to the State of Israel or to the Kingdom of Trans-Jordan but only to the economic union of the two of them.

The second political development which I think is necessary is that Western Union should be raised out of its present state of being an important alliance and projected more along the lines which Churchill has been advocating as the nucleus of an all-European Union. It does not seem to be necessary that detailed plans or projects should be put forward for an actual federation of Europe. I think that Churchill's suggestion of a Council of Europe, which would really technically be a council of Ambassadors or Foreign Ministers would suffice.

In any event, I think we should not fail to make some large advance towards European political union during the next six months, and in making that advance we should not confine our interest to western Europe. We should aim at the union of the whole of Europe as the explicit ideal and not be satisfied with anything less. This was Churchill's position at The Hague[7] and it seems to me the wise and statesmanlike one.

Third, I think it is essential that the Marshall Plan countries should be able to act collectively and not bilaterally with the United States — each separately. It seems to me that if by next winter we have only a series of sixteen separate agreements and sixteen separate relationships with the countries of Europe, the problem will be debated in Congress on the basis of whether we have helped Great Britain too much or too little, whether we have favored Italy too much or too little, and all the pressure groups will become active. The only safety is in dealing with the European countries more or less as a unit. . . .

1. By Democrats opposed to the renomination of Truman, who won that battle easily, as he would have even if Eisenhower had not refused to allow the use of his name. 2. Two senior and influential Republican conservatives in the House of Representatives, Joseph W. Martin of Massachusetts was then Speaker and John Taber of New York, majority leader. 3. During 1948 American policy toward Germany departed fully from the earlier prescription of JCS 1067. In March the United States and Great Britain brought France into their bizonal arrangements, thus creating a common occupation policy that contemplated the reindustrialization of western Ger-

many and led to the inclusion of that part of Germany within the Organization for European Economic Co-operation (OEEC) and the Marshall Plan. It had been those developments that provoked the Soviet departure from the Allied Control Council on March 20. In June the three Western powers announced a major currency reform in western Germany that established the stable Deutsche mark, prevented the Soviet printing of occupation currency from any longer producing an artificial inflation, and abetted the process of economic development. Partly in retaliation, the Soviet Union on July 24, 1948, stopped all rail and road traffic between Berlin and western Germany. In order to surmount that blockade, the United States, assisted by Britain and France, began the prolonged and successful airlift of thousands of tons of essential supplies to Berlin. Further significant changes occurred later in the year. Late in November, the Communists set up a new administration of Berlin that claimed control over the whole city, but in early December an election in the western part of the city put into office a Socialist, anti-Communist government, which the Western powers recognized. On December 28, the United States, Great Britain, France, and the Benelux nations (Belgium, the Netherlands, and Luxembourg), which West Germany later joined, created an International Ruhr Authority with large powers over that vital industrial area.   **4.** During the Republican National Convention there.   **5.** General William H. Draper, the New York investment banker then serving as General Clay's financial adviser. **6.** Economic Co-operation Administration.   **7.** Whatever the long-range implications of Churchill's remarks of early May at The Hague, or elsewhere in 1948, the former prime minister, a committed cold warrior who saw little chance of an early rapprochement with the Soviet Union, likened the crisis over Berlin to that in Czechoslovakia ten years earlier, a comparison at variance with Lippmann's tone in this reference.

To Quincy A. Wright

July 26, 1948

Dear Quincy:

In regard to your letter of July 19 I agree, of course, that the distinction between a symbolic police force and a United Nations Army can not be defined precisely. But there is this important practical distinction to be made which I wonder whether you have considered. A United Nations Army comprising all weapons and composed of contingents from the great powers will require a military treaty which I, myself, think there is no prospect of arriving at. On the other hand, the kind of guard force which Mr. Lie[1] is proposing can be authorized by a resolution of the General Assembly and recruited by Lie without requiring agreement by the General Staffs of all the great powers. It is a much easier thing to do and in my view for the kind of dispute with which the United Nations is now capable of dealing, namely, disputes not involving the great powers, it would probably be a sufficient force.

My hope is that the United Nations can be brought to endorse the guard force plan which might eventually grow into the kind of real force that you have in mind; whereas the attempt now to establish a United Nations Army simply aggravates the differences among the great powers and may prevent us from accomplishing anything. . . .

1. Trygve Lie, of Norway, since 1946 secretary general of the United Nations.

To John Foster Dulles

July 28, 1948

Dear Foster:

I have been somewhat disturbed by repeated statements in the newspapers that Governor Dewey intends to make an issue of the Teheran and Yalta Conferences. On the other hand, I was much reassured by his recent statement that he was concerned not with the past, but with the future.

There are a number of reasons it seems to me why a controversial discussion of Teheran and Yalta is out of place in this campaign. The responsibility for Teheran and Yalta was shared by Roosevelt and Churchill and by their military advisers, including General Marshall and the British Chiefs of Staff. It is a perversion of the historical truth, which many Republicans have indulged in, to make it appear that the aspects of Teheran and Yalta, which they disapprove, were the sole responsibility of Franklin Roosevelt. Certainly on the political side, Churchill's responsibility was at least as great as Roosevelt's and perhaps his influence was stronger. I think a dispassionate examination of the record would show that particularly on the Polish question Churchill was prepared sooner and earlier to concede the Russian demand for a revision of the frontiers than was Roosevelt.

The issue in this election is really whether we are to have a Truman Administration or a Dewey Administration and I can't think of a good political reason, apart from the historical side of it, why Dewey should campaign against Roosevelt and Churchill rather than against Truman who had no responsibility for Yalta and Teheran and who probably doesn't know what happened there even now. It is necessary to remember, too, that Churchill is still alive, that he is writing his memoirs and that some time during Dewey's administration he will publish his account of Teheran and Yalta. It would be a pity, it seems to me, to lay the ground for a controversy over the past between Churchill and Dewey.

There is still another reason why I think it would be unwise to raise this issue in the campaign. If there is to be argument about the diplomatic record of the past, the governor will inevitably open himself to a discussion of the whole record on the war — his own and that of the Republican Party. It will be easy to point out that if Roosevelt and Churchill made greater concessions to Stalin at Teheran and Yalta than we wish they had, the compelling reason was the relative military weakness of Great Britain and the United States and their dependence upon the Red Army. From that it is an easy step to the argument that our military unpreparedness in 1941 was a determining cause of our diplomatic weakness later and, of course, the Republican Party bears a heavy responsibility for our unpreparedness in the early stages of the war.

Putting the matter on the lowest ground, there is no important body of votes to be gotten, I think, by the attempt to prove that Dewey would have been a better war President than Roosevelt. It is much easier for him to prove that he will be a better peace President than Truman and if he sticks to that issue, I am confident he will win without involving himself in controversies that must disturb and may alienate many who are determined to support him. . . .

To Philip Jordan[1]

July 29, 1948

Dear Philip:

. . . It seems to me important that now we should look beyond the problem created by partition, the establishment of an enlarged kingdom of Trans-Jordan,[2] and the establishment of the State of Israel, to a plan for the development of the whole Middle Eastern world. I am sure you are right in what you say about our having torn up the roots of Islam and having failed to replant them, and that we are faced with a half-educated, half-urbanized population which, lacking opportunity to develop, could become a prey to communism or to general anarchy. Quite obviously it is impossible to return to the status quo ante. We must, therefore, go forward and we should make ourselves the sponsors and promoters and supporters of a large scheme of economic development based on irrigation and water power. The one based on the development of the Jordan under the aegis of the economic union of Israel and Trans-Jordan, and the other on the development of Mesopotamia. Would it not be an act of justice and also a wise policy for us to work out a plan for plowing back into the Middle East some considerable part of the immense profit from the oil concessions? Here is a task for your planners and for our own, and if done wisely and boldly, might present to the Middle East something more fruitful to think about than the quarrel between the Zionists and the Arab League.

I am much more troubled about Germany than about any other thing. Without trying to talk about the immediate issues arising in Berlin and our plans for western Germany, I feel that the basic trouble in our official thinking, and in yours too, is that we are not looking at Germany as a European problem. We are in fact trying to find a solution in Germany apart from a solution in Europe and that, I think, will prove impossible. This in strictest confidence is, I believe, the view that Dewey's closest advisers now take and will take when they come into power. Therefore, for all sorts of reasons, including political reasons, involving relations between our two countries it will be wiser to temporize with the German situation so as not to present the incoming administration next January with an accomplished fact about which it can do nothing except choose between an indefinite subsidy for a western Germany that can't be made self-supporting, unlimited guarantees to western Germany which will be exorbitant and, on the other hand, abandoning the whole position in Germany.

I think it may be said that the German problem cannot be solved satisfactorily by the outgoing Truman Administration and that that ought to be the fixed point of our thinking. You must be prepared for spectacular and irrational developments in this country during the next three or four months. The position of Truman is desperate, but unfortunately he is in the state of mind of a man who has nothing to lose and who may try anything in the hope of winning. He has not only ruptured the moral compact under which the bipartisan foreign policy has been conducted, but he has broken away from the leaders of his own party — he no longer consults them, even men like Senator Barkley,[3] who is the Vice Presidential candidate and the leader of the party in Congress. The situation may be quite dangerous because the President of the United States after all has enormous power, and until election that power will be in the hands of a very small clique of men who have no great sense of responsibility, who have no training for high office, and who are quite unpredictable. You will need all the ancient wisdom you have and a good deal of firmness and persistence to see that nothing irretrievable happens. On the other hand, I think you may have a good deal of confidence in Dewey and Warren. They are not only extremely competent men and astute politicians, but, moreover, since they feel certain of election,[4] they will already begin to act in the knowledge that they will have the responsibility for events and must make the situation that they will find as manageable as possible.

1. Philip Jordan, British journalist, first secretary to the British embassy in Washington, 1946–47, at the date of this letter public relations adviser to the prime minister. 2. Lippmann was referring to the section of Palestine that remained under Arab control. Though the Arab League did not recognize Israel as a state, Trans-Jordan (later Jordan) was moving toward a proposal to merge with that Arab section. The Arab League opposed that step, which materialized in 1950. 3. Alben W. Barkley, Democratic senator from Kentucky since 1927, majority leader since 1937. 4. They were wrong, of course, as was Lippmann. To the surprise of most prognosticators, Truman won the election, and the Democrats carried both houses of Congress.

To Dorothy Thompson [1]

September 9, 1948

Dear Dorothy:

. . . I saw your piece on the difficulty of reconciling socialism with European confederation, and I was of course much reassured to see that you and I had come to such similar conclusions. They are not very optimistic, I must say, because it seems extremely difficult to imagine western Europe in any foreseeable near future reverting to a general liberal economy. Back in the 30's I made a study of the whole idea of planning in my book called "The Good Society," and then and there came to the conclusion that planning was unavoidably associated either with war or scarcity and that it could not be reconciled with a free society. I am afraid that conclusion still holds, and that

Europe which is threatened with war and is at the same time poverty stricken is unable to work institutions that depend upon peace and freedom. That's why my obsession continues to grow greater that the objective we must aim at is the expulsion of the Russians from Europe. I can see no hope and no future in a policy of containing them in the middle of Europe. Moreover, I do not believe that a policy aimed at pushing them out of Europe, not of course by an ultimatum and military force but by steady diplomatic pressure and propaganda, is any more dangerous from the point of view of war than the policy of containment.

About Germany and nationalism, my general view is that of course no one can be dogmatically certain as to the future attitude of the Germans, but the safer assumption, it seems to me, is that in the world as it is today they will become again nationalists. I don't doubt that the more thoughtful Germans, from whom you'd naturally hear, don't feel that way. But I cannot believe that they are likely to be the real leaders of the German people once the Germans begin to come out of the shock of defeat and to exert their will to live.

I think about Berlin we are in agreement. The very worst catastrophe of all would be for us to leave Berlin and to abandon the people there. I'd pay almost any price and make almost any concession to remain in Berlin even if remaining there meant that we could only keep a small garrison in the town. . . .

1. Dorothy Thompson, journalist, syndicated columnist for the *New York Herald Tribune*, 1936–41, and thereafter by the Bell Syndicate.

To John Foster Dulles

September 23, 1948

Dear Foster:

I am enclosing a memorandum[1] which I drafted the other day for my own use that might possibly be suggestive to you.

The proposal that we set up a European commission to draft a provisional peace treaty or statute dealing with Germany may have certain other advantages not mentioned in my memorandum:

1. It may provide a constructive way to bring the German question before the United Nations. I think that a proposal of this kind sponsored by the General Assembly would not be in conflict with Article 107 of the Charter.[2]

2. The European commission, which would not include Russia, Britain or ourselves, would be a recognition of a fact which, I think cannot be disputed that if Europe is to be united, the key countries are France, Germany and Poland. I think we must in our own minds accept the fact that Great Britain will not accept the status of a purely European country and enter into a European federation. It will be, perhaps, favorable to a European federation but it will remain somewhat outside of it just as we do. Europe is essentially continental Europe.

3. In my view Europe cannot be federated in the west alone.
  a. Because Great Britain will not enter the federation.
  b. Because western Germany alone cannot be integrated with it.
  c. Because without eastern Germany and Poland the western federation
     would be merely an extremely impotent military alliance.

1. Which directly follows this letter. **2.** "Nothing in the present Charter shall invalidate or
preclude action, in relation to any state which during the Second World War has been an enemy
of any signatory to the present Charter, taken or authorized as a result of that war by the Government's having responsibility for such action."

ON THE NEGOTIATION OF A GERMAN PEACE TREATY

The classic agenda of peace-making consists first in recognizing a government with which to negotiate and then of defining frontiers, reparations and
other matters. This was the procedure adopted by Talleyrand at the Congress
of Vienna.

However, in the case of Germany, the disappearance of government has
created a new problem, different from any before faced by peacemakers. The
disappearance of German government has resulted in the attempt of the Big
Four to agree among themselves on a German settlement. What they have
attempted to agree on primarily, and what has divided them irreconcilably, is
the nature of the German government with which they will make peace.

I tentatively suggest, therefore, that the problem of the nature of the German government be taken from the head of the agenda and that the first
problem considered should be the definition of the frontiers of Germany.

Adopting this procedure will compel the USSR, and also the Western Powers, to take a definite position on the nature of the eastern frontier. (I would
argue that the character of the decision about the eastern frontier will determine fundamentally the character of the German government.)

We may assume that the USSR must support the present Polish boundary.

I shall assume that we support a modification of it.

We may be entirely certain that German nationalism cannot accept the present Polish frontier and that Russian support of it will produce a conflict between German nationalism and Soviet policy and also between Polish policy
and German nationalism.

We must, however, assume as no less certain that German nationalism will
not in the long run accept our position, namely that of a modified Polish
frontier, because that would still entail the loss of much former German territory.

The fact that German nationalism cannot accept either the Russian or the
western version of the eastern boundary of Germany means that Poland must
become dependent on the USSR for maintenance of the frontier. This depen-

dence is of a dual character — Poland depends on the USSR to guarantee the frontier against a German war of revenge, but this guarantee by the USSR to Poland puts Poland at the mercy of the USSR in that a deal between Russia and Germany could always be made at the expense of Poland.

Poland, therefore, cannot be satisfied or secure by the recognition, even in a formal treaty, of her annexations of German territory. She cannot be a truly independent country unless there is a Germany which (a) *can* accept the annexation, or (b) is not *able* to make a deal with the USSR at any time in the future to recover the territory.[1]

Only a German confederation can fill these conditions. For in a German confederation the lost territory would be lost not by Bavaria, not by Westphalia, not by Saxony, but by some of the minor eastern states of the German confederation. Though Germany had been dismembered, though Germany had lost territory, Bavaria would not have lost it, and in so far as German political feeling can be concentrated on Bavaria, Westphalia, etc., etc., an acceptance of the new frontier becomes at least theoretically possible.

A German confederation, which means an association of German states which can act as a unit in foreign affairs only by something approaching unanimity, would be, if not incapable, at least greatly hampered in making a secret deal with the Russians at the expense of Poland. Such a deal can be made only by a central government which has sovereign powers over all Germans.

Moreover, in a confederacy special arrangements can be made with certain of the key states of the confederacy, such as Bavaria or Westphalia, which would give them strong inducements not to enter into a policy of the revival of German nationalism. It will be easier to integrate some of the German states with the west than to integrate Germany as a whole.

II.

This reasoning leads to a tentative suggestion which is that since Four Power decisions as to the future of Germany have failed and seem impossible, they should now be replaced by negotiation in which the three non-European powers — the USSR, Great Britain and the USA — retire into the background and call upon the continental neighbors of Germany to prepare the provisional draft of a German treaty. The neighbors involved would be France, the Benelux countries, Poland, Czechoslovakia, and the German states speaking through their Minister Presidents.

It is conceivable, as a further development of this idea, that the United Nations might propose the establishment of a European commission, minus Great Britain, USSR and USA, to prepare the tentative draft of the German peace treaty. This commission would be the embryo of a European federation, or at least of a European political system. The function of this commission would be to propose a delimitation of the frontiers of Germany and the plan of a European statute governing the relations among the participants, namely the European neighbors of Germany and the German states.

This plan would be the core of the eventual treaty. The core would be surrounded by guarantees of disarmament, of civil liberties and the like, which would be underwritten by the great powers.

1. Both emphases Lippmann's.

To Jean Monnet [1]

September 30, 1948

Dear Jean:

. . . I think that it is important that French thought should be put on the inevitable fact that a military retirement from the center of Germany, if not a withdrawal from the whole of Germany, is, over a time, the only alternative to war. I realize that people in France are afraid of the idea because of the feeling that they will be left defenseless if the American army were withdrawn to the United States. But it does not follow at all that a solution of the German occupation problem requires the withdrawal of American forces to the United States.

I think I am justified in saying that responsible people here are thinking of a withdrawal for the first period to the Rhine and the Oder, and that there is opinion which could be developed, if the French wanted it, for some prolonged military support by Americans over a still longer period. By support I do not mean merely military lend lease; I mean the maintenance of American combat forces at strategic points where their presence would guarantee the automatic support of the United States in case of aggression. Personally, I feel that some arrangement of that sort would be better even than an elaborate rearmament of France which, I should imagine, would put a new and extremely heavy strain upon the French economy. . . .

1. Jean Monnet by this time had become the first statesman of Europe, the leading protagonist of economic cooperation among the Western nations of the continent, and the main intellectual force behind the establishment in 1949 of the European coal and steel authority, which led ultimately to the European Economic Community (the Common Market) in 1957.

To Warren R. Austin

November 1, 1948

Dear Warren:

. . . I am writing to you now . . . to tell you that I have been making some inquiries about this extremely troublesome business of the trusteeship in relation to our own strategic needs in the Pacific. All in all that surely is the most delicate and difficult problem that we shall have to deal with at this session of the U.N. We are caught between our professions under the Atlantic

Charter, and the like, on the one hand, and our own vital needs in an area which no administration can surrender after it was captured at such cost, without turning American public opinion against the United Nations itself.

My suggestion is that we avoid isolating the question of the Jap mandated islands and focusing the attention of the whole world upon our claims. I am afraid we may be tempted to do this because in the settlement of this whole war we are proceeding piecemeal, rather than under some general plan. Here the piecemeal procedure would work to our great disadvantage and to our infinite embarrassment. The alternative is to take the position that the disposition of the mandated islands and of the islands that are to be ceded, namely Okinawa, etc., of the Kuriles and Sakhalin, are part of a general settlement with Japan in the Far East. They should not be the subject of separate agreements. This seems to be the only way we can hope in the end to square our public commitments and our strategical defense.

A general settlement in the Far East will inevitably involve concessions by everyone, and we can hope to obtain concessions in our favor in such an arrangement far better than if we ask for them separately. Moreover, in a general arrangement the Navy may feel that it can make some concessions in the form, if not in the substance, which it will not be very disposed to make now.

It seems to me clear that we must find a way to postpone a showdown on those mandated islands and on Okinawa. To take the position that they are only part of the general settlement of the Far East seems to me inherently true and also an effective way of gaining time.[1]

1. In 1947 the Security Council had made the United States trustee for the Pacific islands formerly under a Japanese mandate. Those islands and others of Lippmann's concern in this letter did not become a subject of important international discussion again until the negotiation of a formal peace treaty with Japan during 1951.

To Jean Monnet

January 10, 1949

Dear Jean:

I am sure you are able to interpret the changes in the State Department for yourself, but you may be interested, nevertheless, in hearing from me about them.

In my view, the clue to the proper interpretation is to note that the appointment of Acheson was accompanied by the appointment of James Webb as Under Secretary.[1] Webb, of course, has never worked in foreign affairs, but as Director of the Budget, he has had an intimate view of the administrative disorganization of the State Department and the other agencies which affect foreign policy, such as the Economic Cooperation Administration, Treasury and the military services. Undoubtedly, the proper interpretation to be put upon these events is not that they herald a sudden dramatic change of policy in the popular sense of the term, but the reorganization of the machinery by which foreign policy is made and operated. In the long run this will affect the tone and the temper of the policy even if it doesn't affect the main objectives.

There are more critical appointments to be made, and much will depend on who is selected. But the plan of reorganization of the State Department calls for another Under Secretary of State, not yet named, who will be the political head of the Department under Acheson; also for the appointment of four Assistant Secretaries of State, who will deal each with one of the great areas of the world. Until these appointments have been made, and the reorganization has been carried out, it is not possible for the State Department to assume real control of foreign policy, taking away the power which has been allowed to drift into the hands of the military forces and into the hands of other agencies of the government.

In connection with the plans for Western European Union, there is visible on the horizon a problem which may become of very great consequence. It is reasonably evident that the western European countries, all of them colonial powers, are working on some kind of secret or tacit arrangement to support each other in Asia. This has been evident in the Indonesian case;[2] it is also evident in Palestine, and there are some other strong indications to that effect.

Responsible people abroad ought not to underestimate the dangers of such a policy under which Western Union assumes to defend democracy in Europe becomes an agreement to maintain old style imperialism in Asia. The obvious advantages that this gives to communist propaganda need not be labored. What should not be forgotten, however, is that the American people are deeply and fundamentally anti-imperialist themselves, and if they get the idea that they are participating in an arrangement to support imperialism, the moral foundations of Western Union will be very greatly imperiled. I wonder if this aspect of the matter is realized at the Quai D'Orsay. I think it would be well if you looked into it, but please do not bring me into the matter at this stage. . . .

1. On January 7, 1949, Truman announced Marshall's resignation as secretary of state and the nomination of Dean G. Acheson to succeed him, with James E. Webb nominated as undersecretary and second in command. By the end of June, other senior State Department officers had come to include Deputy Undersecretary Dean Rusk, Counselor and Director of Policy Planning George F. Kennan, and Ambassador-at-Large Philip C. Jessup, as well as eight assistant secretaries, all of lesser distinction. 2. The Dutch were attempting to sustain their rule in Indonesia, but on January 28, 1949, the UN Security Council called for an immediate cease-fire there and the transfer of sovereignty to the United States of Indonesia by July 1, 1950. The Dutch agreed to negotiate and in November to relinquish sovereignty. Until 1947 British troops had assisted the Dutch in Java, one of the islands of the new republic.

To Sumner Welles

January 28, 1949

Dear Sumner:

. . . I think it is increasingly accepted that Clay will have to be replaced when it can be done without losing face, but no one can think of a successor.[1] I have been talking to a lot of people about the North Atlantic Pact, but I am very much afraid the thing has got considerably confused and distorted by the military people who want to establish bases all over the place. It was their insistence on getting Norway in in order that we could establish air bases and sea bases in southern Norway that caused the whole Scandinavian crisis and may have disrupted the growing prospect of regional unity among the Scandinavians. They are also continuing to meddle with Spain. But the most serious complication is the fact, which will of course be denied vehemently, that eventually the North Atlantic Pact is to include western Germany rearmed.[2]

I hear also that after ratification of the North Atlantic Pact there is a proposal to make a declaration guaranteeing Greece, Turkey, and Iran by the North Atlantic nations. In my view, this would add nothing whatever to the security of those three countries, which are already guaranteed not only by the United Nations Charter but by the de facto attitude of the United States. To bring France, Belgium and the Netherlands into the guarantee is, I think, to confuse matters greatly. Behind it there is, I believe, the dangerous complication that the Western Union powers are also the colonial powers. We have seen that in respect to Indonesia, Palestine and the Italian colonies these powers have had some kind of working agreement to support one another in the Security Council against efforts to make the will of the United Nations prevail. . . .

1. Truman appointed John J. McCloy United States military governor and high commissioner for Germany, a post he held through much of 1952. **2.** The North Atlantic Treaty, signed in Washington on April 4, 1949, included Great Britain, France, the Benelux countries, Italy, Portugal, Denmark, Iceland, Norway, Canada, and the United States. It provided for mutual assistance against aggression in the North Atlantic area and for collaboration under the direction of a North Atlantic council in military training and strategic planning. In January 1950, the United States agreed to provide arms to the other signatories. Germany became a member of the alliance in 1954; Greece and Turkey had joined in 1952.

To George F. Kennan[1]

February 1, 1949

Dear George:

I am one in whom l'esprit de l'escalier is strongest the morning after. Therefore, these few notes.

In regard to the transfer to the State Department of responsibilities for

Germany, it seems to me important that the Department should not merely take responsibility for dealing with the consequences of the present policy. For then if the policy fails, the Department will be blamed for the failure, probably on the ground that it did not carry out the policy effectively and resolutely. The transfer should take place under circumstances in which the general public has been made to understand, what only an informed few now understand, that the existing policy is not successful and that a change is necessary. The Department should not come in to manage an enterprise headed for bankruptcy but to reorganize the enterprise.

For the past few months I have been thinking how the circumstances could develop. It seems to me that given the attitude of Congress, the prestige of General Clay and the army, the division of opinion in the Department itself, it was asking too much to look to civilians like the President, Dean Acheson, and yourself to reorient policy on a subject about which public opinion is so ill-informed and misinformed.

It seems to me that this is a situation calling for independent inquiry and independent judgment by a commission of men who possess personal authority. They should be men taken from private life — not directly from Pentagon, State, or Congress. . . . I am thinking of men like Jessup, McCloy, Allen Dulles, Tom Finletter (when he leaves ECA), and with some question marks, Eisenhower, Conant, Sumner Welles.[2] A report by them could facilitate the transition from Pentagon to State, absorb the extraneous but difficult problems of prestige and of responsibility for the past, and provide the intellectual foundation for a re-orientation.

I feel strongly that when the State Department assumes control it should be on an unequivocal set of principles — namely,

1. That the German problem is soluble only (as per your memorandum) within the framework of a European (not a west European) system. This is essential as respects the Germans, as respects Poland, Czechoslovakia — etc. It is a positive and constructive way of refusing to recognize the permanence of the Iron Curtain. We should never be in the position of accepting the Iron Curtain, always in the position of insisting that it must be lifted.

2. That the partition of Germany and of Europe is, therefore, transitory. We must never allow the Russians to be the champions of German unity. We must be the champions, and put them in the position of preventing it.

3. That the liquidation of military government and the *scheduled*,[3] though gradual, withdrawal of occupation troops is a real and present objective, not a remote and theoretical one. We must put the Russians in the position of being the power which won't evacuate Germany, and therefore won't liberate eastern Europe from the grip of the Red Army. (The western anxiety about *our* leaving Europe and withdrawing across the Atlantic can be met by the North Atlantic Security Pact. In fact that is its chief advantage, that it supplies the juridical basis for remaining in Europe.)

I would now like to summarize what seems to me certain essentials of an interim policy:

1. The formula used last summer in the Moscow negotiation, as respects a C.F.M.[4] meeting when the blockade is lifted, is too generalized. We should say frankly to the Russians that a C.F.M. cannot now make an overall German settlement — because the crucial problem of the character of the German government cannot be solved by the occupying powers. It must be solved by the Germans within an agreed framework. (This is a very strong position vis-à-vis the Germans. It also puts on ice all kinds of questions which divide us from the Russians, and divide the western allies among themselves.)

2. The next C.F.M. should therefore meet *after* discussion has brought agreement on its agenda. The agenda should be devoted to a revision of the Potsdam Protocol in the light of four years' developments. The C.F.M. should aim to agree on a new occupation statute for all of Germany (i.e. your proposal) — 1. withdrawal to the periphery; 2. a neutral commandant of police (number and arms to be stipulated); 3. transfer of authority from military government to the German Laender, jointly and severally; 4. a trade agreement covering exports and imports; 5. a Ten Power pact (Big Four plus contiguous small countries) for the neutralization (under Article 107 of the Charter) of Germany during the period when there is no de jure German government recognized by the great powers and say two-thirds of the Assembly; 6. review of Potsdam Protocol to require that the Council of Foreign Ministers (acting through commissioners) shall be in permanent session until a German peace treaty is ratified.

Forgive the length of this letter. But it covers a lot of ground.

1. Kennan and Lippmann, always respectful of each other's ability in spite of their earlier disagreements about containment, were becoming increasingly good friends and increasingly of a common view about policy in Germany and about Russian intentions, which neither man believed required American military force in Europe as a check. **2.** Of the men listed, all "establishment" figures, Jessup was in the State Department; McCloy about to go to Germany; Allen W. Dulles (Foster Dulles's brother) was head of the Central Intelligence Agency; Thomas K. Finletter, then with the Economic Co-operation Administration, was to become secretary of the air force; Eisenhower was president of Columbia University; Conant, of Harvard; and Welles in retirement living in Washington, D.C. **3.** All emphases in this letter are Lippmann's. **4.** Council of Foreign Ministers.

To Sumner Welles

February 3, 1949

Dear Sumner:

. . . As you have probably seen from the papers, Royall[1] on behalf of the Department of the Army has formally suggested the transfer of occupation authority to the State Department. Entirely between ourselves, the other day

George Kennan told me in a long talk that though the method of transferring responsibility had not been worked out, he would assume from now on that it would be worked out and that he was now responsible for the working out of a German policy. I told him that, desirable as it was for the State Department to take over, there were some questions as to the manner in which the transfer was effected.

It seems to me very important that the Department should not merely take responsibility for dealing with the consequences of the present policy. For then if the policy fails, as it is very likely to, the Department will be blamed for the failure probably on the ground that it did not carry out the policy effectively and resolutely. Therefore, it seems to me imperative that the transfer should take place under circumstances in which the general public has been made to understand, what only an informed few — including Kennan himself — now understand, that the existing policy is not successful and that a change is necessary. Some way must be found for making it clear before the transfer that the change is necessary, so that the change is not carried along on the responsibility of the Department itself. The prestige of the Army in Congress is so great, and the suspicion of the civilians is so strong, that I think Acheson and Kennan would be very unwise indeed to take over a more or less bankrupt enterprise as if they were merely continuing the old management, instead of coming in as receivers in bankruptcy.

I think there is no doubt that the Atlantic Pact was left by Marshall and Lovett in an extremely confused and dangerous condition. My own diagnosis is that the formation of the Pact, which cannot be understood from the mere text but must be interpreted in the light of the military arrangements which would follow it, is dominated by the attempt to fuse two strategical conceptions. These two strategical conceptions were in conflict last spring. On the one hand, there was the Pentagon strategy, which was to abandon the continent of Europe up to the Pyrenees and to fight the war against the heart of Russia by long range bombardment from Scandinavia and from the Middle East. On the other hand, there was the continental, and particularly French insistence, that western Europe be defended against invasion and occupation.

The arrangements being made under Montgomery[2] are a response to this French demand. The French, however, do not really trust him because they will never believe in a continental army commanded by a British general. The memory of Dunkirk is too strong in their minds.

On the other hand, the insistence on our part that Norway and Denmark must enter the Pact, the persistent flirtation with Franco,[3] and some aspects of things we have done in the Middle East, reflect the original strategical conception of the Pentagon. It is this conception that has led to what I think is a most dangerous move on our part in respect to Norway and Denmark.

Under Lovett's management of the negotiations the Pact can hardly be described as anything but a military coalition. It is certainly not a regional arrangement under the United Nations Charter, and I understand that in the drafting of the Pact that theory has been abandoned anyway. It will be very difficult to demonstrate that the Pact, since it is not a regional arrangement, is consistent with the letter or the spirit of the Charter. I get the impression that Acheson is by no means clear as to where he stands or how to proceed with the work which he inherited. In any event, I hope the Senate will insist on a thorough debate.

One of the troubles with a thorough debate is that we have been committed much too far in the negotiations with the European countries before the proposition had been discussed with the leading members of Congress, and put rightly before American public opinion. The situation has been created where the Pact can hardly be amended, or greatly postponed, without opening us to the charge that we have reneged on a commitment made by the Acting Secretary of State and that we are retreating in the face of Russian opposition. I feel that we have lost a good deal of our freedom of choice. . . .

1. Kenneth Royall, then undersecretary of war.   **2.** British Field Marshal Viscount Bernard Montgomery of Alamein.   **3.** Francisco Franco, Spanish Fascist dictator, was eager for a Marshall Plan for Spain, which the United States Congress recommended the next year.

To Quincy A. Wright

February 14, 1949

Dear Quincy:

By the time this letter reaches you, you may have seen my article which will appear in the *New York Herald Tribune* on February 15th, called "The Buffer Belt." You will see from it that my main concern about the North Atlantic Pact is to limit it to nations not in immediate contact with the Soviet orbit. I would like to admit to membership only Iceland, Portugal, and Ireland, if she wishes to come in. Greenland would be included as the Danes are quite willing to say privately on the general theory that Greenland is in the Western Hemisphere and is entitled to have special security arrangements different from those of Denmark itself.

Before arguing my reasons for thinking that this is a better solution than the supplementary treaty under Article 51, let me deal with the point raised in the first paragraph of your letter, namely, the danger that we are underwriting the imperialism of the western powers in Asia. I think, of course, as you do, that it is exceedingly important that we should not do that. But I do not believe that forming the Atlantic Pact will necessarily make it more difficult for us to pursue an independent policy or that not forming it would make it easier. The best way to pursue an independent policy is to pursue it, taking a definite line in Indonesia, Indochina and perhaps later in Malaya, openly associating ourselves with Nehru's India and with Australia in a general Asiatic attitude. Moreover, I believe we shall in the fairly near future be compelled to discuss with the French and the Dutch the fact that so large a part of our aid under the Marshall Plan is syphoned off into the Indochinese and the Indonesian war. In other words, I believe that we must deal directly with the problem of not associating ourselves with the western colonial powers, in their reactionary policies in Asia.

Now I come to my reasons for thinking that the limited pact is preferable to the generalized treaty under Article 51. The limited pact can rationally be defended as a regional arrangement, not different in principle from the network of pacts which the Soviet Union has with the satellite countries (I am sorry to say, however, that in the drafting of the pact we are not making it a regional arrangement under Article 52 because we don't wish to get the Security Council associated with its operation, but are bringing it in under Article 51, with which it is, in spirit at least, not in harmony).

The limited pact that I have in mind combined with a policy of buffer states or neutralized areas in Scandinavia, Germany, Austria, and Italy can honestly be defended as a defensive arrangement without aggressive or provocative features. The same would not be true of the pact if it includes Norway and certainly not if it includes Germany.

The reason I don't like the supplementary treaty under Article 51 is that this scheme was devised to circumvent the Charter of the United Nations, and create a new United Nations with Russia and the satellites left out of it. If the procedure of such a treaty were adopted, and it were opened to signature of all the nations, the western powers would undoubtedly use it as an attempt to form a military coalition all around the periphery of the Soviet Union. It would, I believe, because it lacked any geographical limits and because it had no buffer region between it and the Soviet Union, become a far more dangerous instrument than the limited Atlantic Pact. . . .

I would argue that under the supplementary treaty the bi-polarity would be made absolute. Whereas, with a limited Atlantic Pact, another Scandinavian Pact, perhaps a Southeast Asia Pact, the Rio Pact, and perhaps also a Mediterranean Pact, there would be a greater diffusion of power centers. . . .

To Russell C. Leffingwell

March 1, 1949

Dear Russell:

. . . You must realize that my question arose out of the doubt as to whether a free economy could remain free, if a very large proportion of the product had to be diverted to public or military uses. I think you will agree that in war time the amount that had to be diverted was so large that controls became necessary.

My question was based on the apprehension that if the public expenditures rose very considerably above what they are now, they would again become necessary even though we were not at war.

Leaving the question aside, ... I am convinced that the question of war or peace hangs upon the Soviet willingness to engage in a general war and not on the strength of the local defenses in any particular part of the world. For that reason I have never believed in the policy of containment as preached by the State Department and as practiced here and there, but not everywhere. Above all, I do not believe in the possibility of creating an army in western Europe capable of fighting the Red Army on equal terms, and I feel sure that the attempt to create it will not only exhaust western Europe and strain us, but probably would throw western Europe into political convulsions. Defense of western Europe will not rest, it seems to me, upon the size of the armies created under Field Marshal Montgomery, but upon the overall power of the United States and what it is capable of becoming within a reasonably short time after the outbreak of war.

To Bernard Berenson

March 1, 1949

Dear B. B.:

. . . I find myself increasingly preoccupied with the problem of how Europe, including of course Eastern Europe, can in Churchill's words be delivered from the Soviet power without war. For it seems to me self-evident that if a world war starts, we probably would be able to destroy the Soviet state, but that in the process the remnants of the social order in Europe as a whole would also be destroyed, and that therefore while Soviet power would decline, communism would spread. The lesson of Asia in this respect seems to me clear enough. The spread of communism through China to Southeast Asia is not the result of communist propaganda or of Soviet power. It is the result of the destruction of the old regime, leaving a vacuum which the communists fill. The material cause of the spread of communism in Asia was the early Japanese victories. They destroyed nationalist China, the British, the Dutch and the French imperial positions, and though Japan was completely defeated by the United States, it has never been possible since then to restore British, French and Dutch or Chinese authority.

The same thing, I am convinced, would happen in Europe if war breaks out. The defeat of the Soviets would not prevent the existing order in Europe from being fatally destroyed.

Therefore, we face the extraordinarily difficult task of developing military power sufficient to deter the Russians from aggression, sufficient to exert pressure which will in the end cause them to retire from Europe, and yet not of a kind which would provoke a war of desperation on the part of the Soviet Union. I don't know whether we'll be able to do that, or whether, if we had the power, we would have the wisdom. . . .

I may say that my first instincts during the election which were that a change was necessary are being heavily confirmed by Truman's conduct since the election. The present struggle which he has precipitated in Congress, ostensibly over civil rights for the negroes, really raises the gravest constitutional issues which have been presented in modern times.[1] For if the Senatorial power to filibuster is destroyed, then the Senate can legislate by simple majorities, and our system, as Macauley once said, will be all sails and no anchors. . . .

1. In 1948 Truman had urged Congress to enact legislation recommended by the Committee on Civil Rights he had appointed. He asked for a permanent Fair Employment Practices Committee, federal laws prohibiting lynching and the poll tax, and stronger civil rights statutes. Those courageous proposals, which would have accomplished more for American blacks than any developments since the era of Reconstruction, aroused the anger of the South and provoked the split from the Democratic party in 1948 of the unyielding Dixiecrats. In 1949 Truman again recommended civil rights legislation as part of his Fair Deal. Again he engendered fierce opposition, which was expressed in the successful filibuster in the Senate against the FEPC bill. In this letter, written before that filibuster, Lippmann spoke the counsel of inactive caution that suited the purposes of Southern senators. His anxieties and theirs reflected their dismay at measures the House of Representatives had taken to speed civil rights legislation; see R. J. Donovan, *Tumultuous Years* (New York, 1982), p. 118.

To J. William Fulbright

March 11, 1949

Dear Bill:

It isn't even a question of our insisting or promoting political federation in Europe. What has actually happened is that even the modest amount of economic cooperation and mutual help called for in the ECA legislation has, for all practical purposes, collapsed. Everyone in Europe knows that, but apparently no one in this country has realized it.

What we've got now in Europe are eighteen or nineteen separate programs of self help subsidized by the United States.

There is no reasonable doubt that this is the deliberate policy of Cripps[1] and the British government. They have never liked that aspect of the Marshall Plan which required them to act as one among several European nations. They don't regard themselves as European, they do not wish to stand in the same queue with the others, and they have as a matter of national policy maneuvered themselves out of a collective effort for European recovery. Cripps admitted to me privately that he would much rather go it alone, and not be obligated to make agreements with the other European nations. The fact is that our people have accepted this result without serious resistance.

Now it may be that European cooperation and mutual help, such as Congress thought it was voting for, is not feasible or desirable. I don't agree with that view, but I can see that a man might take that view. What I think is reprehensible is that this major defeat of a declared American purpose should be glossed over and hidden from the American people, and from the Congress. . . .

1. Sir Stafford Cripps was then chancellor of the exchequer in Attlee's government. That government did succeed in preserving a "special relationship" with the United States, though neither that friendship nor Marshall Plan aid to Britain could forestall the necessity in September 1949 to devalue the pound sterling. The devaluation arose in large part because the British in 1949 could find only an inadequate market for their products in the United States, where a recession reduced both consumer and capital spending. The British were not alone at that time in cultivating their nationalism at the expense of cooperation with other countries in OEEC. The force of nationalism was no less strong in France.

To Thomas K. Finletter

April 18, 1949

Dear Tom:

. . . I am, as usual, much more bearish about the famous German solution (the latest of the famous German solutions, I might add) than anyone else seems to be, except that I am glad to say George Kennan agrees. I don't see how that arrangement can last, how anyone can think it could last, and therefore I wonder whether Jack McCloy will, when he faces up to it, really want to undertake a job that is essentially a job of liquidating an entanglement rather than of constructing something on a settled basis.

Here there doesn't seem to be any doubt that the Senate will eventually ratify the Atlantic Pact, but on the question of money for arming Europe there is going to be a great big fight. I think myself that the Administration ought not to ask for additional appropriations, but that it ought to ask simply for an authorization from Congress to distribute arms up to say a billion dollars, paying for them out of their military budget, which is already grossly inflated. I am in favor of that procedure not merely to save money (though there is a limit to what the American Congress ought to be asked to appropriate), chiefly because I think it is psychologically and politically desirable that the ratification of the Pact should not be followed by an increase in the general costs of the cold war. When you add together our military budget and the ECA and all the other foreign subsidies that we are providing, the total should be regarded as sufficient to finance the new commitments by re-allocating the funds, and it should not require an addition to them.

I think that is desirable for all kinds of internal American reasons, and also because if the total cold war budget is no larger than it was before the Pact, and if it could be made symbolically even a little bit smaller, it would be the most convincing evidence we could provide that we regard the Pact as a real accomplishment in the interests of peace. If the budget has to be increased after the Pact, it will be very hard to answer the feeling that it doesn't inaugurate a still more intense phase of the race of armaments — and that rather knocks into a cocked hat the argument that the Pact works for security. I myself am convinced that if the Russians ever intended to start an overt war, they will not start it when it is certain that they cannot win the war unless they defeat the United States. Therefore, the security of all Europe is greater than it was once the Pact has been ratified, and that security ought to be confirmed by not increasing our appropriations, and if possible by reducing them.[1]

On the whole I think Dean is doing well. His greatest omission has been, in my opinion, the failure to present the Pact before the General Assembly of the United Nations in a convincing, dignified and persuasive way. I hate to see the Pact presented in the form of high school rebuttal to Gromyko's[2] arguments. A much better case for it can be made than has been made, and I wish to heaven Dean would put his mind on it and make it. It was also extremely discourteous of the Foreign Ministers, who were all here in Washington when the Assembly met, not go to there and to stay there for at least a week. . . .

1. Though President Truman remained wedded to an austere military budget, he changed his mind in 1950, partly because of the conviction of the chairman of the Council of Economic Advisers, Leon Keyserling, that heavy deficit spending would reinforce the economy, partly because of the militant views of the National Security Council as incorporated in its then secret assessment of American interests and policy, NSC 68. Those two influences and their confluence receive admirable analysis in J. L. Gaddis, *Strategies of Containment* (New York, 1982), ch. 4. The anxieties of the Joint Chiefs derived in major measure from the complete triumph of the Chinese Communists in 1948 and their proclamation of the People's Republic of China on August 1 of that year, to be followed in 1950 by the Sino-Soviet Alliance; from the Soviet success in developing an atomic bomb, which was reported in September 1949; and from reports of extensive Soviet espionage within the United States during World War II, particularly espionage at the Manhattan Project, which had developed the American atomic bomb.   2. Andrei Gromyko, Soviet deputy foreign minister.

To John Foster Dulles[1]

April 25, 1949

Dear Foster:

. . . You are dead right, of course, about the false hopes created at the time the United Nations was founded. I agree entirely with everything you say about world government. I think you are right in saying that the United Nations has been a bulwark against indirect aggression and I like the implications of what you say about the Atlantic Pact.

If there is any part of it that I would like to see developed more and somewhat differently, it is the part where you justify the Pact in relation to the Charter. It seems to me the plain truth that the original Charter did not envisage anything like the Pact. I know that because long before the Dumbarton Oaks Conference, while Hull's experts were working on the subject, I was writing my book, *U.S. War Aims*, and I had many discussions with Pasvolsky[2] and others. I had then come to the conclusion that a universal association of separate sovereign states was an unworkable idea and that the true universal society would be a society of communities of states. That, in fact, is how the thing is developing and the Atlantic Pact is one but not the only one of the communities of states who now participate more or less as political units in the world organization. The Soviet group existed before the Atlantic group recognized its own existence. There is obviously an Arab group. There is probably going to emerge a South Asian group. I think the right way to justify the Pact is not to say that it is in accord with the letter or even with the original spirit of the Charter. But that it is in accord with the historical development of events and that the letter of the Charter will have to adjust itself to these historical developments. I think that line of argument is more candid and also more convincing. . . .

1. Dulles was again to attend a meeting of the Council of Foreign Ministers, scheduled for Paris in May 1949.   **2.** Leo Pasvolsky had been in charge of the State Department's postwar planning during World War II.

Memorandum for John Foster Dulles

May 19, 1949

When I saw Phil Jessup just before he left for Paris I asked him whether we intended to take the initiative by presenting a western program, or whether we would disclose our position in response to offers and proposals of the Soviet government. He said the matter was still unsettled. But in this memorandum I shall assume that the U.K., France, and the U.S.A. will not have had time to agree on a comprehensive program, and that, therefore, we may expect the Soviets to make the initial proposals on the five problems named in Section 8 of the Warsaw Declaration.[1] They are: (1) demilitarization, (2) four power control "for a definite time" of heavy industry in the Ruhr, (3) a government for the whole of Germany, (4) a peace treaty followed by withdrawal of occupation troops within one year, (5) reparations.

On the principle that you cannot beat a horse with no horse, we should, if the British and French will agree, make a statement of purposes and principles which includes, and then transcends and supersedes in men's minds, the attractive and reasonable elements of the Warsaw Declaration. We should not reject it, or rebut it merely on the ground that it is impractical or that we distrust the Soviets. For that would leave us in the impossible position of appearing to wish to perpetuate the status quo — the partition of Germany and of Europe, endless military occupation, no genuine self-government, the abandonment of eastern Europe behind the Iron Curtain, a permanently subsidized western Germany because western Germany is not viable, prolongation of the dangerous anomaly in Berlin. We, not the Russians, must be the champions of a unified Germany in a unified European system, and of a free Europe, which is impossible, indeed a contradiction in terms, as long as Europe is occupied by two, and if you count Britain, three non-European powers.

I think that our reply to the five points of the Warsaw Declaration should in general terms be as follows:

1. *Demilitarization.*

That we favor the demilitarization of Germany, not only in terms of weapons of war but in terms of its right to make alliances; that, therefore, we shall not admit Germany into the Atlantic Pact provided there is a stipulation in the peace treaty that Germany may make no political alliances of any kind and shall participate in no political system except with the consent of all her neighbors. We should say that we favor the demilitarization and neutralization of Germany because we hope to see a free and peaceable Germany take an equal place within the framework of an all-European system.

2. *The Ruhr.*

We should stand for European agreements. To the Russian demand for four power control, we should reply that we regard three power control as provisional and to be superseded by European agreements, perhaps under the aegis of the U.N., perhaps under the aegis of a Council of Europe, within a short time after the conclusion of a peace treaty.

(I think this is the best position because (a) we do not want the Russians in the Ruhr, (b) three power control won't work long or work well, and will concentrate German irredentism against the West, (c) because the principle of co-operation based on reciprocal advantage is better than control by the victors — who will be suspected by the Germans and by each other of being carpetbaggers.)

3. *A German Government.*

Our strongest position is to recognize, not to fudge and conceal these basic principles:

(a) That the victors cannot create a free government for the vanquished, and that no German government formed under military occupation will be accepted by the Germans as a legitimate German government. (I call your attention to the fact that this principle is explicitly incorporated in the Bonn basic law — in the preamble and in the final article.)

(b) That a valid and lasting peace treaty should be one negotiated with a legitimate German government — and not open, therefore, to the charge that like the Versailles Treaty it is a "Diktat."

The problem, therefore, is how to arrive at a legitimate German government. This is the point at which we can most effectively and sincerely contend that the objective of this Council of Foreign Ministers is not the conclusion of a peace treaty but an agreement on a new Protocol, amending and superseding Potsdam, to govern relations with Germany in the period of transition from military government to the formation of a German government.

My own view is that we should say flatly — and that we shall be widely applauded in Germany if we do — that the Council of Foreign Ministers cannot in any sense be a Constituent Assembly for the German nation. Since military government should be liquidated at once in all zones, authority should pass to the de facto German authorities in all zones, and that it will be the task of the German authorities to form a government. When the Germans have a government which they, by a free vote, have recognized as legitimate, which has been recognized by us as legitimate, there shall be a peace conference to conclude a treaty.

The criterion of legitimacy from the Allied point of view shall be:

(1) that it is a government de facto, and that it is by due process — such as free elections and ratification of the Laender — a de jure government;

(2) that it commits the German state to the Charter of the U.N. and makes violation of that charter an offense under German law;

(3) that it accepts demilitarization and neutralization, and makes violation an offense under German law;

(4) that it has a bill of rights, and makes the violation of it an offense both under German and under international law.

[a period of time — at least a year — would be required for the formation of the German government. This Interim Period would be governed by the new Protocol, referred to previously, which I shall discuss more fully in the next section. I call your attention to the advantages of this procedure:

(a) in the Interim Period, freed of military government, the real forces in German political life, which are now obscured and suppressed, will begin to show themselves;

(b) Soviet intentions will be more definitely disclosed and tested;

(c) the West will have time to consolidate its position through ERP, the Atlantic Pact, the Statute of Europe;

(d) the long term economic trends will be much clearer, especially as to the viability of Europe;

(e) the Far Eastern situation will be clearer;

(f) there will have been time to make necessary arrangements for creating confidence and a sense of security in France and western Europe when, as it must eventually, the German occupation ends;

(g) we shall be definitely out of the untenable position of appearing to want to divide Germany and Europe, to perpetuate the occupation and to incorporate Germany as a satellite in the military system of the West;

(h) finally, and above all, it may enable the Council to adjourn with something definite and promising accomplished, and avoid the danger of total disagreement on the ultimate settlement.]

4. *Military occupation and the withdrawal of troops.*

We should take our stand on the need for a military agreement in the Protocol for the Interim Period — proposing for that period (1) a reduction in the size of the occupying armies and (2) a redeployment.

It is greatly to our interest to bring about a reduction in the size of the armies. If the Russian striking force outside the Soviet Union is, (I do not know the exact figures), say, 40 divisions, a reduction to 20 would immediately enhance the security of western Europe. For western Europe can mobilize 20 divisions quickly but not forty. A reduction of the American forces would make no difference. For our forces are token forces anyway, and as respects the Red Army, their function is that of a screen which if penetrated will bring the whole American force into action. This purpose would be served as well by a smaller force as by the present force.

If the American air force doctrine is correct — that it can disrupt a mobilization in Russia — then the size of the Russian forces already mobilized and deployed *outside*[2] of Russia is of critical importance. The smaller it is, the greater the security of Europe.

We should also propose a redeployment following immediately after the liquidation of military government and the recognition of the de facto German authorities. Our first concern here should be to get the Russian troops away from the approaches to Berlin, so that the blockade cannot be re-imposed. We shall not have "won the battle of Berlin" unless we achieve this much. That will mean, I should suppose, at the minimum a withdrawal of all occupation troops (except the equivalent of legation guards for the High Commission offices) from the core of Germany.

After the liberation of Berlin, our next military objective should be to get the Russian troops behind a line where they do not need to have lines of supply running through Poland, where they are not in near contact with Austria and Czechoslovakia. That is the great virtue of the original plan to withdraw the armies to the area of the ports — Stettin, Bremen and Hamburg. The only defect in that plan is that it would in the eyes of the French remove the American screen between them and the Russians and Germans. The plan could therefore be amended by placing some American forces on the left bank of the Rhine and perhaps in the Saar.

Besides the reduction of the forces and their redeployment in the Interim Period, we must provide for German internal security. We should propose giving to the German authorities the right to create police forces and a constabulary — without military aviation or heavy arms — sufficient to liquidate the para-military organizations which the Protocol should outlaw.

If the Russians refuse to liquidate their eastern force, we should tell them we shall authorize and help the western Germans to equip a considerably larger force. The position will not be like Korea, which has no military traditions and no reserve of veterans. As the west Germans are three times as numerous as the east Germans, we have the whiphand in this argument. But our real objective should not be to have competing forces — which might bring about civil war — but a new force created by and owing allegiance to the new provisional government.

5. *The Frontiers.*

Since the eastern annexations are critical for the ultimate relations of Germany, Poland, Russia and Czechoslovakia, our best position for the time being, I believe, is not to share the responsibility of settling an almost insoluble question. The relation between Germany and eastern Europe can never be finally stabilized as long as the frontier question remains. We should by inaction exploit that fact. We should avoid promising the Germans territory which we cannot return to them. We should avoid participating in or conniving at another partition of Poland. We should place the Soviets in the position where they cannot make an alliance with Germany without outraging the world by a partition of Poland.

If we are pressed to state our views, we should say that the problem is in the first instance a German-Polish-Czech-Russian problem, which we hope will be settled amicably and justly, with regard to the general peace of a united Europe, but that we did not create the problem, and do not feel it our duty to solve it.

6. *Reparations.*

I do not have definite suggestions to make beyond saying that our general line should be to submerge the reparations question in generous proposals for the development of East-West trade. I have an impression from the Warsaw Declaration that the Russians no longer regard reparations as a principal objective.

7. *American Withdrawal.*

Preparations must be made by discussion with the French and the British for definite arrangements under the Atlantic Pact against the time when, in order to get all the Russians out of Germany and Poland, we must leave Germany.

We should recognize the French demand for an American screen to make the Atlantic Pact automatic. The problem here is to find a place to quarter our troops permanently — that is to say for 20 years — without infringing on French sovereignty and without incurring a Russian charge that we have not withdrawn. Perhaps we can meet the French need and the French objection by quartering our troops in the Saar, and by arrangements for air forces in Britain, in North Africa, and if they want it, in metropolitan France. We should try to offset the Russian argument by a demonstration that the force is — after the Russian withdrawal — a screen against Germany, not against them.

To rebut the argument that we are withdrawing across the Atlantic, whereas Russia is only withdrawing to the Pripet Marshes, we should say that American forces are in fact withdrawn across the Atlantic now, and that as long as token forces of any kind remain as a screen, the position as respects French security and the Pact would not be altered.[3]

---

1. The Russians had agreed to lift the Berlin blockade (as they did on May 12) in return for an end to the Western counterblockade and the reconvening of the Council of Foreign Ministers.

With that meeting scheduled for Paris, Ambassador Jessup undertook lengthy negotiations with Soviet representatives about Germany. The Russians wanted a return to the status quo *ante* in order to prevent the establishment of separate German states. **2.** Emphasis Lippmann's. **3.** The Truman administration had no intention of adopting the policies Lippmann put forward in this memorandum. Indeed their chief appeal within the administration may have been to George Kennan, who admitted on May 24 that he "had been overruled on all the main proposals for Germany"; from Lippmann diary entry for May 24, 1949. Kennan and Bohlen both also interpreted Soviet policy in Europe as defensive, whereas Acheson viewed it as dangerously aggressive. Before the end of 1949, Kennan resigned his position, to be replaced by the more militant Paul H. Nitze. Earlier the Federal Republic of Germany (West Germany) had come into existence on May 23 under the sponsorship of the Western occupying powers and in counterpoise to the Democratic Republic of Germany (East Germany), which the Soviet Union organized.

To Charles B. Gary

July 7, 1949

Dear Charles:

. . . The question you raise about Germany is one that has preoccupied me almost from the beginning of the war and constituted the theme of a book I wrote during the war, called *U.S. War Aims*. There is no doubt that the Germans have always planned to exploit the conflict between East and West in order to recover their position in Europe. If I differ from your conclusions at all it is in thinking that the Germans will never align themselves honestly and reliably with one side or the other. Therefore, it is unwise to base any policy on the assumption that they would align themselves. I think they will do what you and I would do in their place, which is to exploit the conflict and maneuver themselves into a position where they hold the balance of power in Europe. For that reason I have come to the conclusion that however difficult the only course that promises security is one that has as its principal objective the political neutralization of Germany. By neutralization I mean a western policy which excludes Germany [from] the Western Military Alliance and at the same time threatens her with immediate punishment if she joins the Eastern Alliance. I think we have the power to do that even though our control over Germany is declining rapidly. For Germany in a military sense can be neutralized by military means and it doesn't take great armies to do it. Whatever the limitations of air power in respect to the Russians, there can be no real doubt that the Germans are now vulnerable to air power in a degree which no other great country has ever been.

To Arthur H. Vandenberg

August 8, 1949

Dear Arthur:

I am very pleased indeed to see that you have taken a strong stand against Section 3 of the Administration's Military Aid Bill.[1]

For myself I find it [a] shocking example of utter disrespect for our constitutional traditions and for the very processes of law. Not the least unpleasant aspect of the matter was the way the provisions were glossed over in the official public presentation made by Acheson and others in the Department booklet. It was bad enough to ask for such unlimited powers but to try to get them by hitching them to a measure which commands general support seems to me to be sharp practice.

I wonder if the whole affair doesn't call for a measured but stern lecture from you on the need for a return to recognized standards of conduct in dealing with Congress and with the people. I should think that such a reproof might be made by you, and as a matter of fact only by you, without jeopardizing the support of the avowed purposes of the bill, which we all want to see go through.

1. On signing the NATO treaty, Truman requested $1.5 billion for military aid to the other members of the organization. The discretionary authority he also asked for struck Vandenberg as "almost unbelievable" and Lippmann as "a general license to intervene and to commit the United States all over the globe"; Ronald Steel, *Walter Lippmann and the American Century* (Boston, 1980), pp. 460–61. The Russian detonation of an atomic bomb, however, sent the measure sailing through Congress.

To Russell C. Leffingwell

September 16, 1949

Dear Russell:

. . . I have been giving a good deal of thought to the question we discussed about the political possibility of changing the tariff laws so that we would really take in imports. The more I look around, the more deeply pessimistic I am about the possibility of any serious change in our tariff policy within a future near enough to make a difference in the present situation. The trouble is that while it would be an enlightened policy to reduce the tariff, there is no popular compulsion behind it. Of course, there are no things we have to import from abroad which we want to get cheaply. On the other hand, the impact on particular industries is obvious. In the struggle between these particular interests which are hurt and the great amorphous mass of the people who would be benefited, particular interests will make the most noise and the most effective noise. Perhaps I am a defeatist, and that in the long run we will change our minds about the tariff, as we have about the rest of our foreign policy. But I wouldn't expect very much very soon. There is, moreover, a considerable reaction towards isolationism. I was talking with Senator Vandenberg about it last night, and he tells me that the large majorities he has been able to obtain for the United Nations, the Marshall Plan, etc. could not be obtained today. They would still pass, but by smaller majorities.

To William F. Knowland[1]

September 21, 1949

Dear Bill:

I appreciate your writing me so fully. I wish I could write you as fully as your letter should be answered, but that is not possible as I am just in the throes of getting ready for a trip abroad, which will take me to India via Turkey, Syria, Greece, Italy, France and Germany.

The purpose of this trip is to clarify my own mind about what our Asiatic policy should be. As of the present my general view is as follows: That we should give full scale financial aid to India and Pakistan, based on a condition that the Kashmir dispute[2] (which could lead to war between them) be settled peaceably before the aid is given. I think it is sound strategy to consolidate the friendly base which we might have in Asia, using "base" in its largest political sense, as our primary objective.

Secondly, I would do what high French officials have told me privately they hope we will do, though they cannot say so publicly, insist that the French government grant complete independence to Indochina subject only to the continued presence of the French army for a period of three to five years.[3] I would make the offer of independence subject also to the condition that the Indochinese government have no military or political alliances which are not approved by a council of Asiatic states, which I would try to see have set up to include India, Pakistan, Australia, the Philippines, Siam, and perhaps some others.

I would advise the Philippine government privately to stop playing petty power politics and to concentrate on its domestic problems, in which I think we should give them generous assistance.[4] I would reject completely all nonsense about alliances among straw men, among feeble states such as southern Korea, what is left of Chiang and the Philippines. That is nothing but mischievous meddling, in which they'll get their fingers burnt.

I would find a way of asserting the principle that the crossing of any frontier in Asia by organized military forces is an act of aggression under Article 51 of the Charter, and that the United States would react, by-passing any veto in the Security Council.

That is about all I can see that we should do at the present time, except that I must add, drawing upon the experience of our dealings with the original Russian revolution in 1919, I would not foreclose de facto recognition of a Chinese communist government if and when it is set up. I do not believe in the non-recognition principle of accomplished facts in international affairs. Almost invariably the results are quite contrary to those which it is intended to achieve. . . .

---

1. Senator William F. Knowland of California, elected in 1946, had been since then a consistent, though ambitious and restless, follower of the leadership of Robert Taft.   **2.** India and Pakistan had agreed to a cease-fire in Kashmir which the UN had recommended, but India had rejected UN arbitration of the dispute over that region. That dispute, which remained unresolved for years, had originated in 1947 when the government of India admitted Kashmir into the Indian union, but Pakistan objected because the population of Kashmir was largely Moslem. **3.** The French had recognized the independence of Vietnam within the French union and in an agreement with the anti-Communist Vietnam Nationalists under Bao Dai, the former emperor. That arrangement met the continuing, armed opposition of the Communist Vietminh under Ho Chi Minh. Early in 1950, both the Soviet Union and China recognized the Vietminh regime, while the United States and Britain recognized the Bao Dai government. Both sets of external powers then also provided their preferred Vietnam regimes with military assistance. **4.** In the violent campaign preceding the Philippine elections, the question of American aid to the Liberal party, which won in November, was a major issue.

To Russell C. Leffingwell

December 29, 1949

Dear Russell:

. . . I learned many things abroad, of course, which I am only beginning to digest. . . . The political implications . . . are obvious and they are enormous. For what we are struggling for in Asia, I now realize, is not democracy and not free enterprise, and not allies in the cold war against the Soviet Union, but to maintain some contact between Asia and the West. We have very little power in Asia, and we must not think of ourselves as lords of creation who can fix the terms of the bargain on which relations are to be continued. We have to make connections, we have to seek avenues of contact and of influence, or we shall gradually find ourselves shut out. . . .

To Hanson W. Baldwin[1]

January 3, 1950

Dear Baldwin:

I have been reading your article in the *Atlantic Monthly,* and I wonder whether you could indicate briefly to me the answer to one question which is not dealt with in your argument about the political advantages of the Mediterranean operation as against the cross channel one.

The question is this: Suppose we had invaded the continent from the south, what would the Russian army have been doing in the north, assuming that we could have got into the Danube valley and even into southern Germany before the Russians? Would that not have meant that the Russians got into the whole of northern Germany including Westphalia and into the Low Countries, and perhaps into France itself before we got there? Is there any reason to think that if we were on the Danube, they would have stopped at the Elbe? I can see no reason for thinking so. And if we had not reached the Elbe in force before the defeat of Germany, would we be better off today if we had

Vienna, Budapest and Belgrade while they had Warsaw, Berlin, the Ruhr, the Low Countries and Denmark? . . .

I might say that in 1942 and 1943 I was very much convinced of the soundness of the Churchillian strategy. That was when it seemed improbable that the Russian army could advance into Europe and when we were all suffering from the illusion that Germany would be defeated by air power. Once it became evident that Germany would have to be invaded, I changed my own mind and felt that Stimson and Marshall were essentially right, even from the long range political view as distinct from the immediate military view, in wanting to put powerful Anglo-American forces into western Germany. Of course if we had been able to do both operations, we should have avoided much subsequent trouble, but as we were not strong enough to do that, I can't help feeling that we chose the lesser of two evils. That is to say, the relinquishment of the Balkans and the Danube Valley in order to gain France, the Low Countries and western Germany.

There are a number of other debatable points in your article which I should like some time to talk over with you. In my view you greatly exaggerate the importance of Roosevelt's alleged personal confidence in Stalin. After all, it was Churchill in his broadcast on the day of Hitler's invasion of Russia who committed Great Britain to an all out military alliance with the Soviet Union.

When you accept Bullitt's[2] thesis that the great opportunity of the democracies for establishing a stable peace came on June 22, 1941, I think you give the forgetful reader the impression that on that date we were a full ally of the democracies. Actually, of course, only Great Britain was actively at war and it was Churchill, not Roosevelt, who made the decision at that time. . . .

1. Hanson W. Baldwin, military editor of the *New York Times*, was publishing his "Our Worst Blunder of the War" in three successive issues of the *Atlantic Monthly*, January, February, and March 1950.   2. William C. Bullitt had become a leading voice in the right-wing chorus of disapproval of Franklin Roosevelt's alleged sellout to the Soviet Union.

MEMORANDUM[1]

January 7, 1950

The outstanding fact about the last year's developments is that the Soviet position in Europe has deteriorated and the western position in Asia has deteriorated. This is tantamount to saying that western influence is improving outside Asia, and declining inside Asia.

This basic equilibrium of power rests on the fact that Soviet military power is essentially based on ground forces and the range of Soviet power is the range of the ground forces. On the other hand, Amer. and western power is based on long-range instruments of war which are effective up to the frontiers of Asia, but not within Asia itself.

The Soviet position and our own in Europe turns upon Yugoslavia and Germany. The immediate problem in Asia turns upon China — the issue being whether China is to be a satellite of the Soviet Union or an independent state. The assumption that it is necessarily a satellite and that therefore the problem is to contain it, is false and defeatist. The problem for us in China is not containment, but division between Mao Tse-tung and Stalin. The struggle is waged not on the frontiers of China, but on the frontiers between China and the Soviet Union.

1. Lippmann wrote this memorandum as a kind of reminder to himself.

To Arthur H. Vandenberg

January 18, 1950

My dear Arthur:

. . . I cannot agree that the problem is whether the Senate Foreign Relations Committee is entitled to first-hand information, etc., etc. There is no problem about that. It is entitled to first-hand information. The problem is how it can most properly get genuine first-hand information without invading the prerogatives and the responsibilities of the Executive.

My contention is that the way it should get first-hand information is not through formal proceedings either in executive session or publicly but, necessarily and inevitably in matters of this kind, informally and privately. There is no other way to avoid the dilemma of disclosing too much or telling too little. In other words, the Chiefs of Staff can and should speak confidentially to you, as leader of the minority, leaving it to *you*[1] to pass on to other Senators your own judgment and conclusions without necessarily disclosing all the reasons and all the information. That is the way they do it in England, as I understand it, and the thing works very well.

Mr. Churchill[2] is, I believe, shown all important telegrams wherever the national interest is at stake, but he does not transmit all the information given to him to all the Conservative members of Parliament. They trust him as their leader. In our case the Senate must trust somebody. And in a matter of this kind they ought to trust you to tell them what it is necessary for them to know. It is an absurdity to suppose that each individual Senator can know all the facts about all these difficult subjects and reach his own independent judgment upon each situation.

My answer to your question then is that the contacts between the Senate and the military leaders should, under our system of government, be made through trusted responsible Senators off-the-record and continually. Once you try to formalize the matter, the contact will become spasmodic and at arm's length and in the end the Senate will be less informed, not better informed. . . .

1. Emphasis Lippmann's. 2. As leader of the opposition party, the Conservatives, in the House of Commons.

To Forrest P. Sherman

February 16, 1950

Dear Forrest:

. . . I came back from Asia deeply troubled about our future on that continent. I am afraid we made a decisive and irreparable mistake when we failed to recognize, despite the explicit warnings of all our foreign service officers, that in the contest for the leadership of the Chinese revolution Chiang had no possible chance to win out, no matter how much military or economic help we gave him.

Our only chance of salvaging anything in China lay either in supporting a far more liberal and enlightened regime as an alternative to the communists, or of disengaging ourselves three years ago, and observing a policy of correct neutrality in the Chinese civil war.

Now we are almost hopelessly committed to the support of those elements in Asia that cannot possibly hope to recover the leadership of Asia. All we have in the Far East now are a few beachheads occupied by discredited or puppet regimes.

The worst aspect of this is its effect on that part of Asia where we still have a chance, namely the sub-continent of India and Pakistan. My greatest fear now is that we shall lose Nehru[1] and the Indian Congress Party. They are the greatest forces left which could align themselves on our side. But we are handling them badly, without sufficient understanding, without diplomatic ingenuity and resourcefulness. . . .

The Pakistan-India cold war over Kashmir and other matters is of infinitely greater importance than anything that is happening in southeast Asia, to which our attention is immediately directed. If Pakistan and India can be brought together, all of south Asia can be held, and we shall have a great Asiatic force on our side. If Pakistan and India blow up in communal rioting and civil war, we'll have no position at all left in Asia. The effects of that disaster will spread both to southeast Asia and to the Middle East.

Pardon my speaking so vehemently, but our policy today in the Far East seems to me not much more than the attempt to stick our finger in one or two holes in the dike. . . .

1. Since 1947 Jawaharlal Nehru had been prime minister first of the independent Dominion of India and then, after November 1949, of the Republic of India.

To Andre Visson[1]

April 5, 1950

Dear Andre:

I appreciate your letter more than I may be able to tell you, for I have the deepest respect for your knowledge and judgment, and I approach this whole question with an open mind.

Perhaps the most important question that your letter poses is this: if, as you agree, the policy of military containment has failed — though we are still determined resolutely to prevent the expansion of the Soviet power — what is to be the role of the principal countries still outside the Soviet orbit which, on your own admission, cannot be organized into a military coalition by us?

Your answer, I take it, is that western Germany must be brought into a western system. But you recognize how difficult that is. If I differ with you at all, it is in thinking that it can't be done. I don't mean that Adenauer[2] won't . . . participate in the Marshall Plan. I mean that this will not reflect the real position of Germany. . . .

Just one word about the misleading term "neutrality." I do not envisage the Germans as being neutral in the Swiss sense of playing no part in the power politics of the world. That is impossible for so big a country as Germany. Perhaps I have made a mistake in using the word neutrality, though I intended it technically as defining their military relationship to the two coalitions.

What I really believe is that Germany will occupy her historic position, which is to be in the middle between the Latin world and the Slavic world or, if you like, the western world and the eastern. Such a middle position can be very dangerous to the peace of the world. Our task is to see whether this natural position of the Germans can be made to serve the general cause of peace and stabilization.

As a student of history, I should like just in passing to call your attention to the fact that the western European system which our official policy contemplates is almost identical geographically with Charlemagne's empire. That empire lasted forty-three years. Never before that and never since then has Germany been a part of what we would call "western Europe." Most people don't think that these historical precedents are significant, but I imagine you do think they are, as I certainly do. They lead me to the conclusion that we must come to think of the Germans as they think of themselves — not as a western power, but as a middle European power. . . .

1. Andre Visson, Washington journalist and commentator, author of *The Coming Struggle for Peace* (New York, 1944) and *As Others See Us* (Garden City, 1948).   2. Konrad Adenauer had been elected chancellor of the Federal Republic of Germany in September 1949.

To Alan G. Kirk[1]

April 26, 1950

Dear Alan:

I am writing you . . . to give you my own personal estimate of the attack on the State Department.[2]

It is becoming increasingly clear that this is the postwar isolationist movement now at last under way. Many people have been slow in recognizing it as an isolationist movement because the leaders in the attack — first Senator Knowland and Senator Smith of New Jersey and then later Senator Mc-Carthy — have all appeared to take the non-isolationist line and indeed to talk as if we ought to go on a military crusade against Russia. But if you look at what is behind the attack, and at the behavior of the men behind the attack, the isolationist tack of the thing becomes quite evident. The men behind McCarthy are Taft, Wherry and Bridges in the Senate and their counterparts in the House. While Bridges himself doesn't have an isolationist record, Taft and Wherry of course are the heart and center of Republican isolationism.

Parallel with the great outcry about communism in the State Department and in the administration, they will do their best to cut the heart out of the European aid programs. It looks now as if they had killed Point Four for this session and they are, as I write, trying to reduce the ECA appropriation drastically. Taft has even come out for cutting the British out of it entirely.

I saw at firsthand the rise of the isolationist movement after the first world war. It began, as did this one, not with their demand that we retire from Europe, but with an outcry led by Senator Lodge and Senator Knox that Wilson was appeasing the Germans, that he was planning to make too soft a peace. Under the banner of a hard peace for Germany they went on to destroy the treaty and the League and ended by making a separate treaty of peace with Germany. That was the foundation of the isolationist movement which led to the overthrow of the internationalist Republicans and the rise of the Harding isolationists.

What is happening now is that under the cry of appeasing the Reds and not supporting Chiang Kai-shek and all the rest of it the isolationists — Taft, Wherry and Bridges — are seizing control of the Republican party, taking advantage of Vandenberg's illness and the discredit of Dewey's and Dulles' defeats[3] and they intend to emerge from the whole fracas at this election as the leaders of the Republican party.

That, I think, is the true story of the meaning of this whole winter's confusion in Washington.

If we take a longer view of it, I think you have to come to the conclusion that the stage was set for it by the fact that the collapse of China constitutes a diplomatic defeat which has shaken the confidence in the whole Truman Administration and its foreign policy. The Administration has been going to the Congress and the country for three years, telling them the Truman Doctrine and the measures which were designed to support it were containing the expansion of communism. Then the public realized that communism had not been contained in China and that it would not be contained easily in southeast Asia. The feeling that something is very wrong inside the Administration stems from this defeat which the Administration has not been able to explain as a defeat or to transcend by offering a clear policy as to what is to happen after the defeat. Nothing succeeds like success in foreign policy, and nothing fails like a failure. It has been the failure in Asia which has made possible the whole McCarthy business.

I think the matter was summed up neatly the other day by an English journalist whom I was talking to, who said "the United States is, in the eyes of the American people, by definition incapable of being defeated. The United States has nevertheless been defeated in China. Since the United States cannot be defeated, it must have been defeated by treachery, therefore, somewhere in the high command there must be a Soviet spy to explain the otherwise impossible fact that the United States has suffered a diplomatic defeat." . . .

1. Admiral Alan G. Kirk, U.S.N., retired, had been a senior American naval commander in the European theater during World War II. He served most memorably as commander of the Navy task force in the invasion of Normandy in 1944. Kirk became ambassador to Belgium in 1946 and to the Soviet Union in 1949. 2. Leading Republicans in the Senate had begun to attack President Truman and the State Department, especially Acheson, for the failure of American policy in Asia to prevent the victory of the Communists in China. The attack reflected a genuine concern about the "loss" of China and a related supposition that domestic perfidy within the United States must have occasioned that loss. The attack also revealed the influence of the "China lobby," which was financed in part by Chiang Kai-shek's friends and his government, now established only in Taiwan (Formosa). Resolved to find an issue through which they could revenge Truman's victory in 1948, the Republicans made China that issue. At this time, they focused on the State Department's White Paper on China, which Lippmann also criticized, though on different grounds; see Ronald Steel, *Walter Lippmann and the American Century* (Boston, 1980), pp. 466–67. By this time, Senator Joseph R. McCarthy of Wisconsin — following his irresponsible charges in a speech at Wheeling, West Virginia, on February 9, 1950 — had begun to lead the others in accusations about the alleged presence of Communists in the State Department and elsewhere within the executive branch. In this letter, Lippmann referred also to the other leading Republicans engaged in harassing the State Department: William F. Knowland of California, Howard K. Smith of New Jersey, Kenneth S. Wherry of Nebraska, and (Henry) Styles Bridges of New Hampshire. 3. Dulles had been defeated as Republican candidate for the United States Senate from New York.

To Jean Monnet

June 1, 1950

Dear Jean:

I have made some careful inquiries in very reliable high places as to whether it would be useful for you to pay a quick visit to this country. The net conclusion is that support for the plan[1] is so strong here that your immediate presence is not needed for the purpose of winning support, and that your presence in Europe — in order to see that the negotiations proceed well — is indispensable. After negotiations are well started a visit here might be very useful in order to deal with difficulties that will arise out of details.

I think you would be greatly reassured by the attitude of the Administration here. The offer is regarded by the President and the Secretary of State, Paul Hoffman,[2] by all the top policy people of the State Department and of the Pentagon, by all the leading members of both political parties in Congress, as the most hopeful postwar development in Europe. Instructions have been issued to the technicians that no difficulties are to be raised on technical grounds until the main political purposes are assured. The matter is to be treated as a question of high policy and not as an incident of an economic problem, or of trade ideology.

The situation is better than I thought it was. I was rather afraid that the British had exerted influence successfully at the high levels.

My own belief is that the right policy for your government now is to push ahead quickly for an agreement primarily with the Germans. The other western countries can be negotiated with after that. The decisive event will be the Franco-German agreement.

1. The Schuman plan, devised by Monnet and proposed by French Foreign Minister Robert Schuman in May 1950, called for the integration of the Western European coal and steel industries. In April 1951, representatives of France, West Germany, Italy, Belgium, the Netherlands, and Luxembourg signed a treaty giving substance to the plan by establishing a unitary market for coal and steel among their nations. 2. Paul G. Hoffman, for many years president of the Studebaker Corporation, a Republican and an internationalist, had been appointed the first administrator of the Economic Co-operation Administration (ECA).

To John D. M. Hamilton

June 21, 1950

My dear Mr. Hamilton:

. . . Now as to the attempt to date the inception of what we now call the "cold war." Relations with Russia were difficult even during the hardest parts of the world war, and they had clearly begun to deteriorate after the Yalta Conference of 1945. Nevertheless, the inception of the "cold war" could not in any event be put earlier than the Potsdam Conference of July 1945. It cannot be put earlier, in my view, than Secretary Byrnes' visit to Moscow at, I believe, the end of 1945. It can fairly be said to have begun to break out during the affair over Iran which, I think, was in the spring of 1946. But if I had to pick a date as marking the acceptance of the whole conflict by the United States government, I would select President Truman's message about Greece and Turkey announcing the so-called Truman Doctrine. That, I believe, was in March 1947. That marked the open acceptance of the idea of political warfare and was swiftly followed by the breakdown of any immediate hope of a four-power agreement about Germany and Japan.

By the autumn of 1947 the failure of the Foreign Ministers' conference to agree showed that the break was wide open. There followed the decision to set up a West German Government, which was followed immediately by the Soviet blockade of Berlin. At that point the cold war was in full force. . . .

To John Foster Dulles

July 18, 1950

Dear Foster:

. . . It would never have occurred to me to think you had not drawn a sharp distinction between sanctions up to and including air and sea power and the actual commitment of a land army on the mainland of Asia.

I don't think the country has yet realized that there were two great decisions taken in that first week, not merely one, and that the second decision to commit the land army was a far deeper and a far more momentous and a much more irrevocable commitment than the first.[1]

It seems to me that a diplomatic United Nations handling of the whole Korean question is the only way out of the military situation, even on the most optimistic estimate of our chances to hold a line and to conduct a counteroffensive up to the 38th parallel. Even if we can do all that without becoming involved in a much larger war with the Chinese . . . merely to get to the 38th parallel will simply restore the occupation of southern Korea, which we gave up some time ago, and military government (in which we will be faced with the guerrilla problem of tremendous difficulty). But we have no right to count on being allowed to conduct a counteroffensive up to the 38th parallel without the intervention of at least the Chinese. Therefore, we must hope that the British, with the help of the Indians, will bail us out of the consequences of the decision to land an army. Had we not done that, but had followed your advice, we would be able to take a much stronger diplomatic line in the Far East than we are now.

We have given hostages to fortune which we would have been much stronger without. . . .

1. North Korea had invaded South Korea on June 25, 1950. President Truman, advised by Secretary of State Acheson and the Joint Chiefs of Staff, had committed air and naval forces to the defense of South Korea on June 27 and ground troops on June 30. The United States also put forward a resolution that the UN Security Council — the Soviet Union was boycotting it at the time — adopted on June 25, calling for a cessation of hostilities in Korea and the withdrawal of North Korean forces; on June 27, the Security Council requested members of the UN to send assistance to the Republic of Korea (South Korea). For a detailed account of the onset of the war in Korea and of the war itself, see J. C. Goulden, *Korea* (New York, 1982); on Lippmann's responses to the war, see Ronald Steel, *Walter Lippmann and the American Century* (Boston, 1980), pp. 469–78; and on Dulles, who was in Tokyo negotiating the American peace treaty with Japan when the war began, see also "Conversation with Foster Dulles," September 10, 1950, inf.

To Joseph W. Alsop [1]

July 19, 1950

Dear Joe:

. . . I have been very deeply deeply depressed by the Korean affair, chiefly because of the disclosure that the National Security Council simply hasn't worked at all as it was intended to work. I often talked with Forrestal [2] about it, and in his mind it was primarily intended to make sure that the Pentagon and the State Department worked hand in glove. This is just what did not happen in Korea, and I don't think that all the fault is your friend Louis Johnson's. [3] Truman and Acheson must share the fault, not having clarified the question of our obligation in Korea and insisted on knowing whether we were prepared to support it. They knew and accepted the theory that Korea had been written off and, therefore, that we were not going to be prepared to fight there. [4]

For this reason I am rather gloomy about the quality of the men in charge of our destiny.

1. Joseph W. Alsop, syndicated columnist, major figure in political Washington, great-nephew of Theodore Roosevelt and inheritor of that relation's strenuosity, member of the staff of General Claire Lee Chennault in China during World War II, and emphatic cold warrior.   2. James Forrestal had resigned as secretary of defense in March 1949 and, depressed and anxious about the department's problems and his personal life, committed suicide in May of that year.   3. Louis A. Johnson, Forrestal's successor as secretary of defense.   4. Lippmann was referring to Acheson's speech at the National Press Club in January 1950, in which the secretary of state defined an American strategic defense line in Asia that included Japan and the Philippines but not Formosa or Korea.

To Dorothy Thompson

September 1, 1950

Dear Dorothy:

. . . I am happy to find that we are so much alike in our thinking on the fundamentals. I don't think even on the question of German armament that we are far apart. For while I do strongly favor building up a force similar to, but stronger than, the East German forces, I consider that that is something quite different from recreating a German army under the Atlantic Pact.

I think now that there is reason to believe that the British military people have come to the same conclusion. I notice a sudden switching of the *Economist*, which usually speaks for Whitehall, on this subject, in the issue of August 26th.

I think that the West German police army (or whatever you wish to call it) is necessary in itself, of course, to preserve security, and also as a necessary bargaining instrument for the kind of negotiation which you propose in your letter. I have long believed that the political framework of our policy should be unification, elections and neutralization. The only thing is that now I am regretful that I used the word "neutralization" which confuses people, whereas what I really mean is a policy on a large scale appropriate to a big power like Germany on the Swedish model. I think the true historical role for Germany is to stand not with the West and not with the East, but between the two. My understanding of the Germans, whom you know much better than I do, of course, is that they are at their best only when they have a sense of historical mission. I'd like to give them an historical mission which conforms to their history, their interests and is compatible with the peace of the world, and I think the conception of Germany as the great middle power around which the smaller neutral states (like the Scandinavians) could group themselves, and to which eventually the East Europeans could attach themselves, is an attractive idea.

We've got to give the Germans some place in the world which befits their dignity and which is not necessarily to be interpreted by the Russians as Germany becoming the spearhead of the West. Also we have to provide some place to which the East European countries could go, if they started to separate themselves from Russia, without falling completely into our arms. It is enough for us if they separate from Moscow. We should not expect them, nor even want them, to come all the way over to us. But in that case there must be some strong point around which they can rally, and that strong point in the end should, in my view, be Germany.

I very much like the statement in your letter that it is not a flaw in plans of this sort that the Russians would not accept the plans. I wish you were able to persuade some of our colleagues in the press, and some of the people in Wash ngton to that view. . . .

Conversation with Foster Dulles

September 10, 1950

1. *MacArthur & Korea* — So shielded by his staff that not advised of invasion until Foster brought it to his attention on the evening of June 25 (?). Foster spending weekend of Sat. & Sun. (June 24 & 25) in country out of Tokyo. Called on phone by . . . State Dept. Officer accompanying him & advised attack by N. Koreans had begun. Foster asked pilot of Gen. MacA's plane (who had flown him to country for weekend) to telegraph MacA. at once "in view of developments in Korea, suggest you meet me in Tokyo this eve." Pilot suggested no reference to Korea in communication so as not to disturb Gen. who had not yet been told anything. — Arriving in Tokyo, found staff & MacArthur believing nothing but a raid in force (Was this Sun., June 25?)

Dinner with MacArthur — 4 of them (Gen. & Mrs. MacA) (Think this was Mon. eve, June 26). No mention of Korea — After dinner, a movie (Wild

West) until 11 p.m. In grand ballroom — 3 comfortable chairs and one rocking chair for the Gen. Some enlisted men in rear of room. MacA. entered last — "Good evening gentlemen" "Good eve — sir" a movie started. When Dulles got back to Embassy . . . Seoul being evacuated & help must be sent in form of planes, etc. to take any women & children. Artillery fire at gates of city. Dulles phoned MacArthur at once to horror of his staff who did not wish to disturb him.

Dulles were 3rd set of people ever to have dined with General — Usually receives only at lunch — There he enters last like royalty & with his aide shakes hands with each guest.

MacA. — 12-year old son not allowed to go to school with other American children but brought up & taught by English governess. Breakfasts daily with his father, the only time he sees him.

MacA. great admirer of Chiang — on the whole willing for war with Russia as he sees himself the center & head of it all — This in spite of fact that when he saw Dulles off he said "Anyone who wants to commit U.S. troops to fight in Korea should have his head examined" — But once order has been given him to head such an undertaking, then he must have everything for it — it becomes his project &, consequently, of supreme importance — He sees himself always, everywhere as the leading actor in a great drama.

2. Meeting in White House & other meeting upon his return. The first with only Acheson & Truman to tell T. that MacArthur would take orders only from the Pres. of the U.S. Other meeting Dulles arrived a little late. . . . Talk was re sending 24–25 Divisions altho until then only a few ground units to help aviation — Dulles: Will 2 Divisions do the job? If so — O.K. to commit them — If not, State Dept. will adjust its policy — Pace[1] replied impossible to give guaranty as this would require weeks of evaluation — Important now to reach a decision — "After all, we're only carrying out your foreign policy" — Dulles advised not to underestimate N. Koreans. . . .

3. When Chiang offered 30,000 Chinese soldiers State asked Gen MacA to send military mission to tell Ch——— More important to keep them for defense of Formosa.[2]

---

1. Frank Pace, then secretary of the army. **2.** These notes of Lippmann's conversation with Dulles were probably transcribed during the conversation by Helen B. Lippmann. They were supplemented by the following memorandum of September 11, 1950:

MacArthur was not informed by his staff of the invasion of South Korea until about 12 hours after the news reached Tokyo. It was the belief of his staff, as well as of MacArthur's that the whole thing was a raid in force — similar to earlier border raids — and that the tanks and the rest of the artillery would retire soon because they had run out of gas.

At that time MacArthur said to Dulles that anyone who committed American land forces on the mainland of Asia ought to have his head examined.

MacArthur was summoned to the "telecon" just as Dulles was leaving Tokyo. The message reached MacArthur at the airport where he was seeing Dulles off, and that was the message which told him that he would be the commander-in-chief and that we were going to intervene.

The decision which was reached by 9:45 on the Monday evening here in Blair House had a report from MacArthur saying that at most 2 American divisions would be needed to repel the invasion.

The decision to intervene seems to have been made in three main stages — (1) meeting which culminated in Blair House on Monday, where the actual commitment was limited to sea and air forces south of the 38th parallel; (2) second meeting at the White House on Thursday, at which it was agreed to commit supporting ground units, which were understood at the time to mean teams to . . . signal to the air force to locate targets and to guard the air fields and service the planes. The third (3) decision came, I believe, on Saturday, though the orders may have been issued before the meeting itself — it was the decision to commit the 24th and 25th Infantry Divisions. At this meeting Frank Pace represented the Pentagon. There was a debate between him and Dulles. Dulles raised the question as to whether the Pentagon had a calculation of the size of the American force required for the Korean job. Pace replied that the calculations would take a week and there was no time to make them as a decision had to be made at once about those two divisions. It is probable that the divisions had already received orders when the meeting was held.

To William H. Jackson[1]

December 12, 1950

My dear Jackson:

I had lunch today[2] . . . with the Second Secretary of the Soviet Embassy who is really the Press Counselor, Mr. Alexander I. Zinchuk. Unfortunately a Mr. Davidson of one of the French news agencies was also present, and through what I think was sheer excess of volubility interrupted Zinchuk just when he was beginning to say something interesting.

Despite this, I got certain things out of it all which I thought you might wish me to pass on to you. In the first place, this is the only time since 1945 that I have been able to talk, except at receptions, with any official of the Soviet Embassy. In the second place, Zinchuk came alone, unaccompanied by anyone else from his Embassy. Third, he complained to me in a friendly way that I never came to the Soviet Embassy, adding that it was difficult for the Embassy to make contact with unofficial Americans.

Out of all the various things he said; the following is a kind of summary, put together more logically than it came out of his conversation, of the position he took:

The Soviet Union is concerned by what he called provocative actions. When I asked him to define them concretely, they turned out to be the rearming of Germany, the approach of American forces to the frontiers of the Soviet Union in (and he named the countries) Norway, Iran, Korea. He volunteered the statement that the Soviet Union had no objections to any armament that we made within the United States, to any arming that was done inside Britain or France. "We have a big army ourselves," he said.

Discussing the Prague proposals,[3] I asked him whether he understood the evacuation of Germany to mean the retirement of the Russian army behind the Oder River or to the Soviet Union. He said that his government saw no reason for keeping an army in Poland under the condition of an agreement about Germany.

I asked him what his government's attitude would be to a proposal not to evacuate Germany but to reduce the occupation forces on the basis of equal occupation forces on both sides of the Elbe line both of the big powers and of the Germans. I said that this would mean withdrawing some of the Russian troops, because they now had much more than parity. He said that that was an interesting proposal and he'd never heard of it before. Then I told him I wasn't surprised he hadn't heard it before because it was my own private idea of how to begin.

In regard to Korea, I asked him whether the Chinese would have intervened if we had stopped at the 38th parallel.[4] The question arose in the course of general give-and-take about suspicion and provocative acts on the part of the Soviet Union. He said he didn't think they would have intervened because if they had, "their moral position" would have been not so strong as it is now.

My general conclusion is that the Russians would like to talk, but that it would take a lot of talking before they began to say very much. On the other hand, with patience and some skill on the part of the interviewer they will say something which is worth knowing.

1. William H. Jackson, New York lawyer and investment banker, then deputy director of the Central Intelligence Agency.   2. At the home of an acquaintance.   3. The Soviet-bloc countries, meeting in Prague on October 20–21, 1950, had reasserted their objections to German reindustrialization and militarization and denounced the September decisions of the United States, Britain, and France. Those democratic countries had then agreed to consider any attack on Berlin or on the Federal Republic as an attack against themselves, to relax their economic controls in Germany, to lift limits on steel production, and to permit the Federal Republic to open diplomatic relations with the Austrians. The three powers also began then openly and officially to consider German participation in NATO, a prospect Lippmann deplored.   4. An American and South Korean offensive in September had reached the 38th parallel, the line dividing the two parts of Korea, and under orders from the commanding general, Douglas MacArthur — orders Truman and Acheson had approved — crossed that line on October 9, 1950, and gone on to reach the Yalu River. Though China had warned it would retaliate against such an approach to the Manchurian border, MacArthur and his sponsors in Washington were surprised when Chinese troops joined the North Koreans in an extensive counterattack that drove MacArthur's armies back toward the South. Before the end of November, China had large forces in Korea, and the Americans and South Koreans had fallen back to the 38th parallel. That line collapsed early in 1951.

To Douglas Southall Freeman[1]

December 19, 1950

Dear Mr. Freeman:

    . . . I do not myself believe that Korea, Japan, Okinawa, and Formosa can be held in case of war, or that they would prove to be anything but strategical liabilities in case of war. We cannot defend Japan against atomic attack from the mainland, nor can we defend Formosa or Okinawa. Moreover, the obligation to feed the 80 million people of Japan involves a battle of the Pacific, compared with which the battle of the Atlantic in the Second World War was comparatively easy. The distance is much greater, the contribution of the Japanese as compared with the English would be much smaller. Moreover, the population of Japan is not to be compared with that of the British in its loyalty and its reliability.

In my view, therefore, Japan in case of war could be little more than a staging area for the bombers, and to get even that much out of Japan would call for a permanent investment of a large number of American troops. I think that this is a bad military calculation on our part, and that we would do far better to put our bases farther back where they are really secure against the mainland of Asia and then carry them forward on carriers, which present no targets and can give us tactical initiative and tactical surprise.

Our real defensive line in the Pacific is, I believe, what Admiral Sherman told me last spring he believed it should be — namely, Alaska, Hawaii, Guam, the Philippines. With that line, while we cannot hold Japan, Formosa, Southeast Asia, we can deny them to the enemy in case of war.

I believe our people have not grasped the distinction between holding places yourself and denying them to the enemy. Yet that distinction is crucial both in the Far East and in the Middle East, and I would be inclined to say also in Germany.

My own conclusion after visiting Germany this time (and I have been there every year since the end of the war) is that Germany cannot be made the military outpost of the western world. The Germans won't participate in it, the French will run away from it, the Russians, as they have announced publicly, will not tolerate it.

Therefore, in my view, our true course in Germany is to make a policy based on the idea that Germany must be denied as a military partner to the Soviet Union. A diplomatic expression of that military decision would be the sponsorship of a neutralized Germany. That is the course that the overwhelming majority of Germans wish to take. It is, moreover, the only German solution which, backed by the deterrent power of our strategic air force, the Russians are most likely to acquiesce in. . . .

1. Douglas Southall Freeman, long-time editor of the *Richmond News Leader*, celebrated biographer of Robert E. Lee and his Confederate lieutenants.

To Florence J. Harriman [1]

January 8, 1951

Dear Daisy:

. . . Dean should have resigned long ago, in my view last Spring. No man ought to be, or want to be Secretary of State who does not have the confidence of the substantial majority of Congress. The question of whether the majority of Congress lacks confidence in him for good reasons or bad is quite irrelevant.

It is impossible to conduct foreign affairs and especially to conduct wars without popular confidence in the men who conduct them. The situation which he has tolerated since last spring would be absolutely unthinkable in any parliamentary government. Either he would have got a vote of confidence in some form or other, or he would have resigned. Just staying in office with the majority against him is not admirable and makes the effective conduct of government virtually impossible. This is particularly true in a situation like the present, where the head of the government is at once incompetent and irremovable.

In my view this country is going to go either to a frightful crisis at home, or a catastrophe abroad, or both unless somewhere in the system of high command there are changes of men. . . .

1. Florence J. Harriman (Mrs. J. Borden), "Daisy" to her friends, was a leading Washington hostess, a former American ambassador to Norway, and a prominent figure in Democratic circles in the District of Columbia and in the nation.

To Bernard Berenson

January 22, 1951

Dear B. B.:

. . . Of course I believe in "treating" with the Soviets. How on earth can one ignore their existence, which is what not treating with them would amount to? I am not particularly interested in writing treaties with them, because most of the treaties that we could write they couldn't abide by. But I would be very much interested in the kind of treaty they would have to abide by, and I see no reason to think that such treaties are a priori impossible. For example, they have never violated military agreements, I emphasize the word "military," made at Yalta. . . .

To James B. Conant

February 12, 1951

My dear Conant:

. . . I am troubled by the argument . . . "that the danger of a third global war . . . turns on the fact that a few years hence the handful of men who rule Russia may decide that the power of our strategic air force has been largely canceled out. If at that time Europe is defenseless on the ground, the Russian hordes will begin to move. . . ."

I am familiar with this argument and in fact have used it myself in the past. But I am now no longer sure that it is soundly reasoned.

The doubtful point in my mind is the assumption you are making about command of the air, not over the Soviet Union, but over continental Europe and Great Britain. Does not the argument about the Russian army moving assume (a) that the power of our strategic air force has been largely canceled out not only over Russia but over eastern Europe and (b) that we have substantially command of the air over western Europe including Scandinavia? Are these two assumptions credible, namely that the Russians will have air supremacy on their side of the Iron Curtain and we on ours?

Yet it is necessary to make that assumption, so it seems to me, if the argument that the Russian army will march is correct. For if either of the two assumptions is untrue, the situation will be different from the one you describe. If we have air supremacy approximately up to the frontiers of the Soviet Union, we can exercise immense deterrent and defensive power against any ground invasion of western Europe. And if, on the other hand, we do not have air supremacy over western Europe, then it is not necessary for the Russians to march. They will dominate the western countries and compel them at a minimum to declare their neutrality on penalty of destruction.

My own reasons for supporting the re-creation of ground armies in western Europe with a large American contingent is that this is an indispensable part of the reconstruction of Europe as a political power in the world. Because I take this view of it, I feel that Eisenhower has done a great service in recognizing the fact that political solutions must precede rearmament in Germany.[1]

---

1. Eisenhower was about to assume command of the military forces of NATO. He believed the rearmament of Germany (a prospect the French had opposed) would be possible only if German troops were integrated into NATO forces. He also was "coming to believe," as he later wrote in his diary, "that Europe's security problem is never going to be solved satisfactorily until there exists a United States of Europe, to include all countries now in NATO . . . "; R. H. Ferrell, ed., *The Eisenhower Diaries* (New York, 1981), p. 194.

To Robert Brand

March 2, 1951

Dear Bob:

 . . . I regard the idea of an Atlantic government — as distinct from the Atlantic community, which I have been writing about since 1917 — as nonsense, and dangerous nonsense if it were to be taken seriously.

I consider that surrender of sovereignty to a federal government which, by definition, must be able to tax and conscript the individual person in the new state is absolutely out of the question. The Atlantic nations are bound to remain a league of states, at most a more or less loose confederacy.

Streit is an old friend of mine, but he has built his whole crusade on an hysterical illusion, namely that the Philadelphia Convention of 1787 created a new state out of many separate sovereign states. It did no such thing. The thirteen colonies had always had the same allegiance, and the authors of the federal constitution in Philadelphia knew perfectly well that this was true —

saying in the preamble that they were forming a more perfect union. They were not forming a new union of the kind that Streit is proposing and which, I fully agree with you, has never yet been created except by a conqueror.

I regard the campaign as on the whole well-meaning, but very misguided. Its effect is to mis-educate rather than to educate American opinion, at least. But I never attack it or criticize it publicly because there are so many worse things abroad.

To Russell C. Leffingwell

April 16, 1951

Dear Russell:

Sir Leslie Rowan,[1] who has been called back to London, tells me that he and the economic people in Great Britain are deeply disturbed by the armaments plus rising civilian standard of life program which the Administration and the Pentagon and Wilson have embarked upon.

He says that an increase of over 40 billions in the gross national product, which is what Wilson is aiming at, will be devastating to European economies because of the suction exerted in this country upon raw materials in order to sustain such an enormous and rapidly expanding industrial production.

He says that the world production of important raw materials (of many important raw materials) cannot sustain such a program in the United States except at the expense of armament production or essential production, or both, in many other countries, — and that the production of these raw materials cannot be expanded fast enough to keep pace with our industrial expansion.

Rowan, as you know, is a key official in Britain, very close not only to this government but to Churchill himself, and he spoke in a tone of utmost gravity. I knew that there had been much discussion about raw materials, and that it was Attlee's second greatest preoccupation when he came here on his visit, but I hadn't realized how badly the British felt about it.

Have you encountered this feeling, and have you anything you can tell me about it and your views on it?

Thank you for your note about the MacArthur business.[2] I am clinging in these days to the hope that he may prove to be a bigger man than the lunatic fringe of the Republicans, who wish to play politics with his reputation.

1. Sir Leslie Rowan, private secretary successively to Churchill and to Attlee, 1941–47, later a senior official in the British Treasury, was returning to that department after two years as economic minister at the British embassy in Washington.   2. The "MacArthur business" had been absorbing the attention of the country. The general, believing that the United States had to fight the Korean War to total victory, had chafed under the restrictions that President Truman imposed upon him, restrictions that had the approval of the State Department, the Joint Chiefs of Staff, and the British government, the most important of the nations aligned with the United States. MacArthur demanded the bombing of Chinese bases in Manchuria, the blockade and even nuclear

bombing of China, and the entry into the war of Nationalist China (Taiwan). "In war," he held, "there is no substitute for victory." But Truman was unwilling to commit the United States to an all-out war in Asia, as General Omar Bradley of the J.C.S. put it, "the wrong war, at the wrong place, at the wrong time, and with the wrong enemy." The president intended to limit the war to the objective of restoring the independence of South Korea.

On April 5, Congressman Joe Martin, the Massachusetts Republican leader, produced an insubordinate letter from MacArthur that left Truman with no further choice; he relieved MacArthur of his command. The general reached the height of his temporary popularity on April 19, when he addressed a joint meeting of Congress. The Senate Foreign Relations and Armed Services committees then conducted a hearing that revealed the administration's excellent reasons for overruling MacArthur's advice. Though the general continued for a time to harbor ambitions for the Republican nomination, his star had begun to fade. During the episode, Lippmann in "Today and Tomorrow" observed that MacArthur had tried to exceed his authority, but also criticized Truman and Acheson for losing control of the war in Korea; see Ronald Steel, *Walter Lippmann and the American Century* (Boston, 1980), pp. 474–75.

To Leon H. Keyserling[1]

May 1, 1951

Dear Mr. Keyserling:

. . . I am sorry to hear that you feel I have imperfectly interpreted your view and that, in fact, I have imputed to you views which you do not hold. I am puzzled as to why you think so.

My only reference to your view was in the statement that the official administration doctrine, presumably formulated by you and put into practice by Mr. Wilson,[2] was the thesis that we could rearm on a large scale in the next few years with only comparatively small and passing shortages and at the end be in a position to maintain both the necessary military strength and a civilian production "higher than before Korea." I quoted this from Mr. Wilson's report. Needless to say, I was also familiar with the reports of the Council of Economic Advisers and in this instance I checked these and recent statements and speeches of yours which were available to me.

Since I received your letter, I have checked back through the references you mention. I do not find anything which appears to contradict my original statement. A summing up of the implications of the production effort outlined as feasible (see p. 81 — Economic Report of the President) says GNP should rise at a rate adequate "to absorb a yearly defense effort at the levels to be reached at the end of this year, to maintain and expand our productive plant, and at the same time bring per capita consumption . . . at least up to the level achieved in 1950." In your recent radio broadcast "Production and Strategy for Defense," you say that "total of personal consumption should remain fairly constant between now and the end of 1952 (although) the consumption of durables . . . will need to be cut back sharply but by no means critically." . . .

My main purpose was to stress the importance of relating our objectives to the essential requirements of our allies. I find no more than passing and secondary concern with this problem in any of the recent statements and reports of the administration. The emphasis, it seems to me, is placed almost entirely on the United States defense effort, on the theme that we must and can continue to expand our capacity and production, and that we can build a large defense effort with no real loss in less essential consumption. I do not find, as you indicate in your letter, any frequent or special emphasis (in any of your recent statements) on the importance of contracting the disparity in living standards between the United States and other countries or on the fact that our living standards can take far greater cuts than those of most of our allies.

I do not doubt the importance of expanding our basic capacity or that over the long run the American economy is capable of great expansion. The question in my mind is whether we can expand the production of raw materials sufficiently rapidly during the initial period of mobilization to meet both our targets and the requirements of other countries. Our economic and political power is so great that we inevitably set the terms and my impression to date has been that we may not have fully appreciated the seriousness of the problem. I hope I am wrong.

1. Leon Keyserling was then chairman of the Council of Economic Advisers.   **2.** Charles E. Wilson, former head of the War Production Board and president of General Electric, then director of the Office of Defense Mobilization, the major agency concerned with the domestic economy during the Korean War.

To Harold G. Nicolson

May 2, 1951

Dear Harold:

. . . I belong to the school of thought over here, admittedly not a big one, which feels that the whole situation would be better, including relations between our two countries, if responsible and friendly people had only talked out more frankly about their disagreements. During this past year we have desperately needed the firm advice of candid friends, but we have not gotten it. The effect of British appeasement of American opinion has created a fantastic state of mind in this country, namely the assumption that no one has a right to disagree with us and that if any one doesn't follow us instantly he has a bad motive. You have made a great mistake to leave criticism of American policy for so long a time to the *New Statesman* and the Left Wing. You should not create the impression which we all have in Washington here that you are afraid to talk for fear that Congress won't vote the money. The Canadians have begun to speak up and I wish the British would too.

To Herbert B. Elliston

August 9, 1951

Dear Herbert:

. . . About MacArthur, I would say that on the basis of the . . . passage you quote about the relation of the army to the President, the right course for a journalist is to take off his gloves and swat him with all his might. That is the kind of remark that should not be passed over lightly, coming as it does from a man who stays in uniform and indulges in factional politics.[1] It is hard enough for me to take Gen. Marshall and Gen. Eisenhower coming into politics, but at least both of them have come in by the road that goes above partisanship.[2] But MacArthur has come in, not even through a respectable partisan line but through that of a faction of the Republican party. But when he challenges openly the basic principle of the relation between the military and the civil power, and really announces a doctrine of pure fascism, I would not soon let him hear the end of it if I were writing. . . .

1. "What are we going to do about MacArthur?" Elliston wrote Lippmann on August 3, 1951. ". . . It pains me to read him getting away with the proposition that military commanders are independent of 'the temporary head of the executive branch.' " **2.** Marshall had reluctantly yielded to Truman's request to become secretary of defense, a position he assumed in September 1950. Eisenhower remained in command of NATO but also much in the news as the preferred presidential candidate of prominent Republicans of an internationalist view.

To Arthur H. Vandenberg, Jr.[1]

[November 1951]

Dear Arthur:

If I were asked that question by an historian who had lived abroad and had never known your father personally, but wanted, nevertheless, to write a book about him, I would urge him to give great importance, indeed primary importance, to the influence of a conspicuous personal example.

We do not any of us like to change our minds, particularly in public. And when we have taken a public stand we tend to be stuck in it. Once an issue has been fought over a long time, most of us are too proud and too timid to be moved out of our entrenchments by reason and evidence alone. Nothing then is likely to change quickly, and in time before it is too late, the minds of a whole people accept a collision with the brutal facts and being run over by them, — as in Pearl Harbor.

But when a sudden and tremendous change of outlook has become imperative in a crisis, it makes all the difference in the world to most of us to see a man whom we have known and trusted, and who has thought and has felt as we did, going through the experience of changing his mind, doing it with style and dash, and in a mood to shame the devils of his own weakness. I would argue at the bar of history, if ever I got the chance, that his spiritual experience, which great masses of our people entered into vicariously, was the creative element which made his other political powers so enormously effective.

In all men who lead multitudes of human beings there is a bit of magic. When it is working, then their other powers — such as the ability to see through an argument to the crucial issue, and to know at all times not only what they themselves are thinking but what others are feeling, and the gift of judging what is and what is not feasible, and what has priority, and the gift of eloquence — all these become incandescent with an effective energy that in themselves they would not possess. . . .

1. Arthur H. Vandenberg, Jr., was the son of the late senator, who had died on April 18, 1951, after a long struggle with cancer. The younger Vandenberg edited *The Private Papers of Senator Vandenberg* (Boston, 1952), which on its dust jacket quoted most of the third paragraph of this letter.

To Leverett Saltonstall[1]

January 11, 1952

Dear Lev:

. . . In regard to your question, I thought when I read the General's statement that it was unwise of him to say that under no circumstances would he ask for relief.[2] If he is going to be President of the United States, he has got to learn never to say never! I have a feeling that in saying that he trapped himself, and that Truman took quick advantage of it by saying he wouldn't relieve Eisenhower.

That leaves the matter, technically at least, in such a condition that Eisenhower has to stay in Europe until he is nominated. The political disadvantage of this is that it greatly accentuates what is in my view his greatest political liability, namely that he is a soldier in uniform.

On the other hand, I'd prefer that to his coming back early and making an active, orthodox campaign for the nomination. He hasn't got the political know-how to do it very well, in my view. All his inexperience will, I think, be exposed to the country, and the American people, we must not forget, can turn quickly against their heroes.

I favor a very aloof campaign on his part, one which keeps him in the position of being above the party struggle. But I'd like him to get out of NATO before the nominating convention.

1. Republican Senator Leverett Saltonstall of Massachusetts was then a leader of the movement to draft Eisenhower as the G.O.P. presidential nominee in 1952. Lippmann was working privately with Saltonstall to that end. In "Today and Tomorrow" on January 10, 1952, he wrote that, as a candidate, Eisenhower could "lead to almost certain victory by healing and uniting the nation." 2. From his NATO command.

To Wilmarth S. Lewis[1]

October 13, 1952

Dear Lefty:

Thank you. It certainly will be nice to have the election over. I have been having an awful wrestle with myself, but I finally decided that it isn't safe to have a whole generation of Republicans without any experience of governing.

It has been hard for me because I know Stevenson[2] well and like him so much. Last winter when he was wrestling with himself he asked me, as he did so many others, what he should do. I told him not to run because I would have such a miserable year resisting him, if he did.

---

1. Wilmarth S. Lewis — wartime member of the Office of Strategic Services, enthusiastic author of books about eighteenth-century London, editor of the correspondence of Horace Walpole, fellow of the Yale Corporation, and trustee of several other educational institutions — later persuaded Lippmann, long a friend, to give his papers, scrapbooks, and manuscripts to the Yale University Library.   2. Governor Adlai E. Stevenson of Illinois, the Democratic presidential nominee in 1952 and 1956, had known Lippmann for some years. The two men corresponded on a first name basis. Stevenson's gallant and forthright campaign in 1952 won Lippmann's admiration even though Lippmann continued to support Eisenhower because he believed the country needed a Republican administration to restore national unity.

To Adlai E. Stevenson   TELEGRAM

November 5, 1952

You have won everything that a good man could want except only the election[1] (stop) That was impossible for a Democrat to do this year (stop) You should think of your campaign as the beginning. Affectionate regards.

---

1. Eisenhower won 33.9 million votes to Stevenson's 27.3 million and carried the electoral college 442 to 89. The victory swept the Republicans into control of both houses of Congress.

To Learned Hand

November 28, 1952

Dear B:

. . . I understood perfectly well why you felt so strongly about Dean. Throughout this whole wretched business all my personal inclinations were and still are in his favor. In my job I have found myself faced with this: that it was very difficult and probably impossible to criticize his administration of the State Department without giving aid and comfort to his low down enemies.

My fundamental conclusion about him has been that no man ought to remain Secretary of State who does not have the substantial confidence of the country because he cannot do the business of Secretary of State without it. I believe he should have had a showdown early in the day and either got what amounts to a vote of confidence from at least his own party and some substantial part of the Republicans, or he should have resigned.

It grieves me to have to find myself in this relation to him. I have not written this to anyone else, but I should like you to know it.

To George F. Kennan

January 17, 1953

Dear George:

. . . I have always been unhappy about our German policy and I am in fundamental agreement with your analysis.[1] I agree with your appreciation that the defense of Western Germany is an American vital interest and I would add that its corollary is the brutal but perhaps salutary fact that in case it were lost to the Soviet Orbit it would be an American necessity to deny its use to our adversaries. In other words if Western Germany is not successfully defended, its war potential will have to be scorched.

I agree also with the second appreciation that in the long run the best people to defend Western Germany are the Germans and I would certainly be in favor of the creation of a German armed force on a scale quite sufficient to deal with the armed forces of Eastern Germany, plus the armed forces capable of entering Germany of the satellite states. I would regard it as the business of NATO to neutralize the Soviet forces.

I think I agree with all the rest of the paper and certainly I do not disagree with much of it. But I would say that in my view the paper does not come to grips sufficiently with the most difficult German problem, which is that of the frontiers of the unified Germany. EDC in my opinion is bound to fail because it attempts to ignore both the problem of unification and the problem of frontiers. EDC, therefore, can not represent the national interests of the Germans and the French can never be happy with EDC knowing that it does not represent the true interests of the Germans. Your paper does not, I would say, meet this problem. If I read the paper correctly, you leave the armed Germans of West Germany free to work out their unification with the Eastern Zone and free also to form their policy about their frontiers, both the Saar and beyond the Oder-Neisse Line. I realize that there is no easy way to solve this problem. But within the last year I have come around to the view that what we might do is this: propose the arming of a united Germany within the Potsdam frontiers, a Germany armed as you propose; second, take the position that the occupation of Western Germany can not be ended until a united Germany has negotiated with its neighbors, France and Poland, a frontier agreement which both accept and have ratified; third, since this would take a long time the center of Germany and Berlin the capital of the united Germany should be evacuated by all foreign troops who would retire to peripheral points — as I think you proposed some years ago.

The leading idea in this proposal is that we can not afford not to participate in the delimitation of Germany's frontiers. We can not leave the delimitation of the Eastern frontier to a bi-lateral agreement between united Germany and the Soviet Union. We must reserve our right to participate in it and the only way to do that effectively is to remain an occupying power until negotiations for the frontiers are concluded. I might add parenthetically that I do not think the United States ought to have a position of its own as to what is the right frontier. Our position should be that it must be a frontier negotiated by a united Germany and Poland and approved by the occupying powers as having been the result of a fair and free negotiation.

I might add that I do not think that this policy as you have laid it down and as I have tried to supplement it can be put into effect in any near future. But I do believe that if it became our policy, it would greatly strengthen our influence in Germany, in Europe, and perhaps elsewhere.

I should say also that it is very necessary to have another position prepared in case the turn of events in Europe is such that the present plans and policies become quite untenable. It is not entirely beyond the wit of man, I believe, to draft such a policy on to the existing papers and documents and pacts, thus avoiding the confusion of a drastic about-face. . . .

1. George F. Kennan, then American ambassador to the Soviet Union, was about to retire from the foreign service. He then became a member, later a professor, of the Institute for Advanced Study at Princeton. He had sent Lippmann an eleven-page typescript, single spaced, consisting of his "thoughts about the German problem which depart very drastically from those that have governed our recent policy." In that paper, Kennan advocated the ultimate unity of Germany, viewed NATO as an unsuitable framework for resistance to the USSR in Europe, and opposed placing German troops within the forces of the European Defense Community (EDC) — the forces of the NATO nations.

To James B. Conant

January 19, 1953

My dear Conant:

I am sure I need not tell you how earnestly I wish you well in this brave and difficult work you have agreed to do. You are taking the crucial job in our foreign relations.[1]

May I suggest that you do not identify the success of your mission with the formalities of the ratification of the pacts and agreements in France and Germany,[2] or with the time-table of the recruitment of the German divisions. The holding of Germany within the western community is fundamentally, I believe, the question of Franco-German reconciliation. The pacts, modifications of the pacts and radical revision of the pacts should all be judged, I would say, in reference to the objective of Franco-German reconciliation.

It is my personal view that you may find it necessary to recommend a revision of the forms of our policy as adopted since 1950 in order to attain the objectives of the policy.

In any event, I hope ways can be found so that you are not regarded by the American public as a kind of super-lobbyist for E.D.C.

My other suggestion is that you make it a point to have a long and thorough discussion with George Kennan before you leave for Germany. He is a German expert, perhaps more even than he is a Russian expert, and he has recently been in Germany, as you know and is full of very serious ideas about the future of our policy. . . .

1. Conant was on his way to assuming office as United States high commissioner for Germany.　2. As it worked out, in August 1954 the French national assembly rejected the European Defense Community treaty.

To George F. Kennan

February 12, 1953

Dear George:

. . . My first feeling is that your doctrine about the *de jure* recognition[1] of a government contains within it the implication of sufficient ideological harmony between the two governments to rule out any fundamental irreconcilable conflict of ultimate purposes.

In general I do not like the idea of recognition to carry with it implications beyond the pragmatic rule that the government governs the area under a certain jurisdiction and that it wishes to establish diplomatic intercourse. If no more than that is implied in recognition, then the questions of principle which are troubling you do not, I think, arise. I think that the other view, which attaches implications of morality and political approval to the act of recognition, is inexpedient and unworkable. Consider, for example, the situation after Pearl Harbor if we had found ourselves refusing *de jure* recognition to the Soviet Government, which was the wartime ally of our ally, the British. Even if in 1933 we had refused *de jure* recognition, would we not have granted it hurriedly and not very elegantly, considering the urgency, as a preliminary to the signing of the United Nations Pact right after Pearl Harbor?

May I raise the question whether the position you are taking here is not a throw-back to the kind of moralistic, legalistic thinking which your book attacks? . . .

1. Kennan had sent Lippmann the copy of a letter to McGeorge Bundy, then a professor of government at Harvard, in which he asserted that the United States should never have established de jure political relations with the Soviet government. As Lippmann suggested, that statement

seemed at variance with the case for realism, as opposed to moralism, that Kennan had made in his best-selling book, *American Diplomacy, 1900–1950* (Chicago, 1951).

To Arthur L. Goodhart[1]

February 23, 1953

Dear Arthur:

It occurred to me that you would give me some good advice on what is rapidly becoming the most critical problem the new Administration has to deal with. This is the action of Congressional committees, led by McCarthy and others, to reach way down into the Civil Service, dealing directly with the small people individually and bypassing the responsible ministers at the top. I don't need to say how this destroys the morale and discipline and efficiency of the departments. In the State Department the situation is truly critical.

This sort of thing does not, and I take it could not, be done in England. . . .

The Swedish Ambassador told me the other night that if a civil servant is criticized by name in the Swedish parliament, the speaker immediately rules that the discussion is out of order and that the criticism must be addressed to the responsible minister. . . .

1. Arthur L. Goodhart, American lawyer, barrister in Great Britain, then professor of jurisprudence and master of University College, Oxford.

To Ralph E. Flanders[1]

April 23, 1953

My dear Senator Flanders:

. . . I should like to tell you, rather more explicitly than I felt it wise to do in a newspaper, why I think it inadvisable to proceed rapidly to an attempt to unify Korea by free elections.

It is that I have no confidence or hope that in a general election any Korean government would emerge which would be reliable and reasonably friendly to the United States. Yet, once the country had been united under a Korean government our forces would have to leave. It seems to me in the highest degree improbable that Syngman Rhee could by election establish a general government in all of Korea.[2]

On the other hand, I do not think it safe for the United States to leave the Korean peninsula until the whole Far Eastern position is far more stabilized than there is any prospect of its being.

I would be the first to admit, of course, that I may be taking an unduly pessimistic view of the consequences of a general election. But that at least is the basis of my argument. . . .

1. Senator Ralph E. Flanders, Vermont Republican, one of the most respected members of the liberal wing of his party.   **2.** Discussions of an armistice in Korea, which had stalled the previous December, were about to resume. They concluded in June 1953 with provisions for a demilitarized zone between the two Koreas, each of which retained its previous borders and independence. No general Korean election would have suited the president of South Korea, the authoritarian Syngman Rhee, then serving another four-year term, for he could probably not have won.

To Russell C. Leffingwell

June 3, 1953

Dear Russell:

    . . . I have a piece coming on Monday about the parallelism between Grant and Eisenhower, and how conceivably the awful parallelism might break down in favor of Ike. My real opinion is that the present administration will be an ignominious failure unless Eisenhower reorganizes his Cabinet and brings into the leading positions two or three powerful Republicans who agree with him,[1] probably Dewey and Warren. . . .

1. Lippmann had already concluded that Eisenhower suffered as president from "weakness and indecision," not the least in his apparent unwillingness and inability to restrain the damages inflicted by Senator Joe McCarthy on American civil liberties at home and the American reputation abroad; see Ronald Steel, *Walter Lippmann and the American Century* (Boston, 1980), pp. 480–85.

To Roger D. Lapham[1]

July 1, 1953

My dear Lapham:

    . . . I am rather depressed, if you ask me, about the American state of mind today. There is no leadership in Washington, not even a rallying point. Under those conditions . . . there can be only a kind of chaos of prejudices, fear, half-information, cloudy aspirations, suspicions and a general incoherence.

    I have recently been to Europe and within the twelve months which passed since my last visit the downfall, one might almost say the collapse, of American prestige has been spectacular. I knew that things were not going well for us abroad, but until I got there I did not realize how badly they were going. They will not get better, I am afraid, until the President restores the prestige and the authority of his office. . . .

1. Roger D. Lapham, a San Francisco acquaintance of the Lippmanns', was chairman of the board of the American Hawaiian Steamship Company.

To George F. Kennan

August 24, 1953

Dear George:

. . . Our public life seems, for the time being, incapable of any moderate, considered, discriminating view of any international question. I find our manners — disregarding entirely the substance of our position — in the U.N. and Korean Conference business positively embarrassing in its crudity. Reading Cabot Lodge's remarks the other day, I thought how fearfully odd it would be if Henry Cabot Lodge's grandson had a leading part in the destruction of the United Nations.[1]

Of course, if the United Nations is destroyed, the real responsibility in my view will be with those who expected it to do the impossible and used it for purposes that it was never fitted to achieve and, in fact, tried to treat it as if it were something approaching a world government. . . .

1. Lodge, then American ambassador to the UN, had been attacking the Soviet Union and its policies in speeches at the General Assembly.

To J. William Fulbright

March 13, 1954

Dear Bill:

. . . I have been four times to Europe since McCarthyism became important, and our people over here who have not been there have no idea whatsoever of the damage it has done. . . .[1]

1. Fulbright knew. He was the only senator to oppose the next appropriations for the budget of McCarthy's committee, though other Democrats also attacked McCarthy for his demagoguery and for the book banning by his agents in their visits to European offices of the United States Information Service.

To Allen W. Dulles

April 13, 1954

Dear Allen:

As I informed you on Saturday, the Polish Ambassador came to see me this afternoon by appointment at four o'clock and stayed for about an hour. His secretary telephoned me a week ago asking for the appointment, saying that he would like to call upon me on Monday, Tuesday or Wednesday of this week, and I fixed the date for today.

He began by giving me an album containing photographs of the famous Polish altar piece . . . which belongs to the Cracow Cathedral. Though he did not say so, I assumed that he had remembered my telling him after our return from a visit to Poland in 1947 that I had been to the studio in Cracow, where this altar piece, which had been broken up and hidden during the war, was being reassembled. He brought also a small peasant ornament from his wife for Helen. You will remember our showing you the ikon of the Virgin Mary, which Helen received after a talk they had had about religion. There was no doubt in my mind that he wished to signify his interest in things outside the sphere of the ideological war.

After these preliminaries, and a few remarks about how glad he was not to have spent so much time at the U.N. as he had had to spend last year, he said that the reason he asked for the appointment was that it was his business as Ambassador to get informed about American public opinion and the American attitude, and he was puzzled and troubled and hoped I could help clarify his mind.

I asked him what he wanted me to try to clarify, and he put the case this way: after the Korean armistice and even through the Berlin Conference[1] he had hoped and believed that relaxation of the tension would take place, but that in the last few weeks he had become very much frightened about the possibility of a general war developing out of Indochina. He said this fear was strong in Poland, and that it was accentuated by the reasoning from what he called their "bible," the bible of Marx and Lenin, that capitalist countries when they have a recession tend to become warlike.

I interrupted him at that point to say that I knew that was the Marxist-Leninist theory, but he had lived in this country for eight or nine years and I would like to know whether he believed in that doctrine about America. He hastily disclaimed it and said no, that was not his personal view at all, but it was the view of communists in Poland.

After that digression he went on to give a rather long discourse about how the desire for normalization, in order to raise the standard of life, was very strong in the Soviet Union and in Poland. But now they were very much afraid that the tension, which might lead to war, was rising rather than being reduced.

Up to that point I had no chance to say anything because although he came saying he wanted information, in fact he was doing all the talking.

However, at that point I interrupted and said that I, too, felt the tension was rising and that the question of whether it would rise more or would be reduced depended on what happened at Geneva. So I would like to know what he believed were the terms which the communist powers might propose at Geneva. He said that he did not know and that they were a closely guarded secret in Peiping and in Moscow, but that he himself wondered whether the French agreement with Ho Chi Minh in 1946 might form the basis of an agreement.

I told him that if he wanted my own judgment of American opinion and attitude, it was that any proposal which amounted to turning the country over to Ho Chi Minh would be rejected without negotiation and that, furthermore, if the war were not ended by an honorable and satisfactory armistice at Geneva and during the rainy season, the war might become more extensive and more violent when the fighting was resumed. I said that the communists must not expect to get by negotiation at Geneva anything more than they now have, and that what they now hold is the maximum they can expect to get. He was very much taken back by that, and it was obvious to me that he is not only uninformed about Indochina, but that he is concerned with it only because of a vague and general fear that it would lead to a general war.

After that the conversation drifted off into rather routine arguments on his part about how they were surrounded by our bases and how they were maligned in our press and how they are treated as if they were monolithic, when in fact there are many varieties of opinion.

I learned nothing from the interview, except to have confirmed for me an indubitable anxiety that he feels and which is probably reflected from Poland. I did not think there was any particular feeler which he wanted to put out. My impression was that he wanted to be consoled and reassured that the situation is less dangerous than he thinks it is.

As I think it is both true and useful to insist that it is dangerous, I insisted several times.

1. The foreign ministers of the United States, Great Britain, France, and the Soviet Union met in Berlin in February 1954 and agreed to meet again in April, with a representative from China, to discuss the continuing problems of Indochina. In March 1954, the Vietminh — the Communist and Nationalist forces under Ho Chi Minh — had attacked the French at Dien Bien Phu, which fell on May 7. Meanwhile Secretary of State Dulles had offered the French additional aid, and President Eisenhower had declared the defeat of Communist "aggression" in Indochina and elsewhere in Southeast Asia of crucial importance to the United States. At Geneva talks went on inconclusively until June, when French Premier Pierre Mendès-France and Chinese Premier Chou En-lai, conferring privately, agreed on the provisions for a settlement. In July the Geneva Conference agreed on an armistice in Indochina that divided Vietnam at the 17th parallel, with Ho Chi Minh's government in control of the Democratic Republic of Vietnam north of that line, and the French client state of South Vietnam in control south of that line. The United States refused to accept any responsibility for that armistice, including its provision for a national election in Vietnam, or to be bound by its terms. In December France officially granted independence to the three associated states of Indochina — South Vietnam, Laos, and Cambodia. South Vietnam became a republic under Premier Ngo Dinh Diem in October 1955.

To Allen W. Dulles

April 20, 1954

Dear Allen:

This is for your information: the Indian Ambassador telephoned me Monday afternoon, saying he would like to come and see me today. I told him that I would be glad to go to see him, and I have just been there for tea.

The occasion for his call was my article on Monday, called "The Dulles Trip

and Indo-China," and he was, of course, particularly interested in the suggestion at the end that the proposed pact might become a means of protecting the
independence of the Indochinese states and that it was to be hoped that India
would not shut the door against such a possibility. (Incidentally, Foster telephoned me Monday evening, saying that he liked the article as a whole and
that it reflected what he had in mind.)

When I saw the Ambassador today he asked me to tell him what I was
suggesting. I put it to him this way: that while the Indochinese states are
entitled to independence, they are and will be incapable of exercising full independence for a considerable time to come. They are, and he agreed, unready
for self-government. Therefore, independence as such must create a political
vacuum which would promptly be filled by the communist dictatorship. That
being the situation, the problem is to create a political protectorate of some
sort within which the newly emancipated Indochinese states could learn to use
their independence. Such a protectorate, once the French withdraw, cannot be
created by any Western power alone, and therefore unless the independent
nations of Asia take the lead in creating that protectorate, Indochina will either
fall within the communist orbit or become the battleground of a great war.

He agreed with this and then proceeded to tell me that substantially the
same idea was in the mind of his government and that he expected a proposal
of some sort to come from the forthcoming meeting at Colombo on April 28th,
at which there will be present the Prime Ministers of India, Pakistan, Burma,
Ceylon and Indonesia. This conference has been called by the Prime Minister
of Ceylon.

I assume from this that we shall see discussed at Geneva three Asian pacts:
one from the communists modeled on Molotov's pact for Europe, our own
proposed pact, and a third Asian pact.[1]

The new information in all this, as far as I am concerned, was the probable
action at Colombo.

1. The conference discussed no pacts, but during the meetings Secretary of State Dulles reported
that the United States was continuing to try to form a Southeast Asia defense alliance, an idea
advanced in 1953 by Winston Churchill, who had become prime minister again after the Conservative victory in the British elections of 1951. The Southeast Asia defense treaty was signed
in September 1954, at Manila. SEATO included the United States, Great Britain, France, Israel,
New Zealand, the Philippines, Thailand, and Pakistan in a loose and ineffectual alliance directed
against Communist subversion in the area.

To John Cowles[1]

May 13, 1954
Dear John:

. . . On the general line that there is no use asking for something that
can't possibly be obtained, I would say that as long as we give help to the
French we will not persuade the other side to stop helping the Viet Minh.

Also I think . . . that you do not make enough distinction between our recognition of Red China and admitting Red China to the U.N. These are separate problems. The U.N. matter is not entirely within our control. Recognition is entirely within our own control. It seems probable that the first will happen before the second is even seriously considered.

Frankly I don't agree with what you say about disarmament. Personally I do not favor it and I think there is no possibility that the American people would agree to it. I do not see how the President could propose "complete and universal disarmament, the abolition of all weapons, not just atomic weapons."

I do not like also the form of your warning to the Soviet Union. We are at present committed to regard as a cause of war any external organized military aggression by the Soviet Union across recognized frontiers. Our commitment is as complete and definite on this point as it ever was on the Monroe Doctrine. I would not like to mix it up with the question of disarmament.

There are many weaknesses in the Eisenhower foreign policy, but the basic policy of this warning and our own deterrent power has proved to be effective. . . .

1. John Cowles, president of the Des Moines Register and Tribune Company of the Cowles Broadcasting Company, and of Cowles Magazines, Inc., and chairman of the board of the Minneapolis Star Journal and Tribune Company.

To George F. Kennan

June 10, 1954

Dear George:

. . . If the Administration is to be criticized on the grounds that I did criticize it, namely that it made a security case out of what should have been an administrative decision about its adviser, then Oppenheimer on the other side should not have been in the position where he appears to be fighting to be retained as a high level adviser.[1] There is something false in his fighting for the reinstatement of his clearance as if he hoped to compel the President to continue using him in a top job.

At some point in the proceedings — I don't know exactly where, but early — there should have been no doubt left that he was not seeking a job, and that he did not wish to serve in the job if he was not really wanted in it. This is not entirely hindsight, because I had that feeling very early in the day when I first learned what was up. But, of course, the exact point at which to do that, and exactly how to do it is something I don't venture to have an opinion upon, not knowing enough about the events which led up to this investigation. . . .

1. J. Robert Oppenheimer, the eminent physicist who had been director of the Los Alamos laboratory when the atomic bomb reached final development, had been denied a security clearance to

classified government information. A three-man board had found his friends questionable, though he had had the same friends during his long years of distinguished service to the government. The mood of the time, exemplified by the excesses of McCarthyism, Oppenheimer's earlier opposition to the construction of a fusion bomb — the hydrogen bomb — and the enmity of other scientists constituted a background for the decision, but the immediate cause lay, as Lippmann observed, with the awkward administrative procedures of the Eisenhower administration. For his part, Oppenheimer had often seemed arrogant during the hearings on his case and, as Lippmann also contended, had seemed to demand retention as a policy adviser to a government that did not want his counsel.

To Bernard Berenson

August 23, 1954

Dear B. B.:

. . . About ten days ago I finished my book, the book I have been writing on and off for fifteen years. It will be called *The Public Philosophy*,[1] and it deals, in the main part at least, with the positive ideas that are necessary to make work a free and democratic society. The public philosophy is natural law on which western institutions were originally founded.

There is a lot more to the book than the discussion of natural law in its modern and contemporary application — for example, a discussion of the sudden and steep decline of the Western Society immediately upon the achievement of universal suffrage and the democratic control of war and peace. But you won't suspect me of having become some kind of authoritarian crank. By the time I reach Italy I may have a copy decent enough to show you. I hope you won't dislike the book because some of its spirit, more particularly its appreciation of the great traditions of the West, I owe to you. . . .

1. *Essays in the Public Philosophy* was published by Little, Brown and Company in Boston in 1955 and later reprinted in many paperback editions. Thirty years after its first publication it remained the only one of Lippmann's many books, except *Public Opinion*, still in print. The uneven reception *The Public Philosophy* received contributed to the "nervous exhaustion," in Lippmann's phrase, that occasioned his stay for several weeks in February 1955 in the Massachusetts General Hospital. On the reception of the book and Lippmann's illness, see Ronald Steel, *Walter Lippmann and the American Century* (Boston, 1980), pp. 492–96.

To Iverach McDonald[1]

December 7, 1954

Dear Iverach:

I have been back only a few days, but I have seen a number of people who know what is going on here, and I was at the President's press conference the other day, and I feel that I ought to amend one impression I may have left with you.

When I was in London I did not expect that the President would be able to do more than be the rather helpless victim of the division of his own party. Though the evidence is far from conclusive, there are reasons for thinking that he has crossed the Rubicon in the business of trying to appease the right wing of his party. Friends of mine tell me that he has felt the Democratic victory in Congress[2] not as a defeat but as a liberation. . . .

1. Iverach McDonald was then foreign editor of the *Times* of London. 2. In the November elections, the Democrats had regained control of both houses of Congress by narrow margins.

To Bartley C. Crum[1]

December 13, 1954

Dear Mr. Crum:

. . . In regard to Senator Knowland, the basic consideration for me is that in his position as official leader of the Administration party in the Senate, orderly government requires that he should argue his views confidentially within the Administration circle.[2] I don't deny that his views may be correct, though I don't really fully share them. If he feels that he must argue them publicly, then I think he must divest himself of the authority which goes with his official position. Not to do that is to cause immense confusion in the outer world, arising from the fact that there appear to be two voices speaking for the United States.

1. Bartley C. Crum was then practicing law in New York City. 2. William F. Knowland had become Republican leader in the Senate after the death of Robert Taft in July 1953. He held the position until 1959 but, unlike Taft, was frequently uncooperative with the administration and often of limited influence with his colleagues. Knowland, "the Senator from Formosa," was especially critical of Eisenhower's Asian policy and cool to the prospect of Eisenhower's renomination.

To Robert Brand

December 13, 1954

Dear Bob:

. . . I might say that since I have come back I am more than ever satisfied that the decision to support Eisenhower rather than Stevenson in 1952 was sound. My two reasons were that only under a Republican Administration could the McCarthy problem be dealt with successfully, and only under a Republican Administration could an essentially pacific policy be carried out. There is now pretty good reason for thinking that both of these arguments are being proved correct.[1]

1. Eisenhower's "atoms for peace," which called for an international agency to promote the beneficial use of atomic energy, had won unanimous endorsement of the UN General Assembly on December 4, 1954. Eisenhower had also warned China that any effort to conquer Taiwan would "have to run over the Seventh Fleet," but he had supported General Matthew Ridgeway against the other members of the Joint Chiefs in refusing to authorize the bombing of China or to defend Quemoy (an island off Taiwan) unless an attack on Quemoy or the island of Ma-tsu was part of an attack on Taiwan. Chinese shelling of Quemoy persuaded Eisenhower to sign a defense treaty with Chiang Kai-shek, but he also placed new restraints on the generalissimo to keep him from involving the United States in any Nationalist attack on the mainland. On December 10, 1954, Dulles and the Nationalist ambassador agreed that the use of force from any area under Chiang's control would "be a matter of joint agreement." Eisenhower also ignored Senator Knowland's demand for an American blockade of the Chinese coast. The president's Asian policy receives excellent treatment in R. A. Divine, *Eisenhower and the Cold War* (New York, 1981), ch. 2.

The president had had less influence in the case of Senator McCarthy, though he exhibited a patient dignity in awaiting the senator's eventual self-destruction. That had occurred during televised hearings about alleged subversion within the Army, hearings that revealed McCarthy to the nation as the brutal bully he was. Ralph Flanders of Vermont deserved the greatest credit for pushing his fellow senators to condemn McCarthy for his behavior then and earlier. A select bipartisan Senate committee, formed at Flanders's initiative, heard evidence for and against McCarthy and in September 1954 unanimously urged censure on account of his "contemptuous, contumacious, and denunciatory" treatment of a Senate subcommittee and an Army general. The Senate voted that censure sixty-seven to twenty-two on December 2, 1954, several weeks after the November elections. Thereafter McCarthy's influence waned.

To Quincy A. Wright

January 25, 1955

Dear Quincy:

. . . Let me say that I do, of course, distinguish the public philosophy from the ideology or religion of any particular group. In my discussion of Alexander the Great and the Stoics I tried to make plain that the public philosophy is necessary for a plural society and that it assumes the existence of diversities of belief. It does, however, require that diverse beliefs shall be judged and/or accommodated by rational procedure.

Although I agree with you that the public philosophy must be applicable to the entire community, I do not attempt to define a priori who is in the community and who is not. The community really consists of those who accept and abide by the public philosophy. The ultimate issue with communism in this field is over the willingness to abide by rational procedure in a settlement of or the accommodation of opposing doctrines. . . .

To Henri Bonnet [1]

May 2, 1955

Dear Henri:

. . . There is more bewilderment than anything else here in Washington about the developments in Vietnam. Our two governments do not seem to see eye to eye, perhaps because neither of them really sees clearly what can be done.[2] But then I have long been a pessimist about Vietnam.

During this past week the Administration has probably crossed the Rubicon in relation to Chiang Kai-shek and Senator Knowland. This is due quite as much to the support given by Senator George[3] to the idea of a negotiated truce as to Chou's statement at Bandung.[4] But we have hopes because there is very good evidence that these more conciliatory statements are the result of many weeks of diplomatic discussion in which Eden and Molotov had a leading part.

In our home affairs the crucial question in almost any political discussion is whether or not Eisenhower will run again. The Republicans regard the outlook as hopeless if he doesn't. The Democrats regard it as hopeless if he does. My own feeling has been that in the end he would not run. Certainly he acts more and more like a man who dislikes his office and is unwilling to make the kind of actions which are expected of a candidate. . . .

1. Henri Bonnet had resigned a few months earlier as French ambassador to the United States. **2.** Premier Ngo Dinh Diem, victor in a South Vietnam power struggle with Prince Bau Loa, on May 8, 1955, rejected a French plan for the return of Bau Loa under a reorganized government. The United States nevertheless remained committed to Diem even after France decided to remove its troops from South Vietnam later in May.   **3.** Walter F. George, Georgia Democrat, had been a member of the United States Senate since 1922. A patriarch of that body, he was also chairman of the Committee on Foreign Relations. In April he had called for American negotiations with both the Soviet Union and Communist China.   **4.** Early in 1955, Communist China attacked the Tachen Islands, which lay between the Chinese coast and Taiwan. Eisenhower arranged to assist the Nationalists in evacuating the islands and also asked Congress for a joint resolution authorizing the use of force to protect Taiwan and "closely related localities." He used that ambiguous phrase to keep the mainland Chinese from knowing precisely what he intended about the controversial islands of Quemoy and Ma-tsu. But in March, warned about the possibility of an attack on them, Eisenhower in a press conference hinted that defense of the islands might involve the use of tactical atomic weapons, a message he intended for the Chinese Communists. Two weeks later, he let it be known he expected no war. Still, his implicit threat may have influenced Chinese Foreign Minister Chou En-lai at Bandung on April 23 to say China did not want a war with the United States and to suggest discussions to relax tension in the Taiwan area. Though the State Department rejected that offer, Eisenhower accepted it, and inconclusive discussions were held in Geneva in August. They failed to settle the issue, but Eisenhower's refusal unhesitatingly to embrace Chiang, and his willingness to talk to the Communist Chinese in the absence of Nationalist representation, upset Senator Knowland. Indeed, for a brief period unconfirmed rumors reported Knowland's intention to resign as minority leader.

To Robert Brand

May 9, 1955

Dear Bob:

. . . You are right in saying that the United States suffers more than the United Kingdom from the malady of the legislature that will not permit the executive to govern. I had that in mind and made a reference to it in my book.

I don't however think that parliamentary governments are less susceptible to it than our type. Consider for example, France, where the disease is much further advanced than it is with us. But it is a curious and, I think, significant fact that the most successful representative governments in this century, excepting Switzerland and the United States, have been constitutional monarchies. I think that is because monarchy gives to the executive a status not entirely dependent upon the votes of the assembly. In our system we achieve some of that by making the President not only the chief of the government but the head of the state and giving him a fixed tenure. But under a weak President our system does not work well, and we, and I think our allies, are paying a heavy price because the American executive both under Truman and under Eisenhower has been subject to so much domination from the Congress. . . .

To Robert Hall[1]

May 21, 1955

Dear Robert:
    . . . I would so particularly like to talk with you about . . . the further consequences of full employment. Unfree states use coercion as their final sanction to maintain discipline in production. The older capitalism had as its sanction the fear of unemployment. Without coercion and without fear, discipline will depend upon improving the incentives to work. I don't doubt that this can be done for most people. But there is likely to be a minority who do not respond to them.

    I should like very much to hear how you believe this difficulty can be resolved — that of combining full employment with no coercion. Manifestly it must involve the creation of strong incentives to work. But there will long be a minority who do not respond to such incentives.

    I might say that I think that is only one of the very difficult problems which our new democratic societies have to struggle with. . . .

1. Sir Robert Hall, a leading economist in the British Treasury.

To Paul G. Hoffman[1]

May 25, 1955

Dear Paul:
    I have been thinking a lot about Eisenhower and 1956, and I have come up with the idea that it is very important to build up another man who could run with Eisenhower as Vice President or could run for President, if Eisenhower bows out.

There are now only two men in the running — Nixon and Knowland — and neither of them could expect the independent support that Eisenhower has. In fact either of them will tend to alienate that support. Nixon as Vice President to Eisenhower would be a liability. Nixon on his own would almost surely be defeated.

A third man should be brought forward and built up and it seems to me that the man who fits the role best is Governor Herter of Massachusetts.[2] There is no question that he is a wholehearted Eisenhower Republican. He has been an extraordinarily successful and popular governor of a great and important state. Our history shows that the most effective presidents during this century have been men who learned government as governors of a state. He is a very attractive personality.

There are two things that might be raised against Herter. The one is his arthritis, which makes him lame. But my Boston friends tell me that he is in better health since he became Governor than he was when he was in Congress, and that his health is no problem at all. The other question arises from the fact that he was born in Paris, although of course his parents were American citizens. There would be some argument as to whether this disqualifies him under the Constitution. But Judge Learned Hand, with whom I talked the other day, doesn't feel that it surely would disqualify him. And other lawyers whom I have talked with argued that he is not in the true intent of the Constitution "foreign born."

I am writing this to you in no feeling that you ought to commit yourself about it one way or the other. I would feel more comfortable if the Republicans didn't have only one string to their bow. . . .

1. Paul G. Hoffman had returned to private life in 1950 as chairman of the board of Studebaker-Packard Corporation. **2.** Herter had been elected governor in 1953.

To Bernard Berenson

November 8, 1955

Dear B. B.:

We have now been back a bit over a week and in all my experience I have never seen Washington so inert. We might well have stayed in Europe another month without missing anything here. With Congress away from Washington, and with the President ill,[1] and the Secretary of State in Europe, nothing is allowed to happen in Washington. There ought to be big decisions taken as a result of the Soviet incursion into the Middle East, but there is no one here who can or will make those decisions.

We had a busy five days in London, which included lunch with the Edens, . . . several visits to the Foreign Office, talks with the Treasury people, and a round of parties. My main feeling was that the Churchill influence on the

Conservative Party was wearing out rapidly and that the party was again very much like what it was in the 1930's. It seems pretty evident that Churchill put a face on the Conservative Party which isn't natural to it. It is also pretty clear that Eden was a far better Foreign Minister with Churchill at 10 Downing Street than he is as Prime Minister,[2] with Macmillan at the Foreign Office.

Before London we were a week in Paris where, as you know, the moral and political atmosphere is now most depressing. If France is going to be governed by people like Edgar Faure and Pinay, it seems to me that nothing on earth could prevent France from losing the whole of North Africa. . . .[3]

1. Eisenhower had had a heart attack while in Denver on September 24, 1955. During his illness and early recovery, his immediate entourage retained control of his office, from which they were determined to exclude Vice President Nixon. On November 11, the president returned to Washington in good health.   2. Anthony Eden became prime minister in April 1955, when Churchill resigned because of his advancing age and failing health. Eden retained office after the Conservative victory in the general election in May. Harold Macmillan served in his cabinet.   3. During the last half of 1954, French Premier Pierre Mendès-France was able to obtain the approval of the French assembly for increased self-government for Tunisia and Morocco, but he was unable to resolve the continuing conflicts with insurgent forces there and especially in Algeria. Forced to resign in February, he was succeeded by Edgar Faure, whose new cabinet, more conservative than its Socialist predecessor, included former Premier Antoine Pinay.

To George W. Ball[1]

November 25, 1955

Dear George:

When I saw the Governor on Wednesday evening, I put forward my favorite notion: that, as things stand now, the election will be a contest for possession of the confidence of the voters on two questions — the preservation of prosperity and the preservation of peace. Eisenhower's strength is that he has public confidence on these subjects. The great question for the Republicans is whether any other available Republican can have public confidence on these subjects.

The critical weakness of the Democrats lies, I believe, in their being susceptible to the charge of being a war party — the party of the two World Wars and of the Korean War. . . .

The underlying error, in my opinion, lies in a failure to recognize that Eisenhower's reputation as a defender of peace is solidly established at home and abroad, and that this reputation is not impaired by the mistakes of our foreign policy as administered by Dulles and imposed by Congress. Eisenhower's personal reputation rests on the fact that he ended the Korean War, refused to participate in the Indochinese War, avoided war in the Formosa Straits, and at the Summit Meeting at Geneva played a leading part in a public renunciation of war between East and West.[2]

The attempt to ignore or to deny or to pick faults in these Eisenhower achievements will be a boomerang. It will not diminish Eisenhower's prestige because the people judge by the results. It would permit the Republicans to retort that under the Democrats these great acts for the avoidance of war would not have taken place.

The right line, I believe, is to give Eisenhower full and generous appreciation for the part he has played, and to concentrate criticism on

(1) The administration of foreign policy by Dulles,

(2) The Right-Wing Republican warmongering, and

(3) The fact that Eisenhower has not conducted and controlled his foreign policy. He has rescued it by emergency decisions from the dilemmas and dead ends into which it has been sucked.

This approach puts the Democrats in a position to discuss critically the dead ends and dilemmas such as that

(1) In Germany we have been maneuvered into a position where we are threatened with a German-Russian deal,[3]

(2) In Japan we are threatened with a neutralist reaction against our militarized diplomacy,

(3) The alienation of India,[4]

(4) The political penetration of the Soviet Union into the Middle East. The most immediate dangerous consequence of this is the Egyptian-Israeli tension.[5] The danger of a Palestine War arises from the rivalry of the great powers. This rivalry prevents them from imposing a peaceable settlement. No settlement is possible except one imposed by the United Nations with the support of the great powers.

But the paramount political question in foreign affairs will probably not be any of these concrete problems. It will be, who is going to control foreign affairs after 1956? There is a real majority for a sound policy of peace in Congress. This real majority consists of virtually all the Democrats and about half the Republicans. As we have seen this majority can become a working majority only when the Democrats are in control of Congress.

On the assumption that Eisenhower will not run again, the question then is whether there is a Republican successor who can control the Republican Right Wing and also work effectively with the Democrats.

---

1. George W. Ball, a Washington attorney who had practiced law in Chicago, 1935–42, was an intimate of Adlai Stevenson's. Stevenson did again win the Democratic nomination, but in November 1956 lost the election to Eisenhower in a landslide. 2. At Geneva in July, Eisenhower met with Eden, Faure, and Soviet Premier Nikolai A. Bulganin, who was then still Soviet head of state though less powerful than Nikita Khrushchev, who accompanied him. At Geneva Eisenhower called for ''a basis for accommodation . . . a new spirit that will make possible future solutions.'' None was forthcoming at the conference, where Eisenhower also proposed ''open skies'' for mutual strict inspection, an idea the British and French supported. Bulganin seemed impressed by the proposal, but Khrushchev openly opposed it as a device for espionage. 3. In September 1955, Chancellor Adenauer had visited Moscow, where West Germany and the Soviet

Union agreed to establish diplomatic relations, and the Soviet Union to release German prisoners of war. But German rearmament was proceeding at that time, with the new German forces committed to the West. No "deal" of significance between Germany and Russia materialized. **4.** American military and technical aid to Pakistan offended India, which in June 1955, while Nehru was visiting Moscow, reached an agreement for Soviet economic and technical assistance. In November Bulganin and Khrushchev visited India.   **5.** Egyptian Premier Colonel Gamal Abdel Nasser had agreed in September 1955 to exchange rice and cotton for Czechoslovak arms — evidence of the increasing influence of the Soviet Union in Egypt. The agreement provoked Israel to appeal to the United States for armaments equal to whatever Egypt received from the Soviet bloc. For the while, Israel's chief Western supplier remained France.

To Bernard Berenson

December 3, 1955

Dear B. B.:

. . . About Adlai Stevenson, we spent the night at his country place, north of Chicago, and as we were all alone, just the three of us, and we stayed up late, we had a chance to talk about almost everything. I came away quite happy about him and quite reassured about his reputed indecision. In fact, on public questions, that is simply the result of his having an open mind, his unwillingness to make snap judgments, and his capacity, which is rare in public men, for deliberating. When he has reached a conclusion, he is quite firm and decisive about it.

My own present guess is that he will surely be nominated by the Democrats and that on the Republican side, it will turn out in the end to be Nixon. I just don't believe that Eisenhower will run again and the nomination, therefore, is likely to go to Nixon more or less by default. . . .

To Arnold O. Wolfers[1]

January 27, 1956

Dear Arnold:

I wish we could discuss the theory of deterrence.[2] I do not think that deterrence works automatically except in the sense that both sides are aware of the dangers of nuclear warfare.

My quarrel with Dulles lay in the fact that we failed to say that along with the warnings which were given explicitly or implied, we, quite wisely, took the trouble to convey reassuring information to the other side.

In the case of China and Quemoy, for example, the information was conveyed to Chou En-lai that we would not use the islands as a springboard for Chiang's invasion of the mainland. And that, in fact, we no longer regarded Chiang *de facto* as having any prospects on the mainland. We didn't merely scare off the Chinese, we reassured them and, indeed, through third parties, negotiated with them. I am worried about giving the American people the idea that they can accomplish these things by brandishing the bomb alone. . . .

1. Arnold O. Wolfers had been a professor of international relations at Yale University since 1935. **2.** "Deterrence" implied here the possession and threat to use the atomic bomb, later the hydrogen bomb, or tactical atomic weapons, as John Foster Dulles had meant in his phrase "massive retaliation" of the early Eisenhower years, and as Eisenhower had issued the threat in demanding armistice negotiations in Korea and in the Quemoy crisis. The doctrine receives lucid analysis in J. L. Gaddis, *Strategies of Containment* (New York, 1982), chs. 5, 6.

To Walt W. Rostow [1]

September 26, 1956

Dear Walt:

. . . I am rather troubled about your admonition that we must be prepared for a war anywhere including guerrilla war. Do you really think that is a feasible military objective?

1. Walt W. Rostow was then a professor of economic history at the Massachusetts Institute of Technology and a senior member of that institution's Center for International Studies, which was subsidized by the CIA for classified research about problems in American foreign and military policy. He had sent Lippmann the text of a speech intended for delivery at the Naval War College. Rostow's theories about guerrilla warfare were to have a considerable influence in the 1960s, particularly upon American policy in Vietnam which Lippmann opposed.

To Robert Brand

December 3, 1956

Dear Bob:

. . . I attribute our policy not to any desire on Eisenhower's part to humiliate or punish the allies.[1] For whatever else one may think of him, he has I am told been from the beginning a moderating force in the councils of our government. His great weakness is naivete and a preference for the easiest way. It is, for example, almost inconceivable that with his Secretary just recovering from a very serious operation, he should go off to Atlanta for two weeks of golf. I am supposing that he would not have done that, if he had not been ordered by his doctors to take the rest. He can't possibly have done it just for fun.

With Eisenhower playing a passive part and with Dulles away, there has been nobody to form a policy. The easy way out was to cling to the United Nations and that is how the policy was adopted.

In saying all this, one has to bear in mind the shock caused in Washington by the military action in Egypt which struck them without warning and knocked them off their balance.

In the past week there have been many signs that the balance was being righted. I don't know whether it is too late and whether the new measures are too little. But the first phase which culminated in the resolutions in the United Nations has passed.

In my view what the British government should have done was to deliver its ultimatum not to Egypt but to the United Nations and to have told them eloquently and firmly that if the United Nations did not do something serious about the canal and Palestine, it would be necessary to act outside the United Nations. The things that did the British cause the most harm were ignoring the United Nations, failing to make a convincing case for intervention, and finally in not making a very good job of the military task.

I have been worried about the consequences in Europe of the oil shortage. I have a very strong impression that it is Nasser's policy and also the Soviet policy to keep the canal closed through the winter as a means of pressure on the West. I hope I am wrong about that. . . .

1. The deterioration in Anglo-American relations had occurred in large part because Anthony Eden's distaste for the preachings of John Foster Dulles had prevented full communication between the two countries. Indeed Eden deliberately had not told the United States about British plans for intervention in Egypt after President Gamal Abdel Nasser of that country nationalized the Suez Canal in July 1956. After efforts at negotiation with Nasser failed, the British and French in September agreed to apply economic pressure to force Egypt to accept international control of the canal. The two European nations also referred the dispute to the UN Security Council, where a Soviet veto prevented a compromise resolution on the matter. On October 29, to the surprise of the United States, Israeli forces invaded Egypt, and the next day, rejecting American and Soviet suggestions for a cease-fire, Britain and France issued an ultimatum demanding Israeli and Egyptian withdrawal from a ten-mile strip along the canal. On October 31, Britain and France vetoed UN Security Council resolutions to refrain from force and began bombardment of Cairo and the area around the canal. On November 6, the Soviet Union threatened to act to end the fighting, and Eisenhower ordered an alert of American armed forces. Only then did the British government agree to a cease-fire, with France and Israel following that example. On December 22, with a UN force to supervise the cease-fire in place, the British and French evacuated their troops from Egypt, as soon also did Israel, though it retained the Gaza Strip and the area of Aqaba until March 1957. The following month, the UN completed clearing sunken ships from the canal, which Egypt then opened except to Israeli users. Meanwhile the ineffective military planning that had characterized the British operations in the crisis, and the clash of British with American policy, had damaged the reputation of Prime Minister Eden, who resigned in January 1959, to be succeeded by Harold Macmillan. The new prime minister successfully restored excellent relations with the Eisenhower government.

To Bernard Berenson

December 17, 1956

Dear B. B.:

This is just a note in reply to your letter of the 12th of December in which you say that we disagree "perhaps fundamentally" in the way we think about agreements that require collaboration. But I believe that an agreement, if we could get one, to withdraw troops from a certain region, say back of the Soviet frontier, would not be signed by the Soviet Union unless it intended to comply with it. If it didn't comply with it, the violation would be open and obvious. I have often put it this way: I don't believe in anything like a marriage with the Soviet Union, which is a promise to live together. But I would not feel the same way about a divorce contract which separated the Soviet Union from the Western world. I look upon the military evacuation of Eastern Europe as a most highly desirable agreement. I don't know whether we can reach it. But I am in favor of trying. . . .

To Robert H. Estabrook[1]

July 29, 1957

Dear Bob:

. . . As for Civil Rights, I am troubled about the jury trial business . . . but I haven't been able to make up my mind whether the distinction between civil and criminal contempt can be made to work in cases of refusing to let Negroes vote or to intimidate them if they try to vote. On the whole, I think I'd be satisfied if the injunctive process of the Bill were applicable only to election officials. . . .[2]

1. Robert H. Estabrook, head of the editorial page of the *Washington Post*. 2. The Civil Rights Act of 1957, the first since Reconstruction, was then still pending in the Senate. As passed by both houses in September, the measure, an ineffectual effort to protect the voting rights of Southern blacks, eliminated a controversial section that was designed to speed the desegregation of Southern schools as ordered by the Supreme Court. The act provided for the establishment of a Civil Rights Commission and authorized federal suits in support of blacks denied the right to vote. Those suits were to be settled by the courts in all cases involving charges of civil contempt and in those cases involving charges of criminal contempt if the judge's sentence did not exceed a three-hundred-dollar fine or forty-five days in jail. The measure required trial by jury in cases involving heavier penalties.

To Bernard Berenson

October 17, 1957

Dear B. B.:

. . . Our people here are shocked by the discovery that we do not possess an innate technological superiority over the rest of mankind.[1] And if there were national voices capable of speaking clearly about cultural values, our people would, for the first time in a long epoch, be prepared to listen. But there are no such voices. The President is, by all accounts, a bored and tired man, who does only what he inescapably must do. . . .

1. On October 5, 1957, the Soviet Union had successfully launched into orbit an earth satellite, Sputnik I, which circled the globe at eighteen thousand miles per hour. Startled by that Soviet

achievement, Americans began to question their national programs in science and in military innovation. Lippmann and some others were soon to attack the values of a consumer culture as the source of American indifference to national investment in science, applied science, and education.

To Thomas G. Pullen, Jr.[1]

November 15, 1957

Dear Mr. Pullen:

. . . My reason for saying that the worst place to begin integration is in coeducational schools for teen-agers is that racial integration is difficult enough without adding to its difficulty by raising the problems of adolescence. The reason I prefer to begin integration at the level of higher education is that there there is presumably a much greater sexual maturity. I cannot imagine how this obvious point can have puzzled you.

As for the second question about the responsibilities of leaders of American education, I was obviously referring to their responsibilities in helping to formulate an educational program in connection with the problems of integration. I think we must invite them now because now the problem has arisen. Before the Supreme Court decision began to be enforced,[2] the problem did not exist in its present form. I would assume that that also was obvious. . . .

1. Thomas G. Pullen, Jr., state superintendent in the Maryland Department of Education.
2. Enforcement languished at best, with less than 1 percent of black children in the South then attending public schools with white children. In September 1957, however, at Little Rock, Arkansas, Eisenhower had used federal troops to compel the admission of nine black children to one high school.

To Charles Child[1]

December 17, 1957

Dear Charles:

Did Cassandra scream or was she sad when what she saw would come, did actually come? When Ike let himself be persuaded in the winter of 1956 to run again, the fatal mistake was made, and the country had to be doped with prosperity and phony peace to elect him.

It may take a generation to reverse the decline on which we have entered. For what is wrong now is not this or that official, this or that item in the budget, but the mores we have allowed ourselves to sink into. However, I do not despair. . . .

1. Charles Child, a portrait painter and personal friend of the Lippmanns', had written that "I realize that it must be hard for you to continue . . . in a voice of moderation" in "Today and Tomorrow."

To Ann E. Hurd[1]

October 7, 1958

Dear Ladies:

I have your . . . questions about the Arkansas situation.

I would say that . . . Governor Faubus is in open rebellion against the United States Government and the law of the land. . . .

He probably did not realize what would be the result of closing the schools before he closed them . . . . his eyes are being opened by the indignation of the students and their parents.

1. A group of American women working at the American Pavilion at the Brussels World Fair had designated one of their number, Ann E. Hurd, to write Lippmann with questions about the current crisis in Little Rock, Arkansas. In 1957 Eisenhower had had reluctantly to use federal troops to force the state to admit nine blacks into all-white Central High School of Little Rock. In September 1958, the Supreme Court refused to permit a postponement of integration there, regardless of the threat of violence. Governor Orval E. Faubus, who had backed down in 1957, remained defiant and closed the high schools of the city. They remained closed throughout the ensuing academic year.

To Joseph W. Alsop

October 10, 1958

Dear Joe:

. . . It has been plain enough for quite some time that the bombardment of Quemoy was not the opening phase of a military attack on Formosa and that Peiping has no real intentions of doing anything so absurd as to attempt to conquer Formosa. . . .[1]

It is the Quemoy crisis that I have been addressing myself to primarily and almost entirely. If you . . . are right that the regime in Formosa has a future beyond the lifetime of Chiang himself, it would be a very good thing, more than I had dared to hope.

As to what you say about Chiang having given up the idea of a return to the mainland by military means, all I can say is that I am not convinced that this is true.

I do not laugh at the idea that the Chinese may reject the Peiping regime. I do not feel that I am entitled to express an opinion on that one way or the other. And you may well be right that in twenty years there will be a revolution. All that is reasonably certain is that for the near future there is not likely to be a revolution. . . .

1. In August 1958, Communist China had resumed bombing Quemoy and Ma-tsu. Eisenhower declared the islands more important to the defense of Taiwan than they had been three years earlier and sent an aircraft carrier and four destroyers to the area, but while threatening to fight if necessary, he urged negotiations. They began in Warsaw on September 15, and on October 6 the Communist Chinese ceased firing and called for a settlement. The Nationalists for their part remained resolved to keep the islands, and the cease-fire ended with renewed bombings on October 20; but since no attack on Taiwan was pending, the crisis passed.

To Ellery Sedgwick

December 9, 1958

Dear Ellery:
    . . . I have long been in complete agreement. Soviet policy, strategic and military, is far more Russian than it is Communist. I was speaking about this very point the other day to Dag Hammarskjold,[1] who, being a Swede, has had to keep his mind very much on Russia. I asked him how much of the Soviet policy was Russian, and how much Communist. He replied that it was at least ninety percent Russian. . . .

1. Dag Hammarskjöld, then secretary-general of the UN.

To Eric Boheman[1]

December 13, 1958

My dear Eric:
    . . . We have all settled down to the prospect of two years of deteriorating vision and decision in the handling of our affairs. For in the present case what Shakespeare said about Cleopatra is not so. In these closing years of the Administration age can wither and custom can stale its extraordinary lack of variety.
    You no doubt know as much about our recent elections[2] as I do. But I would say that unless Nixon becomes President during Eisenhower's present term, he has very little prospect of being elected in his own right in 1960. His own position in the Republican Party has declined severely, and the position of the Republican Party in the country as a whole has also declined severely. The Republicans who want to win are likely to try for Rockefeller.[3] But his friends and his wisest advisers are telling him to avoid 1960 and to wait. . . .

1. Eric Boheman had been Swedish ambassador to the United States until the previous March, when he returned to Stockholm and private life. He had written to convey his "interest and admiration" of Lippmann's account of an interview with Khrushchev in Moscow in October 1958. The articles Lippmann wrote about that Russian trip were published by Little, Brown in a small book entitled *The Communist World and Ours* (Boston, 1959). **2.** In November the Democrats had increased their majorities in both houses of Congress. **3.** Nelson A. Rockefeller had just been elected governor of New York. Earlier he had held positions under Eisenhower as undersecretary of health, education and welfare, 1953–54, and as special assistant to the president, 1954–55.

To J. Herman Van Roijen[1]

January 9, 1959

Dear Herman:

I came away from the dinner last night with the uncomfortable feeling that our talk had gotten us at cross purposes and that there was left a misunderstanding. If so, the blame lies in the enormous complexity of the subject, which cannot be talked out successfully in a few minutes.

So, I am writing this note not to argue the whole business, but to make sure that on a few points there is no misunderstanding between us.

The first has to do with the United States fulfillment of the NATO guarantee in relation to the eventual withdrawal of troops from a reunified Germany. I am sure you cannot suspect me of denigrating the NATO guarantee, which has been something that I have advocated continuously since before the First World War, and about which I have written innumerable articles and several books.

My point about the NATO guarantee is that it will be in effect even if there are no United States ground forces on German soil, and that U.S. involvement in a war would be as automatic as anything can be, once a Soviet missile or a bomb were launched against any NATO country. I do not believe that the United States guarantee depends upon the five divisions on German soil. There may be, and I think there are, political reasons for not withdrawing those troops precipitately and until a reunited German government has been consolidated. In my own mind I think of that as meaning anything from five to ten years for the transition.

The second point, which I should like to note here, is that the reunification of the two Germanys should not be postponed indefinitely because of the great danger of an uprising in East Germany which would almost inevitably involve us all . . . I believe we must be prepared to work immediately for reunification, not merely to repeat the old formulas, and that this reunification cannot be achieved without an agreement on the military evacuation of the two Germanys.

This second point is, I realize, highly debatable, and decisions about it involve a complicated calculation of many risks.

1. J. Herman Van Roijen, then Netherlands ambassador to the United States.

To the Editor of the Washington Post

January 15, 1959

In his letter, which you published on Thursday, Senator Barry Goldwater[1] of Arizona, in the course of his argument with your editorial, takes a sideswipe at me: "Recently your Walter Lippmann called me a 'reactionary' but was unable to explain why when I asked him."

The Senator asked me on November 18. Quoting from the dictionary he said "a reactionary being a person who wants to 'return to an older order.' . . . I am exceedingly interested to find out what process you followed" in describing Senator Goldwater not as a conservative but as a reactionary.

I replied on November 22 that "your definition of a reactionary is correct." And "I regard your views on foreign policy, which I have followed with considerable interest, as inspired by an attempt to return to an older order of things in the world."

The Senator would prefer to be called a conservative. But his version of an unreconstructed isolationism is a reactionary attempt to return to the order of things in the world as it was before the two World Wars in this century.

1. Barry M. Goldwater had been elected as a Republican senator from Arizona in 1952.

To Russell C. Leffingwell

September 3, 1959

Dear Russell:

. . . The basic question which worries me, and which I do not know how to answer, is how our Western societies can match the purposefulness of our great adversary. The adversary puts not only guns ahead of butter, he puts education and research and medical care ahead of butter. I do not feel that we can take the view that we must not cut into consumption, into our butter, and that therefore we must keep armaments below the level that the best experts think is prudent, that we must allow public education to be as grossly inadequate as it is, and medical care what it is for the lower middle class and the poor.

We have, I am coming to think, to find ways of allocating to the "public sector" of defense, education, research and medicine and also to other necessary public facilities such as airports and highways, a larger proportion of the national product. How to do this without stifling the energies of our economy is the problem to which I do not know the solution, and it worries me. . . .

To Marquis W. Childs
James B. Reston[1]

September 14, 1959

Dear Mark and Scotty:

I think you know already from what I said to each of you last June that my feeling about the book is one of being overawed. I had not imagined that such a thing could happen to me, and now that it has happened, I am filled with humility and I have a warm feeling in the pit of my stomach.

All summer I have been thinking of how I could say anything at all adequate to each of the contributors. I am stumped, and for the moment I must thank them through you. As I read the printed book, I feel as if trying to write to each of them individually would be rather like trying to hold a serious conversation in a room with mirrors wherever one looks. Seeing so much of oneself in so many aspects makes a man like me incoherent.

But I can collect my wits enough to say that next to the delicious prejudices of my friends, what pleases me most is that they have at the same time done me the honor of being critical.

When I was a young man leaving college, I asked Graham Wallas to inscribe his book for me. He did this and wrote in it a line from "The Vision of Piers Plowman" which runs "I will be Truth's pilgrim at the plow for poor mens' sake." As I read this book and think of the men who wrote it, I know that in spite of all my mistakes and follies, my sins and weaknesses, what I have tried to do has not been misunderstood.

1. Marquis W. Childs and James B. Reston, distinguished columnists and friends of Lippmann's, had edited and contributed to *Walter Lippmann and His Times* (New York, 1959), a collection of essays about Lippmann to commemorate his seventieth birthday. The other contributors to that book, which was by no means pietistic in its treatment of Lippmann, were Carl Binger, George F. Kennan, Allan Nevins, Arthur Krock, Raymond Aron, Iverach McDonald, Frank Moraes, Harry S. Ashmore, Reinhold Niebuhr, and Arthur Schlesinger, Jr.

To William R. Mathews

January 8, 1960

Dear Bill:

. . . You ask me how we can reduce the proportion that goes into consumer goods, etc. etc. The answer is by levying taxes to pay for our national needs, which are now not being met. When did it become an imperative that taxes must always remain at or below the level fixed by George Humphrey in 1954?[1]

As to the other part of your letter about our comparative strength with the Soviet Union, . . . what I think is not debatable is that the strength of the Soviet Union in the fields that it has chosen to be strong in is not a bluff, and we shall deceive ourselves if we think so. . . .[2]

1. George M. Humphrey, Eisenhower's first secretary of the treasury, a staunch conservative, had kept a portrait of Andrew Mellon behind his desk and had stood, like Mellon, for minimizing federal spending and reducing federal taxes, especially income taxes on the rich and on corporations. The budget for 1954–55 and the revenue legislation of 1954 — both reflecting Humphrey's influence — took steps in those directions. 2. The Soviet Union, it was widely believed at that time, was far ahead of the United States in its production and stockpile of missiles.

To John F. Kennedy [1]

January 22, 1960

Dear Senator Kennedy:

Thank you for taking the trouble to write to me about the primaries. . . .

I construed your remarks on "Meet the Press" as meaning that the conventions should surrender their judgment if a candidate had not submitted to some primary contest. You said on "Meet The Press" that "as a Democratic delegate, I would not take their candidacy seriously." If that does not mean what I understood it to mean, what does it mean?

You go on to say in your letter that "all serious candidates should be willing to submit their record, views and vote-getting abilities to the electorate." Where I differ from you is that I do not consider a few primaries, selected by the candidate himself, as submitting to the electorate. [2]

If these primaries are the kind of test that you say they are, on what ground do you pick and choose among them? Why don't you enter them all without question? The fact is, is it not, that the criterion by which you pick and choose is not that of submitting to the electorate, but where you believe you stand to make the best showing?

I have a general dislike of the primary system as it has developed in the past forty years, and I do not think matters would be improved by having a nation-wide primary as advocated by Woodrow Wilson. That would amount to having two national elections, and would put an exorbitant premium on the candidacy of one who has the most money, the greatest access to the mass media and the general ability to manipulate blocs and organizations.

The 1956 primaries had a devastating effect on Stevenson, and I must tell you that I do not look forward with any pleasure to the contest between Humphrey and you. You both will be doing and saying things that as President you would wish you hadn't had to say and do.

I hope you will not interpret this disagreement as anything more than a disagreement on a particular point in political discussion. . . .

---

1. Senator John F. Kennedy of Massachusetts had announced his candidacy for the Democratic presidential nomination. His foremost liberal rival was obviously to be Senator Hubert H. Humphrey of Minnesota. Though Adlai Stevenson would have liked the nomination, he would not declare his candidacy or campaign; and at this time Lyndon B. Johnson of Texas, the party's majority leader in the Senate, had yet officially to begin his campaign. **2.** Kennedy did not select necessarily easy states for his campaign. Humphrey had a strong following in Wisconsin, which Kennedy won. He also then won in West Virginia, where his Catholicism was expected to constitute a handicap. Those victories knocked Humphrey out of the race. In July Lippmann began to praise Kennedy; in October he endorsed him.

To Lewis W. Douglas

February 4, 1960

Dear Lew:

. . . I find it very hard to believe that the Soviet rate of growth is not considerably greater than our own.

I myself am particularly concerned about the comparative rates of growth in those elements which constitute national power, not only armaments but technology and science and the education of men in those fields.

I have talked with a number of our own scientists in these fields and I don't think the pessimism I have been showing is exaggerated or unfounded. . . .

To John A. Davenport[1]

March 15, 1960

Dear John:

. . . Of course I know Colin Clark,[2] have met him and talked with him, and know his theory about the amount of the national product that a government may take without necessarily causing inflation. The 25% measure is probably a good rule of thumb, and I for one always bear it in mind in discussing what we can afford to do. We have not yet reached the 25% mark. The latest figures I have available are from the Rockefeller Brothers Report, and these figures show that for the year 1957, taking all federal, state and local expenditures for goods and services, they came to 20% of the GNP. If we can increase our rate of growth to 4%, a rate which we have frequently attained in the past, we can afford to spend for defense and for public services all that any reasonable person is proposing and still stay under the 25% rule.

As to Hayek, I have read your review with great interest, but I have not yet read the book.[3] I have known Hayek a long time, and when I wrote my own *The Good Society* in the 30's, I made use of his analyses of the market economy. I, too, agree with the concept of liberty under law, but I am very much dissatisfied with his working out of that concept. Most especially I feel that he has never ventured to confront the problem of the corporation in the modern capitalistic society. . . .

1. John A. Davenport, then a member of the Board of Editors of *Fortune*. **2.** Colin Clark, British economist then supervising research at the Econometric Institute in New York. **3.** Friedrich A. von Hayek's *The Constitution of Liberty* (Chicago, 1960) developed views the author had expressed in previous books. Davenport reviewed it as unrepentant Whiggery in the March 1950 issue of *Fortune*. As another reviewer wrote, and Lippmann agreed, it was a learned effort to turn back the clock.

To Harris L. Wofford[1]

April 22, 1960

Dear Mr. Wofford:

. . . In the first place, I don't think I said, and I certainly didn't mean to say, that Kennedy was avoiding the hard public issues. What I did say is that in the conditions of a primary such as Wisconsin no one would know about these public issues. This may be the fault of the press for not reporting his speeches, but it is also the fault of the primary which diverts attention from the issues themselves.

Second, I did not suggest that a Stevenson-Kennedy ticket could be elected to the Presidency this fall. I was not prophesying. I was saying that this would be the strongest ticket. Whether it would be strong enough to defeat Nixon is both for you and for me purely speculative at this time.

I would like to see Kennedy run as Vice President for two reasons. First, I believe that while he has the qualifications to be President, he lacks the experience which is necessary and he is not, as I felt his speech to the Newspaper Editors yesterday showed, as yet sufficiently mature. I think he will mature, and I would not favor him for Vice President if I did not think so.

My second reason for wishing Kennedy to be nominated for Vice President is that with these qualifications and these limitations we could, if he were nominated and elected, smash the taboo on a Catholic in the White House. As the Editor of the *New York World* at the time when it promoted the candidacy of Governor Smith, I don't need to tell you that I have a great desire to see that taboo smashed.

1. Harris L. Wofford, then an associate professor at the Notre Dame Law School on leave to assist in the Kennedy campaign, became an assistant to President Kennedy and an influential adviser on civil rights.

To H. Alexander Hetherington[1]

May 12, 1960

Dear Mr. Hetherington:

. . . The discussion of Kennedy's being a Roman Catholic is inevitable and necessary. It raises the kind of problem that will be raised in England if the Prince of Wales should somehow become a Roman Catholic.

I am confident that this country can and will within the fairly near future, perhaps in this election, elect a Roman Catholic. But it constitutes a very great break with tradition and there is no use disguising this fact.

I did not mean to imply by my letter that you are not right to be concerned about our elections. I thought I detected in this particular editorial acceptance of the Kennedy thesis, which is much resented among Democrats, that if he wins a few primaries, he is entitled to the nomination and that only his Catholicism would prevent his getting it. This is not true and it consists of a subtle form of blackmail which is, of course, unacceptable.

My own view is that Kennedy is not yet certain of the nomination, but that if he is nominated, he will be infinitely preferable to Nixon. . . .

1. H. Alexander Hetherington, since 1956 editor of the *Manchester Guardian*, which on April 21, 1960, had run an editorial about the Catholic issue in the Kennedy campaign.

To John D. Miller[1]

May 24, 1960

Dear Johnnie:

Who was it — it was some diplomat, I think an Englishman — who said of something that it was worse than a crime, it was a blunder? . . .

Of course, that is what happened. It was monumental stupidity. One example of it, which I have not seen anyone talk about, was this. Eisenhower knew on Sunday that Khrushchev was going to break up the conference and denounce him personally. Why on earth he subjected himself to such a public beating on Monday I cannot imagine. I would have supposed that he would have asked on Monday for an adjournment of the meeting and for direct confidential talks. There is no reason I can think of why he should have subjected himself, after full notice, to the public tongue-lashing. . . .[2]

1. John D. Miller, a close friend of Lippmann's who was then residing in Paris. 2. Eisenhower had stumbled badly in his handling of Khrushchev's announcement of May 5 that the Soviet Union had shot down an American U-2, a high-altitude spy plane engaged in aerial photography. First the United States asserted that the aircraft had strayed while on a meteorological mission. Then when Khrushchev produced the pilot's confession on May 7 and said that he was willing to believe that Eisenhower had known nothing about the flight, the president accepted full responsibility. His secretary of state, Christian A. Herter, who had been appointed to that office after Dulles's resignation in 1959, maintained that the United States had been entitled to conduct espionage flights to protect the "free world" and implied, as did Vice President Nixon, that the flights would continue. Those were awkward statements to make less than a week before the scheduled summit meeting in Paris. There Khrushchev demanded that Eisenhower apologize and punish those responsible for the flights. Eisenhower refused, and the summit meeting broke up. Under pressure from the Chinese, Khrushchev may have intended in any case to sabotage the summit conference; but if that was so, Eisenhower at the best walked into the Russian trap.

To Carl A. L. Binger[1]

September 29, 1960

Dear Carl:

. . . I agree with you entirely about future aid to the underdeveloped countries and the U.N. As a matter of fact, you may have noticed that that is what Eisenhower has come around to, at least in regard to Africa.[2] This is a very great step in the evolution of our own policy. I am sure the principle is correct, and ought to be applied in the Middle East, in South Asia and in Latin America, although it is not essential that the mediating agency in each case must be the U.N. It should be some international institution which takes the curse off individual power politics. . . .

1. Carl A. L. Binger, a noted psychiatrist, had been a friend of Lippmann's since their childhood and college days.   2. On September 22, Eisenhower had called for the settlement of the world's problems through the United Nations and specified disarmament and economic aid to the underdeveloped nations of Africa as appropriate for that treatment.

To George F. Kennan

October 21, 1960

Dear George:

. . . Kennedy's position has been much misrepresented by the press and of course by Nixon. He has never said that he would not defend Quemoy and Ma-tsu. What he has said is that he would try to persuade Chiang Kai-shek to evacuate the islands. The only trouble with that is I am afraid he will find it almost impossible to do that. . . .

To W. C. Naude[1]

November 7, 1960

Dear Mr. Ambassador:

. . . I do not think there was anything unfair in coupling your country with the Soviet Union since you are the two leading exporters of gold. Nor can it be denied that as exporters of gold, it would be very profitable to you both if the official price were raised.

Since in my view raising the price of gold would nullify itself,[2] almost immediately, I see no advantage to the United States but a very considerable advantage to your country and to the Soviet Union. . . .

1. W. C. Naude, then South African ambassador to the United States.   2. There had been some discussion about raising the price of gold because of the increasingly unfavorable American balance of trade that was drawing down the gold held by the United States. An artificial increase in the dollar price of gold would have inflated the value of the American holdings without remedying the unfavorable trade balance.

To Allan Nevins

December 9, 1960

Dear Allan:

. . . As to the U-2, there have been a very large number of such flights over the Soviet Union over a period of four years. The original plane was devised so that if for any reason it descended to 40,000 it blew itself up and there was nothing that the pilot could do about it. For some reason, which I do not know, the plane was later modified, giving the pilot control over the automatic self-destroying explosives and this was the reason why Powers[1] and the plane landed virtually intact.

I have talked with some of the CIA men about why the flight was permitted on May 1st. They tell me that they debated it anxiously and decided in favor of it if the weather on any particular day proved to be good for photography because it would be very nearly their last chance before the cloudy summer weather to find out about the new missile sites in the Soviet Union. So far as I know, Herter did not participate in the decision, nor I think did Eisenhower himself. You may remember that when the whole thing came out Dulles[2] offered to accept the responsibility for the affair and to resign, and that Eisenhower refused the resignation.

I don't think the State Department has any active control over Dulles since the death of John Foster Dulles, and one of the things Kennedy is going to have to go into is the relationship between the Foreign Service and the CIA.

The real tragedy of the whole affair, however, was the decision made by the President, not by Herter, under the direct influence of Hagerty,[3] to assume personal responsibility for the U-2 flight and to justify it. This was the thing which upset Khrushchev. In the week following the capture of the plane he said at least once, and I think twice, that of course the President couldn't have known about this flight and he didn't hold him responsible for it. It was when the President insisted that he was responsible that Khrushchev blew up, feeling that he had been humiliated by the man he had told the Russians they could trust. . . .

This week I had an hour's talk with Kennedy, who was still uncertain about the Secretary of State. And I had a talk yesterday with Adlai Stevenson, who is very unhappy at Kennedy's decision not to appoint him. Kennedy was leaning to Fulbright when I spoke to him, aware that Fulbright's signing the Southern Manifesto[4] and some injudicious remarks he made about the Zionists were a liability. But with Stevenson eliminated, because Kennedy believed the Republicans would make him a second Acheson, with Bowles[5] eliminated as too fluent, the choice really lies between Fulbright and two younger men — one Dean Rusk and the other McGeorge Bundy of Harvard.[6]** For myself, I think Fulbright would do well enough under Kennedy's leadership, but I advocated his appointing Bundy and taking a chance on the fact that he was so young and not well known. Now I am beginning to hope it will be Fulbright. . . .

** or it may be Bruce for a year.

1. Gary Powers. 2. Allen Dulles of the CIA. 3. James C. Hagerty, Eisenhower's press secretary. 4. The Southern Manifesto condemned the decision of the Supreme Court — *Brown v. Board of Education of Topeka*, 1954 — that had called for the desegregation of public schools. Fulbright had signed it, but Lyndon Johnson had not. Johnson's position on the race issue helped

to assure the narrow margin of victory of the Kennedy-Johnson ticket in 1960. The president-elect in any event was eager not to offend either American blacks or the new nations of Africa. **5.** Kennedy appointed Stevenson ambassador to the United Nations and Bowles senior undersecretary of state. **6.** Kennedy appointed Dean Rusk, formerly an assistant secretary of state and then president of the Rockefeller Foundation, secretary of state; and McGeorge Bundy, then dean of the Harvard faculty of arts and sciences, special assistant for national security. David K. E. Bruce, veteran and distinguished foreign service officer, became ambassador to Great Britain.

Memorandum for Chester Bowles

December 20, 1960

At his request, I lunched with the Soviet Ambassador[1] on Monday, December 19th. It was at once clear that he wants to open up as many channels of communication as he can with the Kennedy Administration. Having made it as plain as I could that I had no official connection whatever, I said I would, of course, be glad to hear what he had to say and to read a memorandum, which he said he had prepared for me but which is obviously intended to be passed on to you.

The interesting points in the interview were as follows:

1. Mr. Khrushchev is particularly concerned to enter into discussions about West Berlin and the German question. According to Mr. Menshikov, he is worried about being pushed into dangerous positions by the East German state. It is apparent that he greatly fears having to sign a separate peace treaty.

2. Mr. Khrushchev has realized, it would appear, that no summit meeting is in prospect, and is, therefore, seeking to open better communications through more normal diplomatic channels. Mr. Menshikov himself hopes to break out of the diplomatic isolation in which the Eisenhower Administration has contained him. A certain amount of sitting around informally with a drink or a private luncheon apparently would mean a great deal to him.

3. It is a fair conclusion, I believe, that if there is a certain amount of personal intercourse in Washington at the higher levels of the Administration, this would make it somewhat easier for our Ambassador in Moscow to communicate with Mr. Khrushchev.

1. Ambassador Mikhail Menshikov later helped to arrange a second interview for Lippmann with Khrushchev in April 1961.

To John D. Miller

January 24, 1961

Dear Johnnie:

. . . I am happy about the beginning. I think the Cabinet is excellent, although Rusk was not my first choice. The country is absolutely astonished at having a President who works in the afternoon as well as in the morning. . . .

To Raymond Moley[1]

September 23, 1961

My dear Ray:

. . . I have had your figures examined carefully, and it is evident on the face of it that there is something strange about them. You speak about what has happened to the population and to the gross national product and expenditures on the public sector in the years from 1953 to 1961. You are the only man in the world who has seen the Eisenhower figures for 1961. They do not exist. The last Eisenhower year for which the record is complete is 1959.

Between 1953 and 1959 calendar years the total public expenditure, as recorded by the Department of Commerce, rose by 29% in money terms. However, correcting for the inflation change in the price level, the total of real public spending in terms of 1959 prices rose by only 6.3%. During the same period the population increased by 11%, and real gross national product by 15.6%.

However, you do not allow for the fact that the substantial fraction of total public spending is irrelevant to the argument about public vs. private shares, — namely, transfer type spending which included interest on the public debt, social security payments, cash benefits to veterans, etc. If we make deductions for these shares, as in honesty we must, the government purchases of goods and services between 1953 and 1959 by all levels of government taken together declined by 4.8%.

You say, moreover, that "private consumption" between 1953 and the unknown year 1961 increased one-half, while the federal spending for civilian purposes has gone up almost two and a half times. In fact between 1953 and 1959 personal consumption in real terms increased not by one-half, but by 23.4%. During this same period federal purchases of goods and services, far from rising, declined by 25%. . . .

1. Raymond Moley, a critic of Kennedy's policies, was then contributing a regular column to *Newsweek*.

To Theodore C. Sorensen[1]

October 6, 1961

Dear Mr. Sorensen:

In setting down, as you requested, some random ideas, I should like first to ask you to read the enclosed passage from Churchill, setting forth his conclusions on the Munich tragedy. It is taken from the "Second World War," Volume I, page 319, of the American first edition. This is a classic statement of the moral principles at stake in the issue between compromise and appeasement.[2]

I am writing what follows in the first person, as if the President himself were speaking, because that is the easiest way to do it. But I am not attempting to make the judgments which he alone can make as to what is expedient for the President to say out loud at this stage in the international conflict.

MEMORANDUM FOR THEODORE C. SORENSEN

The burdens of these times are very great. They are being made much heavier by confused men who go up and down the land crying out that any peaceful solution of the problems we face in Berlin, in Southeast Asia, and in Cuba, is appeasement and surrender. They ask us to bow our heads in shame. They tell the world that it need no longer believe that we will do what we say we will do. They destroy the confidence of our people at home and confidence in us abroad. Why? Because we are not at war in Southeast Asia, because we are not at war in Cuba, because we are working out ways of protecting the freedom of West Berlin without a war of annihilation.[3]

I call upon our people to turn against those who are saying that there is nothing between surrender and war, against those who are talking as if there were no difference between appeasement and negotiation. We are not appeasers, and we have never done appeasement, we do not intend to start being appeasers. For appeasement, since the tragedy of Munich before the Second World War, has meant selling out another country in order to save yourself. We are not selling out anybody to save ourselves. When we are committed and have vital interests, as in the political and economic freedom of West Berlin, we have not and we shall not welsh. But we shall do our best to reinsure that freedom. We believe it does need to be reinsured because we do not wish to have a Berlin crisis the rest of our lives. In order to reinsure it we are talking with the Soviet government, and we are prepared to negotiate about all sorts of things, though not about the freedom of West Berlin. No responsible and honest man has a right to call that appeasement. It is sheer, practical common sense in a world where we cannot dictate our own solutions of all international questions.

I do not believe that the hysterical oversimplifiers have any realization of what are the real problems of the United States Government in this highly troubled world. I am speaking of those who say that there is nothing between the two extremes, that there is only a choice between war and surrender, that we must all be dead or all be Red, that we must have total victory or we will have total defeat, that all men are divided into hard ones and soft ones. My Countrymen, the world is not like that. It is not that simple, and the decisions which I, as President, must make are not that easy.

The ladies and gentlemen who make the issue so simple and so resounding have not yet learned what it is like to conduct the foreign affairs of a great power in this age of nuclear weapons. But I am sure that Mr. Khrushchev knows, and I am sure that I know, that in a nuclear war both the Soviet society and the Western society would be ruined, that communism would be destroyed, but so would the free enterprise system and democracy as we know it, that the destruction would be greater and the calamity would be more enormous than any in the whole history of man.

My duty is to protect our vital interests around the world without destroying the world. If we do our duty, which requires the understanding and the support of our people, we shall not be Red and we shall not be dead. We shall not surrender, and we shall not have a nuclear war.

But if we are not to have a nuclear war, our people must keep cool, they must keep calm, they must not listen to the agitators, they must not be upset by the rumor-mongers. They must look at it all with a cold eye and a quiet heart.

Looking over this, which I have written rather hastily, I think the most useful idea in it — which could, of course, be very greatly improved — is that the President begin to make our people realize what they don't realize at all, what it means to conduct great diplomatic affairs like Southeast Asia, Cuba and Berlin in the new and revolutionary nuclear age which has just begun.

He is the first President in history who has had to deal with the old issues and with American commitments in terms of nuclear parity. No other President in history has had to do it, not Truman in the Korean War, not Eisenhower until the aftermath of the U-2. The President should find ways of making our people realize how primitive and romantic are men like Goldwater, who talk as if war today would be like the Alamo, like San Juan Hill, or even like World War II.

1. Theodore C. Sorensen, special counsel to President Kennedy and, except for Attorney General Robert F. Kennedy, the president's closest adviser. **2.** The statement concluded with a warning that an exaggerated code of honor could lead to vain and unreasonable deeds. **3.** During the six months before this letter was written, the administration had agreed to increase military aid to South Vietnam and to send more observers there, had undertaken to support the abortive invasion at the Bay of Pigs in Cuba by refugees supplied by the CIA, and had increased the armed forces and defense spending — in response especially to the Soviet threat to sign a separate peace treaty with East Germany that would exclude the West from Berlin and to the East German decision, Soviet inspired, in August to construct the Berlin Wall to stop the flow of refugees from east to west. Kennedy had met with Khrushchev in June. They had then discussed a nuclear test ban and resolved the problems their nations faced in Laos, but otherwise the conference had proved disheartening, particularly because of Khrushchev's blustering manner and their disagreements about Germany. In "Today and Tomorrow," Lippmann had criticized the Bay of Pigs operation, urged negotiations with the Soviet Union about Berlin, and questioned the utility for American interests of military involvement in Southeast Asia; see Ronald Steel, *Walter Lippmann and the American Century* (Boston, 1980), pp. 527–33.

To Edward Engberg[1]

November 7, 1961

Dear Mr. Engberg:

I had received my regular copy of the *Commonweal* several days before your letter came. You may well believe that I was astonished to see your article, and enormously pleased when I had read it. I thank you for the best gift anyone can give an author, which is to understand him.

In response to your question, I have re-read Arthur Schlesinger's assessment. He is, of course, a better judge than I could be, and I can say that his description of a long search and much turmoil is entirely plausible, and of course most generous. I think he has not wholly understood or sympathized with — no doubt the fault of mine — where the search ended in Part II of *Public Philosophy*, particularly Chapter 10.

1. Edward Engberg, editor of the *Insider Newsletter*, had interpreted Lippmann's book as the product of a convinced and consistent moralist, a position Engberg held himself. That interpretation contrasted especially with that of Arthur Schlesinger, Jr., who in *Lippmann and His Times* had viewed Lippmann as a commentator who regularly took a stance in opposition to the prevailing mood of the nation as it had changed over the years since 1910.

To McGeorge Bundy

March 15, 1962

Dear Mac:

I had a wild idea in bed the other night. Here it is:

If all else fails about testing and no treaty to ban it can be agreed upon, might it not be a last resort measure to propose: —

The reduction and limitation of nuclear testing instead of its abolition. I have in mind some such thing as an agreement to allow each of the two nuclear powers to make a specified number of tests of a specified magnitude within a limited period of time every five years.[1]

The advantage I see in this is that it would introduce into an irrational rivalry an element of order and regulation and rationale. And at the same time, it would take care of the people on both sides who are afraid that if no testing is done, the know-how will be lost.

I get lots of crazy letters, and you may throw this one in the wastebasket, as I do so many I receive.

1. The previous September, President Kennedy and Prime Minister Macmillan had proposed to Khrushchev an agreement among their nations to cease testing nuclear weapons in the atmosphere so as to prevent radioactive fallout, a matter of increasing concern all over the world. For its part, the United States resumed testing nuclear weapons but not in the atmosphere. But after months of futility, in January 1962, conversation among the three powers came to an unsuccessful conclusion. Concerned about potential Soviet gains in military technology, Kennedy decided the

United States had to resume atmospheric testing, as he informed the nation in a speech of March 2, 1962. He also called again for a modified test ban treaty before late April, when American testing was scheduled to begin again. Nevertheless the impasse persisted until 1963, when a limited test ban treaty, negotiated in July, became effective in October after winning approval from the United States Senate. It prohibited nuclear testing in outer space, in the atmosphere, and underwater, but allowed continued testing underground.

To Barbara W. Jackson[1]

May 22, 1962

Dear Barbara:

. . . You will find that I came back very much impressed with de Gaulle's hostility to the admission of Great Britain and to any serious partnership with the United States.[2]

I am beginning to think that just as in the World War the rivalry within the anti-Hitler coalition broke out as soon as there was reason to think it would win, so today, when we are on the stronger side in the balance of forces, rivalries in the Western camp are becoming acute. De Gaulle intends to take the leadership of the Western Alliance away from what he calls the Anglo-Saxons in a slightly sardonic voice. And if I am any judge of how Kennedy's mood has turned, he is not going to have it taken away from him.

We have put our minds somewhat on what should be done by the British and the Americans in case the British application for membership is rejected. My present mood is to take an increasingly strong stand against de Gaulle, designed especially to detach his German satellite — and I hope and believe Jean Monnet and his friends eventually will come out on top. But we will have to do more than sit and wait, and we must have some plans of action. . . .

1. Lady Barbara W. Jackson, formerly Barbara Ward, was the celebrated British author of many articles and books about the relations between East and West, between poor nations and rich. From 1957 to 1968 she held the position, among others, of visiting scholar at Harvard University.   2. Charles de Gaulle, first president of France under the constitution of the Fifth Republic adopted in 1958, retained a lifelong commitment to the grandeur of his nation and a suspicion of almost equal duration of the Anglo-American powers, a suspicion intensified by his wartime disappointments with British and American policy. He was antagonistic to developing plans, favored by the United States, for British entry into the European Economic Community (Common Market). De Gaulle officially declared his opposition to that possibility in January 1963. With Britain effectively excluded, he also rejected an American proposal for France to join a multilateral nuclear force within NATO, and in July refused to sign the test ban treaty.

To Walter W. Heller[1]

June 12, 1962

Dear Walter:

. . . I have begun to think that our direct taxes have reached a point where they put too great a strain on the political bonds of our society. I began to

realize this more clearly last winter when I paid a visit to Texas and looked to
see what the real grievance was. You will understand that I am not suggesting
that we abolish the income tax, but only that we follow the practice which, I
think, is common in Europe — except in Great Britain — of not counting on
it for so large a proportion of the revenue. . . .

1. Walter W. Heller, then chairman of Kennedy's distinguished Council of Economic Advisers.

To Barbara W. Jackson

September 17, 1962
Dear Barbara:

. . . Our best-informed people here think that in spite of Menzies and
Diefenbaker and de Gaulle, Great Britain will join the Common Market.[1] If
that does happen, our own optimists around Kennedy think that, armed with
the rather good trade extension bill, they can negotiate something like a general fifty per cent reduction in tariffs with the enlarged Common Market.[2] I
hope they are right because I think if the present effort is broken off it will be
almost impossible to resume it. The divisive forces will take charge all over
the continent and in Great Britain. . . .

1. To the satisfaction of Prime Minister Robert G. Menzies of Australia and Prime Minister John
G. Diefenbaker of Canada, Great Britain did not join the market at that time. 2. The tariff
legislation that the Kennedy administration had persuaded Congress to adopt did permit extensive
reductions in international tariff schedules among the nations subscribing to the General Agreement on Tariffs and Trade (GATT). The previous July, those nations, meeting at Geneva, had
agreed upon some 4400 concessions involving overall about five billion dollars in world trade.

To Samuel Lubell[1]

October 3, 1962
Dear Mr. Lubell:

. . . My own view is that the President's problem is less difficult than it
may look. If Castro commits an overt act, the President will have a casus belli.
If he doesn't commit an overt act, no serious interests of the United States
will be injured. . . .[2]

1. Samuel Lubell, publicist and political analyst, author of the incisive and influential *The Future
of American Politics* (New York, 1952). 2. Though President Kennedy in September had warned
the Soviet Union against placing offensive missiles in Cuba, and though Khrushchev had disclaimed any intention of doing so, some Republicans during the congressional election campaign
claimed that the Russians were engaged in a dangerous arms build-up on the island and called for
an invasion or blockade. Republican Senator Kenneth B. Keating of New York asserted that he
had verifiable proof that offensive missiles were in place. But the first actual verification came

from photographs taken from a U-2 plane on October 16, 1962 — the day, as the president's brother Attorney General Robert F. Kennedy later recalled, that the missile crisis began; see R. F. Kennedy, *Thirteen Days* (New York, 1969).

To Christopher Emmet[1]

December 20, 1962

Dear Mr. Emmet:

. . . It pleased me to think that anyone remembers my criticism of the army I. Q. tests after World War I. I don't think I ever took part in a journalistic fracas which I enjoyed more. Now, alas, the subject itself has become infinitely more complicated than it was at that time, and my own job has become such that I do not have the time to study the subject.

I would like, however, to say that I am quite open-minded about the use of the tests, especially as they have developed since World War I, except on one crucial point. To my mind it is intolerable that the individual student should be tagged for life by any test. The tests are at best a statistical device which could be used confidentially by education authorities for general planning and administration. But never under any circumstances should they become judgments on the intellectual capacity and future performance of any individual. . . .

1. Christopher Emmet, a frequent correspondent who had sometimes disagreed with Lippmann, had written on December 1, 1962, about a program on public television devoted to a discussion of IQ tests, then still a subject of controversy.

To George F. Kennan

February 16, 1963

Dear George:

. . . I wrote a gloomy book about democracy some years ago called *The Public Philosophy*, and one of the main themes of it was that free societies were unworkable without predominant executive leadership. We are in one of those bad periods of our history which Woodrow Wilson complained about when he was young, a period of Congressional government.[1] I don't mean to throw up my hands but, allowing for a certain amount of exaggeration, that's about the way I feel. . . .

1. Kennedy's proposals for civil rights, fiscal, and other major legislation were tied up in congressional committees.

To Harold Macmillan

November 21, 1963

[Dear Mr. Macmillan] [1]
    . . . I am very much pleased about what you say about the philosophy of my writings.

It confirms me in what I have been saying fairly recently during the strange controversy in this country over "conservatism" and "liberalism," — that a civilized man was a conservative in his attachment to the constitutional foundations, a liberal in his beliefs about the interpretation and administration of the Constitution, and a progressive in his efforts to fit the needs of the age he lives in. . . .

1. The copy of this letter in the Lippmann papers contained no greeting at all, though the addressee was clearly Macmillan. It may have been a draft.

To Camille A. Gutt [1]

January 29, 1964

My dear Camille:
    . . . If it is a matter of talking out loud about de Gaulle and his policy in the Far East, I suppose I am just about completely isolated in this country. But between what is said out loud, and what is not said out loud, there is on the China question an enormous gap, and I think I can say there is no popular resentment against de Gaulle though there will be plenty of conventional disapproval. There is much more sympathy with him in higher quarters than anyone feels it politically expedient to express. . . .

1. Sir Camille Gutt, a former Belgian minister of finance, then president of the Banque Lambert, Brussels, in a letter to Lippmann had deplored the amount of "bunk" in European and American newspapers about France's official recognition of the Republic of China on January 27, 1964. Some of the "bunk" interpreted de Gaulle's action as a deliberate affront to the United States, especially in the light of his disapproval of widening American involvement in the war in Vietnam.

To Erik Wensberg [1]

March 6, 1964

Dear Mr. Wensberg:
    . . . I may say that I have been advocating the repeal of the 1947 law so as to restore the line of succession through the Secretary of State. This is what General Eisenhower has been advocating. [2]

There may be other solutions. But the essential point is that the line of succession should be cleared up *immediately*,[3] and that cannot be done by Constitutional amendment. It must be done by a Congressional statute.

1. Erik Wensberg, then articles editor for *Esquire*.   **2.** After the assassination of President Kennedy in November 1963, and the swearing in of Lyndon B. Johnson, there was again no vice president in office, as had been the case so often before in American history. The law of succession at one time had placed the secretary of state next in line, but it had been altered to substitute the Speaker of the House, an elected official, as the secretary of state was not. Yet the secretary of state during the twentieth century had ordinarily been a more substantial statesman than had the Speaker.   **3.** Emphasis Lippmann's.

To John M. Mecklin[1]

April 10, 1964

Dear Mr. Mecklin:

. . . I agree with your remark that we have learned since 1945 that settlements can be negotiated with the Communists only if there is a military and political stalemate. That's exactly what I think we should have as our objective in Southeast Asia — the creation of a stalemate. That means not only strengthening the Saigon government so that it doesn't run out on us, but it involves also some very careful planning, which I think is actually under way, to strengthen our sea and air power in that part of the world. The proposal for a task force in the Indian Ocean is part of that planning.

As for defeating guerrilla warfare, frankly, I don't believe it's possible for the United States to do that kind of thing on the mainland of Asia. . . .

1. John M. Mecklin of Chevy Chase, Maryland, had heard Lippmann, during a television interview, call for a negotiated peace in Vietnam. Mecklin, who had previously served two years as public affairs officer at the American embassy in Saigon, disagreed. "History showed," he argued in his letter to Lippmann, that only with a "military-political stalemate" could successful negotiations with the Communists take place. That was, of course, an argument Lippmann had heard and answered often before during his years of criticism of American policy in Vietnam; see Ronald Steel, *Walter Lippmann and the American Century* (Boston, 1980), chs. 43–44.

To David Astor[1]

July 16, 1964

Dear David:

. . . I would say that I don't know whether I am the only journalist whom Khrushchev allows to write his account of a conversation with him. The fact is not only do I never submit what I am writing to the Soviet officials, but I have not even written what I did write until after I had left the Soviet Union. The only discussion of this matter that ever came up was at the end of my first interview with Khrushchev in 1958, when, after two hours of talking, during which my wife took as full notes as she could, and I took brief notes, I turned to him and said, "Is there any part of this conversation that you don't want used?" He waved me aside and said "I am sure you mean well for peace and write what you like."

As a matter of fact, this is not as free as it sounds because Khrushchev is a very shrewd man and I am sure doesn't say anything in these interviews that he is not perfectly willing to have known publicly. In other words, he is his own censor. The only thing, in my case, he has as a safeguard is that I do not publish a verbatim account and often his actual text is, if reproduced literally, too earthy for printing in a family newspaper. . . .

1. David Astor, editor of the *Observer* of London.

To Dean Rusk

September 22, 1964

Dear Dean:

I had lunch with Ambassador Dobrynin[1] on Monday at the Soviet Embassy. After some chat about our election campaign, I told him that what was worrying me was the effect of the Soviet-Chinese quarrel on Soviet relations with this country and with the Western powers. Would Moscow feel that, to preserve its position in the Communist world, it had to move closer to the hard Chinese line?

His immediate retort was to ask me what would be the American line about agreements with the U.S.S.R. after the election was over. I said I supposed we would want to go on with the search for agreements which would lessen the tension. But why did he not answer my question? He then said that co-existence with the United States was an unchangeable Soviet policy — it was "the law" — but it would mean a great deal to the government whether we in our turn showed ourselves willing to negotiate further agreements.

About everything? I asked. Well, he replied, we have "principles" which we cannot give up. Such as? "We cannot let Cuba be attacked . . . we are on the side of peoples fighting colonial rule."

Then I asked him if he thought the Sino-Soviet conflict could be composed. He was non-committal and appeared to be puzzled about this. And then I asked him if it were composed, would it be on Chinese or Soviet lines. "It would be composed," he said, "only on the Soviet policy of coexistence." He then asked me whether I thought the U.S.A. would ever change its attitude towards China by changing its policy in Taiwan. I told him he must know that we would never abandon Taiwan, but that, personally, I thought it conceivable that eventually there could and would be some arrangement for the guaranteed independence and neutralization of Taiwan.

My net impression was that he very much wants resumption of the improving relations which had evolved since October 1962,[2] but that on the record, the U.S.S.R. will oppose us verbally and by parliamentary maneuvers in the UN on issues affecting Southeast Asia, Cyprus, Cuba, the Congo,[3] etc.

I enjoyed our talk the other day.

1. Anatoly F. Dobrynin, then Soviet ambassador to the United States. **2.** With the peaceful resolution of the Cuban missile crisis. **3.** The United States had at this time increased the size of its forces in South Vietnam; the Greeks and Turks, both members of NATO, were contending for increased control in Cyprus; relations between the United States and Cuba, still the recipient of continual Soviet aid, remained tense and suspicious, particularly because of Cuban intentions to expand the revolution elsewhere in the Americas; and rival factions continued to struggle in the Congo, where the parties preferred by the West were gaining the upper hand.

To Zbigniew Brzezinski[1]

March 29, 1965

Dear Mr. Brzezinski:

. . . I do not think . . . that the concrete proposal you make . . . is feasible or, in present conditions, even desirable. I think that the Europeans will tend to work out their own community in the course of a generation — a generation because it will take that long for the survivors of the Second World War to disappear. But I think such a grandiose plan proposed by an American president today would be rejected almost everywhere, and would be suspected even where it wasn't rejected. It is too grandiose a role for the United States at this period of history. . . .

1. Zbigniew Brzezinski, at that time a member of the Research Institute on Communist Affairs at Columbia University, had sent Lippmann a brochure advocating an American role as an intermediary, along with the Soviet Union, in the politics of Europe, particularly Eastern Europe. The "peaceful engagement" of the two superpowers, Brzezinski contended, was necessary so that neither side would feel it had "lost" in a movement for a united Europe.

To McGeorge Bundy

April 23, 1965

Dear Mac:

I am grateful for your letter about my column of April 20, and moreover, I am relieved to find that the points you raise do not go to the basic propositions of the article.

On the question of fact, you are quite right. Eisenhower was not the authority to have cited — if, indeed, any citation was necessary — for my observation that Ho Chi Minh would have won the 1956 elections.

And I ought not have allowed the implication of relevance of the juridical status of the 17th parallel to Security Council action to creep into the article.

The explanation of it is that my attention and my intention were concentrated on the argument that, contrary to the Geneva Agreements, we had declared the two states to be sovereign and separate, and that, acting on our own say-so, we declared one of them to be the aggressor. Under the Charter it is, I believe, the function of the Security Council to determine the existence of an aggression.

These are trying times for all of us, and I am very conscious of the heavy burden which you bear.[1]

1. As President Johnson increased American forces engaged in the war in Vietnam, Lippmann increased his criticisms of Johnson's policy. Bundy, at this time still the president's national security adviser, as long as he held that office continued to defend his chief.

To Allan Nevins

October 14, 1965

Dear Allan:

. . . You ask about the breakthrough in legislation.[1] My view is that Johnson, whose great specialty is legislative leadership, took very skillful advantage of the confluence of a number of elements — among them, the desire to make amends for the legislative frustration of John F. Kennedy, the accumulated force of twenty years of education and propaganda for the welfare state, the devastation of the Republican opposition and indeed of the conservative bloc by the Goldwater disaster, and the demonstration that the key principle of the new welfare state, which is Keynesian economics, was a brilliant success, etc., etc. All those ideas are already present in your mind, and I'm sure I am adding nothing to your enlightenment.

I am much more deeply concerned about Southeast Asia than you seem to be, for it could well happen that the entanglement in Vietnam will divert attention from our domestic problems. They have only been sketched out. The Johnson bills are merely the beginning. I have called them myself architect's plans and a few holes in the ground, but no building.

I do not doubt Johnson's sincerity and fervor for these domestic reforms, but when he looks abroad, he is filled with a simple-minded chauvinism of the good-guy, bad-guy thought, and I doubt very much if he has the kind of moral courage which it takes to liquidate an unprofitable war. . . .

1. Following Johnson's election by a landslide over Goldwater in 1964, the large Democratic majorities swept into office in both houses of Congress enacted the president's "Great Society" program, including important statutes pertaining to his commitment to civil rights and his "war" on poverty. In 1964 Congress had enacted a major civil rights bill and the president's Keynesian revenue measures, earlier introduced in substantially the same form during Kennedy's presidency.

To Chester Bowles[1]

January 31, 1966

Dear Chet,

I agree entirely. . . . As I would put it, it is impossible for the United States to deal with China unilaterally, and the eventual equilibrium in Asia in which China is peaceably contained must come from the Asian powers, from India, Japan and the Soviet Union.

The principal vice of our present Asian policy is that our unilateral military presence on the mainland of Asia is preventing rather than promoting a true balance of power through the actions of the Asian nations themselves. However, I would go further and say that our military presence in Southeast Asia is provoking Chinese military intrusion into that area. Now if we were gone, the crucial military problems of China would lie along the Soviet frontier and with Japan. . . .

1. Bowles was then American ambassador to India.

To Richard H. Rovere[1]

January 23, 1967

Dear Dick,

. . . I don't think your comment on me is quite fair. I've reread my own article and there is no suggestion in it that Lyndon Johnson started the Vietnamese War. What I quarrel with him about in that article is that he transformed it into an American war. That was his decision, sharply different from the position by Kennedy and Eisenhower. . . .

1. Richard H. Rovere, then at work on an authorized biography of Lippmann, was also the regular contributor of "A Letter from Washington" to *The New Yorker*. The most recent edition of that magazine provoked this letter. Rovere later gave up the biography, which Ronald Steel then agreed to undertake.

To Arthur M. Schlesinger, Jr.[1]

September 25, 1967

Dear Arthur:

I have read your piece on the "Origins of the Cold War" with gratitude for much of the detail but I must say with considerable disappointment. I am not a revisionist as you define the word, far from it, and I agree with you that an analysis of the origins of the Cold War is incomplete if it leaves out the Leninist ideology, the dynamics of a totalitarian state and the madness of Stalin.

But in my mind your analysis is incomplete in that it ignores the strategic consequences of the First and Second World Wars. I mean the destruction of all the imperial powers which lay between Russia and America: not only the German and Japanese Empires but also the French, the British, the Belgian and the Dutch. And in the First World War, Austria, Hungary and Turkey. The two world wars destroyed the buffer powers and laid open between them a no-man's land in which the Soviet-USA confrontation has taken place.

The creation of this political and strategic vacuum has at once provoked and lured Moscow and Washington to fill it. Because of the fall of Germany the Red Army went West until it met the allies. Because of the fall of Japan, of the Chinese Empire, of the British and the French Far Eastern Empires, the United States was lured forward onto the off-shore islands and the peninsulas of Eastern Asia, — to Japan, to the thirty-eighth parallel in Korea, to Okinawa, to Formosa. You exaggerate, I think, Soviet motives and pay no attention, as the criminal law requires, to opportunity. Furthermore, you fail to take notice of how often the search for security and the assembling of an empire are two sides of the same coin.

My own personal dissent from the official theory of the cold war has sprung from the belief that the strategic consequences of the two world wars are the cause of the confrontation, which is particularly dangerous not only because there are two opposing ideologies but that they are held by two very great powers. . . .

1. Arthur M. Schlesinger, Jr., had become a professor of history at the graduate center of the City University of New York not long after resigning as a special assistant to the president following the death of John F. Kennedy. His "Origins of the Cold War" appeared in the October 1967 issue of *Foreign Affairs*.

To George H. Gallup [1]

October 31, 1967

Dear Ted:

. . . One point you raise is, of course, a very real one that Johnson is in a better strategic position than Hoover in that he could do something about the war whereas Hoover could do little about the depression. My own conviction, which must, of course, be tentative is that he can't do anything about the war because he is trapped by his own feeling that he can settle for nothing less, something which is called a victory for him. He has gone out on that limb quite unnecessarily and I don't think there is any way back for him. But, of course, events will show. [2]

1. George H. Gallup, a journalist and advertising executive in his early career, had become a prominent — perhaps the most prominent — American statistician of public opinion, which he analyzed regularly in the polls that bore his name.   2. Events drove Johnson and Lippmann further and further apart. In 1968 Lippmann applauded the candidacy of Senator Eugene Mc-

Carthy of Minnesota and encouraged the candidacy of Senator Robert F. Kennedy, both Democratic opponents of the Vietnam War and of Johnson. Lippmann also supported Richard M. Nixon, the Republican nominee, in preference to Johnson's chosen successor, Hubert H. Humphrey; see Ronald Steel, *Walter Lippmann and the American Century* (Boston, 1980), ch. 45.

To Palmer Hoyt[1]

February 26, 1968

Dear Palmer:

I did indeed write the columns you speak about and I felt at the time great anguish at doing it. My reason was a belief that in a state of war hysteria after Pearl Harbor, Japanese, who are easily identifiable by mobs, would not be safe. As there were continual threats, and rumors of Japanese submarines landing on the Pacific coast, I felt that very great popular trouble might result. There is no doubt that the rights of the citizens were abridged by the measure, but I felt then, and I still do, that the temper of the times made the measure justified. . . .

1. Palmer Hoyt, editor and publisher of the *Denver Post.*

To Donna M. Reichel[1]

December 15, 1969

Dear Miss Reichel:

. . . There is no denying the general truth that life in the modern world is far from being the good life. The question you are asking yourselves is whether "revolution" is not the only way of achieving the good life.

I had asked myself that question when I, too, was a student in college. My conclusions have come from watching the many revolutions of this century and also from a study of the great revolutions of the past, notably the French, the English and the American. These revolutions have always begun with the belief that they would create new men in a new society and none of the revolutions were ever radical enough and creative enough to achieve such a transformation of men and their social world.

In the advanced nations in the modern age, the old conception of revolution — the overthrow and the replacement of an established governing class — is, I believe, antiquated. It belongs to the horse-and-buggy age, to the time before the great technological achievements, which have produced, among other things, an affluent majority, which is able and ready to put down the activist rebels of the minorities.

In a way, I believe that society can be improved and reformed but not transformed by disruption of the established institutions, in which and on which and through which all of us have to live. . . .

1. Donna M. Reichel, an undergraduate at the University of Maryland at College Park, had written Lippmann on behalf of a group of "concerned" students to solicit his opinion about their conviction — characteristic of so many students at that time — that reform had failed and the moment for revolution had come. The students who inquired had participated in the civil rights movement in the South, worked in the unsuccessful presidential campaign of Eugene McCarthy, and joined antiwar protests in Washington, D.C. But, as she put it, the war in Vietnam continued, the "military-industrial complex" kept on absorbing funds needed for domestic programs, and colleges (according to a pamphlet she enclosed) offered an education without "relevance" to the great issues of the day.

*

Lippmann lived until December 14, 1974. In the years after his retirement in 1967 from the regular grind of "Today and Tomorrow," he had written fewer and fewer letters, as well as fewer and fewer articles. During the summer of 1974, he entered a nursing home in New York after a serious heart attack, and thereafter he made no effort to sustain even routine correspondence.

Appendix

A LIPPMANN CHRONOLOGY[1]

1889 September 23. Born in New York City; son of Jacob and Daisy (Baum).

1896 May 16. First of more than forty Atlantic crossings.

September. Entered Sachs Collegiate Institute, New York City.

1903 February. Wrote first editorial for school paper, the *Record*, as editor in chief.

April 25. Awarded the Arnold B. Horwitz prize "for faithful devotion to school duties and for general excellence."

1904 May 20. Confirmed as a member of Temple Emanu-El.

May 22. Awarded the Lewis May pin and medal, Temple Emanu-El.

1906 April 28. Awarded the Arnold B. Horwitz prize.

June. Graduated from Sachs Collegiate Institute. Awarded the Arnold B. Horwitz prize. Had been a member of the debating, football, hockey, and tennis teams.

September. Entered Harvard College.

1907 December. One of the winners of the Harvard College prize for academic distinction.

1908 January 9. Elected to the Circolo Italiano Society.

October. Taught evening classes at the Cambridge Social Union as an instructor in fine arts.

December. One of the winners of the Harvard College prize for academic distinction.

Active in Harvard Chapter, Intercollegiate Socialist Society.

1909 Elected to the Cosmopolitan Club. Member of the debating, philosophical, and political clubs. Joined the Harvard Socialist Club and later became president.

Active in Harvard Chapter, Intercollegiate Socialist Society, attending conventions and organizing chapters at other colleges.

[1] Prepared by Robert O. Anthony and adapted and published with his permission.

One of the winners of the Deturs prize for academic excellence.

June 30. Completed requirements for A.B. degree (three years), cum laude. Phi Beta Kappa, Alpha Chapter of Massachusetts.

1910 Assistant to Professor George Santayana, Department of Philosophy, teaching history of philosophy. Also studied for master's degree. Active in Harvard Chapter, Intercollegiate Socialist Society.

April. Elected to Board of Editors, the *Harvard Monthly*.

May. Within three weeks of earning master's degree, left Harvard, and was hired as a reporter on the *Boston Common* by his first employer and future father-in-law, Ralph Albertson.

June. Took A.B. degree.

Engaged by Lincoln Steffens for *Everybody's Magazine*.

1911 April 1. Elected to Executive Committee, Intercollegiate Socialist Society.

Regular contributor to the *International Magazine* through 1912.

1912 January 1. Appointed executive secretary to the Reverend George R. Lunn, Socialist mayor of Schenectady, New York. Resigned four months later.

Wrote articles for the Intercollegiate Socialist Society publication.

1913 Joined the Socialist party, New York County, and the Socialist Press Club of New York City.

First book, *A Preface to Politics*, published.

Invited by Herbert Croly to become one of the six members of the editorial board of a new weekly, *The New Republic*. The other four members were Francis Hackett, Philip Littell, Charlotte Rudyard, and Walter Weyl.

1914 November 7. First issue of *The New Republic*.

Book, *Drift and Mastery*, published.

1915 Book, *The Stakes of Diplomacy*, published.

Wrote series "Today and Tomorrow" for *Metropolitan* magazine.

1917 May 24. Married Faye Albertson, daughter of Ralph and Irene (Mulford) Albertson.

July 18. Appointed assistant to Newton D. Baker, secretary of war.

September 24. Invited by Colonel House to become secretary of the Inquiry, an organization created by order of President Wilson to prepare data for the Paris Peace Conference.

1918 June 28. Commissioned captain, Military Intelligence, and assigned to the staff of General Pershing and sent to France. Prepared propaganda leaflets for dropping behind the German lines and interrogated prisoners.

July 3. Assigned to the staff of Colonel House and to the American Mission to Negotiate Peace. Interpreted President Wilson's Fourteen Points to the British and Italians.

1919 January 23. Resigned and returned home.

February 3. Honorably discharged from the U.S. Army.

Book, *The Political Scene*, published.

1920 Regular contributor to *Vanity Fair* magazine.

Book, *Liberty and the News*, published.

1922 January 1. Joined the editorial staff of the *New York World* in the capacity of editorial and special writer.

Book, *Public Opinion*, published.

1924 March 10. Became chief editorial writer in charge of the editorial page of the *New York World*.

1925 January 12. Gave the Bloch Foundation Lecture at Yale University.

Book, *The Phantom Public*, published.

1926 June 4. First honorary degree, LL.D., conferred by Wake Forest College.

1927 April. Appointed to National Panel of Arbitrators by the American Arbitration Association.

August. Death of father.

Book, *Men of Destiny*, published.

1928 Book, *American Inquisitors*, published. Lectures delivered at the University of Virginia for the Barbour-Page Foundation.

1929 Became editor of the *New York World*.

Appointed to Committee to Visit the Department of Government at Harvard; served through 1961.

Book, *A Preface to Morals*, published. A Book-of-the-Month Club selection.

1930 Appointed to Committee to Visit Harvard College; served through 1936.

1931 February 25. Last issue of the *New York World*.

September 8. First "Today and Tomorrow" column for the *New York Herald Tribune*.

1932 Book, *U.S. in World Affairs: 1931*, published; written in collaboration with William O. Scroggs.

Book, *Interpretations: 1931–1932*, published from "Today and Tomorrow" columns selected and edited by Allan Nevins.

1932–1935 Regular contributor to the *American* magazine.

1933 June 22. Elected to the Board of Overseers, Harvard University, for a six-year term.

Appointed to Committee to Visit the Department of Economics at Harvard; served through 1937.

Book, *U.S. in World Affairs: 1932*, published.

1934 May. Delivered the Godkin Lectures at Harvard.

Appointed to Committee to Visit the Department of Philosophy at Harvard; served through 1957.

Book, *The Method of Freedom*, published. Godkin Lectures delivered at Harvard.

Book, *U.S. in World Affairs: 1933*, published.

1936 Book, *Interpretations: 1933–1935*, published from "Today and Tomorrow" columns selected and edited by Allan Nevins.

1936–1937 Regular contributor to the *Atlantic Monthly*.

1937 December 9. Divorce decree from his wife, Faye.

Book, *The Good Society*, published.

Book, *The Supreme Court: Independent or Controlled?* published from reprinted "Today and Tomorrow" columns.

1938 February 16–18. Gave series of three lectures at the University of Chicago.

March 26. Married Helen Byrne Armstrong. Moved to Washington, D.C.

September 5. Decoration conferred: Officier de l'Ordre National de la Légion d'Honneur.

1940 Book, *Some Notes on War and Peace,* published from four reprinted "Today and Tomorrow" columns.

1943 Book, *U.S. Foreign Policy: Shield of the Republic,* published.

1944 Autumn. Trip to Europe as a war correspondent.

Book, *U.S. War Aims,* published.

1945 January 26. Gave the Bergen Lecture at Yale University.

1946 April. Attended the Nürnberg trials.

Appointed to the Committee to Visit the Graduate School of Arts and Sciences at Harvard.

1947 February 1. Elected a member of the American Society of International Law.

April 26. Elected a member of the American Philosophical Society.

Book, *The Cold War,* published from a series of articles that appeared in the *New York Herald Tribune.*

1949 May 11. Elected a Fellow of the American Academy of Arts and Sciences.

July 27. Death of mother.

1950 February 22. Gave the Newton D. Baker Memorial Lecture, Cleveland, Ohio.

March 1. Presented with the Knight Cross of First Class of the Order of St. Olaf (Norway).

1951 January 22. Death of father-in-law, Ralph Albertson.

January 23. Elected a member of Sigma Delta Chi.

November 7. Elected a Fellow of the American Geographical Society.

1952 March 13. Elected commandeur, Orde Van Oranje-Nassau (The Netherlands).

May. Gave Sulgrave Manor Board Lecture in England.

Book, *Isolation and Alliances,* published.

1955 Book, *Essays in the Public Philosophy,* published.

1957 January 27. Gave the Gideon D. Seymour Memorial Lecture at the University of Minnesota.

1958 May 5. Awarded the Pulitzer Prize for editorial comment.

1959 March 2. Named Associe de sa Section des Sciences Morales et Politiques, Academie Royale des Sciences, des Lettres et des Beaux-Arts de Belgique.

September 23. Awarded the National Press Club Certificate of Appreciation in recognition of meritorious service to correspondents of press, radio, and television in the nation's capital.

Elected member of the American Military Institute.

Book, *The Communist World and Ours,* published from reprinted "Today and Tomorrow" articles following his trip to Russia in 1958.

1960 July 7. First TV appearance; CBS Reports, "Walter Lippmann on Leadership."

October 27. Testimonial of Appreciation and Esteem, Hall of Fame for Great Americans, New York University.

1961 June 15. Second TV appearance; CBS Reports, "Walter Lippmann, 1961."

November 14. Appointed a member of the Advisory Committee on the Arts, National Cultural Center, by President John F. Kennedy.

December 21. Third TV appearance; CBS Reports, "Walter Lippmann, Year End."

Book, *The Coming Tests with Russia,* published from reprinted "Today and Tomorrow" articles following his second trip to Russia in 1961.

1962 April 18. George Foster Peabody Broadcasting Award presented to Walter Lippmann and CBS for the programs that did most to promote international understanding during 1961.

May 7. Awarded Pulitzer Prize for distinguished reporting of international affairs.

May 16. Appointed a member of the Woodrow Wilson Memorial Commission by President John F. Kennedy.

June 7. Fourth TV appearance; CBS Reports, "Walter Lippmann, 1962."

December 13. Elected corresponding member of the Massachusetts Historical Society.

1963 January 1. Changed "Today and Tomorrow" syndicate from the *New York Herald Tribune* to the *Washington Post.*

January 21. First of the biweekly articles for *Newsweek.*

May 1. Fifth TV appearance; CBS Reports, "Walter Lippmann, 1963."

1964 April 8. Sixth TV appearance; CBS Reports, "Walter Lippmann, 1964."

September 14. Recipient of the Presidential Medal of Freedom from President Lyndon B. Johnson.

1965 February 22. Final TV appearance; CBS Reports, "Walter Lippmann, 1965."

March 1. Addressed the United Nations.

April 26. George Foster Peabody Broadcasting Award presented to CBS Reports, with special mention of interview with Walter Lippmann televised on April 8, 1964.

May 27. Addressed the International Press Institute, London.

December 22. Named Grand Officier de l'Ordre National du Mérite by President Charles de Gaulle.

Awarded the National Institute of Arts and Letters Gold Medal for eminence in essays and criticism.

1967 May 25. Final "Today and Tomorrow" article.

May. Moved from Washington, D.C., to New York City.

1971 January 11. Final article for *Newsweek.*

June 11. Elected a charter member of the Washington Hall of Fame, Sigma Delta Chi.

1974 February 16. Death of Helen Byrne Lippmann.

December 14. Death of Walter Lippmann.

December 18. Memorial service at the Ford Foundation, New York City.

1975 January 8. Memorial service at the Washington Cathedral, Washington, D.C.

Index